LEASE
ENFRANCHISEMENT – THE NEW LAW

LEASEHOLD ENFRANCHISEMENT – THE NEW LAW

D N Clarke MA, LLM, Solicitor
Senior Lecturer in Law
University of Bristol

The chapters on valuation have been contributed by
Andrew Wells BSc, ARICS,
Director of Residential Professional, Chesterton

JORDANS
1994

Published by
Jordan Publishing Limited
21 St Thomas Street
Bristol BS1 6JS

Reprinted October 1994

British Library Cataloguing-in-Publication Data
A catalogue record for this book is available from the British Library.

ISBN 0 85308 211 1

Typeset by Pentacor PLC, High Wycombe, Buckinghamshire
Printed by Hobbs The Printers Limited.

DEDICATION

For my parents, Joan and Ron Clarke,
who taught me so much.

PREFACE

The rights of leasehold enfranchisement granted by the Leasehold Reform, Housing and Urban Development Act 1993 ('the 1993 Act') may be viewed as a culmination of a process which began with the Leasehold Reform Act 1967. Once the right to acquire the freehold of their homes had been given to the long leaseholders of houses, it was difficult to justify the exclusion from similar rights of tenants with long leases at low rents of flats. The right to buy given to tenants in the public sector during the last decade only served to highlight the more limited rights available to flat dwellers with private landlords. The provisions of the Landlord and Tenant Act 1987, granting a right of first refusal on the disposal of an interest by an immediate landlord and an ability to acquire the landlord's interest when management obligations were not being fulfilled, have proved to be transitory. They may not be totally obsolete but they are now overshadowed by the much heralded right of collective enfranchisement. In practice, however, the collective right may not be taken up where it is available. Many tenants may prefer the individual right to a new lease, obtaining a virtual freehold since it is a potentially indefinite estate free of rent.

This book is an exposition of this new law, primarily covering collective enfranchisement, the right to a new lease and the extension of enfranchisement to houses previously excluded. However, the text also deals with all the landlord and tenant changes contained in Part I of the 1993 Act. The decision to exclude consideration of Parts II and III of the Act, on Housing and Urban Development respectively, was taken at an early stage in preparation of this book. The 1993 Act is really three pieces of separate legislation in one Act for the convenience of the promoting Government Department. The establishment of the Urban Regeneration Agency was not likely to be of interest to the reader seeking assistance on leasehold enfranchisement. The changes to public sector housing made by Part II of the Act are more closely related to enfranchisement in the private sector. However, half of those housing provisions make changes to Scottish law and the amendments to English law made by the 1993 Act can only be fully understood in the light of the framework of the Housing Act 1985. It was considered that the amendments in Part II would be rapidly incorporated into texts on public sector tenancies and the right to buy where they belong.

The exclusion of Parts II and III of the Act also enabled the second aim to be realistically possible. That aim has been to go further than a mere guide to new legislation and, within the time restraints, to produce a book which discusses some of the many difficulties with the implementations of the legislation and offers some practical solutions. It was appreciated that such an approach meant that the book would not be available within weeks of Royal Assent but it was hoped to have the work in print by the time the Act came into force. However, the speed with which the legislation has been implemented – Part I was largely in force on 1 November 1993 – and my own shortcomings has meant that that hope has not been fulfilled. However, the beneficial side-effect has been the ability to incorporate into the text the provisions of relevant statutory instruments and print them in full as appendices in addition to the text of the Act.

The draftsman of the legislation drew on the provisions and experience of the Leasehold Reform Act 1967 but the procedure and, often, the detailed wording of the 1993 Act differs from its predecessor. Nevertheless, reference is made to the comparable position under the 1967 Act and decisions of the courts or tribunals on applications under that Act wherever it was considered helpful. Similarly, reference has been given to the parliamentary debates in both the House of Commons and the House of Lords and there is a table detailing where the discussion in Parliament of Part I of the Act is to be found in the appendices. Neither this preface nor this text is the proper place for a discussion of the decision in *Pepper v Hart* [1993] AC 593; suffice to say that that ability of the courts to have reference to parliamentary material as an aid to statutory construction has resulted in more detailed reference and discussion of material from Hansard than might otherwise have been appropriate. The decision in that case permits reference only in situations where the statutory wording is ambiguous or obscure and then only to clear statements by the minister or other promoter of the Bill. Inevitably, statements in Hansard are highlighted where I considered that there may be some ambiguity or difficulty in the future; only time will tell if these cases are the ones where future litigation is focused. Most of the reference is to the detailed discussion either in the Commons Standing Committee or in the legislative stages in the House of Lords where many amendments were introduced. The Lords sit as a committee of the whole House so that all the legislative stages are covered in the numbered volumes of Hansard. The Committee stage in the Commons was in Standing Committee B; unfortunately, reports of such committees are only held in a few specialist libraries and it will be more difficult for a researcher to obtain access to them.

A successful enfranchisement, whether collective or by an individual obtaining a new lease, will require the close co-operation of the lawyer and valuer acting for the parties. This book has been written with both solicitor and surveyor in mind. I have been fortunate in securing the assistance of Andrew Wells, a chartered surveyor with Chesterton, who has contributed chapters 18–21 on the valuation aspects of the new legislation. His valuation insight has been invaluable and my especial thanks are due to him.

With Andrew Wells, I was privileged to conduct a series of lectures and seminars on the new legislation during 1993. The discussions and feedback from these sessions stimulated a number of passages in this book and we thank the delegates for their contributions.

My thanks are also due to my colleagues at the University of Bristol who have covered my teaching duties while I was given study leave for the Autumn Term 1993; to Professor Stephen Cretney for his encouragement to undertake the project and to Professor Martin Partington who read part of the manuscript and made helpful comments. Susan Bright of St Hilda's College, Oxford, generously offered time out of a busy schedule and contributed some incisive comments on the first draft of many chapters and thus I obtained the benefit of her own study of this legislation. The published texts of lectures given on the proposed legislation by Jennifer Israel and by Gerald Sherriff stimulated my consideration of a number of issues and I acknowledge my indebtedness. Melanie Plimmer acted as my research assistant last June and assisted in the analysis of the parliamentary debates. Of course, such errors and omissions that remain in chapters 1–17 and 22–25 are my responsibility alone. For chapters 18–21, contributed by Andrew Wells, we accept joint liability since the final product was the result of careful consideration by both of us. The opinions stated by Andrew in those chapters are his own and not necessarily those of his firm, Chesterton.

I could not have asked for a better publisher than Jordans. Martin West has been unfailingly encouraging and Mollie Dickenson and her team have turned the word-processed manuscript into a book in an amazingly short period of time. The forbearance of my family in tolerating prolonged absences was vital to completion of the project – thanks to Judy, and to Johanna, Lizzie and Naomi.

The law is stated as at 30 November 1993 when the text was completed.

D N CLARKE,
University of Bristol
31 December 1993

CONTENTS

TABLE OF CASES

References in the right-hand column are to paragraph numbers.

TABLE OF STATUTES

References in the right-hand column are to paragraph numbers.

TABLE OF STATUTORY INSTRUMENTS

References in the right-hand column are to paragraph numbers.

PART ONE

AN OVERVIEW OF PART I OF THE LEASEHOLD REFORM, HOUSING AND URBAN DEVELOPMENT ACT 1993

CHAPTER ONE

AN OUTLINE OF THE NEW LAW

1.1 Scope of the text

This book is an analysis and commentary on the provisions contained in Part I of the Leasehold Reform, Housing and Urban Development Act 1993 ('the 1993 Act' or 'the Act'). Although, for the sake of convenience, those provisions are referred to in the title to this book as relating to leasehold enfranchisement, in fact Part I of the Act contains seven Chapters, only the first three of which specifically relate to new or extended provisions relating to leasehold enfranchisement.

1.2 The Leasehold Reform, Housing and Urban Development Act 1993 – Part I

1.2.1 Leasehold enfranchisement

The term 'leasehold enfranchisement' describes the principle whereby leaseholders are entitled to obtain the freehold of their property.[1] However, in this book a slightly wider meaning is adopted to include the provisions of Chapter II of the Act whereby a tenant with a long lease at low rent is given the right to an extended lease of a residential flat at a peppercorn rent. The freehold continues to exist but the landlord has relinquished all interest of value in the flat to the tenant.[2] Even under the provisions of Chapter I – which the Act itself terms 'the right to collective enfranchisement' – the leasehold framework of individual tenants and a freehold estate is preserved. Moreover, the freehold will not necessarily be vested in all the tenants. The right to acquire that freehold collectively is only available to those tenants who qualify for the right of collective enfranchisement and participate in its acquisition.[3]

---

1 See Hague, *Leasehold Enfranchisement*, 2nd edn, 1987, Sweet & Maxwell, p 1.

2 Except redevelopment value (see 16.8.1).

3 For a full consideration of how a tenant qualifies for the right and the meaning of 'participating tenants', see 3.2.1 and 5.6.1.

1.2.2 Collective enfranchisement – Chapter I

Part I of the Act, which is headed 'Landlord and Tenant', is centred largely on the new rights of leasehold enfranchisement contained in Chapters I and II. Chapter I[4] contains the new right of collective enfranchisement which is given to qualifying long-leaseholders of residential properties. The tenants qualify to enfranchise collectively if they hold long leases and pay a low rent in a building which is predominantly residential. Such qualifying tenants obtain a collective right to purchase the freehold of their building at a market value as defined by the Act. That right becomes exercisable if at least two-thirds of the flats in the relevant building are let on long leases within the Act, and then at least two-thirds of those long leaseholders, who together must also constitute one half of the total number of flats, jointly give a notice of their wish to acquire the freehold. At least one half of the tenants who give the initial notice to exercise the claim must satisfy a residence condition.[5]

The new collective right can be seen as an extension to long leaseholders of the right already given to long leaseholders of houses under the Leasehold Reform Act 1967. Once the principle had been established in relation to houses, the only basis for denying similar rights to flat owners could be the practical and legal obstacles which had to be overcome. Further political pressure to extend enfranchisement arose after the 'right to buy' principle had been applied to public sector tenancies. Tenants in the private sector did not wish to be excluded from this move towards greater home ownership. The 1993 Act can also be seen as a necessary prelude to the promised introduction of a new form of freehold for owners of residential flats, to be known as commonhold.[6] By giving long leaseholders the right to enfranchise collectively, future developers will have more incentive to adopt the commonhold legislation when it is introduced and less incentive to continue to develop with long leaseholds if tenants can immediately exercise their rights under the 1993 Act. Moreover, leaseholders who have either taken advantage of their right to enfranchise collectively or who have secured an extended lease at a peppercorn rent should find that they will be less disadvantaged by any subsequent introduction of commonhold and perhaps be able to convert their arrangement more easily to that new status should they wish to do so.

1.2.3 The individual right to acquire a new lease (or 'individual enfranchisement') – Chapter II

The second major provision, contained in Chapter II of Part I of the Act[7] is to give a right to a new and extended lease to long leaseholders of flats paying a

4 Sections 1–38.

5 For full details of the qualifying conditions, see chapter three and 6.1.6.

6 This argument is more fully developed at 2.4.4.

7 Sections 39–62.

low rent who have occupied the flat as their only or principal home. Such leaseholders are given the individual right to acquire a new lease for a term of 90 years, plus the outstanding period on the old lease. This new lease will be granted to them at a peppercorn rent for the entire term and will be purchased from the freeholder, again at a market value as determined by the Act. The original draft of the Bill only gave extended new lease rights to tenants in a block which did not qualify for collective enfranchisement. The right was amended and widened to be made available to all long leaseholders of flats at a low rent, but they must satisfy a residence requirement.[8]

1.2.4 Amendments to the Leasehold Reform Act 1967 – Chapter III

Chapter III of the 1993 Act contains a short but important series of sections[9] which amend the Leasehold Reform Act 1967. The 1993 Act brings the enfranchisement rights given to long leaseholders of houses under the 1967 Act into line with the new rights for long leaseholders of flats in the 1993 Act. It extends the rights to obtain the freehold by removing the rateable value limits so as to mirror the rights given to long leaseholders of flats. The 1993 Act does not, however, give long leaseholders of houses under the Leasehold Reform Act any further right to an extended lease. The overall result is that long leaseholders of houses, who prior to the 1993 Act were excluded by the tests under the 1967 Act, will now be able to buy their freehold.

1.2.5 Estate management schemes – Chapter IV

The remainder of Part I of the 1993 Act contains provisions largely consequent upon or relating to the right of collective enfranchisement and to an extended new lease. Thus, in Chapter IV of the Act,[10] provisions are made so that landlords who now face the prospect of tenants making claims for either collective enfranchisement or for an extended lease will be able to apply to the leasehold valuation tribunal for the approval of an estate management scheme. When the tribunal considers that it is in the general interest that the landlord retains powers of management, then the tribunal may approve a scheme in respect of houses, flats or premises in a particular area to maintain standards of appearance, amenity and to regulate redevelopment. By this means, it is hoped that the uniform appearance and amenity of flats in estates or areas which had been previously under the control of a single freeholder will continue to be able to be managed under an estate management scheme,

8 See 11.2.3.
9 Sections 63–68.
10 Sections 69–75.

notwithstanding the fact that the freeholds of many such properties may now be acquired.

1.2.6 Tenant's right to management audit – Chapter V

Not every long leaseholder of a flat will be able to benefit from the right to collective enfranchisement. There may be insufficient tenants who qualify under the Act in the block; or, even if a claim is possible in theory, there may be insufficient tenants willing to participate – for reasons of cost and finance or otherwise. For some, there will be the substantial alternative right of an extended new lease but others may find that they do not even have that right – perhaps because they do not fall within the terms of the legislation because the rent they pay is above that fixed for the low rent test. Corporate tenants cannot satisfy the residence requirement – they cannot qualify for a new lease. In such circumstances, Chapter V of Part I[11] may provide a little consolation. It makes provision for the all long leaseholders in residential dwellings to have a right of management and financial audit of the service charge and other management accounts maintained by their freeholder or landlord. This important practical right will give leaseholders an important source of information in cases where they have reason to believe that their landlord is not carrying out his obligations efficiently or effectively.

1.2.7 Supplementary provisions – Chapters VI and VII

Chapters VI and VII[12] of Part I contain a number of supplemental jurisdictional matters consequent upon the major provisions of the 1993 Act, including amendments to the Landlord and Tenant Act 1987 so as to bring it more closely into line with the 1993 Act's provisions.[13] Section 89 stands alone – after the Act came into force,[14] it renders void agreements which have the effect of prohibiting or restricting occupation of dwellings by persons with mental disorders.[15]

1.2.8 Parts II and III of the Act

The remainder of the 1993 Act is concerned with public sector housing and urban development. Indeed, the 1993 Act is really three separate pieces of legislation contained, for the convenience of the promoting Government Department, in one statute. Those provisions in Parts II and III of the Act are not covered in this book; nor are the later sections of the Act (ss 104–185)

---

11 Sections 76–84. The right to management audit must also be considered in the light of the provisions of the Landlord and Tenant Act 1987. (See 24.1.1).

12 Sections 85–103.

13 These amendments are fully noted at 25.1.1.

14 The Act received Royal Assent on 20 July 1993 (see 1.2.9 for commencement).

15 See further 25.2.

reproduced. The relevant supplemental ss 186–188 of Part IV and all the Schedules to the Act which relate to Part I are printed in full in Appendix 1.

1.2.9 *Commencement*

By virtue of s 188(2), Part I of the Act was to come into force on such day as the Secretary of State might by order appoint. By the Leasehold Reform, Housing and Urban Development Act 1993 (Commencement and Transitional Provisions No 1) Order 1993,[16] the sections of Part I permitting the making of rules of court and those conferring power on the Secretary of State to make orders, regulations or declarations were brought into effect on 2 September 1993.[17] The same Order brought nearly all the remainder of Part I, including all the provisions relating to collective enfranchisement and the right to a new lease, into force on 1 November 1993. The only sections in Part I not in force on that date are the subject of transitional provisions.[18] They are:

1 ss 67 and 68 (new exceptions to the Leasehold Reform Act 1967); and
2 ss 85 and 86 (alterations to the Landlord and Tenant Act 1987).

1.3 Secondary legislation

1.3.1 *Power to prescribe procedure*

The Act envisages that some of the detailed procedure relating to both the right of collective enfranchisement and the right to acquire a new lease should be made by statutory instrument. The procedure for giving effect to the initial notice or tenant's notice[19] and the rights and obligations of all parties in relation to investigation of title and other matters arising in giving effect to the notice are to be such as may be prescribed by regulations.[20]

1.3.2 *The Leasehold Reform (Collective Enfranchisement and Lease Renewal) Regulations 1993*

These regulations,[21] made on the 30 September 1993, came into force on 1 November 1993. As envisaged by the Act,[22] they make provision for the

16 SI 1993/2134, made on 1 September 1993.

17 Namely, ss 26(9), 98, 100 and so much of ss 75, 88, 91 and 99 as confer power on the Secretary of State to make orders, regulations or declarations.

18 SI 1993/2134, Sch 1, paras 1, 2 and 3.

19 For an explanation of these terms, see 6.1.1 and 13.1.1 respectively.

20 Section 98(1). Section 100 specifies the extent of the power to make orders and regulations under Part I; these are to be laid before Parliament subject to the negative resolution procedure by either House. Regulations as to form or particulars of notices are not subject to the procedure (s 100(2)). See also 1.3.3.

21 SI 1993/2407.

22 See s 98(2); the regulations are framed to mirror the position, as nearly as may be, in the case of a contract of sale or leasing freely negotiated between the parties.

payment of a deposit in connection with both a collective enfranchisement and a claim to acquire a new lease; and deal with the investigation and proof of title and the conveyancing details. The regulations are set out in Appendix 2.

1.3.3 The form of notices

The Secretary of State may by regulations prescribe the form of any notice required or authorised to be given under Part I and the particulars which any such notice must contain. It is specifically provided that those particulars may be by way either of addition to or in substitution for the particulars set out in Part I.[23] However, forms have not been prescribed as to do so is considered to be inconsistent with current Government policy to deregulate as far as possible.[24]

1.3.4 Application to a leasehold valuation tribunal

The form of applications, or particulars to be contained in such applications, to a leasehold valuation tribunal must comply with any requirements in regulations made by the Secretary of State.[25] These regulations are now the Rent Assessment Committee (England and Wales) (Leasehold Valuation Tribunal) Regulations[26] which are set out in Appendix 2.

1.3.5 Variation of estate management schemes

An application to vary an existing estate management scheme under the Leasehold Reform Act 1967 before a leasehold valuation tribunal shall comply with any requirements made by regulations.[27]

1.4 Extent

Part I of the Act extends to England and Wales only and to the Isles of Scilly subject only to any modification directed by order of the Secretary of State.[28]

---

23 Section 99(6).

24 Although the 1993 Act gave the Secretary of State the power to prescribe the form of any notice required to be given under the Act, no regulations have been made nor are any expected. However, forms which can be used for all notices which may be given under the Act are available from law stationers.

25 Sections 91(6) and 88(5).

26 SI 1993/2408.

27 Section 75(5).

28 Sections 188(4) and 103.

CHAPTER TWO

BACKGROUND AND INTRODUCTION TO THE LEGISLATION

2.1 Context

The provisions of the 1993 Act can be viewed in two contexts. First, there has been a long-term legal and political dissatisfaction with the arrangements for residential long leaseholders. The new rights given by the Act seek to provide further remedies for much of that dissatisfaction while retaining the existing leasehold framework. Secondly, the new legislation can also be seen as a response to the political difficulties of introducing a new planned form of land holding for future developments, namely commonhold, without providing a solution for the problems of existing residential leaseholders where there was growing political demand for action. In this chapter, therefore, the background and rationale of the legislation is set out.

2.2 Practical problems with the present arrangements

2.2.1 The inability to use freehold

The inability of English property law to permit, for all practical purposes, the freehold horizontal division of property is the root cause of the problems which have subsequently plagued the law. Although there are examples of 'flying freeholds' both in the old common law[1] and in flat developments,[2] these examples have been the subject of interest for legal historians and stand as a warning of the resultant legal and practical difficulties[3] rather than being the basis for any modern development of the concept. The basic rule is that the

1 'Flying freehold' titles do exist, the most well known being those in Lincoln's Inn. See also Tolson (1950) 14 Conv (NS) 350.

2 The Nugee Committee, using the 1981 census figures, suggested that freehold owner-occupiers in purpose-built blocks of flats were more numerous than might be imagined. Both Aldridge, *Law of Flats*, 2nd edn, 1989, Longman and George and George, *The Sale of Flats*, 5th edn, 1984, Sweet & Maxwell include precedents for the sale on freehold title of flats or maisonettes.

3 The freehold flat or maisonette is not attractive to many lending institutions; their reluctance to accept freehold properties 'in the air' as security ensures that few exist.

common law does not allow positive obligations to be attached to the ownership of land; but where property is horizontally divided, there is a vital and absolute necessity for the property so divided to be subject to mutually enforceable positive obligations to repair, maintain and provide services to and over each others' property. Horizontal division leads, inevitably, to mutual interdependence. The legal arrangements for horizontally divided property must guarantee that the owner for the time being of each property within a block can enforce the obligations on which the enjoyment and marketability of each property depends.

2.2.2 Suggested possible solutions found wanting

Over the years, lawyers have suggested a number of possible solutions to try to achieve this satisfactory mutual interdependence in freehold tenure. The rock on which all such attempts have foundered is the decision in *Austerbury v Oldham Corporation*[4] where it was held that the burden of positive obligations does not pass from the original owner of the land who entered into them to successors in title of the same property. Some of the attempts to get round that rule have had limited success. The doctrine of mutual benefit and burden[5] may provide a remedy in some basic situations but it is hedged ground with limitations.[6] Furthermore, its development is relatively recent – too recent for the common law now to develop the principle sufficiently for it to provide any answer to modern problems of residential developments of flats. Some believe the use of an estate rent charge could have been developed in the same way[7] but there is little evidence of practitioners having sufficient confidence in the device to adopt it very widely. The full list of the suggestions to get round the rule in *Austerbury v Oldham Corporation* is well known and need not be repeated here.[8] Suffice to say that the widely adopted practical solution to horizontally divided property is to use leasehold tenure.

2.2.3 The necessity for leaseholds

The legal estate between the landlord, who retains the freehold, and the group of tenants in a block whose properties are horizontally divided, creates the relationship of landlord and tenant within which obligations can be enforced.

4 (1885) 29 Ch D 750, 781.

5 *Halsall v Brizell* [1957] Ch 169.

6 See *Tito v Waddell* [1977] Ch 106, 289ff and the recent decision in *Rhone v Stephens* (1993) *The Times*, January 21.

7 See Bright [1988] Conv 99; and Aldridge, *Law of Flats,* 2nd edn, 1989, Longman, chapter 13.

8 A summary of the devices can be found in Cheshire and Burn, *Modern Law of Real Property*, 14th edn, Butterworths, pp 580–581. The most practical solution, for registered land only, is to covenant with the first proprietor and insist upon protection by land registry entries prohibiting registration of transfers without first obtaining a direct covenant from the transferee. In a flat situation, this could require direct covenants with other flat owners. It is inconvenient and still not guaranteed to achieve the objective.

This enables suitable leasehold covenants for repair and maintenance and obligations to insure and pay a suitable service charge to be inserted into the lease of each property and, as leasehold covenants, to become binding on the leaseholder for the time being. The mutual interdependence which is required is achieved indirectly. Precedents for the modern, long residential lease, developed and adapted for this situation, will now ensure the presence of all the required covenants for management and mutual enforceability.[9] Nevertheless, nothing can disguise the fact that the leasehold arrangement remains inadequate for the purpose for which it has been adopted and adapted. Most significantly, there is no direct right of enforceability by one tenant against another. All action must be through the freeholder or immediate superior leaseholder. Many standard lease covenants sit uncomfortably in the context of a long residential lease at low rent. The conveyancing solicitor may strive to achieve an arrangement which, in many circumstances, will leave the residential leaseholder untroubled by the legal complexities, but it can never be guaranteed that any particular long leaseholder will not suffer from the inadequacies of the law.

2.2.4 The inadequacies of leaseholds

The leasehold device is used for the horizontal division of property because of its ability to permit covenants entered into by one party to the original lease to be enforced not only by the other party to the lease but by all successors of title to either the lease or the freehold reversion. However, the rules relating to the enforceability of leasehold covenants are technical, archaic and unduly complex. If it has been difficult for generations of lawyers to come to terms with those rules, then it is hardly a surprise if the lay clients who have to live within and sometimes operate the provisions of the lease are dissatisfied with the legal provisions applicable to the property which is their home. The utilisation of leasehold tenure also opens the risk of forfeiture, however long the term and however minor the breach. The risk is not illusory if the leaseholder, for example, refuses to pay a service charge and then fails to respond to all communications. It is a potentially powerful weapon in the hands of a freeholder. Although an application for relief from forfeiture can always be made[10] the leaseholder does have to take action to avoid the risk of losing a substantial capital asset. It is difficult to justify the existence of such a draconian remedy in the case of long leases at low rents.[11]

---

9 For precedents see, for example, those in Aldridge and George and George (cited in fn 2 above).

10 Even after a peaceful re-entry (*Howard v Fanshawe* [1895] 2 Ch 581; *Abbey National Building Society v Maybeech* [1985] Ch 190; *Billson v Residential Apartments* [1992] 1 All ER 141).

11 The best-known case is perhaps *Di Palma v Victoria Square Property Company* [1986] Ch 501 where the lease with an estimated value of £30,000 was forfeited for non payment of arrears of rent of £299. The subsequent amendments to the County Court Act 1984, in s 138(9A), make the result less likely but still possible if there is no application within six months of possession.

2.2.5 Inadequacies of the management company

The problem, however, is more fundamental than just the technical and difficult rules which apply. Quite simply, the leasehold arrangement, however well set up by lawyers who draft the original documentation, does not achieve the desired result directly. One leaseholder cannot force the obligations direct against a defaulting fellow leaseholder who owns a flat within the same block. This can only be done through the medium of the person or corporate personality which holds the freehold or an intermediate leasehold interest of the whole. This had led to the development of the management company concept and, in ideal situations, the management company will itself be the freeholder. Even in the situation where the leaseholder has a 999-year lease and is a shareholder in the management company which owns the freehold, the arrangement is essentially inappropriate. The management company is subject to corporate rules designed to operate in very different circumstances and can lead to unfortunate results if they are not observed.[12] The successful arrangement depends on a degree of co-operation between the leaseholders which, if it is not forthcoming voluntarily, will depend for success on the ability of the draftsman of the original documentation. In some situations, flat developments have so refined the long leasehold device that a degree of success has been achieved. In such situations, a developer will grant 999-year leases at nothing more than a peppercorn or nominal rent and, on completion of the development, immediately transfer the freehold reversion and freehold over the common parts to a management company set up for the purpose in which each of the leaseholders have either an equal share or a share which is proportional to the nature of the property which they hold. In some parts of England and Wales this has now become the normal and accepted practice. The vital point is that the leasehold arrangements are only being used as a vehicle of mutual interdependence and the freehold reversion has little value except for that purpose. The residential leaseholders do not have a wasting asset and there is no fear of the property reverting to the freeholder by the passage of time.

2.2.6 Part I of the Act – a partial solution

A collective enfranchisement, when successfully concluded, will place the tenants – or at least some of them – in the position similar to that already achieved in developments where there was a grant of 999-year leases and the

---

12 The requirements imposed on companies for annual returns (Companies Act 1985, s 362) and audit of accounts can be onerous for tenants running a management company. The annual return (current fee £32) must be sent; and though declaring a 'dormant company' may obviate the need for an annual audit, the new statutory penalties for late returns (s 242A) may give rise to fresh dissatisfaction with the utilisation of a management company device for holding the freehold.

transfer of the freehold to a management company. After a collective enfranchisement, there will no longer be an outside investment interest in the property and the control and operation of the management of the block will be in the hands of tenants. The difference may be that not all tenants in a block subject to a successful claim for collective enfranchisement will necessarily have an interest in the freehold. Only those who qualify and participate will gain a full say in management decisions. The right to a new lease will only terminate the investment interest in the particular flat. Although the extended new lease terms will be shorter[13] than those assumed on a collective enfranchisement, when all or a large majority of tenants in a block have new leases a landlord may decide to sell the remaining freehold value to the tenants and so may achieve an enfranchisement 'by the back door'.[14]

2.3 Identifying the issues of concern

2.3.1 Three main issues

It is submitted that the broad concerns with long residential leases of flats can be seen as three main issues which are the basis of the difficulties.

2.3.2 The investment issue

The first of these may be termed the **investment issue** relating to the inevitable division of ownership implicit in any leasehold relationship. In many situations, the freeholder chooses not to relinquish the investment interest. Leases granted in such situations are frequently of 99 years' duration, the annual rent reserved is more than merely a nominal figure and if a leaseholders' management company does exist it will, at best, only have an intermediate leasehold interest in the property. Any lease involves a division of ownership between the landlord with the longer-term freehold interest, and the tenant with the fixed duration leasehold interest but in such a case both parties regard the property as an investment. The landlord gains two returns on its financial investment, namely the receipt of the annual rent (with, perhaps, some benefit from the service charge) and the longer-term capital investment in the reversionary interest. The tenant's investment may also be financial in the sense that a substantial premium will have been paid for the long lease of a residential property. However, the tenant's overriding interest, in the vast majority of cases, is in using the property as a home and as a capital investment which can be realised to allow the monies to be used for the provision of a different home. The interests of the landlord and tenant are at variance. With only a 99-year lease, the leaseholders have a wasting asset and, with the passage of time, they will experience problems in obtaining mortgages or other finance secured on

13 Unless there is agreement to extend them (see 16.5.2).

14 See further 12.5.1.

their properties as the term reduces in length and therefore is increasingly difficult to sell. Leases with less than 40 years to run are not attractive to lending institutions.[15] This has led to a need to negotiate, at some point in the term, a fresh lease from the reversioner who is in a position to drive a hard bargain. If no fresh lease can be negotiated, the leaseholder may be trapped and face the loss of a capital asset at the end of the lease. The security of tenure rights[16] on expiry are poor consolation – especially as the landlord has some rights to repossession and the tenant has to pay a rack rent. The trend of English statutory intervention is to favour the tenant's investment in his home above the long-term investment interests of the landlord. The 1993 Act takes this development substantially further and, in the new right to the extended lease at a peppercorn rent, a residential tenant occupier can force a landlord to relinquish his investment interest in the flat, the tenant effectively buying the capital investment out.

2.3.3 The management issue

The second major issue addressed by the 1993 Act, as well as by earlier legislation, is the **management issue**. Inevitably, and almost by a consequence of the definition, wherever a horizontally divided property exists, two or more persons have an interest in the repair, maintenance and management of the block. The traditional leasehold arrangement places the responsibility for the repairs, maintenance and management with the landlord or, if not with the landlord, with a management company or managing agent who may have an intermediate leasehold interest in the whole block. Inevitably, the cost of providing such repairs, maintenance and management is recouped from the tenants as a whole by means of a service charge. Although the tenants end up paying a proportionate share of the cost, individual tenants may have very little say in the decisions on the level of repairs and the type of maintenance. Even the tenants as a whole acting in consort may lack control. This division of responsibilities and payment between landlord and tenant has caused discontent among tenants, which has led to statutory intervention both before and in the 1993 Act. The problem can stem from a number of different factors. In some instances, the landlord may be insolvent or disappear and be unable to carry out management functions; in others the landlord is unwilling to undertake the repairs and maintenance which is necessary and a very poor

---

15 The exact date when the lease will become difficult to mortgage or market may depend on the area; much shorter terms retain marketability in central London. Elsewhere, terms with more than 40 years left to run may suddenly become unmarketable.

16 Currently, under Part I of the Landlord and Tenant Act 1954 a long leaseholder may remain in occupation as a Rent Act tenant. Leaseholders under long tenancies at a low rent whose leases expire after January 1999 will become assured tenants under the Housing Act 1988 (Local Government and Housing Act 1989, s 186(3)). Leases entered into after 1 April 1990 are already within the new regime.

standard of maintenance results; in others the very opposite may be the case, and the tenants may feel that the landlord and/or his managing agents are making a substantial profit at their expense because of the particular terms written into the leases relating to repair and maintenance. The pressure from tenants (who have more votes than the landlord and therefore greater political pressure) has been for remedies and for substantive changes which will enable them to control the maintenance and repair of their own blocks of flats. Even in the cases of good management, the tenants may still wish to have a say in the decisions because they will eventually pay for the consequences through the service charge. In 1985, the Nugee Committee report[17] proposed improvements to the system of management of blocks of flats and the main recommendations were implemented by the Landlord and Tenant Act 1987[18] ('the 1987 Act'). The provisions of the 1987 Act do not solve the underlying tension – a recent DOE study suggests that leaseholders continue to experience problems about how the services in their block are paid for.[19]

2.3.4 The 1987 Act – A response to the management issue

The 1987 Act took the first tentative steps towards giving tenants the right to buy the freehold of a block but only in two limited circumstances.

1 There is a right of first refusal[20] where the landlord decides to sell his interest but the time periods specified in the legislation may be too short for the leaseholders to have time to act, particularly where there is a large number of leaseholders in the block.[21]

2 Where the landlord has failed to discharge its obligations and the appointment of a manager would not be a sufficient remedy, or where a manager has been appointed for at least three years, then a majority of leaseholders may apply to the court for an order to secure the interest.[22] In practice, this often means a three-year wait until compulsory acquisition is possible and procedures are felt to be lengthy and costly – a complaint which will, doubtless, also be made about the 1993 Act.

The 1993 Act builds on the tentative steps taken in 1987 by introducing a general right of collective enfranchisement which secures to the participating tenants the control of the freehold and thereby of management of the block. The framework of the lease will be retained and only tenants who can and choose to participate obtain a share of management control. The rights under

17 *Report of the Committee of Inquiry on the Management of Privately Owned Blocks of Flats*, 1985.

18 The 1987 Act contains provisions relating to levying of service charges.

19 Department of the Environment, *The Landlord and Tenant Act 1987: Awareness, Experience and Impact*, HMSO, May 1991.

20 Landlord and Tenant Act 1987, Part I, ss 1–20.

21 See the DOE study referred to in fn 19 above.

22 Landlord and Tenant Act 1987, Part III, ss 25–34.

the 1987 Act remain available. In some circumstances, the compulsory acquisition rights under Part III of the 1987 Act may be cheaper and therefore more attractive.

2.3.5 The legal inadequacies issue

The third issue may be termed the **legal inadequacies issue**. Practical problems have exacerbated what was already recognised to be an unacceptable legal framework. Pressure for reform and proposals for change has come from both lawyers, who have sought a more appropriate legal framework to be used for residential flat developments, and from consumers, dissatisfied leaseholders who suffer from the inadequacies of the law and arrangements under which they have to live. The consumer pressure is for the right to have a freehold flat; collective control of the freehold is the next best, and perhaps only, solution for existing long leaseholders. The 1993 Act does not address the legal inadequacies of leases – the potential solution, for future developments at least, lies with the concept of commonhold.

2.4 The place of leasehold enfranchisement in the future legislative scheme

2.4.1 A longer-term objective?

The 1993 Act, which retains and operates within the leasehold framework, should also be seen as part of a longer-term objective to change completely the form and the use of leasehold tenure for the development of horizontally divided properties.

2.4.2 Proposals to reform legal inadequacies

Proposals for fundamental change are not new. As long ago as 1965, the Wilberforce Committee[23] recommended that the law should provide for the running of positive covenants with the land, thus enabling freehold title to be used for divided buildings. No action was taken on their recommendations, notwithstanding that other common law jurisdictions before and since 1965 have introduced schemes of management and statutory provision for mutually enforceable obligations between owners of properties in the same block. Statutory schemes in North America (known as condominium) and in Australia and New Zealand (known as strata-titles) have now been operating for a number of years.[24] In 1985 the Law Commission, in Report 127,[25]

---

23 Report of the Committee on Positive Covenants affecting Land, Cmnd 2719, 1965.

24 See, eg the Strata Titles Act 1973, replacing the Conveyancing (Strata Titles Act) 1961 (New South Wales); the Strata Titles Act 1967 (Victoria); and the Unit Titles Act 1972 (New Zealand).

25 Law Commission Report on Positive and Restrictive Covenants 1984, Law Com No 127.

rejected piecemeal change and, adopting the ideas of the Wilberforce Committee, recommended comprehensive reform and the introduction of a new, enforceable land obligation as a new legal interest in land. These obligations would cover both restrictive and positive obligations and thus include the carrying out of repairs of provisions of services and could also cover reciprocal payments to cover the payment of service charge and expenditure incurred within blocks of flats. Once again, these proposals received a wide measure of support but the success of condominiums and strata-titles in other jurisdictions meant that an even more fundamental reform was proposed, namely the introduction of a similar form of land holding introduced by statute into English law.

2.4.3 *The commonhold proposals*

In 1990, the Lord Chancellor's Department produced a consultation paper on the proposals to introduce that form of new land holding which was termed 'commonhold'.[26] This consultation paper made concrete proposals for a commonhold scheme of freehold ownership and communal management for flats and other interdependent buildings with shared services and common parts. The freehold of a flat or other horizontally divided property could be purchased with the security of a statutory system of enforceable mutual obligations where the common parts would be owned and managed by a statutorily regulated association comprising the block's residents. A detailed draft bill was annexed to that consultation paper. The proposals received a broad measure of support across the political spectrum[27] and the proposals built on the Law Commission's concept of land obligations. The draft legislation there proposed would introduce both the land obligation and commonhold together[28] but envisaged that, for mutually interdependent properties such as residential flats, the new commonhold tenure would be the standard form of land holding. The commonhold proposals, however, involved some difficult issues of principle on which views were sought in the consultation paper.

2.4.4 *Enfranchisement – preparing the way for commonhold?*

The first difficulty, although not specifically addressed in the commonhold consultation exercise, is perhaps the most significant in practical terms. The introduction of a new framework for residential flats and other mutually, horizontally divided property will only be a success if developers decide to use that framework in future. If the arrangements for long leasehold tenure had

26 *Commonhold – a consultation paper with draft bill annexed*, Lord Chancellor's Department, Cm 1345, 1990.

27 See the House of Commons debates on 8 March and 16 April 1991.

28 The latest view of the DOE appears to be that land obligations and commonhold are sufficiently separate to be treated independently.

been permitted to continue then there is a risk of the commonhold tenure being relatively little utilised if the developers decided that the leasehold arrangements continued to be more attractive to them as developers in terms of cost, convenience and future investment. There is little point in introducing a complex and detailed scheme of commonhold if it is not used by developers of new units. It is suggested that the leasehold enfranchisement provisions now enacted make that result less likely, once commonhold is ultimately introduced. A developer will be less inclined to wish to retain the freehold if, on completion of the development, he may receive an immediate claim for collective enfranchisement. A grant of a lease for 99 years at a low but not inconsiderable ground rent is less likely if the developer knows that a claim to a right to an extended lease at a peppercorn rent may follow at any time. The existence of the rights to enfranchise collectively and to an extended lease will make it less likely that developers of blocks of flats will be tempted to retain long leases for each flat sold in the future. If the market for them exists, they may grant leases which are outside the terms of the 1993 Act (for example at a rent which exceeds the low rent limits) but it will be a different market.

2.4.5 The problem of converting leasehold to commonhold

The second difficulty, which the consultation paper on commonhold specifically addressed, was the key issue of whether any commonhold legislation should include provision enabling the conversion to commonhold of residential long leasehold flats at other developments against the wishes of, in particular, the freeholder. The legal and political difficulty is that, if the statutory commonhold framework becomes the standard form of land holding for new developments then the marketability of residential units currently held on long leasehold will or may, in the long run, become more difficult.

Unfortunately, the legislative framework which would be necessary to enable existing long leaseholders to convert direct to commonhold seems to raise substantial difficulties. Potentially, such legislation would have been very complex, even more so than the 1993 Act. Not only would the formula for ascertaining price be very difficult (more formidable even than the method of obtaining the price set for collective enfranchisement in the 1993 Act[29]) but there would also be substantial problems where some of the long leaseholders were unwilling or financially unable to participate in the conversion to commonhold. Could a majority insist that they be involved?[30] On the other hand, to require all the tenants to participate would have meant that, in practice, very few (if any) conversions from long leasehold direct to commonhold would occur.

There are not only these legal difficulties. It is suggested that it would have been politically unacceptable for a government to introduce commonhold for

29 One grave difficulty would be the lack of a market by which to measure value.

30 A part conversion to commonhold would not be possible.

the future without making some provision for existing long leaseholders. Given the extent of current dissatisfaction and the pressure for change, the provisions for collective enfranchisement contained in the 1993 Act can be seen as a necessary preliminary to the promised introduction of commonhold.[31]

2.4.6 Enfranchisement a commonhold substitute for existing leases?

The right of collective enfranchisement can also be seen as the preferred solution to the problem of conversion of long leasehold units direct to commonhold. Instead of giving the leaseholders that right, they are given the collective right to buy the freehold as long leaseholders. This, in particular, meets the problem of non-participating long leaseholders. Any non-participating tenant in a block of flats remains unaffected (at least as far as the legal position is concerned) – so instead of being a leaseholder of, for example, a development company he becomes the leaseholder of those of his co-tenants who join in to collectively enfranchise and secure the freehold. Moreover, the mortgages on the existing flats will not be affected, as the leases will remain in operation.

Having secured the freehold, the leaseholders who collectively enfranchise will secure the ability to grant themselves 999-year leases at a nominal rent.[32] The need to convert their units to commonhold will not then be as great because they will already have a greater control over their affairs. If, however, they choose to convert their legal arrangements to the commonhold tenure when it is brought into operation it should be very much easier for them to do so because, having secured the freehold, there will be no dissenting freeholder or intermediate long leaseholder to object to the conversion and no further price to pay to such persons – although the participation of all leaseholders may well be needed.

2.5 Conclusion

2.5.1 The end of investment in long leases

By giving rights of collective enfranchisement and the right to an extended lease, the legislation adopts the principle that the retention of an investment interest by a landlord in a freehold of long residential flats at a low rent is inappropriate. Leaseholders who take advantage of enfranchisement obtain a greater stake in their property, with the power to grant new leases and overcome

---

31 The commitment to introduce commonhold was reiterated in the debates on the 1993 Act (for example by the then Secretary of State for the Environment, Mr Michael Howard, HC Deb, Standing Committee B, col 155, 3 Nov 1992. An Opposition attempt to introduce substantive commonhold provisions into the Bill failed (see HC Deb, Standing Committee B, cols 339–370, 1 Dec 1992). In that debate, Mr Dudley Fishburn pointed out the difficulties of introducing commonhold before or without enfranchisement (at cols 352–353)).

32 This is the assumed basis for the valuation formula (see 19.3.2) but the grant of replacement 999-year leases is not a requirement if the parties are content with their present leases.

the problem of depreciation while also gaining management control; the extended lease, while leaving the management provisions in the leases largely unaffected, at least removes the freeholder's investment interest in the flat and secures the tenant's capital investment.[33]

2.5.2 *A major change*

The right of collective enfranchisement should be seen as the first part of what could be a major revolution in land holding in English law. It is the prelude to the still promised introduction of commonhold legislation which will enable future developments of flats and horizontally divided property to be held of a form of freehold tenure and thus bring English law closer to the reforms and developments which have already taken place in North America and Australasia. The remaining provisions in Part I of the 1993 Act are also designed to ensure that existing long leaseholders who are not able either to enfranchise collectively or make the move to any future commonhold tenure are not substantially disadvantaged. Thus, the right to a new lease will enable the residential long leaseholder, who may have neither the right nor the ability to participate in collective enfranchisement, to secure a new extended term at a peppercorn rent. The tenant's right to management audit will likewise give a greater scrutiny of management to tenants who have to remain within the leasehold framework, and ensure that they can have a financial and management audit of the service charge, and other obligations undertaken by a freeholder, carried out.

2.5.3 *A prelude to further change?*

The Leasehold Reform, Housing and Urban Development Act 1993 is undoubtedly a most important change in property law in England and Wales. It is also a prelude to what could well be a really fundamental change, namely the introduction of commonhold legislation and freehold ownership of flats and other interdependent buildings.

33 New developments of flats in the future are likely either to adopt 999-year terms at low rents with a transfer of the freehold to a management company on completion of the development or, if a market exists, to grant leases not caught by the Act.

PART TWO
COLLECTIVE ENFRANCHISEMENT

CHAPTER THREE

THE STATUTORY REQUIREMENTS

3.1 A suggested approach

When a possible claim to collective enfranchisement is first raised, it will be necessary to assess whether the right exists for the particular block of flats or premises in question. Initially, this may have to be done on the basis of some assumed factual information, for example the exact terms of the flat leases. Once a decision in principle is taken to proceed, then before the initial notice is served it will be necessary to check again, in the light of the full information obtained, to ensure that the preliminary assessment of eligibility was correct.[1]

3.2 The nature of the right to collective enfranchisement

3.2.1 The right defined

'The right to collective enfranchisement' is a right given to qualifying tenants of flats contained in premises to which the Act applies to have the freehold of those premises acquired on their behalf by an appointed person or persons and at the price determined in accordance with the Act.[2] The date for ascertaining whether the right exists is the date on which the initial notice of claim is made.[3] Any block of flats or premises where this right to acquire the freehold collectively exists is given the shorthand title of 'the relevant premises'.[4]

---

1 The practical steps which need to be considered before a claim to collective enfranchisement is commenced are considered in the next chapter (see 4.1.1 ff).

2 Section 1(1).

3 See ss 1(1) and (8); the initial notice of claim is under s 13 (see 6.1.1).

4 Section 1(2). It is possible that more than one right to collective enfranchisement can exist at any time. Thus, where two or more terraced houses have been converted into a jointly managed block, the existence of the vertical division may mean that the flats in one of the former houses can have a right; or there may be a right for a larger number or all in the jointly managed block (see 3.3.2). In such cases, it is expressly provided that a claim to collective enfranchisement may be made even if the premises are less extensive than the entirety of the premises in relation to which those tenants are entitled to exercise that right (s 1(5)).

3.2.2 The right extends to appurtenant property

The right extends[5] beyond the freehold of the relevant premises to certain other associated freehold property – provided the freehold of such property is owned by the person who is also the freeholder of the relevant premises. This extension is, first, an entitlement[6] to freehold appurtenant property which is demised by the lease held by one of the qualifying tenants.[7] Appurtenant property is any which belongs to or is usually enjoyed with the flat and is expressly defined to include garages, outhouses, gardens or yards which are so enjoyed.[8] There are two significant limitations. The right does not extend to appurtenant property let to a non-qualifying tenant. Perhaps, more significantly, a garage, garden or other appurtenant property enjoyed with the flat but let to the tenant by a separate lease would not appear to be included – it must be demised by *the lease* held by the qualifying tenant of a flat.

3.2.3 The right extends to common parts

Secondly, there is an entitlement to acquire property which any tenant is entitled, under the terms of his lease, to use in common with other occupiers of other premises.[9] The right of acquisition in respect of property used in common is, however, taken to be satisfied if comparable permanent rights over such common parts are granted by the freeholder at the time of the acquisition of the relevant premises.[10] Such permanent rights must ensure that the occupier of the flat after enfranchisement will enjoy, as nearly as may be, the same rights as those enjoyed by the qualifying tenant under the terms of his lease. In some situations, there may be property used in common (a staircase or a communal garden perhaps) which is used by other flats not in the premises which are the subject of enfranchisement. If a claim to collective enfranchisement is made by the tenants in one set of premises then it appears to be possible, while that first initial notice is in force, for tenants of another set of premises to serve an initial notice which includes the same appurtenant property or property used in common.[11]

5 Section 1(2)(a).

6 Not a requirement; so the participating tenants may choose to specify in the initial notice less than that to which they are entitled.

7 Section 1(3)(a).

8 Section 1(7).

9 Section 1(3)(b). The occupiers of the other premises which have common rights to use do not have to be contained in the relevant premises. In the case of a garden, for example, more than one block of flats might have rights of use in common.

10 Section 1(4). Although it is the reversioner's right to choose to grant permanent rights in lieu of the freehold to the appurtenant property, the nominee purchaser and the participating tenants may well prefer this alternative.

11 Section 13(8) and (9) apply only to the premises containing the flats and not to appurtenant property and common parts (s 13(10)). In such a case the grant of appropriate rights will be a better solution.

There is a potential problem with communal access ways, gardens and other common parts shared by a number of blocks of flats and currently maintained by a single service charge. It is not possible for blocks of flats to join together to enfranchise collectively; probably the first block of flats would prefer not to include the freehold of such communal areas and may exclude it from their claim. The landlord may seek to require it to be included; but even if rights are granted instead, it will be more difficult to arrange to cover the cost of maintaining the common access ways and securing payment after an enfranchisement.

3.2.4 *Intermediate leasehold interests*

The acquisition of the freehold might be of little value if the tenants were not able to acquire intermediate leasehold interests; conversely, the rights of those lessees might be prejudiced if they are not acquired. Consequently, the right to collective enfranchisement carries the right and duty to acquire superior leasehold interests.[12] If there are any intermediate leases superior to the leases of the qualifying tenants, then the qualifying tenants shall also acquire the interest of the current lessee of that superior lease;[13] there is an obligation to acquire that interest and no choice not to do so. The tenants are also entitled (but, by contrast, are under no obligation) to acquire the interest of any superior lessee in any common parts or appurtenant property if the acquisition of those interests are reasonably necessary for proper management or maintenance of those common parts.[14]

The rights to acquire superior leasehold interests are limited in two respects. First, they do not extend to other property or premises contained in any intermediate lease which is not a flat, any common parts or any appurtenant property.[15] Thus, where there is an intermediate lease of two separate blocks of flats, the right of acquisition only extends to those parts of the relevant premises – in this example, the block of flats where a claim to collective enfranchisement is being made. Secondly, the right does not extend to an intermediate interest held by a public sector landlord[16] where the qualifying tenant of the flat is also a public sector landlord and where the flat is let by that public sector landlord to a secure tenant.[17]

---

12 Section 1(2)(b).

13 Section 2(1)(a) and (2).

14 Section 2(1)(b) and (3).

15 Section 2(4).

16 Defined as any of the persons listed in s 171(2) of the Housing Act 1985, s 38(1). These are a local authority, a new town corporation, an urban development corporation, a housing action trust, a registered housing association, the Housing Corporation, Scottish Homes, Housing for Wales and the Development Board for Rural Wales. See also 9.5.2.

17 Section 2(5). This exception seeks to ensure that the 1993 Act provisions do not prejudice the position of a secure tenant of a flat. For it to apply, the qualifying tenant must be a public sector landlord and be either the immediate landlord under the secure tenancy or landlord of a superior tenancy where every intermediate tenant is public sector landlord, s 2(6).

3.2.5 Minerals

The freeholder can require any mineral rights to be excepted from any acquisition provided that proper provision is made for the support of the property as it is enjoyed on the date the initial claim is made.[18]

3.3 The premises

3.3.1 The definition

The first step is to ascertain whether the premises in which the long leases are contained are premises to which the 1993 Act applies. To be subject to enfranchisement, the premises must:[19]

(a) consist of a self-contained building or part of a building and the freehold of the whole of the building or that self-contained part must be owned by the same person;
(b) contain two or more flats which are held by qualifying tenants; and
(c) the total number of the flats held by qualifying tenants is not less that two-thirds of the total number of flats contained in the premises.

3.3.2 Self-contained building

A 'self-contained building' is defined, for the purposes of the Act, as 'one which is structurally detached'.[20] A part of a building can be self-contained if it constitutes a vertical division of the building and the structure of the building is such that that part could be redeveloped independently of the remainder of the building.[21] Thus, where there are flats in what was originally a row of, for example, four terrace houses, it is probable that there may continue to be sufficient vertical division to allow a collective enfranchisement claim to be made by only some of the flats in those four former houses – those in houses 1 and 2, for example. In such a case, the premises seeking collective enfranchisement must be physically linked; entirely separate parts of one group of flats (eg, houses 1 and 3 in the row of 4) cannot join together. A further requirement for part of a building to be self-contained is that the relevant services

18 Section 1(6).

19 Section 3(1). Even if premises fall within this definition, they may be excluded if they fall within one of the exemptions, for example, the internal floor area devoted to non-residential use exceeds 10 per cent (see 3.4.1).

20 Section 3(2). 'Building' is not defined but this should not cause difficulty. In the context of other legislation, it means a permanent, man-made structure (see eg *Tandon v Trustees of Spurgeons Homes* [1982] AC 755; *Cheshire County Council v Woodward* [1962] 1 All ER 517 at 519; and the Town and Country Planning Act 1990, s 336(1)).

21 Section 3(2)(a).

provided for the occupiers of such parts must either be provided independently of services provided for occupiers of the remainder of the building or could be so provided without involving the carrying out of any works likely to result in a significant interruption in the provision of any such services for occupiers of the rest of the building.[22] Services, for this purpose, are services provided by the means of pipes, cables or other fixed installations.

In terms of numbers of flats and types of buildings, the definition is widely drawn. A conversion of two flats will qualify for collective enfranchisement if both occupiers are qualifying tenants; and unless the premises are excluded by one of the exceptions[23] there is no upper limit on the number of flats in a block except the practical difficulties of a large number of tenants acting in consort.

3.3.3 Owned by the same person

To qualify, the freehold of the premises must be owned by the same person; any appurtenant property must be owned by that same person.[24] Once the tenant has commenced the statutory procedure by an initial notice, the freehold interest cannot be severed.[25] However, prior to that time a landlord could sever the freehold and thereby prevent a collective enfranchisement or confine it to a smaller section of the freehold. On the face of it, this offers a clear opportunity for avoidance;[26] but a landlord must consider the following issues carefully before severing the freehold.

1 If the Landlord and Tenant Act 1987 applies, it may be necessary to comply with the procedures of that Act and give the tenants an opportunity to acquire the freehold.[27]
2 Severance of appurtenant property or part of the curtilage of a block of flats from the flats themselves may be feasible but would not prevent a collective enfranchisement of the premises remaining; and the freeholder might be left with a reduced price on that enfranchisement and a useless part of the freehold.
3 Severance of and within the building poses difficulties. A vertical severance may well allow the tenants to place claims for collective enfranchisement of the two parts instead of the whole – and perhaps at a price combined for the two at less than the whole. A severance involving a horizontal division may well succeed in stopping a claim – but there may be a price to pay. Tenants in such a situation will still have their right to a new lease[28] and when exercising

22 Section 3(2)(b).
23 See 3.4.
24 Sections 3(1)(a) and 1(3). 'Same person' includes reference to an interest owned by joint tenants; s 101(4) and cf the Interpretation Act 1978, s 6(c).
25 See s 19(1)(a) and 6.2.1.
26 More fully discussed in 10.4.2.
27 Under the 1987 Act, Part I, ss 1–20. A severance by an immediate landlord would trigger the requirement to serve a notice of the right of first refusal.
28 Provided that they establish their residence requirement (see 11.2.3).

that right may argue that the value of the freehold reversion has been reduced by the severance and creation of a 'flying freehold'. If this argument is successful, the premium paid for the new lease may be significantly reduced.

3.3.4 Flat and unit

A 'flat' means a separate set of premises (whether or not on the same floor) which forms part of a building and which is constructed or adapted for use as a dwelling and either the whole or a material part of which lies above or below some other part of the building.[29] A maisonette or dwelling on two or more floors is included provided that some part of it is above or below another part of the building. For the purposes of collective enfranchisement, the 1993 Act also refers to 'units' within a building. A unit is more widely defined[30] and means a flat, any other set of premises which is constructed or adapted for use for the purposes of the dwelling or a separate set of premises let or intended for letting, on a business lease.[31] A flat will always be a unit; a garage or store used for the purposes of a dwelling may be a separate unit; any premises let on a business lease within the building will be a unit. A dwelling will not be a flat if neither the whole nor a material part of it lies above or below some other part of the building but if otherwise part of a building it will be a unit. The freehold of units may be included in a claim for collective enfranchisement[32] but only the qualifying tenant of a flat can participate in the claim.

3.3.5 Two-thirds of flats held by qualifying tenants

The two-thirds requirement is a minimum requirement. Where there are only two flats, for instance, then both must be held by qualifying tenants; where there are three flats it will be sufficient if two are held by qualifying tenants; where there are four flats it will be necessary for three to be held by qualifying tenants; where there are five flats it will be necessary that four are held by qualifying tenants; and so forth. Various attempts were made in the Committee Stages of the Bill to alter the balance of these provisions.[33] Some concern was expressed that the requirement of two-thirds of the flats held by qualifying

---

29 Section 101(1). The definition which emerged in the Act differs from that in the original Bill, which was identical to the definition in the Landlord and Tenant Act 1987, s 60(1) and which referred to horizontal division and might have resulted in some premises being outside both the Leasehold Reform Act 1967 and the 1993 Act.

30 Section 38.

31 A business lease means a tenancy to which Part II of the Landlord and Tenant Act 1954 applies (s 101(1)).

32 But will be subject to the reversioner's option to take a leaseback (see 9.5.3).

33 The requirement is of two-thirds of the *flats* not the *units*. An alteration was made to change the draft of the Bill from two-thirds of the units to two-thirds of the flats (HC Deb, Standing Committee B, col 64, 12 November 1992). This ensures that flats above a number of small retail units are not disadvantaged. It also prevents an avoidance device; a landlord might have been able to create more units to bring the percentage occupied by qualifying tenants down.

tenants was too high but an attempted amendment to reduce the percentage to 50 per cent failed.[34]

3.4 Premises which do not qualify for collective enfranchisement

3.4.1 Exception where non-residential use exceeds 10 per cent

The most important of the exceptions is where business or commercial use in the premises exceeds 10 per cent of the internal floor area. The statutory wording excludes premises which contain any part or parts occupied, or intended to be occupied, otherwise than for residential purposes where the internal floor area of that part, or of those parts taken together, exceeds 10 per cent of the internal floor area of the premises taken as a whole.[35] In calculating the 10 per cent and the balance between residential and non-residential use, the common parts of the premises are disregarded.[36] Those parts used or intended for use in conjunction with a particular dwelling are to be taken to be occupied, or intended to be occupied, for residential purposes.[37] Garages, parking spaces and storage areas are specifically cited as examples in this context. Further assistance in making the calculation is provided; in determining the internal floor area of a building, or of any part of a building, the floor or floors are to be taken to extend (without interruption) throughout the whole of the interior of the building or part.[38] Business units currently vacant or unoccupied will, it is submitted, still be considered as part of the non-residential element within the premises, provided that the intention is that they be occupied in due course for other than residential purposes.[39]

This exclusion of premises where more than 10 per cent of the total internal floor area is taken up by business, professional, commercial or any other non-residential use may have the effect of excluding a considerable number of blocks of flats which would otherwise qualify for collective enfranchisement.[40] In particular, wherever a block of flats is constructed so that the whole of the ground floor consists of retail use, then the block will need to have nine further floors to qualify for enfranchisement. For this reason, there was considerable controversy on the level of non-residential use which would exclude the right to collective enfranchisement. However, attempts during the Committee Stage of

34 HC Deb, Standing Committee B, col 63, 12 November 1992.

35 Section 4(1).

36 Section 4(1)(a)(ii) and 4(3).

37 Section 4(2).

38 Section 4(3).

39 If this were not the case, a forfeiture or surrender of a business lease could tip the percentage balance – perhaps temporarily – in favour of a collective enfranchisement.

40 The qualifying tenants who meet the residence requirement will be able to claim a new lease (see 11.3.2).

the Bill to increase the level to 25 per cent or 50 per cent failed.[41] Consultations then took place on the figure of 20 per cent. In the end, no change was made to the Bill as drafted. The 10 per cent rule is a compromise and reflects the view that where there is any substantial non-residential use it may be inappropriate for residential flat owners to become the reversioners of the commercial element in the block of flats. Even if the percentage had been higher than 10 per cent it is likely that few tenants of such blocks could have afforded the purchase anyway.

3.4.2 Resident landlord exception

Where premises are premises with a resident landlord, and do not contain more than four units, then there is no right of collective enfranchisement.[42] However, this exception is defined as limited to premises which are not, and do not form, part of a purpose-built block of flats, and the freeholder (or an adult member of the freeholder's family) must, at the time, occupy one of the flats or units in the premises as his only or principal home, and must have so occupied such flat or unit throughout a period of not less than 12 months ending with that time.[43] It should be noted that there is no similar limitation to the right to an extended lease. Consequently, tenants who have a resident landlord within this exception will be able to seek an extended lease even if collective enfranchisement is not available.

3.4.3 Limits of the resident landlord exemption

Certain features of the resident landlord exemption should be borne in mind.

1 A resident landlord can only be a freeholder.[44] An intermediate lessee of the whole who is resident in part and has let the rest of the premises on long sub-leases may find that those sub-tenants have rights to enfranchise collectively. In some circumstances, that intermediate resident lessee may have rights to acquire the freehold under the Leasehold Reform Act 1967. There is no guidance in such cases as to which piece of legislation takes priority; it is likely that the first notice in time will take precedence.

2 A purpose-built block of flats is defined as meaning a building which, as constructed, contained two or more flats.[45] Such a building is not exempted from collective enfranchisement.

3 The limitation is to not more than four *units* and not flats. The exception will not apply if there are five units or more in the premises.[46]

---

41 HC Deb, Standing Committee B, col 88, 17 November 1992.

42 Section 4(4).

43 Section 10(1).

44 Section 10(6).

45 Ibid.

46 The distinction between flat and unit in this context is not likely to be significant except in rare cases; for example, four flats and a business unit would be excluded under the previous exemption if the business unit exceeded 10 per cent of the internal floor area.

4 If a previous freeholder of the premises occupied as a resident landlord as defined, then the current freeholder, or adult member of the freeholder's family, may also be a resident landlord even if they have not occupied for the previous 12 months, provided that they entered into occupation within a 28-day period from the date of acquisition of the interest and have occupied the flat as only or principal home since then.[47]

5 The resident freeholder or member of the family may occupy a unit (other than a flat) which is used as a dwelling. Thus, if the part the freeholder occupies is not itself a flat, the exception may still apply.[48]

6 A person is an adult member of another's family if that person is the other's wife or husband; or a son, daughter, son-in-law or daughter-on-law of either the freeholder or the spouse who has attained the age of 18; and the father or mother of either the freeholder or the spouse. The definition is expressly extended to include any stepson or stepdaughter.[49]

7 If the freehold interest is held on trust the reference to a freeholder is taken to be a reference to any person having an interest under the trust (whether or not also a trustee).[50]

It was originally provided in the Bill as drafted that the Secretary of State might, by order, alter both the relevant percentage of the internal floor area which is to be occupied other than for residential purposes (from 10 per cent) and the number of units applicable to the resident landlord exemption (to more or less than four). This 'Henry VIII' clause was deleted during the passage of the legislation.

3.4.4 *Exception where compulsory purchase notices exist*

An initial notice is of no effect if, when it is given, any acquiring authority has, with a view to acquisition of whole or part of the specified premises, served a notice to treat on either the freeholder or a person who owns any leasehold interest in the premises specified in the initial notice; or entered into a contract for the purchase of the interest of such a person.[51] The extent of the exception is more fully discussed in chapter eight.[52]

3.4.5 *Inheritance tax designation; gifts for public benefit*

An exclusion was introduced during the Act's passage through the House of Lords and then redrafted by the Government. Property of outstanding historic

---

47 Section 10(2).

48 Section 10(3). In such a case, collective enfranchisement may be possible by excluding the freeholder's unit; because it is a unit, there may be sufficient vertical division between the unit and the flats for this to be done.

49 Section 10(5).

50 Section 10(4).

51 Section 30(1) and (2).

52 See 8.4.2.

or architectural or aesthetic interest and subject to a designation under s 31 of the Inheritance Tax Act 1984 or belonging to a body not conducted for profit and subject to a direction under s 26 of that Act is excluded from the collective enfranchisement provisions.[53] Where the premises specified in the initial notice are such property, termed by the Act 'qualifying property', then the initial notice is of no effect.[54] Even if the specified premises are not 'qualifying property', an initial notice which proposes to acquire other freehold appurtenant property or property used in common[55] where that other property is 'qualifying property' is also of no effect.[56] For a fuller discussion of the meaning of 'qualifying property', see chapter eight.[57]

3.4.6 National Trust and cathedral precincts

The above exceptions only apply to a collective enfranchisement; the right to a new lease may be available.[58] There are, however, some premises which are exempted completely from the provisions of both collective enfranchisement and the right to an extended lease.

1 There is no right to acquire any interest vested inalienably in the National Trust.[59]
2 There is no right to acquire any interest or lease of any property within the precinct of a cathedral church.[60]

3.4.7 Crown leases

Where there is a lease from the Crown[61] the right to collective enfranchisement arises only if there has ceased to be a Crown interest in the land subject to it.[62] However, indication has been given[63] that, in many cases, tenants under Crown leases may be given the opportunity to acquire the freehold collectively if, but

53 Section 31.
54 Section 31(1)(a).
55 Within s 1(3).
56 Section 31(1)(b).
57 See 8.5.3.
58 But not if there are compulsory acquisition procedures in respect of the flat (see 15.4.1).
59 Section 95.
60 Section 96. A property falls within the precinct of a cathedral church if it is so considered for the purposes of the Care of Cathedrals Measure 1990.
61 A 'lease from the Crown' is defined to mean interests comprised in the Crown Estate, those belonging to Her Majesty in right of the Duchy of Lancaster, those belonging to the Duchy of Cornwall and any other interest belonging to a government department (s 94(11)). 'Appropriate authority' is to be construed accordingly.
62 Section 94(1).
63 Written Reply, 2 November 1992. The argument is based on the constitutional difficulties of binding the Crown to dispose of land. The agreement to dispose of freeholds on a voluntary basis does not apply to property related or associated with the Royal Parks and Palaces. Tenants of such properties will be offered lease renewals, but subject to an estate management scheme.

for the statutory exclusion, the tenants would have had the right under the Act. There are provisions designed to facilitate the acquisition of the freehold by or with the consent of the appropriate authority in relation to that Crown interest as if the right to collective enfranchisement was available. It is envisaged, therefore, that tenants may be proceeding with a view to acquiring the freehold of premises in circumstances in which, but for the existence of the Crown interest, there would be an entitlement to do so. In such a case the parties[64] may agree that the decision of any question relating to the acquisition, such as the price payable, should be determined by the leasehold valuation tribunal. If there is such agreement, the leasehold valuation tribunal has jurisdiction.[65] Similarly, the appropriate Crown authority may make application for an estate management scheme.[66]

3.5 The qualifying tenants

3.5.1 Definition

Once it has been ascertained that the premises is one to which the Act applies, the next stage is to ascertain whether a sufficient number of flats are held by qualifying tenants. A person is a qualifying tenant if he is a tenant of a flat under a long lease at a low rent.[67] However, a tenant cannot be a qualifying tenant if:[68]

(a) the lease is a business lease;[69] or
(b) the intermediate landlord of the lease is a charitable housing trust[70] and the flat forms part of the housing accommodation provided by it for the pursuit of its charitable purpose; or
(c) the lease was granted by a way of sub-lease out of a superior lease where that superior lease itself is not a long lease at low rent and the grant of the sub-lease was made in breach of the terms of the superior lease and the breach has not been waived by the superior landlord.

3.5.2 One qualifying tenant per flat

There can be only one qualifying tenant at any one time in respect of each flat.[71] Thus, if a flat is subject to two or more successive leases the tenant of any

64 That is, the appropriate authority, the tenants and all other persons such as other relevant landlords who would otherwise be entitled to be represented before a leasehold valuation tribunal.
65 Section 94(9) and (10) and s 88.
66 Under s 70 (see s 94(6),(7) and (8)).
67 Section 5. Reference to a lease of a flat means reference to a lease where the demised premises consist of or include the flat (s 101(3)).
68 Section 5(2)(a)–(c).
69 A tenancy to which Part II of the Landlord and Tenant Act 1954 applies (s 101(1)).
70 'Charitable housing trust' means a housing trust within the meaning of the Housing Act 1985 which is a charity within the meaning of the Charities Act 1993 (s 5(2)).
71 Section 5(3).

of the superior leases shall not be a qualifying tenant if any other tenant is, in fact, a qualifying tenant. Similarly, where a flat is let, for the time being, to joint tenants those joint tenants jointly constitute the qualifying tenant for the flat.[72]

3.5.3 Qualifying tenant of three or more flats

If one person is a qualifying tenant of three or more flats contained in premises which consist of the whole or part of a building, then for the purposes of collective enfranchisement[73] there is no qualifying tenant for any of those flats.[74] Joint tenants can be caught by this provision; if a parent was a tenant of one flat and a joint tenant of two other flats with two children, there would be no qualifying tenant for any one of the three flats. The aim of this provision is to prevent a single person, whether an individual or a company, from profiting by means of ownership of a considerable number of flats; and the exclusion of any such multiple owner from the body of qualifying tenants may make it much less likely in any individual case that there will be sufficient number of qualifying tenants able to proceed. If a body corporate is the qualifying tenant then any flat let to an associated company is treated as let to the body corporate.[75] A company with three or more flats in a block cannot, therefore, attain qualifying tenant status by vesting flats in an associated company; but vesting in a company which is not associated as defined may allow each to become a qualifying tenant. Similarly, an individual with three or more flats could achieve the same result by divesting sufficient flats to other individuals or persons, perhaps other family members.[76]

3.6 Qualifying tenants satisfying the residence condition

3.6.1 Applies at initial notice stage

A tenant does not have to be resident to be a qualifying tenant and participate in a collective enfranchisement. However, when an initial notice is given, one half

72 Section 5(4).

73 The right to acquire a new lease will exist for those flats which satisfy the residence condition (see 11.2.2).

74 Section 5(5). If a person would be regarded as a qualifying tenant, or among those constituting the qualifying tenant, of a flat and would also be, or among those constituting, the qualifying tenant of two or more other flats in the same premises, there is no qualifying tenant of any of those flats.

75 Section 5(6). For this purpose, associated company means another body corporate, within the meaning of s 736 of the Companies Act 1985, which is that body's holding company, a subsidiary of that body or another subsidiary of that body's holding company.

76 Although it may be possible to increase the number of qualifying tenants in this way, it is unlikely that any new qualifying tenants so created will satisfy the residence condition immediately (unless, as in the example postulated above, the new tenant had previously been one of the joint tenants) (see 3.6.1). Corporate tenants can never satisfy the residence condition.

of the qualifying tenants giving that notice must satisfy the residence condition.[77] This requirement, inserted into the Act at a late stage,[78] is intended to ensure that at least half of the tenants seeking the freehold collectively are using the flat as their principal home.

3.6.2 The condition

To satisfy this condition, a tenant must have occupied the flat as his only or principal home[79] either for the last 12 months or for periods amounting to three years in the last 10 years.[80] It does not matter if the flat has been used for other purposes as well in that time; and occupation of part of it as a residence will suffice.[81] The occupation does not need to have been under the current lease; it can be in right of some other or earlier lease.[82] Thus, a qualifying tenant might have been granted the lease fairly recently after previous occupation as a periodic tenant at a full market rent. In such circumstances, the earlier periods of occupation can count towards meeting the residence condition. Where a lease is held by joint tenants the residence condition need only be satisfied in respect of one of them.[83] There is no express provision to cover the situation of a flat in the name of a trustee and occupied by a beneficiary. In the absence of such provision the better view must be that a beneficiary cannot satisfy the residence condition.

3.6.3 Corporate tenants cannot meet the condition

Occupation by a company or other artificial person is not regarded as occupation sufficient to satisfy the residence condition;[84] and if the tenant is a corporation sole (for example a rector or bishop) occupation by that corporator is not occupation for these purposes.

---

77 Section 13(2) and see 6.1.6.

78 In the House of Lords at Report Stage of the Bill. The Government had resisted a number of amendments proposing a residency requirement but eventually accepted the present test which prevents a majority of non-resident long leaseholders purchasing the landlord's interest (see HL Deb, Vol 545, col 1262, 11 May 1993).

79 'Principal home' is not defined, but compare the Housing Act 1985, s 81, where it was held that it is inherent in the phrase that it is possible to occupy as a home two places at the same time, *Crawley Borough Council v Sawyer* (1987) 20 HLR 98, CA at 101 (Parker LJ). See also *Poland v Cadogan* [1980] 3 All ER 544, CA.

80 Section 6(2). The qualifying tenant will satisfy the residence condition at any time when these statutory conditions are met (s 6(1)). The 12-month period is shorter than that specified for the residence requirement in connection with the grant of a new lease (see 11.2.3).

81 Section 6(3)(a).

82 Section 6(3)(b).

83 Section 6(4)(a). Similarly, s 6(3)(a) and (b) can apply where there are joint tenants constituting the tenant, so that one joint tenant's residence of part will suffice and one joint tenant's earlier occupation under an earlier lease can satisfy the residence condition s 6(4)(b)).

84 Section 6(3), proviso. 'Artificial person' is not defined but probably includes any legal person who is not an individual.

3.7 A long lease

3.7.1 The requirement

The qualifying tenant must have a long lease. A long lease, for the purpose of collective enfranchisement, means, primarily, a lease granted for a term of years certain exceeding 21 years, whether or not it is, or may become, terminable before the end of the term granted by notice given by or to the tenant or by re-entry, forfeiture or otherwise.[85]

3.7.2 Extended definition of a long lease

Section 7 contains further alternative additional definitions of 'long lease',[86] each ensuring that in other situations where the lease actually extends, or will extend, beyond 21 years, there will be a lease which qualifies under the Act. Those situations, defined as being a long lease for the purpose of the Act, are as follows.

1 A lease granted for a term fixed by law, containing a covenant or obligation for perpetual renewal. This includes a lease taking effect under s 149(6) of the Law of Property Act 1925 which deals with leases terminable after a death or remarriage. The only such perpetually renewable lease excluded is a lease by sub-demise, which contains a covenant or obligation for perpetual renewal which was granted out of a lease which was not itself a long lease as defined.[87]

2 A lease granted in pursuance of the right to buy which was conferred by the Housing Act 1985, Part V, or in pursuance of the right to acquire on rent to mortgage terms conferred by that Part of that Act.[88]

3 A shared ownership lease where the tenant's total share is 100 per cent.[89]

---

85 Section 7(1)(a). Compare the definition to that in the Leasehold Reform Act 1967, s 3 and the Housing Act 1985, s 115. 'Lease' and 'tenancy' have the same meaning and include sub-leases and agreements for leases but not a tenancy at will or at sufferance (s 101(2)).

86 A long lease period includes any period during which the lease is or was continued under either the Leasehold Property (Temporary Provisions) Act 1951, Part I of the Landlord and Tenant Act 1954 or under Sch 10 to the Local Government Housing Act 1989 (s 7(5)).

87 Section 7(1)(b). A lease terminable by notice after a death or remarriage is not to be treated as a long lease if the notice is capable of being given at any time after the death or marriage of the tenant, the length of the notice is not more than three months and the terms of the lease preclude both assignment and sub-letting of the whole of the premises comprised in the lease (s 7(2)). Permissible assignments by way of exchange under the Housing Act 1985, s 92 do not prevent assignments being precluded.

88 Section 7(1)(c). The reversioner in such a case may well be the local authority. The rent to mortgage provisions are introduced, by way of amendment, by Part II of the 1993 Act.

89 Section 7(1)(d). There is a statutory definition of a shared ownership lease in s 7(7), and total share is also defined. The initial year, for the purpose of determining whether such shared ownership lease is at low rent, is calculated as if the commencement date was the date when the tenant's total share became 100 per cent (see s 8(6)).

4 Any tenancy of a property which is a subsequent tenancy to a long lease at low rent, which has now expired; such subsequent tenancy, whether by express grant or by implication of law, is deemed by the Act to be a long lease irrespective of its terms.[90]
5 Leases originally granted for a term of years certain which do not exceed 21 years but which contain a covenant or obligation for non-perpetual renewal provided that no premium is paid.[91]
6 Leases which have been renewed on one or more occasions so that the total of the terms so granted is more than 21 years, the period to include any interval between the end of a lease and the grant of a renewal.[92]

3.7.3 Two or more leases of a flat between the same parties

There is a special provision[93] for situations where there are two or more separate leases but the same landlord and the same tenant. In such cases, provided those separate leases are long leases, and provided that the property in one of the leases consists of the flat or a part of it[94] and in the other of part of the flat or appurtenant property only, then the Act applies to them as if they were a single lease of that flat, and as if the lease was a long lease. This anti-avoidance provision ensures that division of a flat into separate leases will not prevent there from being a single long lease of the flat for the purposes of collective enfranchisement.

3.8 A lease at low rent

3.8.1 The requirement

The qualifying tenant's long lease must be a lease of a flat[95] at a low rent. It differs from previous statutory definitions of low rent by being based on the rent in the initial year and ignores any subsequent increase.[96]

3.8.2 The low rent test

For the purposes of the Act, a lease of a flat is a lease at a low rent under any of the following circumstances:[97]

---

90 Section 7(3).
91 Section 7(4)(a).
92 Section 7(4)(b).
93 Section 7(6). Leases treated as a single lease by virtue of s 7(6) are 'let with other property' under the Act (s 101(7)).
94 A lease of the flat or part of it may be with or without appurtenant property.
95 Any appurtenant property (as defined, see 3.2.2) let with the flat to the tenant under the lease is included (s 8(7)).
96 It therefore differs from the Leasehold Reform Act 1967, s 4, which is amended by the 1993 Act (see s 65 and 17.3.1).
97 Section 8.

(a) where no rent was payable under it in respect of the flat during the initial year;[98] or

(b) where the lease was entered into before 1 April 1963, the aggregate amount of rent so payable during the initial year did not exceed two-thirds of the letting value of the flat (on the same terms) on the date of commencement of the lease;[99]

(c) where the lease was either entered into on or after 1 April 1963 but before 1 April 1990 (or on or after 1 April 1990 if in pursuance of a contract made before that date) and the flat had a rateable value[100] at the date of commencement of the lease or at any time before 1 April 1990, the aggregate amount of rent so payable during the initial year did not exceed two-thirds of the rateable value of the flat on the appropriate date;[101]

(d) in any other case, the aggregate amount of rent payable during the initial year did not exceed £1000 if the flat is in Greater London or £250 if elsewhere.[102]

The low rent test, as defined, caused considerable opposition during the passage of the Bill through Parliament. In particular, it was felt that the considerable number of long leaseholders might find that their right to collective enfranchisement was not available because their rent was just above the defined level. However, attempts to increase the limits to bring more leases within the statutory definition was resisted by the Government.

3.8.3 Scope to avoid the Act in future

The definition offers limited scope to landlords to avoid the provisions of the Act – at least in the future. No doubt freeholders who wish to avoid collective enfranchisement will ensure that new leases within blocks are granted at rents above the statutory limit but existing leases will not, of course, be affected.[103]

3.8.4 Definition of terms

Section 8(2) contains a definition of the following terms.

'*Initial year*', which means a period of one year beginning at the date of commencement of the lease.[104]

98 Section 8(1). This provision means that, in new leases, particular care must be taken when rent-free periods, for whatever reason, are being considered.

99 Section 8(1)(a).

100 For the purpose of determining the amount of rateable value of a flat on a particular date, the Rent Act 1977, s 25 applies (s 8(2)(c)).

101 Section 8(1)(b).

102 Section 8(1)(c).

103 See also 10.1.1.

104 A lease commences when it is executed and dated and not on the date from which the term is calculated (*Roberts v Church Commissioners for England* [1972] 1 QB 278 , confirmed by the declaratory definition in s 101(5)).

'*Appropriate date*', which means the date of commencement of the lease or the date on which the flat first had a rateable value if it did not have a rateable value when the lease commenced.

'*Rent*' which means rent reserved as such and there shall be disregarded any part of the rent expressed to be payable in consideration of services, repairs, maintenance or insurance to be affected by the landlord; and any provision for suspension or reduction of rent in the event of damage is disregarded for these purposes.

The reference to *letting value* is to be construed in the same way as under the proviso in s 4(1) of the Leasehold Reform Act 1967 where low rent is defined for the purposes of that Act.[105] Regard should be had to whether a premium might have been lawfully demanded as the whole or part of the consideration for the letting.[106]

Where a lease which has been renewed on one or more occasions is to be treated as a long lease[107] then, for the purposes of determining whether it is at a low rent, the lease is deemed to have been entered into on the date of the last renewal and that date is deemed to be the date of commencement of the lease.[108]

---

105 Section 8(3). Unfortunately, that proviso does not define 'letting value' and has been described by one experienced practitioner and author as 'ill-considered and poorly drafted' (Hague, *Leasehold Enfranchisement*, 2nd edn, 1987, Sweet & Maxwell, pp 3–15 where there is a valuable discussion of the proviso). Letting value under the 1967 Act has been construed in *Johnson v Duke of Westminster* [1986] AC 839 to mean 'the best annual return obtainable in the open market for a grant of a long lease on the same terms whether this is achieved by letting at a rack rent or letting it at a lower rent plus the payment of a premium'. If this involves 'decapitalising' the premium and expressing it in annual terms, 'letting value' may exceed the market rent.

106 Section 8(4).

107 By virtue of s 7(4) (see above).

108 Section 8(5).

CHAPTER FOUR

COLLECTIVE ENFRANCHISEMENT – PRELIMINARY STEPS

4.1 Outline of the preliminary work required

4.1.1 The need

Before any right of collective enfranchisement can be commenced by the service of an initial notice under s 13 of the 1993 Act, a considerable amount of detailed preliminary work is necessary by the professional advisers, solicitor and surveyor or valuer, acting for those tenants who are considering exercising their right. Of the suggested steps below, only preliminary inquiries are the subject of specific statutory provision; but unless a claim is meticulously prepared in advance, there may be problems in meeting the procedural timetable or in otherwise seeing the enfranchisement to a successful conclusion. The necessary preliminary work may fall into the categories suggested below; this chapter then analyses these aspects in more detail[1] in the order in which, logically, they are likely to be considered by the proposed enfranchisees and their advisers.

4.1.2 Are the statutory requirements satisfied?

The solicitor will need to ensure that the tenants satisfy all the statutory requirements for a claim to be made. These requirements have been analysed in the preceding chapter.[2] A preliminary assessment of whether the premises qualify will have to be made by the solicitor when first consulted; the assembling of information during preparation for a claim will show if the assessment was correct, but before an initial notice is given, a final evaluation to make sure all the requirements are met will be advisable.

4.1.3 Preliminary assessment of the cost

The valuer acting for the tenants will need to make a preliminary assessment of the likely value of the freehold and any intermediate leasehold interests to be acquired. This will enable the tenants to decide whether they can afford and

---

1 On the assumption that there is sufficient basis to assume the premises qualify for a claim to collective enfranchisement to be made, see chapter three.

2 See 3.2.1.

wish to proceed with the enfranchisement. If the tenants agree to proceed in the light of the preliminary assessment of the sums involved, the detailed statutory valuation required by the Act will need to be completed by the tenant's valuer before the initial notice can be served.

4.1.4 A participator's agreement

Ideally, the solicitor should address the issue of preparing a written agreement between the participating tenants who are exercising the right of collective enfranchisement. This agreement, which will probably be termed the 'participators' agreement', will address the division between them of the respective sums to be paid to secure the freehold and of the costs of the acquisition. The possibilities of one participating tenant selling a flat or the death of a tenant during the enfranchisement process could be addressed. A prudent solicitor will also make provision for the situation where one or more of the participating tenants later discovers that they will have difficulty in raising their share of the finance. There is no statutory guidance in the 1993 Act on these issues but tenants will be ill-advised to proceed without a clear and comprehensive agreement between them. Where an agreement has not been reached there are potential conflict of interest problems for professional advisers to a group of tenants. Difficult differences of opinion, perhaps on the current market value of each flat, may have to be resolved by separate advice from other solicitors or surveyors. An alternative would be for the collective enfranchisement to be postponed while the individual tenants exercise their right to a new lease which may make the agreement on a later acquisition of the freehold easier since the value of that freehold will be much reduced by the new leases granted.[3]

4.1.5 Costs fund

A 'costs fund' will usually be required. The costs to be covered will include both those eventually due to the reversioner as required by the Act and the costs paid to the tenants' own advisers, which will include their solicitor and valuer. The expense of initial preparation may in itself be considerable – for example, full office copies of all the registered titles and all the leases may be needed and the cost of these alone will soon mount up.

4.1.6 Financing the transaction

The financing of the proposed transaction will not be easy but it must be established prior to the giving of the initial notice. An individual tenant's share may be raised prospectively by the agreement of the mortgagee bank or building society to grant a fresh mortgage on a 999-year lease to be granted by the nominee purchaser after enfranchisement. Such funds will only be available at completion and would necessitate the grant of those 999-year leases

3 See 12.5.1.

simultaneously with completion of the collective enfranchisement. Such mortgage funds will not cover the purchase of reversions to flats or units of non-participating tenants and are unlikely to cover costs. Access to other sources of funding or loans may be required. The financing arrangements will also need to cover provision of the deposit on entering into a binding contract.

4.1.7 The nominee purchaser

The participating tenants must decide upon a nominee purchaser. The negotiations to secure the freehold are carried out on behalf of the tenants by the nominee purchaser. It is, therefore, necessary, prior to commencement of the claim, to secure agreement on whom the nominee purchaser is to be. In most situations, this will involve the creation of a suitable corporate personality such as a management company in which the participating tenants will have appropriate shares.[4]

4.1.8 Preparing the initial notice

The solicitor will need to assemble all the information and details required when the initial notice exercising the right is served on the reversioner.[5]

4.1.9 Preparing for the subsequent procedure

The solicitor will need to assemble in advance the information which may be required later in the procedural steps taken in the process of collective enfranchisement. Since the procedure is subject to strict time-limits, it is very important that the tenants' advisers have to hand the information which they will need to respond to steps taken during the process by the reversioner's solicitor or advisers.

4.1.10 Local search

An early local search should be carried out as standard procedure. It should be checked particularly to see whether a compulsory purchase notice to treat has been given.[6]

4.2 Preliminary assessment of the cost

4.2.1 Involvement of a qualified surveyor at the outset

An early assessment of the likely cost of enfranchisement is essential, given that a group of tenants is unlikely to take the first steps of the process unless they

4 The status, duties and responsibilities of the nominee purchaser, and the considerations to be taken into account in deciding whether this should be a company, individual or some other mechanism is discussed at 5.7.3 below.

5 For full details of what an initial notice must contain, see 6.1.10 below.

6 Service of a notice to treat will prevent an enfranchisement (see 3.4.4).

have a clear idea of the expense involved, and consider that they have the means to raise the necessary finance. Indeed, an over-zealous group of tenants who plan to proceed without the ability to finance the premium and costs and a clear basis for division of that expense must be advised to be more patient and cautious. By the time the initial notice commencing the procedure is started,[7] it will be necessary to have obtained a valuation prepared by a qualified surveyor, prepared in conformity with the provisions of Sch 6 to the Act. Consequently, the involvement of the surveyor right from the outset of the preliminary procedure is essential.

4.2.2 General assessment or statutory valuation?

The tenants will have a choice at this early stage either to ask the surveyor immediately to prepare the necessary valuation in accordance with the Act or, alternatively, they could ask the surveyor to do the more simple preliminary valuation to give them some idea of the costs involved and only ask for the more detailed specific valuation for the purposes of the Act once they have decided to proceed.

The statutory requirements for a valuation within s 13 and Sch 6 are considered later.[8] What will be necessary at this stage of the process is for the surveyor to make a preliminary assessment of the value of the freehold interest (and of any intermediate leasehold interests which will have to be acquired) in the premises. To do that, he may have to work on certain assumptions until full information about the freehold title and the details of all the leases have been obtained. For this reason, the better approach would be to delay the statutory valuation until all the information on which it is based is confirmed. The surveyor may also need to make a valuation judgment in respect of the flats of the tenants involved to enable advice on the sharing of the costs of acquisition. In many instances, however, the preliminary valuation may be able to be assessed on the basis of the expectation that the flat leases (or a group of them) are in similar or identical form, and the leases have the same specified number of years remaining. A value will also have to be placed on any superior leasehold interests which are to be acquired under the Act[9] and of any appurtenant freehold property which must be acquired by virtue of s 1(2)(a) which is included in the property granted by any of the leases held by any of the qualifying tenants.

4.3 Preliminary meeting of qualifying tenants

4.3.1 Not a statutory requirement

At an early stage in the process it will be advisable to notify all the qualifying tenants (or those believed to be qualifying tenants) within the block of flats of

7 See 6.1.1.

8 For which see 19.1.

9 See 19.6.1.

the right of collective enfranchisement which is believed to exist and the intention of the prime movers to consider whether that right should be exercised. No doubt a meeting, to which all such potential qualifying tenants should be invited, will be held at an early stage of the process. However, it is one of the features of the legislation that there is not only no necessity for such a preliminary meeting but that there is also no requirement that every potential qualifying tenant should be informed of the intention to make a claim – let alone be given the opportunity to participate.[10] In many cases, it will be in everyone's interest to involve as many of the qualifying tenants as possible to ensure both that the statutory requirements are met and also to reduce the percentage of the cost borne by each individual tenant. One can envisage situations, however, where it is desired to exclude one or more individuals or persons. There appears to be no clear basis on which an excluded qualifying tenant could obtain a court order to insist on participation.[11]

4.3.2 Role of professional advisers

It may be advisable for the solicitor and surveyor to be present at any preliminary meeting to explain the legal process and the valuation method. It will be important to secure a preliminary agreement to proceed or to make further progress in preparing a claim for collective enfranchisement from a sufficient number of the qualifying tenants to satisfy the requirements of the Act. The involvement of the minimum number of two-thirds of the qualifying tenants (half of whom must satisfy the residence condition) in the premises is essential if the claim is to proceed. Once a tentative agreement to be involved has been made, the professional advisers will assist in moving towards a firm commitment from those qualifying tenants who expressed an interest. It may be necessary only to advise generally; advice to an individual qualifying tenant may have to be considered on each occasion in the light of any potential conflict of interest arising from acting for the group of tenants as a whole. Once the initial notice is served, then those qualifying tenants who are participating in the claim are defined by the Act as 'participating tenants'.

4.3.3 Qualifying tenants by whom the initial notice is given

Those qualifying tenants who commit themselves to giving the initial notice are referred to in the Act as 'the qualifying tenants by whom the notice is given'. This is the body of tenants who are the clients of any solicitor and surveyor dealing with a claim. They become the participating tenants; in turn defined[12]

10 A tenant will probably hear about the proposal or initial notice in other ways – such as when a right of access is exercised (see 6.3.1).

11 The problem of an excluded qualifying tenant is discussed more fully at 5.2.3.

12 Section 14. The status, rights and obligations of a participating tenant is considered at 5.6.1.

first, as the qualifying tenants by whom the initial notice is given; but secondly in relation to any time after the notice, such of the qualifying tenants giving the initial notice who remain a qualifying tenant of a flat contained in the specified premises. Although the participating tenants will make their collective claim for enfranchisement through the medium of the nominee purchaser[13] that nominee purchaser may be a corporate personality without assets formed for the purposes of the claim. Consequently, it will be to the participating tenants that the solicitor and surveyor primarily look for the not inconsiderable costs of proceeding with the claim, and it will be the participating tenants who, in the event of a successful claim, will finance the purchase of the freehold through the nominee purchaser and will be liable, not only for their own legal and valuation fees and costs, and those of the nominee purchaser, but also the relevant costs of the reversioner in dealing with the claim.[14] In turn, no doubt, the participating tenants, once they have secured the freehold, will look to their solicitors to grant to them fresh 999-year leases on their flat and so secure the individual benefits of collective enfranchisement.[15]

4.4 Apportioning the cost

4.4.1 Sharing the price and cost's burden

Once the meeting of qualifying tenants has agreed, in principle, to make a claim for collective enfranchisement in the light of the preliminary assessment of the overall cost, the next question which will be asked is what the relevant share of each participating tenant will be. The larger the percentage of qualifying tenants who participate (above the statutory two-thirds limit) the more there will be to share the burden and the less each participating tenant will have to pay. The vital question, though, is the percentage that each participating tenant has to bear.

4.4.2 Equal division?

In many instances, the solution which may be both equitable and straightforward will be equal shouldering of the burden of costs between each of the participating tenants. Each can then have an equal share in the value of the freehold so acquired, but this may only be possible where the participating tenants have flats of very similar value and held for identical terms. A good guide may be to look at the leases and consider the contribution which is required from each tenant towards the service charge. In many instances, the

13 The choice of a nominee purchaser is considered at 5.7.1.

14 Section 33. For full details, see 9.2.2.

15 There is no requirement to grant fresh leases, although the valuation basis assumes this. If the existing leases are satisfactory to the participating tenants, they do not have to be changed.

levying of the service charge will be of an equal percentage in each case, so a block of 20 very similar flats may each provide, for example, a five per cent service charge. A minimum of 14 such flats within that block will need to be let to qualifying tenants for a claim for enfranchisement to be made, and a minimum of 10 will need to be ready to be involved as participating tenants, five of whom must satisfy the residence condition.[16] If 16 tenants make a claim for collective enfranchisement then it would be reasonable to assume that they will be ready to agree to share the burden of the costs equally and take a 6.25 percentage share of the costs.

4.4.3 *A matter for negotiation*

The Act gives no guidance as to this division of the costs between the participating tenants. It is entirely a matter for agreement between them. Thus, where one or more flats in a block, perhaps a penthouse flat, contributes a larger proportion of the service charge to reflect the flat size or amenities, then it is probably right that the tenant of that particular flat should take on the greater share in the acquisition of the freehold. In such cases, division of expense in accordance with the service charge provisions may still be possible. However, a more complex calculation may have to be made based on the market value of the flat of each participating tenant and, perhaps, the likely value of each flat with a 999-year lease after enfranchisement.

4.4.4 *Covering the cost of non-participating flats and of units*

Where the successful claim will result in the participating tenants taking the reversion to flats of non-participating tenants or commercial units, further adjustments will need to be considered. In some cases, the value of such reversions may be shared equally and, therefore, the cost of acquisition of, and the benefit of reversion to, those parts will be shared equally. In others, it may be that the collective enfranchisement can only proceed if one or two more wealthy participating tenants take on the burden (and the investment benefit) of acquiring those valuable reversionary elements. In such circumstances, the relevant part of the costs of such acquisition would be borne by those individuals.[17]

4.4.5 *Resolving disputes*

There is undoubtedly room for dispute here. There may be situations where leases provide for equal contribution to the service charge but some of the flats enjoy greater amenities, such that the value of their current leases are higher

16 This example assumes that there are only 14 qualifying tenants. If all 20 were qualifying tenants then at least 14 must give the notice. If, for example, 16 gave the initial notice, then eight must satisfy the residence condition. See, further, 6.1.7.

17 An agreement entirely between participating tenants does not have to be revealed under the duty of disclosure. See s 18 and the discussion at 6.5.1.

because of those amenities (rather than because of the state of repair or the improvements made to the property). One example might be a block of four flats where only one flat has the benefit of the garden. It may be difficult for a professional, whether solicitor or valuer, who is retained by the group as a whole to advise on the resolution of such issues. If a conflict of interest arises, either separate advice for each tenant will be required or those tenants meeting the residence requirement may choose to pursue a new lease first and return to a collective enfranchisement later.[18]

Given that each of the participating tenants will secure not only the ability to grant to themselves the 999-year lease of their own flat at a nominal peppercorn rent but may also acquire an equal share in the reversion of the flats which are occupied by qualifying tenants who are not participating,[19] it may be sensible to operate, where possible, on the basis that the participating tenants will share equally the burden of the cost of acquiring the freehold and the costs involved.

4.5 Participators' agreement

4.5.1 The need

It is anticipated that all but the most straightforward and simple claims will require some sort of agreement among the participating tenants; even in a case of a few tenants in a block where all are participating and the money required from each has been made available in advance, it will be prudent to record what is proposed in formal written terms.

4.5.2 Parties to the agreement

All participating tenants should agree on the basis to proceed with a collective enfranchisement and sign an agreement to that effect. Just as with the necessity to sign the initial notice, the formality will highlight the obligations being undertaken and give an opportunity to explain the commitment. The nominee purchaser should also be a party. If the nominee purchaser is an individual who is also a participating tenant, that person should be a party to the agreement in both capacities. In cases where a non-qualifying tenant, whether a tenant in the premises, such as a business tenant or a complete outsider, is involved in the acquisition in some financial capacity, that involvement will be better reflected in a separate agreement[20] with the nominee purchaser rather than as part of a participator's agreement.

---

18 As discussed at 12.5.1.

19 The reversion to flats of qualifying tenants must be purchased; they may also have to acquire the reversion to some leases of flats where the tenants are not qualifying tenants and to all units if the reversioner's optional right of leaseback is not exercised (see 9.5.3).

20 Which will be subject to the duty of disclosure (see 6.5.1).

4.5.3 *When required*

Some sort of agreement will be needed prior to the entry into a binding contract between the reversioner and the nominee purchaser. However, it may be inadvisable to leave an agreement until after the enfranchisement process has commenced; it will be important that the extent of the commitment of each participating tenant is known and secured as far as possible before the procedure commences and the costs liability arises.

4.5.4 *Contents of the agreement*

This will need to be tailored to the individual situation but the following suggestions for inclusion are put forward.

1 To assist in meeting the statutory requirements, each participating tenant should warrant that they rank as a qualifying tenant and they are not disqualified from participating in any way.[21] Those participators who so qualify should equally warrant that they meet the residence condition. Although improbable, each participating tenant should agree not to acquire another flat lease without consent of the others or the nominee purchaser.[22] In a case where one joint tenant participates on behalf of the other(s), it will be important that there is a warranty that the authority of each joint tenant has been given. A better solution where there are joint owners is for all to sign the participators' agreement.

2 To enable the financing of the enfranchisement, the percentage share agreed of each participating tenant should be specified and an obligation imposed to pay and to take up that share in the nominee purchaser where appropriate.

3 The percentage share of a participating tenant will increase if one or more of the others is unable to meet their obligations. To reduce that possibility, each participating tenant could be obliged, on an assignment of an interest in the flat while a claim is current, to require any purchaser to elect to participate at completion of the sale of the flat.[23] If this is not done the purchaser of a flat from a participating tenant has the right to elect to participate, but has no obligation to do so. Similarly, the death of a participating tenant could be very inconvenient since personal representatives have a period of 56 days to elect to withdraw from participation.[24] It may be possible for the lives of all the

---

21 See 5.6.2.

22 To avoid ceasing to be a qualifying tenant by virtue of being a tenant of three or more (see 3.5.4).

23 See s 14(2) and 5.6.5. Such a requirement may be resisted by one or more individuals. It is exactly the sort of issue where there may be issues of a conflict of interest. The term may be in the interests of the participating tenants as a whole but could work to the detriment of an individual tenant who finds a sale of the flat on these terms difficult.

24 See s 14(4) and 5.6.6.

individual participating tenants to be insured for the period of the claim, at least for any loss incurred through delay or inability to proceed as a result of a death.[25]

4 Since, at completion, participating tenants must pay any arrears of service charge and rent due under their existing leases, an obligation so to do should be in the participators' agreement.

5 The nominee purchaser will usually be a company controlled by the participating tenants.[26] However, notwithstanding the fact that it may be pointless for the tenants to sue their own company, the nominee purchaser should be under a duty to proceed with the claim with all due diligence, register the estate contract after service of the initial notice, observe all time-limits, observe the duty of disclosure and complete the purchase of the freehold. Where appropriate, the nominee purchaser should also be under a duty to grant to each participating tenant new leases, prospective mortgages of which may be financing the transaction. The terms of the new leases should be agreed in advance.

6 Decisions may have to be taken by the nominee purchaser during a collective enfranchisement claim in the light of the response of the reversioner to the claim. This may relate to the proposals for leaseback, whether to challenge or accept the reversioner's proposals on the price payable, whether to appeal against decisions of the court or leasehold valuation tribunal, and so forth. The participators' agreement should set out clearly how such decisions are to be reached.

7 A nominee purchaser who is an individual or trustee acting on behalf of others will need suitable indemnities from the participating tenants.

8 The services of a lawyer and valuer will almost certainly be required throughout the claim. The participators' agreement should name the agreed solicitors and surveyors and provide that they should only be removed or changed by a specified procedure, such as a majority vote at a meeting called for the purpose. Such a procedure could also be used to deal with any future disputes among the participators.

9 The participators' agreement could establish a costs fund, providing for the initial contribution of each participator and for further calls for payments when required, with an obligation to make such payments. In view of the joint and several liability on withdrawal,[27] and because the nominee

25 It will almost certainly be too great an added complication to get all the participating tenants to make a will or a codicil seeking to instruct the executors not to withdraw from participation; advising each tenant on the implications and drawing up details of how it might be possible to continue to participate after a death in each individual case would be a substantial undertaking.

26 See 5.7.3.

27 See 8.2.3.

purchaser will need to be put in funds for costs at completion, a costs fund is desirable to minimise the risks associated with one or more participating tenants not meeting their share of the costs. The mode of financing the deposit payable at exchange of contracts needs to be addressed.[28]

4.6 Financing the transaction

4.6.1 Finance through security of new long leases

The finance of each collective enfranchisement will depend so much on the particular circumstances that only a few general principles can be put forward.

It is anticipated that the use of the security offered by new long leases to be granted after the enfranchisement is likely to be an element, if not a substantial element, in most cases. Individual participators will arrange for loans to be secured upon the new long leases of each participator's flat for 999 years at a peppercorn or nominal rent;[29] such leases to be granted after the completion of the enfranchisement. This will be complex conveyancing, necessitating the completion of the enfranchisement, the grant of the new leases, and the new mortgages all on the same day. The funds so made available will cover the value of that participator's share but it is unlikely that it will cover costs and certainly not the cost of covering the reversions to flats and units not held by participating tenants.

The arrangements for such financing should be by way of the participators loaning a sum, to the value of the new lease, to the nominee purchaser who will then grant the new lease for the same amount, thus clearing the loan. A purchase of a share in the nominee purchaser, who then grants the new lease for a nominal sum, could have adverse tax complications.[30]

Some participating tenants may have difficulty in servicing the necessary loan on their new lease. In such cases, for example with a retired tenant, another family member could guarantee such a loan; or private financing, for example involving a second mortgage or the grant of a shared interest in the new lease, may be possible.

4.6.2 Financing the purchase of reversions to other units

The financing through the medium of security of long leases granted after completion will not cover the element of value in the freehold represented by reversions to flats and units which are not participating in the enfranchisement. If these are subject to mandatory leaseback, the value will be retained by the landlord; similarly if the choice is made by the reversioner to take a leaseback of

28 See 7.6.3.
29 See 9.6.2 for a brief discussion of whether a rent is desirable.
30 The risk would be that the grant of the leases could be taken as a distribution giving rise to advance corporation tax.

other units such as commercial lettings or flats not let to qualifying tenants. However, the reversioner's decision on leaseback will not be known until the counter-notice stage – unless a position can be reached by private negotiation in advance.[31] Thus, finance may have to be arranged to cover such elements. The security of the freehold may be available – provided it has value after the grant of new long leases to the participating tenants. This will only be the case if there are commercial units at a market rent or flats with Rent Act or assured tenants. The value may still, even then, be insufficient to secure the full balance required.

4.6.3 Other sources of finance

Resort may then be required to other sources of finance. One or more participating tenants may be able to find resources to put into the purchase and be rewarded accordingly with a greater share. Such contributions could be covered by a reversionary lease on non-participating flats and units and a proportionate increase in shares in the nominee purchaser company.

4.6.4 Financing the reversions to flats of non-participating qualifying tenants

The reversioner has no right to a leaseback of the flats of qualifying tenants who do not participate. The participating tenants will always need to cover the cost of this element in the purchase. One way is for all participators to put in equal amounts by way of loan to the nominee purchaser. When the qualifying tenant of that flat elects to participate, or applies for a new extended lease under the Act, the premium then received can be used to repay those loans.[32] However, a participator who later sells his or her own flat before recoupment of the investment will be left with that investment outstanding, unless it can be sold to the purchaser of the flat. An alternative is for one or more of the participating tenants, perhaps those with a long-term interest in the block of flats, individually to cover the cost, taking a reversionary lease of the flat concerned as security.

4.7 Obtaining information

4.7.1 Assembling the information

A considerable amount of information will need to be collected both to serve the initial notice and to satisfy the probable riposte of the reversioner seeking verification of the right to participate of all the tenants.[33] Much of this

31 Such agreement to leaseback may result in a full agreement to purchase the freehold without resort to the statutory procedure. The terms of the leaseback would have to be agreed to tie in with any new leases to be granted to the participators.

32 At such repayment, it will be necessary to consider any capital gains tax implications.

33 Under s 20. See 6.4.1.

information can be obtained without recourse to the statutory procedure for inquiries. Thus, tenants may be able to produce the necessary copies of their title deeds and leases. Good plans may be obtainable from the Ordnance Survey or other sources. Where the titles in the block of flats are all registered, the public right of inspection will enable office copies of the titles and copies of leases to be obtained from the land registry. Although the cost will not be insignificant,[34] it may be cheaper and certainly more convenient than seeking early production of title deeds from a large number of mortgagees.[35] Index map searches should reveal if any relevant land or premises remains unregistered title. The statutory procedure to obtain information will, however, usually have to be resorted to.

4.7.2 Preliminary inquiries by tenants

The Act contains comprehensive provisions enabling tenants to obtain information about the title to their block of flats. These provisions are contained in ss 11 and 12 of the Act. A preliminary inquiry under s 11 is the only formal stage of the process which a tenant or tenants can take which does not commit them in any way to costs or to any further action – in contrast to the proceedings following an initial notice under s 13.[36] The time for instituting any formal initial inquiry under s 11 will depend very much on the particular situation – it will be a tactical decision. In some cases, the tenants will have sufficient information amongst themselves to make the preliminary assessments necessary, as discussed above, to ascertain whether there are sufficient qualifying tenants to enable a claim for collective enfranchisement to be made, and to provide the surveyor with sufficient information to proceed to make some preliminary valuations. In those cases, the preliminary inquiries under s 11 may be delayed until just before an initial notice is given, and their purpose may be to ensure that the initial notice under s 11 is given to the reversioner in respect of the premises and that the assumptions on which the calculations have proceeded are exactly correct.

In other situations, it may be important to use the rights under s 11 to ascertain details at an early stage; for example, to obtain details of the tenancy of other persons within the relevant premises and thereby calculate whether there is a sufficient number of qualifying tenants entitled to proceed with the claim.

The giving of any notice under s 11 will have the effect of alerting the recipient, and thereby probably the freeholder and any superior leaseholder, that a claim is being considered under the Act, and in some situations the advisers to the tenants may wish to delay such a notice as long as possible.

---

34 The current cost for a set of office copies of a title is £16.00.

35 The deeds to each flat will almost certainly eventually be required except in a case, perhaps, of existing 999-year flat leases where no fresh leases are to be granted after acquisition of the freehold and there are no valuation issues which depend upon details from the deeds.

36 See 6.1.1.

4.7.3 May be initiated by a single qualifying tenant

The preliminary inquiries which can be given under s 11 can each be given by any single qualifying tenant[37] but the inquiries may, of course, be activated on behalf of a group of tenants acting together. An individual interested in pursuing a claim for collective enfranchisement may, therefore, make a number of inquiries on his or her own account before ever involving either the other tenants or the professional services of a solicitor or surveyor.

The preliminary inquiries which can be given fall into three main categories. Two are straightforward; the third gives rise to more complex consequences and therefore needs more careful analysis.

4.7.4 Obtaining the name and address of the freeholder – s 11(1)

A qualifying tenant of a flat may give a notice requiring the recipient to give to that tenant (so far as is known) the name and address of the person who owns the freehold of the relevant premises.[38] Such a notice may be given either to the immediate landlord of the tenant or to any person receiving rent on behalf of the immediate landlord.[39] Thus, if the only person the tenant knows of is the person receiving the rent then that is the person who can initially be served with a notice to require this information.

A notice requiring the name and address of the freeholder may also ask for the name and address of every other person who has an interest either in the freehold of any property not contained in the relevant premises but which is demised by the lease held by the tenant, or the freehold of property which the tenant is entitled, under the terms of the lease, to use in common with other persons.[40] Such property might, for example, be a garage situated away from the flat or property over which the tenant has rights of access. The notice can, and should, also ask for the name and address of any leasehold interest in the relevant premises which is superior to that of the immediate landlord of the tenant.[41]

When giving a request under s 11(1), it will be advisable to always ask for the details of any superior leasehold interest, as the tenant may not know whether such a leasehold interest exists. The tenant's lease should be checked to see if it does contain the freehold of any other property not in the relevant premises or if the tenant is entitled to use property in common and, if that is the case, then that information would be requested as well.

---

37 Section 11(1), (3) and (4).

38 For the purposes of s 11, 'relevant premises' is defined in s 11(9) by reference to the person who has the ultimate freehold interest in the flat of the qualifying tenant who gives the notice. Therefore, the relevant premises is the whole of the building in which the flat is contained if the person owns the freehold of the whole of that building but if the person owns the freehold of only part of the building then the relevant premises is that part.

39 Section 11(1)(a) and (b).

40 Section 11(2) (a).

41 Section 11(2) (b).

4.7.5 Requiring the name and address of other tenants – s 11(3)

Once the tenant has ascertained the name and address of the person who owns the freehold (by notice if necessary), a notice may be given to that freeholder requiring the freeholder to give to the tenant (so far as it is known to him) the name and address of every person, apart from the tenant giving the notice, who is a tenant or licensee of the whole or part of the relevant premises. Under this provision,[42] the tenant can ask for the name and address of a tenant of the whole of the relevant premises, or the tenant or licensee of every separate set or sets of premises, or the tenant or licensee of the whole or a part of the common parts demised by the lease or which the tenant is entitled to use (whether contained in the relevant premises or not). Such a notice can, therefore, require the name and address of the tenants of each of the flats and units in the block.

4.8 Ascertaining details of interests in the premises – s 11(4)

4.8.1 Nature of the inquiry

The third, most complex and most important preliminary notice, is ascertaining the nature of each interest, freehold and leasehold, within the relevant premises. A clear and correct understanding of all the existing interests is necessary if decisions to make a claim for collective enfranchisement and undertake the necessary valuations are to be made on a sound basis. It is important to understand that:

(a) the notice must or may require the recipient to supply up to four pieces of information;[43]
(b) the notice provides for the qualifying tenant giving the notice to have three rights which can be exercised;[44]
(c) the notice may result in the recipient having one or more of three different duties of subsequent notification to the qualifying tenant.[45]

4.8.2 Obtaining information about interests held by recipient of the notice

After obtaining, where necessary, the names and addresses of each of the persons who have a freehold or leasehold interest in the relevant premises, the qualifying tenant can give to the freeholder or to any person who is a tenant or licensee of the whole or any part of the premises a notice requiring him to give to the tenant such information relating to his interest in the premises as

42 Section 11(3).
43 As detailed in 4.8.2 and 4.8.3.
44 Discussed at 4.8.4.
45 See 4.8.5–4.8.7.

specified in the notice.[46] The information requested must be reasonably required by the tenant in connection with the making of a claim to exercise the right of collective enfranchisement in relation to the whole or part of the relevant premises. It is not possible, therefore, to use the right under s 11(4) to get general information; the information must be needed to ascertain whether a claim to collective enfranchisement could be made or is needed in connection with such claim. The notice may also require the recipient to give to the tenant such information relating to any interest which is derived, whether directly or indirectly, out of that interest. Such notices should, therefore, ask for details of any intermediate leasehold interest or any sub-tenancies in relation to any part or the whole of the relevant premises. Possible recipients are not only the freeholder and superior lessees but any tenant or licensee of any flat, unit, premises or common parts within the relevant premises.

4.8.3 Information which the notice shall require to be given

In addition to the information relating to the interests, any s 11(4) notice shall require the recipient to give to the tenant two additional pieces of information.[47] These are:

(a) whether the recipient has received, in respect of any premises containing the tenant's flat, an initial notice or a copy of such notice relating to a claim which is still current.[48] If so, the date such initial notice was given and the name and address of the nominee purchaser appointed for that claim must be supplied;
(b) whether the tenant's flat is comprised in property designated under the Inheritance Tax Act 1984 within s 31 of the 1993 Act.[49]

4.8.4 Rights which become exercisable

When a qualifying tenant does give a notice under s 11(4) asking for details of the interest of the recipient then the Act gives, to the qualifying tenant, certain rights which are exercisable in relation to the recipient of the notice.[50] These rights are as follows.

---

46 Section 11(4).

47 Section 12(1). Because of the nature of the preliminary inquiry, it is not thought that failure to require this additional information results in an invalid inquiry despite the terminology of the statute 'shall require'. The context is not imperative (cf *United Scientific Holdings v Burnley Borough Council* [1978] AC 904).

48 Section 12(2). A claim is current (s 12(6)) if either the notice continues in force in accordance with s 13(11), or a binding contract remains in force pursuant to that notice or a court order for vesting the freehold in the nominee purchaser has been made (under s 24(4)(a) or (b) or s 25(6)(a) or (b)) but the interests have not yet been vested.

49 Section 12(3). For details of this specialised exemption which, if applicable, makes the initial notice of no effect, see 3.4.5. and 8.5.1.

50 Section 11(5).

1 A right, on giving reasonable notice, to be provided with a list of documents where the sight of those documents is reasonably required by the qualifying tenant in connection with the making of a claim. The document must be one which, on a proposed sale by a willing seller to a willing buyer, the seller would be expected to make available to the buyer whether at or before contract or completion.[51] The documents, therefore, cover documents of title, searches and inquiries usually supplied in a conveyancing transaction, but in all cases the sight of a particular document in question must be required in connection with the making of the claim to collective enfranchisement.
2 A right to inspect, at any reasonable time and on giving reasonable notice, any of those relevant documents.
3 A right, on payment of a reasonable fee, to be provided with a copy of any of the relevant documents contained in any list or inspected.

The right is one to be supplied with a list; and then a subsequent right either to inspect, or obtain copies, or both. The period of reasonable notice and the amount of a reasonable fee are not further defined in the Act.

4.8.5 Notification duties: giving notice of disposal

A person receiving a notice under s 11(4),[52] ie a notice asking for information relating to the interest of the recipient in the relevant premises, is under a duty to notify the qualifying tenant who gave the notice of any subsequent disposal of any interest in the relevant premises[53] unless the disposal has already been notified earlier. This duty applies for a period of six months beginning with the date of receipt of the notice from the qualifying tenant and applies to the disposal of any interest, whether legal or equitable, in the relevant premises except the creation of an interest by way of security for a loan. Similarly, the acquisition of any further interest must also be notified. The notification must be given to the qualifying tenant of the disposal or acquisition within a period of 28 days from the date when it occurred.

This provision is likely to be a headache for conveyancers. It is not only the freehold interest which may be affected; the tenant of any long lease in a block may have received a notice from one of his fellow tenants under s 11(4). Consequently, on the disposal of any interest within the premises which are subject to the Act the vendor may need to seek, from his client, details of any notices served. The purchasers' solicitor may raise a preliminary enquiry on the point.

4.8.6 Notification duties: subsequent receipt of an initial notice

Where the recipient of a s 11(4) notice subsequently, within a period of six months beginning with the date of receipt of the notice from the qualifying

51 Section 11(6).
52 It does not apply to notices under s 11(1) or (3).
53 Section 11(8).

tenant, receives an initial notice[54] in respect of premises which include the tenant's flat, or a copy of such notice, there arises another duty of notification[55] – unless, naturally, the qualifying tenant is one of those giving the initial notice. Once again, the notification must be given to the qualifying tenant within a period of 28 days beginning with the date of the receipt of the initial notice or copy. The notification must include the name and address of the nominee purchaser appointed in relation to that claim.

4.8.7 Notification duties: decision on inheritance tax designation

If the response to a s 11(4) notice informed the tenant that an application for designation under the Inheritance Tax Act 1984 or an application for a direction is pending, there is a duty of notification of the result of such pending decision; within 28 days of the decision the qualifying tenant must be notified if the application was granted, refused or withdrawn.[56]

4.9 Preliminary inquiries – time-limit for response

4.9.1 Twenty-eight days to respond

The recipient of any notice under this section,[57] whether the notice asks for information or asks for a list of documents or inspection of copies thereof, shall comply with the requirement in the notice within a period of 28 days beginning with the date of the giving of the notice or of requiring inspection of copies.[58]

4.9.2 No sanction for non-compliance

There is no specified penalty for non-compliance and, in default, the main remedy for the qualifying tenant is to make an application to the court.[59] The application would be for an order requiring the person who has failed to comply with the request in the notice to comply with the requirements imposed in the Act and make good the default within such time as the court specifies in the order. However, before making an application to the court, a further notice must be given requiring the person failing to comply to make good the default, and a period of 14 days must elapse from that second notice requiring compliance before the court application can be made.[60]

There is the prospect that some landlords may choose not to supply the information and prevaricate for some time. Too long a delay in response might

54 Under s 13 (see 6.1.1).
55 Section 12(4).
56 Section 12(5).
57 Ie, under s 11(1), (3) or (4).
58 Section 11(7).
59 Under s 92.
60 Section 92(2).

prompt tenants to ignore the remedy of seeking a court order to comply and to make a claim on the basis that the landlord cannot be found.[61] Such a move might place a landlord, who then makes his identity known, at a disadvantage.[62]

---

61 See s 26 and 7.8.1.

62 Because of the court's power under s 26(5)(b) – discussed at 7.8.5.

CHAPTER FIVE

THE PARTIES TO A CLAIM – AND THOSE OUTSIDE

5.1 The persons involved

A collective enfranchisement claim demands a clear appreciation of the different categories into which individuals and persons fall and the position, rights and duties of each. This chapter provides an analysis of the *dramatis personae*; not only the parties to a claim – the qualifying tenants, the participating tenants, the nominee purchaser, the reversioner and other relevant landlords – but also those necessarily outside the process but who may have a very real interest in the outcome of proceedings.

5.2 The qualifying tenants

5.2.1 Definition summarised

A qualifying tenant is a person who is the tenant of a flat under a long lease at low rent.[1] There is a full discussion of this definition and the exceptions in a previous chapter,[2] but the following essential features are worth recalling in this context.

1 There can only be one qualifying tenant for any flat at any one time.[3]
2 A qualifying tenant may be a corporate body.
3 A person may be a qualifying tenant of two flats within the same relevant premises but where a person is a qualifying tenant of three or more there is no qualifying tenant for any of those flats.[4]
4 If the lease is a business lease, there can be no qualifying tenant; but since a business lease is a tenancy to which Part II of the Landlord and Tenant Act

1 Section 5(1). Joint tenants of a flat together constitute the qualifying tenant (s 101(4)).
2 See 3.2.1–3.8.4.
3 Section 5(3).
4 Section 5(4) and see fuller discussion at 3.5.4.

1954 applies[5] there may be a qualifying tenant in those cases of mixed user which fall outside the 1954 Act.[6]

5.2.2 No guaranteed right to participate

The right to collective enfranchisement is available only if there is a sufficient number of qualifying tenants in the premises and it is only if the total number of flats held by qualifying tenants is at least two-thirds of the total number of flats that there are premises to which the Act applies.[7] Not every qualifying tenant has to participate for a claim to be made; although there are detailed requirements as to the minimum number of tenants necessary to proceed.[8] What the Act omits to provide is a right or opportunity to participate for a qualifying tenant who wishes to do so. Although there may be a financial benefit in involving all the qualifying tenants, or as many as possible, and although there may be risks in proceeding with the absolute minimum of qualifying tenants required,[9] there is no obligation either to inform every qualifying tenant of the intentions of other tenants in the premises or to give any opportunity to each qualifying tenant to be involved in any claim.[10]

5.2.3 A remedy for an excluded qualifying tenant?

For financial reasons, in most cases a qualifying tenant who wishes to participate will be welcomed; but the deliberate exclusion of one or more appears possible. There is no clear basis on which a court order could be made to require other qualifying tenants to allow an excluded qualifying tenant to join in. A bold court might, before an initial notice is given, allow an election to participate on the basis of s 14(3), which permits an election to participate after the initial notice only with agreement of all the persons who are then the participating tenants. It could be argued that such a provision implies a right to participate at the earlier date. Since it might also be thought contrary to the rationale of collective enfranchisement if one qualifying tenant could be excluded from participation by the others, it is possible to envisage a successful action by an excluded tenant.

---

5 Section 101(1).

6 For example, this will be the case if the lease of the flat was originally for residential purposes and the business use is incidental to the continuing use of the flat as a residence (*Cheryl Investments Ltd v Saldanha* [1978] 1 WLR 1329, CA). See also *Gurton v Parrott* [1991] 1 EGLR 98.

7 Section 3(1)(c) and see 3.3.1 ff.

8 See s 13 and 6.1.7.

9 In case one or more are found not to qualify or are excluded for some reason (see 6.1.9 below).

10 In the House of Lords, an amendment was proposed giving all tenants the right to participate in the initial notice. It was not accepted, the Minister arguing that it would be impracticable unless each tenant had a right to be part of the nominee – which would constrain the freedom of the tenants (see HL Deb, Vol 543, cols 1281–1286, 15 March 1993).

5.3 Qualifying tenants satisfying the residence condition

5.3.1 A minimum number at initial notice stage

For the purposes of collective enfranchisement it is sufficient if one half of the qualifying tenants who give the initial notice satisfy the residence condition.[11] This ensures that at least 50 per cent of those starting the claim have their only or principal home in their flat[12] but, apart from that crucial threshold, there is no other significance to the collective enfranchisement process between qualifying tenants who satisfy the residence condition and those who do not.

5.3.2 An example

The residence condition threshold should not be difficult to satisfy. If an example is postulated of 18 flats in premises, then a collective enfranchisement claim could be made with as few as five flats occupied by qualifying tenants who satisfy the residence condition. There would need to be 12 flats occupied by qualifying tenants (two-thirds of the total number of flats). If there are only 12 such flats the claim would need to be made by at least nine of those 12 (two-thirds of 12 is eight, but there is an overriding minimum of half the total number of flats) of whom five (the closest to half of nine) must satisfy the residence condition.

5.3.3 Temporary exclusion to permit a claim?

The residence condition could lead to the enforced temporary exclusion of some qualifying tenants who wish to participate to allow a claim to be made. In the example of 18 flats in premises, let us assume that all 18 are occupied by qualifying tenants but 12 of those flats are let to different corporate tenants and only six tenants are individuals satisfying the residence condition. If all 18 qualifying tenants gave the initial notice, nine need to satisfy the residence condition – which cannot be done. However, if only 12 of the qualifying tenants, including the six meeting the residence condition, give the initial notice,[13] the statutory minimum is met. The excluded qualifying tenants could, by agreement, be admitted as participators after the initial notice is given or at any later stage.

---

11 Section 13(2); and see 3.6.2 and 6.1.7.

12 For a detailed analysis of the residence condition requirement, see 3.6.1.

13 This is the minimum on this example, being two-thirds of the total number of qualifying tenants.

5.4 Qualifying tenants who do not participate

5.4.1 No compulsion

There is no compulsion on a qualifying tenant to participate in the collective enfranchisement process. Such a tenant may remain aloof and allow the other tenants to proceed and bear the costs. Such a qualifying tenant, if they satisfy the residence requirement for lease renewal,[14] will have the right to a new extended lease under Chapter II of the Act, a right which can be exercised before or after a collective enfranchisement claim but which will be suspended if still in train when an initial notice is served.[15]

5.4.2 Disadvantage of not participating

Qualifying tenants who do not participate may do so either by choice, practical necessity (eg they do not have the financial resources to contribute) or by exclusion by the participating tenants. Such qualifying tenants may find that they become second or even third class tenants after the conclusion of the enfranchisement. They will still enjoy all the rights as tenant given by the general law and their lease but they may be excluded from a full part in management which a share in the freehold would bring. For such tenants not participating, the enfranchisement may bring no benefits but only a set of potential new problems. A freehold controlled by only some tenants could be a powerful weapon or factor in management or other disputes between tenants.

'Second class tenants' could be the designation given to those non-participating qualifying tenants who satisfy the residence requirement for lease renewal. They can secure the investment value in their home at a later date by exercising the right to a new lease but they may lose their voice or be denied a full involvement in the management decisions by those tenants who have completed a collective enfranchisement claim and secured the freehold. Moreover, any later extended lease will be for a term of 90 years, plus the residue of their original lease, whereas the qualifying tenants who secured the freehold will have purchased on the assumption, usually a fact, that they will grant themselves 999-year leases of their flats. The excluded qualifying tenants, with original or new extended leases will be subject to the possibility of redevelopment[16] but the participating tenants will have secured any development value for themselves.

'Third class tenants' might be the term given to those qualifying tenants who are excluded from the collective enfranchisement and do not satisfy the residence requirement for lease renewal – perhaps because the tenant is a corporate body. Such tenants have no right to a new lease and so, as the term of

14 See 11.2.3.

15 Section 54 (discussed at 12.2.2 and 15.3.1).

16 See s 61 and 16.8.1.

their existing lease draws to an end, can only negotiate privately with the participating tenants, through the medium of the nominee purchaser (now the freeholder), for a new lease. Negotiation of a new lease by an existing tenant who has no rights to renew has always been a situation of unequal bargaining, with the freeholder able to impose terms or withhold a new lease. If a tenant has to go 'cap in hand' to fellow tenants, other factors could influence the decision whether to grant or withhold a new lease. At worst, one can envisage situations where a corporate or other qualifying tenant not satisfying the residence condition is deliberately excluded from the collective enfranchisement process in order, eventually, to remove that tenant – either when their existing lease expires or at an earlier date when the lease becomes practically unassignable. A forced surrender to the nominee purchaser freeholder controlled by the participating tenants may occur. Less dramatically, for example, the participating tenants controlling the freehold may make management decisions which are considered by those excluded to be contrary to the interests of all. There is undoubtedly the potential for disputes and litigation after an enfranchisement.[17]

5.5 Non-qualifying tenants

5.5.1 Residential non-qualifying tenants

Non-qualifying tenants of residential flats are those who have no right to participate in the statutory process. They may not have long leases; or the rent may exceed the low rent limits.[18] In whatever way they fail to meet the statutory requirements, they will normally be only interested observers of the enfranchisement. A secure tenant who has a public sector landlord will be least affected because of the mandatory leaseback provisions;[19] but all non-qualifying residential tenants will face the prospect of an ultimate change in the freeholder owner if the collective enfranchisement claim succeeds.[20] A change to the level and method of management control may follow.

5.5.2 Business tenants in the premises

A tenant under a business lease cannot be a qualifying tenant and, equally, has no statutory part to play in an enfranchisement. However, there is always the prospect of an agreement between the nominee purchaser (controlled by the participating tenants) and any such business tenant who may be interested in

17 One interesting scenario is a second collective enfranchisement, perhaps initiated by qualifying tenants originally not participating, who join with a group who did but are dissatisfied with the new management.

18 As discussed at 3.7 and 3.8.

19 See ss 2(5), 36 and Sch 9 (discussed at 3.2.4 and 9.5.2).

20 If the current freeholder exercises the right to leaseback, the non-qualifying tenant may retain that former freeholder as immediate landlord at the conclusion of the enfranchisement. See 9.5.3.

sharing in the acquisition of the freehold and thereby securing a long lease, at a peppercorn rent, of the business premises within the premises. The participating tenants may be favourably disposed to such financial participation as it may relieve them of the possibly onerous burden of the cost of the reversion to that commercial element. However, any such agreement is likely to be covered by the duty of disclosure[21] to the reversioner and so will be a factor in the valuation of the interests to be acquired. Moreover, the reversioner will be able to prevent a tenant of a business lease taking part in this way by opting in the counter-notice for a leaseback of the business unit.

5.6 Participating tenants

5.6.1 Definition

'Participating tenants' are those qualifying tenants who gave the initial notice and remain qualifying tenants of flats in the premises after the initial notice has been given.[22] They are the group – necessarily all of whom will be qualifying tenants – who will acquire the freehold through the medium of the nominee purchaser and will bear the costs – both of success and failure. There must be the necessary minimum number at the date the initial notice is given – so that they constitute two-thirds of the total number of qualifying tenants and not less than one half the total number of flats. One half of them at least must satisfy the residence condition.[23] The commitment of participation in a claim is emphasised by the requirement that the initial notice must be signed by each of the tenants by whom it is given,[24] together with the inability of a participating tenant to later resign or withdraw from the group on an individual basis in the absence of mutual agreement.[25]

5.6.2 Restriction on participation at the outset

In the following instances, a qualifying tenant may not participate in giving a relevant notice.[26] These are as follows.

1 Where the tenant has given notice terminating the lease.[27]

21 Section 18. See the discussion at 6.5.1.

22 Section 14(1). A 'participating tenant' and 'a tenant by whom the initial notice is given' are identical at the date of the initial notice; but not necessarily at a later date because the body of participating tenants may enlarge or contract, as discussed below.

23 Section 13(2).

24 Section 99(5)(a).

25 See s 28 and the discussion at 8.2.2.

26 These restrictions are more fully elaborated at 6.1.9.

27 Unless the notice is superseded by the express or implied grant of a new tenancy (Sch 3, para 1(a)). Similarly, the qualifying tenant cannot participate when the tenancy is due to terminate by reason of an agreement for a future tenancy not at a low rent, to which the Local Government and Housing Act 1989, Sch 10, para 17, applies (Sch 3, para 1(b)).

2 Where a landlord's statutory[28] notice terminating the tenant's lease of the flat has been given more than four months before the initial notice, whether or not the notice had effect to terminate the lease. A notice given less than four months before the initial notice ceases to have effect and does not prevent participation.[29]
3 Where the tenant is obliged or will be obliged at a specified date to give up possession of the flat in pursuance of a court order.[30]
4 Where proceedings are pending to enforce a right of re-entry or forfeiture terminating the lease of the flat, unless the court gives leave. Leave can only be granted if the court is satisfied that the tenant does not wish to participate solely or mainly for the purpose of avoiding the consequences of the breach of the terms in the lease, but if leave is given the lease is then deemed to be subsisting.[31]
5 Where a compulsory purchase notice to treat or contract remains in force on the date notice is given.[32]

Of these restrictions, forfeiture proceedings are likely to be the most significant in practice. Where the number of participating tenants are likely to be close to the statutory minimum a landlord seeking to make collective enfranchisement more difficult might commence speculative forfeiture proceedings,[33] thus forcing one or more tenants to get leave to participate and delaying the commencement of the enfranchisement.[34] In such situations the courts should be willing to grant the necessary leave.

5.6.3 Election to participate during the currency of a claim

A qualifying tenant who did not give the initial notice and is not an assignee of a participating tenant can only become a participating tenant later by electing to do so and with consent of *all* the persons who are currently participating tenants.[35] Any such election, which will no doubt have to be accompanied by an agreement on the sharing of costs and the purchase price, must be notified to the nominee purchaser forthwith. The effect of such an election on a qualifying tenant in a case where the landlord has served a statutory notice to terminate

28 Under the Landlord and Tenant Act 1954, s 4, or the Local Government and Housing Act 1989, Sch 10.

29 Schedule 3, para, 2(1) and (2). If the initial notice does not result in collective enfranchisement, the landlord can revive the statutory notice by a further notice within one month of the expiry of the currency of the claim. See Sch 3 para 2(3)–(5) for details.

30 Schedule 3, para 3(1).

31 Schedule 3, para 3(2)–(4). If the enfranchisement claim is later effective, the court dealing with the forfeiture proceedings has power to set aside or vary any order which it has made.

32 Schedule 3, para 4(1).

33 Perhaps in respect of service charge arrears or relatively minor alleged breaches of covenant.

34 See 10.4.5 for a fuller discussion.

35 Section 14(3).

within the last four months is similar to the position relating to qualifying tenants who gave the initial notice.[36]

5.6.4 Restrictions on electing to participate

There are restrictions on electing to participate during the currency of a claim.[37] These cover the same grounds as those which prohibit participation in the first place,[38] for example where there is a court order for possession or where proceedings are in train to forfeit. In these cases, if a tenant was prohibited from participation when the initial notice was given, a later election to participate is not possible even if the relevant restriction has ceased to apply; nor can he elect to participate if any of those restrictions apply at the time of the election.[39] If proceedings are pending to enforce a right of re-entry or forfeiture, then election to participate is only possible with leave of the court – which will, again, only be granted if the court is satisfied that the tenant does not wish to make the election solely or mainly to avoid the consequences of the breach of the terms of the lease.[40] The new participating tenant is regarded as such from the date of the agreement allowing participation.[41]

5.6.5 Participation by assignees of a flat

Assignees of the lease of a flat[42] may take the place of a participating tenant who sells by assigning the interest in the flat to another person. In such a case, the assignee shall give notice of the assignment within 14 days, notifying the nominee purchaser of the assignment and indicating whether or not the assignee is electing to participate in the proposed acquisition.[43] The agreement of the other participating tenants is not required in this case but the time-limit is (as so many are in the Act) vital. Once the 14 days have passed the *automatic* right to take the place is lost. If notice is given within that time, the assignee is regarded as a participating tenant from the date of the assignment and for so long as he remains a qualifying tenant.[44]

5.6.6 Death of a participating tenant

Personal representatives of a participating tenant who dies are under a similar duty of notification to the nominee purchaser. In this case, they are allowed a

36 Schedule 3, para 9 (see 5.6.2).
37 Schedule 3, para 8.
38 See 5.6.2 and Sch 3, paras 1–4.
39 Schedule 3, para 8(1)(a) and (b) which set out the details.
40 Schedule 3, para 8(2)–(4) contains the full details.
41 Section 14(4).
42 References to an assignment include an assent and an assignment by operation of law to a trustee in bankruptcy or to a mortgagee by way of foreclosure (s 14(10)).
43 Section 14(2).
44 Section 14(4).

period of 56 days to give notification of the death, and of their decision whether or not to withdraw from participation. In the absence of such notification the personal representatives are regarded as being the participating tenant of the flat from the date of the death and until the lease ceases to be vested in them.[45]

The death of a participating tenant may give rise to practical difficulties. It is an eventuality which may have been allowed for in the participator's agreement[46] but, even so, may result in the other participators having to shoulder the burden of the deceased tenant's share of the purchase price if the personal representatives elect to withdraw. The 56-day period may be considered rather short by the solicitor seeking to apply for probate but too long from the viewpoint of the other participating tenants awaiting a decision.

5.6.7 *Impact of a change in participating tenants*

Where an assignee or the personal representatives become a participating tenant then any contract, agreement or other arrangement between the nominee purchaser and the participating tenants subsisting at the date of the assignment or death is modified to substitute the assignee or personal representatives for the tenant which they replace. In the case of an assignment by a person who remains a participating tenant of a flat in the premises, the arrangements are modified to add the assignee or personal representatives.[47] The Act does not cover new participating tenants who join by an election to participate. Since such an election requires the consent of all the existing participating tenants, the terms on which he or she joins in is a matter for agreement between them.

5.6.8 *Notification of changes in participants*

When a qualifying tenant elects to participate after an assignment or by consent of the participating tenants, or when personal representatives elect to continue or withdraw from participation, the nominee purchaser will be notified. On receipt of any such notification, the nominee purchaser must give a notice to the reversioner within 28 days of being notified, with a copy to every other relevant landlord, giving details of the new participating tenant.[48] All notifications which state that a particular person is to be regarded as a participating tenant must be signed by the person or persons in question,[49] so the nominee purchaser will need to have the co-operation of that new participating tenant. As with the initial notice, this reflects the commitment of participation and seeks to ensure that the implications of participation are known. Only notices that an assignee

45 Section 14(5).
46 See 4.5.4 and 5.6.7.
47 Section 14(6).
48 Section 14(7). It may be useful to get the new participating tenant to sign a copy of the initial notice and send it with the notification.
49 Section 14(9)(b).

or the personal representatives have not elected to participate can be signed by a solicitor or agent. The details of the content of these notices to the reversioner are as follows.

1 In the case of a qualifying tenant joining by agreement, the notification must identify the flat and give the name and address of the person who has become a participating tenant.[50]
2 In the case of a qualifying tenant joining after assignment, the notification must identify the flat, give the date of the assignment and the name and address of the assignee, state whether or not election has been made to become a participating tenant and state that such participation is in place of the assignor.[51]
3 In the case of a qualifying tenant joining as personal representatives, the notice must identify the flat, give the date of death of the deceased tenant, the names and addresses of the personal representatives and whether or not they are electing to withdraw and are or are not to be regarded as a participating tenant.[52]

Once a binding contract has been entered into pursuant of the initial notice, the duties of notification no longer apply.[53]

5.6.9 Compulsory cessation on participation

A qualifying tenant who is participating ceases to be a participating tenant if an authority, with the power so to do, serves a compulsory purchase notice to treat in respect of the flat;[54] but the initial notice is not invalidated. This is in contrast to the position where a notice to treat is served on the freeholder or owner of a leasehold interest which it is sought to acquire.[55]

5.7 The nominee purchaser

5.7.1 Definition

The nominee purchaser is the person who conducts, on behalf of the participating tenants, all proceedings arising out of the initial notice with a view to eventual acquisition of the freehold.[56] The acquisition will be of the freehold and all other interests which fall to be acquired under the statutory provisions.

---

50 Section 14(8)(b) and (9)(a).

51 Section 14(8)(a) and (9)(a); the only instance where it is not necessary to state that the assignee has taken the place of the assignor is in the case of an assignor who remains a participating tenant by virtue of being a qualifying tenant of one other flat (s 8(a)(iii) and see s 6(1)(b)).

52 Section 14(8)(c) and (9)(a).

53 Section 14(11). By Sch 5, para 5 the reference to a binding contract includes a reference to a vesting order under ss 24 and 25.

54 Schedule 3, para 4(2).

55 Section 30(4)–(6); and see 8.4.3.

56 Section 15(1).

5.7.2 Appointment of nominee purchaser

The nominee purchaser is the person or persons appointed for the time being by the participating tenants. In the first instance, it is the person or persons specified in the initial notice.[57] The nominee purchaser may be one or more individuals but some form of corporate body will usually be desirable as the nominee purchaser. A corporate body will not die and is less likely to need to be replaced. It will enable shares to be taken in it by the participating tenants in proportion to their agreed contribution. Indeed, in Parliament, the Opposition sought to restrict who could be a nominee purchaser to a company in which each participating tenant had a share.[58] This was rejected in favour of maximum flexibility.

There appears to be no restriction on who may be appointed. Although it is likely that the tenants will agree on a corporate body as nominee purchaser which they will control, they are able to enter into an agreement with an outsider – perhaps a property company or developer – as nominee purchaser if they wish to do so. There might be a reason for this if there are assured or Rent Act tenancies or commercial units in the premises and the qualifying tenants do not wish to purchase the value of the reversions to these flats or units. However, the reversioner may exercise the right of leaseback[59] on such flats or units, at which point the property company will have little incentive to continue. It may, therefore, be preferable for the tenants in such a situation to have control of the nominee purchaser and enter into an agreement[60] with the property company in the event of the reversioner not exercising his right of leaseback.

5.7.3 Nominee purchaser – the alternatives

In most situations, the corporate vehicle will be the preferred alternative – a management *company* either *limited by shares* or by *guarantee*. This may be the only possibility in cases of a block of a large number of flats. An acceptable choice where the interests of all the participators are equal is a company limited by guarantee since problems of share transfers are avoided; but preferences will differ and a share structure may be needed if the participants have differing financial stakes in the purchase. An existing management company could be used but probably only if all the tenants who are members of the company are participating.

The disadvantage of a company as a nominee is the necessity of annual returns, the costs of the annual audit, usually resented by tenants, and the statutory duties and administration which usually falls upon one tenant. For such reasons, practitioners sometimes adopt alternatives for flat management and there is no reason why these alternatives could not be used as a nominee purchaser. A *tenant's trust*, whereby the freehold is held by individuals as

57 Section 15(2).

58 HC Deb, Standing Committee B, cols 161–167, 19 November 1992.

59 See 9.5.3.

60 Which will be subject to the duty of disclosure (see 6.5.1).

trustees upon trust for sale is a solution put forward for a small block of flats.[61] If this was adopted, the individuals chosen as trustees could constitute the nominee purchaser. An *industrial or provident society* or the appointment of a *professional agent* are other possibilities but neither are recommended and a professional person is unlikely to accept appointment.

In a building with only two flats, management is sometimes by *cross vesting of reversions* not only because a corporate vehicle is unwieldy in such a case but also because of the potential problems of an unresolvable dispute.[62] If such an eventual solution was desired, the two tenants pursuing the collective enfranchisement would be the nominee purchaser. After the acquisition, and when they granted themselves new leases, the reversion could be separated so that the freehold to each flat was vested in the lessee of the other.

5.7.4 Termination of appointment and replacement of nominee purchaser

There are detailed provisions for the termination of the appointment of the nominee purchaser and the replacement of it by the participating tenants.[63] These provisions will rarely be required; indeed their very complexity is another reason for using a corporate vehicle as a nominee purchaser which does not die or have to be replaced. Any adviser dealing with a termination and replacement of a nominee purchaser will need to refer to the exact provisions of s 15. Its main features are as follows.

1 Termination is by notice given by the participating tenants to the nominee purchaser and the reversioner (with copies to every relevant landlord)[64] specifying the date of termination.[65]

2 The notice must either specify a replacement nominee purchaser with an address[66] for service or state that full replacement details will be contained in a further notice.[67]

3 The appointment of a replacement nominee purchaser is not valid unless specified in such a notice; and, if not specified in the notice of termination, a failure to replace the nominee purchaser[68] and notify the reversioner within 28 days of the notice of termination leads to a deemed withdrawal.[69]

---

61 See *Precedents for the Conveyancer*, Sweet & Maxwell, Forms 5-86 (for premises with three or four flats) and 5-86A (for premises with five or more flats).

62 See *Precedents for the Conveyancer*, Sweet & Maxwell, Form 5-62.

63 Section 15(3)–(12).

64 Section 15(11).

65 Section 15(3) and (4).

66 In England and Wales.

67 Section 15(5).

68 Except where two or more persons constitute the nominee purchaser. The termination of appointment of one or some without replacement results in the remaining person(s) continuing as and constituting the nominee purchaser (s 15(8)).

69 Section 15(10).

4 While there is no nominee purchaser, the running of any time period is suspended.[70]
5 Acts of the original nominee purchaser are to be treated as being done by the replacement nominee purchaser;[71] but the liability for costs of the nominee purchaser whose appointment is terminated ceases after the date of termination.[72]
6 None of the provisions relating to termination applies once a binding contract is entered into;[73] as far as the statutory provisions are concerned, all references to the nominee purchaser after that time are to the person who was the nominee purchaser at the time of the contract.

5.7.5 Resignation and death of the nominee purchaser

The nominee purchaser may resign his appointment by giving, to each of the participating tenants and the reversioner, a notice of resignation taking effect 21 days after the date of the notice.[74] In such a case, and in the case of the death of the nominee purchaser or of one of the persons constituting the nominee purchaser,[75] the participating tenants have 56 days to appoint a new nominee purchaser and give notice of that appointment to the reversioner. Without such notice the appointment of a replacement is not valid.[76] Once again, the running of time is suspended while there is no nominee purchaser.[77] A failure to give notice to the reversioner can lead to a deemed withdrawal.[78] The provisions of s 15 relating to anything done by the former nominee purchaser, costs and the effect on two or more persons constituting the nominee purchaser apply equally to termination by resignation or death.[79] These requirements no longer apply after a binding contract is entered into.[80]

5.8 The reversioner

5.8.1 Definition

The reversioner is the person who conducts, on behalf of all owners of interests which it is proposed to acquire under a claim for collective enfranchisement, all

70 Section 15(9).
71 Section 15(6).
72 Section 15(7); except in relation to a failure to supply documents in its custody or control which relate to the acquisition after a request for their supply.
73 Section 15(12).
74 Section 16(1) and (2).
75 Section 16(5).
76 Section 16(3) and (5). Once again, the notice must give the name and address of the nominee purchaser, the date of appointment and an address for service in England and Wales.
77 Section 16(7).
78 Section 16(8).
79 Section 16(4) and (6).
80 Section 16(10).

proceedings arising out of an initial notice.[81] The reversioner receives the initial notice and is responsible for giving the counter-notice and copies of notices to other relevant landlords. The reversioner resists or gives effect to the claim and is the medium through whom negotiations are normally conducted.[82]

5.8.2 Power to bind other landlords

In order to enable the reversioner to conduct the proceedings effectively, there are provisions to ensure that the other relevant landlords are bound by the acts of the reversioner.[83]

1 Any notice given after receipt of the initial notice is given on behalf of all relevant landlords.
2 The reversioner may, on behalf and in the name of all or any of the relevant landlords deduce, evidence or verify the title relating to any property, negotiate and agree with the nominee purchaser the terms of the acquisition, execute any conveyance needed to transfer any interest to the nominee purchaser, receive the price payable for the acquisition of any interest, and take or defend any legal proceedings in respect of matters arising out of the initial notice.[84]
3 The reversioner is not liable to any other relevant landlord for any loss or damage in the exercise of his authority if he acts with good faith and with reasonable care and diligence.[85]

Unless a relevant landlord takes steps to act independently, the acts of the reversioner and the determination of the court in proceedings between the reversioner and the nominee purchaser bind all other relevant landlords.[86] There is a power to apply to the court for directions in the event of a dispute between the reversioner and relevant landlords. The reversioner shall also apply to the court for directions where a relevant landlord cannot be found or ascertained. Subject to those directions though,[87] he can proceed as normal and execute a conveyance on behalf of a relevant landlord who cannot be found, paying any sum received into court.

5.8.3 Reversioner is normally the freeholder

The reversioner will normally be the freeholder;[88] and this will certainly be the

81 Section 9(3).
82 Once an initial notice is given, the reversioner cannot sever the freehold interest. For the impact of a disposal of the whole of the interest, see 6.2.2.
83 Schedule 1, para 6. These provisions are without prejudice to the generality of the power to conduct proceedings in s 9(3).
84 Except those under s 23 (see 5.9.2 and 7.3.2).
85 Schedule 1, para 6(4).
86 Schedule 1, para 6(3).
87 The court can make such order as it thinks proper to give effect to the rights of the participating tenants and protect the interests of other persons.
88 Schedule 1, para 1.

case where it is not proposed to acquire any interests other than the freehold or interests owned by the freeholder.[89]

Even where there are intermediate landlords or other persons whose interests the nominee purchaser proposes to acquire, the reversioner will be the freeholder unless steps are taken to substitute a replacement.[90]

5.8.4 *Replacement of freeholder as reversioner*

The freeholder may be replaced as reversioner by application to the county court.[91] Such an application can only be made by a relevant landlord and the replacement must be a relevant landlord.[92] If all the relevant landlords apply, the court will appoint as reversioner whoever they all agree upon as the reversioner. If there is no such agreement, then on application of any relevant landlord the court may appoint such person, and upon such terms and conditions, as it thinks fit to be the reversioner. The court will only make such an appointment of a person other than the freeholder if:

(a) the freeholder is unwilling to act as the reversioner; or
(b) the absence or incapacity of the freeholder require another person to act; or
(c) the respective interests of the relevant landlords or other special circumstances require another person to act.

Unless the freeholder is unwilling to act, absent or incapacitated, the burden of proof on a relevant landlord seeking to replace the freeholder appears high – replacement must be 'required'. If, however, the freeholder has only a nominal reversion (for example a 999-year lease of the whole to an intermediate landlord) and the real investment value in the block of flats is with that intermediate landlord, then the case for replacement would be strong. Similarly, if the tenants had already effectively secured control of the freehold and the purpose of the collective enfranchisement claim was really to secure the intermediate interests, it is very likely that a replacement of the reversioner would be desirable.

There is no reason why an application to replace the freeholder should not be made before the receipt of an initial notice. Indeed, if a relevant landlord considers that a collective enfranchisement claim may be made and that the freeholder is not the right person to be the reversioner, it may be advisable to make an application to replace in anticipation of the claim.

5.8.5 *Removal of the reversioner*

On the application of any relevant landlord, the court may remove the reversioner from that position and appoint another person, who must be a

89 Section 9(1).
90 Section 9(2)(a) and Sch 1, para 1.
91 The details are contained in Sch 1, paras 2, 3 and 5.
92 For the definition of a relevant landlord, see 5.9.1.

relevant landlord, in his place. Such removal will only be ordered if it appears to the court proper to do so by reason of any delay or default on the part of the reversioner, whether actual or apprehended.[93] During the collective enfranchisement process, therefore, a reversioner can either be *replaced* (if required as set out above) or *removed* under this provision, which will be done on the basis of delay or default.

5.9 Relevant landlords

5.9.1 Definition

A relevant landlord, in relation to a particular block of flats or premises, is the person who owns the freehold and every person who owns any leasehold interest which it is proposed to acquire by virtue of collective enfranchisement.[94]

5.9.2 The rights of relevant landlords

Although the reversioner conducts the proceedings arising out of the initial notice, relevant landlords who are not the reversioner are given some rights to act independently.[95] At any time after the reversioner gives a counter-notice, a relevant landlord may give notice to both the reversioner and the nominee purchaser of his intention to act independently. On giving such notice in relation to all or any of the following, the relevant landlord is entitled:[96]

(a) to deal directly with the nominee purchaser in connection with deducing, evidencing or verifying title relating to the acquisition of any interest of his, negotiating and agreeing with the nominee purchaser the terms of the acquisition, or executing any conveyance;[97]
(b) to be separately represented in legal proceedings relating to his title or terms of acquisition of any of his interests;
(c) to require the reversioner, by notice, to apply to the leasehold valuation tribunal for the determination of the terms of acquisition relating to his interest;

93 Schedule 1, paras 4 and 5.
94 Section 9(2)(b). They must be leasehold interests within s 2 (see 3.2.4). References to a landlord mean reference to all persons jointly constituting the landlord as joint tenant (s 101(4)).
95 Schedule 1, para 7.
96 Schedule 1, para 7(1),(3) and (4).
97 Once the relevant landlord has given such a notice, the regulations relating to requiring proof of that relevant landlord's title and dealing with requisitions on title (see 6.7.1), apply to substitute that relevant landlord in place of the reversioner – Leasehold Reform (Collective Enfranchisement and Lease Renewal) Regulations 1993, SI 1993/2407, Sch 5.

(d) to require that the price to be paid by the nominee purchaser be paid, instead of to the reversioner, direct to him or to a person (such as a solicitor) authorised by him to receive it.[98]

The reversioner cannot bring proceedings by way of opposition to an initial notice on the grounds of an intention to develop[99] on behalf of any other relevant landlord; but any other landlord may commence such proceedings on his own behalf.[100]

5.9.3 Duties of relevant landlords

Relevant landlords may find that some duties are imposed upon them during the collective enfranchisement process. Thus, the nominee purchaser can require by notice to the reversioner and the relevant landlord that that landlord shall deal directly with the nominee purchaser for the purpose only of deducing, evidencing or verifying title.[101] It is the general duty of each of the other relevant landlords to give the reversioner all such information and assistance as he may reasonably require.[102] In particular, a copy of any notice from a qualifying tenant exercising the right to a new lease[103] must be furnished to the reversioner as soon as possible after receipt.[104] Unless the option to act independently has been exercised then, on being given proper notice of the arrangements for completion, a relevant landlord must ensure that the land certificate, deeds and all documents necessary to perfect title are delivered to the nominee purchaser.[105] If the reversioner incurs costs and expenses not recoverable or recovered from the nominee purchaser, then the other relevant landlords must make such contribution as shall be just.[106]

5.10 Special categories of landlords

5.10.1 Detailed provision made

Special and detailed provision is made for certain special classes of landlords.[107] Some relate to mortgagees in possession so as to give them notice or, in some

98 If, after being given notice of completion, the relevant landlord fails to notify or implement arrangements for completion, the reversioner is authorised to receive payment for him (Sch 1, para 7(4)).

99 Section 23 (see 7.3.2).

100 Schedule 1, para 9.

101 Schedule 1, para 7(2).

102 Schedule 1, para 8(1)(a).

103 Under s 42.

104 Schedule 4, para 3. A copy of a notice of withdrawal by such a tenant or a copy of any counter-notice given in response must also be supplied.

105 Failure to comply gives rise to a right of indemnity for any liability incurred by the reversioner (Sch 1, para 8(1)(b)).

106 Sch 1, para 8(2).

107 By virtue of s 9(4) and Sch 2. For parallel provisions, see the Leasehold Reform Act 1967, ss 25, 26 and 31.

cases, power to take the place of the relevant landlord. Another provides for a receiver to take the place of a landlord under a disability. There is clarification where an interest is vested if held by a custodian trustee and there is provision as to how the price or compensation received is to be treated in the hands of trustees for sale, university or college landlords or ecclesiastical landlords. The following is a precis of those provisions but if any of these situations apply the exact wording of the relevant provision of Sch 2 should be consulted.

5.10.2 Mortgagees in possession

Where the interest of a relevant landlord is subject to a mortgage:[108]

(a) if the mortgagee is in possession, then all proceedings which would have been conducted by that landlord are conducted by the mortgagee, including any application to prevent enfranchisement on the grounds of redevelopment;[109]
(b) if the mortgagee has appointed a receiver or is in receipt of the rent and profits by order of any court, then any application to prevent enfranchisement on the grounds of redevelopment cannot be made without the consent of the mortgagee and the mortgagee can by notice assume the rights of a mortgagee in possession;[110]
(c) if the mortgagee is either in possession or has appointed a receiver or is in receipt of the rent and profits by order of any court, then notices are regarded as duly given if given to the mortgagee or receiver; but whoever receives the notice out of landlord, mortgagee or receiver must give a copy to the others.[111]

It should be noted that a landlord, whose interest is subject to a mortgage to secure the payment of money, must inform the mortgagee on receipt of an initial notice that notice has been given and give such other further information as the mortgagee may from time to time reasonably require.[112]

5.10.3 Landlord under a disability

If a relevant landlord is incapable by reason of mental disorder of managing his property and affairs the landlord's receiver or person authorised in that behalf shall take the place of the landlord.[113]

108 Mortgage includes a charge or lien (Sch 2, para 1).

109 Schedule 2, para 2(1) and (2); these provisions do not affect the operation of s 35 relating to discharge of the mortgage at enfranchisement (see 9.4.1).

110 Schedule 2, para 2(3).

111 Schedule 2, para 2(4). Notice may also validly be given to trustees for debenture holders under a debenture holder's charge (see Sch 2, para 2(1) and (5)).

112 Schedule 2, para 2(6). This does not apply to a debenture holder's charge (para 2(7)).

113 Schedule 2, para 4. This is done under an order of the Court of Protection or other authority having jurisdiction under Part VII of the Mental Health Act 1983.

5.10.4 *Interests vested in custodian trustee*

An interest vested in a custodian trustee is deemed to be vested in the managing trustees or committee of management for all purposes of collective enfranchisement except execution of any instrument.[114]

5.10.5 *Interests held on trust*

Where an interest of a relevant landlord is held on trust for sale, sums payable to the landlord are dealt with as if it were proceeds of sale.[115] There are no other express provisions to assist where an interest is held on trust. For the purpose of the giving and receiving of notices, the trustees of any interest held on trust for sale would appear to be the relevant landlord as the holder of the legal estate in the land. In the case of an interest of a relevant landlord held under a strict settlement, under the Settled Land Act 1925, the tenant for life would be the relevant landlord, but the provisions of that Act as to the price payable for an enfranchisement will need to be observed.

5.10.6 *University or college landlords*

Any sum payable to a university or college subject to the University and Colleges Estates Act 1925 by way of price is dealt with as if payable by way of consideration on a sale under that Act.[116]

5.10.7 *Ecclesiastical landlords*

Certain ecclesiastical landlords, as defined, are subject to the consent of the Church Commissioners for some decisions and the Commissioners have rights of appearance in proceedings. There are provisions as to how sums payable are to be treated.[117]

---

114 Schedule 2, para 3.

115 Schedule 2, para 5(1).

116 Schedule 2, para 7(1).

117 Full details are set out in Sch 2, para 8. Ecclesiastical landlords are capitular bodies under the Cathedrals Measure 1963 and, in relation to glebe land, a diocesan board of finance.

CHAPTER SIX

PROCEDURE – INITIAL NOTICE AND COUNTER-NOTICE

6.1 The initial notice

6.1.1 Commences the claim; the relevant date

The claim to exercise the right to collective enfranchisement with respect to any premises is made by the giving of notice of the claim under s 13 of the 1993 Act.[1] The giving of this notice is the critical watershed for the whole process. The date on which the initial notice is given is defined by the Act as the 'relevant date'[2] and it is from this date that the strict timetable for the various procedures are ultimately calculated.

The 'relevant date' is also important because it is the date on which the right of the participating tenants to a collective enfranchisement will be judged.[3] At that date, there must be a sufficient number of qualifying tenants in the premises and those participating and signing the initial notice must meet the minimum required of two-thirds of the total number of qualifying tenants, amounting to one half of the total number of flats with half of those giving the notice satisfying the residence condition.[4] It does not matter if more tenants join in by election later;[5] nor, more significantly, if one or more participating tenants loses that status by ceasing to be a qualifying tenant.[6] The result is that if the absolute minimum give the initial notice then, providing all those who sign the notice do in fact meet the statutory requirements, the collective enfranchisement can be completed even if one or more of the qualifying tenants who gave the initial notice has ceased to participate. It is also submitted that providing

1 Section 13(1).
2 Section 1(8).
3 Thus, if the reversioner challenges the entitlement to enfranchisement by serving a counter-notice not admitting the right which results in a s 22 application by the nominee purchaser (see 6.6.4 and 7.2.1), then the court considers the right to entitlement at the relevant date (s 22(1)(b)).
4 Discussed more fully at 6.1.6 and 6.1.7.
5 By virtue of s 14(3) (see 5.6.3).
6 See the definition of participating tenant in s 14(1) and 5.6.1; this will most commonly happen if a tenant who signed the initial notice assigns his lease (see 5.6.5 for the right of the assignee to take over the place).

there is a sufficient number of tenants meeting the residence condition[7] among those who give the initial notice, it does not matter that other qualifying tenants, none of whom satisfy the residence condition, later elect to participate[8] – even if the result is that the group of tenants proceeding to complete the enfranchisement could not have qualified as a group to give the initial notice.[9]

6.1.2 *The commitment of an initial notice*

The giving of the initial notice is also a watershed because it marks the point at which the participating tenants commit themselves to proceed with their claim to enfranchise. From this point, the participating tenants are committed to paying the relevant costs[10] wherever the initial notice is later deemed to have been withdrawn or where the participating tenants choose to withdraw. Each of the participating tenants is liable to the reversioner and any other relevant landlord for all of the relevant costs incurred pursuant to the initial notice down to the time of either notice of withdrawal or the deemed withdrawal.[11] It is vital, therefore, that all participating tenants recognise, before the initial notice is given (and this matter must be specifically drawn to their attention), that such liability is a joint and several liability of the persons concerned.[12] For this reason, it may be prudent to establish a costs fund into which the participating tenants contribute equally or otherwise provide security for costs, to ensure that the later liability for costs which will arise whether or not the collective enfranchisement claim succeeds is evenly distributed amongst the participating tenants. The participating tenants should also understand that it is not possible for one participator to unilaterally elect to withdraw.[13]

6.1.3 *Restriction on subsequent initial notices*

There is a further reason to ensure that the documentation in connection with the claim is fully prepared before the initial notice is given. Once premises have been specified in an initial notice under s 13, and that notice is later withdrawn or is deemed to have been withdrawn under the Act,[14] then no subsequent notice specifying either the whole or part of the same premises can be given

---

7 See 3.6.2.
8 Under s 14(3) (see 5.6.3).
9 See also the discussion at 5.3.3.
10 As defined (see s 33 and 9.2.2).
11 Sections 28 and 29 (see 8.2.3 and 8.3.4).
12 See 8.2.3 for the direct costs liability in the event of a withdrawal or deemed withdrawal; if the enfranchisement is completed, the nominee purchaser will pay the costs but each tenant will no doubt have an agreed contribution.
13 It may be possible with the consent of all the others; this might be covered by a participator's agreement (see 4.5.4).
14 Or it is proved that the landlord has an intention to redevelop (see s 23).

under s 13 within a period of 12 months beginning with either the date of withdrawal or the deemed withdrawal of the earlier notice. It is also provided that, where any premises has been specified in a notice, no subsequent notice specifying the whole or part of those premises can be given in any event, so long as the earlier notice continues in force.[15]

6.1.4 Power to amend initial notices

An initial notice should not be withdrawn if there is an error or mistake in it; such withdrawal will necessitate a wait of 12 months until a fresh notice can be given. Instead, advantage should be taken of the court's power to amend inaccuracies or misdescriptions.[16] For the 12-month restriction to apply, 'the premises must have been specified in a notice under this section'. A purported notice which is so defective that it cannot operate at all, such as one not given to the reversioner, or specifying entirely incorrect premises, is probably not given under the section to prevent a further valid initial notice being given within the 12-month period.

6.1.5 To whom is the notice given?

An initial notice is given to the reversioner[17] as defined in the Act. The reversioner is the freeholder of the premises in all those cases where it is not proposed to acquire any other interests except the freehold or any other interests of the person who owns the freehold.[18]

In those cases where it is proposed to acquire interests of persons other than the person who owns the freehold, such as intermediate leaseholders, the reversioner, for the purposes of the Act, is defined by s 9(2) and Part I of Sch 1 to the Act. Once again, the reversioner in respect of any premises is prima facie the person who owns the freehold of those premises.[19] However, in such cases, the freeholder can be replaced as the reversioner by any other relevant landlord, defined for this purpose as not only the freeholder but every person who owns any leasehold interest which it is proposed to acquire under and by virtue of s 2 of the Act. Only a relevant landlord may be a reversioner, and a freeholder will only be replaced by one of the relevant landlords on application to the court by one or more of the relevant landlords.[20]

Normally, therefore, the reversioner will be the freeholder whose details can, if necessary, be ascertained by preliminary enquiries under s 11.

---

15 Section 13(8). This provision applies to the premises specified so that not only are the participating tenants under the withdrawn notice affected but also it prevents any other qualifying tenants giving an initial notice specifying those premises during that period.

16 Schedule 3, para 15 (see 6.1.12).

17 Section 13(2). See 5.8.1.

18 Section 9. For a full discussion of who the reversioner is or may be, see 5.8.3 ff.

19 Schedule 1, para 1.

20 In accordance with Sch 1, paras 2–4 (see 5.8.4).

6.1.6 Who gives the notice?

The initial notice is given by the initial participating tenants[21] who, by definition, must be qualifying tenants. Three separate conditions must be met by them when the initial notice is given.[22]

1 The notice must be given by not less that two-thirds of the qualifying tenants of the flats contained in the premises at the relevant date, ie the date of the initial notice.
2 They must be qualifying tenants of flats which must amount to not less than one half of the total number of flats contained in the premises.
3 One half of the qualifying tenants giving the notice must satisfy the residence condition.

6.1.7 Meeting the minimum requirement

The resultant requirements are rather untidily related. The format is the result of late amendments in Parliament – originally the only one of the three was that the qualifying tenants proceeding should be two-thirds of the total number of qualifying tenants.[23] The addition of the residence condition was to ensure that a majority of non-residential tenants could not qualify to enfranchise;[24] the requirement of one half the total number of flats was to prevent a minority of tenants proceeding.

The interrelationship can be best understood by a series of examples. Although it will always be possible to calculate, from the number of flats in the premises, the absolute minimum number of qualifying tenants who must be present to make a claim, it is important to grasp the principle that the actual number of qualifying tenants who must give the initial notice in any given case depends on the total number of such tenants in the premises.

Consider premises which contain 18 flats. For a valid claim to collective enfranchisement to be made, at least 12 (two-thirds) of those tenants must be qualifying tenants. If there are exactly 12 tenants, then, in the Bill as drafted, eight of those (two-thirds of two-thirds) would have had to give the initial notice; but the added requirement that they constitute 50 per cent of the flats increases that number to nine. This means that five of those nine (one half, rounded up), as an absolute minimum, must satisfy the residence condition. If

21 Referred to in the Act as the 'qualifying tenants by whom the notice is given'. The persons in the two groups will be the same at the giving of the initial notice (s 14(1)(a)) but may diverge later because at any given time participating tenants must remain qualifying tenants of flats in the specified premises.
22 Section 13(2).
23 Since there had to be a total of two-thirds of all the tenants as qualifying tenants, this meant two-thirds of two-thirds or 45 per cent. The prospect of a minority proceeding against the wishes of the majority, or two 45 per cent rival groupings, was a prime reason for one of the amendments, to ensure 50 per cent minimum.
24 But note the discussion at 6.1.2 and 5.3.3.

there are fewer than half the flats occupied by qualifying tenants (nine in this example), a collective enfranchisement is never possible. However, if there are more than 12 qualifying tenants in premises consisting of 18 flats, there is a corresponding increase in the number required to give the initial notice and the number who must meet the residence condition. Thus, again in premises with 18 flats, the following calculations can be made.

1 Where all 18 flats, or 17 of the 18, are occupied by qualifying tenants, a minimum of 12 must give the initial notice and six must satisfy the residence condition.
2 Where 16 flats are occupied by qualifying tenants, a minimum of 11 must give the initial notice and six must still satisfy the residence condition.
3 Where 14 or 15 flats are occupied by qualifying tenants, a minimum of 10 must give the initial notice and only five need satisfy the residence condition.
4 Where 12 or 13 flats are occupied by qualifying tenants, the absolute minimum of nine must give the initial notice and five must satisfy the residence condition.

6.1.8 All to sign

All those proceeding must each sign the initial notice,[25] either personally or through their attorney, since the notice is given by them. Since the giving of the notice gives rise to financial liabilities, clear advice as to the consequences of participating should be given. Where joint owners constitute the qualifying tenant of a flat, both should sign.[26]

6.1.9 Restrictions on participation

There are some restrictions on participation by individual tenants in the giving of the initial notice. These restrictions are set out in Sch 3 to the Act. The following qualifying tenants of a flat shall not participate in the giving of an initial notice of a claim.

1 If the relevant tenant has given a notice terminating the lease of the flat, unless that notice has been superseded by the grant, express or implied, of a new tenancy.[27]
2 If the tenant occupies during the subsistence of an agreement for the grant of a future tenancy.[28]
3 Where the initial notice is given more than four months after a landlord's notice terminating a qualifying tenant's lease of a flat if that notice is given

---

25 Section 99(5)(a).
26 The better view of the provision that joint tenants jointly constitute the qualifying tenant (s 5(4)(b)) is that both must elect to participate; s 99(5)(a) requires both to sign.
27 Schedule 3, para 1(a).
28 Where that agreement is one under para 17 of Sch 10 to the Local Government and Housing Act 1989 (Sch 3, para 1(b)).

under s 4 of the Landlord and Tenant Act 1954, or under para 4(1) of Sch 10 to the Local Government and Housing Act 1989. This restriction applies whether or not the notice has effect to terminate the lease. If the landlord's notice was given less than four months before the initial notice then the landlord's notice ceases to have effect.[29]

4 Where a tenant is obliged to give up possession of his flat in pursuance to an order of the court[30] or will be so obliged in a date specified in the court order. This restriction extends to a qualifying tenant when proceedings are pending to enforce a right of re-entry or forfeiture which will have the effect of terminating the lease although, in such circumstances, leave of the court to participate can be obtained if the court is satisfied that the tenant's wish to participate in the initial notice was not solely or mainly for the purposes of avoiding the consequences of a breach of the terms of his lease in respect of which those forfeiture proceedings are pending.[31] If leave is granted and an initial notice is then given, the tenant's lease is deemed to subsist notwithstanding the forfeiture proceedings and any order made. The court making any forfeiture order can then set aside or vary its order if the claim for collective enfranchisement is effective.[32]

5 Where any person or body of persons has, or could be authorised to, acquire the whole or part of a flat compulsorily for any purpose and has, at the date of the initial notice, served a notice to treat or entered into a contract with the purchaser of the interest in the flat and the notice to treat or the contract remains in force.[33]

It will be necessary to check that the qualifying tenants who are participating in giving the initial notice do not fall foul of any of these provisions, particularly where the number who intend to be involved are close to any of the limits.[34]

6.1.10 What must the initial notice contain?

The requirements of the initial notice are set out in s 13(3) of the Act. Under that subsection, the initial notice must meet the following requirements.[35]

---

29 Schedule 3, para 2(1) and (2). The wording of this provision would appear to apply to a notice given in the last four months to any qualifying tenant – even those not participating.

30 In such a case, neither the tenant nor a mortgagee in possession could be a qualifying tenant.

31 Schedule 3, para 3. It should be noted, however, that once the initial notice is given, there is a restriction on proceedings by the landlord to enforce any right of re-entry or forfeiture; the court will only give leave to proceed if the court is satisfied that the tenant is participating solely or mainly to avoid the consequences of the breach of the terms of the lease in respect of which proceedings are brought.

32 Schedule 3, para 4.

33 Schedule 3, para 4.

34 If it later transpires that one of the qualifying tenants is prohibited from participation under the provisions of Sch 3, the initial notice is not invalidated so long as the notice was in fact given by not less than two-thirds of the qualifying tenants (Sch 3, para 16).

35 These requirements are set out in s 13(3)(a)–(g) and 13(5).

1 It must specify, and be accompanied by, a plan which shows the premises of which the freehold is proposed to be acquired including, where appropriate, the freehold of any appurtenant property[36] which it is proposed to acquire within s 1(3) of the Act. The extent of the proposed acquisition is a matter for the participating tenants to decide. A claim may be made to premises less extensive than that to which the participants are entitled.[37] There is therefore no need to seek to acquire the freehold to access roads, gardens or garages; even part of the building could be excluded provided that what is claimed is a self-contained part of the building.[38] The plan must also show, where appropriate, any property of the person who owns the freehold over which it is proposed that any rights should be granted by him in connection with the acquisition of the freehold.

2 It must contain a statement of the grounds under which it is claimed that the specified premises are, on the relevant date, the premises to which the Act applies. In other words, it must clearly show that the premises are premises to which the Act applies within s 3 of the Act,[39] showing that the building is self-contained and that the requisite number of flats are held by qualifying tenants on long leases at low rent; and that the requisite number meet the residence condition.

3 It must specify, where appropriate in the particular case, any leasehold interests proposed to be acquired under s 2 of the Act and the flats contained in the specified premises in relation to which it is considered that the mandatory lease back provisions of Sch 9, Part II apply. These are the situations in which it is mandatory for the nominee purchaser to lease back to the freeholder flats let under secure tenancies and flats let by housing associations under other tenancies.[40]

4 It must specify the proposed purchase price of each of the interests which it is proposed to acquire. This will be the freehold interest and the freehold interest on any property which is specified in the notice and any further leasehold interest specified in the notice. The proposed price does not have to be the sum reached by the surveyor in his valuation but any departure from that valuation may need to be explained when the terms of acquisition are being negotiated.

5 The notice must state the full names of all the qualifying tenants[41] of the flats contained in the specified premises and the addresses of those flats. The

36 See 3.2.2.

37 Section 1(5).

38 See 3.3.2; the landlord in the counter-notice may respond by seeking to require the nominee purchaser to take the freehold of property ceasing to be of useful benefit (see 6.6.3).

39 See 3.3.1.

40 See 9.5.2.

41 This means all the qualifying tenants and not just those who are participating.

particulars must be sufficient in relation to each of the tenants so to identify the lease and include the date on which the lease was entered into, the term for which it was granted and the date of the commencement of the term. It will be necessary to include further particulars if it is necessary to show that the lease is, in fact, a lease at low rent. For all those tenants where it is claimed that the residence condition is satisfied, the particulars of the period or periods of occupation as the only or principal home will need to be set out.

6 The initial notice must state the full name or names of the person or persons appointed by the qualifying tenants giving the notice as the nominee purchaser for the purposes of the Act. In this regard, an address[42] at which notices may be given to the nominee purchaser must also be stated.

7 The initial notice must specify the date by which the reversioner must respond to the notice by giving a counter notice under s 21 of the Act. The date so chosen and specified must be a date which falls not less than two months after the relevant date,[43] which is, of course, the date of the giving of the initial notice.

8 Finally, the initial notice must contain a statement which confirms that the participating tenants have obtained a valuation, prepared by a qualified surveyor, in respect to both the freehold interest in the specified premises and any other freehold or leasehold interest which is specified in the notice. They must state the name of the surveyor in question. For these purposes, a qualified surveyor is a fellow or professional associate of the Royal Institution of Chartered Surveyors or of the Incorporated Society of Valuers and Auctioneers.[44] Regulations may be made which impose further requirements in respect of such qualified surveyors. The qualified surveyor so chosen must be reasonably believed by the qualifying tenants to have ability in, and experience of, the valuation of premises of the particular kind and in the particular area in question. The valuation will have been prepared by the surveyor in accordance with the provisions of Sch 6 to the Act.[45]

The preparation of an initial notice should be a matter of great care and should only be given when all practical and financial arrangements are in place and the participating tenants are confident that the various hurdles in the procedure can be overcome.

6.1.11 Copies of the notice to relevant landlords

In addition to giving the initial notice to the reversioner, the qualifying tenants by whom the initial notice is given must give a copy of the notice to every

42 Which must be one in England or Wales.
43 Section 13(5).
44 Section 13(7).
45 See 19.2.1.

person known or believed by them to be a relevant landlord,[46] that is a person with any leasehold interest which it is proposed to acquire under the Act. Where it is appropriate to give such copies, the initial notice must itself state whether copies are being given and, if so, to whom.[47]

A reversioner or relevant landlord receiving an initial notice must give a copy of it to every person believed by the recipient to be a relevant landlord who is not stated in the initial notice to have received a copy.[48] Any such persons must be added to the initial notice and the qualifying tenants by whom the notice was given informed. A landlord whose interest is subject to a mortgage must inform the mortgagee that the notice has been given.[49]

A failure to serve the copies of the initial notice on all the relevant landlords without reasonable cause or because of unreasonable delay results in the person failing to serve being liable for any loss which results. If, however, the failure to serve a copy of the initial notice was on a relevant landlord who had notified any of the qualifying tenants by whom the initial notice was given that he had an interest, the consequence is more serious. The initial notice ceases to have effect on the date specified in the initial notice for the counter-notice to be given.[50]

6.1.12 Inaccuracies or misdescription in the initial notice

To be valid, an initial notice must be given to the reversioner, and must be given by a sufficient number of the qualifying tenants to meet the statutory requirements,[51] but an initial notice is not invalidated by any inaccuracy in any of the particulars required by s 13(3) or by any misdescription of the property to which the claim extends.[52] Consequently, if a notice specifies a property not liable to acquisition or fails to specify a property or interest which is liable to acquisition then the notice may be amended with leave of the court and on such terms as the court thinks fit, so as to exclude or include the property or interest in question.[53] Amendments may exclude or include any property or interest and such amendments are treated as if their acquisition had been proposed at the date of the initial notice.[54]

If it later transpires that one or more of the persons by whom the initial notice was given is not a qualifying tenant of a flat contained in the premises or is such a qualifying tenant but prohibited from participating under Sch 3, or did not satisfy the residence condition when it was claimed that he did, then a notice is not invalidated on that account as long as the notice was in fact properly given

46 Schedule 3, paras 11–14.
47 Schedule 3, para 12.
48 Schedule 3, para 13.
49 Schedule 2, para 2(6); this does not apply to a debenture holders' charge.
50 Schedule 3, para 14.
51 See 6.1.7.
52 Schedule 3, para 15(1); cf the Leasehold Reform Act 1967, Sch 3, para 6(3).
53 Schedule 3, para 15(2).
54 Schedule 3, para 15(3).

by a sufficient number of the qualifying tenants of the flat contained in the premises as at the relevant date and not less than one half by whom it was given then satisfied the residence condition.[55]

6.1.13 Registration as if an estate contract

Immediately on serving an initial notice, the solicitor should register the initial notice[56] as if it were an estate contract, either by registration as a land charge in the case of unregistered land or by a notice or caution in the case of registered land. Registration is vital to secure the position against a subsequent purchaser of the freehold.[57]

6.2 Effects of an initial notice

6.2.1 Paralysing the freehold

Once the initial notice has been registered then, as long as the initial notice remains in force, the freeholder shall not make any disposal *severing* his interest in the premises or in any property specified in the initial notice.[58] Further, the freeholder cannot *grant a lease* out of his freehold interest in circumstances where the interest of the tenant of that lease would be liable to acquisition.[59] If there are other relevant landlords, they, too, are prevented from granting new leases which would be liable to acquisition out of their interest in the specified premises or any property covered by the initial notice.[60] Any such attempted transaction shall be void to the extent that it purports to make such disposal or grant such a lease.

6.2.2 Disposal of the freehold subsequent to an initial notice

A disposal *of the whole* of the freehold or the whole of any relevant landlord's leasehold interest is not prevented or rendered void by the Act. However, if such a disposal takes place and the initial notice has been registered in accordance with s 97(1), then all parties are placed by the Act in the same position as if the person acquiring the interest had become its owner before the initial notice was served.[61] The acquiring purchaser, therefore, becomes a relevant landlord, replaces the person making the disposal and is treated as if he had been given a notice or copy of notice and had taken all the steps which the vendor had taken prior to the disposal. The same position applies to every

55 Schedule 3, para 16.
56 Under s 97(1). The rights arising from an initial notice are not an overriding interest under the Land Registration Act 1925.
57 See 6.2.2.
58 Section 19(1)(a)(i).
59 Section 19(1)(a)(ii).
60 Section 19(1)(b).
61 Section 19(2) and (3).

subsequent disposal of the interest. Some such disposals will in any event be subject to the provisions of the Landlord and Tenant Act 1987 and require a notice offering first refusal to the qualifying tenants under that Act.

6.2.3 Suspension of contracts

If, when the initial notice is given, there is in force at that date a binding contract providing for the disposal to any extent of the freehold interest or the leasehold interest of any relevant landlord then the service of the initial notice suspends the operation of that contract, and it remains so suspended as long as the initial notice continues in force.[62] It is therefore provided that in the case of such a suspended contract, and without prejudice as to the general law as to the frustration of contracts, the freeholder or relevant landlord who then enters into a binding contract in pursuance of the initial notice is discharged from the further performance of the suspended contract so far as it relates to the disposal of the interest in the specified premises.[63] There is, however, an important qualification. A contract disposing of a freeholder's interest can make specific provision for the eventuality of the receipt of a subsequent initial notice. A contract which does provide for this eventuality is not suspended.[64] It is important, therefore, that the issue is addressed in any contract to dispose of an interest which might be subject to a collective enfranchisement claim.[65] If the purchaser agrees to proceed in the eventuality of an initial notice before completion, that will be valid but the purchaser will become the reversioner or relevant landlord as if he had been the owner before the initial notice was given.

6.2.4 No limitation on dealings prior to the initial notice

Section 19 ensures that, once an initial notice is served and registered, no disposal or dealing with the interest by the freeholder or by the other relevant landlords can frustrate the completion of the collective enfranchisement. What is more significant, perhaps, is that there is no such limit on the action which the landlords can take prior to the service of the initial notice, and severance of an interest or a granting of a lease will be valid if done before the initial notice is served and registered.[66]

---

62 Section 19(4). The suspension is only so far as it relates to the disposal. This provision would appear to apply to a contract even if the procedures imposed by the Landlord and Tenant Act 1987 have been observed and a notice giving right of first refusal has been served under that Act and there has been no response.

63 Section 19(5). A contract, for this purpose, includes a contract made in pursuance of an order of any court.

64 Section 19(6).

65 Provision should also be made in cases of contracts which may be subject to the 1987 Act.

66 However, any transaction after 20 July 1993, the date of the passing of the Act, which involves the creation or transfer of an interest superior to that of a qualifying tenant or an alteration of the terms on which any superior interest is held cannot increase the value of the freeholder's interest in the specified premises (Sch 6, para 3(5)).

6.2.5 Restrictions on termination of the lease

Once an initial notice is given, there are restrictions on the termination of the lease of a participating tenant.

1 Any notice terminating a lease of a participating tenant, whether given by the tenant or by the landlord under the Landlord and Tenant Act 1954, s 4 or the Local Government and Housing Act 1989, Sch 10, para 4(a), is of no effect if given or served during the currency of a claim.[67] If the claim is not successful, any notice caught by this provision would not revive; a fresh notice would be required.

2 A lease of a participating tenant cannot terminate by effluxion of time, by landlord's notice to quit or by the termination of the lease of a superior landlord during the currency of a collective enfranchisement claim and for three months thereafter. If the claim is not effective, it will terminate at the end of the three-month period if, but for this provision, it would have terminated earlier.[68]

3 Proceedings to forfeit the lease of a participating tenant or to exercise any right of re-entry cannot be brought during the currency of a claim without the leave of the court. Leave will only be granted if the court is satisfied that the tenant is participating in the making of a claim solely or mainly for the purpose of avoiding the consequences of the breach of the terms of the lease.[69] This test, identical to the one applied to a tenant seeking to participate after forfeiture proceedings are in train,[70] is likely to be a difficult one for a landlord to satisfy.

6.3 Rights of access

6.3.1 Access for reversioner and landlords

The service of the initial notice upon the reversioner, or the service of a copy of this notice on any other relevant landlord, triggers a right of access.[71] This right of access is given to the reversioner and all the relevant landlords or to persons authorised to act on their behalf. It allows them access to any part of the specified premises in which the landlord has either a freehold or leasehold interest which is included in the proposed acquisition. If the initial notice includes notice to acquire appurtenant property included in the lease of any of

---

67 Schedule 3, para 5.

68 Schedule 3, para 6(1). Termination of the lease by any other means is not prevented; and the tenant's right to relief under the Law of Property Act 1925, s 146, the Landlord and Tenant Act 1954, s 16 or the Local Government and Housing Act 1989 is not affected (Sch 3, para 6(2)–(3)).

69 Schedule 3, para 7.

70 See 5.6.2.

71 Section 17.

the qualifying tenants or includes the acquisition of any property used in common with occupiers of other premises,[72] then the landlord also has a right of access to the part of any of that property in which he has a freehold or leasehold interest. The right of access is for the purpose of enabling any of the relevant landlords to obtain a valuation of that interest in connection with the claim.

6.3.2 Access for nominee purchaser

The nominee purchaser, or any person acting on its behalf, has a similar right of access to any part of the specified premises or property specified in the notice.[73] The access must be reasonably required by the nominee purchaser in connection with any matter arising out of the initial notice. A further right of access in favour of the nominee purchaser may arise after a reversioner's counter-notice if that counter-notice requires the nominee purchaser to acquire property which the reversioner considers to cease to be of practical use or benefit.[74]

6.3.3 Exercise of access rights

All rights of access are exercisable at any reasonable time, and on giving not less than 10 days' notice to the occupier of the premises to which access is sought.[75] If the premises are unoccupied, then notice is given to the person entitled to occupy. Thus occupiers and tenants who are not participating may have to yield rights of access.

On or before giving the initial notice, therefore, the solicitor acting for the nominee purchaser and the participating tenants should draw his clients' attention to the rights of access. More importantly, he should consider giving due warning of the right of access to those qualifying tenants who are not participating and any other occupiers of flats in the block who may receive a request for access under s 17.

6.4 Reversioner's right to require evidence of right to participate

6.4.1 Right to require title to be deduced

In addition to the right of access, the reversioner has the right to give the nominee purchaser a notice which requires the nominee purchaser to deduce the title of any person by whom the initial notice was given.[76] The requirement

72 See s 1(2) and (3).
73 Section 17(2).
74 Section 21(5) and see 6.6.3.
75 Sections 17(3) and 21(5). In the Bill as drafted, only three days' notice was required.
76 Section 20(1).

will be to deduce the title of that person to the lease by virtue of which the claim is made to be a qualifying tenant. Such a request for evidence may be given by the reversioner within a period of 21 days from the date of the initial notice. The purpose of the provision is that the reversioner may thereby secure evidence from the title deduced that each person who claims to be a qualified tenant is in fact so qualified.

6.4.2 Tenant must be ready to respond

It is likely that landlords will give a notice under s 20 as a matter of standard practice and they are likely to give such notice in respect of each and every person by whom the initial notice was given. They have only 21 days to give the notice and are likely to do so by way of immediate riposte to the initial notice. For this reason, it has already been suggested in a previous chapter[77] that prior to giving the initial notice the solicitor for the nominee purchaser should have already prepared sufficient proof of title in respect of each of the participating tenants.

6.4.3 Meaning of deducing title

In the absence of guidance in the Act as to the meaning of deducing title, it would be advisable to deduce title in each case to the same standard as that required in a normal conveyancing transaction. It is suggested that this need not extend to include deducing title to any outstanding current mortgages on the property as such details are not relevant to the issue of whether the tenant is a qualifying tenant, but in the absence of guidance a prudent solicitor may choose to do so.

6.4.4 Potential deemed withdrawal in the event of non-compliance

The nominee purchaser has only 21 days from the date the reversioner gives notice under s 20 to comply with the requirement of deducing title.[78] If, as may be the usual practice, the reversioner asks for evidence in respect of all the participating tenants and the nominee purchaser then fails to comply within that time period by complying with the requirement to deduce title then the initial notice is deemed to have been withdrawn at the end of that period.[79] This rather draconian provision terminates the enfranchisement process and, being a deemed withdrawal, prevents the service of another initial notice within a period of 12 months. It is to avoid such a possible consequence that the solicitor should have the title to each participating tenant prepared in advance and ensure that he complies promptly with any notice under s 20.

---

77 See 4.1.9.

78 Section 20(2).

79 Section 20(3).

The potentially draconian nature of this provision was noted and some measure of alleviation introduced.[80] If there is a failure to deduce title in respect of only one or some of the participating tenants but sufficient qualifying tenants remain among those giving the notice (so that the initial notice would have been valid without those where title has not been deduced), there is no deemed withdrawal – and no other penalty. The more major problem, however, is not dealt with at all. If the nominee purchaser fails to respond within 21 days to the landlord's notice under this section at all, or with insufficient evidence of title so that there does not remain enough qualifying tenants, the process is terminated. It is to avoid this consequence of a deemed withdrawal, necessitating one year's wait to start again, that it is necessary to ensure the titles are ready to be given to the reversioner. It is to be noted that it is not necessary to deduce title to qualifying tenants who do not participate in the initial notice.[81]

6.4.5 Right to require evidence that the residence condition is satisfied

The reversioner may require the nominee purchaser to give him evidence of the occupation on which a qualifying tenant who is claimed in the initial notice to satisfy the residence condition relies.[82] This may be done within the period of 21 days beginning with the date the initial notice was given. It is likely, therefore, that a reversioner will require this evidence of each and every qualifying tenant who is stated to meet the residence condition at the same time as requiring title to be deduced. The nominee purchaser must comply by producing a statutory declaration made by each qualifying tenant in respect of whom the notice was given within 21 days.[83] However, because this requirement appears in regulations, there is no deemed withdrawal or other penalty for failure to comply with the time-limit.[84]

6.5 The duty of disclosure

6.5.1 The nature of the duty

The duty of disclosure, added to the Act at a late stage in the parliamentary process,[85] requires that the reversioner be notified of certain agreements relating to the disposal of interests in the premises which are the subject of the enfranchisement. The agreements covered by the duty are any agreements, of whatever nature, made between the nominee purchaser and any other person

80 HC Deb, Standing Committee B, cols 167–168, 19 November 1992; s 20(3)(b).
81 Section 20(1).
82 Leasehold Reform (Collective Enfranchisement and Lease Renewal) Regulations 1993, SI 1993/2407, Sch 1, para 2(1).
83 Schedule 1, para 2(2).
84 The difference is probably accounted for by the fact of the very late introduction of the residence conditions into the legislation.
85 HL Deb, Vol 543, cols 1314–1323.

except a participating tenant providing for the disposal of a relevant interest.[86] If the nominee purchaser is a company, the duty of disclosure also applies to revealing a shareholding in that company which is held by a person other than a participating tenant by virtue of which a relevant interest may be acquired.[87] 'Relevant interest' means any interest in the whole or any part of the premises subject to the enfranchisement claim or in any other property specified in the initial notice.[88]

The motivation behind the introduction of this amendment, the rationale of which was accepted by the Minister, was to prevent a group of qualifying tenants proceeding with a minimum number of participants in an attempt to pay only marriage value on the flats of such participants and obtain the whole at a lower price.[89] The duty of disclosure is designed to ensure that agreements with other qualifying tenants who are not participating are disclosed, so that the price payable for the freehold is calculated in the light of the 'hope value' represented by those agreements.

However, the duty will cover not only an agreement with other qualifying tenants who are not participating in the giving of the initial notice;[90] and will clearly also include agreements with tenants of any commercial units within the premises or any outside persons. However, the creation of an interest by way of security for a loan is not covered by the duty to disclose.[91] Agreements which are purely for financing purposes and create mortgages or other security interests do not have to be disclosed.

6.5.2 *When the duty arises*

The existence of an agreement or shareholding subject to the duty of disclosure shall be notified to the reversioner by the nominee purchaser as soon as possible after the agreement or shareholding is made or established. A majority of such agreements or shareholdings may be created prior to the giving of the initial notice. In such a case, the duty to notify arises as soon as possible after the giving of the initial notice.[92]

The duty of disclosure continues to apply in respect of an agreement or shareholding made or established after the initial notice is given until the valuation date,[93] ie the agreed date for acquisition of the freehold interest from

86 Section 18(1)(a).

87 Section 18(1)(b).

88 Section 18(3).

89 As to whether marriage value is indeed affected by the number of participants, see the discussion at 19.3.5.

90 See the discussion at 5.3.3.

91 Section 18(4).

92 Section 18(1). Although the initial notice is given by the participating tenants, there is no reason why the nominee purchaser should not give notification at the same time as the initial notice.

93 As defined by Sch 6, para 1.

the reversioner or until the date determined by the leasehold valuation tribunal for that acquisition.

6.5.3 Consequences of a failure to disclose

If the nominee purchaser is required to give notification but fails to do so before the price is paid in respect of the enfranchisement, the remedy is a liability for any shortfall in the price as a consequence of the non-disclosure. The liability is a joint and several liability on the nominee purchaser and the participating tenants to pay to the reversioner any amount by which the price might reasonably be assumed to have increased by reason of the notification.[94]

6.5.4 Difficulties with the duty of disclosure

It is suggested that the main value of the duty to a reversioner is one of providing information. It should reveal not only if some qualifying tenants are not participating but have an agreement to join in later but also what outside parties are involved and the nature of the involvement. The information revealed may be a factor in whether the reversioner decides to exercise the right to a leaseback of units and the flats held by non-qualifying tenants. If, for example, a tenant of a commercial unit has agreed to buy the value of that unit, that may be a factor in settling the price of the acquisition of the freehold. However, the consequences of a failure to notify is only a potential liability to pay more if it can be shown that the price would have been increased by an amount referable to that agreement or shareholding. The price agreed or determined may be unaffected by the failure to disclose. If the nominee purchaser and participating tenants believe this to be the case (and are prepared to argue this position later if necessary), there will be no penalty for a failure to notify. There may be some cases as a result where a nominee purchaser and the participating tenants decide to deprive the reversioner of information which would be revealed by notification under s 18 and argue (if necessary) later that the price would be unaffected. In view of the joint and several liability and the uncertainty as to the proper interpretation of the marriage value provisions, observance of the duty of disclosure is always advisable.

6.6 Reversioner's counter-notice

6.6.1 The necessity for a counter-notice

The first two responses of a reversioner to an initial notice, namely seeking access to the premises for valuation purposes and requiring evidence of the right to participate, are responses which, although likely in many circumstances

94 Section 18(2).

if not in nearly every case, are, in fact, optional. The first step the reversioner *must* take in response to the initial notice is to serve a counter-notice, specifying an address for service in England and Wales,[95] on the nominee purchaser by the date which the nominee purchaser has specified in its initial notice.[96]

6.6.2 *The alternative forms of counter-notice*

The Act provides that there are three alternative counter-notices which the reversioner may give, although in the vast majority of cases the third alternative will not apply. These three possibilities are as follows.[97]

1 The reversioner can serve a counter-notice stating that he admits that the participating tenants were, on the relevant date (that is on the date of the initial notice), entitled to exercise the right of collective enfranchisement in relation to the premises.
2 The reversioner can serve a counter-notice which states that the reversioner does not admit that the participating tenants were so entitled. If this counter-notice is served the reasons for not admitting the right must be specified in the counter-notice.
3 The reversioner can serve a counter-notice which either admits or does not admit the right, as in either (a) or (b) but, additionally, states that in any event an application for an order under s 23 of the Act will be made by the reversioner. By such application, the reversioner will be declaring the intention to redevelop the whole or a substantial part of the premises. A counter-notice of this sort will only be possible when the reversioner can meet the strict requirements of s 23 and, in particular, it will only apply when not less than two-thirds of all the long leases contained in the premises are due to terminate within a period of five years from the date of the initial notice.[98]

6.6.3 *Admitting the right to collective enfranchisement*

When a counter-notice is served admitting the right of the participating tenants to exercise the right to collective enfranchisement, the counter-notice must contain a full response to the claim as set out in the initial notice. The statutory requirements are as follows.[99]

1 Such a counter-notice must state which, if any, of the proposals in the initial notice are accepted by the reversioner and which, if any, of the proposals are

95 Section 21(6).
96 Section 21(1).
97 Section 21(2).
98 The redevelopment defence is fully discussed at 7.3.1.
99 Section 21(3).

not accepted. If any of the proposals are not accepted the reversioner must state his counter-proposals. If the reversioner considers that further parts of the property or flat should be subject to additional leaseback in favour of the reversioner the counter-notice must say so.[100] It is therefore at the counter-notice stage that the decision on optional leaseback should be notified to the nominee purchaser.[101]

2 In a case where the initial notice states entitlement to the freehold of property which is used in common by any qualifying tenant under the terms of the lease of his flat or which is used in common with occupiers of other premises[102] the reversioner has the choice of whether to agree to the disposal of that freehold interest or to offer to grant permanent rights instead. The counter-notice can, therefore, give the counter-proposal of the reversioner in which the reversioner specifies the nature of the permanent rights which he is willing to grant when enfranchisement takes place. Such permanent rights will have to be extensive enough to ensure that the occupier of the flat will enjoy as near as maybe the same rights as those enjoyed by the qualifying tenants under the terms of his lease. They do not have to be identical to those that currently exist under the lease.

3 The reversioner may require the nominee purchaser to acquire, on behalf of the participating tenants, the interest of either the freeholder or any other relevant landlord in any other property if, in the event of collective enfranchisement, that other property would, for all practical purposes, cease to be of useful benefit to him or would cease to be capable of being reasonably managed or maintained by him. If the reversioner considers that such property exists then the counter-notice must state what those interests are which the nominee purchaser is to be required to acquire.[103] It is interesting that the statutory wording does not require the property objectively to cease to be of use and benefit but introduces a subjective element. A freeholder could argue that, whatever another owner might

---

100 These leaseback proposals are a reference to leaseback within s 36 and Sch 9 (see s 21(7)).

101 By virtue of Sch 9, para 6(2), the nominee purchaser shall grant a leaseback 'if the freeholder by notice requires him to do so'. In 9.5.5, the view is taken that this permits a freeholder to give notice after a counter-notice and at any time prior to a binding contract to require a leaseback. This view is consistent with s 21 which only refers to leaseback proposals. However, the reversioner will usually be the freeholder and it may be that a court would decide that the proposals on leaseback must be put in the counter-notice where the freeholder is the reversioner and the decision cannot be changed by a later notice under Sch 9. A reversioner freeholder should therefore be advised to put all his leaseback requirements in the counter-notice.

102 Within the terms of s 1(3)(b) (see 3.2.3).

103 Section 21(3)(c) and (4). Where a counter-notice specifies an interest which the nominee purchaser is to be required to acquire, then the nominee purchaser is given a right of access to that property for the purposes of enabling him to obtain a valuation of the interest (s 21(5)).

consider, the property has ceased to be of use and benefit *to him*. Since adding property to that which the nominee purchaser has to acquire will increase the cost of enfranchisement, this is an argument that may well be put forward by the reversioner.

4 In some circumstances, the freeholder or any other relevant landlord may wish to retain an interest over the property to be acquired by the nominee purchaser where necessary for the proper management or maintenance of other neighbouring property, in which he retains a freehold or leasehold interest. An example might be rights of access to an adjoining block of flats, or the grant of an easement for services passing through the soil of the premises to be acquired. In such cases, the counter-notice must state the rights which the landlord or freeholder desires to retain.[104]

5 Finally, the counter-notice must address the terms of the conveyance to the nominee purchaser on enfranchisement. The details of that conveyance and the terms to be included are subject to detailed provision in the Act.[105] There are provisions to ensure the nominee purchaser is bound by existing restrictive covenants or to secure further restrictions to the extent allowed by the Act.[106]

6.6.4 *Counter-notices which do not admit entitlement to enfranchise*

A counter-notice under s 21(2)(b) which does not admit that participating tenants were entitled to the right to collective enfranchisement only has to state the reasons for such a statement. Such a notice is likely to be contested by the nominee purchaser by application to the court under s 22, although the reversioner who is unsuccessful before the court may have to pay the costs of those particular proceedings. It is possible that some reversioners will choose to give such a counter-notice to test the resolve of the nominee purchaser and participating tenants. It does put the ball back into the tenant's court by requiring them to apply for an order under s 22 within a period of two months beginning with the date of the giving of the counter-notice.[107] A failure to meet that time-limit will result in a deemed withdrawal.[108]

6.6.5 *Redevelopment counter-notice*

A redevelopment counter-notice under s 21(2)(c), even if it admits the right to enfranchise, does not have to contain all the additional requirements of a counter-notice under s 21(2)(a) which admits the right. Instead, the reversioner will need to ensure that there is a realistic prospect of sustaining a claim within

---

104 Section 21(3)(d).

105 See s 34 and Sch 7. See 9.3.1 for a full review.

106 See Sch 7, para 5.

107 Section 22(2) (see 7.2.1).

108 See s 29(1) and discussion at 8.3.1 ff.

s 23 which enables the initial notice to be defeated on the grounds of redevelopment.[109]

6.6.6 *Duty to furnish further information*

If the reversioner or other relevant landlord has received a notice (or a copy of one) exercising the right of a qualifying tenant to acquire a new lease,[110] then a copy of that notice must either be sent with the counter-notice or given to the nominee purchaser as soon as possible after receipt.[111] The duty to keep the nominee purchaser informed is a continuing one, so that if a notice exercising a right to a new lease, or notice of withdrawal is received after the counter-notice has been given, a copy must again be sent to the nominee purchaser. The duty continues until the collective enfranchisement procedure is complete or terminates.[112]

6.6.7 *Failure to give a counter-notice in time*

If the reversioner fails to give a counter-notice by the date specified in the initial notice, the better view is that a late notice cannot be given. This view is based on the straightforward terms of s 21(1) which impose a duty to act in the time-limit. The moral is clear – the advisers to a reversioner should always seek to ensure that a counter-notice, or further counter-notice, is given in time.

If a late counter-notice is indeed not possible, the nominee purchaser must apply to the court in accordance with s 25 for the court to determine the terms of acquisition.[113] If s 25 had permitted a consideration of the terms of acquisition proposed by the nominee purchaser, a reversioner would not have been substantially disadvantaged. However, providing that the court is satisfied that the initial notice was given validly and all requisite notices were given to any relevant landlords,[114] it seems that the court has no discretion as to the terms of acquisition and must make an order in accordance with the proposals in the initial notice.[115] If this is correct, then, although there may be no criminal penalties for failing to give a counter-notice, the potential for loss to all the relevant landlords and not just the reversioner may be considerable, especially if the proposed price in the initial notice[116] is a low figure designed as a negotiating starting point.

---

109 This matter is further discussed at 7.3.1.

110 Under s 42 (see 13.1.1).

111 Schedule 4, para 1.

112 Schedule 4, paras 2 and 3.

113 See 7.4.1.

114 In the case of the further counter-notice, requisite notices do not have to be shown as they will have been proved in the earlier court applications (s 25(1)(b) and (3)).

115 Section 25(1). This may not have been the impression held by the Under-Secretary of State, Mr Baldry, in his reply in HC Deb, Standing Committee B, col 172, 19 November 1992 when he referred to an application 'for terms to be determined'.

116 Which need not be the price as set by the surveyor in the statutory valuation.

The possible courses of action open to a reversioner who has not given a counter-notice in time are limited. However, it does seem possible that a later notice can be given where an optional leaseback is required by the reversioner of any units or flats not occupied by qualifying tenants.[117]

What may be argued is that a late counter-notice may be given, at least before the court makes an order under s 25. The basis of such an argument would be that potential detriment to all the relevant landlords if a late counter-notice cannot be given and a consideration of the scheme of the Act as a whole. In particular the following points could be considered.

1 There is no indication in the parliamentary debates that a strict time-limit is to apply.[118] Indeed, the Minister indicated that the reason that there were no criminal sanctions was because, whereas the advisers to the tenant can take as long as they like to prepare the initial notice and 'ensure that their attack is in order' the freeholder may receive an initial notice 'out of the blue' and 'might be out of the country'. The ability for the nominee purchaser to apply under what is now s 25 was said to be provision for 'when a reversioner proves to be unco-operative'.[119]

2 There is no express provision preventing a later counter-notice, nor a deemed acceptance of the proposals in the initial notice – in contrast to specific provisions in relation to other parts of the procedural timetable. Yet, if the court must accept the proposals in the initial notice when making an order under s 25, it amounts to such deemed acceptance by the reversioner. If the intention had been to deprive the reversioner and all the relevant landlords of the opportunity to argue the terms of acquisition before the leasehold valuation tribunal, one could have expected a clearer provision. To hold that a late counter-notice is not possible may well result in the reversioner relinquishing the freehold on less favourable terms and at a price considerably less than a leasehold valuation tribunal would determine as the price payable under the Act.

3 There is no statutory power to amend a counter-notice to correct inaccuracies or misdescriptions, while such a power is given in relation to an initial notice.[120]

4 A late counter-notice can marginally delay the procedure but cannot prevent it. If a tenant applies for an order under s 25 and a late counter-notice is allowed, the reversioner would have to give the counter-notice before a s 25 order is made. Once given, a late counter-notice would then enable the subsequent procedure to operate.

---

117 See Sch 9 and 9.5.3 and 9.5.5.

118 Reference to *Hansard* is now possible after the decision in *Pepper v Hart* [1992] 3 WLR 1032, [1993] 1 All ER 42, HL.

119 See HC Deb, Standing Committee B, cols 171–172, 19 November 1992.

120 See Sch 3, para 15.

The alternative, or additional argument, for a reversioner who has missed the time-limit is to argue that the court does have a discretion under s 25 and need not adopt the proposals in the initial notice. It is harder to find any cogent statutory basis for such an argument except by giving a very limited meaning to the phrase 'in accordance with the proposals in the initial notice' in s 25(1). Any discretion would involve the court referring the terms of acquisition to a leasehold valuation tribunal for determination.[121]

It is submitted that the interrelationship of ss 21 and 25 may work injustice on a reversioner who, perhaps for justified reasons, did not give a counter-notice within the two-month time-limit. There is room for litigation and perhaps for legislative amendment if landlords are disadvantaged.[122]

6.7 Proof of title and requisitions

6.7.1 Applies in default of agreement

The conveyancing procedure subsequent to a reversioner's counter-notice is provided by statutory instrument.[123] It applies to all transactions to give effect to an initial notice unless the reversioner, nominee purchaser and any relevant landlord otherwise agree. Delivery of proof of title and requisitions thereon may be done prior to entering into a binding contract. It may be appropriate for the nominee purchaser to require title to be deduced as soon as a counter-notice or further counter-notice has been given admitting the right, because if the title appears defective this may have an impact on valuation. Much of the matter covered by the Regulations would be dealt with by conditions of sale in a privately negotiated transaction.[124]

6.7.2 Delivery of proof of title

Once the reversioner has given a counter-notice or a further counter-notice admitting the right to collective enfranchisement, or if the nominee purchaser has applied to the court for an order where there has been a failure to give such a notice, the nominee purchaser may by notice require the reversioner to deduce title. Within 28 days of such notice, the reversioner shall comply by supplying the necessary office copies in the case of registered land or an

---

121 Section 91(4) would give jurisdiction to order such a transfer.

122 Reference to corresponding provisions in the Leasehold Reform Act 1967 do not assist as the procedure is not really comparable – although failure to serve a notice of reply within two months under that Act did not prevent a landlord making a challenge on validity (see 1967 Act, Sch 3, para 7 and Hague, *Leasehold Enfranchisement* 2nd edn, 1987, Sweet & Maxwell, 5–18).

123 The Leasehold Reform (Collective Enfranchisement and Lease Renewal) Regulations 1993, SI 1993/2407, made on 30 September 1993 and in force on 1 November 1993.

124 The empowering section (s 98(1)) provides that they shall be as nearly as may be the same as in the case of a contract for sale freely negotiated between the parties.

epitome of title in the case of unregistered interests.[125] Title is to be deduced to the interests that the nominee purchaser proposed to acquire in the initial notice, both freehold and leasehold. If, in the counter-notice, the reversioner required the nominee purchaser to acquire additional property, title to that must also be deduced. Where the leasehold valuation tribunal has already determined the property to be acquired, or the extent of it has been agreed, then title is to be deduced to that. A reversioner may need to obtain some title details from another relevant landlord.[126] Although the regulations only apply to giving the reversioner notice to deduce title, there is express provision in the Act allowing a nominee purchaser to give notice and then deal direct with any relevant landlord for the purpose of deducing title.[127]

6.7.3 Requisitions on title

Within 14 days of receipt of the proof of title, the nominee purchaser may give a statement of any objections or requisitions; there is a further period of 14 days for the statement of the reversioner's answer to those requisitions; and a period of seven days for the nominee purchaser to give a further statement of objections or comments.[128] These time-limits should be observed; any requisition or objection not given by the nominee purchaser in such statement or further statement is deemed to be waived; and any matter not raised cannot be deemed to be a defect in title for valuation purposes.[129] If the nominee purchaser does not respond with a further statement, the reversioner's answer is considered satisfactory.

6.7.4 Relevant landlord's title

A relevant landlord can give notice of an intention to deal directly with the nominee purchaser in deducing, evidencing or verifying title; a nominee purchaser can require a relevant landlord to deal directly in these matters.[130] In such a case, the notices and statements requiring proof of title or in respect of requisitions are to be given to the relevant landlord, who then has the duty of response.[131]

---

125 Ibid, Sch 1, para 3. In the case of registered interests the landlord must supply the particulars and information which have to be given on a sale pursuant to s 110 of the Land Registration Act 1925.

126 Schedule 1, para 8 imposes the obligation to assist.

127 Schedule 1, para 7(2).

128 Schedule 1, para 4.

129 See Sch 6, para 3(3).

130 See Sch 1, para 7(1)(a) and (2); and see 5.9.2.

131 Sch 1, para 5.

CHAPTER SEVEN

RESOLVING DISPUTES AND DIFFICULTIES

7.1 The potential problems

There are a number of potential disputes and difficulties which may arise during the collective enfranchisement process. The landlord may dispute the tenants' right to enfranchise or challenge the validity of the procedure; the landlord may resist the claim under the redevelopment defence which the tenants do not accept; or the landlord may not fulfil the statutory requirement to give a counter-notice. In many cases the right of the tenants may be accepted but the parties cannot agree the price or the other terms of the acquisition. Naturally, the Act makes detailed provision for such situations. A dispute about the validity of the right or procedure is referred to the county court;[1] valuation issues are dealt with by the leasehold valuation tribunal, which is a rent assessment committee constituted for the purposes of the Act.[2] Valuation appeals will be taken to the Lands Tribunal.[3]

7.2 Challenge to the validity of an initial notice – s 22

7.2.1 Nominee purchaser to apply

Where the reversioner does not admit the entitlement of the tenants to collective enfranchisement and serves a counter-notice to that effect,[4] the nominee purchaser may make an application to the court for a declaration that the participating tenants were entitled, at the date of service of the initial notice, to exercise the right of collective enfranchisement.[5] Such an application must be made within two months of the giving of the counter-notice to the nominee

---

1 Section 90(1). The county court exercises any jurisdiction conferred by Part I of the Act on the court. See 22.2.1.

2 Section 91. See 22.3.2.

3 Section 91(10) applying the Housing Act 1980, Sch 22, para 2.

4 The counter-notice will have stated that the reversioner does not admit that the participating tenants were entitled to the right of collective enfranchisement and given reasons; the notice will have been served under either s 21(2)(b) or (c) (see 6.6.4).

5 Section 22(1).

purchaser;[6] and the consequence of missing this time-limit is severe – there is a deemed withdrawal.[7] In effect, therefore, the nominee purchaser must make this application within the time-limit if the claim is to progress.

7.2.2 *Powers of the court*

The issues argued under this section are likely to be to establish whether the participating tenants meet all the statutory requirements[8] with the burden of proof on the nominee purchaser. If the court is satisfied that the tenants were entitled to the right it will make a declaration to that effect. If the court makes such a declaration, it will also declare that the reversioner's counter-notice shall be of no effect and require the reversioner to give a further counter-notice by such date as the court specifies in the order.[9] If such a counter-notice is ordered to be given by the court the reversioner is again subject to the statutory requirements for the giving of a counter-notice which admits the right of collective enfranchisement.[10]

If the nominee purchaser does not succeed in establishing the right to collective enfranchisement, the court will dismiss the application. The initial notice then ceases to have effect at the time when the order dismissing the application becomes final.[11] A landlord may also seek to take advantage of procedural lapses but the court's power to deal with inaccuracies or misdescription[12] suggests that the landlord is only likely to be successful on procedural issues if there is a fundamental blunder – such as serving the notice on the person who is not the reversioner.

7.2.3 *Validity application heard first*

In a situation where the reversioner has both made an application to challenge the effect of an initial notice and also indicated an intention to take advantage of the redevelopment defence and make an application under s 23,[13] the challenge on validity will be argued first.[14] If the tenants successfully obtain a declaration of their right to collective enfranchisement the court will not declare the counter-notice to be of no effect or require a fresh counter-notice if a s 23 application is still pending or the time-limit for making such application has not

6 Section 22(2).
7 Section 29(1).
8 As discussed in the previous chapters, especially at 3.3.1 ff and 6.1.7.
9 Section 22(3).
10 As required by s 21(3)–(5) and s 22(5). See further 6.6.3.
11 Section 22(6). This will give the nominee purchaser the opportunity to appeal against the refusal of a declaration.
12 Schedule 3, para 15 (see 6.1.12).
13 By giving a counter-notice under s 21(2)(c).
14 Section 23(3).

expired.[15] Instead, the next stage will be to dispose of the redevelopment issue and if the tenants are again successful, a fresh counter-notice will be required at that stage.[16]

7.3 Defence of an intention to redevelop – s 23

7.3.1 Prevents a collective enfranchisement claim

The claim to collective enfranchisement is liable to be defeated if the appropriate landlord applies to the court and establishes a sufficient intention to redevelop the whole or substantial part of the premises. It must be a redevelopment plan for the premises; redevelopment of appurtenant property (such as a block of garages) will not suffice. The statutory requirements are such that it is thought that there will be relatively few cases where the requisite intention can be established.

7.3.2 Who makes the application?

The application can only be made after the *reversioner* has given a counter-notice under s 21(2)(c);[17] but the application is made by any *appropriate landlord.* Although an appropriate landlord is either the reversioner, or any relevant landlord or any two or more acting together,[18] an application to defeat the tenants' claim can only be made by or with the authority of the landlord who wishes to establish the requisite intention. This is one area where the power of the reversioner to bind other relevant landlords is limited.[19] The reversioner does not have authority in this instance to act on behalf of a relevant landlord but the relevant landlord can bring proceedings on his own behalf. Since it is the reversioner who gives the counter-notice, a degree of co-operation is required at an early stage if the reversioner and the landlord who wishes to establish the intention are not the same person.

7.3.3 Time-limit to apply

An application must be made within two months of the giving of the counter-notice to the nominee purchaser;[20] although if there is also a challenge to the

---

15 Section 22(4).
16 See 7.3.5.
17 Section 23(1).
18 Section 23(10).
19 Schedule 1, para 9.
20 Section 23(3).

validity of the initial notice,[21] any such s 22 application is proceeded with first and the s 23 application is not proceeded with until such time as an order under s 22 becomes final.[22]

If the reversioner gives a counter-notice stating that an application will be made under s 23 but does not make an application within the time-limit, or withdraws an application duly made, then the opportunity is lost and the reversioner is under a duty to give a further counter-notice[23] within the period of two months.[24] The duty to give a further counter-notice does not arise if an application by the nominee purchaser to establish the validity of the claim has been made but not yet disposed of.[25]

7.3.4 *What must be established?*

To make an order under this section the court must be satisfied that:[26]

(a) not less than two-thirds of all the long leases on which flats in the premises are held are due to terminate within five years of the initial notice;
(b) for the purposes of redevelopment, the applicant intends, once the leases have terminated, to demolish or reconstruct, or carry out substantial works of construction on the whole or a substantial part of the premises; and
(c) the applicant could not reasonably do so without obtaining possession of the flats demised by the long leases.

The requirement of two-thirds of the long leases expiring within five years will be infrequently found – except in genuine cases where a landlord has refused all pleas for privately negotiated new leases and had a policy of accepting surrenders and no fresh grants of long leases. It is in precisely those cases that a genuine intention may be established. The ability to oppose a claim on redevelopment grounds was described as a loophole by the Opposition[27] during the passage of the legislation but has limited scope. The burden of proof is on the landlord and the requisite intent must be established even if the long leases are due to terminate in five years.

The test to be applied has some very distinct similarities to that applicable under s 30(1)(f) of the Landlord and Tenant Act 1954.[28] As a result, it is

21 See 7.2.
22 See s 101(9) and 24.4.
23 Section 23(6). It must be a counter-notice admitting the right (s 23(9)).
24 The two-month period is calculated from either the expiry of the time-limit for an application or from the date of withdrawal (s 23(7)).
25 Section 23(8).
26 Section 23(2).
27 HC Deb, Standing Committee B, cols 173–178; their proposal to reduce to a three-year period in which the leases were to expire was rejected.
28 The wording does not differ in substance; under the 1993 Act, the applicant will have to show that the work is for purposes of redevelopment. See also the Housing Act 1985, Sch 2, Ground 10 and the Housing Act 1988, Sch 2, Ground 6.

certain that the not insubstantial case-law on the 1954 Act will be of relevance if similar issues arise under the 1993 Act. Thus, to establish the requisite intention, the applicant will need to show some firm decision and a reasonable prospect of being able to redevelop,[29] which may be a considerable task. It may well be necessary to have obtained outline planning permission[30] and works of reconstruction falling short of demolition and rebuilding have to be substantial so that work to the structure may be needed and substantial refurbishment may not suffice.[31] Work which the applicant could do without obtaining possession, perhaps under rights of access and entry in the lease, will not count as works for this purpose.[32] Where the landlord fails to establish this defence, any realistic separate development value which exists should be reflected in the price paid.

7.3.5 Orders by the court

In dealing with an application, the court will either:

1 dismiss the application if the applicant landlord fails to satisfy the statutory requirements, in which case the court will declare the counter-notice to be of no effect and the court will require a further counter-notice;[33] or

2 declare that the right to collective enfranchisement shall not be exercisable. If such an order is made the initial notice ceases to have effect on the order becoming final.[34] This will give an opportunity for an appeal against the court's decision.

7.4 Failure to give a counter-notice

7.4.1 The power of the court

Once the nominee purchaser has served an initial notice, the statutory procedure depends upon the receipt of a counter-notice which, if it disputes the claim, allows applications to contest validity; while if it admits the claim, will contain the reversioner's proposals on terms and price allowing negotiation to

---

29 *Cunliffe v Goodman* [1950] 2 KB 237 where it was said (at 254) that the project must move 'out of the zone of contemplation – out of the sphere of the tentative, the provisional and the exploratory – into the valley of decision'; *Reohorn v Barry Corporation* [1956] 1 WLR 845.

30 *Cappocci v Goble* [1987] 2 EGLR 102; *Edwards v Thompson* [1990] 2 EGLR 71. In the case of the 1993 Act, the court might choose to relax the requirements, particularly in the case of planning consent, given that the time for commencing the redevelopment may be five years away and any existing permission would expire before that time. A reasonable prospect of obtaining consent at the time of the proposed redevelopment, as evidenced by discussions with the planning authority, may suffice.

31 *Barth v Prichard* [1990] 1 EGLR 109.

32 *Heath v Drown* [1973] AC 498, HL.

33 Section 23(5). Once again, it must be a counter-notice admitting the right (s 23(9)).

34 Section 23(1) and (4).

proceed. If a counter-notice, or further counter-notice, is not given to the nominee purchaser, the court may, on application of the nominee purchaser, make an order determining the terms on which the nominee purchaser is to acquire the interests and rights specified in the initial notice.[35] An order determining the terms of the acquisition will only be made if the court is satisfied that the participating tenants were entitled to enfranchise collectively when they gave the notice and that all requirements for giving copies of that initial notice[36] were complied with.[37] Such terms determined by the courts must include any mandatory leaseback,[38] but in other respects will be in accordance with the proposals in the initial notice. The reversioner's failure to give a counter-notice may therefore prejudice the position of the reversioner and any other relevant landlord by depriving them of the right to insist on an optional leaseback of units and certain flats and result in an imposition by the court of the terms as to price, conditions or the provisions in the conveyance in accordance with the proposals in the initial notice.[39]

7.4.2 Time-limit

An application for an order to determine terms must be made within six months beginning with the date by which the counter-notice or further counter-notice should have been given.[40] Unless there are good reasons to the contrary, an application under this section should be made as soon as the date for giving the counter-notice or further counter-notice expires.[41]

7.5 Negotiation – and failure to agree contract terms

7.5.1 Negotiation

Once a counter-notice has been given admitting the claim, the statute envisages negotiation. The nominee purchaser and reversioner will have set out their

---

35 Section 25(1). For a discussion of the possibility of a late counter-notice, see 6.6.7.

36 See 6.1.11.

37 Section 25(3).

38 Section 25(2) and in accordance with Sch 9, Part II (see 9.5.2).

39 For the definition of 'the terms of acquisition', see s 24(8) and the discussion at 7.5.2. A reversioner who did not give a counter-notice in time may still be able to give a late notice requiring leaseback (see 9.5.5 for a full discussion). Unless a late counter-notice is possible (see 6.6.7), it would seem that the court has no discretion but will make an order incorporating the terms proposed in the initial notice.

40 Section 25(4).

41 It may be possible for a counter-notice to be validly given late, even after an application under s 25 (see the discussion at 6.6.7). If this is right then such a counter-notice will allow a restoration of the normal procedure although the reversioner should be left with the costs in making the application.

respective cases in the two notices. They will be joined in the negotiations by any relevant landlord who has given the requisite notice[42] of a wish to negotiate the terms of acquisition of his interest directly with the nominee purchaser.[43] If an agreement can be reached to compromise any differences, perhaps on price, conditions, or the terms of the conveyance or leaseback, the parties can conclude a binding contract and proceed to completion. The time for negotiation is, however, strictly limited and a nominee purchaser who delays too long may find the next time-limit has passed and the initial notice is deemed withdrawn.

7.5.2 *Agreeing terms of acquisition*

What needs to be agreed are the 'terms of acquisition'. In relation to a collective enfranchisement claim, this means all the terms of the proposed acquisition by the nominee purchaser. The statutory definition particularly refers to the interests to be acquired, the extent of the property to which those interests relate, the rights granted over any property, the price payable for such interests and the provisions to be contained in any conveyance.[44] It will also include matters relating to the reversionary interest if it has to be severed, rights granted over appurtenant property which the reversioner chooses to retain and the terms relating to property which the reversioner insists the nominee purchaser should acquire on the basis that it ceases to be of use and benefit or capable of reasonable management.[45]

7.5.3 *Determination of disputed matters*

There is a two-month period, beginning with the date the counter-notice or further counter-notice was given, for negotiation – during which no further steps in the process can be taken. If, however, any of the terms of acquisition remain in dispute at the end of that period, then either the reversioner or the nominee purchaser can apply to the leasehold valuation tribunal for a determination of those disputed matters.[46] Any such application must be made within six months from the date of the counter-notice[47] – so there is a four-month window of opportunity for an application to be made. The burden of meeting that time-limit is effectively on the nominee purchaser. If the six-month period slips by the claim will be deemed to be withdrawn.[48] The

---

42 Under Sch 1, para 7 (see 5.9.2).

43 For the purposes of s 24, 'parties' includes such relevant landlords as well as the reversioner and the nominee purchaser (s 24(7)).

44 Section 24(8).

45 In accordance with ss 1(4) and 21(4).

46 Section 24(1). A relevant landlord involved in the negotiation cannot apply.

47 Section 24(2).

48 Section 29(2).

leasehold valuation tribunal, and not the court, will determine the disputed matters.[49]

7.6 The contract and deposit

7.6.1 Required once the terms of acquisition are settled

By one route or another, the position will be reached, after service of the initial notice and the counter-notice, that the terms of the acquisition are settled. This may come about through agreement, or the terms of acquisition may have been determined by the leasehold valuation tribunal. Alternatively, the terms may have been determined by order of the court if no counter-notice was given. In all three sets of circumstances there should be no further hindrance to the parties entering into a binding contract and proceeding to complete the enfranchisement – and this will be the normal procedure.[50]

7.6.2 Preparation of the contract

The draft contract is prepared by the reversioner and given to the nominee purchaser within 21 days of the terms of acquisition being agreed or determined. The draft is deemed to be approved unless the nominee purchaser gives proposals for amendment to the reversioner within 14 days. Unless the reversioner responds within the same time period with an answer to the amendment proposals, the amendments are deemed agreed.[51]

7.6.3 Payment of the deposit on exchange of contracts

Once the draft contract is agreed, the contracts will be signed by and exchanged between the reversioner and nominee purchaser. On exchange, the reversioner can require a deposit to be paid to the reversioner's solicitor or licensed conveyancer as stakeholder. Unless otherwise agreed, this is to be £500 or 10 per cent of the purchase price, whichever is the greater.[52]

---

49 For a full discussion of the determination of the price, see 19.2.1.

50 The requirement of a contract makes a collective enfranchisement very different to the procedure under the Leasehold Reform Act 1967 and that for a new lease under Chapter II. Once the contract is entered into, the general principles and rules will apply.

51 These provisions are in the Leasehold Reform (Collective Enfranchisement and Lease Renewal) Regulations 1993, SI 1993/2407, Sch 1, para 6. There are therefore no penalties for non-observance except the deeming provisions on acceptance. The provisions will not apply if the parties agree not to be bound by the regulations (see s 2).

52 Leasehold Reform (Collective Enfranchisement and Lease Renewal) Regulations 1993, Sch 1, para 7.

7.7 Failure to enter binding contract and power to make vesting orders

7.7.1 Application for a vesting order

The Act makes detailed provision for those situations where the terms have been agreed or determined but no binding contract has been entered into.[53] Either the reversioner or the nominee purchaser can apply within two months of the appropriate period as defined to the court which can make such order as it thinks fit.[54] The appropriate period in this context is normally a period of two months.[55]

7.7.2 Calculating the time-limit to apply

The calculation of when the two-month period commences depends on the 'route' taken.

1 If the parties agreed terms, it will be two months from the date the terms were finally agreed.[56] There is potential for dispute here. By definition a *binding* contract does not yet exist. Where terms are settled in open correspondence, but there is no contract signed by the parties,[57] it is submitted that the terms are finally agreed; but where the agreement remains 'subject to contract' a final agreement is not yet made.
2 If all or any of the terms have been determined by the leasehold valuation tribunal, it will be a period of two months beginning with the date when the decision of the tribunal becomes final. The leasehold valuation tribunal does, however, have power to fix a period other than two months when making its determination.[58]
3 Where the terms of acquisition have been determined by court order after failure to give a counter-notice, it will be a period of two months beginning with the date when the order of the court becomes final. The court does, however, have power to fix a period other than two months when making its order.[59]

7.7.3 Risk of a deemed withdrawal

If these time-limits for application are missed then, once again, the nominee purchaser will suffer a deemed withdrawal of the initial notice and the collective

53 These provisions are contained in ss 24(3)–(6) and 25(4)–(8) depending on whether a counter-notice was given or not. They are virtually identical in wording and are therefore considered together.

54 Sections 24(3) and 25(5).

55 Sections 24(5) and 25(7).

56 Section 24(6)(a).

57 Within the provisions of the Law of Property (Miscellaneous Provisions) Act 1989.

58 Section 24(6)(b).

59 Section 25(8).

enfranchisement procedure will terminate.[60] This is notwithstanding the agreement on, or the determination of, the terms of acquisition. Until a binding contract exists, time-limits continue to run against the nominee purchaser. If these time-limits are missed then, on application to the court, no doubt by the reversioner, the court may order that the initial notice is deemed to have been withdrawn.[61]

7.7.4 Vesting orders – taking the place of a binding contract

A vesting order is effectively a substitute for a binding contract – it does not itself vest the freehold or other interest in the nominee purchaser. It may provide for the interest to be acquired by the nominee purchaser to be vested in him on the terms agreed, determined by the leasehold valuation tribunal or by order of the court (as the case may be).[62] The terms can only be modified if a separate prior application is made[63] to the leasehold valuation tribunal which has determined, and specified in an order, that modifications are required by reason of a change in circumstances since the time the terms were agreed or determined earlier.[64] For the purposes of the Act, a reference to a binding contract includes a reference to a vesting order.[65] For example, all the provisions relating to the procedure on the election by a qualifying tenant to particpate or the death of, or assignment by a participating tenant do not apply once a binding contract is entered into;[66] so they will equally not apply after a vesting order.

7.7.5 Vesting order procedure

Schedule 5 of the Act sets out the details of the vesting order procedure.[67] The nominee purchaser will pay into court the appropriate sum, namely the amount fixed as the price together with any outstanding amounts determined by the leasehold valuation tribunal as due from the tenants, such as in respect of rent or service charges.[68] On payment into court, he will receive a conveyance, executed by a person designated by the court and in a form approved by the leasehold valuation tribunal, giving effect to the terms of acquisition.[69] The

60 Section 29(2)(b) and (3).
61 Sections 24(4)(c) and 25(6)(c).
62 Sections 24(4)(a) and 25(6)(a).
63 On the application of either nominee purchaser or the reversioner.
64 Sections 24(4)(b) and 25(6)(b).
65 Schedule 5, para 5.
66 Section 14(11); Sch 5, para 5(2).
67 When ordered under s 24(4)(a) or (b) or 25(6)(a) or (b). Note that a vesting order ceases to have effect if a compulsory purchase notice to treat is served (Sch 5, para 3). See s 30 and 8.4.3.
68 Schedule 5, para 2(1) and 3(1).
69 Schedule 5, para 2(1).

conveyance is effective to vest in the nominee purchaser the interests expressed to be conveyed[70] and the payment into court satisfies any claims in respect of the price against the nominee purchaser or the participating tenants.[71]

7.8 Procedure where a landlord cannot be found

7.8.1 Applies if any relevant landlord cannot be found

The collective enfranchisement procedure depends upon service of an initial notice on the reversioner and copies of the notice on every relevant landlord. If one or more of these relevant landlords cannot be found or their identity cannot be ascertained, the usual procedure cannot be commenced. Sections 26 and 27 contain detailed provisions to cover the contingency that the identity of freeholder or other relevant landlord cannot be ascertained, or, even if ascertained, they cannot be found.[72]

7.8.2 Procedure where there is at least one relevant landlord

If at least one relevant landlord can be ascertained and found by the nominee purchaser, the usual procedure can be followed, although with necessary changes. The first step will be for the qualifying tenants who wish to proceed with a claim to apply for an order dispensing with the need to give an initial notice, or serve a copy of it, upon the unavailable landlord.[73] The court can only make such an order if it is established that the requisite two-thirds of the qualifying tenants desire to make an enfranchisement claim and that the identity of one or more (but not all) of the relevant landlords cannot be ascertained or cannot be found so that the initial notice, or copy of it, cannot be given.[74] If one of the persons whose identity is unknown or cannot be found is the freeholder then, in the same application, the qualifying tenants may seek an order substituting any other relevant landlord as the reversioner.[75] Notice of an application to appoint another relevant landlord as reversioner will be served, under rules of court, upon any person known or believed to be a relevant landlord; and such persons will have a right to be joined as parties to the proceedings.[76]

A subsequent initial notice must contain a statement of the effect of an order dispensing with the need to give notice – so that those landlords who do receive

70 Schedule 5, para 2(2).

71 Schedule 5, para 4.

72 The procedure is not dissimilar to that under the Leasehold Reform Act 1967, s 27 (See *Re Robertsons Application* [1969] 1 WLR 109, [1969] 1 All ER 257, and Hague, *Leasehold Enfranchisement*, 1987, Sweet & Maxwell, 17–17 to 17–26).

73 Section 26(2).

74 Section 26(2)(a)–(c).

75 Section 26(3).

76 Section 26(9).

it will be fully informed.[77] Provided the initial notice contains such a statement, the requirements of giving the notice or copy to the particular person named in the order is deemed to have been complied with.[78]

7.8.3 Procedure where no relevant landlords can be found or ascertained

In a situation where the identity of the freeholder is unknown and there are no other relevant landlords, or where the identity of all relevant landlords cannot be ascertained, it is not possible to adopt the usual procedure because there can be no reversioner to conduct the proceedings and negotiation. In such a case, it is open to not less than two-thirds of the qualifying tenants who desire to make a claim to exercise the right of collective enfranchisement to apply to the court for a vesting order.[79] The court may make an order vesting the interest of the freeholder or of the relevant landlords, if any, which are liable to acquisition under the Act.[80]

7.8.4 Requirements for the making of an order

The court can only make an order on the application of not less than two-thirds of the qualifying tenants. It must be satisfied that on the date of making the application the premises were subject to the Act and that the applicants would not have been precluded from giving a valid initial notice.[81] Before making the order, the court can require the applicants to take further steps to trace the freeholder or landlord concerned. This can be by way of advertisement or otherwise as the court thinks proper.[82] To avoid this delay, it may be prudent to ensure that all reasonable steps to trace the missing landlord, including advertisement in appropriate cases, has been taken before making an application.

7.8.5 Subsequent tracing of the missing landlord

There remains a possibility, remote no doubt in many cases,[83] that the person who cannot be found or identified is subsequently traced, as a result of the advertisement or other action taken, after the application for a vesting order but before the interest is vested in pursuance of the application. In such

77 Section 26(7).

78 Section 26(8).

79 Section 26(1). Where the property has become bona vacantia (for example, the freeholder was a company which has been struck off the register) and is vested in the Official Solicitor, the tenants may be able to negotiate a purchase without going through the statutory procedure.

80 Section 26(1)(i) and (ii).

81 Section 26(4).

82 Section 26(5).

83 Although, if a landlord has been deliberately concealing its identity, the truth may emerge at this stage.

circumstances, no further steps or proceedings can be taken with a view to vesting and the rights and obligations shall be determined as if the applicants had given an initial notice at the date of their application.[84] Normally, this will then mean the statutory procedure commences and the traced landlord will become the reversioner and under a duty to give a counter-notice. There could be some difficulties at this stage. Not only is there no guidance as to the meaning of 'traced' but there can be no certainty that the person so traced becomes aware of the situation to enable a counter-notice to be given. However, the court can give such directions as it thinks fit to give effect to the rights and obligations of the parties and these can include modifying or dispensing with any of the requirements of Chapter I of the Act and the regulations made thereunder.[85]

7.8.6 *Withdrawal of an application*

An application for a vesting order can be withdrawn at any time before execution of a conveyance.[86] If it is withdrawn after a landlord is traced but before any further steps are taken, the application is no longer to be regarded as if an initial notice has been given. However, when a landlord is traced, a group of applicant qualifying tenants cannot proceed as if an initial notice has been given and then at a later stage withdraw the application for a vesting order. Such later withdrawal is only possible with consent of every owner of any interest and with leave of the court.[87] Leave will only be given if it appears to the court just to do so by reason of matters coming to the knowledge of the applicants in consequence of the tracing of the landlord. The idea is to give an opportunity to withdraw without further liability as soon as the landlord is traced; but if the applicants then choose to proceed or delay and thus permit a counter-notice to be given, the withdrawal must be by notice of withdrawal as participating tenants[88] with consequent liability for relevant costs.

7.8.7 *Vesting order procedure*

The procedure for vesting interests of a landlord who cannot be found has some similarities to that where there is a failure to give a counter-notice or enter a binding contract.[89] There are, however, differences reflecting the fact that in this instance there has been no initial notice and therefore no nominee purchaser or statutory procedure and no opportunity for anyone to put forward

---

84 Section 26(5)(a).
85 Section 26(5)(b).
86 Section 26(6) – even if a vesting order has been made.
87 Section 26(6)(a) and (b)).
88 Under s 28(1) (see 8.2.1).
89 Section 27(3), (5) and (6) are almost identical in effect to Sch 5, paras 2, 3(1) and 4 respectively. It is not clear why one set of provisions is in the body of the statute and the other set is relegated to a Schedule.

the interests of the reversioner or other landlord. Despite the terminology, the order similarly does not vest the interests in the nominee purchaser – that is done by the conveyance once the procedure is complete.

The court will make the order providing for vesting of the interests of the freeholder or relevant landlord whose identity is unascertainable, not in the nominee purchaser – there isn't one – but in the person or persons appointed for that purpose by the applicants.[90] That may be a company set up for the purpose; indeed the choice of the person to accept the vesting interest will involve similar considerations to that of choosing the nominee purchaser. The court will also designate the person to execute the conveyance.[91]

The leasehold valuation tribunal will determine appropriate terms. In doing so, the tribunal will attempt, so far as circumstances permit, to reflect what the result would have been had the applicants been able to give an initial notice.[92] It will assume that the person whose interest is being conveyed has no interest in the property other than that being conveyed, and the mineral rights which will be exempted from the conveyance.[93] The interest so vested may be less extensive than was specified in the application[94] – enabling the tribunal to consider what the landlord might have done by way of proposals in any counter-notice. The tribunal will also approve the form of the conveyance.[95]

The person appointed by the applicants will pay into court the appropriate sum, namely the amount determined by the tribunal as the price – that which would have been payable if acquired pursuant to an initial notice – together with any outstanding amounts determined by the tribunal as due from any tenants, such as in respect of rent or service charges.[96] On payment into court, the conveyance giving effect to the terms of acquisition will be executed. The conveyance is effective to vest in the nominee purchaser the interests expressed to be conveyed[97] and the payment into court satisfies any claims in respect of the price against the applicants, their personal representatives or assigns.[98]

The Act makes no express provision as to how any sums paid into court are to be paid to any person who claims to be the proper recipient.

---

90 Section 27(1)(a).

91 Section 27(3).

92 Section 27(1)(b).

93 Section 27(4).

94 Section 27(2).

95 Section 27(3)(a); the conveyance will as far as possible give effect to the statutory requirements for the conveyance contained in s 34 and Sch 7.

96 Section 27(3) and (5). The outstanding amounts will include sums due from *any* tenants of the person whose interests are to be conveyed, defined as the 'transferor'.

97 Section 27(3).

98 Section 27(6). This section only refers to 'the price' and not to any amounts due and paid as outstanding under s 27(5)(b).

CHAPTER EIGHT

TERMINATION OF THE ACQUISITION PROCEDURE – WITHDRAWAL AND DEEMED WITHDRAWAL

8.1 How a claim may terminate

A claim for collective enfranchisement can be terminated before its conclusion. Rarely, this will be the result of events beyond the control of the participating tenants, such as the institution of compulsory purchase procedures. More frequently, such termination will result from either an express withdrawal by the participating tenants or a deemed withdrawal, where the nominee purchaser will have failed to meet a relevant time-limit or otherwise fallen short of the requirements of the Act. In either case, a costs liability is incurred and a 12-month delay is imposed before a fresh initial notice can be given. Both an express withdrawal and a deemed withdrawal can be viewed as an expensive failure; and in many such cases more careful preparation of the claim or a proper observation of the time-limits would have prevented such termination.

8.2 Express notice of withdrawal

8.2.1 Withdrawal by notice

At any time before a binding contract is entered into, the participating tenants may withdraw the initial notice by giving a notice of withdrawal.[1]

8.2.2 The form and giving of the notice

A notice of withdrawal must be given to all the key parties to a claim to collective enfranchisement – namely to the nominee purchaser, the reversioner, and to every relevant landlord known or believed by the participating tenants to

1 Section 28(1).

have given a notice[2] to the nominee purchaser.[3] If the nominee purchaser is one of the participating tenants or a company controlled by them, they should have the requisite knowledge of all the relevant landlords. However, to cover the possible situation that not all the relevant landlords are known to the participating tenants, it is provided that the notice must state the name of every relevant landlord to which the notice of withdrawal has been given – except the reversioner. The nominee purchaser, on receipt of the notice of withdrawal, is then under a duty to give a copy of the notice of withdrawal to every relevant landlord not stated in this notice.[4] By such means, every relevant landlord should receive a notice or copy of it.

The Act does not permit a single participating tenant to withdraw but refers to the participating tenants as a body. A notice of withdrawal should therefore be signed by or on behalf of each of the participating tenants.[5] Where there is a dispute between them and some wish to withdraw but others wish to proceed, the matter is likely to be resolved by a deemed withdrawal if the dispute is not settled and the next stage in the procedure does not take place. The method of reaching a decision to withdraw should be covered by the participator's agreement if one has been drawn up.[6]

8.2.3 Costs liability

Where a notice of withdrawal is given by the participating tenants a liability for all relevant costs[7] arises. The liability is to the reversioner and every other relevant landlord.[8] The liability falls on all existing participating tenants and every other person who has at any time been such a tenant except where that person ceased to be a participating tenant on the assignment of the lease and the assignee became the participating tenant by way of substitution.[9] The liability is a joint and several liability of each of the persons concerned and, unlike the position at completion of an enfranchisement, the nominee purchaser is not liable for costs.[10] If a costs fund has been established[11] the sums due can be paid from this fund.

2 Under Sch 1, para 7(1) or (4).

3 Section 28(2)(a)–(c).

4 Section 28 (3). The nominee purchaser will be aware of each relevant landlord who has given notice to the nominee purchaser under Sch 1, para 7(1) or (4).

5 Section 99(5)(b). Unlike the initial notice, which must be signed by each of the tenants, it is sufficient to sign a notice of withdrawal on behalf of each tenant.

6 See 4.5.4.

7 This means the costs for which the nominee purchaser would otherwise be liable under s 33; s 28(7). For a discussion of the meaning and extent of these costs see 9.2.2.

8 Section 28(4)(i) and (ii).

9 Section 28(4) and (5); the substitution is by way of election after an assignment under s 14(4) and (10) (see 5.6.5).

10 Section 28(6). The nominee purchaser is not liable either under this section or s 33.

11 See 4.5.4.

8.2.4 Twelve-month moratorium

Where an initial notice is expressly withdrawn, another subsequent notice specifying the whole or any part of those premises can only be given after the expiry of a period of 12 months beginning with the date of withdrawal.[12]

8.3 Deemed withdrawal

8.3.1 Nature

A deemed withdrawal of an initial notice occurs where there is a failure to take the appropriate next step in the time-limit available; the initial notice then ceases to have effect and the acquisition procedure is at an end. In the case of a deemed withdrawal, where it may be that the participating tenants have a clear right to enfranchisement and are ready to proceed but there has been a procedural error, a claim for professional negligence may follow if the failure was that of a professional adviser.

8.3.2 When a deemed withdrawal occurs

A deemed withdrawal will occur in the following instances.[13]

1 Where the appointment of a nominee purchaser is terminated without appointment of a replacement at the same time and no notice giving the name of the new nominee purchaser is given to the reversioner within 28 days.[14]

2 Where the nominee purchaser has resigned or died and the participating tenants fail to give notice of a replacement within the period of 56 days.[15]

3 Where the reversioner has given notice requiring the nominee purchaser to deduce title to each qualifying tenant giving the initial notice but the nominee purchaser has not responded within the period of 21 days.[16]

4 Where the reversioner has given a counter-notice challenging the validity of the initial notice but no application for an order declaring the entitlement to proceed has been made within a period of two months beginning with the date of the counter-notice.[17]

---

12 Section 13(9).

13 They are either referred to or provided for in s 29.

14 Sections 15(10) and 29(5)(a).

15 Sections 16(8) and 29(5)(b).

16 Sections 20(3) and 29(5)(c). It is only a deemed withdrawal if there are insufficient participating tenants for the initial notice to be valid after the exclusion of those tenants whose title is not deduced (see 6.4.4).

17 Section 29(1)(a). There is also a deemed withdrawal if an application is made within the time-limit but is subsequently withdrawn (s 29(1)(b)).

5 Where any of the terms of acquisition remain in dispute at the end of two months from the giving of the counter-notice but no application has been made to a leasehold valuation tribunal before the end of the six-month period from the counter-notice.[18]

6 Where the terms of acquisition have been finally agreed or determined by the leasehold valuation tribunal but no binding contract entered into; and no application for a vesting order has been made within a period of two months from such agreement or determination;[19] and the court may make an order deeming withdrawal at that date.[20]

7 Where the reversioner has failed to serve a counter-notice but no application for a order to determine the terms has been made within a period of six months from the date by which the counter-notice was to be given.[21]

8 Where the terms of acquisition have been determined by an order of the court after the reversioner failed to serve a counter-notice but no binding contract has been entered into; and no application for a vesting order has been made within a period of two months from such determination;[22] and the court may make an order deeming withdrawal at that date.[23]

8.3.3 Notice ceasing to have effect

In addition to these cases of deemed withdrawal, an initial notice will cease to have effect in the following instances:

1 if a copy of it is not served on a relevant landlord who had previously notified any of the qualifying tenants by whom the notice was given of his interest in the premises.[24] The time-limit for giving that copy is the period ending with the date specified for the reversioner's counter-notice;
2 if compulsory acquisition procedures are commenced[25] in relation to the whole or a part of the premises specified in the initial notice;
3 if a court makes an order that the right of collective enfranchisement shall not be exercisable by reason of the landlord's intention to redevelop;[26] the notice ceases to have effect when the order of the court becomes final;[27]

---

18 Section 29(2)(a).
19 Section 29(2)(b).
20 Sections 24(4)(c) and 29(5)(d).
21 Section 29(3).
22 Section 29(4).
23 Sections 25(6)(c) and 29(5)(e).
24 Schedule 3, para 14(1).
25 See 8.4.2 and 8.4.3 for details.
26 Within s 23(1).
27 Section 23(4).

4 where the premises become 'qualifying property' designated under the Inheritance Tax Act 1984.[28]

8.3.4 *Effect of a deemed withdrawal*

A deemed withdrawal operates as if there had been an express notice to withdraw at the time the initial notice is deemed to be withdrawn.[29] Consequently, the participating tenants have the same joint and several liability for the relevant costs[30] as in the case of an express withdrawal.[31] The nominee purchaser also remains liable but is not liable for the costs in those situations where the deemed withdrawal is the result of failure by the participating tenants.[32] There is, again, in all cases a 12-month wait before the procedure could start again with the service of another initial notice.[33]

8.4 Compulsory purchase

8.4.1 *Rationale*

The commencement or existence of compulsory purchase procedures in respect of any of the interests which the participating tenants seek to acquire will prevent or terminate the acquisition process.[34] There would be little point in proceeding if before or soon after acquisition the freehold or other superior interest would pass to an acquiring authority. A collective enfranchisement does not 'revive' where compulsory purchase procedures are terminated; the procedure must be recommenced.

8.4.2 *Existing compulsory purchase procedures*

An initial notice is of no effect if on the date when it is given any acquiring authority,[35] with a view to acquisition of the whole or part of the premises for an authorised purpose,[36] it has served a notice to treat on either the freeholder or a

---

28 See 8.5.2.
29 Section 29(6).
30 This means the costs for which the nominee purchaser would otherwise be liable under s 33 (s 29(8)). For a discussion of the meaning and extent of these costs, see 9.2.2.
31 Sections 29(6) and 33(7).
32 Under ss 15(10) and 16(8) which relate to replacement, retirement or death of the nominee purchaser (s 29(7)).
33 Section 13(9); and see fn 12 above.
34 Section 30. This section only relates to compulsory acquisition of a relevant landlord's interest; for the impact of a notice to treat in respect of the interest of any participating tenant, see 6.1.9, para 5 above.
35 Defined by s 30(7)(a) to include anybody authorised to acquire the whole or part of the premises compulsorily.
36 Defined to cover any purpose authorised in relation to the acquiring authority (s 30(7)(b)).

leaseholder whose interest is specified in the initial notice.[37] This is also the result if the acquiring authority has entered into a contract for the purchase of the premises or part of them; in both cases the notice to treat or contract must, of course, remain in force.[38] Consequently, no collective enfranchisement is possible if a notice to treat or contract is in force in respect of the freehold or superior leasehold interest in any of the flats.

By way of contrast, if the existing notice to treat or compulsory acquisition contract only affects the freehold of superior leasehold interest in appurtenant property or common parts, an initial notice can be validly made but it must not specify for inclusion in the enfranchisement any such appurtenant property or common parts while the notice to treat or contract remains in force.[39]

8.4.3 Notice to treat subsequent to an initial notice

The service of notice to treat on a freeholder or superior leaseholder will invalidate an initial notice which has already been given and a binding contract is discharged. Thus, an initial notice ceases to have effect if an acquiring authority serves a notice to treat with a view to acquisition of the whole or part of the premises.[40] Where a binding contract has been entered into pursuant to an initial notice but before completion of the collective enfranchisement by the nominee purchaser, the service of a notice to treat discharges the parties to the contract from further performance of the contract.[41] In each case, the compensation payable on the compulsory acquisition for the interest shall be valued subject to and with the benefit of the rights and obligations arising from the initial notice or contract (as the case may be).[42]

8.5 Inheritance tax designation; gifts for public benefit

8.5.1 Rationale

Under pressure in Parliament,[43] an amendment was admitted to the Act to allow for exemption from a collective enfranchisement property designated

37 Section 30(1)(a)(i) and (2).

38 Section 30(1)(a)(ii) and (b).

39 Section 30(3).

40 Section 30(4).

41 Section 30(5). This is without prejudice to the general law on frustration of contracts.

42 Section 30(6).

43 At Report stage in the House of Lords, HL Deb, Vol 545, cols 1240–1251, 1 May 1993, the Government was defeated by a substantial majority and an amendment was inserted into the Bill. What is now s 31 is a redrafted version of that forced amendment. It was introduced at Third Reading, HL Deb, Vol 546, cols 186–187, 207–209, 25 May 1993 and limited the effect to collective enfranchisement only (the original amendment would have also prevented any right to a new lease). See also s 68 and 17.2.5.

under the Inheritance Tax Act 1984 or parallel legislation or for property where a direction has been given under the same legislation. Exemption from inheritance taxes is given for property of outstanding historic merit in return for reasonable public access and undertakings to maintain. Where premises are so designated or a direction has been given,[44] the property becomes 'qualifying property'. Where premises are already 'qualifying property' when the initial notice is given, the initial notice is of no effect.[45] Most such properties will be country houses and the aim is to keep the freehold intact and under common control and prevent a collective enfranchisement of a converted stable block, dower house or other part of the main house. The Government's view that estate management schemes could provide a sufficient safeguard did not find favour with the House of Lords.

8.5.2 Effect on an initial notice

Where the whole or any part of the specified premises in an initial notice, or any freehold property specified in the initial notice as appurtenant property or property which the tenant is entitled to use, becomes 'qualifying property' then the initial notice ceases to have effect.[46] Such a result is entirely beyond the control of the participating tenants or the nominee purchaser; therefore neither are liable for any costs.[47] Moreover, since the premises will have only become 'qualifying property' after the initial notice by reason of an application for designation or a direction, the person so applying (usually the freeholder) is liable to the qualifying tenants by whom the notice was given for all reasonable costs in preparing and giving the initial notice and to the nominee purchaser for all reasonable costs incurred in pursuance of the initial notice.[48]

Once a binding contract is entered into pursuant to the initial notice, the fact that the premises become 'qualifying property' will not prevent completion of the enfranchisement.

8.5.3 What is 'qualifying property'?

'Qualifying property', in relation to the whole or any part of either the specified premises or any freehold property which the initial notice proposes to acquire if one of the following is satisfied.[49]

1 It has been designated under the Inheritance Tax Act 1984 or the Finance Acts 1975 or 1976 provided that no chargeable event has subsequently occurred;

---

44 See 8.5.3.

45 This has already been noted (see s 31(10) and 3.4.5).

46 Section 31(4).

47 Section 31(5)(a).

48 Section 31(5)(b).

49 The full definition is in ss 31(2), (7) and (8) which includes the appropriate section numbers of the 1984, 1975 and 1976 Acts.

2 An application to the Board of Inland Revenue to be so designated is pending.
3 It is the property of a body not established or conducted for profit where a direction has been given to it under the Inheritance Tax Act 1984 or the Finance Act 1975.
4 An application to the Board of Inland Revenue for a direction to be given in relation to it is pending.

8.5.4 Claiming 'qualifying property' status

It is not enough for the reversioner, or other person, to claim that a property is designated or an application for a direction has been made. When making a claim of 'qualifying property' the person making the claim must furnish the nominee purchaser with evidence in support of it;[50] if this is not done, there is a liability for any costs which are reasonably incurred by the failure to substantiate the claim. No doubt a nominee purchaser will want the claim verified; if the evidence is not given then the nominee purchaser can seek verification, probably from the Board of Inland Revenue, at the expense of the person claiming that the premises are 'qualifying property'. To make out a case based on a pending application to the Board of Inland Revenue the application must be sufficiently made – which will only be done when the applicant has submitted to the Board all such information in support of the application as the Board requires.[51] There is an outside chance of an unseemly race; the nominee purchaser seeking to complete the collective enfranchisement procedures – perhaps by application for a vesting order – while the reversioner struggles to produce sufficient information to satisfy the Board and so achieve pending application status. Once duly made, however, an application is pending until granted or refused by the Board.

8.6 Cancellation of land charge

When an initial notice has been registered as a land charge or a notice or caution has been registered in respect of it – and registration will have been done in nearly every case – the registration will need to be cancelled in the event of a withdrawal, a deemed withdrawal or in any other situation when the notice ceases to have effect. At the request of the landlord, the nominee purchaser shall, without delay, take all steps necessary to procure cancellation of the registration.[52]

---

50 Section 31(6).
51 Section 31(3).
52 Leasehold Reform (Collective Enfranchisement and Lease Renewal) Regulations 1993, SI 1993/2407 Sch 1, para 8.

CHAPTER NINE

DETERMINATION OF PRICE AND COMPLETION OF AN ACQUISITION

9.1 Price

9.1.1 A market value basis

The price payable by the nominee purchaser for the freehold and other interests to be acquired by him is determined in accordance with Sch 6[1] to the 1993 Act. This Schedule is at the heart of the legislation; the direction on price there set out will guide the valuation by the qualified surveyor in connection with the initial notice; it will be the basis of any negotiations, of any agreement on price or determination by a leasehold valuation tribunal. Even if the application of that Schedule results in no payment or only in a nominal payment, the nominee purchaser paying the price is treated for all purposes to be a purchaser for valuable consideration in money or money's worth.[2]

9.1.2 The price basis in outline

In outline, the price payable for the freehold will be the aggregate of three matters.[3]

1 The value of the freeholder's interest. The valuation is on the basis of an open market sale of the fee simple subject to all leases and disregarding improvements and the right of enfranchisement.[4]

2 The freeholder's share of the marriage value.[5] This will be *either* the proportion agreed or determined by the leasehold valuation tribunal as the proportion which would be agreed in the open market, *or* 50 per cent,

1 Section 32(1).
2 Section 32(5).
3 Schedule 6, para 2.
4 Schedule 6, para 3.
5 Determined in accordance with Sch 6, para 4.

whichever is greater. The freeholder will never receive less than 50 per cent and may receive more if the market evidence so warrants. Marriage value is defined as the increase in the aggregate value when acquired by the nominee purchaser and includes the ability to have new leases granted to the participating tenants by the nominee purchaser.

3 Any compensation for loss suffered by the freeholder, particularly diminution in value of other property or loss of development value.[6]

There are complex formulae for the valuation of intermediate leasehold interests; and for valuation of interests with negative values.

The details of the valuation are dealt with separately in Part Five of this book as the principles and concepts to be applied are common to valuations for collective enfranchisement, a new lease and for the extended rights under the Leasehold Reform Act 1967.[7]

9.1.3 *The price controversy*

The overall valuation formula is controversial and the debate shows that there is a philosophical divide. Some argue that it is confiscatory to landlords since no amount of money can compensate for the forced transfer of interests which may have been retained over many years. The 50 per cent minimum for marriage value is a political compromise. The alternative view that is not generous enough to tenants is based on the concern that the burden on tenants will be too great so that, in practice, few claims for collective enfranchisement will be completed. Certainly, there will be cases where the marriage value may be prohibitively expensive.

9.1.4 *An example*

An example of the operation of the formula was given in Standing Committee during passage of the legislation.[8] If 10 flats with 50 years left to run are valued at £160,000 each and the freehold interest for ground rents of £60 plus reversion is £30,000, then the total value is £1,630,000. If, after enfranchisement, the value of 10 leases with new 999-year leases and control of the freehold is £2,000,000, then the marriage value is £370,000. The qualifying tenants would pay at least half, £185,000, plus £30,000: a total of £215,000 or £21,500 per flat as a minimum price assuming all were qualifying tenants and participating in the enfranchisement.

---

6 Schedule 6, para 5.

7 See chapters eighteen to twenty-one.

8 HC Deb, Standing Committee B, cols 186–187, 19 November 1992.

9.1.5 Date for valuation

The relevant date for calculation of the price is that at which the price is determined either by agreement or by the leasehold valuation tribunal.[9] This differs from the valuation date under the Leasehold Reform Act 1967. Under the 1967 Act, the relevant time for valuation is the date of the service of the tenants' notice of claim[10] which gives incentive for a tenant to delay the procedures in a rising market. The date under the 1993 Act changes the balance between the parties; in a rising market the landlord has the incentive to delay agreement on the price.

9.1.6 The vendor's lien and service charge arrears

The owner of any interest on the specified premises[11] being acquired has a lien, as vendor, on the premises for the price as agreed or determined.[12] The lien extends not only to the price but to the relevant costs due and to all other amounts due at the date of conveyance from any tenants of his in the premises in which his interest subsists except where due in respect of premises which are to be the subject of leaseback.[13] The participating tenants must not only pay their own service charge or other arrears[14] but also take over the sums due from any tenants where the nominee purchaser becomes the new landlord. The lien further extends to cover any costs due from the nominee purchaser[15] and (if appropriate) any sums due after a breach of the duty of disclosure representing the increase in price which would otherwise have been payable.[16]

9.2 Costs

9.2.1 Not all costs are recoverable

The costs liability of the nominee purchaser (and, through the nominee purchaser, the shared liability of the participating tenants) is, essentially, a liability for the reasonable procedural, valuation and conveyancing costs borne by the reversioner. Not all costs incurred by the reversioner will be recoverable.[17]

---

9 Schedule 6, para 1(1).
10 Leasehold Reform Act 1967, ss 9(1) and 37(1)(d).
11 Or part thereof (s 32(4)).
12 Section 32(2).
13 Section 32(2(a) and (3)).
14 Whether due under the lease or collateral agreement.
15 Section 32(2)(c).
16 Section 32(2)(b).
17 See 9.2.4.

9.2.2 The extent of the liability

The nominee purchaser is liable to pay the reasonable costs of the reversioner or relevant landlord which fall within the statutory definition and which have been incurred in pursuance of the initial notice.[18] These costs[19] are the reasonable costs of and incidental to the following matters:[20]

(a) any investigation reasonably undertaken of any question arising out of the initial notice, including whether any interest is liable to acquisition;
(b) deducing evidencing and verifying the title to an interest being acquired;
(c) making out and furnishing such abstracts and copies as the nominee purchaser may require;
(d) any valuation of any interest in the specified premises or other property;
(e) any conveyance of any interest.

In an attempt to avoid the reversioner deliberately incurring high professional valuation and legal fees, it is provided that costs incurred by the reversioner or other relevant landlord in respect of professional services shall only be regarded as reasonable to the extent that those costs might be reasonably expected to be incurred by him if he was personally liable for those costs.[21] The exact meaning of this provision may prove controversial. It is submitted that a nominee purchaser cannot object if the landlord engages a large firm to give specialist assistance on valuation and the response to an initial notice, even where a cheaper local firm has been used by the landlord for other legal or valuation work. On the other hand, the landlord would not be able to agree with a solicitor and surveyor a higher hourly rate than would otherwise have been agreed and claim payment from the nominee purchaser at that higher rate.

9.2.3 Liability of nominee purchaser and participating tenants

The nominee purchaser[22] is liable for these costs in every case where a collective enfranchisement claim proceeds to a completion and also in some cases where the initial notice ceases to have effect, where the liability is for costs incurred down to that time.[23] However, where an initial notice does not

18 Section 33(1).

19 In other sections of the Act, eg ss 28(7) and 29(8), the costs liability is referred to as the 'relevant costs'.

20 Section 33(1)(a)–(e).

21 Section 33(2). The nominee purchaser is not liable for any costs if, on a voluntary sale, a stipulation that they would be borne by the purchaser would be void (s 33(1), proviso).

22 The liability not only falls on a existing nominee purchaser but also upon one whose appointment has been terminated by replacement, retirement or death, subject to the limitation in s 15(7) so that the liability is normally only for costs incurred up to the date of termination (s 33(6)).

23 Section 33(3); for example by virtue of Sch 3, para 14(1) where a copy of the initial notice is not given to a relevant landlord who has notified one of the qualifying tenants by whom the notice is given of his interest. See also 9.2.4 and s 33(4).

eventually result in an enfranchisement, it is much more likely that there will have been an express or a deemed withdrawal. In the case of an express withdrawal, the liability for the relevant costs falls jointly and severally upon the participating tenants[24] and not on the nominee purchaser; in cases of deemed withdrawal, there is also a joint and several liability on the participating tenants as well as the nominee purchaser[25] and in two such instances, there is no liability on the nominee purchaser.[26]

9.2.4 *Where there is no liability for costs*

There is no liability on the nominee purchaser for any costs if the initial notice ceases to have effect either because the freeholder has established a successful defence of an intention to redevelop[27] or because the premises are subject to a compulsory acquisition.[28] There will be no power for either party to get an award of costs in respect of proceedings before the leasehold valuation tribunal;[29] the statutory liability for costs does not extend to any costs incurred in connection with proceedings before a leasehold valuation tribunal[30] and the costs incurred by either party before that tribunal are not recoverable by the order of any court.[31] The costs of any proceedings before the county court will be a matter for the court in accordance with standard procedure; a reversioner who uses court applications as a delaying tactic or without any real prospect of success is likely to be condemned in costs.

9.2.5 *No security for costs*

There is no statutory provision for security for costs. In the case of a successful enfranchisement the costs recoverable will be paid at completion and the reversioner or relevant landlord has a vendor's lien to secure recovery.[32] In the case of an express withdrawal or a deemed withdrawal, there is a joint and several liability on the participating tenants who, by definition, will be tenants of flats on long leases which, in effect, provide some sort of security for recovery. Only in the relatively rare case, where an initial notice ceases to have effect and the liability falls upon the nominee purchaser alone who may be a limited

---

24 See s 28(6) and discussion at 8.2.3.
25 Section 33(7).
26 See s 29(6) and (7) and discussion at 8.3.4.
27 Section 33(4); and see s 23(4).
28 Section 33(4); and see s 30(4).
29 The Tribunals and Inquiries Act 1992 contains no general power to award costs; any power must be specifically granted.
30 Section 33(5).
31 Section 91(8).
32 Section 32(2); and see 9.1.6.

company with few assets, may lack of security for the recovery of costs be a problem.

9.3 Completion

9.3.1 Grant and form of the conveyance

Any conveyance to the nominee purchaser giving effect to a collective enfranchisement claim will be a grant of the fee simple absolute in the premises subject only to incumbrances permitted by the Act.[33] If intermediate leasehold interests are being acquired, the conveyance will provide for the disposal of those interests to the nominee purchaser.[34] The Act therefore envisages one conveyance or transfer vesting the freehold free of all intermediate leasehold interests being acquired.[35] The freeholder is not bound to convey any better title than that which he has or could require to be vested in him and will convey as trustee or mortgagee.[36] If an interest is being acquired from a local authority or other public sector landlord, certain statutory requirements for obtaining ministerial consent or consultation do not apply.[37] Any settled interest will be overreached.[38] Any conveyance under the Act must contain a statement that it is a conveyance executed for the purposes of Chapter I of the 1993 Act and comply with such requirements as may be prescribed.[39]

9.3.2 Easements and rights

There are certain easements for which provision must be made in the conveyance. The first is in respect of rights of support for, or rights of access of light and air to, a building or part of it; rights to the passage of water or piped fuel, drainage or disposal rights, and rights to the use and maintenance of pipes

---

33 Section 34(1). The conveyance is to conform with the provisions of Sch 7, which closely follows s 101(1)–(4) of the Leasehold Reform Act 1967 (s 34(9)). See also Hague, *Leasehold Enfranchisement*, 2nd edn, 1987, Sweet & Maxwell, 6–16 to 6–29.

34 Section 34(2).

35 Only the reversioner will execute the conveyance, although he will do so where appropriate on behalf of and in the name of the other relevant landlords (Sch 1, para 6(b)(iii)) although other relevant landlords may by notice require the price for their interest to be paid direct (see 5.9.2).

36 Schedule 7, para 2(2); the reversioner is not bound to enter into any covenant for title other than that implied in the case of a person expressed to convey as trustee or mortgagee, as under the Law of Property Act 1925, s 76(1)(F).

37 Section 37 and Sch 10, para 1(1). The full list of disapplied statutory provisions is in Sch 10, para 1(2).

38 Section 34(3); the conveyance will be treated as made under the powers of the Settled Land Act 1925 and payment as the 1993 Act provides will satisfy the requirements of the 1925 Act as to payment of capital money.

39 Under the power to make general rules in respect of registered land in pursuance of s 144 of the Land Registration Act 1925.

and cables.[40] A grant must be included of such easements and rights over property as are necessary to secure as nearly as may be, for the benefit of the relevant premises,[41] the same rights as exist for their benefit immediately before the conveyance or which are necessary for the reasonable enjoyment of them.[42] Similarly, such easements and rights must be reserved for the benefit of other property where appropriate.[43] Finally, the conveyance cannot exclude the general words implied by virtue of s 62 of the Law of Property Act 1925 except with the consent of the nominee purchaser in the case only of preserving existing interests of the freeholder or other person.[44]

Rights of way shall be included where necessary to the reasonable enjoyment of property. These may be required by the nominee purchaser to secure rights over other property or by the freeholder to make the conveyed premises subject to rights of way for the benefit of property in which the freeholder retains an interest.[45]

9.3.3 Restrictive covenants

There are three sorts of restrictive covenant which one or other party may require to be included or covered in the conveyance.

1 In the case of existing restrictive covenants which affect the relevant premises[46] and are enforceable for the benefit of other property, provisions to bind the nominee purchaser and secure an indemnity shall be included.[47]
2 A freeholder may require new further restrictive covenants which would materially enhance the value of other property in which the freeholder has an interest but will not interfere with the reasonable enjoyment of the premises as enjoyed previously under the leases.[48]
3 Where existing restrictions arise by virtue of a lease which is to continue and subject to which the relevant premises are being acquired, either party may in some cases require the continuance of those restrictions. Where those restrictions affect the relevant premises and are capable of benefiting adjoining property, continuance may be required by the freeholder only if the restrictions materially enhance the value of the other property. Such

40 Schedule 7, para 3(1).
41 Ie, the premise of which the freehold is to be conveyed (Sch 7, para 1(a)).
42 Schedule 7, para 3(2).
43 Schedule 7, para 3(3).
44 Schedule 7, para 2(1). Exclusion of the all-estate clause implied under s 63 of the Law of Property Act 1925 is similarly restricted.
45 Schedule 7, para 4.
46 Except those affecting the premises by virtue of a lease subject to which the relevant premises are to be acquired.
47 Schedule 7, para 5(1)(a).
48 Schedule 7, para 5(1)(c).

restrictions which affect the other property can be required to be continued if they materially enhance the value of the relevant premises.

9.3.4 *Incumbrances*

A conveyance shall not be made subject to any incumbrance which is capable of being overreached;[49] so such interests arising under a settlement or trust for sale will be met from the price paid. Incumbrances are defined to include rentcharges and personal liabilities attaching in respect of ownership of land, although not charged on that land or interest.[50] A conveyance can be made subject to burdens originating in tenure or in respect of property for the benefit of a locality,[51] but such cases will be rarely found.

A conveyance shall be made subject to rentcharges.[52] However, the freeholder may choose to release the land from the rentcharge; and if it affects other land, may be apportioned or charged exclusively on other land affected by it.[53]

9.4 Discharge of mortgages

9.4.1 *The statutory discharge*

Provided that the nominee purchaser observes the requirements of the Act as regards payment of the price towards discharge of mortgages,[54] the conveyance acquiring any interest shall be effective to discharge the interest from the mortgage.[55] The interest is also discharged from the operation of any court order to enforce the mortgage and any terms of years created for mortgage purposes is extinguished. This is done without any mortgagees becoming a party to the conveyance.[56] The discharge does not affect the personal liability of the landlord nor the enforcement of obligations against other property comprised in the security.[57]

9.4.2 *Mortgages covered*

Unless the mortgage would be overreached, the discharge provisions apply to any mortgage, however created or arising, which secures the payment of money

49 Section 34(6).
50 Section 34(4). Mortgages are dealt with separately (see 9.4).
51 Section 34(5).
52 If redeemable under the Rentcharges Act 1977 or estate or statutory rentcharges under s 2(3) of that Act (s 34(6)).
53 Section 34(7) and (8).
54 The details are considered at 9.4.3.
55 Section 35(1).
56 However, a mortgagee may join the conveyance to discharge the interest from the mortgage without payment or for a lesser payment (Sch 8, para 5(2)).
57 Schedule 8, para 5(2).

or the performance of any other obligation.[58] A charge or lien is included; but not a rentcharge.[59] However, the nominee purchaser may wish to acquire the freehold or other interest subject to the existing mortgage to assist in the financing of the enfranchisement; the reversioner, nominee purchaser and (where applicable) any relevant landlord may agree that the interest in question may be acquired subject to the existing mortgage.[60]

9.4.3 *Payment to redeem mortgages*

In order to take advantage of the statutory discharge, the nominee purchaser must observe the duty in the first instance to apply the consideration payable to the redemption of any mortgage[61] and, if more than one, in order of priority. If this duty is not met, the interest remains subject to the mortgage for the sum not paid.[62] In determining the amount due, a mortgagee cannot consolidate a mortgage with a mortgage on other property; and, if a landlord or participating tenant happens to be a mortgagee, it ranks for payment as if another person was entitled.[63] A mortgagee cannot insist on longer than three months' notice to redeem even if the mortgage makes different provision for repayment; but, in addition to interest, a reasonable further payment can be required by a mortgagee in respect of costs of reinvestment, incidental expenses or in respect of a reduction in the rate of interest on reinvestment.[64]

9.4.4 *Payment into court*

Difficulties may arise in ascertaining how much is repayable on any mortgage. In other cases, the person entitled to payment may be unknown or cannot be found; the mortgagee may be unco-operative and refuse to make out title or accept payment; or title complications may cause unreasonable costs or delay. In all such instances, the nominee purchaser may pay into court on account of the consideration due,[65] the sum payable to discharge the mortgage if known. If it is not known, the whole of the consideration can be paid in or such lesser sum to provide for payment as the nominee purchaser thinks proper.[66] Payment

---

58 Section 35(2).
59 Section 35(4).
60 Section 35(3). The consent of the mortgagee would appear to be required unless permitted by the terms of the mortgage.
61 This duty does not apply to a debenture holder's charge, unless it is a specific and not a floating charge in favour of trustees for debenture holders, and these are also disregarded in determining priorities (Sch 8, para 2(3) and (4)).
62 Schedule 8, para 2(1) and (2).
63 Schedule 8, para 3(1).
64 Schedule 8, para 3(2).
65 That part of the price which represents the consideration for the acquisition of the interest subject to the mortgage (Sch 8, para 1).
66 Schedule 8, para 4(1) and (2). Payment of the whole is likely to be the safer course of action.

into court can also be required by notice to the nominee purchaser where court proceedings for enforcement are in progress, for reasons related to the bankruptcy or winding up of the landlord or to protect the rights of persons entitled to the benefit of the mortgage.[67]

9.5 Leaseback requirements

9.5.1 Two types of leaseback

At completion, the nominee purchaser is required to grant back to the freeholder leases of certain flats and units within the premises of which the freehold is being acquired.[68] Such leasebacks will be of two types – either mandatory or optional. The latter are those permitted by the Act where due notice requiring a leaseback has been given, usually by the reversioner in the counter-notice.[69] All such grants by way of leaseback are to be granted so as to take effect immediately after the acquisition by the nominee purchaser of the freehold.[70] If the flat or unit subject to leaseback is subject to a lease or tenancy not being acquired, the lease granted is a lease of the freehold reversion in respect of the flat or unit.[71]

9.5.2 Mandatory leaseback

A mandatory leaseback will be required in two circumstances, neither of which will be frequently found.

1 Where any flat or unit used as a dwelling is let on a secure tenancy and either the freeholder is the secure tenant's immediate landlord, or the freeholder is a public sector landlord[72] and every intermediate landlord is also a public sector landlord,[73] the nominee purchaser must grant to the freeholder a lease on the terms set by the Act.[74] Such cases may occur especially where the reversioner is a local authority.

2 A mandatory leaseback must also be granted to a housing association[75] which owns the freehold of the premises in respect of any flat or unit used as a dwelling let to a tenant who is neither a secure tenant nor a qualifying tenant.[76]

---

67 Schedule 8, para 4(3).

68 The details are covered by Sch 9 (s 36(1) and (4)).

69 In accordance with s 21(3)(a)(ii) (see 6.6.3 and also the discussion at 9.5.5).

70 Section 36(2).

71 Section 36(3).

72 Within the meaning of the Housing Act 1985, s 171(2) (s 38(1)) and see 3.2.4, fn 16.

73 Even if that public sector landlord is also a qualifying tenant.

74 Schedule 9, para 2.

75 Which has the meaning given by the Housing Associations Act 1985, s 1(1) (Sch 9, para 1(1)).

76 Schedule 9, para 3.

The statutory wording and purpose indicate that a reversioner is obliged to accept a leaseback in these cases.

9.5.3 Optional leaseback

Optional leaseback, those situations where the freeholder has exercised the right to require the leaseback of certain flats and units,[77] will be more common. The freeholder has to give due notice to the nominee purchaser.[78] Usually, such leaseback proposals will have been made in the counter-notice so that due notice will have been given.[79] The nominee purchaser shall then grant to the freeholder a lease on the terms set by the Act.

9.5.4 Flats and units which may be subject to optional leaseback

There are two types of flat or unit which are subject to optional leaseback. The more important is any unit in the premises which is not, immediately before the time when the freehold is acquired, a flat let to a qualifying tenant.[80] This therefore covers all units let on a business lease and all residential flats or units let to non-qualifying tenants, such as Rent Act tenancies, assured tenancies – indeed any tenancy which is not a long lease at low rent. By exercising the right to a leaseback, the freeholder secures the investment or capital value of the reversionary interest since the leaseback will be for a term of 999 years at a peppercorn rent. Alternatively, by declining to give notice, the freeholder thereby requires the nominee purchaser to buy out that value – which may be substantial.

There is to be no leaseback of flats which are let to qualifying tenants who are not participating.[81] One limited exception is the second situation where the freeholder can require a leaseback.[82] This will be where the premises have a freeholder as a resident landlord and that freeholder occupies a flat or other unit and is a qualifying tenant of that flat or unit.[83] The most common situation will be where premises have been converted and the freeholder has retained a flat or unit as a home after conversion. Alternatively, one flat owner may have purchased the freehold reversion. In such cases a lease in accordance with the provisions of the Act is granted back to the resident freeholder and in this case the lease held by the freeholder prior to the leaseback is deemed to have been surrendered.[84]

---

77 Within Part III of Sch 9.

78 See the discussion in 9.5.5 on the issue of due notice.

79 See s 21(3)(a)(ii) and (7).

80 Schedule 9, para 5.

81 Although such a leaseback could be privately negotiated.

82 Schedule 9, para 6.

83 Strictly, only a flat can have a qualifying tenant but for this purpose a unit is subject to the tests in ss 5, 7 and 8 of the Act (see Sch 9, para 6(3)).

84 Schedule 9, para 6(2)(b).

The right to require leaseback only extends to units and specified types of flat. There would therefore appear to be no right of leaseback to a roof void which did not constitute a separate unit, even where planning permission exists to convert that space to a penthouse flat.[85] There could certainly be no right where the permission is for construction by way of additional floors or a penthouse flat built on top of the roof. The value of the planning permission, or even potential permission, should, however, be reflected as development value in the price.

9.5.5 Notice to require an optional leaseback

For an optional leaseback, the freeholder must give notice to the nominee purchaser requiring the grant of a lease in accordance with the Act.[86] Normally, notice will be given by the proposal in the counter-notice; indeed the Act requires any leaseback proposals to be set out.[87] A potentially important issue is whether a freeholder who is the reversioner (as will usually be the case) has to give his proposals for leaseback in the counter-notice or whether a later, written[88] notice prior to the binding contract[89] will suffice. On the statutory wording, the better view is that a later notice suffices; the counter-notice need only contain leaseback 'proposals' whereas Sch 9 states that the reversioner 'shall grant' the leaseback on notice being given. Moreover, the counter-notice is given by the reversioner who will usually be the freeholder but may not be. The right to leaseback includes any unit not occupied by a qualifying tenant before completion of the acquisition of the freehold; so a unit might have a qualifying tenant (not participating) at the date of the counter-notice but cease to have a qualifying tenant before completion.[90] It would therefore seem that a notice requiring leaseback could be given subsequent to a counter-notice but before the terms of acquisition[91] are finally agreed or settled and incorporated into the contract. An argument could easily be made for the contrary view which ensures that a nominee purchaser will know the extent of the property to be acquired by the time the counter-notice is served and avoid the difficulties discussed. Caution would indicate that a reversioner who is the freeholder should put all leaseback requirements as proposals in the counter-notice.

---

85 A leaseback might be negotiable in return for some concession on the price.

86 Schedule 9, para 5(2) and 6(2)(a).

87 See s 21(3)(a)(ii) and (7).

88 Written notice is not specified but must be essential as a matter of practice.

89 It is submitted that the wording of Sch 9, para 5(2) is not wide enough to override the provisions of the binding contract entered into by the reversioner and the nominee purchaser.

90 In this particular instance, Sch 9 appears to allow for a notice to require a leaseback even after contract stage and at any time before completion. As this would necessitate a complete readjustment of the price payable, it is suggested that this point is the result of a statutory oversight.

91 As defined by s 24(8).

9.5.6 *Terms of the lease*

The terms of all leases granted by way of leaseback are subject to the terms of Part IV of Sch 9.[92] The full details of those provisions need not be set out in full but the following should be noted.

1 Leases must conform to the provisions of Part IV of Sch 9; a departure from these terms can only be by consent of both the nominee purchaser and the freeholder or with the approval of the leasehold valuation tribunal.[93] Such a departure will only be approved if it appears to the tribunal to be reasonable in the circumstances having particular regard to the interests of the secure tenant or any inferior tenant to the lease granted to the freeholder. Any agreed clause must also satisfy the reasonableness criterion.
2 The lease shall be for a term of 999 years at a peppercorn rent.[94]
3 The provisions relating to rights of support, passage of water, rights of way and the limitation on excluding or restricting the general words provision[95] are similar in substance to the provisions relating to the conveyance of the freehold.[96]
4 Rights to use the common parts as are enjoyed by any tenant immediately before completion must be granted.[97]
5 The lessor will covenant to keep in repair and insure and the lessee shall covenant to undertake interior and decorative repair;[98] the lease may require the lessee to bear by way of service charge contributions to cover a reasonable part of the costs incurred by the lessor.[99]
6 Except in the case of a leaseback of a business unit, the lease cannot include any restrictions on assigning or sub-letting the whole or part. A unit intended for letting or let as a business unit shall contain a covenant against assigning or sub-letting the whole or part or altering the user of the unit, but such covenant must be fully qualified so that consent cannot be unreasonably withheld.[100]
7 Standard form covenants to secure and indemnify in respect of existing restrictive covenants, and for forfeiture for breach, can be included but not any other provision for termination.[101]
8 Where the lease is to a public sector landlord, the provisions of Sch 10, para 2 apply.

---

92 Schedule 9, paras 8–18
93 Schedule 9, paras 4 and 7.
94 Schedule 9, para 8.
95 In Sch 9, paras 9,10 and 11.
96 In Sch 7, paras 2–4; and see 9.3.2.
97 Schedule 9, para 12.
98 Schedule 9, paras 14 and 15.
99 Schedule 9, para 16.
100 Schedule 9, para 17.
101 Schedule 9, paras 13 and 18.

9.5.7 New mortgages of freehold

Where the nominee purchaser is acquiring the freehold with the assistance of a mortgage, or, indeed, taking over an existing mortgage from the reversioner, there may be problems of priority. Although any leaseback is to be granted to take effect immediately after acquisition,[102] it is submitted that this must be prior to any mortgage of the freehold. It will be advisable to inform any mortgagee of a leaseback and obtain an acknowledgement from such mortgagee that the mortgage is subject to such leaseback.

9.6 Grant of new leases to the participating tenants

9.6.1 May be required in practice

The price paid by the nominee purchaser will include an element in respect of marriage value.[103] The increase in value is calculated on the basis that the participating tenants have the ability to have new leases granted to them without any payment of premium and without restriction on the length of term.[104] In order to secure the full value of their purchase, in most cases the tenants will wish to have new leases granted to them. For financing reasons, this may need to be done at the completion of the enfranchisement.[105]

9.6.2 Not a statutory requirement

There may be good reasons not to grant new leases. The participating tenants may already hold perfectly adequate 999-year leases. In other cases, fresh leases for a long term may be needed to secure the value of the flat to each participating tenant but the length of term and amount of rent will be a matter for agreement. There may be good reasons to have a rent which is more than a peppercorn or other nominal sum; the rent so paid can be put towards meeting maintenance and other charges and so reduce the quantum of the annual service charge.

---

102 Section 36(2).

103 See 19.3.1. This may represent by far the most significant element in the price paid.

104 Schedule 6, para 4(2)(a).

105 See 4.6.1.

CHAPTER TEN

AVOIDANCE AND ANTI-AVOIDANCE

10.1 The extent to which avoidance is possible

10.1.1 For the future

A landlord or property developer who wishes to ensure that the provisions of the Act do not apply to new developments will be able to do so. Flats in new developments may be let on leases where the term is too short or (more likely) the rent too high for there to be a qualifying tenant. Even if some flats are already let to qualifying tenants,[1] there may be a sufficient number of flats currently let on shorter leases to prevent the right of collective enfranchisement ever arising provided that no more flats are let on long leases within the Act. Whether there will be a sufficient market for leases of a shorter duration or at a rent exceeding the low rent limits will no doubt vary according to the locality.

Although it may be possible to avoid the Act's provisions by agreeing lettings which do not fall within the definition, it is not possible to opt out. The Act contains provisions which ensure that it is not possible to exclude or modify rights which are given by the Act.[2]

10.1.2 For existing situations

Where a landlord is unwilling to relinquish the freehold of premises already subject to the right of collective enfranchisement and would like to take action to prevent an enfranchisement, there will be a very limited number of possible options available.[3] In some cases, it may be possible to prevent a collective enfranchisement but it may be unwise to do so if the right to a new lease remains and the premium payable for the new lease may be reduced by the action taken.

---

1 Who may then be able to claim for a new lease (see 11.2).

2 See 10.2.

3 Discused at 10.3.1 ff.

10.2 Anti-avoidance provisions

10.2.1 Rights cannot be excluded or modified

It is not possible to agree to exclude or modify the rights given by the Act, subject to very limited exceptions. Any agreement relating to a lease shall be void insofar as it purports to exclude or modify any entitlement to participate in the making of a claim to exercise the right to collective enfranchisement.[4] This applies to agreements made both before and after the creation of the lease and it does not matter whether the agreement is within the lease or independent of it. A provision which provides for the termination or surrender of the lease in the event of the tenant becoming a participating tenant or one which provides for the imposition of any penalty or disability on the tenant in that event is also void.[5]

10.2.2 Exceptions arising after the initial notice is given

An agreement excluding or restricting the entitlement to participate in the making of a claim to exercise the right of collective enfranchisement may be made for a period not exceeding three years – but only after a tenant has already become a participating tenant.[6] Such a provision is therefore limited and can only be concluded in a case where a group of tenants have commenced a claim – it may not be used in advance, for example by way of a clause in a new lease. It is more likely to be used in a situation where a group of participating tenants discover that they are unable to finance or otherwise proceed with the enfranchisement. In return, perhaps, for a concession on costs, the tenants[7] will agree not to participate in a further claim for a period of three years.[8]

Once a tenant has become a participating tenant, an agreement that an initial notice shall cease to have effect can be made.[9] Such an agreement, which will

---

4 Section 93(1)(a).

5 Section 93(1)(b) and (c). A lease which provides for termination or surrender in the event of the tenant becoming a qualifying tenant, or, more importantly, in the event of a qualifying tenant satisfying the residence condition, would not appear to be covered (see 10.5.4).

6 So an initial notice must have been given before this exception can apply (s 93(2)(b)(ii)).

7 To terminate a claim it will be necessary to agree with all the participating tenants as part of an agreement to withdraw (see 8.2.1); an agreement with one or a few such tenants will not legally prevent completion of the enfranchisement by the others since the right to proceed is tested on the relevant date, when the initial notice is given (see 6.1.1). If this were not the case, it would permit a landlord to stop an enfranchisement by a payment to a sufficient number of tenants to enter into this agreement to reduce the number of participating tenants below the minimum requirement. However, by detaching some tenants from participation, the remainder may have insufficient resources to continue.

8 This will, in effect, extend the moratorium for a period of two years as they would not be able to give another initial notice for a period of 12 months in any event (see 8.2.4).

9 Section 93(2)(b)(i).

need to be between the reversioner, nominee purchaser and the participating tenants, can allow a compromise of the claim or an agreed acquisition of the freehold without going through all the procedures of the Act. In such a case, the nominee purchaser will be acquiring the freehold and any intermediate interests which are superior to the leases of the participating tenants. It is expressly provided that such acquisition on behalf of a tenant of an interest which is superior to the lease is not void.[10]

10.3 Avoidance ideas for the unwilling landlord

10.3.1 Limited scope for manoeuvre

Although there are many possibilities and ideas for making collective enfranchisement more difficult, it will not be easy for a landlord to prevent a determined group of tenants from exercising their collective rights under the Act. Some of the possible options may be more costly to implement than the potential benefit to the landlord may warrant.

10.3.2 The general difficulties

There are three general problems which are faced by such unwilling landlords.

1 The anti-avoidance provisions in s 93[11] prevent any agreement being made which purports to exclude or modify any entitlement to participate in the making of a claim to exercise the right to collective enfranchisement.
2 Care must be taken that any action taken to avoid the provisions of the 1993 Act is not itself a disposal of an interest caught by the Landlord and Tenant Act 1987[12] giving the qualifying tenants the right of first refusal to purchase that interest in any event.
3 A number of steps can be taken to make collective enfranchisement more difficult and an unwilling landlord will be able, at a cost, to use the procedural requirements of the Act in such a way as to ensure that the processes are drawn out and as fraught as possible for the nominee purchaser and participating tenants. However, such action may lead in consequence to individual qualifying tenants deciding to exercise their right to a new lease under Chapter II instead of their collective rights under Chapter I. Some landlords may prefer this because although they will have to grant the

10 Section 93(2)(a).
11 See 10.2.1.
12 See the Landlord and Tenant Act 1987, ss 1–4.

extended new lease at a peppercorn rent they will still retain the freehold, management control and any redevelopment potential. On the other hand, other landlords may not want to manage premises where there is eventually going to be a majority of tenants with new leases and very little or no financial return or capital value in the freehold. To that extent, the right to the new lease may be equally unpleasant to them. However, the possibilities of avoiding a claim for a new lease are very limited indeed[13] unless a large number of such tenants do not satisfy the residence requirement.

With these warnings in mind, the possibility of action by a landlord is briefly considered in a number of different situations.

10.4 Active avoidance steps within existing situations

10.4.1 Various possibilities

A landlord may be able to consider in particular circumstances some of the following steps which may make a collective enfranchisement more difficult in some cases. Not all or even many may be available in a particular case.

10.4.2 Severance of the freehold

Prior to the receipt of an initial notice, the freeholder might choose to sever the freehold of the premises. This would prevent a collective enfranchisement if the result was that there were no premises as defined which were owned by a single freeholder.[14]

Severance of the building may pose particular difficulties. A horizontal severance will create one or more 'flying freeholds'. The consequent necessary arrangement of the mutual positive maintenance obligations between the freehold estates created will be very difficult.[15] Severance of the property vertically may be possible in some situations. In such case, however, a vertical severance may not extinguish the right to collective enfranchisement; if the vertical severance creates two or more parts of a building each of which is self-contained, separate claims to collective enfranchisement will be possible in respect of each part.[16] Moreover, the tenants are unlikely to lose their rights to a new lease. In addition, if the creation of a severed freehold reduces the value of the freehold[17] on the open market, the landlord could find that the tenants

13 See 12.8. and 16.3.2.

14 Section 3(1)(a) (see 3.2.1 and 3.3.3).

15 See 2.2.1.

16 See 3.3.2. It may be easier in practice to proceed with such separate claims since a smaller number of tenants will have to reach agreement to proceed in each case.

17 The argument for reduction would be based primarily on the lack of a market for part of a building and the reluctance of purchasers and lenders to accept title to a flying freehold.

successfully argue on the grant of their new lease that a lower premium is payable in consequence.

There is more scope for severing, from the freehold of the flats, any appurtenant property[18] – those parts of the freehold other than the building in which the flats are situated. A separate block of garages, where each is let with a flat, could be severed from the ownership of the freehold of the flats. A similar severance could easily be done for gardens or access roads. However, the claim for collective enfranchisement could proceed in respect of the flats alone, and the price received will be reduced as the new lease will not include the garages or other severed property. The freeholder considering such severance will need to assess carefully the long-term benefits of retaining the freehold of garages, gardens or other appurtenant property once the freehold to the building containing the flats has been acquired.

10.4.3 Consolidation of properties

If two separate blocks of flats share a common vertical dividing wall, both qualify as separate premises for the purposes of the Act. If one, but not the other, has sufficient qualifying tenants for a potential enfranchisement claim, it may be possible to consolidate the two groups of flats into one set of premises which does not permit a collective enfranchisement. This might be done by creating, out of two separate adjoining units within the two premises, one combined unit by breaking through the vertical dividing wall. There may then be insufficient qualifying tenants for the one enlarged premises to be enfranchised.[19] The freeholder would argue that neither, former, separate block remained with a sufficient vertical division to allow a claim for collective enfranchisement on its own.[20] There are likely to be some substantial difficulties for this course of action. The two units to be combined must be vacant to enable them to be joined and the building and structural cost of the work might be substantial. The legal work of creating the title and fitting in new lease of the combined units to the service charge of the two separate blocks may not be easy. Once again, the qualifying tenants in the premises who satisfy the residence condition will still have their rights to a new lease.

10.4.4 Expand the business-user in the premises

By increasing the number of commercial or other non-residential units within any premises beyond the 10 per cent limit set by the Act,[21] a claim for collective

18 See s 1(2) and (3).

19 If the two buildings are owned by different freeholders, and the work successfully combined the two buildings, no collective enfranchisement would be possible. See, however, 10.4.2.

20 See s 3(2)(a) and 3.3.2. A risk would be that on the facts of any such case, a court decided that the two buildings remained vertically divided. Much would depend on the extent to which the two buildings had been consolidated.

21 See s 4(1) and 3.4.1.

enfranchisement will no longer be possible. It may therefore be possible to seek to change the use of any vacant flats or units to some form of non-residential use. The utility of such an approach in any situation would depend upon whether planning consent would be forthcoming.[22] Even if successful, the remaining qualifying tenants who met the residence requirement would keep their right to new leases.

10.4.5 Action against defaulting tenants

If any tenants within premises where a landlord fears a claim to collective enfranchisement will shortly take place[23] are in arrears with the service charge or otherwise in breach of covenant, the landlord could commence actions against the defaulting tenants for forfeiture or for possession. Whilst such action was being taken, those tenants would not be able to participate in a claim for collective enfranchisement.[24] Such action, unless well founded, is likely to prove expensive[25] in the long run and only have temporary effect.[26] It will only work in any event if the action so reduces either the number of qualifying or participating tenants below the statutory minimum to prevent a claim proceeding. Nevertheless, there is the prospect of an increased incidence of proceedings claiming forfeiture and tenants may be well advised to ensure that there are no service charge arrears in existence as they prepare to give an initial notice.

10.4.6 Inheritance tax designation

In appropriate cases, landlords could seek designation under the Inheritance Tax Act 1984 or apply for a direction under that Act.[27] This would prevent an enfranchisement and any initial notice would cease to have effect.

10.4.7 Estate management schemes

Landlords could consider application for an estate management scheme[28] in advance of the receipt of any initial notice. This would at least allow retention of

---

22 An application for change of use might alert the tenants and precipitate a claim for collective enfranchisement before consent was obtained. Without such consent, it may be difficult to show the requisite intent to occupy for non-residential purposes.

23 A landlord may be alerted to a potential claim by receiving inquiry notices (see s 11 and 4.7.2).

24 By virtue of Sch 3, para 3 (see 6.1.9).

25 Although the cost of the forfeiture action may be recoverable under the service charge provisions in the lease.

26 The tenants may seek leave to participate notwithstanding the forfeiture action (Sch 3, para 3(2) and 3(3)); if it is shown that the main purpose of the landlord's action is to hinder a claim, leave is likely to be given. Even if the tenants do not seek leave, they will almost certainly be entitled to relief from forfeiture.

27 By virtue of s 31(2)(a) and (c) (see 8.5.1).

28 As discussed at 23.2.1.

repairing and other obligations where the scheme is accepted and the existence of an approved scheme may discourage tenants from making a claim for collective enfranchisement.

10.4.8 Cross-restrictive covenants

Where two freeholders have adjacent premises, both of which may be subject to a claim for collective enfranchisement, those freeholders might consider entering into an agreement with cross-restrictive covenants so drafted to discourage the tenants from exercising their rights. Once again, the difficulty with such an action is that on valuation either of the price for collective enfranchisement or of the premium for new leases the tenants may argue that the market value of those freehold interests has been reduced by the creation of those covenants.

10.5 Avoidance techniques to use in future situations

10.5.1 Greater scope

There is more scope for landlords who wish to avoid the collective enfranchisement provisions of the Act and so arrange their affairs that a claim becomes less likely in the future. The possibilities are as follows.

10.5.2 Units or flats becoming vacant

Whenever a flat or unit becomes vacant within a set of premises a landlord can consider so dealing with that flat or unit so as to make collective enfranchisement less likely. A new lease of a flat could be at a high initial rent for the first year and so not qualify as a lease of low rent or the annual rent may be permanently set above the low rent limit.[29] Such leases will not be occupied by qualifying tenants either for a collective enfranchisement claim or for the purpose of any new lease. There is less scope for granting leases of terms of less than 21 years – mainly because the leases so granted may be assured tenancies with security of tenure. Vacant flats or units could also be so used in the future to take the premises above the threshold for non-residential use.[30]

10.5.3 Buying in leases

Another strategy for a landlord with substantial financial resources to circumvent the legislation might be to consider buying in leases which come onto the open market for sale, particularly in a recessionary period. Such action

29 One possibility is to arrange that part of the premium payable for the grant is paid as rent in advance for the initial year.

30 See 10.4.4.

would thereby reduce by one the number of flats within the premises which could count towards meeting the requirements to proceed with a collective enfranchisement claim. This would be a costly strategy because a fresh lease granted at a higher rent to avoid the Act would probably command a lower premium than one which carries the rights under the Act.

10.5.4 Company lettings

There will be room in the future for a greater number of leases where the original tenant is a company and there is a restriction in the lease on an assignment to an individual.[31] It would appear possible to provide for termination or surrender of the lease if the lease became vested in an individual who could satisfy the residence condition.[32] Such company lets could be granted when existing leases are bought in or when a flat becomes vacant. The tenant under such leases may be a qualifying tenant but could not satisfy the residence condition. Such action will not completely prevent a collective enfranchisement unless the minimum number of qualifying tenants meeting the residence condition for an initial notice to be given is not possible.[33] Such company tenants will not qualify for a new lease.[34]

10.5.5 Resist assignment by company tenants to individuals

Where consent to assignments has been sought of the leases of houses subject to the Leasehold Reform Act 1967, a landlord has successfully been able to refuse consent to assign the lease to the house from an existing company or other tenant who does not qualify under the 1967 Act to an individual who, in due course, may so qualify.[35] The existence of this authority will undoubtedly lead to similar arguments being put where the consent of the landlord or freeholder is needed under the terms of the lease[36] and consent to assignments are sought of flats within premises which could become the subject of a collective enfranchisement claim. Landlords will seek to oppose an assignment from a company to an individual since the company cannot satisfy the residence condition. The action will also be based on the desire to prevent that individual

---

31 In view of such cases as *Hilton v Plustitle* [1989] 1 WLR 149, CA, it is unlikely that a court would overturn such arrangements or hold that they were a sham.

32 See s 93(1)(b) and 10.2.1.

33 See 6.1.7 and 5.3.3. As few as 25 per cent of tenants in premises as a whole meeting the residence condition may suffice. Thus in a block of 20 flats, with 14 qualifying tenants, only 10 would need to participate in a claim of whom only five would need to satisfy the residence condition.

34 See 11.2.3.

35 *Norfolk Capital Group v Kitway* [1977] QB 506, CA; *Bickel v Duke of Westminster* [1977] QB 517, CA.

36 It is thought that only a minority of residential long leases, perhaps mainly in London, will contain a provision that assignment requires consent, such consent not to be unreasonably withheld.

being able to exercise a right to new lease in due course once residence for the requisite period has occurred.[37] It is, however, by no means clear that the established position in relation to the 1967 Act will necessarily apply to an application for consent where the 1993 Act is a factor. Unlike the position in the 1967 Act, a company can be a qualifying tenant and participate in an enfranchisement. By refusing consent to assign to an individual, there is a potential detriment to other tenants in the premises as well as to the tenant seeking to assign. A court might consider that Parliament has indicated that the right to collective enfranchisement should be available once a minimum number of qualifying tenants meet the residence condition and the court should not assist a landlord in preventing that happening. The fact that the price for an enfranchisement is fixed according to the market and not by a formula which might be considered confiscatory may be a factor. For these reasons, the issue is not clear-cut and is likely to be litigated.

10.6 Resistance to collective enfranchisement within the statutory procedure

10.6.1 Has the initial notice been registered?

Following receipt of an initial notice, landlords will undoubtedly check immediately as to whether the initial notice has been registered, either (in the case of unregistered land) as if it were an estate contract or (where the land is registered) by notice or caution.[38] If this has been omitted, a disposal of the freehold could enable a purchaser for money or money's worth of a legal estate to claim that they take free of the initial notice.[39] If this was established, the participating tenants and the nominee purchaser would have to give a fresh notice. Since the first notice would have been valid when given, it continues in force until withdrawn; once withdrawn, no subsequent notice can be given for a period of 12 months from the withdrawal.[40] Thus, failure to register followed by a sale of the legal interest could result in a landlord successfully putting back an enfranchisement for a year. However, in many cases the 1987 Act provisions[41] would apply to the disposal, thus requiring notice of the intended sale and enabling the tenants to acquire under the provisions of that Act. The period of notice required to be given[42] should also enable the advisers to the

37 Note the different time periods within which a tenant must reside to participate in a collective enfranchisement as compared with qualifying for a right to a new lease (see 3.6.2 and 11.2.3).

38 Section 97(1).

39 Land Charges Act 1972, s 4(6); and see *Midland Bank v Green* [1981] AC 513.

40 See s 13(8), (9) and (11).

41 The right of first refusal (see the Landlord and Tenant Act 1987, s 1). However, the 1987 Act applies only to a disposal of an interest by an immediate landlord of the qualifying tenants (as defined by that Act) (see s 2(1)(a)).

42 Two months (ibid, s 5(2)(c)).

nominee purchaser to remedy the omission and register the initial notice before completion of the disposal can occur.[43]

10.6.2 Taking advantage and getting the best deal

Few of the active steps which can be taken, as set out above, can guarantee to prevent a collective enfranchisement claim and may only result in a larger number of claims for a new lease. Many involve substantial expenditure by the reversioner or relevant landlord. It may not be worthwhile in financial terms for such steps to be considered. Instead, a strategy of passive resistance may be adopted with the procedures of the Act being used to ensure the best possible price.

10.6.3 Testing the time-limits

The procedure for collective enfranchisement involves a considerable number of time traps for the nominee purchaser[44] and the participating tenants standing behind it. No doubt many landlords will wait passively and see whether each time-limit is met and take advantage of any lapse.

10.6.4 Demanding evidence of title

Landlords will almost certainly wish to exercise their rights in every case by requiring tenants to deduce title to each of the flats held by qualifying tenants by whom the initial notice is given. A failure to respond within 21 days with sufficient evidence will lend to a deemed withdrawal.[45]

10.6.5 Leaseback options

In many planned collective enfranchisement claims the potential participating tenants will seek from the landlord some idea whether he would insist on leaseback of any commercial, vacant or rack-rented flats or units within the premises. An unwilling landlord may choose to exercise the right not to co-operate and to wait until after the initial notice is served before indicating in the counter-notice whether leaseback is required.[46] Landlords may adopt the high-risk strategy of insisting that such units be bought out, thus hoping that the increased price would be beyond the means of the participating tenants.

Alternatively, where the landlord decides to take a leaseback of the commercial, vacant or rack-rented units, the present landlord will become the

---

43 Even if a contract to dispose of the interest exists, it is the date of completion of the purchase which is important for the purposes of the Land Charges Act 1972, s 4(6); a search could not give a sufficient priority period to cover the whole two-month delay necessitated by giving notice under the 1987 Act.

44 See generally chapters six and seven.

45 See 6.4.1 and 8.3.2.

46 It is possible that a decision could be taken at an even later date (see the discussion at 9.5.5).

tenant of the nominee purchaser after completion of the enfranchisement and therefore might seek to impose substantial repairing and management obligations in the lease – although he will end up paying for the proportion of these by way of the service charge.

10.6.6 Argument on price

Unwilling landlords will undoubtedly seek to argue for the maximum possible price before the leasehold valuation tribunal, particularly to try to increase the marriage value from the minimum of 50 per cent to a higher figure. Market evidence will be required for this to be substantiated.[47] Both sides will bear their own costs before leasehold valuation tribunal; but arguing the terms of acquisition will test the tenants' resolve and may produce a much better offer to conclude the enfranchisement than that contained in the initial notice to avoid the costs of the hearing before the leasehold valuation tribunal.

10.6.7 Arguing on completion details

A landlord will always be able to seek the best possible terms at a completion of collective enfranchisement including the terms for any rights over retained property and the terms of any leases granted to him by way of leaseback. He will undoubtedly seek to ensure that the burden of all outstanding service charge claims are settled or passed to the nominee purchaser as new landlord.[48] The tenants may wish to challenge the amount of the relevant costs[49] claimed on completion. The cost burden will not be inconsiderable especially if each of the landlords chooses to act separately in deducing title, as they are entitled to do.

---

47 In many cases, it may be available. See 19.3.1. Landlords may also wish to test the difficulties in interpreting market value. See 19.3.4 and 19.3.5.

48 As he is entitled to do (see s 32(2)(a)).

49 See 9.2.2.

PART THREE

THE RIGHT TO A NEW LEASE (OR 'INDIVIDUAL ENFRANCHISEMENT')

CHAPTER ELEVEN

THE NATURE OF THE RIGHT

11.1 General

11.1.1 An alternative right to collective enfranchisement

The individual right of a tenant of a flat to acquire a new extended lease is contained in Chapter II of Part I of the 1993 Act. As previously described,[1] this right began very much as subsidiary to the general right of collective enfranchisement. However, it now stands quite separately to the collective right in Chapter I of the Act; indeed, wherever the right of collective enfranchisement exists then, almost certainly, some of the tenants exercising the right of collective enfranchisement, but not necessarily all, will have the alternative of deciding to proceed individually and extend their leases instead of jointly proceeding with collective enfranchisement.[2]

Moreover, the right of collective enfranchisement is not lost when one, some, or indeed all of the tenants in a block of flats decide to exercise their individual rights to acquire a new lease. At any time in the future the right of collective enfranchisement to secure the freehold remains available. Conversely, when some qualifying tenants have successfully exercised the right of collective enfranchisement, an excluded qualifying tenant may exercise a right to an extended lease.

11.1.2 A more attractive right

It is submitted that in many instances the individual right to extend the lease will be more attractive than the collective right to enfranchise. This will be the case particularly where the management of the block of flats is conducted satisfactorily and there is no great pressure from tenants to take over the management functions. Indeed, there will be cases where the burden of management may be too burdensome to contemplate and there is no incentive

1 See 1.2.3.

2 It is theoretically possible that none of the qualifying tenants meeting the residence condition (minimum 12 months) for a collective enfranchisement satisfy the residence requirement for a new extended lease (three years) but this will be very rare in practice.

to enfranchise collectively. The main attraction of the right to a new lease under Chapter II is that an individual can exercise the right independently of their fellow tenants and the resulting financing of the transaction is entirely within the control of that one tenant. Additionally, even where a group of tenants would like to enfranchise collectively, there may be circumstances where it is preferable for each of them to begin individually by claiming a new lease extended under the Act. If all or most of the tenants in the block of flats took such action, the freehold value of the reversion which remained after the leases have been extended might be nil or very small unless there was some development potential. It might then become possible to negotiate with the freeholder outside the Act's procedures, and without embarking on the complex procedures of Chapter I, for a transfer of management functions and the freehold to a management company set up by the tenants for that purpose.[3]

11.2 The requirements to be satisfied

11.2.1 The statutory definition

The statutory right is a right given to a qualifying tenant of a flat to acquire a new lease of the flat on payment of a premium, that premium to be determined in accordance with the provisions of the Act.[4] It should be noted that the definition of 'flat' throughout Chapter II carries the extended meaning of including any garage, outhouse, garden, yard or other appurtenance belonging to or enjoyed with the flat and let to the tenant on the relevant date.[5] The basic or unamended definition of a flat continues to apply in the context of any premises containing the flat and, in particular for the purposes, an intention to redevelop or compulsory purchase under ss 47 and 55.[6]

11.2.2 Must be a qualifying tenant

When any individual tenant gives notice of a claim to exercise the right, which is the relevant date for the purposes of the statutory requirements,[7] the tenant must be a qualifying tenant of the flat concerned.[8] The definition of a qualifying

---

3 See further 12.5.1.
4 Section 39(1).
5 Section 101(1), as modified by s 62(2). The relevant date is the date that the tenant's notice is given; in the case of an application where a landlord cannot be found under s 50, the relevant date becomes the date that the application is made.
6 Section 62(3) (see 14.3.1 and 15.4.1).
7 Section 39(8).
8 Section 39(2)(a).

tenant is the same as that for collective enfranchisement and therefore a person is a qualifying tenant of a flat if that person is a tenant of the flat under a long lease at low rent. The relevant sections of Chapter I of the Act relating to the definition and meaning of qualifying tenant, long lease and low rent, namely ss 5, 7 and 8, apply for the purposes of determining the meaning of qualifying tenant, long lease and low rent respectively.[9] Reference should therefore be made to the earlier discussion of those questions in any case to decide whether a person is a qualifying tenant.[10] For the purpose of deciding whether a flat is at a low rent, the modified meaning of flat is to be used although the difference in this context is minimal and the result is likely to be the same.[11]

If an individual is a tenant under a long lease at a low rent of two or more flats then, for the purposes of the right to a new lease, such a tenant can be a qualifying tenant of each or all of those flats.[12] This contrasts with the right to collective enfranchisement where a person cannot be a qualifying tenant of any of three or more flats.[13] An individual with three or more such flats in one block may choose to transfer one or more to others to obtain the right to participate in a collective enfranchisement; but the right to a new lease remains as an alternative – but only of course in respect of the flat or flats where the residence requirement is satisfied.[14]

11.2.3 The residence requirement[15]

The other major statutory requirement is that the qualifying tenant must have occupied the flat as his only or principal home for the last three years or for periods amounting to three years in the last 10 years.[16] Whether the flat has been so occupied will be a question of fact.[17] It does not matter that the flat has

9 Section 39(3). Thus, a business tenant and tenants with a charitable housing trust as immediate landlord cannot be qualifying tenants (s 5(2)).

10 See 3.5.1, 3.7.1 and 3.8.2.

11 Section 62(4) applying s 62(2) instead of s 8(7).

12 Section 39(4).

13 Section 5(5) (see 3.5.4).

14 Since the residence must be by the tenant, it is unlikely that the residence condition will be satisfied in respect of more than one flat, although it is possible in the case of joint tenants who have lived in separate flats or where a tenant has lived for three years in one flat and then moved to another. Under the Leasehold Reform Act 1967, it has been held that a husband and wife can each have a main residence (*Fowell v Radford* (1969) 21 P & CR 99, CA).

15 There was orginally no residential requirement in the Bill as drafted (see 1.2.3). The present requirement was introduced in the House of Lords (HL Deb, Vol 544, cols 101–105), fulfilling a pledge made to the House of Commons.

16 Section 39(2)(b). It must be the tenant, or one of joint tenants, who has occupied the flat; occupation by a member of the family does not suffice. 'Only or principal home' is not defined (cf the Housing Act 1985, s 81 and the Housing Act 1988, s 1(1)(b)).

17 See *Byrne v Rowbotham* (1969) 210 EG 823; *Baron v Phillips* (1978) 38 P & CR 91, CA, on similar wording in the Leasehold Reform Act 1967.

also been used for other purposes. Unlike collective enfranchisement, where a qualifying tenant may still be a qualifying tenant notwithstanding the fact that they do not satisfy the residence condition, for the purposes of claiming a new lease the residence requirement is a primary one. Consequently, if the flat is occupied by a company or other artificial person, or if the tenant is a corporation sole and the occupation is by the corporator, there can be no qualifying tenant because occupation by that corporate person is not regarded as occupation for purposes of the Act.[18] However, it is sufficient that the occupation as the only or principal home is of only part of the flat rather than the whole.[19] It is immaterial whether at any particular time the tenant's occupation was in right of the lease by virtue of which he is now a qualifying tenant[20] – the occupation may have been under some other lease or otherwise. Thus, for example, if a qualifying tenant has recently already negotiated a new extended lease before the Act came into force and now wishes to take advantage of the statutory right in Chapter II, the occupation under the earlier lease can count to satisfying the residence period. Moreover, in the case of a lease held by joint tenants the residence condition need only be satisfied with respect to any one of the joint tenants.[21]

11.2.4 Purchasers and beneficiaries under a trust

A purchaser of the lease cannot rely upon the residence of the vendor; at the relevant date when the notice is given, the existing tenant must have occupied for the three-year period. Consequently, a purchaser who wishes to secure a new lease should require the vendor to give the initial notice prior to exchange of contracts and take an assignment of those rights at completion.[22]

More significantly, there is no provision, as in the Leasehold Reform Act 1967, for the residence by a beneficiary under a trust to count as residence by the trustees.[23] The absence of such a provision is probably explained by the late introduction of the residence requirement into the legislation. In view of the express provision in the 1967 Act, beneficiaries under a trust would appear to have no rights to claim a new lease and little prospect of the legislation being interpreted in their favour. Only amending legislation would appear to offer a solution.

---

18 Section 39(5), proviso.

19 Section 39(5)(a). Thus, if the tenant of the flat has allowed another person into possession of part as sub-tenant or licencee, the residence requirement will still be satisfied (cf *Harris v Swick Securities* [1969] 3 All ER 1131).

20 Section 39(5)(b).

21 Section 39(6). Where joint tenants own two or more flats, the residence requirement could be satisfied by one joint tenant in respect of one flat and by another in respect of a second.

22 See 13.2.2.

23 Cf the 1967 Act, s 6(1).

11.3 Extent of the right

11.3.1 Wider than originally envisaged

It is important to note that the right to acquire a new lease under s 39 is much wider than was drafted in the Bill as presented to Parliament. In particular, the requirement which then existed in the Bill, that an extended lease right could only be exercised if there was no right to collective enfranchisement exercisable in respect of the building in which the flat is contained, was deleted during the passage of the Bill in the House of Lords.[24] This change was one of the most fundamental to the legislation. As originally envisaged, the right to acquire a new lease was only available to those tenants who did not have the right to collective enfranchisement. It would have had the unfortunate result that in those cases where the right of collective enfranchisement was technically available, but for one of many practical reasons, financial or otherwise, the tenants were unable to exercise that right, they would not have individually been able to acquire a new lease with an extended term as an alternative. The change can only be welcomed, but it does mark a major shift in the policy of the legislation and effectively gives individual tenants the choice of either taking an extended lease or partaking in a collective enfranchisement or indeed both, but not at the same time. Where an attempt is made to give notice by some tenants to enfranchise collectively and by one or more other tenants to extend their leases then, as we shall see, the right to collective enfranchisement is dealt with first.[25]

11.3.2 Excepted premises

Unlike the position with collective enfranchisement, there are relatively few premises which are excepted from the right to a new lease. In particular, qualifying tenants of flats on long leases who cannot make a claim for collective enfranchisement because the premises have an internal floor area exceeding 10 per cent devoted to non-residential use or because of a resident freeholder,[26] are able individually to make a claim for a new lease. Qualifying tenants whose flats are in premises designated or subject to a direction within the scope of s 31[27] may also qualify for a new extended lease.

24 The Government long-resisted any change (see HC Deb, Standing Committee B, cols 214–240, 24 November 1992; HL Deb, Vol 545, cols 86–101) despite all-party pressure and detailed argument; but it then introduced its own amendment deleting this requirement (HL Deb, Vol 546, col 209). There was no debate; one can only surmise that the concession was made because of the prospect of defeat. A change in the Secretary of State may have been a factor.

25 See 12.2.2.

26 See ss 4 and 10 and 3.4.1 and 3.4.2.

27 See 3.4.5 and 8.5.1.

However, there is no right to acquire a new lease of a flat where the interest of that property is vested inalienably in the National Trust[28] or to acquire a new lease of any property within the precinct of a cathedral church.[29]

11.3.3 Crown land

The basic principle is that the right to acquire a new lease only applies to a lease from the Crown[30] if (and only if) there has ceased to be a Crown interest in the land.[31] However, there is one instance where there is a right to acquire a new lease notwithstanding a subsisting Crown interest and there are provisions designed to facilitate the grant of fresh leases by or with the consent of the appropriate authority in relation to that Crown interest as if the right to acquire a new lease was available.

The right to acquire a new lease arises when the Crown interest is superior to that of another person who would be the landlord in relation to the grant.[32] If that landlord is entitled either to grant the new lease without the concurrence of the appropriate Crown authority or is notified that the authority will concur in granting the lease, the right to acquire a new lease arises.[33] Provision is also made to allow the appropriate Crown authority to decide to grant a fresh lease as if the Act did apply. Thus the Crown Estate Commissioners are not bound by the restriction on the length of term for which a lease may be granted in a case where, but for the existence of the Crown interest, there would be a right to acquire a new lease.[34] Similar authority to grant leases out of Crown interests is given in the case of land belonging in right of the Duchy of Lancaster or to the Duchy of Cornwall.[35] It is envisaged, therefore, that tenants may be proceeding with a view to acquiring a new lease of a flat in circumstances in which, but for the existence of the Crown interest, there would be an entitlement to acquire a new lease. In such a case, the parties[36] may agree that the decision of any question relating to the acquisition, such as the amount of the premium, should be determined by the leasehold valuation tribunal; if there is such agreement, the leasehold valuation tribunal has jurisdiction.[37]

28 Section 95.
29 Section 96.
30 A 'lease from the Crown' is defined to mean interests comprised in the Crown Estate, those belonging to Her Majesty in right of the Duchy of Lancaster, those belonging to the Duchy of Cornwall and any other interest belonging to a government department (s 94(11)). 'Appropriate authority' is to be construed accordingly.
31 Section 94(1).
32 That other person will be a landlord within the meaning of s 41(1) and have a term of sufficient duration to grant the new lease.
33 Section 94(2).
34 Section 94(3).
35 Section 94(4) and (5).
36 That is, the appropriate authority, the tenant and all other persons such as other landlords who would otherwise be entitled to be represented before a leasehold valuation tribunal.
37 Section 94(9)(b) and (10). See also s 88 and 22.3.6.

11.3.4 Minerals

In the unusual case of a lease extending to underlying minerals, the right to acquire a new lease will not extend to those underlying minerals if the landlord requires the minerals to be excepted and provided also that proper provision is made for the support of the premises granted by that existing lease as they are enjoyed on the relevant date when the claim is made.[38]

11.4 The new lease

11.4.1 A binding obligation

Where the right to acquire a new lease exists and provided that the correct procedure is followed,[39] the landlord is bound to grant to the tenant, and the tenant is bound to accept in substitution for the existing lease on payment of a premium in accordance with the Act, a new lease of the flat at a peppercorn rent for a term expiring 90 years after the term date of the existing lease.[40] The procedure makes no provision for a later binding contract and therefore differs from that for a collective enfranchisement; it is more similar in this respect to the notice by a tenant under the Leasehold Reform Act 1967. Although a tenant may withdraw the notice, or it may be deemed to be withdrawn, a tenant's notice otherwise creates contractual obligations.[41]

11.4.2 The landlord's investment interest bought out

The new lease will add 90 years to the current term of years held by the tenant and the existing ground rent will be bought out. Thus, if a particular tenant has 44 years left to run on their current long lease the term of the new lease acquired under the Act will be 134 years. The second key feature is that the rent will be a peppercorn rent for the whole of that term, whatever the amount of the rent in the existing lease. These two features ensure that as far as the landlord is concerned the investment interest in the flat is very much reduced if not virtually extinguished by the premium paid on the grant of the new lease.[42] There is no future annual income by way of rent and the addition of 90 years, to the term which the tenant already has, will ensure that the reversion to the new lease will have nil or very little capital value. Moreover, in the absence of

---

38 Section 39(7).

39 Section 56(1) and see 13.1.1 and 16.1.1.

40 For calculations of the premium payable and for the exact terms of the new lease, see 20.2 and 16.3.1. 'Peppercorn' is not defined and may be understood as a nominal rent by virtue of its common use for that purpose in private leases.

41 See 13.2.1 below.; and cf the Leasehold Reform Act 1967, s 8(1) and *Collin v Duke of Westminster* [1985] QB 581.

42 Although redevelopment potential in the future may be a factor (see 16.8.1).

development potential, the reversion will not gain value with the passage of time since a further 90-year extension at a peppercorn rent can be claimed at any time. The tenant thereby obtains a 'virtual freehold' – which is why the right to a new lease may be termed 'individual enfranchisement'.

11.5 The landlord granting the new lease

11.5.1 The basic principle

In accordance with general property principles, the new lease to be granted under the Act can only be done by a person whose own interest in the property is either a freehold interest or a leasehold interest long enough to grant the relevant term of years.

11.5.2 The competent landlord

Accordingly, by s 40, the landlord, called the competent landlord,[43] is defined as the person in relation to the lease held by the qualifying tenant as the person who is the owner of that interest in the flat which, for the time being, fulfils the following three conditions:[44]

(a) it is an interest in reversion and expectant (whether immediately or not) on the termination of the tenant's lease; and
(b) it is either a freehold interest or a leasehold interest whose duration is such as to enable that person to grant a new lease of the flat; and
(c) it is not itself expectant (whether immediately or not) on an interest which fulfils those conditions.

What this means is that the competent landlord who grants the extended lease is either the holder of the lowest intermediate leasehold interest which is held for a long enough period to enable the grant of the new lease under the Act, or, if none, the freeholder. Significantly, this means that the value of any intermediate leasehold interest which is of too short a duration must itself be purchased by the tenant exercising the right. For example, if the freeholder has granted a 99-year lease of the whole premises to an intermediate lessee, say a management company and the relevant flat leases are for 99 years less 10 days, then the value of that interest of the management company (if any) in a particular flat will be purchased by the tenant by payment of a premium[45] representing the value of that intermediate leasehold interest.[46] However, the

---

43 Section 40(4)(b).

44 Section 40(1). The definition is similar to that in s 44 of the Landlord and Tenant Act 1954.

45 Calculated in accordance with Sch 13 to the Act.

46 Section 56(2). In the particular example, the value, if any, would be in the net ground rent recoverable.

intermediate leaseholder does not lose the interest completely. Any subsisting intermediate lease is deemed to be surrendered and re-granted.[47] In the example given above, the 10 days' reversion of the management company probably has nil capital value; the deemed surrender and re-grant preserves the important management provisions in the intermediate lease.[48]

11.5.3 Powers of the competent landlord

The competent landlord will conduct on behalf of all other landlords, if any, all proceedings arising out of any notice given by the tenant to claim a new lease[49] whether those proceedings are to resist or give effect to the claim. Normally, this person conducting the proceedings will be the freeholder; it is only when an intermediate leaseholder has a term of sufficient duration that they will be conducting the proceedings and granting the new lease.

11.5.4 'Other landlords'

An 'other landlord' means any person, other than a tenant or a trustee for him, in whom there is vested a concurrent tenancy intermediate between the interest of the competent landlord and the tenant's lease.[50] Such other landlords, probably better described and understood as intermediate landlords, will have the value of their interest purchased as part of the premium paid for the grant of the new lease;[51] but their intermediate lease will continue to exist between the interest of the competent landlord and the tenant's new lease by virtue of a deemed surrender and re-grant of their lease.[52]

11.5.5 Special categories of landlord

If the competent landlord is a mortgagee in possession, a university or college landlord or an ecclesiastical landlord, if the landlord is under a disability, or the interest is vested in a custodian trustee or held upon trust for sale or subject to a settlement, Sch 2 to the Act applies. These provisions have been discussed in relation to Chapter I of the Act.[53] Some of the paragraphs apply specifically and only to Chapter II;[54] they ensure that any sums paid to the landlord are dealt with as capital receipts and any future payment of compensation for either redevelopment or for the modification or excluding the statutory rights[55] is

---

47 Schedule 11, para 10, discussed further at 16.2.2.
48 See further 16.2.3.
49 Section 40(2).
50 Section 40(4)(c).
51 This will represent the value of the net income received under the existing lease and the capital value, if any, of the reversion to the existing lease.
52 Schedule 11, para 10; and see 16.2.1.
53 See 5.10.1.
54 Schedule 2, paras 5(2), 6 and 7(2).
55 Under s 93(4).

treated as authorised under the appropriate statute. Except in the case of a custodian trustee under Sch 2, para 3, the trustees of any landlord's interest held upon trust for sale would appear to be the landlords for the purpose of receiving and giving notices and the grant of a new lease. In the case of landlords' interests subject to a strict settlement within the Settled Land Act 1925, the tenant for life has the legal estate vested in him and is the proper recipient of any notice but the premium on the grant of any new lease should be paid to the trustees.[56]

11.5.6 Competent landlord and intermediate landlords

There are full and complex provisions relating to those situations where the landlord dealing with a tenant's claim to a new lease is not the tenant's immediate landlord. These provisions are contained in Sch 11 to the Act; the provisions in that Schedule relating to the giving of the tenant's notice are considered later.[57]

Provision is made for the competent landlord to conduct the proceedings after a tenant's notice of claim so that any counter-notice given by the competent landlord must specify the other landlords on whose behalf he is acting[58] and the acts of the competent landlord become binding on those other landlords.[59] In the event of a dispute between them the competent landlord or any of the other landlords may apply to the court for directions. If any of the landlords cannot be found the competent landlord can apply to the court for directions and the court may make such order as it thinks fit with a view to giving effect to the rights of the tenant and protecting the interests of those other persons.[60] Unless such directions are sought the competent landlord shall proceed as in other cases. The competent landlord acting in good faith and with reasonable care and diligence is not liable to any of the other landlords for any loss or damage caused by any act or omission by him.[61]

11.5.7 Rights and duties of intermediate landlords

Those landlords who are not competent landlords do have some rights. They can choose to act independently in respect to any legal proceedings in which title to any property comes into question or in any proceedings relating to the determination of the amount payable by virtue of Sch 13; and they may give notice to require the amount due to be paid to them.[62] As in the case of collective enfranchisement, any proceedings to resist the claim on the grounds

56 There is no express provision in the Act dealing with property held on trust.
57 See 13.1.6.
58 Schedule 11, para 5.
59 Section 40(2); and Sch 11, para 6.
60 Schedule 11, para 6(3).
61 Schedule 11, para 6(4)
62 Schedule 11, para 7.

of an intention to redevelop[63] are brought by the landlord wishing to establish the defence and not by the competent landlord on behalf of others.[64] Those other landlords have a duty to the competent landlord to give all such information and assistance as may be reasonably required of them and there is a right of indemnity for the competent landlord against them in consequence of the failure. There is a duty also for those other landlords to make such contribution as shall be just to the cost and expenses which are properly incurred by the competent landlord in dealing with the tenant's claim but are not recoverable or not recovered from the tenant.[65]

63 Under s 47.
64 Schedule 11, para 9.
65 Schedule 11, para 8.

CHAPTER TWELVE

PREPARING FOR A CLAIM TO A NEW LEASE

12.1 The importance of the right

The individual right of a tenant of a flat to acquire a new lease is a 'Cinderella' right, apparently very much secondary to the right of collective enfranchisement, especially in the Bill as drafted, but likely to prove, in practice, to be the most important new right granted by the Act. The substantial amendments to the requirements for the right to be exercised during the passage of the legislation have transformed this right into one which will be of considerable practical value to residential long leaseholders. The statutory requirements which need to be satisfied if a claim is to be commenced have been considered in the previous chapter; in this chapter, the considerable preparatory work necessary before a notice exercising and claiming a right to a new lease is given are discussed.

12.2 Relationship to collective enfranchisement

12.2.1 The choice – collective enfranchisement or new extended lease?

In considering whether either to join in a claim for collective enfranchisement or individually to exercise the right to a new and extended lease term, a tenant must appreciate that it is not a pure either/or situation. A tenant who has exercised the right to a new lease and obtained an extended term 90 years longer at a peppercorn rent can still, at a later date, join in a claim with other qualifying tenants and make a claim to collective enfranchisement. A tenant in such a situation will have already purchased the investment value in the flat occupied and therefore the share then paid to join the collective enfranchisement should be reduced by a similar amount to take into account that other participating tenants may be in a position of not having an extended term. However, there may be a potential but usually small further cost in relation to the flat because the tenant who already has an extended lease will share in buying out any development value in his flat and any such value in the rest of the freehold being acquired. However, the cost of further extending at a later collective enfranchisement what might be, for example, a new term of 145 years (90 years plus the original term of 55 years) to the assumed term of 999 years when the rent is already a peppercorn rent may be of very little and probably nil value. The tenant will have to contribute by taking a share of the cost of the freehold,[1] but that may be relatively small compared to the cost already paid to obtain the extended lease.

12.2.2 Suspension of a new lease claim during a collective enfranchisement

The one thing which cannot be done, however, is to pursue a claim to a new lease at the same time as a claim to collective enfranchisement is proceeding. A claim to acquire a new lease cannot be made if a collective enfranchisement claim is current and an initial notice has been given;[2] and if an initial notice to enfranchise collectively is given after a claim for a new lease has been commenced by notice but before the claim is completed then the collective enfranchisement will take precedence and the individual claim to a new lease will be suspended.[3] If the collective enfranchisement is successful, the individuals not partaking in the collective enfranchisement claim can resume their claim for a new lease against the new freeholder who will be the nominee purchaser. If the initial notice is withdrawn, or there is a deemed withdrawal, the claim for a new lease can be resumed.

12.3 Advantages of a claim to a new lease

12.3.1 No need to act with others

There may be considerable advantages for a tenant deciding to pursue a claim for new and extended term rather than partaking in a collective enfranchisement. The principle advantage will be that the tenant will be acting alone and not in concert with other tenants and will not be relying on an agreement with them. There will be no need to make decisions on the nominee purchaser or a participators' agreement; there will also be no need to finance the purchase of the reversion to flats of qualifying tenants who are not participating. Instead, the individual will be merely securing the investment value in his or her own flat by eliminating the annual rent and reducing it to a peppercorn rent and extending the term by a period of 90 years.

12.3.2 Financing more straightforward

The financing of the transaction, when a tenant does not have sufficient funds, will be easy in comparison to a collective enfranchisement claim. Very often,

---

1 There may also be the shared cost of the reversion to other units or the value of flats of qualifying but non-participating tenants.

2 Section 54(1).

3 Section 54(2). See 15.3.1.

this will be by re-mortgage of the new lease of the flat to cover the cost of purchasing the extended term. There may be no need to take a fresh mortgage if the current mortgagee is willing to lend the money since the security can be transferred automatically to the new lease.[4] All that may be required, therefore, is a further advance. Since other parties are not involved, a mortgagee may even be willing to advance sufficient monies to cover the costs of the transaction, provided that there is sufficient security in the value of the lease as extended.

12.3.3 *No change to satisfactory management arrangements*

It may be an advantage to secure the flat as the home for the future without a change in the management arrangements. The management of the block in which the flat is contained may be managed efficiently and successfully perhaps through a resident's management company and those arrangements need not be disturbed in any way by the grant of a new lease.

12.3.4 *Available when no right to collective enfranchisement*

Finally, the right to a new lease may be the only opportunity available if the flat is in premises which do not qualify for collective enfranchisement. The resident landlord exemption preventing a collective enfranchisement does not apply to a lease renewal. If there is commercial business used in more than 10 per cent of the internal floor area of the premises, the right to an extended lease will be available to qualifying tenants of flats in those premises who satisfy the residence requirement.

12.4 Disadvantages in comparison with collective enfranchisement

12.4.1 *No change to management arrangements*

The grant of the extended lease will not, of itself, make any change to the management and service charge arrangements to the block of flats in which the flat is situated – and this may be a prime concern of the tenants. The service charge arrangements will be repeated in the new lease[5] but substantial change will not be possible. If the tenant is concerned that the management charges are too high or the management of the block is not being efficiently conducted, the

4 Section 58(4); and see 16.4.2.
5 Subject to certain modifications (see 16.3.6).

remedy would be to gather sufficient support from other qualifying tenants to make a claim for collective enfranchisement or to use the rights of management audit as part of a campaign to remedy poor or inadequate management.[6]

12.4.2 Development potential remains with the landlord

The second major difference, which may be a disadvantage, is that the term obtained by exercising the right to acquire a new lease is a 90-year extension added to the number of years left on the existing lease. If there are 25 years left on that existing lease the term of the new lease would be 115 years, and this must be compared with the assumed valuation basis of a grant of new leases to the participating tenants after a collective enfranchisement with a term of 999 years at a peppercorn rent. In many cases the capital value of a 115-year lease at a peppercorn rent may be very similar if not identical to the market value of a 999-year lease on the same terms at a peppercorn rent; but the tenants under an extended lease always have to face the prospect of losing the lease by means of a successful re-development claim. If the landlord can establish an intention to demolish or reconstruct a whole or substantial part of the premises then there is a right of termination of the extended new lease at any time during the period of 12 months ending with the term date of the existing lease, as well as any time during the five years ending with the term date of the new extended lease.[7] Very few tenants will be concerned about the redevelopment at the end of the 115 years; but if there is a real redevelopment prospect at the end of the term date of the existing lease, in our example 25 years, then the market value of the extended lease may be affected, at least in the future.

12.5 Collective enfranchisement 'by the back door'

12.5.1 Resolving disagreement among participating tenants by a lease renewal

The right to a new lease could be used as an alternative route to an eventual collective enfranchisement. The ultimate aim of tenants, or a majority of them, may be control of the freehold and management, but the spectre of the cost and complexity of the statutory collective enfranchisement procedure may be too much to contemplate. More significantly, there may be disagreement between the tenants about the sharing of the price. Thus, in a medium-sized block of flats there may be some with a larger floor area, others with additional amenities

6 The remedies afforded by the Landlord and Tenant Act 1987 also remain available.
7 Section 61, discussed at 16.8.1.

or a better view or some who have already paid in the private market for an extended lease. It is very probable that agreement on respective values and consequent shares in the cost of a collective enfranchisement may be difficult to achieve and the solicitor and valuer instructed to act for the tenants as a body may face conflict of interest problems in attempting to resolve these difficulties.

12.5.2 An alternative route to enfranchisement?

An alternative approach in such situations would be for each tenant to pursue a claim for an extended lease – using their own solicitors and valuers and each negotiating separately. Differences in sizes of flats, lengths of terms or amenities will be reflected in the premiums paid in each case. If, for example, all 12 tenants in a block eventually secured such new leases, financing each transaction independently, the freehold would then be subject to 12 extended leases of terms probably well in excess of 90 years and all at a peppercorn rent. The cost of then securing the freehold, especially in the absence of development potential on the whole site in the near future, will be minimal. Moreover, the freeholder will have little incentive to retain the interest. The freehold may then be secured by negotiation and without ever commencing a formal claim to collective enfranchisement. Even if not every flat has obtained a new extended lease, the fact that a majority have done so may make a formal collective enfranchisement or an agreed purchase of the freehold by negotiation with the freeholder more feasible.

12.6 Preliminary inquiries by a qualifying tenant

12.6.1 Inquiry notice to immediate landlord

A qualifying tenant who wishes to consider making a claim to acquire a new extended lease under the Act may give to his immediate landlord, or to any person receiving rent on behalf of his immediate landlord, a notice requiring the recipient to state whether the immediate landlord is the owner of the freehold interest in the flat.[8] If that immediate landlord is not the freeholder then, on receipt of that notice, the landlord or recipient of the notice must give, so far as is known, the name and address of the person who does own the freehold interest in the flat, the duration of the leasehold interest in the flat of the tenant's immediate landlord and the extent of the premises in which it subsists; and the name and address of every other person who has a leasehold interest in the flat, if any, which is superior to that of the tenant's immediate landlord.[9] If there are such further intermediate leasehold interests then the duration of such interest and the extent of the premises in which they subsist must also be given.

8 Section 41(1).

9 Section 41(2). In this way, a tenant's adviser can determine who is the competent landlord (see 11.5.2).

Where the qualifying tenant knows his immediate landlord is not the freeholder, a similar notice can be given requiring the same information as to the duration of the lease and the extent of the premises in which it subsists.[10]

12.6.2 *Notice to other persons with a leasehold interest*

Any other person known to have a leasehold interest in the tenant's flat can be asked to give such details of their interest and the name and address of the freeholder or any other leaseholder.[11]

12.6.3 *Requesting details of any collective enfranchisement claim*

Any inquiry notice given by a qualifying tenant must also ask and require the recipient of the notice to state whether he has received, in respect of any premises containing the tenant's flat, an initial notice claiming collective enfranchisement or a copy of such a notice. The recipient is only required to give information if the initial notice is still current[12] and, if so, he must give the date on which the notice was given and the name and address of the nominee purchaser for the time being appointed for the purposes of the claim.[13] Such information will of course prevent a claim being pursued for acquisition of a new lease while the collective enfranchisement claim and initial notice are still valid.

12.6.4 *Time for response*

The information and response to a notice must be given within a period of 28 days which begins with the date of the giving of the notice. The failure to respond to the notice can be enforced by application to the court.[14]

12.6.5 *Alternatives to formal inquiry*

As with collective enfranchisement, in the case of registered titles most if not all of the information can very often be obtained in an alternative way by applying to the Land Registry for office copies of the freehold title and any intermediate leasehold titles. This alternative will only assist where all or some of those titles are registered. Where the tenant's own existing lease is registered the tenant's title may give the title details of the superior leasehold or freehold interests and, if it does not, a suitable index search can be carried out. However, even when the Land Registry gives the necessary information it may still be prudent to give a notice under s 41 to ensure that the provisions as revealed by the Land

10 Section 41(3)(a).

11 Section 41(3)(b).

12 A claim is current if the notice or a binding contract continues in force or a vesting order has been made (s 41(5)(b)).

13 Section 41(4).

14 Section 41(6) (s 92(1) and see 22.5).

Registry are still correct and that a recent transfer has not taken place. In the case of unregistered land, recourse to the right to obtain information may be the only way of obtaining the necessary details for the tenant's notice.

12.7 Practical preparations

12.7.1 The deposit

Since the landlord can give a notice at any time requiring the payment of a deposit,[15] it is likely that this will be requested immediately after the giving of the tenant's notice. The tenant should be prepared to pay 10 per cent of the amount proposed as the premium – which is to be a minimum of £250.

12.7.2 Evidence of right

A request for payment of the deposit is likely to be accompanied by a requirement to deduce title and give evidence by statutory declaration of the occupation on which the tenant relies to satisfy the residence requirement.[16] Although there is a period of 21 days to comply, it may be convenient to prepare the title evidence and declaration in advance.

12.7.3 Registration of tenant's notice

A tenant's notice is registrable as an estate contract under the Land Charges Act 1972 and may be the subject of a notice or caution under the Land Registration Act.[17] It is important to register the tenant's notice immediately it is given and thereby bind any person purchasing a reversionary interest. The form of registration should be prepared in advance and dispatched on the day the tenant's notice is given.

12.8 Preparation by a landlord: avoidance and anti-avoidance

12.8.1 Rights cannot be excluded or modified

As in the case of collective enfranchisement, it is not possible to agree to exclude or modify the rights given by the Act, subject to very limited exceptions. Any agreement relating to a lease shall be void insofar as it purports to exclude or modify any entitlement to participate in the making of a claim to exercise the right to acquire a new lease.[18] This applies to agreements made

15 Leasehold Reform (Collective Enfranchisement and Lease Renewal) Regulations 1993, SI 1993/2407, Sch 2, para 2 (see 13.5.1).

16 Ibid, para 4 (see 13.3.3).

17 See 13.1.7 and s 97(1).

18 Section 93(1)(a)(ii).

both before and after the creation of the lease and it does not matter whether the agreement is within the lease or independent of it. A provision which provides for the termination or surrender of the lease in the event of the tenant giving a notice under s 42 or one which provides for the imposition of any penalty or disability on the tenant in that event is also void.[19] These anti-avoidance provisions mean that there is relatively little scope to prevent a tenant who is already a qualifying tenant and can satisfy the residence requirement from claiming a new lease.

12.8.2 Exceptions arising after the tenant's notice is given

An agreement excluding or restricting the entitlement of a new lease may be made for a period not exceeding three years – but only after a tenant has already given a tenant's notice.[20] Such a provision is therefore limited and can only be concluded in a case where a tenant has commenced a claim – it may not be used in advance, for example by way of a clause in a new lease. It is more likely to be used in a situation where a tenant decides for whatever reason not to proceed with the claim for a new lease. In return, perhaps, for a concession on costs, the tenant will agree not to make a fresh claim for a period of three years.[21]

Once a tenant has given the tenant's notice, an agreement that that notice shall cease to have effect can be made.[22] Such an agreement can allow a compromise of the claim or an agreed acquisition of a new lease without going through all the procedures of the Act. It is expressly provided that such acquisition on behalf of a tenant of a new lease on terms different to that provided by the Act is not void.[23]

12.8.3 Action against a defaulting tenant

Taking action against a defaulting tenant who otherwise has the right to a new lease is one of the few actions which can be taken in respect of existing qualifying tenants. If a tenant is thought to be about to make a claim for a new lease[24] and is in arrears with the service charge or otherwise in breach of covenant, the landlord could commence a forfeiture action against the tenant for possession. Whilst such action was being taken the tenant would not be able

---

19 Section 93(1)(b) and (c). A lease which provides for termination or surrender in the event of the tenant becoming a qualifying tenant or, more importantly, in the event of a qualifying tenant satisfying the residence requirement, would not appear to be covered (see 12.8.5).

20 So a tenant's notice must have been given before this exception, in s 93(2)(b)(ii), can apply.

21 This will, in effect, extend the moratorium for a period of two years as a tenant will not be able to give another notice for a period of 12 months in any event (see 13.2.3).

22 Section 93(2)(b)(i).

23 Section 93(2)(a). The power to agree terms to a new lease different from those set out in the Act is considered at 16.3.2.

24 A landlord may be alerted to a potential claim by receiving an inquiry notice (see s 41 and 12.6.1).

to make a claim for a new lease.[25] Such action, unless well-founded, is likely to prove expensive[26] in the long run and only have temporary effect.[27] It is not, therefore, thought to be an action worth taking by a landlord except in cases where forfeiture proceedings would be justified in any event. Nevertheless, a tenant may be well-advised to ensure that there are no service charge arrears in existence or other obvious breaches of covenant when an inquiry notice is given prior to giving a tenant's notice.

12.8.4 Resisting assignment by company tenants

In those cases where a qualifying tenant is a company, the residence requirement cannot be satisfied. If the existing lease is one where the consent of the landlord is needed for an assignment, it is almost certain that landlords will now refuse such consent where the proposed assignee is an individual who could, in due course, satisfy the residence requirement after three years. Litigation on the issue of whether such refusal of consent is reasonable is very probable.[28]

12.8.5 Avoidance for the future

A landlord will be able to so arrange affairs to limit the ability of tenants to make claims for a new lease in the future. Such measures will centre on ensuring that either tenants are not qualifying tenants or that they cannot satisfy the residence requirement. As with collective enfranchisement,[29] new lettings may be at rents which are not low rents as defined, particularly by having a high rent in the initial year. Since a company cannot satisfy the residence requirement, a lease at a low rent with a restriction on assignment to an individual with termination in that event would appear to be valid.[30]

12.8.6 Preparing to use the statutory procedure to best effect

Where a claim for a new lease is made, a landlord will wish to prepare to use the statutory procedures to the best advantage. The issues of whether the tenant's notice has been registered and observing time-limits will apply as they do in

---

25 By virtue of Sch 12, para 3 (see 13.1.4).

26 Although the cost of the forfeiture action may be recoverable under the service charge provisions in the lease.

27 The tenant will probably seek leave to make the claim notwithstanding the forfeiture action (Sch 12, para 3(2) and 3(3)); if it is shown that the main purpose of the landlord's action is to hinder a claim, leave is likely to be given. Even if the tenant does not seek leave, they will almost certainly be entitled to relief from forfeiture.

28 See 10.5.5 for a full discussion of the issues in the context of collective enfranchisement; the same considerations will apply if a tenant is claiming a new lease.

29 See 10.5.2 and 10.5.3.

30 See 10.5.4 for a fuller discussion; s 93(1)(b) is limited to excluding or modifying the right to give a notice.

collective enfranchisement.[31] In the end, however, in a majority of cases the main issue will be ensuring that the best possible premium is obtained for the grant of a new lease and that the terms of any new lease remedy any defects or inadequacies in the existing lease.[32]

---

31 There is a discussion at 10.6.1 and 10.6.3.

32 See further 16.3 and especially 16.3.4 and 16.3.6.

CHAPTER THIRTEEN

THE PROCEDURE

13.1 The tenant's notice

13.1.1 Claim commenced by notice

The procedure for claiming a new extended lease is similar to that for a claim for collective enfranchisement but simplified by virtue of the involvement of fewer parties. A claim to exercise the right to a new lease is made by the qualifying tenant giving a 'tenant's notice' to the landlord.[1] If there is a third party to the existing lease, such as a guarantor or management company,[2] the notice must be given to that person as well.[3] The notice must be signed by the tenant personally and not by an agent or on behalf of the tenant.[4]

13.1.2 Contents of the notice

The tenant's notice must satisfy the following requirements.[5]

1 It must state the full name of the tenant and the address of the flat in respect of which the claim is made.

2 It must contain sufficient particulars to show that the tenant is qualified to make the claim. Those particulars must:

(a) identify the property to which the claim extends;
(b) give enough details of the lease to identify it (in particular the date of the lease, the term granted and the date the term commenced);
(c) provide details to show it is a lease at low rent; and
(d) state the period or periods in the last 10 years for which the tenant has occupied the whole or part of the flat as his only or principal home. If the

---

1 Section 42(1) and (2); the landlord is the person able to grant the new lease as defined (see 11.5.1).
2 A third party is any party to the lease other than the tenant and the immediate landlord (s 62(1)).
3 Section 42(2)(b).
4 Section 99(5)(a). All joint tenants should sign as they jointly constitute the tenant.
5 Section 42(3); the requirements are set out in sub-paragraphs (a)–(f) inclusive.

lease is held by joint tenants, the residence period may be satisfied by any one of them.[6] Such period must encompass either the last three years[7] or three years in the last 10.

These details need to be set out in the notice rather that just sending a copy of the lease attached to it. However, enclosing with the notice a copy of the lease and, where registered, office copies of the title will make it less likely that a claim will be delayed by the landlord seeking verification of the title.[8]

3 It must specify the premium which the tenant proposes to pay for the grant of a new lease. Unlike collective enfranchisement, there is no requirement to have had a valuation and state the name of the valuer in the notice but, in practice, such a valuation will be needed in most cases. The premium will be calculated in accordance with Sch 13 and, if sums are to be paid to holders of intermediate interests, the amount proposed for those must be stated in the notice.

4 It must specify the terms which the tenant proposes should be contained in the new lease. In particular, any alterations from the terms of the existing lease[9] will need to be considered in advance and summarised in the notice.

5 If the tenant has an agent appointed to act in connection with the claim, such as a solicitor or valuer, then the name of that agent and an address in England and Wales for service of notices should be stated.

6 It must specify the date by which the landlord must respond to the notice by giving a counter-notice. The date specified must be a date not less than two months after the notice is given.[10]

13.1.3 Mistake or inaccuracy

A tenant's notice is not invalidated by any inaccuracy in any of the particulars which are required to be included in the notice; nor by any misdescription of any of the property to which the claim extends.[11] Such minor matters can be clarified and the claim may proceed. In the case of the more major error of specifying a property which the tenant was not entitled to have demised to him under a new lease or, conversely, failing to specify property to which the tenant is entitled, the notice may be amended with leave of the court. The notice can

6 Section 42(4).

7 This is a longer period than that required to satisfy the residence condition for collective enfranchisement but is the same as the qualifying occupation period under the Leasehold Reform Act 1967.

8 See also 13.3.3.

9 See 16.3.4.

10 Section 42(5).

11 Schedule 12, para 9(1).

be amended to include or exclude property on such terms as the court may think fit.[12]

13.1.4 Situations where a tenant's notice is of no effect

In the following situations, a tenant's notice, even when given by a qualifying tenant, will be of no effect.

1 Where the tenant has given a notice terminating the lease of the flat, unless that notice has been superseded by the grant, express or implied, of a new tenancy.[13]

2 Where the tenant occupies during the subsistence of an agreement for the grant of a future tenancy, where that agreement is one to which para 17 of Sch 10 to the Local Government and Housing Act 1989 applies.[14]

3 Where a landlord's statutory[15] notice terminating the tenant's lease of the flat has been given more than two months before the tenant's notice, whether or not the notice had effect to terminate the lease; but a landlord may consent in writing to a tenant's notice being given after the end of that two-month period. A statutory notice given less than two months before the tenant's notice ceases to have effect and does not invalidate the tenant's notice.[16] A tenant who, in proceedings to enforce a right of re-entry or forfeiture or a right to damages, has applied for relief under s 16 of the Landlord and Tenant Act 1954 is not precluded from making a claim for a new lease.[17]

4 Where the tenant is obliged to give up possession of his flat in pursuance to an order of the court or will be so obliged in a date specified in the court order.[18]

5 Where proceedings are pending to enforce a right of re-entry or forfeiture to terminate the lease of the flat, unless leave of the court is obtained. Leave will only be granted if the court is satisfied that the tenant does not wish to give the notice solely or mainly for the purposes of avoiding the consequences of a breach of the terms of his lease in respect of which those forfeiture

12 Schedule 12, para 9(2).
13 Schedule 12, para 1(a).
14 Schedule 12, para 1(b).
15 Under the Landlord and Tenant Act 1954, s 4, or the Local Government and Housing Act 1989, Sch 10.
16 Schedule 12, paras 2(1)–(3). The period is half that applicable under Sch 3 in the case of collective enfranchisement. If the tenant's notice does not result in the grant of a new lease, the landlord can revive the statutory notice by a further notice within one month of the expiry of the currency of the claim (see Sch 12, paras 2(4)–(6) for details).
17 Schedule 12, para 7(1).
18 Schedule 12, para 3(1).

proceedings are pending.[19] If leave is granted, and a claim is made, the tenant's lease is deemed to be subsisting.[20]

6 Where a tenant, faced with an action for forfeiture or damages gives a statutory notice[21] to be relieved from any order of possession or recovery of damages but the tenancy is thereby cut short.[22]

7 Where, in response to a preliminary inquiry, a tenant is informed that a particular person has an interest as landlord, but the tenant fails to give a copy of the tenant's notice to that person by the date specified for the counter-notice, the notice ceases to have effect at that date.

13.1.5 Recipient of the notice

The tenant's notice is given to the competent landlord.[23] In perhaps a majority of cases, this person will be the tenant's immediate landlord – and perhaps also the freeholder. However, in those cases where the immediate landlord has an interest too short to grant the new lease, service of the tenant's notice may be more complicated.

13.1.6 Procedure on giving a notice where the competent landlord is not the immediate landlord

There are full and complex provisions relating to those situations where the landlord dealing with a tenant's claim to a new lease is not the tenant's immediate landlord. These provisions are contained in Sch 11 to the Act.[24] In summary, the position in such cases relating to the giving of the tenant's notice is as follows.

1 The tenant's notice exercising the claim may be given to any of the landlords and shall be regarded as given to the competent landlord.[25]

2 Copies of the tenant's notice shall be given by the tenant to every person known or believed by him to be one of the other landlords and if such copies

---

19 Schedule 12, para 3(2)–(3). It should be noted, however, that once the tenant's notice is given, there is a restriction on proceedings by the landlord to enforce any right of re-entry or forfeiture; the court will only give leave to the landlord to proceed if the court is satisfied that the tenant is participating solely or mainly to avoid the consequences of the breach of the terms of the lease in respect of which proceedings are brought. If, however, leave is granted, the tenant's notice ceases to have effect (Sch 12, para 6).

20 Schedule 12, para 3(4). If the claim is later effective, the court dealing with the forfeiture proceedings has power to set aside or vary any forfeiture order it has made.

21 Under the Landlord and Tenant Act 1954, s 16(2).

22 Schedule 12, para 7(1).

23 In accordance with s 40(1) (see 11.5.2).

24 Section 40(3).

25 Schedule 11, para 1.

are given the tenant's notice shall state to whom those copies are being given.[26] There is a risk to a tenant giving notice in such a situation. If he has made preliminary inquiries and in response to those inquiries under s 41 has been notified of a particular person's interest in the flat as landlord, but that landlord has not received a copy of the tenant's notice by the date by which the landlord must respond by giving a counter-notice, the tenant's notice ceases to have effect.[27]

3 A recipient of a tenant's notice of claim shall give a copy of that notice to any person known or believed by him to be either the competent landlord or any one of the other landlords provided that it is not stated in the notice that a copy has been sent to them. A recipient of the notice who either knows who is, or believes himself to be the competent landlord must give notice to the tenant stating who is the person thought by him to be the competent landlord and a copy of it to every other person known or believed by him to be one of the other landlords.[28]

13.1.7 Registration of a tenant's notice

A notice given under s 42 is registrable under the Land Charges Act 1972 and may be the subject of a notice or caution under the Land Registration Act 1925 as if it were an estate contract.[29] It is important, therefore, to register a caution, or an estate contract in the case of unregistered land, immediately upon the tenant's notice being given. The notice gives rise to contractual rights and obligations but these do not constitute an overriding interest.[30] Therefore, the registration is essential to ensure that any purchaser of any reversionary interest affected by the notice is bound by it. It is suggested that the registration should be effected on the day that the tenant's notice is given.

13.2 Effect and impact of the tenant's notice

13.2.1 Gives rise to contractual obligations

Unlike the position in the case of a collective enfranchisement, the procedure does not provide for a binding contract to be entered into. Instead, the giving of a tenant's notice imposes rights and obligations on both the tenant and the landlord. Provided that the procedure and time-limits are observed, the tenant has a right to the new lease and the landlord has an obligation to grant it. In the

26 Schedule 11, para 2.
27 Schedule 11, para 4.
28 Schedule 11, para 3.
29 Section 97(1).
30 See 13.2.1 and s 97(1).

event of default by either party in carrying out the obligations arising from the tenant's notice, the other party has all the remedies and rights which would be available if there was a contract freely entered into;[31] to that extent, a tenant's notice brings a form of contract into effect.[32] Where there is more than one landlord involved,[33] those contractual rights and obligations apply to each landlord so far as their interests are affected.[34]

13.2.2 Rights are assignable

Once notice has been given by the tenant, the rights and obligations which arise from the notice enure for the benefit of successors in title. They are enforceable by and against both personal representatives and assigns in the same way and to the extent of rights and obligations arising under a contract for leasing freely entered into between landlord and tenant.[35] Provided that the notice is duly registered[36] this means that the standard principles relating to an agreement for a lease will normally allow rights and obligations to be enforced.[37]

However, the rights and obligations of the tenant are not capable of subsisting apart from the lease of the entire flat. Therefore, on an assignment of the lease while the notice is still current, the benefit of the notice must be assigned with the flat. If this is not done, the tenant's notice is deemed to be withdrawn at the date of the assignment.[38] Where a purchaser of a flat by assignment wishes to claim a new lease but the vendor has not served a tenant's notice, the purchaser should seek to agree that the current tenant serves a notice relying on the vendor's residence and then take an assignment of those rights at completion. If this is not done, the purchaser will have to wait three years to satisfy the residence requirement.[39]

13.2.3 Limitations on a further notice

Once a tenant's notice has been given, it remains in force until a new lease is granted, or until the date the notice ceases to have effect or is withdrawn or

---

31 Section 43(4).

32 The position is not dissimilar to a tenant's notice under the Leasehold Reform Act 1967, ss 5(1) and 8(1) (see *Collin v Duke of Westminster* [1985] QB 581).

33 Ie, the competent landlord is not the tenant's immediate landlord.

34 Section 43(5). This is without prejudice to the general power of the competent landlord to conduct all the proceedings on behalf of all other landlords (s 43(6)).

35 Section 43(1). References throughout Chapter II to landlord and tenant consequently include reference to their personal representatives and assigns insofar as the context permits (s 43(2)). However, since a tenant when giving notice, must personally occupy the flat, a personal representative cannot give the notice (see 11.2.3).

36 See 13.1.7.

37 By virtue of the doctrine of *Walsh v Lonsdale* (1882) 21 Ch D 9, CA.

38 Section 43(3). If a purchaser of a flat fails to secure an assignment of the benefit of the notice, a further notice will not be possible for 12 months (see 13.2.3).

39 See 11.2.4.

deemed to be withdrawn.[40] While it remains in force, a subsequent further notice cannot be given;[41] and if the notice is withdrawn, deemed to have been withdrawn, or the landlord has obtained an order showing an intention to redevelop,[42] there is, as with collective enfranchisement, a 12-month moratorium. During this period a subsequent, further tenant's notice cannot be given.[43]

13.2.4 Restrictions on termination of the lease

Once an tenant's notice is given, there are restrictions on the termination of the lease of the tenant.

1 Any notice terminating a lease of a tenant who has made a claim to a new lease, whether given by the tenant or by the landlord under the Landlord and Tenant Act 1954, s 4 or the Local Government and Housing Act 1989, Sch 10, para 4(a), is of no effect if given or served during the currency of a claim.[44] If the claim is not successful, any notice caught by this provision would not revive; a fresh notice would be required.

2 A lease of a tenant who has made a claim to a new lease cannot terminate by effluxion of time, by landlord's notice to quit or by the termination of the lease of a superior landlord during the currency of the claim and for three months thereafter. If the claim is not effective, the lease will terminate at the end of the three-month period if, but for this provision, it would have terminated earlier.[45]

3 Proceedings to forfeit the lease of the tenant or to exercise any right of re-entry cannot be brought during the currency of a claim without the leave of the court. Leave will only be granted if the court is satisfied that the tenant is making a claim solely or mainly for the purpose of avoiding the consequences of the breach of the terms of the lease.[46] This test, identical to the one applied in the case of collective enfranchisement,[47] may be a difficult one for a landlord to satisfy.

---

40 Section 42(8). During the currency of the notice, it may be suspended by the commencement of a collective enfranchisement (s 54).

41 Section 42(6).

42 Under s 47(1) (see 16.8.3).

43 Section 42(7). The 12-month period is calculated from the date of withdrawal or the date the notice ceases to have effect.

44 Schedule 12, para 4.

45 Schedule 12, para 5(1). Termination of the lease by any other means is not prevented; and the tenant's right to relief under the Law of Property Act 1925, s 146 or the Landlord and Tenant Act 1954, is not affected (Sch 12, para 5(2)).

46 Schedule 12, para 6.

47 See 5.6.2.

13.3 Rights of the landlord on receipt of tenant's notice

13.3.1 Access for valuation

Once a tenant's notice has been given to the landlord, or a copy served on any other landlord,[48] a right of access arises for valuation purposes. The landlord, or a person authorised to act on behalf of the landlord, has a right of access to the flat to which the notice relates for the purpose of valuing the landlord's interest in the flat.[49]

The right is exercisable at any reasonable time on giving notice to the tenant. This must be not less than three days' notice.[50] Since, by definition, a tenant giving notice will be resident, the short period of notice should not cause undue difficulty; but the tenant will need to be forewarned to afford access to any landlord or his surveyor or other agent.

13.3.2 Payment of deposit

At any time when the tenant's notice continues in force, the landlord may give to the tenant a notice requiring a deposit to be paid on account of the premium payable for the lease.[51] This request for a deposit is likely to be given immediately on receipt of a tenant's notice by most landlords. The deposit payable is to be 10 per cent of the amount proposed in the tenant's notice or £250, whichever is the greater. The deposit is to be paid to the landlord's solicitor or licensed conveyancer within a period of 14 days beginning with the date the notice is given. The deposit will be held as stakeholder. Failure to pay does not lead to a deemed withdrawal as the requirement is imposed by regulation but a landlord could seek a court order, after giving further notice to remedy the default, requiring compliance.[52] Although the tenant has a right to give notice for a return of the deposit in the event of a withdrawal or the notice ceasing to have effect, the landlord can deduct from the deposit any costs due.[53]

---

48 These will be all of the landlords whose interests are affected by the notice and who have a concurrent leasehold interest between that of the tenant and the competent landlord (s 40(4)).

49 Section 44(1).

50 Section 44(2). This is shorter than the comparable rights of access in connection with a collective enfranchisement claim under s 17(3). Both sections specified three days' notice in the original Bill; but the period was extended for a collective enfranchisement. See 22.1 for the form of notices generally.

51 The details are in the Leasehold Reform (Collective Enfranchisement and Lease Renewal) Regulations 1993, SI 1993/2407, Sch 2, para 2 which apply unless the parties otherwise agree.

52 Under s 92 (see 22.5).

53 Leasehold Reform (Collective Enfranchisement and Lease Renewal) Regulations 1993, Sch 2, para 3.

13.3.3 *Evidence of the tenant's right to the new lease*

Within a period of 21 days from the giving of the tenant's notice, the landlord may require the tenant to deduce title to the tenancy and give evidence by statutory declaration of the occupation which is relied upon to satisfy the residence requirement.[54] The tenant has 21 days to comply – although failure to do so will cause delay and perhaps costs but will not cause the tenant's notice to cease to have effect.[55]

13.4 Landlord's counter-notice

13.4.1 *Necessity for a counter-notice*

The landlord shall give a counter-notice to the tenant by the date specified in the tenant's notice.[56] This will be a date at least two months after the tenant's notice was given.[57] Failure to give a counter-notice may result in the court, rather than the leasehold valuation tribunal, determining the terms of the acquisition.[58] If the landlord fails to give a counter-notice by the date specified in the tenant's notice, then the better view is that a late counter-notice cannot be given. This view is based on the straightforward terms of s 45(1) which impose a duty to act in the time-limit. The moral is clear – the advisers to a landlord should always seek to ensure that a counter-notice, or further counter-notice, is given in time. The possibility of the legislation being interpreted to allow a late counter-notice is discussed in relation to an initial notice; similar arguments can be made for a counter-notice in response to a request for a new lease.[59] There was no substantial separate discussion of this section in the committee stage of either House.[60]

13.4.2 *Types of counter-notice*

A counter-notice must conform to the statutory requirements. There are three types which can be given.[61]

1 The counter-notice may state that the landlord admits that the tenant had, on the date the tenant's notice was given, the right to acquire a new lease. In a

---

54 Ibid, para 4.

55 Failure to respond may mean that a landlord services a counter-notice denying the right on the ground that evidence has not been given; the tenant may have to pay the costs of such an application.

56 Section 45(1).

57 Section 42(5).

58 Under s 49 (see 14.5.1).

59 See the discussion at 6.6.7.

60 The section was, in both Houses, agreed to without discussion (see HC Deb, Standing Committee B, col 241, 24 November 1992; and HL Deb, Vol 544, col 106, 22 March 1993).

61 Section 45(2)(a)–(c)).

majority of cases, the right of the tenant will be clearly established and this will be the appropriate counter-notice. However, unlike the position in connection with a collective enfranchisement, such an admission shall be binding on the landlord so far as the issue of whether the tenant is a qualifying tenant and has satisfied the residence condition is concerned.[62] Only if the admission of the right to a new lease was induced by misrepresentation or the concealment of material facts will it be possible to challenge the right at a later stage. The admission does not conclude the question as to whether the particulars of the flat as stated in the tenant's notice are correct.

2 The counter-notice may state that, for such reasons as are specified in the counter-notice, the landlord does not admit the right to a new lease. Such a counter-notice will be appropriate where there are grounds to argue that the lease is not a long lease at low rent or to challenge the residence requirement. Proceedings before the court on validity are then likely where the costs may fall on the unsuccessful party.[63] Such a counter-notice should only be given if a landlord is prepared to take the issue to a court hearing. Failure to proceed or a withdrawal of an application will result in the landlord being treated as failing to give a counter-notice.[64]

3 The counter-notice may admit or deny the right to a new lease but state that the landlord intends to make an application on the grounds that he intends to redevelop the premises in which the flat is contained.[65] Such a counter-notice will only be possible if the tenant's lease is due to terminate within five years of the date of the tenant's notice.

13.4.3 Contents of a counter-notice

Counter-notices which do not admit the right to a new lease must state the reasons for that view. They need contain only one additional piece of information – an address in England and Wales at which notices may be given to the landlord.[66] If, however, the redevelopment defence is also raised and the landlord who intends to establish that defence is not the competent landlord giving the counter-notice, then the name of the landlord intending to make the application on the grounds of redevelopment must be stated in the counter-notice.[67]

Notices admitting the right, which must also include an address for service, must state which of the proposals of the tenant in the notice are accepted.

---

62 Section 45(5).
63 See s 46 and 14.2.1.
64 See 14.2.2 and 14.5.
65 Within s 47 (see 14.3.1).
66 Section 45(4).
67 Schedule 11, para 9(2).

Thosc which are unacceptable must be identified and, in relation to each of these, the counter-notice must specify the landlord's counter-proposal.[68] The most usual dispute may be on the proposed premium – the landlord will have to state the amount which would be acceptable and the figures so specified in notice and counter-notice will be the basis for later negotiation. The tenant's proposals on the terms of the proposed new lease will also need to be scrutinised and counter-proposals made if these are not acceptable.

13.4.4 Further counter-notices

A further counter-notice may be needed in any case where an unqualified admission of the right to a new lease has not been made. Thus, a court shall order a further counter-notice where a landlord's challenge to validity is dismissed or where an application to defeat the right to a new lease on redevelopment grounds is unsuccessful.[69]

13.5 The subsequent conveyancing procedure

13.5.1 Applies in default of agreement

The conveyancing procedure subsequent to a landlord's counter-notice is provided by statutory instrument.[70] It applies to all transactions to give effect to a tenant's notice unless the landlord and tenant otherwise agree. Some steps in this procedure can only be taken after the terms of acquisition have been agreed or determined by the leasehold valuation tribunal;[71] but it is convenient to summarise the main features of the procedure at this stage. Delivery of proof of title and requisitions thereon may be done prior to agreement of the premium or other terms and it may be appropriate to do so if the title appears defective in a way which could have an impact on valuation. Much of the matter covered by the Regulations would be dealt with by conditions of sale in a privately negotiated transaction.[72]

13.5.2 Delivery of proof of title

Once the landlord has given a counter-notice or a further counter-notice admitting the right to a new lease, or the tenant has applied to the court for an

68 Section 45(3).
69 Sections 46(4)(b) and 47(4)(b).
70 The Leasehold Reform (Collective Enfranchisement and Lease Renewal) Regulations 1993, SI 1993/2407, made on 30 September 1993 and in force on 1 November 1993.
71 See 14.4.1.
72 This is intentional and the result of the direction in s 98(1).

order where there has been a failure to give such a notice, then the tenant may by notice require the landlord to deduce title. Within 28 days of such notice, the landlord shall comply by supplying the necessary office copies in the case of registered land or an epitome of title in the case of unregistered interests.[73] A landlord who is not the freeholder must use best endeavours to obtain an epitome of any unregistered freehold or reversionary leasehold title superior to the landlord's title to give to the tenant.[74]

13.5.3 Requisitions on title

Within 14 days of receipt of the proof of title the tenant may give a statement of any objections or requisitions; there is a further period of 14 days for the statement of the landlord's answer to those requisitions; and a period of seven days for the tenant to give a further statement of objections or comments.[75] These time-limits should be observed; any requisition or objection not given by the tenant in such statement or further statement is deemed to be waived; and any matter not raised cannot be deemed to be a defect in title for valuation purposes.[76] If the tenant does not respond with a further statement, the landlord's answer is considered satisfactory.

13.5.4 Preparation of the lease

Once the terms of acquisition are agreed or determined by the leasehold valuation tribunal, the landlord prepares the draft lease and gives it to the tenant within 14 days.[77] The tenant then has 14 days to submit proposals for amendment; the lease is deemed to be approved if there is no response within the time-limit. In a similar manner, the landlord has 14 further days to object or comment on any proposals; failure to respond results in deemed approval of the proposed tenant's amendments. To avoid falling foul of these provisions, it may be advisable, if possible, to agree the exact wording of the new lease as part of the agreement of the terms of acquisition. Once the draft is agreed, the lease is engrossed by the landlord with as many counterparts as are reasonably required. The counterpart or counterparts are given to the tenant for execution a reasonable time before completion.

---

73 The Leasehold Reform (Collective Enfranchisement and Lease Renewal) Regulations 1993, SI 1993/2407, Sch 2, para 5. In the case of registered interests, the landlord must supply the particulars and information which have to be given on a sale pursuant to s 110 of the Land Registration Act 1925.

74 There is no need to show title to interests between that of the tenant and the landlord; these are subject to a deemed surrender and re-grant (see 16.2.1).

75 The Leasehold Reform (Collective Enfranchisement and Lease Renewal) Regulations 1993, SI 1993/2407, Sch 2, para 6.

76 See Sch 13, para 3(5).

77 The details of preparing the lease are contained in the Leasehold Reform (Collective Enfranchisement and Lease Renewal) Regulations 1993, SI 1993/2407, Sch 2, para 7.

13.5.5 Completion of the new lease

Completion takes place at the office of the landlord's solicitor or licensed conveyancer when the executed lease and counterpart(s) are exchanged.[78] Unless otherwise agreed, the tenant may, after the draft lease is approved or deemed to be agreed, give notice requiring completion on the first working day after the expiration of 21 days beginning with the date notice is given. This does not apply if the date for completion would fall after the appropriate period in cases of applications where the terms of acquisition are in dispute, there is a failure to enter into a new lease or an application in respect of a failure to give a counter-notice.[79]

If there is an intermediate landlord who has given notice of intention to act independently, the landlord has the responsibility of giving notice of the date of completion.[80]

---

78 The Leasehold Reform (Collective Enfranchisement and Lease Renewal) Regulations 1993, Sch 2, para 7(7) and 8(1).

79 Under ss 48 and 49 (see 14.4–14.6); the Leasehold Reform (Collective Enfranchisement and Lease Renewal) Regulations 1993, Sch 2, para 8(2).

80 Ibid, Sch 2, para 8(3).

CHAPTER FOURTEEN

RESOLVING DISPUTES

14.1 General

14.1.1 Timetable for subsequent procedure

The procedure following the service of the landlord's counter-notice in relation to disputes and disagreements is similar to that for collective enfranchisement. There are sufficient and significant differences of detail, partly because there is no separate stage of entering into a binding contract, to require separate treatment.[1]

14.1.2 Challenges to the right to a new lease

Two challenges are possible to the right to the new extended lease, either or both of which must be asserted in the landlord's counter-notice.[2] In each case, there is a period of two months[3] from the date of the giving of the counter-notice to take the objection forward for determination. Within that two-month period, the landlord must make application to the court either to challenge the validity of the tenant's claim or to establish the intention to redevelop or both.[4] If no such application is made within the time-limit, or the application is withdrawn, or the court dismisses the application, a further counter-notice, admitting the right and containing the landlord's proposals, must be given.[5]

14.1.3 Opportunity for negotiation

Once a counter-notice has been given admitting the tenant's right, either as the only counter-notice or as a further counter-notice when the challenge of the landlord has been unsuccessful, there is an opportunity for negotiation. The

---

1 However, cross-reference to a fuller discussion of some issues in chapter seven is made where this avoids duplication.

2 As discussed at 13.4.2.

3 Sections 46(2) and 47(3).

4 See 14.2 and 14.3.

5 Sections 46(4) and 47(4) and (5); but note s 46(2) which does not actually require or permit a further counter-notice after a failure to apply to challenge the validity of the tenant's notice or a withdrawal of such application. In such cases, a further counter-notice by the landlord may not be possible (see 13.4.1 and 14.2.2).

tenant's notice and counter-notice will state the proposals of each party; if the terms of acquisition can be agreed, the new lease can be granted in accordance with the Act.

There is a minimum period of two months before further action can be taken in default of agreement; and a maximum period of six months within which an application must be made to the leasehold valuation tribunal to determine matters in dispute;[6] failure to make this application where terms have not been agreed will result in a deemed withdrawal.[7]

Where the landlord cannot be found and so counter-notices and negotiation are not possible there is a separate procedure permitting the court to vest the new lease in the tenant.[8]

14.2 Challenge to the validity of a tenant's notice

14.2.1 Landlord applies within time-limit

Where the landlord does not admit the entitlement of the tenant to a new lease and serves a counter-notice to that effect,[9] the landlord may make an application to the court for a declaration that the tenant had no right to a new lease of the flat.[10] The application must be made by the landlord and therefore the burden of meeting the two-month time-limit is not one which falls on the tenant. Such an application by the landlord must be made within two months of the giving of the counter-notice to the tenant.[11] Action is only likely by the landlord if there is a genuine doubt as to whether the tenant is a qualifying tenant and satisfies the residence requirement.[12] These matters will usually be issues of fact which the tenant will either have established in the notice or in response for a request for evidence of the right to a new lease.[13] Proceedings are therefore less likely than in the case of a collective enfranchisement. A landlord may also seek to take advantage of procedural lapses but mere inaccuracies or misdescription do not invalidate the tenant's notice and the court has the power to amend a notice which fails to specify the property correctly.[14] This suggests

6 Section 48(1) (see 14.4).
7 Section 53(1) (see 15.2).
8 Sections 50 and 51 (see 14.5).
9 The counter-notice will have stated that the landlord does not admit that the tenant was entitled to a new lease and given reasons; the notice will have been served under either s 45(2)(b) or (c) (see 13.4.2).
10 Section 46(1). By way of comparison, in the case of a collective enfranchisement, the duty of making an application to establish the validity of the initial notice, and therefore of meeting the time-limit, falls on the nominee purchaser (see 7.2.1).
11 Section 46(2). The exact wording is 'not later than the end of the period of two months beginning with the date of the giving of the counter-notice to the tenant'.
12 As discussed above, especially at 11.2.2 and 11.2.3.
13 See 13.3.3.
14 Schedule 12, para 9 (see 13.1.3).

that the landlord is only likely to be successful if there is a fundamental procedural blunder, such as serving the notice on the person who is not the landlord.[15]

14.2.2 *Failure to apply within time-limit*

The consequence of missing the time-limit and making no application, or of making an application in time and then withdrawing it, is potentially serious. The landlord will lose the opportunity of challenging the right of the tenant and the landlord is treated as not having given a counter-notice.[16] The tenant is then free to make an application to the court to determine the terms of an acquisition.[17] The landlord may be well-advised to attempt to serve a further counter-notice admitting the right to a new lease and putting any counter-proposals but this may not be possible.[18]

14.2.3 *Orders which may be made*

If the court is satisfied that the tenant was not entitled to the right to a new lease, it will make a declaration to that effect.[19] If the court makes such a declaration, the tenant's notice ceases to have effect on the order becoming final.[20] If the court dismisses the landlord's application and thereby upholds the right to a new lease, it will also declare that the landlord's counter-notice shall be of no effect and require the landlord to give a further counter-notice to the tenant by such date as the court specifies in the order.[21] If such a counter-notice is ordered to be given by the court, the landlord is again subject to the statutory requirements for the giving of a counter-notice which admits the right of a new lease.[22]

14.2.4 *Counter-notices which also stated an intention to redevelop*

In a situation where the landlord has both made an application to challenge the validity of a tenant's notice and also indicated an intention to take advantage of the redevelopment defence and make an application under s 47,[23] the challenge on validity will be argued first.[24] If the court dismisses the landlord's application

15 Or not one of the relevant landlords to whom giving of notice suffices (see 13.1.6).
16 Section 46(2)(a) and (b).
17 Under s 49 (see 14.5.1).
18 See 13.4.1 and the fuller discussion at 6.6.7.
19 Section 46(1). The court is primarily concerned with the tenant's right to claim a new lease and not the form of notice; any errors or inaccuracies do not invalidate it (see 13.1.3).
20 Section 46(3). This gives an opportunity to appeal against the decision of the court (see s 101(9) and 22.4).
21 Section 46(4).
22 As required by s 45(3)–(4) (s 46(6)). See further 13.4.3.
23 By giving a counter-notice under s 45(2)(c).
24 Section 47(3).

on validity thereby upholding the right of the tenant to a new lease, the court will not declare the counter-notice to be of no effect nor require a fresh counter-notice if a s 47 application is still pending or the time-limit for making such application has not expired.[25] Instead, the next stage will be to dispose of the redevelopment issue and, if the tenant is again successful, a fresh counter-notice will be required at that stage.[26]

14.3 Landlord's redevelopment defence

14.3.1 Limited scope of the defence

The tenant's claim to a new lease is liable to be defeated if the landlord applies to the court and establishes a sufficient intention to redevelop the whole or substantial part of the premises. As with collective enfranchisement, the statutory requirements are such that it is thought that there will be relatively few cases where the requisite intention can be established.

14.3.2 Who makes the application?

The application can only be made if the landlord[27] has given the requisite counter-notice;[28] but the application may be made by any other landlord.[29] Although this means an application can be made by the competent landlord, by any other landlord or by any two or more acting together,[30] an application to defeat the tenant's claim can only be made by or with the authority of the landlord who wishes to establish the requisite intention and the name of any landlord intending to make the application must be stated in the counter-notice.[31] This is one area where the power of the competent landlord to bind the other landlords is limited. Since it is the competent landlord who gives the counter-notice, a degree of co-operation is required at an early stage if the competent landlord and the landlord who wishes to establish the intention are not the same person.

14.3.3 Time-limit to apply

An application must be made within two months of the giving of the counter-notice to the tenant; although if there is also a challenge to the validity of the

25 Section 46(5).

26 See 14.3.5.

27 Who will be the competent landlord within s 40 (see 11.5.2).

28 Under s 45(2)(c) (s 47(1)).

29 As defined by s 40(4)(c); any landlord who has a concurrent tenancy intermediate between the interest of the competent landlord and the tenant's lease.

30 Schedule 11, para 9(2).

31 Schedule 11, para 9(1) and (2).

tenant's notice, any such s 46 application is proceeded with first and the s 47 application is not proceeded with until such time as an order under s 46 becomes final.[32]

If the landlord gives a counter-notice stating that an application will be made under s 47 but does not make an application within the time-limit, or withdraws an application duly made, then the opportunity is lost and the landlord is under a duty to give a further counter-notice[33] within a period of two months.[34] The duty to give a further counter-notice does not arise if an application by the landlord to establish the validity of the claim has been made but not yet disposed of.[35]

14.3.4 *What must be established?*

In order to make an order under this s 47, the court must be satisfied that:[36]

(a) the tenant's lease of the flat is due to terminate within five years of the date of the tenant's notice;
(b) for the purposes of redevelopment, the landlord intends, once the lease has terminated, to demolish or reconstruct, or carry out substantial works of construction on the whole or a substantial part of the premises;
(c) he could not reasonably do so without obtaining possession of the flat.
The burden of proof is on the landlord and the requisite intent must be established even if the lease is due to terminate in five years.[37]

14.3.5 *Orders by the court*

In dealing with an application, the court will make one of two orders.

1 It will dismiss the application if the applicant landlord fails to satisfy the statutory requirements, in which case the court will declare the counter-notice to be of no effect and the court will require a further counter-notice;[38] or

2 It will declare that the right to acquire a new lease shall not be exercisable. If such an order is made, the tenant's notice ceases to have effect on the order becoming final.[39] This will give an opportunity for an appeal against the court's decision.

---

32 Section 47(3).
33 Section 47(5). It must be a counter-notice admitting the right (s 47(8)).
34 The two-month period is calculated from either the expiry of the time-limit for an application or from the date of withdrawal (s 47(6)).
35 Section 47(7).
36 Section 47(2).
37 For a discussion, on the identical wording in s 23(2), of the circumstances where the defence might be established and the proof of intention, see 7.3.4.
38 Section 47(4). Once again, it must be a counter-notice admitting the right (s 47(8)).
39 Section 47(1); see 22.4.

14.4 No agreement on terms

14.4.1 Determination of disputed matters

There is a two-month period, beginning with the date the counter-notice or further counter-notice was given, for negotiation – during which no further steps in the process can be taken. If, however, any of the terms of acquisition remain in dispute at the end of that period, then either the tenant or the landlord may apply to the leasehold valuation tribunal for a determination of those disputed matters.[40]

14.4.2 Time-limit

Any such application must be made within six months from the date of the counter-notice[41] – so there is a four-month window of opportunity for an application to be made. The burden of meeting that time-limit is effectively on the tenant. If the six-month period slips by the claim will be deemed to be withdrawn.[42] The leasehold valuation tribunal, and not the court, will determine the disputed matters.[43]

14.5 Failure to give a counter-notice

14.5.1 Order to determine the terms of the acquisition

Once the tenant has served a tenant's notice, the statutory procedure depends upon the receipt of a counter-notice which, if it disputes the claim, allows applications to contest validity while if it admits the claim, will contain the landlord's proposals on terms and premium allowing negotiation to proceed. If a counter-notice, or further counter-notice, is not given to the tenant, the court may, on application of the tenant, make an order determining the terms of acquisition of the new lease.[44] An order determining the terms of the acquisition will only be made if the court is satisfied that the tenant was entitled to acquire a new lease when the notice was given and that all requirements for giving copies of that tenant's notice[45] were complied with.[46] The terms will be

---

40 Section 48(1). Any other landlord involved cannot apply. A leasehold valuation tribunal may specify in its determination property which is less extensive than that claimed in the notice (s 91(9)). This provision was stated as one to correct errors and not to limit rights to which tenants are entitled (HC Deb, Standing Committee B, col 241, 24 November 1992).

41 Section 48(2). These time-limits are the same as those applicable to a collective enfranchisement under s 24(1)–(2).

42 Section 53(1).

43 For a full discussion of the determination of the premium, see 20.3.1.

44 Section 49(1).

45 See 13.1.6.

46 Section 49(2).

in accordance with the proposals contained in the tenant's notice.[47] The landlord's failure to give a counter-notice may therefore prejudice the position of the landlord and any other relevant landlord by depriving them of the right to contest the terms which the tenant proposes and result in an imposition by the court of the terms as to price and the provisions in the lease.

14.5.2 Time-limit

An application for an order to determine terms must be made within six months beginning with the date by which the counter-notice or further counter-notice should have been given.[48] Unless there are good reasons to the contrary, it will be sensible for an application under s 49 to be made as soon as the date for giving the counter-notice or further counter-notice expires.

14.6 Failure to enter into new lease

14.6.1 New lease follows settlement of terms of acquisition

By one route or another, the position will be reached, after service of the tenant's notice and the counter-notice, that the terms of the acquisition are settled. These terms will be the terms on which the tenant is to acquire a new lease of the flat, including both the terms to be contained in the new lease or to the premium or any other amount payable in connection with the grant.[49] This may come about through agreement; or the terms of acquisition may have been determined by the leasehold valuation tribunal. Alternatively, the terms may have been determined by order of the court if no counter-notice was given. In all these sets of circumstances there should be no further hindrance to the parties concluding the grant of the new lease. This will be the normal procedure.

14.6.2 Application for a court order

However, the Act makes provision for those situations where a counter-notice has been given and the terms have been agreed or determined but no new lease has been entered into. Either the tenant[50] or the landlord can apply within two months of the appropriate period, as defined, to the court which can make such order as it thinks fit with respect to the performance or discharge of the obligations arising out of the tenant's notice.[51] The appropriate period in this

47 Section 49(1).
48 Section 49(3).
49 See s 48(7).
50 It is the tenant who has the incentive to apply and complete the last stage of the procedure; a landlord will probably only apply if and when the tenant is out of time.
51 Section 48(3) (s 49(4)).

context is normally a period of two months.[52] The calculation of when the two-month period commences depends on the 'route' taken.

1 If the parties agreed terms, it will be two months from the date that the terms were finally agreed.[53] Where terms are settled in open correspondence it is submitted that the terms are finally agreed; but where the agreement remains 'subject to contract' a final agreement is not yet made.

2 If all or any of the terms have been determined by the leasehold valuation tribunal, it will be a period of two months beginning with the date when the decision of the tribunal becomes final. The leasehold valuation tribunal does, however, have power to fix a period other than two months when making its determination.[54]

3 Where the terms of acquisition have been determined by court order after failure to give a counter-notice, it will be a period of two months beginning with the date when the order of the court becomes final. The court does, however, have power to fix a period other than two months when making its order.[55]

14.6.3 Deemed withdrawal if no application

If these time-limits for application are missed, then once again the tenant will suffer a deemed withdrawal of the initial notice and the collective enfranchisement procedure will terminate.[56] This is notwithstanding the agreement on, or the determination of, the terms of acquisition; until the new lease is granted, time-limits continue to run against the tenant. If these time-limits are missed, then on application to the court, no doubt by the landlord, the court may order that the initial notice is deemed to have been withdrawn.[57]

14.7 Landlord cannot be found or ascertained

14.7.1 Extent of contingency

The procedure to acquire a new lease depends upon service of the tenant's notice on the landlord and copies of the notice on any other landlord. If the landlord cannot be found the usual procedures cannot be commenced or followed. Section 50 contains detailed provisions to cover the contingency that the landlord cannot be found or his identity ascertained.[58] The procedure will

52 Sections 48(5) and 49(6).
53 Section 48(6)(a).
54 Section 48(6)(b).
55 Section 48(7).
56 Sections 48(5) and 49(6); and 53(1)(b) and 53(3).
57 Sections 48(4) and 49(5).
58 Cf the Leasehold Reform Act 1967, s 27.

also be appropriate in those cases of a persistent refusal to answer inquiry notices[59] so that the competent landlord cannot be identified.

14.7.2 Order dispensing with need to serve copies

A qualifying tenant who wishes to make a claim to exercise the right to a new lease may apply for an order dispensing with the need to give a copy of the tenant's notice upon a landlord whose identity cannot be ascertained.[60] The court can only make such an order if it is established that, although the identity of the competent landlord is known, the identity of one or more of the other landlords cannot be ascertained so that a copy of the notice cannot be given.

A subsequent tenant's notice must contain a statement of the effect of an order dispensing with the need to give notice – so that those landlords who do receive it will be fully informed.[61] Provided the initial notice contains such a statement, the requirements of giving the notice or copy to the particular person named in the order is deemed to have been complied with.[62]

14.7.3 Vesting order

In a situation where the identity of the competent landlord is unknown or his identity cannot be ascertained, it is not possible to adopt the usual procedure because there is no landlord able to grant the new lease and conduct the procedure and negotiation. In such a case, a qualifying tenant who wishes to make a claim to acquire a new lease may apply to the court for a vesting order.[63]

14.7.4 Requirements for the making of an order

The court can only make an order on the application of the tenant. It must be satisfied, in both the case of dispensing with the need to serve copies and for a vesting order, that on the date of making the application the tenant had the right to acquire a new lease of the flat and on that date would not have been precluded from giving a valid tenant's notice.[64] Before making the order, the court can require the tenant to take further steps to trace the person in question. This can be by way of advertisement or otherwise as the court thinks proper.[65] To avoid this delay, it may be prudent to ensure that all reasonable steps to trace the missing landlord, including advertisement in appropriate cases, has been taken before making an application.

---

59 Under s 41.

60 Section 50(2).

61 Section 50(6).

62 Section 50(7).

63 Section 50(1). A vesting order under this section is not a substitute for the new lease but rather an order declaring the right to have a new lease in the absence of a tenant's notice.

64 Section 50(3).

65 Section 50(4).

14.7.5 Subsequent tracing of the missing landlord

There remains a possibility, in many cases remote,[66] that the person who cannot be found or identified is subsequently traced, as a result of the advertisement or other action taken, after the application for a vesting order but before the interest is vested in pursuance of the application. In such circumstances, no further steps or proceedings can be taken with a view to vesting and the rights and obligations shall be determined as if the tenant had given a tenant's notice at the date of the application.[67] Normally, this will then mean that the statutory procedure commences and the traced landlord will be under a duty to give a counter-notice. However, the court can give such directions as it thinks fit to give effect to the rights and obligations of the parties and these can include modifying or dispensing with any of the requirements of Chapter II of the Act and the regulations made thereunder.[68]

14.7.6 Withdrawal of an application

An application for a vesting order can be withdrawn at any time before execution of a lease.[69] If it is withdrawn after a landlord is traced but before any further steps are taken, the application is no longer to be regarded as if a tenant's notice has been given. However, when a landlord is traced a tenant cannot proceed as if a notice has been given and then at a later stage withdraw the application for a vesting order. Such later withdrawal is only possible with consent of the landlord and with leave of the court.[70] Leave will only be given if it appears to the court just to do so by reason of matters coming to the knowledge of the tenant in consequence of the tracing of the landlord. The idea is to give an opportunity to withdraw without further liability as soon as the landlord is traced; but if the tenant then chooses to proceed or delay and thus permit a counter-notice to be given, the withdrawal must be by notice of withdrawal[71] with consequent liability for the procedural and valuation costs.[72]

14.7.7 Vesting order procedure

The procedure for vesting interests of a landlord who cannot be found has distinct similarities to that relating to the same situation in a collective

66 Although, if a landlord has been deliberately concealing its identity, the truth may emerge at this stage.

67 Section 50(4)(a). As in the case of a collective enfranchisement there is no statutory guidance as to the meaning of 'traced', which might cause difficulty (see 7.8.5).

68 Section 50(4)(b). One situation where this might be used would be against a very unco-operative landlord and so remove the benefits which might otherwise accrue from a delay in some cases.

69 Section 50(5).

70 Section 50(5)(a) and (b).

71 Under s 52(1) (see 15.1.1).

72 Within s 60 (see 16.7.1).

enfranchisement.[73] There are, however, differences reflecting the fact that in this instance the vesting is of the grant of a new lease to a single tenant and not the vesting of the freehold.

The court will make the order providing for vesting of the interests of the landlord whose identity is unascertainable in the tenant. It will provide for the surrender of the existing lease of the flat and for the grant of a new lease to the tenant.[74] The court will also designate the person to execute the lease.[75]

The leasehold valuation tribunal will determine appropriate terms. In doing so, the tribunal will attempt, so far as circumstances permit, to reflect what the result would have been had the tenant been able to give a tenant's notice.[76] It will assume (unless the contrary is shown) that the person whose interest is being conveyed has no other interest in the property other than that to be demised – except mineral rights, which will be exempted from the lease.[77] The interest so vested may be less extensive than was specified in the application[78] – enabling the tribunal to correct any error in the property specified and to consider what the landlord might have done by way of proposals in any counter-notice. The tribunal will also approve the form of the lease[79] and the terms included will need to conform to the requirements of the Act relating to the grant of new leases generally.[80]

The tenant will pay into court the appropriate sum, namely the amount determined by the tribunal as the premium – that which would have been payable if acquired pursuant to a tenant's notice – plus any other amounts, if any, determined to be payable by virtue of Sch 13, together with any outstanding amounts determined by the tribunal as due from the tenant to the landlord, such as in respect of rent or service charges.[81] On payment into court, the lease giving effect to the terms of acquisition will be executed. The lease is effective to vest in the tenant the interests expressed to be demised by it[82] and the payment into court satisfies any claims in respect of the premium and other amounts payable under Sch 13 against the tenant, his personal representatives

---

73 Section 51(2)–(6) are very similar in effect to ss 27(2)–(6) (and see also Sch 5, paras 2, 3(1) and 4); except that they relate to the grant of a new lease to a single tenant rather than vesting the freehold in a nominee purchaser.

74 Section 51(1).

75 Section 51(3).

76 Section 51(1).

77 Section 51(4).

78 Section 51(2). See HC Deb, Standing Committee B, col 241, 24 November 1992.

79 Section 51(3)(a); the lease will as far as possible give effect to the statutory requirements for the lease contained in ss 56 and 57 (s 51(3)(b)).

80 A lease vested under s 51 is subject to ss 57–59 and s 61 and Sch 14 (s 51(7) and (8). See 16.3.1.

81 Section 51(3) and (5). Sums due to the landlord under a collateral agreement can be included but sums due to an intermediate landlord are not included, unlike the normal position under s 56(3)(c) (see 16.1.2).

82 Section 51(3).

or assigns.[83] As in the case of collective enfranchisement, there is no express provision as to how any sums paid into court are to be paid to a person claiming to be the landlord and a proper recipient.

---

83 Section 51(6). The Act does not however state that the payment satisfies sums due to the landlord from the tenant under the lease or a collateral agreement.

CHAPTER FIFTEEN

TERMINATION AND SUSPENSION

15.1 Express withdrawal

15.1.1 Notice of withdrawal

Notwithstanding the fact that the giving of a tenant's notice creates contractual obligations,[1] there is a statutory power given to the tenant to unilaterally withdraw from the process. The tenant may withdraw at any time before a new lease is entered into by giving a notice of withdrawal.[2]

15.1.2 To whom given

A notice of withdrawal must be given to the landlord, every other intermediate landlord (if any) and to any third party to the tenant's lease.[3] Since the notice is to be given under s 52, it may be prudent to specify that it is given under this section.

15.1.3 Effect of withdrawal

The effect of withdrawal is that the tenant becomes liable for the reasonable procedural, valuation and conveyancing costs[4] of each and every person to whom the notice of withdrawal is given.[5] No subsequent or further tenant's notice can then be given for 12 months from that date of withdrawal.[6]

15.2 Deemed withdrawal

15.2.1 The concept

A deemed withdrawal of a tenant's notice usually occurs where there is a failure to take the appropriate next step in the time-limit available; the notice is then

1 See 13.2.1.

2 Section 52(1).

3 Section 52(2). The landlord is the person who would have granted the lease as defined by s 40(1) and the other landlords are those who have a concurrent tenancy within s 40(4)(c) (see 11.5.2 and 11.5.4).

4 As specified and set out in s 60 (see 16.7.1).

5 Section 52(3).

6 Section 42(7).

deemed to be withdrawn and the acquisition procedure is at an end. In the case of a deemed withdrawal, where it may be that the tenant had an unambiguous right to a new lease and is ready to proceed but there has been a procedural error, a claim for professional negligence may follow if the failure was that of a professional adviser.

15.2.2 When a deemed withdrawal occurs

A deemed withdrawal will occur in the following instances.[7]

1 Where the tenant assigns his lease without the benefit of the tenant's notice; the deemed withdrawal occurs at the date of such assignment.[8]

2 Where any of the terms of acquisition remain in dispute at the end of two months from the giving of the counter-notice but no application has been made to a leasehold valuation tribunal before the end of the six-month period from the counter-notice.[9]

3 Where the terms of acquisition have been finally agreed, or determined by the leasehold valuation tribunal, but a new lease has not been entered into; and no application for a court order has been made within a period of two months from such agreement or determination;[10] and the court may make an order deeming withdrawal at that date.[11]

4 Where the landlord has failed to give a counter-notice or further counter-notice but no application for an order to determine the terms has been made by the tenant within a period of six months from the date by which the counter-notice was to be given.[12]

5 Where the terms of acquisition have been determined by an order of the court after the landlord failed to serve a counter-notice but a new lease has not been entered into; and no application for a court order has been made within a period of two months from such determination;[13] and the court may make an order deeming withdrawal at that date.[14]

In addition to these cases of deemed withdrawal, a tenant's notice will cease to have effect in the following instances.

---

7 They are either referred to or provided for in s 53.
8 Sections 43(3) and 53(4)(a).
9 Section 53(1)(a).
10 Section 53(1)(b).
11 Sections 48(4) and 53(4)(b).
12 Section 53(2).
13 Section 53(3).
14 Sections 49(5) and 53(4)(c).

1 If a copy of it is not served on a landlord who had previously notified the tenant by whom the notice was given of his interest in the flat.[15] The time-limit for giving that copy is the period ending with the date specified for the landlord's counter-notice.

2 If a court makes an order that the right to a new lease is not exercisable by reason of the landlord's intention to redevelop;[16] the notice ceases to have effect when the order of the court becomes final.

3 If compulsory acquisition procedures are commenced in relation to the flat after a tenant's notice has been given.[17]

These situations do not count as deemed withdrawals so the costs liability does not arise.[18]

15.2.3 Effect of a deemed withdrawal

There is, as in the case of an express withdrawal, a 12-month wait before the procedure could start again with the service of another tenant's notice.[19] This moratorium will not apply to cases where the tenant's notice has ceased to have effect, although in the case of compulsory acquisition or the landlord successfully establishing an intention to redevelop there will be little point in recommencing the procedure unless the situation has changed.

15.3 Suspension in the event of collective enfranchisement claim

15.3.1 The principle

It would not be possible for a claim to collective enfranchisement in respect of premises and an individual claim to a new lease relating to a flat in those premises to continue at the same time. A collective enfranchisement takes priority. During the currency of any collective enfranchisement claim, all claims to a new lease are suspended. They are not, however, lost. Once the outcome of the collective enfranchisement is settled, the new lease claim can be reactivated either against the landlord or against the nominee purchaser where the collective enfranchisement has succeeded.[20]

---

15 Schedule 11, para 4(1)(b).
16 Within s 47(1).
17 Section 55(2) (see 15.4.3).
18 Section 60(4).
19 Section 42(7) (and see fn 6 above).
20 If the tenant giving the notice then participated in the successful collective enfranchisement, there will be no need to reactivate the tenant's claim as the nominee purchaser will, no doubt, be granting the tenant a new term of 999 years.

15.3.2 *When a tenant's notice is suspended*

A tenant's notice is suspended immediately it is given if an initial notice has already been given in respect of the premises containing the tenant's flat and providing that the claim is still current.[21] Similarly, if the tenant's notice was the first in time, but continues in force and the new lease has not been granted, a later initial notice suspends the tenant's notice from the date on which the notice of claim was given.[22] A collective enfranchisement claim is current if it is still in progress but the freehold has not been conveyed; in other words, the initial notice is still in force, or a binding contract has been entered into or a vesting order made but not yet completed.[23] In both cases, suspension is total; no further notices can be given and no application can be made in relation to the tenant's claim.

15.3.3 *Giving notice of suspension*

It is likely that a tenant will be aware of a collective enfranchisement claim; indeed he might be participating and have no need to reactivate the new lease proceedings if the collective enfranchisement succeeds. However, it is possible that a tenant could be in ignorance. The landlord in respect of the new lease application will either be a freeholder or relevant landlord in connection with the collective enfranchisement and will receive notice of it. Therefore, it is a requirement that the landlord shall give the tenant notice of the suspension. Notice is to be given not later than the date specified for giving the counter-notice where the initial notice was first; or as soon as possible after the initial notice is given if the tenant's claim to a new lease is underway first. Such notice must inform the tenant of the date that the initial notice was given and the name and address of the nominee purchaser.[24]

15.3.4 *Revival when a tenant's notice was immediately suspended when given*

As soon as the collective enfranchisement ceases to be current, the tenant's notice revives and is in force again. If it was suspended immediately on being given, no action will have been taken on it. The date specified in the tenant's notice will be changed; for the date specified, there shall be substituted a date which allows the same period of time for the landlord's response.[25] Once again,

21 Section 54(1).
22 Section 54(2).
23 Section 54(11)(b).
24 Section 54(3).
25 Section 54(4); the period is defined in this section, using terms defined elsewhere, as such new date as results in the period of time intervening between the date when the enfranchisement claim ceases to be current and the new date being equal to the period of time between the date the tenant's notice of claim was given and the date originally specified in the notice. It is hoped that the summary in the text is both clearer and correct.

there is duty on the landlord to give the tenant notice, as soon as possible, that the tenant's notice is no longer suspended.[26]

15.3.5 Revival when a tenant's notice was suspended during the claim

The suspension of a tenant's notice by virtue of a later initial notice may occur at any stage of the process of claiming a new lease. So, although the tenant's notice is revived when the initial notice ceases to be current, the manner and timing of its revival depends on what stage had been reached when it was suspended.

1 The suspension may have occurred at an early stage, before the landlord gave any counter-notice at all or before the giving of an unqualified counter-notice admitting the right to acquire a new lease. Such cases therefore include the situation where a counter-notice has been given contesting validity or showing an intention to oppose on redevelopment grounds and a court application is still pending; and where the court has ruled against the landlord in either of those cases and a further counter-notice has not yet been given. In all such cases, at the time of the suspension, the landlord has not given a counter-notice under s 45(2)(a) and a time-limit would be running to complete the next stage of the process – to give a notice or to make an application in connection with the tenant's claim.[27] The relevant period in respect of that time-limit is deemed to have begun on the date that the initial notice ceases to be current and the tenant's notice revives.[28] In effect, the person subject to the time-limit gets the benefit of the full period, however close the time-limit was to being met at the date of suspension. There is, again, the duty on the landlord to inform the tenant as soon as possible after becoming aware of the circumstances by virtue of which the tenant's notice has revived.[29]

2 At any later stage of the process, after an unqualified counter-notice[30] has been given, the tenant's notice is only revived from the date on which the landlord gives the tenant notice that the claim to a new lease is no longer suspended. As before, this notice must be given as soon as possible after becoming aware of the circumstances by virtue of which the tenant's notice ceased to be suspended. To ensure that a landlord could not delay the claim by not giving the notice, it is provided that the claim is also revived by the tenant giving notice to the landlord informing the landlord of the

---

26 Section 54(8).
27 See s 54(10).
28 This is a summary of the combined effect of s 54(5),(6) and (10).
29 Section 54(8).
30 Given under s 45(2)(a).

circumstances by virtue of which the operation of the tenant's notice is no longer suspended.[31]

15.4 Compulsory acquisition

15.4.1 Prevents or terminates the new lease procedure

The commencement or existence of compulsory purchase procedures in respect of the flat will prevent or terminate the statutory process.[32] If the compulsory acquisition is not completed, there is no automatic revival of the claim for a new lease.

15.4.2 Existing compulsory purchase procedures

A tenant's notice is of no effect if, on the date when it is given, any person or body authorised to acquire the whole or part of the premises compulsorily, with a view to acquisition of the whole or part of the premises, have served a notice to treat on either the landlord or the tenant.[33] This is also the result if that person or body has entered into a contract for the purchase of the flat or part of it; in both cases, the notice to treat or contract must, of course, remain in force.[34] Therefore, if a notice to treat or contract is in force in respect of the flat, any tenant's notice is of no effect.

15.4.3 Notice to treat subsequent to a tenant's notice

The service of notice to treat on the landlord or the tenant will invalidate a tenant's notice which has already been given. Thus, a tenant's notice ceases to have effect if a person or body who could be authorised to acquire the flat serves a notice to treat with a view to acquisition of the whole or part of the flat.[35]

15.4.4 Compensation payable

In the case of a notice to treat being served after the tenant's notice, the compensation payable on the compulsory acquisition in respect of any interest in the tenant's flat shall be determined on the basis of the value of the interest subject to and with the benefit of the rights and obligations arising from the tenant's notice.[36] Thus, where a compulsory purchase is a possibility, a tenant

---

31 Section 54(7) and (8). Once the tenant has given such a notice, the landlord is, naturally, no longer required to inform the tenant that the tenant's notice is revived (s 54(9)).

32 Section 55.

33 Section 55(1)(a)(i).

34 Section 55(1)(a)(ii) and (b).

35 Section 55(2).

36 Section 55(3).

may benefit financially by serving the tenant's notice before any compulsory acquisition procedures commence.

15.5 Return of the deposit

15.5.1 Notice to require return

At any time after a tenant's notice is withdrawn, deemed to have been withdrawn or otherwise ceased to have effect, a tenant may give to a landlord a notice requiring him to procure the return of the deposit.[37] Since the deposit will have been paid to the landlord's solicitor as stakeholder this will involve authorisation to repay to the tenant.[38] The landlord has a period of 14 days to comply from the date such notice is given.[39]

15.5.2 Entitlement to deduct costs

Before repayment, the landlord is entitled to have deducted from the deposit any amount due from the tenant for costs.[40] These are the costs for which the tenant is liable under s 60.[41]

15.6 Cancellation of land charge

When a tenant's notice has been registered as a land charge – and it will have been done in nearly every case – it will need to be cancelled in the event of a withdrawal, deemed withdrawal or in any other situation when the notice ceases to have effect. At the request of the landlord, the tenant shall, without delay, take all steps necessary to procure cancellation of the registration.[42]

---

37 Leasehold Reform (Collective Enfranchisement and Lease Renewal) Regulations 1993, SI 1993/2407, Sch 2, para 3(1).

38 See 13.3.2.

39 Leasehold Reform (Collective Enfranchisement and Lease Renewal) Regulations 1993, SI 1993/2407, para 3(2).

40 Ibid, para 3(3).

41 See 16.7.1.

42 Leasehold Reform (Collective Enfranchisement and Lease Renewal) Regulations 1993, SI 1993/2407, Sch 2, para 9.

CHAPTER SIXTEEN

GRANT OF A NEW LEASE

16.1 The obligation to grant a new lease

16.1.1 Nature of the obligation

The landlord is bound to grant a new lease of a flat to a tenant who has the right to acquire a new lease and has given the requisite notice.[1] This new extended lease is in substitution for the existing lease and is granted on payment of the premium and other sums due. The new lease is at a peppercorn rent for the entire term which is calculated to expire 90 years after the term date of the existing lease.[2] If, therefore, the tenant has an existing lease of 99 years from 1 July 1960 and expiring on 30 June 2059, the new lease at a peppercorn rent will commence on the date of the grant and expire on 30 June 2149.

The obligation to grant the new lease is not limited by the fact that any subsisting head-lease contains a provision prohibiting, restricting or otherwise relating to a sub-demise. Any such provision has no effect as far as the grant of a new lease under the Act is concerned.[3] Where the landlord granting the new lease is a local authority or other public sector landlord, certain statutory requirements as to consent, consultation or by way of restriction on disposal do not apply to the grant of the new lease.[4]

16.1.2 The premium and other sums payable for the grant

The premium payable is calculated in accordance with the Act.[5] In addition to the premium due to the landlord, the tenant must pay in connection with the grant the proper amount due to the owners of any intermediate leasehold interests.[6]

---

1 In accordance with s 42.

2 Section 56(1).

3 Section 56(5).

4 Section 56(6) and (7); this is a similar provision to that relating to collective enfranchisement in Sch 10. The statutory provisions concerned are those listed in para 1(2) of Sch 10 with the exception of s 79(2) of the Housing Act 1988.

5 The details are set out in Sch 13 (see 20.3 and 20.4).

6 Section 56(2).

A tenant is only entitled to the grant if, in addition to those sums due to the landlords, there is paid and tendered at the execution of the lease the appropriate amounts to cover arrears and costs. All sums due by way of rent or recoverable as rent (such as service charge or insurance premiums if so reserved) in respect of the flat must be paid up to the date of tender plus any other sums due and payable by the tenant under or in respect of the lease to any of the landlords.[7] The costs which must be paid are those for which the tenant is liable under s 60.[8] It is possible that exact amount of some of the sums due cannot be ascertained – such as some service charge items. In such a case, the tenant must offer reasonable security for the payment of such amount as may afterwards be found to be payable in respect of them. Such security could be the deposit of an estimated sum with the tenant's solicitors until the correct amount is known.

16.1.3 To whom the premium is payable

All sums due and payable for the grant will normally be payable to the landlord making the grant even if ultimately due to another person.[9] It will then be the responsibility of that landlord to pay the correct proportion to the other landlords to whom amounts may be due. However, any of the other landlords may, prior to the grant, by notice require the tenant to pay direct to him or someone duly authorised any amount due to him.[10]

16.2 Surrender and re-grant of existing intermediate leases

16.2.1 The principle

Although the value of any intermediate leases between that of the tenant and the interest of the competent landlord granting the lease is purchased, such intermediate leases normally remain in existence. They will have no further monetary value – for the rent payable under the new lease is a peppercorn rent

---

7 Section 56(3)(a) and (c). In the unusual case of the new lease being granted after the term date of the existing lease, the tenant is liable to pay by way of an addition to the rent payable an amount to cover any shortfall on the service charge for repair maintenance and insurance for the period between expiry of the existing lease and the grant of the new one (see s 57(5)).

8 Section 56(3)(b); and see 16.7.1.

9 Section 56(4). This is the competent landlord as defined by s 40 (see 11.5.2).

10 Schedule 11, para 7(2). If one of the other landlords gives such a notice, he must notify the competent landlord of the arrangements to receive payment and implement them; if this is not done, the competent landlord remains authorised to receive payment and give the tenant a receipt which will be a complete discharge of the obligation.

and there will be no reversionary value since the term of any intermediate lease will by definition expire before that of the new lease; but the integrity of intermediate leases of the whole block of flats and any service charge arrangements contained in them is thereby preserved.

16.2.2 Surrender and re-grant at time of the grant of a new lease

This result is achieved by a deemed surrender and re-grant of the subsisting intermediate leases between the tenant's lease and the interest of the competent landlord whenever a new lease is executed under the Act.[11] The deemed surrender is necessary to allow the competent landlord to grant the term of the new lease; the re-grant effectively continues the intermediate lease in existence until its contractual date for expiry. The covenants and other provisions of the new lease are to be framed and take effect subject to that surrender and re-grant.[12] The only exception to a deemed surrender and re-grant will be in the rare circumstance where the intermediate lease is vested in the tenant or a trustee for the tenant. In such a case there is to be an actual surrender of the superior lease and no re-grant.[13]

16.2.3 An example

Thus, in the not uncommon situation of a 99-year lease by a freeholder to a management company and flat sub-leases of 99 years less 10 days, the intermediate interest of the management company is preserved for the remainder of that 99-year term. A tenant of one of the flats with a right to a new lease will obtain the grant from the freeholder, the competent landlord in this case. At the grant, there will be a deemed surrender and re-grant of the intermediate lease to the management company. The tenant will remain subject to the covenant's obligations and service charge provisions in the intermediate lease with the management company. At the end of the 99-year term of the intermediate lease, the tenant will still have 90 years, less 10 days, under the new lease.[14] Unless by that time there has been a collective enfranchisement or a negotiated purchase of the freehold by the tenants and fresh 999-year leases, there will need to be provisions in the new lease to ensure that the freeholder then takes over any management provisions and lessor's covenants which are currently contained in the intermediate lease in return for a suitable service

---

11 Under either s 56(1) or s 93(4) (Sch 11, para 10). It is perhaps unfortunate that this important provision is contained in a schedule under s 40 of the Act and not in terms related to s 57. The rent payable under the subsisting intermediate lease will remain unchanged – a point which will affect the valuation of that interest and the division of the premium paid. A concurrent lease is, it is submitted, 'intermediate' for these purposes. See also s 101(8).

12 Schedule 11, para 10(1) (see 16.3).

13 Schedule 11, para 10(3).

14 Unless the landlord has successfully exercised the redevelopment option under s 61 (see 16.8.3); the tenant will have the right, if not already exercised, of further extended terms.

charge.[15] This may be an interim arrangement; in practice, when the date when the existing lease would have expired arrives, the tenants with long leases may all have exercised their rights to a new lease and be able to set up new management arrangements – or will have purchased the freehold by then.

16.3 The terms of the new lease

16.3.1 To be on the same terms as the existing lease

Apart from the peppercorn rent payable and the extended duration, the terms of the new lease are to be primarily the same as the existing lease.[16] The Act, however, requires that some changes be made and some matters excluded or added to the terms of the new lease.

16.3.2 Power to agree terms

The requirements of the Act as to the terms of the new lease take effect subject to any agreement between the landlord and the tenant.[17] The parties are at liberty, therefore, to agree to some changes which would otherwise not be permitted. However, unless those changes are parts of terms of acquisition approved by the leasehold valuation tribunal, the court has power to set aside or vary terms which do not adequately compensate the tenant for his statutory rights. This may be done on application by the tenant to a county court or in any court in which proceedings on the agreement are brought where the court has a power to give such relief as appears to the court to be just having regard to the situation and the conduct of the parties.[18] This is a powerful and long-term deterrent to incorporating terms which do not conform to the statutory requirements or which do not have prior court approval;[19] parties considering a grant of a new lease on terms which depart from the statutory requirements may be well-advised to seek approval of the details of the terms of acquisition from the leasehold valuation tribunal.

16.3.3 Extent of the property included

The tenant's right is only to a new lease of the flat.[20] As a result, any property included in the existing lease but not comprised in the flat will not be included

15 See s 57(2)(b) and the discussion at 16.3.6.
16 Section 57(1).
17 Section 57(5).
18 Section 93(3).
19 For example, a tenant could raise the issue much later in an action to recover service charges due or in forfeiture proceedings.
20 Sections 39(1) and 56(1).

in the new lease and the new lease will be modified as required or appropriate to take account of the omission.[21] However, for this purpose, flat is widely defined for the purpose of the claim to a new lease and includes any garage, outhouse, garden, yard or appurtenances belonging to or usually enjoyed with the flat and let to the tenant with the flat on the date the claim was made.[22] If, therefore, the lease includes a garage, even if in a separate block, this will be included in the new lease. It is thought that it will be rare for an existing lease of a flat to include property which does not qualify for inclusion in the new lease.

16.3.4 Changes and modifications which may be required

Certain modifications to a term of the existing lease may be insisted upon when settling the terms of the new lease.

1 Modifications will be required or will be appropriate to take account of any alterations to the property demised since the grant of the existing lease.[23] Thus, if the lease includes, for example, a demise of a separate coal store since demolished with the advent of gas central heating, the new lease may not include the grant of the piece of land on which the coal store stood.[24]

2 Either party can require modification or exclusion of a term insofar as it is necessary to remedy a defect in the existing lease.[25] The interpretation of 'defect' may be crucial.[26] It may be interpreted narrowly and thus prevent 'modernisation' of any terms of the lease which are outmoded but serviceable and do not amount to a defect – unless both parties agree.[27] If a wider view were adopted, it will allow the inclusion of lease covenants in a form normally found in modern leases by way of replacement of covenants or wording of covenants which are now less acceptable and which a conveyancer would consider 'defective'. Some difficulty in agreeing such changes may be encountered if the defect is also contained in the existing leases of other flats and the change or modification will disadvantage one or other of the parties while defects remain in the other flat leases.

3 Either party can require that for the purposes of the new lease any term of the existing lease shall be excluded or modified insofar as it would be unreasonable to include the term in question in view of changes occurring

21 Section 57(1)(a).
22 Section 62(2). See 11.2.1.
23 Section 57(1)(b).
24 Unless the piece of land can still be included as an appurtenance (see 16.3.3).
25 Section 57(6)(a).
26 There is no similar provision in s 15 of the Leasehold Reform Act 1967; 'defect' is not defined.
27 This would accord with the approach of the House of Lords in *O'May v City of London Real Property Co* [1983] 2 AC 726 where the alteration of terms of commercial leases on a statutory renewal under the Landlord and Tenant Act 1954 were considered.

since the date of commencement of the existing lease. The changes must affect the suitability on the date that the claim was commenced of the provisions in the existing lease.[28] Thus, if the lease includes the right to use a separate coal store but which is no longer used by the tenant and has fallen into disrepair, there has been no alteration as such to the property demised but the landlord may argue that it is unreasonable to include the right to use the coal store in the new lease.

4 Where the existing lease of the flat is in fact two or more separate leases with the same landlord and tenant,[29] modifications can be required or may be appropriate to take account of the combined effect of those leases and of any differences in their terms.[30]

5 In a case where there is an agreement collateral to the existing lease, provision shall be made by the terms of the new lease for the continuance of that agreement with any suitable adaptations.[31]

16.3.5 Exclusions from the new lease

The new lease gives the tenant a substantial extended term at a peppercorn rent and the statutory right to a further renewal.[32] The matters to be excluded from the new lease are a consequence of that fact. Any term of an existing lease or collateral agreement shall be excluded from the new lease insofar as that term:[33]

1 provides for or relates to the renewal of the lease;

2 confers any option to purchase or right of pre-emption in relation to the flat demised by the existing lease;

3 provides for the termination of the existing lease before its term date otherwise than in the event of a breach of its terms.

Where such terms are excluded, modifications shall be made where required or appropriate to take account of the exclusion.

The exclusion of any break clause or power to determine is a necessary consequence of the nature of the new lease; any value which attached to it and is lost as a consequence of the grant should be reflected in the premium payable.[34] Provisions for renewal, options to purchase or rights of pre-emption would also

28 Section 57(6)(b); 'changes' are not otherwise defined.
29 See ss 7(6) and 39(3).
30 Section 57(1)(c).
31 Section 57(3). There is no elucidation of what is a collateral agreement. Cf the Leasehold Reform Act 1967, s 15(4).
32 See s 59 and 16.5.2.
33 Section 57(4)(a)–(c); cf the Leasehold Reform Act 1967, s 15(5).
34 This view accords with that of the author of the leading text on the 1967 Act in respect of the similar provision (see Hague, *Leasehold Enfranchisement*, 2nd edn, 1987, Sweet & Maxwell, para 9–02).

exist uncomfortably with the new lease terms. However, in some cases existing rights of renewal or purchase in the existing lease might possibly be more advantageous than exercising the statutory right to a new lease. This may need to be assessed, preferably before giving the tenant's notice.

16.3.6 Service charge provisions

Normally, existing service charge provisions will be the same as in the existing lease.[35] Any defect or inadequacy in them can be subject to either agreement for change or can require modification on the grounds of necessity to remedy a defect or unreasonableness.[36] This principle is clear but the proper interpretation of the detailed provisions relating to service charges is not easy.

Where the terms of the existing lease do not include provision for the making of service charge payments in consideration for the provision by the landlord of services, repairs, maintenance or insurance, or include provision only for the payment of a fixed amount then, from the term date of the existing lease, the new lease shall make such provision as may be just for the making of payments from time to time to cover the cost to the landlord of the provision of services or for repairs, maintenance or insurance. The liability for such payments are to be made enforceable by provision permitting distress, re-entry or otherwise as if it were a liability for payment of rent.[37] On this interpretation, s 57(2)(b) permits the tenant, prima facie, to retain any advantage of non-existing or inadequate service charge provisions until the date of the expiry of the existing term. This view gives primacy to the general rule that existing terms are carried over into the new lease.[38] It is also consistent with a not dissimilar provision in the Leasehold Reform Act.[39] However, the problem may be academic; it will be possible to argue strongly for changes to any existing but inadequate service charge arrangements carried over into the new lease for the period until the expiry of the existing term. This can be done on the grounds either of necessity to remedy a defect or that it would be unreasonable to include the existing term without modification in view of changes occurring since the date of commencement of the existing lease.[40] It is submitted that a landlord who is granting a new lease at a peppercorn rent for effectively an indefinite period will be able to argue that the new lease should not result in a burden of any costs in the provision of services which is not recoverable from the tenant. On this view,

---

35 In accordance with the general principle in s 57(1). If the current service charge is paid as rent, the new lease may continue to require such payments as rent (s 57(2)(a)).

36 See 16.3.4.

37 Section 57(2)(b).

38 An alternative view is that s 57(2)(a) requires payments to be made for any obligation for the provision of services in the new lease but it is submitted that this cannot be fitted into the wording of s 57(2) as a whole; see also fn 44 below.

39 Leasehold Reform Act 1967, s 15(3) which section is concerned with the terms of a new tenancy granted under that Act and is interrelated to s 15(2).

40 By virtue of s 57(6) discussed at 16.3.4.

whatever the position in the existing lease, a landlord should be able to establish either necessity to remedy a defect, or unreasonableness to include the existing term, or both.[41]

Where the existing lease is with an intermediate landlord, the mutual obligations to provide services and to repair, maintain and insure may lie with the intermediate landlord and the liability of the tenant will be to make payment to that person. Those intermediate interests continue, by virtue of a deemed surrender and re-grant,[42] and the new lease, although granted by the competent landlord, will carry over the obligations to make service charge payments to intermediate landlord. Account is to be taken of the obligations imposed on the other landlords for this purpose.[43]

The intermediate leases, although subject to a deemed surrender and re-grant, are not extended and will therefore expire by effluxion of time before expiry of the new lease. At that point, the landlord may become under an obligation, if this is not already the case, to provide services or for repairs maintenance or insurance. Thus if, during the continuance of the new lease, the landlord will be under any obligation for the provision of services or for repairs maintenance or insurance, the new lease may require payments to be made by the tenant (whether as rent or otherwise) in consideration of those matters or in respect of the cost thereof to the landlord.[44]

16.3.7 Third parties to the existing lease

Many flat leases may have a third party to the flat lease.[45] This may be a guarantor or surety but is more likely to be a management company or residents' association which does not have a legal or equitable interest in the block of flats but joins in the lease to undertake management or other functions.

41 Section 57(6)(a)–(b). It may not be clear-cut however. In a situation where a landlord currently suffers a loss providing services because the recovery is of a fixed amount, the stronger argument would be that this is a defect in the existing lease – but can a defect be shown? It may not always be 'unreasonable . . . in view of changes' unless inflation and a fall in the value of money are such changes.

42 See 16.2.2.

43 Schedule 11, para 10(2).

44 Section 57(2)(a). The proper interpretation of s 57(2) as a whole may be open to dispute, but it is submitted that giving a wide general view of s 57(2)(a) as requiring the inclusion of an absolute minimum service charge provision in a new lease, even where there is none in the existing lease or the existing mechanism is inadequate to reimburse the landlord, is not possible. The subsection applies 'during the continuance of the new lease' and this is better understood as referring to the period after the expiry of the existing lease; and the wording is that the lease 'may require' payments, not that it 'shall'. Sub-paragraphs (a) and (b) are also linked. This view also accords with the interpretation of a not dissimilar provision (s 15(3)) in the Leasehold Reform Act 1967 in Hague, *Leasehold Enfranchisement*, 2nd edn, 1987, Sweet & Maxwell, 7–12. Any alternative view would mean that s 57(2)(b) is more narrowly confined to additional specific and more detailed provision applicable from the term date of the existing lease.

45 A third party, in relation to any lease, means a person who is a party to the lease other than the tenant and the immediate landlord (s 62(1)).

Where any such person is a third party to the existing lease or a party to any agreement collateral to the lease, that person is also to be a party to the new lease or replacement collateral agreement and shall join in its execution.[46] This is subject to contrary agreement between that third party and the landlord and the tenant – it may be more convenient to alter the arrangements. In any event, the third party cannot normally be required to discharge any function after the term date of the existing lease. If it is expedient or necessary in connection with the proper enjoyment by the tenant of the flat for provision to be made for the continued discharge of that function after that date, then the lease is to make provision for the function to be discharged after that date either by the third party, with its consent, or by some other person;[47] if the third party does not agree then the responsibility may have to be taken by the freeholder or competent landlord, with payments by the tenant to cover the cost.[48]

16.3.8 Covenant for title

The tenant cannot require an extended covenant for title. In granting the new lease, the landlord is not bound to enter into any covenant for title beyond that implied in the grant. If a covenant is required of the landlord in that capacity, a landlord is entitled to limit expressly his personal liability to breaches of that covenant for which he is responsible.[49]

16.3.9 Statutory additions to the new lease

There are three important matters contained in every new lease granted under the Act which may affect later holders of the lease and so must appear as part of its terms.

First, the terms of the new lease shall reserve to the person who is for the time being the tenant's immediate landlord the right to obtain possession of the flat on grounds of redevelopment in the future.[50] Any purchaser of the lease will see from the face of the lease that this right is in the lease and when this right may become exercisable.

Secondly, provision shall be made that no long lease created by way of sub-lease out of the term of the new lease shall confer on the sub-tenant any right to acquire a new lease under the 1993 Act.[51]

Finally, the new lease must contain a statement which is granted under s 56 of the Act. Rules may be prescribed to which such statements must comply.[52]

---

46 Section 57(9).
47 Section 57(10).
48 See s 57(2)(a) and 16.3.6.
49 Section 57(8). The matter may well be covered by the covenants for quiet enjoyment and non-derogation carried over from the existing lease.
50 Section 57(7)(b); and in accordance with s 61 see 16.8.1.
51 Sections 57(7)(a) and 59(3).
52 Under s 144 of the Land Registration Act 1925 (s 57(11)).

For the purpose of excluding future security of tenure,[53] this statement is conclusive in favour of any person who is not a party to the lease.[54]

16.4 Mortgages

16.4.1 Mortgages of the landlord's interest

A mortgage of the landlord's interest cannot prevent the grant of the new lease. A qualifying tenant shall be entitled to a new lease even if the grant of the existing lease was subsequent to a mortgage of the landlord's interest and was not authorised by it. A new lease granted under the Act is deemed to be authorised as against any person interested in the mortgage, however created or arising, and binds those persons.[55] The only exception is in respect of a mortgage granted after 1 November 1993[56] and where the existing long lease was granted subsequent to the mortgage and does not bind the mortgagee.[57] If a mortgage of the landlord's interest remains in force after the grant of the new lease and the mortgagee is entitled to the documents of title, the landlord shall deliver the counterpart lease duly executed by the tenant within one month of the execution of the lease.[58] Failure to do so gives rise to mortgage remedies since the obligation to deliver a counterpart applies as if it were included in the terms of the mortgage.[59]

16.4.2 Mortgages of the existing lease

One of the advantages of taking a new lease as an alternative to joining in a collective enfranchisement is the simplicity of dealing with any mortgage of the lease of the flat. Where the existing lease is, immediately before its surrender on the grant of the new lease, subject to any mortgage, lien or charge, the new lease takes effect subject to the mortgage in substitution for the existing lease.[60] The terms of the mortgage apply to the new lease as to the existing lease. This will enable the new lease to be granted without disturbing any existing financing and with the minimum procedure; and where the premium for the new lease is

53 See 16.6.1.

54 Section 59(5).

55 Section 58(1). A mortgage includes a lien or charge (s 62(1)).

56 The date of commencement of Chapter II of Part I of the Act.

57 Section 58(2). A landlord in such a case shall be bound to take such steps as may be necessary to secure that the lease is not liable to be defeated by any persons interested in a mortgage of his interest, although the landlord is not obliged to acquire a better title than he has or could require to be vested in him (s 58(7)). What this means in practice is unclear; Sch 11, para 11 would suggest that the premium paid for the new lease to the landlord who is liable under the mortgage should be used to discharge the tenant's flat from the mortgage.

58 Section 58(3).

59 Section 58(6)(a).

60 Section 58(4).

being provided by the existing lender, all that may be necessary is a further advance on the existing mortgage. Where a lease takes effect subject to any existing mortgage and the mortgagee is entitled to the documents of title, that mortgagee is naturally entitled to possession of the documents of title relating to the new lease. Thus, the tenant shall deliver the new lease to the mortgagee within one month of the date on which the lease is received from the Land Registry following its registration.[61] Once again failure to do so gives rise to mortgage remedies since the obligation to deliver the new lease applies as if it were included in the terms of the mortgage.[62]

16.5 The right to further renewal

16.5.1 'Virtual freehold' concept

Once granted, the new lease confers on the tenant an estate in land which is perhaps best described as virtual freehold – at least as far as duration and rent are concerned. The rent is a nominal peppercorn and, by providing for further renewal and separating the new lease away from security of tenure provisions which relate to other leaseholds, the new lease is marked out as a special sort of leasehold estate.

16.5.2 Further renewal at any time

The right to acquire a new lease may be exercised in relation to a lease of a flat despite the fact that the lease itself is a lease granted under the Act.[63] Exactly the same provisions apply in connection with such a claim as they do to the first new lease granted under the Act, with any necessary modifications. There is no time-limit on when such an application could be made;[64] so a tenant could make a further application immediately on the conclusion of the grant of the new lease.

The premium payable on the grant of the further new lease is likely to be nil or a nominal sum – at least for the next few decades. The tenant may have little incentive to go through the procedure again; but equally a landlord has little interest in resisting a further new lease. The main impact of an early grant of a further lease will be that a further right of termination on the grounds of redevelopment will appear in the further lease at the term date of the first new lease.[65]

---

61 Section 58(5).

62 Section 58(6).

63 Section 59(1).

64 Even s 42(7), which imposes a year's moratorium, only applies to impose a 12-month delay when a notice is withdrawn, deemed to be withdrawn or rendered of no effect by a successful application by a landlord on the grounds of an intention to redevelop under s 47.

65 In accordance with s 61 (see 16.8.2).

It is, perhaps, unfortunate that the Act did not permit or insist that the new term could be or was to be one of 900 years expiring after the term date of the existing lease with the landlord's right to terminate on the grounds of redevelopment arising every 90 years – which is what the tenant would have if 10 further leases were sought in quick succession. However, it is open to the parties to agree on this solution and make the new lease granted in the first instance in this form. If other terms of acquisition were being settled by the leasehold valuation tribunal, then the approval of the tribunal could be sought by consent. Even without such approval, the agreement of terms different from those set by the Act is permitted[66] and is hardly likely to come within the definition of an agreement which could be later challenged.[67]

16.5.3 No security of tenure

The new lease granted under the Act does not attract the existing security of tenure provisions which would otherwise apply at the conclusion of the term – none of the statutory provisions applies to the lease.[68] This is clearly of no concern to the existing tenant who has a term in excess of 90 years – and in years to come, later successors can put in a claim to a further lease.[69]

16.6 Sub-leases

16.6.1 Long sub-leases

A long lease created by way of sub-demise out of a new lease granted under the Act does not give rise to rights to a new lease in favour of the sub-tenant as against the tenant's landlord.[70] Rights could in theory arise against the tenant if the tenant grants the long sub-lease and has a term under the new lease of sufficient duration to provide a reversion to any new extended sub-lease.

16.6.2 No security of tenure after term date

During the term of the new lease, any sub-tenant will have such security of tenure as is normally applicable; so, for example, any assured tenancy will operate in the normal way in the case of a residential sub-lease and the

66 Section 93(2)(a).

67 See s 93(3) and 16.3.2. Once the term of the new lease reaches 300 years or more (perhaps on the third renewal) an interesting possibility is the right under s 153 of the Law of Property Act 1925 to enlarge the lease into a fee simple. This might be attractive, given the continuing enforceability of covenants, but may not be possible in view of the right to terminate on the grounds of redevelopment under s 61 (see the Law of Property Act 1925, s 153(1)(a)).

68 Section 59(2)(a).

69 Assuming that there has not been a collective enfranchisement by then or indeed more fundamental changes!

70 Section 59(3). For this purpose, a long lease has the meaning given by s 7 (see 3.7.1).

Landlord and Tenant Act 1954, Part II, will apply as appropriate to any business sub-tenancy. However, after the term date of the new lease, none of the core security of tenure provisions apply to a sub-lease or allow a person to remain in possession;[71] but are unlikely to be of concern to prospective sub-tenants for some years. If a sub-lease is granted which will be so affected or is being negotiated, the person so granting or negotiating must inform the other party.[72]

16.7 Costs

16.7.1 The extent of the liability

The costs liability of the tenant is, essentially, a liability for the reasonable procedural, valuation and conveyancing costs borne by the landlord. Not all costs incurred by the landlord will be recoverable.

The tenant is liable to pay the reasonable costs of the landlord, other landlord or any third party to the lease which fall within the statutory definition and which have been incurred in pursuance of the tenant's notice.[73] These costs are the reasonable costs of and incidental to the following matters:[74]

(a) any investigation reasonably undertaken of the tenant's right to a new lease;
(b) any valuation of the tenant's flat obtained for the purpose of fixing the premium or other amount payable in connection with the grant;
(c) the grant of a new lease.

In an attempt to avoid the landlord deliberately incurring high professional valuation and legal fees, it is provided that costs incurred by the landlord or other relevant person[75] in respect of professional services shall only be regarded as reasonable to the extent that those costs might be reasonably expected to be incurred by him if he was personally liable for those costs.[76]

In a case of withdrawal by the tenant, or a deemed withdrawal, the liability is for costs incurred up to that time.[77]

---

71 The statutory provisions are listed in s 59(2)(b)–(c).

72 Unless he knows that the other party is aware of it or is unaware of it himself (s 59(4)). Since the lease contains a statement it is granted under s 56 the fact should become clear. The duty to inform may fall upon the solicitor or other agent of the proposed grantor.

73 Section 60(1).

74 Section 60(1)(a)–(e).

75 Defined in s 60(6) to mean the landlord, any other landlord and any third party.

76 Section 60(2). The tenant is not liable for any costs if, on a voluntary sale, a stipulation that they would be borne by the purchaser would be void (s 60(1), proviso).

77 Section 60(3).

16.7.2 No liability for costs

There is no liability on the tenant for any costs if the tenant's notice ceases to have effect either because the freeholder has established a successful defence of an intention to redevelop[78] or because the premises are subject to a compulsory acquisition.[79] The statutory liability for costs does not extend to any costs incurred in connection with proceedings before a leasehold valuation tribunal and costs incurred in connection with any application to the court will be a matter for the court in accordance with usual procedure.[80]

16.7.3 No security for costs

There is no statutory provision for security for costs. In the case of a successful claim for a new lease, the costs recoverable will be paid at the grant of the new lease. In the case of an express withdrawal or a deemed withdrawal, there is a liability on the tenant whose flat will provide some sort of security for recovery. If a deposit has been paid, costs can be recovered from it before repayment.[81]

16.8 The redevelopment right in the new lease

16.8.1 Rationale

As we have seen, the new lease must contain a reservation of the right to obtain possession of the flat on grounds of an intention to redevelop in favour of the person who is for the time being the tenant's immediate landlord.[82] This right is available at the term date of the existing lease and at the term date of the new lease. The reason is that although the tenant, by paying the premium, has bought out the rent and capital value of the reversion to the existing flat, any residuary redevelopment value in the premises or the site as a whole has not been included and remains with the freeholder or intermediate landlord. Only a collective enfranchisement or other purchase of the freehold will transfer any redevelopment value to the tenants – by that redevelopment value being included in the price paid. In the absence of the 1993 Act, a landlord could have allowed all existing leases to expire and then redevelop on that expiry. The Act allows that right to be retained, subject to payment of compensation, and if not so exercised at the term date of the existing lease, may also be exercised at the term date of the new lease.[83]

78 Section 60(4) (and see s 47(1)).

79 Section 60(4) (and see s 55(1)).

80 Section 60(5).

81 By virtue of the Leasehold Reform (Collective Enfranchisement and Lease Renewal) Regulations 1993, SI 1993/2407, Sch 2, para 3(3).

82 See s 57(7)(b) and 16.3.9.

83 If all existing leases in a block expire at the same date, the term date of any new leases to those flats will also be identical.

16.8.2 Time for application

A landlord[84] may only make application in a period ending with the term date of either the existing or new lease. The first opportunity will be at any time in a period of 12 months ending with the term date of the lease in relation to which the right to acquire the new lease was exercised.[85] How soon that will be depends of course on how many years remained on the existing lease at the time of the grant. It is unlikely in any event to be exercised in the first five years of the new lease as a landlord is likely to have taken advantage of defeating the claim for a new lease under s 47. Once the first opportunity has passed, the next occasion will be at any time in the period of five years ending with the term date of the new lease.[86] By definition, this must be at least 85 years after the term date of the existing lease and probably over 100 years after the grant of the new lease. For valuation purposes, and in practical terms, only the right to terminate in the 12-month period ending with the term date of the original lease will be of significance – and then only in some cases.

If a further lease is granted under the Act, the right to apply to terminate is preserved at the term date of the original lease and of the term dates of the first and any subsequent leases granted.[87] It will therefore arise every 90 years calculated from the term date of the original lease.

16.8.3 What must be established

In order to make an order under on application by the landlord, the court must be satisfied that:[88]

(a) for the purposes of redevelopment, the landlord intends to demolish or reconstruct, or carry out substantial works of construction on the whole or a substantial part of any premises in which the flat is contained; and
(b) he could not reasonably do so without obtaining possession of the flat.[89]

The burden of proof is on the landlord and the requisite intent must be established at the time of the application in relation to the date on which the lease is due to terminate.[90] If the case is made out, the court will order that the landlord is entitled as against the tenant to obtain possession of the flat and that the tenant is entitled to compensation.[91]

---

84 Who will be the tenant's immediate landlord for the time being (s 57(7)(b)).
85 Section 61(2)(a).
86 Section 61(2)(b).
87 Section 61(3).
88 Section 61(1).
89 Possession must be required of the flat and not just of premises such as a garage let with the flat (s 61(5)).
90 For a discussion, on the very similar wording in s 23(2), of the circumstances where the defence might be established and the proof of intention, see 7.3.4. See also 14.3.4.
91 Section 61(1).

16.8.4 The date of termination

If the landlord establishes the case for redevelopment and the court makes an order the lease will determine on a date fixed by the court order.[92] This date cannot be earlier than the term date of the original lease – the lease in relation to which the right to acquire a new lease was exercised or first exercised[93] – and, in fixing the date, the court will have regard to the extent to which reasonable preparations to proceed with the redevelopment have been made.[94] Any immediate or derivative sub-lease will also terminate and the occupying tenant, who has a right to be heard with leave, is bound to give up possession since there will be no entitlement to statutory rights of security of tenure.[95]

16.8.5 The right to compensation

The tenant has a right to compensation for the loss of the lease which becomes payable on the date fixed for termination.[96] Prior to such termination, the amount of compensation will be as agreed between the landlord and the tenant or may be determined by the leasehold valuation tribunal. The whole or part of the compensation shall be paid into court if the court so orders.[97] There is special provision for division of the compensation between the tenant and a sub-tenant of a business lease.[98]

The amount of such compensation is the vacant possession market value of the new lease but on the assumption that there is no right of collective enfranchisement and no right to any further new lease and on the assumption of a restriction to the actual uses to which the flat has been put.[99] In effect, the valuer will be putting a market value on a 90-year term at a peppercorn rent. The valuation date is the date of determination.[100] The compensation, from which the landlord can deduct sums such as service charges recoverable as rent, is payable to the tenant whose receipt is a complete discharge to the landlord.[101]

---

92 Section 61(4); Sch 14, para 2(1)(a).

93 Schedule 14, para 2(2). It can also not be earlier than the date of fixing the amount of compensation either by agreement or as determined by the leasehold valuation tribunal (see 16.8.6).

94 Schedule 14, para 2(3).

95 Schedule 14, para 3. The same or another county court deals with any subsequent actions for possession pursuant to the order (Sch 14, para 4).

96 Section 61(4) and Sch 14, para 2(1)(b)).

97 For whatever purpose but particularly for discharging any mortgage or for division between tenant and sub-tenant (Sch 14, para 2(4)).

98 Schedule 14, para 6(2)–(3). This is because the business tenant loses the right for compensation for improvements and has no right to request a new tenancy under the Landlord and Tenant Act 1954 (Sch 14, para 6(1)).

99 Schedule 14, para 5(1). Other assumptions which may be appropriate to market valuation in a particular case can be made (Sch 14, para 5(2)–(3).

100 Schedule 14, para 5(4).

101 Schedule 14, para 7. However, payment into court may be directed (see fn 97 above) and statutory requirements as to payment of capital money have to be observed.

The court has power to revoke, vary or direct repayment in cases of unreasonable delay or default by either party and a power to restrict further applications in the case of bad faith or misrepresentation by the landlord.[102] There are detailed provisions for the payment of the compensation where the new lease is held on trust for sale and in respect of certain special categories of tenant.[103]

16.8.6 *Right to compensation cannot be excluded*

The right to compensation cannot be excluded. Any agreement relating to a lease, whenever made, shall be void insofar as it purports to exclude or modify any right to compensation under s 61.[104]

102 Schedule 14, para 8.
103 Schedule 14, paras 9–12.
104 Section 93(1)(a)(iii).

PART FOUR

AMENDMENTS TO THE LEASEHOLD REFORM ACT 1967

CHAPTER SEVENTEEN

EXTENSION OF ENFRANCHISEMENT UNDER THE LEASEHOLD REFORM ACT 1967

17.1 The 1967 Act – a sketch of the major provisions

17.1.1 The right conferred

Chapter III of the 1993 Act, ss 63–68, makes amendments to extend the scope of the Leasehold Reform Act 1967 ('the 1967 Act'). It is not possible, within the scope of this book, to give more than an outline sketch of the major features of that legislation or of the other changes made to it since 1967 but before the 1993 Act. For detailed discussion and analysis the reader is referred elsewhere.[1]

The right conferred by the 1967 Act permits a tenant of a leasehold house, who occupies it as his residence, to acquire on fair terms the freehold of that house and premises or to have an extended lease.[2] The 50-year lease extension does not of itself give the right to acquire the freehold and is subject to the freeholder's power to determine for redevelopment. It is not attractive as security for mortgagees. Despite the greater capital outlay, the right to acquire the freehold is the usual choice. The 1993 Act does not amend or extend the right to an extended lease in the 1967 Act and need not be discussed in this text.

17.1.2 The conditions to be satisfied prior to 1993

The following conditions which must be satisfied for a tenant to claim the freehold of a house are unaffected or substantially unaffected by the 1993 Act.

1 There must be a tenancy, legal or equitable.[3]

---

1 The most comprehensive study is Hague, *Leasehold Enfranchisement*, 2nd edn, 1987, Sweet & Maxwell. There are also more concise summaries in the books on landlord and tenant, the most recent being Evans and Smith, *The Law of Landlord and Tenant*, 4th edn, 1993, Butterworths, pp 346–364.

2 1967 Act, s 1.

3 Ibid, s 37.

2 The tenancy must be a long tenancy as defined.[4]
3 The tenant must occupy the house as his residence either for the last three years or for periods amounting to three years in the last 10 years.[5]
4 The tenant must be a tenant of a house.[6] This is defined as including any building designed or adapted for living in and reasonably so called, even if it is not structurally detached. However, a residence which is not structurally detached and has a material part above or below a structure which is not comprised in the residence is not a 'house' within the 1967 Act. In the vast majority of cases there will be no overlap between the 1993 rights to collective enfranchisement and to a new lease of a flat and the enfranchisement rights under the 1967 Act. This is because where a building is divided horizontally, the flats or units are within the 1993 Act[7] but are not houses.[8] Some possible problems of inter-relating the two pieces of legislation are briefly raised below.[9]

The following conditions have been substantially affected by the 1993 Act.

1 Until 1 November 1993, when the 1993 Act came into force, the house had to fall within the relevant rateable value limits on the appropriate day, as defined. These provisions are complex and need not be summarised here.[10] They remain relevant for houses which are below those limits and qualify for enfranchisement under the 1967 Act prior to the 1993 amendments. This is because the approach to valuation and the consequent price payable will depend upon the appropriate rateable value.[11] The rateable value limits have now been removed as far as the right to acquire the freehold is concerned.[12]
2 Under the 1967 Act, the tenancy had to be a tenancy at a low rent at all times during the qualifying occupation period.[13] A low rent is one which does not exceed two-thirds of the rateable value on the appropriate day. There is now

4 Ibid, s 3. The 1967 Act definition of 'long tenancy' differs in wording from the definition of 'long lease' in s 7. However, the basic definition of a term certain exceeding 21 years is the same. The relatively minor amendment to the definition of long tenancy in relation to tenancies determinable by death or remarriage (see 17.2.4) makes a similar provision for the 1967 Act as that in relation to flats.
5 1967 Act, s 1(1), as amended by the Housing Act 1974. This is the same period as the residence requirement in respect of the right to a new lease under the 1993 Act (see 11.2.3).
6 1967 Act, s 2.
7 See 3.3.4.
8 1967 Act, s 2(1)(a) – 'where a building is divided horizontally, the flats or other units into which it is divided are not separate "houses" although the building as a whole may be'.
9 See 17.5.1.
10 See Hague (above) 2–16 to 2–22, or Evans and Smith, (above) p 353.
11 See 18.2.3 and 18.3.3.
12 See 17.2.1. For the valuation approach for houses receiving the right to enfranchise under the 1993 Act amendments, see 21.1.
13 1967 Act, ss 1(1)(b), (4); see Hague (above) 3.14.

an alternative low rent test which will have the effect of giving a right to acquire the freehold where it was not previously available.[14]

17.2 The extended right to enfranchisement

17.2.1 Removal of upper rateable value limits

The 1967 Act, prior to the 1993 Act coming into force, gave a right to a tenant of a house to acquire the freehold of the house and premises provided that certain limits on rateable value were not exceeded.[15] The 1993 Act effectively removes the upper limit on rateable values so that enfranchisement is considerably extended.[16] The method to achieve this result is not straightforward but rather tortuous.[17] A new section is inserted into the 1967 Act[18] which confers upon a tenant of a house the right to acquire the freehold of the house and premises under the 1967 Act if the only reason for previous exclusion is that the applicable rateable value financial limit was exceeded. This new right is also extended to tenancies which were not tenancies at a low rent as originally defined but do qualify under the extended low rent test introduced by the 1993 Act.[19]

17.2.2 All houses acquire enfranchisement rights

The result of the amendment is that there is no longer a rateable value limit in respect of notices of desire to enfranchise and acquire the freehold under the 1967 Act given after 1 November 1993. In the last few years, fewer claims have been made under the 1967 Act as a majority of tenants who had the right had chosen to exercise them. The extension afforded by the 1993 Act is likely to lead to an increased number of claims in respect of houses previously excluded.

17.2.3 No new rights to an extended lease

Long leaseholders of houses are not given further rights to an extended lease. For this purpose, the various rateable value limits[20] remain applicable. However, it was rarely sensible to choose an extended lease rather than

---

14 See 17.3.1.

15 See previous section.

16 Section 63.

17 This is because the changes only extend and relate to the right to acquire the freehold of the house and do not apply to lease extension (see 17.1.1 and 17.2.3). Additionally, a simple removal of the limits would have made it more difficult to ensure that houses being given enfranchisement rights by the 1993 Act were subject to the new provisions as to price and compensation which mirror those for flats.

18 1967 Act, s 1A(1) by s 63.

19 Section 1A(2); and see s 65 (inserting s 4A of the 1967 Act as amended) and 17.3.1.

20 Contained in s 1(1)(a), (5) and (6) of the 1967 Act.

acquisition of the freehold for houses which qualified before the 1993 Act.[21] The lack of an extended lease option in respect of houses which receive enfranchisement rights for the first time is, therefore, unlikely to be a problem. The legislative decision not to make an extended lease available to a wider group of tenants of houses accords with the overall policy of promoting freehold home ownership.

17.2.4 Enfranchisement extension to tenancies terminable after death or marriage

Prior to 1 November 1993, certain tenancies, commonly known as those containing 'Prince of Wales' clauses, were not treated as long tenancies as defined by the 1967 Act.[22] These were tenancies which were terminable by notice after a death or marriage and granted before 18 April 1980 or in pursuance of a contract entered into before that date. The 1993 Act removes the restriction in relation to tenancies granted before 18 April 1980, insofar as acquisition of the freehold is concerned. Thus, a tenancy terminable by notice after a death or remarriage and granted before 18 April 1980[23] is to be treated as a long tenancy for the purpose of conferring the right to acquire the freehold of a house and premises.[24] There is some consequential redrafting to the 1967 Act.[25] A tenancy terminable after death or remarriage will not be a long tenancy only if the notice is capable of being given at any time after the death or marriage of the tenant, the length of the notice is not more than three months and where the terms of the tenancy preclude both assignment and subletting of the whole of the premises.[26]

17.2.5 Exclusions from enfranchisement

There are two exceptions applicable to tenancies created before the commencement of the 1993 Act[27] which would otherwise enjoy the right to acquire the

---

21 See Hague (above) 7–02 and 7–15.

22 Between 1967 and 1980, tenancies were granted avoiding the 1967 Act by making them terminable after the death of the Prince of Wales, or by reference to other Royal marriages or lives. The use of this device was terminated for leases after 18 April 1980 by s 141 of the Housing Act 1985. The 1993 amendment now permits leases containing such clauses granted before 18 April 1980 to enfranchise, thus remedying what was termed a 'blatant avoidance device' (HC Deb, Vol 218, cols 833–834).

23 Or in pursuance of a contract entered into before that date.

24 1967 Act, s 1B, inserted by s 64. This means that there is no right to an extended lease in such cases (see 17.2.3).

25 In s 3(1) of the 1967 Act (see s 64 (2)).

26 1967 Act, s 3(1) and proviso. By earlier amendment to that proviso, assignments by way of exchange by virtue of s 92 of the Housing Act 1985 were permitted without giving rise to rights under the 1967 Act. The use of this type of tenancy in genuine cases, such as tenancies to former employees for the rest of their life, is still possible.

27 1 November 1993 (see 1.2.9).

freehold given by the 1993 Act. These reflect exceptions accorded in the case of collective enfranchisement of flats. First, where there is a charitable housing trust[28] as the immediate landlord of the tenant of the house and the house forms part of the housing accommodation provided by the trust in pursuance of its charitable purposes, there is no right to enfranchise in respect of tenants of houses who would otherwise have received the right to enfranchise under the 1993 Act.[29] Secondly, the exclusion of enfranchisement in the case of property transferred for the public benefit, introduced during the passage of the 1993 Act, has been applied to enfranchisement of houses. Thus, where a tenancy obtains the right to enfranchise by virtue of the 1993 Act, a designation or a direction under the Inheritance Act 1984 will result in a notice of desire to acquire the freehold ceasing to have effect.[30]

Both these exceptions are extended so as to apply generally to tenancies created after 1 November 1993, the date of commencement of the 1993 Act.[31] This will permit the creation of new long tenancies of houses at a low rent by charitable housing trusts and freeholders of properties subject to the Inheritance Tax Act which will not obtain rights to acquire the freehold.[32]

17.3 The new low rent test

17.3.1 Rent in the initial year

The low rent test introduced for enfranchisement of flats[33] is added as an alternative low rent test to the Leasehold Reform Act 1967[34] – again only in respect of the right to acquire the freehold of a house and premises. The new low rent test is identical to that for collective enfranchisement.[35] So, for the purposes of acquiring the freehold of a house, a tenancy of any property is treated as a tenancy at a low rent in the following circumstances:[36]

---

28 'Charitable housing trust' means a housing trust within the meaning of the Housing Act 1985 which is a charity within the meaning of the Charities Act 1993 (1967 Act, s 1(3A), inserted by s 67(3)) (see also s 5(2)).

29 Section 67(2) and (3), inserting an additional exception into s 1(3) of the 1967 Act and a new s 1(3A)(b). The provision is not therefore retrospective and will not affect tenants with rights under the 1967 Act before 1 November 1993.

30 1967 Act, s 32A, inserted by s 68. See 8.5.3 and 8.5.4 for a discussion of the similar provisions relating to collective enfranchisement. For the Parliamentary history of this clause, see HL Deb, Vol 543, cols 1050–1054, Vol 545, cols 1240–1251 and Vol 546, cols 212–213.

31 See 1967 Act, ss 1(3A)(a) and 32A(1)(a), inserted by ss 67 and 68.

32 Although the right of lease extension may apply if the relevant rateable value limit is not exceeded.

33 Discussed at 3.8.2.

34 Section 65, introducing s 4A into the 1967 Act.

35 The relevant wording of s 4A(1)(a) is the same as that in s 8 (see 3.8.2).

36 1967 Act, s 4A(1).

1 where no rent was payable under it in respect of the flat during the initial year; or

2 where the lease was entered into before 1 April 1963, the aggregate amount of rent so payable during the initial year did not exceed two-thirds of the letting value of the property (on the same terms) on the date of commencement of the tenancy;

3 where the lease was either entered into on or after 1 April 1963 but before 1 April 1990 (or on or after 1 April 1990 if in pursuance of a contract made before that date) and the property had a rateable value at the date of commencement of the tenancy or at any time before 1 April 1990, the aggregate amount of rent so payable during the initial year did not exceed two-thirds of the rateable value of the flat on the appropriate date;

4 in any other case, the aggregate amount of rent payable during the initial year did not exceed £1,000 if the flat is in Greater London or £250 if elsewhere.

17.3.2 An alternative test

If this test is satisfied then a tenancy is to be treated as one at low rent for the purposes of the 1967 Act.[37] It is the rent in the initial year – which means the period of one year beginning with date of the commencement of the tenancy[38] – which needs to be a low rent. This amendment will have the effect of giving the right to the freehold of a house in cases where the rent was not a low rent because it was fixed at fluctuating levels to prevent enfranchisement but there was a low rent in the initial year.

17.4 Price payable on enfranchisement

17.4.1 'New method' of valuation applies

Where the right to enfranchise a house arises by virtue of the 1993 Act,[39] the price payable is to be determined largely in accordance with the 'new method' of valuation added to the 1967 Act in 1974[40] and contained in s 9(1A) of the 1967 Act.[41] This valuation approach is discussed further in chapter twenty-one below. However, there are two qualifications to the valuation process which apply to houses which qualify by virtue of the 1993 Act, both designed to accord substantially with the valuation guide-lines in respect of flats.

37 1967 Act, s 1A(2), inserted by s 63.

38 1967 Act, s 4A(2)(a).

39 Under s 1A or 1B of the 1967 Act, inserted by ss 63 and 64.

40 By the Housing Act 1974, s 118.

41 1967 Act, s 9(1C), inserted by s 66(1).

17.4.2 Tenants share of marriage value not to exceed one half

In determining the price for enfranchisement of a house, it will be usual to take account of marriage value arising from the coalescence of the freehold and leasehold interests.[42] Where the enfranchisement right arises because of the 1993 Act amendments, the tenant's share is not to exceed one half.[43] This ensures that the reversioner or landlord receives a minimum of one half of any marriage value, as in the case of a collective enfranchisement or the grant of a new lease.[44]

17.4.3 Compensation for loss or damage is payable

If the landlord can show a diminution in the value of any interest held in other property which results from the enfranchisement of the house, or any other resulting loss or damage which is referable to ownership of an interest in other property, then reasonable compensation is payable.[45] The loss may include the loss of potential development value in the house or premises to the extent that it is referable to ownership of the other property interest.[46] Once again, the purpose is to place the tenants of houses gaining enfranchisement rights by virtue of the 1993 Act in a similar position to tenants of flats.[47] Any compensation which is payable is to be regarded as part of the price to be paid for the enfranchisement of the house.[48] For the complete, amended text of s 9 of the 1967 Act, see Sch 15 to the 1993 Act.

17.5 The inter-relationship between the 1967 and 1993 Acts

17.5.1 Some possible problems

In a vast majority of situations, there will be no overlap or conflict between the provisions of the 1967 Act and those in the 1993 Act. The definitions of 'house' and 'flat' respectively will normally mean that residential premises will be

---

42 This is a statutory recognition of validity of the decisions of the Lands Tribunal in *Norfolk v Trinity College, Cambridge* (1976) 32 P & CR 147, LT; and *Lloyd-Jones v Church Commissioners for England* (1981) 261 EG 471, LT, which held that the valuation under s 9(1A) of the 1967 Act must reflect the existence of any marriage value.

43 1967 Act, s 9(1C)(a).

44 See Sch 6, para 4(1) and Sch 13, para 4(1); and see also 19.3.1 and 20.4.1.

45 1967 Act, ss 9(1C)(b) and 9A (not to be confused with s 9(1A)!), inserted by s 66(1) and (3).

46 Section 9A(3).

47 The provisions are similar to Sch 6, para 5 and Sch 13, para 5 (see 19.4.1 and 20.5).

48 Section 9A(5).

subject to one Act or neither, but not both. However, it is possible to postulate cases, no doubt rare in practice, where:

1 residential premises qualify as a house for the purposes of the 1967 Act but may also be a flat or a unit for the purposes of the 1993 Act;
2 situations where the premises as a whole is a house for the purposes of the 1967 Act but which contains flats or units which qualify for rights under the 1993 Act.

17.5.2 Is it possible to have a 'house' which is also a 'flat' or 'unit'?

It is difficult to conceive of a situation where residential premises were both a 'house' for 1967 Act purposes and a 'flat' within the 1993 Act at the same time. To be a flat, the whole or a material part of the premises must be above or below some other part of the building;[49] the premises cannot be a house if it is not structurally detached and a material part lies above or below a part of the structure not comprised in the premises.[50] Perhaps a 'house' could be two 'flats' since it has been held that a building which looked like a house but had separate front and rear entrances and was occupied by two families was still a 'house reasonably so called'.[51] A change is certainly possible. A building consisting of two floors, with a flat on each floor but used as a single dwelling with access between the two floors, was held to be a 'house';[52] clearly, a change to separate occupation on the two floors could produce two 'flats' for the purposes of the 1993 Act.

Can a 'house' also be a unit for the purposes of collective enfranchisement? A unit includes a separate set of premises which is constructed or adapted for use for the purposes of a dwelling.[53] Unless a narrow interpretation is given to this definition,[54] so that purposes of a dwelling means purposes of another dwelling, then a unit may also be a house if it is designed or adapted for living in and reasonably called a house. A large Victorian house may have been converted into flats and a new maisonette constructed alongside, perhaps sharing services and contributing to the service charge. If no part of the maisonette is above or below some other part of the building, it is not a flat within the 1993 Act but since it is linked to the flats and perhaps shares use of the garden it could be held to be a unit. If so, the freehold of the maisonette could be included in a collective enfranchisement – yet as a house it may have separate rights under the 1967 Act if other conditions are satisfied.[55] The problem may be solved in

49 Section 101(1) (see 3.3.4).
50 1967 Act, s 2(2).
51 *Malpas v St Ermin's Property Co Ltd* [1992] 1 EGLR 109, CA.
52 *Sharpe v Duke Street Securities NV* [1987] 2 EGLR 106, CA.
53 Section 38(1).
54 Which would be very difficult since exactly the same wording is used in the definition of a flat in s 101(1).
55 It will not have rights under the 1993 Act unless it is a flat.

practice by the maisonette being excluded, by reason of the vertical division, from any collective enfranchisement.[56]

17.5.3 Is it possible for a dwelling to be neither a 'house' nor a 'flat'?

Normally, a dwelling which is not a 'house' will be a 'flat'. Thus, it seems that a dwelling on stilts or platforms cannot be a house since a material part is above part of the structure not comprised in the house.[57] In such a case, it should be a 'flat' since it is likely to be held to form part of a building only. However, the wording and approach of the two definitions are different and it may be that neither will apply. For example, if a property let to a tenant included garages below some of the rooms of the property which had then been sub-let by him, there may be no 'house' since the garages are not structurally detached and the overhang is a material part of the structure;[58] but it does not necessarily follow that what was clearly not a 'flat' within the 1993 Act prior to the sub-letting has become a 'flat' by reason of the sub-letting.

17.5.4 Is it possible for a 'house' also to be 'relevant premises'?

Logically, premises which contain a number of flats and which are relevant premises and subject to collective enfranchisement[59] should not also be a house for the purposes of the 1967 Act. Consider, however, a case of a house which is subject to a long lease and which would qualify for enfranchisement under the 1967 Act as amended by the 1993 Act. The tenant has converted the house and let the basement and top floors as flats on long sub-leases, those leases meeting the conditions for the 1993 Act to apply. The tenant continues to live in the house on the ground and first floors. The two sub-tenants, if they are both qualifying tenants, may have the right of collective enfranchisement;[60] the resident landlord exemption does not apply since the tenant is not the freeholder.[61] The whole building may be a 'house', notwithstanding the flats[62]

---

56 The flat owners will have a financial incentive to exclude the maisonette. Alternatively, they may agree with the owner of the maisonette for the grant of a 999-year lease of the maisonette from the nominee purchaser at the conclusion of the enfranchisement in return for the maisonette owner contributing to the cost. Such an agreement would be subject to the duty of disclosure.

57 1967 Act, s 2(2) (see *Woodfall*, para 3–0960, and *Cresswell v Duke of Westminster* [1985] 2 EGLR 151, CA (a dwelling, part of which was above an archway, was a house since the demise included all the structures above the land lying beneath the archway)).

58 See *Parsons v Viscount Gage (Trustees of Henry Smith's Charity)* [1974] 1 WLR 435, [1974] 1 All ER 1162, HL.

59 See ss 1(2), (7) and 3 and 3.3.1.

60 They would take the freehold and their landlord's interest; the freeholder and the tenant of the whole might argue about who was to be the reversioner; and the tenant of the whole, not being the freeholder, does not have the statutory right to require a leaseback under Sch 9, para 6.

61 See s 10 and 3.4.2.

62 *Peck v Anicar Properties Ltd* [1971] 1 All ER 517, CA; *Wolf v Crutchley* [1971] 1 WLR 99, [1971] 1 All ER 520.

and the tenant may also be entitled to the freehold under the 1967 Act which, if completed, would bring the resident landlord exception into play and prevent a collective enfranchisement. There is no statutory guidance as to which right would prevail in such a case. Perhaps 'first in time prevails' and the first to give notice would be permitted to proceed.

PART FIVE
THE VALUATION ISSUES

CHAPTER EIGHTEEN

VALUATION PRINCIPLES

18.1 The role of the valuer

The 1993 Act gives the valuation surveyor an important role whether instructed by tenant, landlord or intermediate landlord. This may not simply consist of proffering a written valuation; in many circumstances, it will involve assisting the client through the entire enfranchisement process in conjunction with other professional advisers. Certainly, the procedure allows ample room for negotiation on price and other dependent terms. The legal adviser, for that matter, will wish to be acquainted with the valuation principles, if not the detail, as it is the price which will dictate ultimately whether enfranchisement succeeds or fails. This part of this book is written with both valuer and legal adviser in mind and attempts to strike a balance between a basic outline of the valuation provisions of the Act and excessive valuation detail.

Before examining the directions for value given in the 1993 Act, it is helpful to consider the principles behind residential valuation where there is more than one legal interest held in the property in question. These principles flow from accepted market practice and statutory intervention prior to 1993.[1]

18.2 The concept of market value

18.2.1 The definition of market value

In its simplest form, market value is the price agreed for the sale of an interest in property, assuming that the vendor and purchaser are entering into the transaction as willing parties. By definition, the use of the word 'market' implies that there is a market place for such an interest with both parties to the transaction being 'willing'[2] and that there may indeed be more than one willing purchaser.[3] The competition created by a collection of willing purchasers has a

1 For example, the Leasehold Reform Act 1967 and the Landlord and Tenant Act 1987.

2 Even in the case of an open market valuation required by a rent review clause, it has been held to be implicit to an open market valuation that a willing lessor and a willing lessee are assumed (*Dennis & Robinson v Kiossos Establishment* [1987] 1 EGLR 133).

3 See *F R Evans (Leeds) Ltd v English Electric Co Ltd* (1977) 36 P & CR 185.

direct uplifting effect upon the price, whereas the absence of willing purchasers will have a contrary effect.

Market value is often prefixed by the word 'open', and in this context it is assumed that the market place is not closed to those who may be interested in acquiring, nor restricted to persons having only a special interest in acquiring, the property in question. Open market value is the basis of valuation for most transactions in the market place and its definition is accepted widely by valuers, funders, buyers and sellers.[4]

The vast majority of residential property in England and Wales is owner occupied on a freehold basis without any intermediary or sub-interests. The open market value of these properties is dictated by a matrix of factors which can normally boil down to demand and supply. The willing vendor/willing purchaser scenario is fundamental to value since neither party could be expected to proceed if the price were lower or higher than their respective expectations. In a successful transaction, therefore, the price finds a level and the art (as opposed to science) of valuation is about estimating the level of price which would be agreed in a hypothetical negotiation but in a real market place.

18.2.2 The impact of legislation on market value

Legislation adds a third dimension to the willing vendor/willing purchaser, open market valuation sequence of events. If statute dictates that parties to a transaction be given powers as of right, it can be argued that not all the parties to the transaction are willing. The Land Compensation Act 1961 is a prime example of how a purchase of an interest in land is imposed upon a non-willing vendor, yet where, paradoxically, the cost of acquisition to the purchaser (normally the State) is at 'market value'. The paradox is that the parties to the transaction must place themselves in a hypothetical market place, being entirely contrary to the state of affairs they both find themselves in. The Leasehold Reform Act 1967 offers a not dissimilar concept and to an extent this is followed through into the 1993 Act.

18.2.3 The hypothetical valuation in the notional market place

As we shall see, the 1993 Act specifically refers to the open market in which a 'willing' seller is offering his interest. The valuer is asked to place himself in this notional market place; a task which may seem difficult given the compulsion for one party to sell his interest and the limited market place in the real world which exists for that same interest because of the existence of another person having a different interest in the same property. The ability or otherwise for the valuer to reflect market circumstances in a statutory valuation process has exercised many expert minds. The 1993 Act does not disappoint in this regard.

---

4 See the definition of 'open market value' in the Statement of Asset Valuation Practice 2, prepared by the Assets Valuation Standards Committee of the Royal Institution of Chartered Surveyors.

18.3 Valuation under the Leasehold Reform Act 1967

18.3.1 The principle behind the valuation

There are a number of excellent commentaries on the valuation approach under the 1967 Act.[5] This chapter seeks only to highlight the evolved methodology insofar as it is relevant to consideration of the 1993 Act.

The 1967 Act was drafted on the principle that the lessee of a residential dwelling qualifying under the Act should compensate his freeholder for the loss in value of the site only because the lessee was morally entitled to ownership of the building which had been put on the land.

18.3.2 How the 'old method' of valuation under the 1967 Act works

The original enfranchisement valuation method seeks to compensate the freeholder only for the lost value of the land and the income from it. The 'market' which the valuer was entitled to assume existed for the property was specifically defined[6] to exclude the tenant and his family. In a free market, and assuming that the freeholder's interest became available openly, the lessee of the house could always be expected to bid more than anyone else in order to secure the property.

The valuer is therefore faced with a statutorily imposed valuation which ignores what might actually happen in a willing vendor/willing purchaser scenario. The following example puts the valuation approach at its simplest for houses which have a rateable value under £1,000 (London) or £500 elsewhere.[7]

WORKED EXAMPLE ONE

Valuation under s 9(1) of the Leasehold Reform Act 1967

Enfranchisement of houses – 'the old method'

A semi-detached leasehold house in Tunbridge Wells with an unexpired term of 22 years at a fixed ground rent of £20 per annum. The house has a 1973 rateable value of £125. The vacant possession value, freehold, is £75,000.

---

5 See Hague, *Leasehold Enfranchisement*, 2nd edn, 1987, Sweet & Maxwell; also Baum and Sams, *Statutory Valuations*, 2nd edn, 1990, Routledge & Kegan Paul for good legal and valuation commentaries respectively.

6 Leasehold Reform Act 1967, s 9(1), as amended by the Housing Act 1969, s 82.

7 These rateable value limits were imposed by the Housing Act 1974, s 118. Only houses under these limits have the benefit of this valuation method which is particularly generous to the tenant.

Ground rent		£20 pa	
Years purchase for 22 years @ 7%	×	11.06	
			£ 221.20
Freehold vacant possession value		£75,000	
Site value @ 30%		£22,500	
Modern ground rent @ 7% of site value		£ 1,575 pa	
Years purchase in perpetuity, deferred for 22 years @ 7%	×	3.22	
			£5,071.50
			£5,292.70
Enfranchisement price		say	**£5,300**

The valuation compensates the dispossessed freeholder for his rights to receive the ground rent for the remaining term of the lease, capitalised at an investment rate of seven per cent. The sum of £221 therefore reflects the value in today's terms of the right to receive £20 for the next 22 years. The freeholder is then compensated for the loss of what would be a modern ground rent ('MGR') upon expiry of the 22-year term. This is arrived at by calculating what the site value of the house would be (£22,500)[8] and then establishing what an MGR per annum would be for that site in perpetuity.[9]

The generally adopted investment rate is seven per cent although some lower percentages of six per cent and 5.5 per cent have been used.[10] Tribunal decisions have again supported the use of these low investment rates and it has been accepted that, in practice, the amounts involved are relatively small and the adoption of different rates of return usually results in only insignificant variations on the overall enfranchisement price.

18.3.3 The 'new method' of valuation under the 1967 Act

The Housing Act 1974[11] brought a long-overdue amendment to the 1967 Act, enabling the freeholder to take into account the added value resulting from the tenant's participation in the notional marketplace for the freeholder's interest being sold. Political compromise diluted the acceptance of the tenant's bid in the case of lower value houses because this would mean a significant uplift in the

8 This method of arriving at site value is known as the 'standing house' approach (see *Farr v Millersons Investments Ltd* (1971) 22 P & CR 1055, [1971] JPL 523, LT). The percentage of vacant possession value adopted (here, 30 per cent) can vary depending on location. In central London, 40 per cent has been adopted (see *Middleton-Smith v Harrow School Road Trust* (1981) 262 EG 73, LVT). Comparable evidence will always be of assistance.

9 By decapitalising the site value at seven per cent to arrive at a modern ground rent.

10 A range of investment rates between six per cent and eight per cent have been consistently agreed by Tribunal decisions; only rarely has a Tribunal departed from this custom (see *Janering v English Property Corporation Ltd and Nessdale Ltd* (1977) 33 P & CR 523, [1977] JPL 378, (1977) 242 EG 388). Despite valiant attempts by many valuers, tribunals have been reluctant to accept current market evidence on appropriate investment rates.

11 Section 118 of that Act inserted s 9(1A) into the 1967 Act as the second form of valuation.

tone of enfranchisement prices generally. Accordingly, what has become known as the 'new method' applies only to houses with a rateable value in excess of £1,000 in London or £500 elsewhere. The 1993 Act removes the rateable value limits entirely so far as acquisition of the freehold is concerned such that any house which meets the qualifying criteria may now be enfranchised.[12]

The 'new method' of valuation under s 9(1A) has been fine-tuned since 1974 and the example below demonstrates the approach.

WORKED EXAMPLE TWO

Valuation under s 9(1A) of the Leasehold Reform Act 1967

Enfranchisement of houses – the 'new method'

A terraced house in St Johns Wood with an unexpired term of 18 years at a ground rent of £150 per annum. The house has a 1973 rateable value of £1,350. The vacant possession value of the freehold is £650,000. The vacant possession value of the unexpired 18-year lease is £225,000. Both of these capital sums are established by market evidence.

(a) Freeholder's interest				
Ground rent		£150 pa[13]		
Years purchase for 18 years @ 7%	×	10.06		
				£ 1,509
Freehold vacant possession value		£650,000		
Less risk for rights under the 1954 Act, Part I (10%)		£ 65,000		
			£585,000	
Deferred for 18 years @ 7%	×		.2959	
				£173,101
				£174,610
(b) Marriage value				
Freehold vacant possession value		£650,000		
Less freeholder's interest		£174,610		
Less lessee's interest		£225,000		
Gain on marriage		£250,390		
Share at 50%[14]				£125,195
				£299,805
Enfranchisement price		say	**£300,000**	

12 See 17.2.1, subject to special provisions for houses which obtain the right to enfranchise under the 1993 Act (see 17.4.2 and 17.4.3).

13 The ground rent may rise at periodic review. If it merely keeps pace with the level of modern ground rents, then it is not normally necessary to reflect increases in the enfranchisement valuation.

14 A 50/50 share of the marriage value is most commonly adopted but there is no direction in the 1967 Act which insists upon it, unlike the provision in s 9(1C)(a), inserted by the 1993 Act (see 17.4.2). Comparable evidence is useful.

The valuation of the freeholder's interest in the first part of the valuation is not dissimilar to the valuation under the old method in **Worked Example One**. The difference, however, is that there is no reversion to a modern ground rent, rather a reversion to the vacant possession value less an element for the risk that the lessee could claim rights of continued occupation. The 10 per cent deduction[15] is a reflection of the practical fact that few lessees of properties in the higher rateable value brackets allow their tenancies to expire. At long last, market factors such as this were able to be reflected in the statutory valuation for higher value houses.

The necessity to take into account the tenant's bid results in a 'marriage value' calculation which is seen in the example and merits detailed analysis.

18.4 Marriage value

18.4.1 The meaning of marriage value

Marriage value is the difference between the combined and separate values of different interests in the same property. The leasehold system in England and Wales admits a strata of interests in property of which only one is likely to be occupational. Each constituent part of the strata may be of worth in the marketplace even though it does not carry with it the right to enjoy physical occupation. Instead, the interest may bring with it the right to receive rent and/or the right to the reversion at the end of the lease which will then bring a significant uplift even if the occupation is still protected. The aggregate of the individual open market values of all the interests in property will rarely add up to the open market value of the property if it was subject to no other interest than the freehold and was available with vacant possession.

For example, a house freehold with vacant possession may be worth £70,000. If it is occupied by a lessee who has a leasehold interest worth, say, £40,000[16] and the value of the freeholder's present interest (subject to the occupying lease) is worth £10,000, there is a latent value in the property of £20,000, ie £70,000 – (£40,000 + £10,000). This £20,000 is known as the marriage value. The marriage value cannot be realised by either party without the co-operation of the other and it seems right, therefore, that each party should share in this released value upon merger of the interests. Often, through custom and practice, the released value is split on a 50/50 basis but much will depend on the negotiating strengths of each side and evidence of other settlements.

The amendments to the 1967 Act acknowledged the release of this 'latent' value on enfranchisement and most settlements and tribunal decisions have been on the basis of an equal share of the uplift. As we shall see, the principle of

15 This deduction was first accepted in *Lloyd-Jones v Church Commissioners for England* (1982) 261 EG 471, LT, and has broadly been adopted since then.

16 Ignoring the right to enfranchise.

marriage value is an important part of the 1993 Act, not only for collective enfranchisement but also for individual lease extension, and also in the 'new method' of valuation under the 1967 Act.[17]

18.4.2 *Market practice in the case of marriage value*

Outside the statutory framework for compulsory acquisition of freehold title, marriage value exists in the day-to-day market place. Particularly in London, the dominance of the landed estates has brought with it a common acceptance of shortening leases, privately negotiated premiums for lease extension and surrenders of existing leases, renewals of leases and 1967 Act acquisitions in the case of houses.

Until the 1993 Act, lessees of flats within blocks relied entirely upon the co-operation of their landlord for lease extension. Understandably, many landlords have seen this as an opportunity to supplement their rental income with capital payments in return for extending the term of the lease. Other landlords have taken a less co-operative standpoint, refusing requests for extensions, thus causing the wasting leasehold asset to waste still further with the consequence for the tenant of much reduced marketability.

The price which lessees have been asked to pay for lease extension has followed no accepted valuation principle. Essentially, many landlords have adopted the marriage value argument and split this latent value on a 50/50 basis. Others have required a much greater share of the latent value, including a requirement in some cases that 100 per cent of the marriage value represents the price for extension. Here the landlord exploits his dominant position, knowing that in many instances the tenant has no option but to meet the landlord's request. Opportunistic tenants, on the other hand, will realise that the landlord has little other opportunity for capital receipt other than the extension of the lease. This 'cat and mouse' game is a unique feature of the English and Welsh residential property market. Practitioners will be well-versed in the idiosyncrasies of local markets depending on whether the cat or mouse has the upper hand.

Whilst negotiation on lease extension is nothing new to those in the market place, collective enfranchisement and the ability to demand a new lease at a peppercorn rent do bring a very new dimension. The Landlord and Tenant Act 1987 which might be thought to offer some valuation evidence on the issue of tenants acquiring the freehold collectively has had limited application in the market and the statutory directions for valuation are minimal. The 1987 Act envisages that the qualifying group of tenants have nothing to rely on other than their own valuer's expertise. That Act offers tenants merely a right of first refusal and not a mechanism for acquiring the freeholder's interest at a pre-directed price. Transfers to the nominee purchaser under the 1987 Act have

---

17 See 19.3.1, 20.4.1, 17.4.2 and 21.2.

been at a price freely negotiated between a vendor and a would-be purchaser. The artificial 'open market value' as discussed earlier is not a feature here because, technically, the vendor freeholder is able to take into account open market bids when arriving at the price at which he offers his interest to the qualifying residents.[18]

The 1993 Act arrives in a marketplace, therefore, which is used to enfranchisement valuation of houses under the 1967 Act, but otherwise free to deal with lease extension and freehold sale of blocks of flats in a manner which local practice directs.

18 In practice, the price under a 1987 Act sale may reflect the fact that the freehold interest is worth more to the tenants than it is to a third-party purchaser.

CHAPTER NINETEEN

COLLECTIVE ENFRANCHISEMENT – VALUATION

19.1 The three elements of the valuation

Schedule 6 to the 1993 Act sets out, over some 13 pages, the directions for calculation of the price payable on a collective enfranchisement. The price payable by the nominee purchaser for the freehold of the premises specified in the initial notice is the aggregate of three elements:[1]

1 the value of the freeholder's interest in the premises;[2]
2 the freeholder's share of the marriage value;[3]
3 any amount of compensation which is payable to the freeholder as compensation for loss and resulting from the enfranchisement.[4]

The basic valuation direction does not make any contingency for the existence of any intermediary leasehold interests between those belonging to the nominee purchaser and that of the freehold. Separate directions are given for the valuation of any such intermediate leasehold interests and these are discussed later.[5]

The three constituent parts of the valuation of the freehold are now considered in turn.

19.2 The value of the freeholder's interest in the premises

19.2.1 A market valuation

The freeholder's interest[6] is valued at what it might be expected to realise if sold on the open market by a willing seller, but with the proviso that no special value

1 Schedule 6, para 2. The date at which no valuation is to be calculated is the date when the price is agreed or determined (see 9.1.5).
2 As determined in accordance with Sch 6, para 3.
3 As determined in accordance with Sch 6, para 4.
4 Under Sch 6, para 5.
5 Under Sch 6, para 6 (see 19.6.1).
6 The freeholder is defined as the person who owns the freehold in the premises specified in the initial notice (Sch 6, para 1(1)).

is created by virtue of the nominee purchaser or any of the participating tenants being in the marketplace and seeking to buy.[7] It is valued on the assumption of the acquisition of an estate in fee simple subject to all of the occupying and intermediary leases.[8] If they have valuation implications, the rights and burdens required in the conveyance[9] are to be assumed.[10] If an allowance on the price in the open market would be made for any defect in title, this amount is to be deducted from the valuation price.[11]

19.2.2 A disregard of the 1993 statutory rights

There is an assumption that there is no right to enfranchise and no right to a lease extension. Thus, the impact on the market of the 1993 Act is to be ignored, avoiding obvious circular arguments. However, the valuer is entitled to take into account any actual notices which have been received by the landlord in respect of tenants requiring lease extensions. Thus, except in respect of an actual existing tenant's notice under s 42 given by a person other than a participating tenant,[12] the general right for tenants to take a lease extension under Chapter II of the 1993 Act must be disregarded.[13] The intended effect of this was to exclude any addition to the value of the freeholder's interest for the prospect of capital receipts from lease extension premiums. However, it seems that the door has been left open for an additional sum to be added to the valuation, if appropriate, which reflects the value of the future right to receive capital sums from privately negotiated lease extensions which may have been forthcoming in any event before any statutory rights were envisaged.[14] An addition for this 'hope value' is likely to be more relevant in cases where leases are particularly short.

19.2.3 Disregard of improvements

The valuer is also required to ignore any increase in value of a flat held by a participating tenant which is attributable solely to an improvement carried out

---

7 Schedule 6, para 3(1).
8 Schedule 6, para 3(1)(a).
9 In accordance with Sch 7 (see 9.3).
10 Schedule 6, para 3(1)(d).
11 Schedule 6, para 3(3).
12 Which will be suspended during the collective enfranchisement procedure (see 12.2.2).
13 Schedule 6, para 3(1)(b). Since such notices are merely suspended the impact of the capital sum expected to be paid and anticipated by way of premium for the lease extension will be a valuation factor – unless, of course, the lease extension notice is by a tenant who is now participating in the enfranchisement.
14 If the freeholder's interest was offered in the market, it may be reasonable to expect some 'hope value' in addition to the value of the income and the reversion, particularly if the occupying leases are short.

by the tenant or any predecessors in title of the tenant.[15] This can be expected to generate a good deal of argument and work by the tenant's valuer in establishing what is an improvement (as opposed to a repair) and at whose expense it was executed. A central heating system will be an improvement but it may be difficult to establish by whom it was installed, especially in the case of an old system. The replacement of rotting wooden window-frames by modern double-glazed units may give an improving benefit but might be regarded primarily as part of the repairing obligation.

19.2.4 Other market assumptions may be made

The assumptions which are set out in Sch 6 are not in themselves exclusive. It is declared that other assumptions can be made as the valuer deems appropriate for determining the amount which the freeholder's interest might be worth in the open market.[16] This is an important consideration and enables, at least, some market circumstance to be reflected in this constituent element of the enfranchisement valuation. It is to be hoped, however, that it will not act as an invitation to valuers inserting multifarious assumptions which are plainly not accepted as market practice.

19.2.5 Valuing those parts subject to a leaseback

Those parts of the freehold interest which the landlord is entitled to take on leaseback (perhaps rack rented flats, vacant units or commercial units) are also to be included in this part of the enfranchisement valuation. In this instance, the value of the freeholder's interest in those premises is the difference between, on the one hand, the value of his freehold interest in it and, on the other hand, the value of his interest in it under a new 999-year lease.[17] Alternatively, the freeholder is entitled to insist on conveying the entire freehold without leaseback which may include such valuable elements as shop units. Their open market value will have to be reflected in this part of the enfranchisement valuation.

19.2.6 Transactions after 20 July 1993

In order to nullify the effect of transactions made by the freeholder which are designed to have the effect of increasing the value of the freehold, the valuer is directed to ignore certain transactions entered into on or after 20 July 1993.[18] If

15 Schedule 6, para 3(1)(c).

16 Schedule 6, para 3(2).

17 Schedule 6, para 3(4) and Sch 9.

18 This is the date the Act was passed. Transactions after that date but pursuant to a contract entered into before that date can be taken into account.

such transactions create a new interest superior to that of any qualifying tenant or alter the terms under which any such superior interest is held, then the value of the freeholder's interest is not to be increased.[19]

19.3 The freeholder's share of the marriage value

19.3.1 The freeholder's share

The second constituent part of the enfranchisement valuation is the share of marriage value payable by the nominee purchaser. The concept of marriage value has been discussed in chapter 18 and should be familiar to practitioners in the marketplace. Here, there is an attempt to put market perspective upon the enfranchisement valuation and it can be expected to be the most contentious and largest element in the price paid for freeholds. Freeholders will argue that the 'willing vendor/willing purchaser' relationship does not exist because the vendor is not willing and that through the compulsory procedure the tenant is able to derive a 'profit'.

Lessees, for their part, will argue that the enfranchisement gives the freeholder an immediate right to a substantial capital sum. In the absence of the 1993 Act, he would have had to wait until every tenant came forward with successive requests for lease extension. They could also argue, with some justification, that the freeholder is obtaining more from the tenants than he would if they were absent from the market.

The freeholder's share of the marriage value (which is to be added to the value of the freeholder's interest) is:[20]

> 'a) Such proportion of (the marriage value) as is determined by agreement between the reversioner and the nominee purchaser or, in default of agreement, as is determined by a leasehold valuation tribunal to be the proportion which in its opinion would have been determined by an agreement made at the valuation date between the parties on a sale on the open market by a willing seller, or
> b) 50% of that amount
> whichever is the greater.'

Accordingly, the freeholder will always be guaranteed 50 per cent of the marriage value and if he can show that in the open market he could have obtained more and proves this, the proportion of marriage value may be higher. It cannot be less than 50 per cent. The directions for valuation of freeholder's existing interest as part of this marriage value calculation state that it shall be on the same basis as valuation of the freeholder's interest under Sch 6, para 3.[21]

---

19 Schedule 6, para 3(5). A leasehold interest with a negative value may be so increased (see Sch 6, para 3(6) and 19.8).

20 Schedule 6, para 4(1).

21 Schedule 6, para 4(3) and see above.

19.3.2 The definition of marriage value

The definition of marriage value in the Act is not the same as valuers have become used to in other contexts.[22] Schedule 6, para 4(2) is likely to be the principal source of disagreement and is already subject to varied interpretation and disagreement as to its meaning and effect. It is therefore worth setting out in full.

> 'The marriage value is any increase in the aggregate value of the freehold and every intermediate leasehold interest in the specified premises, when regarded as being (in consequence of their being acquired by the nominee purchaser) interests under the control of the participating tenants, as compared with the aggregate value of those interests when held by the persons from whom they are to be so acquired, being an increase in value –
>
> a) which is attributable to the potential ability of the participating tenants, once those interests have been so acquired, to have new leases granted to them without payment of any premium and without restriction as to length of term, and
>
> b) which, if those interests were being sold to the nominee purchaser on the open market by willing sellers, the nominee purchaser would have to agree to share with the sellers in order to reach agreement as to price.'

Since the passing of the Act, there has been debate on the proper interpretation of important parts of this marriage value definition.

19.3.3 Is the marriage value definition defective?

It has been suggested that Sch 6, para 4(2) contains a significant drafting error.[23] The argument concludes that the form of wording will not produce any increase in value of the freehold. It is argued that the new leases to be granted at no cost to the participating tenants reduces the value of the freehold and that tenants will be able to deprive the freeholder of the share which the legislation intended should accrue to the freeholder. It is submitted that this view is erroneous and is unlikely to find favour with the leasehold valuation tribunals.

What lies at issue is whether valuers should reflect the increase (or decrease) in value of the freehold interest only when assessing marriage value, or whether it was intended that the uplift in value of the individual leases should also be taken into account. The wording of the Act refers only to the 'potential ability'[24] of participating lessees to exchange new longer leases for their existing shorter leases in the valuation of the freehold; it does not ask the valuer to value the actual increase in the value of occupational leases. Accordingly, on this interpretation of the Act it is argued that the freehold value diminishes because those lease extensions are to be assumed to take place at nil premium.

---

22 Particularly when compared with the marriage value on houses.

23 See the correspondence pages of the *Estates Gazette* between August and October 1993 (32 EG 25, 35 EG 49, 36 EG 57, 41 EG 59 and 42 EG 60 and in particular Daiches, 'Marriage Value and Flats' (1993) 9343 EG 104.

24 Schedule 6, para 4(2)(a).

19.3.4 A suggested interpretation of the statutory definition

The state of affairs and possible interpretation highlighted in the previous section is clearly not what the legislation envisaged.[25] No doubt, the early decisions of the Tribunals will provide better guidance as the issue is certain to be litigated.

It is submitted that there is a better interpretation of Sch 6, para 4(2) which not only accords with the legislative purpose but makes better sense of the paragraph as a whole. First, the wording says that marriage value is 'any increase'. The Daiches view of the meaning of the wording would always result in a decrease in value. This suggests that a different view must be found.

Secondly, the increase in value is to be found by valuing the freehold in two contrasting situations. The first is the value as it stands as held by the persons from whom it is to be acquired. This value specifically disregards the presence in the market of the nominee purchaser and the participating tenants.[26] The second situation to be valued is the freehold now in control of the participating tenants, still subject to the original leases existing when the enfranchisement commenced[27] but with the potential ability to grant new leases to themselves without payment of a premium. The valuation is to be *before* that presumed grant of the new leases.[28] Attention has been focused upon the fact that there will be no premium for such grant; therefore, it is argued, the freehold value is reduced. The better view is that the freehold has the extra value precisely because the participating tenants control it and have the ability to grant themselves new leases without payment of a premium or restriction as to length of term. The potential capital value of all those new leases exists, before the grant, in the freehold which is being acquired.[29] It is for this reason that the freehold is valued; and for this reason that the capital value of the freehold in the hands of the participating tenants will normally be higher than the value in

---

25 The Secretary of State (Mr Michael Howard) defined marriage value as 'the difference between aggregate of the values of the freehold and leasehold interests before and after enfranchisement. In other words, it represents the increase in value when the freehold and leasehold come under the same control' (HC Deb, Vol 218, col 874).

26 See above and Sch 6, para 3(1).

27 Schedule 6, para 4(4)(a). The same assumptions are made but with the vital addition that the participating tenants control the freehold and have the potential ability to grant themselves the new leases. Any merger or circumstances affecting the interest on its acquisition is to be disregarded (Sch 6, para 4(4)(b)).

28 It is to be at the valuation date (Sch 6, para 4(3)(b)). Daiches, in his article (see fn 23 above) refers to the valuation of the freehold on the basis that 'the participating tenants have granted themselves new long leases at no cost' (at p 105, col 2). This is the error in his view. The valuation is clearly directed to be of the freehold before the new leases are granted. See also HC Deb, Vol 218, col 874 where the Secretary of State referred to marriage value as the way the market put monetary value on the fact that the tenants collectively can grant themselves new leases for little or no premium.

29 After the grant, the freehold in the flats subject to those new leases will have little or no value.

the hands of those from whom it is acquired. There will invariably be an increase in value; this is the marriage value as defined and in which the freeholder is entitled to share.

The valuation examples in this chapter are based on this interpretation that the freehold interest increases in value by the same amount as the participating tenants' own interests increase. Valuers should, however, consider the marriage value definition carefully and acquaint themselves with the recent argument.

19.3.5 The problem of flats of non-participating qualifying tenants – 'hope value'

It is only the flats of the participating tenants which are taken into account in calculating marriage value. This seems clear from the statutory wording and was the interpretation espoused by the Ministers in debates on the legislation in Parliament. Although it can be argued that it is not patently clear in Sch 6, para 4(2) whether it is the increase in value of the occupational interests of the participating tenants only which should be taken into account in the valuation, the sense of the wording, which refers only to the participating tenants and their ability to have new leases granted 'to them', suggests that the potential value in leases of other qualifying tenants, arising from them either later joining the participating tenants or by taking a lease extension,[30] is not added to the marriage value. To include the value of the flats of non-participating tenants as marriage value was said not to be possible. They are not brought under the same control as the freehold and therefore no marriage value is released. A landlord could not, in the open market, claim marriage value where none exists.[31] The alternative view stresses the forced sale; in the open market, the landlord would be unlikely to sell unless he obtained an element of marriage value.

In the Parliamentary debates,[32] it was explicitly stated that 'the landlord will receive marriage value only on the flats of tenants who participated in giving the initial notice'.[33] If this is right, there is an incentive for a collective enfranchisement to proceed with the minimum number of participants. If, however, there is an agreement for other tenants to remain outside the enfranchisement but to take advantage[34] and join in later, the duty of disclosure will apply and the lost marriage value may be able to be clawed back.[35]

---

30 Where the residence requirement is satisfied.

31 See the arguments of Lord Strathclyde, HL Deb, Vol 543, col 1322.

32 For example, HC Deb, Vol 218, cols 872–877, especially col 876 (Mr Michael Howard); HL Deb, Vol 543, cols 1314–1323, and Vol 544, cols 40–51, especially col 42 (Lord Strathclyde).

33 Lord Strathclyde, HL Deb, Vol 543, col 1322.

34 An agreement will be required – otherwise the participating tenants could later decide not to allow those other qualifying tenants to join in and share their good fortune.

35 See s 18 and the discussion at 6.5.1. Indeed, it was because of the possibility of arrangements being made to reduce the marriage value by limiting the participants to the minimum that s 18 was introduced into the Act.

The doubts were raised on the question of marriage value as it relates to those flats belonging to non-participating qualifying tenants because it was feared that landlords will lose a substantial element in the price. There will normally be considerable value in the future potential for capital income from lease extension premiums[36] from non-participating tenants as and when they come forward. By negotiation or by a later participation by agreement in the control of the freehold and grant of a 999-year lease, those non-participating tenants may later obtain exactly the same position as the original participating tenants – but without the freeholder having an opportunity to receive any marriage value in relation to these flats. The intention appears to be that such value should be added to the value of the freeholder's existing interest as 'hope value', rather than in the marriage value calculation.

Where side agreements are made and disclosed as the Act requires, the valuer may add to the value of the landlord's interest the hope value represented by those agreements. The scope for real argument is whether a valuer can add hope value to the value of the freeholder's interest even where there is no agreement disclosed. It may be difficult to assume this and make an addition to the valuation in view of the explicit direction to assume that there are no statutory rights; but a valuer can argue that there would be hope value in the prospect of privately negotiated lease extensions.[37] The issue is another which is likely to be litigated; there appears to be less room in this case for the leasehold valuation tribunal to adopt a solution which gives the freeholder a substantial share of the potential marriage value in the flats of non-participating qualifying tenants.

19.4 Compensation for loss

19.4.1 Extent of the right

The third constituent element of the collective enfranchisement valuation is such amount as is reasonable to compensate the freeholder for any loss or damage arising out of the freehold sale.[38] It applies to any diminution in value to any interest of the freeholder in other property resulting from the acquisition

36 Either from premiums paid for statutory extensions under Chapter II or for agreements to join the participators in a share of the freehold and the grant of a 999-year lease at a peppercorn rent.

37 See 19.2.2 and paras 3(1) and (2) of Sch 6. The valuer must assume that Chapters I and II of the Act confer no rights and the open market is one where neither the nominee purchaser nor any participating tenant is buying or seeking to buy. This would permit a non-participating qualifying tenant being considered as being in the market for a privately negotiated lease. See HL Deb, Vol 545, cols 1676–1680, where Lord Strathclyde said (at col 1679): 'When valuing the landlord's present interests, any hope value element in the open market value of the non-participating tenants' flats is included as it is only nominee and participating tenants who are assumed not to be in the market'.

38 Schedule 6, para 5(1).

of his interest and to any other loss or damage which is referable to that ownership in other property.[39] Thus, any diminution in value of any of the landlord's retained interests would be an acceptable claim – if the landlord can prove that it results from the forced sale on enfranchisement. The loss only applies to interests in other property. Lost development value in relation to a roof void or the airspace above the roof of the specified premises in respect of a proposed penthouse flat would not give rise to compensation under this head but would, where relevant, be a factor in the valuation of the freeholder's interest.

Diminution in value of retained interests is pertinent to many of the Central London Estates which are likely to have retained adjoining property. Whether a freeholder would go so far as to argue that his retained interest is less valuable because the adjoining property is no longer in his control or management (perhaps implying that those acquiring his interest will be less commendable in their stewardship of the building) remains to be seen, but it should not be discounted. Claims under this head are more likely for lost development rights[40] of garage blocks or spare parcels of land which, for some reason or other, the landlord decides not to take on a leaseback although he is entitled to do so under s 36. It is immaterial to the issue of determining the amount of compensation that the loss or damage could be avoided or reduced if the option of a leaseback of part of the premises had been exercised.[41]

19.4.2 Valuation difficulties

The concept of compensation is perhaps easier to deal with than the other two parts of the valuation. However, proving and quantifying loss in value will be another matter. In the case of lost development value, if planning consent exists, this will make respective valuers' jobs far easier; if all that exists is 'hope' value, there is likely to be much negotiation on a fair interpretation of 'hope'.

19.5 The enfranchisement valuation

19.5.1 The date for valuation

Bringing together these three necessary parts, a single valuation can be formulated. The date of valuation is the date of acquisition of the interest, effectively being the date at which the price is determined, either by agreement

---

39 Schedule 6, para 5(2).

40 Loss of development value, defined as any increase in value which is attributable to the possibility of demolishing, reconstructing or carrying out substantial works of construction on the whole or a substantial part of those other premises, is specifically included as a kind of loss which can give rise to compensation (Sch 6, para 5(3) and (4)).

41 Schedule 6, para 5(5).

or by the leasehold valuation tribunal.[42] This is different to the valuation date under the 1967 Act, where this was taken as being the date upon which the tenant served his notice. The impact of delay upon agreement of price is therefore not an issue under the 1993 Act, although in a rising or falling market, diversionary tactics by one side or the other may be employed in an endeavour to see benefit.

19.5.2 A straightforward example

The following worked example sets out the culmination of the three component parts in as straightforward a manner as possible.

WORKED EXAMPLE THREE

Indicative valuation under proposed enfranchisement

Blocks of flats

'Straightforward case'

A 1960s-built block of 12 similar flats in Bromley. All flats have 67 years unexpired on their leases at ground rents of £50 per annum each. Flats have current values of £45,000. On a 999-year lease they would have values at around £65,000. Both capital values established by comparable evidence. All 12 tenants wish to join in the enfranchisement.

(a) *Value of freeholder's interest:*

12 × £50 ground rent	£600 pa		
Years purchase for 67 years @ 13%[43]	× 7.69		
		£ 4,614	
Capital value of reversion			
Flats will have statutory protection			
12 × £65,000 × 60%[44]	£468,000		
Present value £1 for 67 years @ 13%[45]	× .0002	£ 93	
			£4,707

42 Schedule 6, para 1(1).

43 The investment yield used should reflect market evidence. Here, 13 per cent is intended to match the yield from pre-1993 Act freehold sales.

44 In this example, it is assumed that all flats would revert to assured tenancies upon expiry of existing leases. The traditional method of valuing residential property subject to protected occupancy is by taking a percentage of vacant possession value rather than capitalising the rent. Sixty per cent is used in this example, but higher or lower percentages could be justified depending upon location and evidence.

45 A case could be argued for adopting a different yield on the reversion to capital income because it brings a quite different balance of risk and opportunity.

(b) Marriage value:[46]			
Proposed interests			
(i) New freehold	£ Nil		
(ii) New occupying leases (999 years) 12 × £65,000	£780,000		
Aggregate A	£780,000		
Existing interests			
(i) Freehold	£ 4,707		
(ii) 12 × existing leases	£540,000		
Aggregate B	£544,707		
Aggregate A less Aggregate B	£235,293		
Share at 50%		£117,646	
			£122,353
(c) Compensation:			£Nil
Enfranchisement price		say	**£122,500**

Clearly, in practice, not all the 12 flats would have identical accommodation and the valuer would be expected to reflect their individual peculiarities or amenities. Additionally, the value of tenants' improvements (if any) will be taken off the £65,000 average valuation per flat.

The marriage value calculation is very similar to the 1967 Act valuation as set out at **Worked Example Two**.[47] Here, the marriage value has been split on a 50/50 basis, producing an enfranchisement price at £122,500. This represents a cost to each of the 12 lessees at £10,208. Added to this will be sums for the landlord's relevant costs[48] and, of course, the tenant's own valuation and conveyancing costs.

By paying just over £10,000 each, the lessees gain an interest which is £20,000 more than their existing interest. On the face of it there may seem considerable incentive to enfranchise, but one must take into account that not all of the lessees may wish to, or could afford to, join in the purchase. Assuming that the pre-requisite number of tenants have elected to participate,[49] one could envisage a situation where perhaps three of the 12 did not want to acquire and yet an element of hope value would normally be attached to the prospect of

46 It is stressed that this example adopts the traditional interpretation of marriage value and that espoused at 19.3.4 and not the view highlighted at 19.3.3.

47 Set out at 18.3.3.

48 See 9.2.2.

49 See 6.1.6.

lease extension premiums from the non-participating lessees in the future.[50] The remaining nine participating lessees would therefore be paying a price each in excess of the simple pro-rata £122,500 divided by 12. How this would be funded depends entirely upon the participating lessees' financial arrangements.[51] The apportionment of the overall price between the nine participants to reflect any agreement reached as to the basis of the financing will be a task for the lessees' valuer.

Lessees will no doubt wish to consider the mortgagability of that part of the purchase price which is not directly attributable to the flat which they occupy.[52] In other words, mortgagees may not be prepared to lend what amounts to 'venture finance' on an interest over which they do not presently have a first legal charge.

In these 'straightforward cases', there is a fair chance that enfranchisement will succeed and that the appetite amongst lessees may be high. Not only does freehold acquisition bring with it the ability to extend their leases, but also control of their own destiny and the ability to take important management decisions for the benefit of their own interests.

19.5.3 Valuing more complex cases

Looking at a more complex case, the appetite for enfranchisement is likely to be vastly reduced and the take-up of individual lease extensions under the Act more prevalent. It is appropriate, however, to show the application of differing lease lengths within a block upon the valuation and, in the following example, the inclusion by the landlord of Rent Act flats in the disposal.

WORKED EXAMPLE FOUR

Indicative valuation under proposed enfranchisement

Blocks of flats

'More complex case'

A Victorian mansion block of 150 flats in Marylebone. Twenty-five flats are let to tenants enjoying the protection of the Rent Act 1977. Thirty-five flats are on leases having an unexpired term of 25 years. The remainder (90 flats) are on leases having an unexpired term of 87 years.

Average vacant values of 87-year leases are £200,000, 25-year leases are £80,000 and 999-year leases are £205,000.

---

50 The prospect of privately negotiated lease extensions with tenants with non-qualifying leases and no statutory rights may be a factor (see 19.3.5).

51 See 4.6.2.

52 The value attributable to the freehold if it contains commercial property, rack rented flats etc, or alternatively a high proportion of compensation.

(a) Value of freeholder's interest:			
35 × £150 pa ground rents	£5,250 pa		
Years purchase for 25 years @ 13%	× 7.33	£38,482	
Plus			
90 × £50 pa ground rents	£4,500 pa		
Years purchase in perpetuity 13%	× 7.69	£34,605	
Plus			
Capital value of reversion of 90 flats		£Nil	
Capital value of reversion of 35 flats			
35 × £205,000 × 60%	= £4,305,000		
Defer 25 years @ 13%	× .047	£202,335	
			£ 275,422
Plus			
25 Rent Act unmodernised flats			
25 × 160,000 × 40%[53]		£1,600,000	
			£1,875,422[54]

(b) Marriage value:			
Proposed Interests			
(i) New freehold (unmodernised flats)	£ 1,600,000		
(ii) New occupying leases 125 × £205,000	= £25,625,000		
Aggregate A		£27,225,000	
Existing Interests			
(i) Freehold	£ 1,875,000		
(ii) Lessees existing interests			
90 × £200,000	= £18,000,000		
35 × £80,000	= £ 2,800,000		
Aggregate B		£22,675,000	
Aggregate A less Aggregate B		£ 4,550,000	
Share at 50%			£2,275,000
(c) Compensation:			£ Nil
			£4,150,422
Enfranchisement price		say	**£4,150,000**

The enfranchisement price at £4,150,000 equates to a price per long leasehold flat (of which there are 125) of £33,200. The vast majority of flats in

53 Rent Act flats are valued at a lower percentage of vacant possession to reflect the existence of a 'fair rent' and the biennial reviews.

54 In the open market, an addition to this sum would normally be made for the 'hope value' from capital income on future lease extensions. Valuers dealing with the 1993 Act should make this addition if circumstances are appropriate.

this block have perfectly saleable 87-year leases which, in this estimation, only have a £5,000 differential between that and a 'freehold' value. The per unit value is so high because the lessees are having to 'carry' the £1.6 million worth of value of the 25 Rent Act flats.

Unless lessees wish to enter into the residential investment market, it is unlikely that they will acquire the block unless they seek the co-operation of a friendly residential investor. Assuming that the landlord took a leaseback of the 25 Rent Act flats, the enfranchisement price would fall from £4,150,000 to £2,550,000. This is still a price per long leasehold unit of around £20,000. If the lessees were still interested in acquiring, the minority 35 flats holding 25-year unexpired leases would have to bear a much greater pro-rata price because it is their short leases which are generating the main quantum of value. How lessees will deal with this and the inevitable number of non-participating lessees adds a complicating dimension to enfranchisement and is expected to result in low take up. This has certainly been the experience in voluntary sales under the 1987 Act. A more likely occurrence will be that many of those qualifying tenants in the 35 flats who satisfy the residence requirement will take up lease extensions. Some or a majority of those with 90 years may do so as well in order to buy out the ground rent. A collective enfranchisement at a later date will then be much cheaper as the value of many flats will have been bought out separately and acquiring the freehold may become a realistic option, especially if a leaseback of the Rent Act flats and other units can be negotiated.

19.5.4 Apportioning the enfranchisement price

The valuer acting on behalf of the tenants will normally accept responsibility for apportioning the enfranchisement price between the participating tenants.[55] This should ideally be carried out on an individual appraisal of each flat and the proportionate gain. Less precise approaches could include a split based on rateable value, service charge percentage or floor area.

19.6 Intermediate leasehold interests

19.6.1 The price payable

The existence of head lessees and head underlessees are a characteristic of many blocks of flats, particularly large ones where the head lessee has a maintenance role. Any such intermediate leasehold interest must be brought into the valuation process. They are defined as those interests in the specified premises under a lease which is superior to that of any qualifying tenant in the premises to the extent that the interest is being acquired by the nominee

---

55 Unless there is an agreement to and an acceptance of such apportionment, there could be conflict of interest issues for the professionals involved.

purchaser.[56] Where the nominee purchaser is to acquire one or more of such interests, a separate price is payable for each one[57] which is an aggregate of its value[58] and any amount of compensation for loss or damage.[59]

19.6.2 Valuation of minor intermediate interests

Many of these intermediate leases are of inconsequential capital value because they are co-terminus with the occupying leases.[60] In such a case, the 1993 Act provides for a formula based on the gilts market[61] and this will need to be followed in any case where the expectation of possession is less than one month and the profit rent in respect of the intermediate lease is no more than £5 per year.[62] If the minor intermediate lease is the immediate reversion to two or more leases then the formula is applied to each sub-lease and the value is the aggregate amount.[63]

19.6.3 Valuation of other intermediate interests

For more valuable intermediate interests, the price must be calculated along similar lines to the valuation of the freeholder's interest, subject to such modifications as are appropriate for the sale of a lease.[64] What is being acquired is normally a lease with a term of years longer than the occupying lessees term but less than a 999-year lease. In such circumstances, the value of the intermediaries' interest takes into account the normal considerations on marriage value and compensation for lost rights. Marriage value will only comprise the latent value which would accrue from the participating lease merging into the intermediary lease. For example, if the occupying leases have 45 years unexpired, and the intermediary has a headlease of 70 years, the marriage value will take into account the assumed right for the acquiring lessees to grant themselves a 25-year lease extension (70 years less their existing 45-year term).

---

56 Schedule 6, para 1(1).

57 Schedule 6, para 6(1).

58 As determined in accordance with Sch 6, para 7 (see 19.5.2).

59 This is payable by virtue of Sch 6, para 8; it is determined in the same way as compensation for a freeholder (see 19.4).

60 There will often be a nominal reversion of 10 days.

61 Schedule 6, para 7(2),(7) and (8). It is similar to that used in the 1967 Act and based on the yield from two-and-a-half per cent consolidated stock.

62 Such an interest is defined as a minor intermediate lease (Sch 6, para 7(3)). Profit rent, as might be expected, is the amount received by the intermediate lessee less the amount paid under that lease (Sch 6, para 7(5)). Expectation of possession is defined in Sch 6, para 7(9) and (10).

63 Schedule 6, para 7(4).

64 Schedule 6, para 7(1).

19.6.4 Apportioning marriage value

In calculating the intermediate interest, any marriage value will be apportioned. Where the price payable for the freehold includes an amount for marriage value and an intermediate leasehold is being acquired by the nominee purchaser, the freeholder's share of marriage value must be divided between the freeholder and the owners of the intermediate leasehold interest in proportion to the value of their respective interests.[65] It follows, therefore, that the valuer must first undertake the valuation to ascertain the price payable for the freehold in accordance with Sch 6, para 2 (which will take into account the existence of an intermediate interest), then undertake a valuation of the intermediate interest in accordance with Sch 6, para 6, but in an attempt to avoid double counting of marriage value, make an apportionment in accordance with Sch 6, para 9. It is up to the freeholder to compensate the head lessee for his share of the marriage value as so determined.[66]

19.7 Valuing other interests which are to be acquired

19.7.1 The nature of other interests which may be acquired

In addition to the freehold of the specified premises and any intermediate leasehold interests, the nominee purchaser may acquire other property. This may be appurtenant property which the nominee purchaser has chosen to acquire and which has been specified in the initial notice;[67] or the reversioner may have successfully required the nominee purchaser in the counter-notice to acquire other property which has ceased to be of practical use or benefit or would cease to be capable of being reasonably managed.[68] Such property may be freehold or leasehold.

19.7.2 Valuation basis

As might be expected, any other property which is freehold is valued in a similar manner to the freehold of the premises. The price is the aggregate of the value of the interest, any share of the marriage value and any compensation.[69] The value of the interest is determined by exactly the same valuation guidelines.[70] Any leasehold interest which is not an intermediate interest is valued in the same manner and any compensation added to find the price payable. If there is a minor intermediate lease, it is valued by the gilts market formula.[71]

---

65 Schedule 6, para 9.
66 Schedule 6, para 9(3).
67 See 3.2.2.
68 Within s 21(4) (see 6.6.3).
69 Schedule 6, para 10. These are the same three elements (see 19.1).
70 Those contained in Sch 6, paras 3–11. See 19.2 for a discussion.
71 Schedule 6, para 10(2) and 11; and see 19.6.2.

The manner of determining marriage value and any compensation for loss is likewise to be done by applying the provisions which apply to the freehold of the specified premises.[72]

19.8 Valuation of interests with negative values

19.8.1 Principles to be applied

The provisions relating to the valuation and treatment of interests in the specified premises which have negative values are drawn out and complicated.[73] It is not proposed to discuss these in full but to highlight the basic principles to guide a practitioner who has to apply these provisions.

19.8.2 Negative amounts result in a nil price or value

If the valuation of a freehold or intermediate leasehold interest, or the valuation of other property to be acquired, when all the aggregate amounts of value, marriage value and compensation are added together, results in a negative amount, then the price payable by the nominee purchaser for the freehold shall be nil.[74]

Similarly, when the value of the freeholder's interest or that of an intermediate landlord is determined as a negative amount, the value of that interest shall be nil.[75] The same principle applies to the calculation of marriage value and the apportionment of marriage value.[76]

19.8.3 Reduction in value of superior interests

Where an intermediate leasehold interest has a negative value, the value of the freehold or other superior interest is reduced in value until the reduction is equal to the negative amount in question but without reducing the value of any interest to less than nil.[77] This ensures that the nominee purchaser does not pay a sum greater than the total value of all the interests to be acquired by reason of the existence of one or more interests with negative values.

72 Schedule 6, paras 12 and 13 which apply the provisions of paras 4 and 5, with such modifications as are appropriate (see 19.3 and 19.4).

73 Contained in Parts V and VI of the Schedule, paras 14–21, they occupy nearly half the length of Sch 6. They are designed to ensure that the presence or creation of negative value leases does not increase the enfranchisement price by taking only interests with positive values into account, while negative value interests count as nil.

74 Schedule 6, paras 2(2), 6(2) and 10(3).

75 This applies for determining the value under Sch 6, paras 2(1)(a) and 3, and 6(1)(b)(i) and 7 respectively (Sch 6, para 14(1)).

76 Schedule 6, paras 15(1) and 16(1).

77 Schedule 6, paras 14(2–5) and 15(2–3).

19.8.4 Reduction in share of marriage value or compensation

If all the interests being acquired – freehold and any intermediate leaseholds – have negative values there is a proportionate reduction in the reversioner's share of any marriage value; provisions also ensure that it is any reduced value which is taken into the apportionment calculation.[78] Similarly, there is an adjustment to any compensation payable to take account of the negative or reduced values.[79]

19.8.5 Other interests with negative values

Similar provisions apply the same principles where the valuation of other interests result in negative values.[80]

78 Schedule 6, para 16(2–4).
79 Schedule 6, para 17.
80 Schedule 6, paras 18–21.

CHAPTER TWENTY

TAKING AN EXTENDED LEASE – VALUATION

20.1 Valuing a leasehold interest

20.1.1 More straightforward than collective enfranchisement

The previous chapter will have demonstrated the complexity of collective enfranchisement except in the most straightforward cases. Unless there is overwhelming support for collective action with the majority of qualifying tenants participating, the cost of acquiring the freehold may prove to be prohibitively expensive. Many residents' groups will recognise that enfranchisement of the freehold not only brings with it the benefit of the ability to grant new 999-year leases, but also the obligations of management and the potential for disquiet amongst those residents who did not join in the collective purchase. The general right to an individual lease extension, as we have seen, was a late amendment to the Act[1] and will be welcomed by all tenants and most neutral observers. Landlords, for their part, may also see this as a better alternative to the dispossession of their freehold interest. The more straightforward valuation will be an attraction.

20.1.2 The wasting asset problem

The residential long leasehold interest is a commonly occurring one in England and Wales but is unusual in other jurisdictions. It has a finite lifetime; the further it ages, the less attractive it becomes.

Unlike commercial tenancies, long residential leases have not until now had any statutory rights for renewal and in this sense it has always been regarded as a 'wasting asset'.[2] In real terms, the marketability of a long residential lease (and thus its value) declines, initially on a shallow gradient but steepening particularly when it has under 50 years unexpired. Ignoring movement in the

1 See 11.3.1.

2 Security of tenure provisions are little compensation.

housing market, a flat with a 99-year unexpired term may be worth, for example, £75,000; with a 70-year unexpired term, £62,000; but with a 35-year unexpired term, £32,000. The rapid decline in value arrives at an earlier point in the term of the lease in the provinces than in London. Why this should be so is a result of a large number of complex, inter-related issues peculiar to the London residential market.

In the provinces, the availability of mortgages is restricted largely to flats having an unexpired lease term of in excess of 50 years (25 years more than the term of the mortgage) and following the experience of the poor housing market in the last four to five years, most lenders would shy away from anything under 75 years. With many residential blocks built in the 1960s and let then on 99-year leases, it can be seen that there are a large number of flats which have unexpired terms of between 65 and 75 years. From a political viewpoint, dealing with these wasting assets was seen as a justifiable vote winner, particularly at a time when the housing market was facing difficult times. Before the recent recession, the wasting nature of shortening leases had more than been compensated for by a buoyant and rising housing market in the mid to late 1980s. Pressure from lenders was also a critical factor in the political decision.[3]

In London, shortening and short leases are a characteristic part of the market place and have been for a longer period of time than in the provinces. The historic estates have had differing policies on the grant of lease extension. In some parts of Central London, leases with a term of a decent length on particular types of property may simply not be available. Most purchasers in the market accept that if one wishes to live in a particular street, then one has to take what is on offer and, in any event, the neighbours are in the same boat.

The acceptability of short leases in London is also a function of the higher values, particularly in the centre. Shorter leases (because they are less valuable) permit entry into the marketplace at a lower value level by those who perhaps could not afford to live in that location on a longer lease. Owning a 25-year unexpired term on a lease in Mayfair may have an equivalent cost to a freehold terraced house in Clapham. Less reliance, at the higher end of the market, on traditional Building Society finance, has also assisted the short lease market. It should be noted, however, that the values of short and shortening leases have fared worse than their longer leasehold counterparts during the housing market slump as purchasers realise that falls in value through declining years will not be matched by an equivalent or better opposite force in terms of house price inflation.

The 1993 Act therefore comes at a critical time in the housing market cycle and gives leaseholders of flats the opportunity to solve the wasting asset problem. It has a cost, and this is now examined.

---

3 See, for example, the Building Societies Association Report, *Leaseholds – Time for a Change*, July 1974.

20.2 The elements of a lease extension valuation

The new lease is to be for a term of 90 years in excess of the term left unexpired on the existing lease at the date of the grant[4] and Sch 13 to the 1993 Act sets out the directions for calculation of the premium on the grant of the new lease. There are three constituent elements of the premium calculation.[5] The premium payable by the tenant in respect of the grant of the new lease shall be the aggregate of:

(a) the diminution in value of the landlord's interest in the tenant's flat;[6]
(b) the landlord's share of the marriage value;[7] and
(c) any amount of compensation payable to the landlord as compensation for any loss arising out of the grant of the new lease.[8]

Each of these composite parts will be considered in turn.

20.3 Diminution in value of landlord's interest

20.3.1 Definition

The diminution in value of the landlord's interest is defined as the difference in value between, on the one hand, the value of the landlord's interest in the tenant's flat prior to the grant of the new lease and, on the other hand, the value of his interest in the flat once the new lease has been granted.[9] The valuation basis is the same for both the before-and-after situations, except that the before valuation is subject to the existing lease and the after valuation is subject to the new lease.[10]

20.3.2 Assumptions

In valuing the landlord's interest at the valuation date[11] on the basis of an open market sale by a willing seller, similar assumptions as those applicable on a collective enfranchisement must be made.[12] The valuation of the landlord's interest prior to the grant proceeds on the basis of a sale of the fee simple subject to the existing lease and ignoring the statutory rights given by the 1993

---

4 Section 56(1)
5 Schedule 13, para 2.
6 As determined in accordance with Sch 13, para 3.
7 As determined in accordance with Sch 13, para 4.
8 In accordance with Sch 13, para 5.
9 Schedule 13, para 3.
10 Schedule 13, para 3(3).
11 This is the date the terms of acquisition are agreed or determined by a leasehold valuation tribunal (Sch 13, para 1).
12 The wording of Sch 13, para 3(2) is identical in effect to that in Sch 6 (see 19.2.1–19.2.6 for a fuller discussion of these assumptions). It is submitted that it is not necessary to postulate a sale of the freehold fee simple in the flat alone – such sales of 'flying freeholds' do not occur in the open market – but the wording of Sch 13, para 3(2)(a) may cause difficulties.

Act. Tenants improvements are to be disregarded. If there is a defect in title, a deduction can be made if the defect would result in such an allowance on the open market.[13] The valuer takes into account the effect of any intermediate leasehold interests but the value is not to be increased by any transaction entered into after 20 July 1993[14] which involves the creation of any interest superior to the interest held by the tenant or any alteration on or after that date of the terms on which any superior interest is held.[15] This measure seeks to prevent artificial transactions designed to increase the value of the landlord's interest.

20.3.3 An example of valuation of the landlord's interest

A tenant wishing to exercise his rights under the Act but having an existing lease with 60 years unexpired at a fixed ground rent of £50 per annum would be entitled to an additional 90 years, making a new lease term of 150 years at a peppercorn rent. The open market value of the 60-year unexpired term may be, for example, £62,000 and of the extended new lease, £75,000. The diminution in value of the landlord's interest would be represented as follows.

WORKED EXAMPLE FIVE

Diminution in value of landlord's interest

(a) Before				
Capitalised income value of the ground rent		£50 per annum		
Years purchase for 60 years @ 13%[16]	×	7.68[17]		
			£384	
Capital value of the reversion to tenanted value in 60 years				
£75,000 × 60%		£45,000		
Deferred for 60 years @ 13%	×	.0006	£ 27	
				£411
(b) After				
Income value: peppercorn ground rent		£ Nil		
Capital value of reversion to tenanted value in 150 years		£ Nil		
				£ Nil
Diminution in value (a) – (b)				£ 411

13 For this reason, title will normally be deduced before the terms of acquisition are agreed (see 13.5.1).

14 The date of the passing of the Act.

15 Schedule 3, para 6. Transactions entered into after 20 July 1993 but pursuant to a contract entered into before that date will be treated as one entered into before that date.

16 The comments on investment yield appropriate to collective enfranchisement made at 19.5.2. are relevant here.

17 These multipliers are taken from a standard set of valuation tables.

Here it can be seen that the 'before' valuation puts a capital sum on the right to receive ground rent at £50 per annum for the next 60 years, capitalised at 13 per cent and a reversion at the termination of the lease to tenanted value because the lessee will enjoy rights of continued occupation, but on a statutory tenancy. The 'after' valuation is effectively nil because, in the marketplace, no one would acquire an interest where all that exists is a right to receive a peppercorn for 150 years and then a reversion to tenanted value at that time. The diminution in value is therefore £411.

We have seen in chapter sixteen,[18] that the landlord retains a redevelopment right at the term dates of the existing and new leases. This right[19] to vacant possession brings with it, however, an obligation to pay compensation in accordance with Sch 14. Since the compensation payable will be broadly equivalent to the value of the interest which the tenant is relinquishing, its effect upon the enfranchisement valuation can, in most cases, be ignored.[20]

Added to the diminution in value must be the landlord's share of marriage value.

20.4 Landlord's share of the marriage value

20.4.1 Definition

The landlord's share of the marriage value is the proportion which the parties agree or the sum determined by the leasehold valuation tribunal. The share shall be not less than 50 per cent and will be more if it can be shown that more would be obtained between parties on a sale in the open market by a willing seller.[21] Marriage value for the purposes of an extended new lease is, however, calculated slightly differently than in the case of collective enfranchisement. It is the difference between two aggregate amounts.[22] The first aggregation to make comprises the following three elements.

1 The value of the interest of the tenant under his existing lease.
2 The value of the landlord's interest in the tenant's flat prior to the grant of the new lease.
3 The values prior to the grant of that lease of all intermediate leasehold interests (if any).

The second aggregation to be made is of the following composite parts.[23]

1 The value of the interest to be held by the tenant under the new lease.

18 See 16.8.1.
19 Schedule 13, para 4(2)(a).
20 Schedule 13, para 4(2)(b).
21 Schedule 13, para 4(1).
22 Schedule 13, para 4(2).
23 Except perhaps in the case of extensions where the existing lease is less than 10 years unexpired.

2 The value of the landlord's interest in the tenant's flat once the new lease is granted.
3 The values of all intermediate leasehold interests (if any) once that lease is granted.[24]

20.4.2 Marriage value – an example

If we continue to use the sample valuation figures from **Worked Example Five** above,[25] the two aggregations would appear as follows.

WORKED EXAMPLE SIX

Landlord's share of marriage value

First aggregate

(i)	Value of tenant's existing lease	£62,000	
(ii)	Value of landlord's existing interest	£411	
(iii)	Value of intermediate landlord's interest	£Nil	
			£62,411

Second aggregate

(i)	Value of tenant's new lease	£75,000	
(ii)	Value of landlord's new interest	£Nil	
(iii)	Value of intermediate landlord's new interest	£Nil[26]	
			£75,000
	Difference (marriage value)	=	**£12,589**

It will be seen that in a straightforward case such as this, the calculation is not all that complex even though it may appear so from the statutory wording. This is because, in this example, the tenant has a reasonable, marketable existing 60-year term and there are no intermediate leasehold interests. If there is only 10 years to run on the tenant's existing lease, the value of the landlord's existing interests would be greater and the value of the existing lease very much lower; the landlord's proposed interests may have some value with the overall result of a much higher marriage value.

20.5 Compensation for loss

In the same vein as the collective enfranchisement, the third constituent element of the valuation is compensation for loss arising out of the grant of the

24 These intermediate interests are subject to a deemed surrender and re-grant (see 16.2.2).
25 See 20.3.3.
26 These 'after values' are usually going to be nil values as there will be no rental income and no capital value to the reversion – unless there is a residual redevelopment value which exists and is exercisable at the term date of the existing lease in the near future.

new lease. The compensation is to be such sum as is reasonable to compensate for the loss or damage which can be shown.[27] It applies to any diminution in value of an interest of the landlord in any property other than the tenant's flat which results from the grant of the tenant's new lease or any other loss or damage which results to the extent that it is referable to the ownership of that other interest.[28]

It is more difficult for a landlord to claim compensation for the reduced control and management of the block as a whole because the freehold is retained with the benefit of all the rights and privileges in a residential long lease. If anything, the granting of new statutory long leases under the 1993 Act in a block of flats will have a downward push on the value of the remaining shorter leases, thus increasing the potential for added marriage value on those shorter leases where they seek extension. Compensation for lost development rights and other similar matters on surrounding property[29] would fall under this head of claim.

20.6 Calculating the premium payable on the grant of an extended lease

Pulling these three parts together and using the example of the flat with an existing value of £62,000 and a proposed value of £75,000, the premium payable would be calculated as follows.

WORKED EXAMPLE SEVEN

Lease extension premium

Diminution in value of landlord's interest	£411	
Marriage value share		
£12,589 × 50%	£6,295	
Compensation	£ Nil	
		£6,706
Premium payable	say	**£6,700**

The premium payable at £6,700 would result in a notional 'profit' to the tenant of £6,300 (ie £75,000 less £62,000 less £6,700). However, one must take into account the fact that the tenant is responsible for the landlord's relevant costs[30] in the matter and that, in this example, a 50/50 split has been

27 Schedule 13, para 5(1).
28 Schedule 13, para 5(2).
29 An example might be in the case of lease renewal of a top floor flat where the loss is of a chance of redevelopment of a roof space above the flat which would only be possible when the existing term of the top floor flat had expired and the lease reverted to the landlord. See Sch 13, para 5(3) and (4).
30 See 16.7.1.

used whereas a case may be made on market evidence in any given case for a greater share to the landlord.

The valuation figures at £62,000 and £75,000 have been arrived at having regard to what the valuer can obtain from comparable sales evidence in the vicinity. It may not always be easy to establish the value of the extended new lease because there may not be, quite simply, any similar leases close by. Furthermore, with particular short leases, it may also be difficult to place a comparative valuation on the unexpired term because of the lack of comparable evidence locally. The valuer will therefore have only his judgment to rely on, perhaps with assistance from a calculation of what the short leasehold flat may be worth to an investor acquiring it only for rental purposes and applying an appropriate yield.

It is also worthy of note that, since the introduction of the 1993 Act, there have already been signs of lessees paying more for short leasehold property than they would have done prior to any knowledge of the Act. This is in anticipation of the fact that the value of a short lease need not be discounted to its historic extent because of the ready availability of a statutory right to extend a lease.

For example, the £62,000 value attached to the unexpired 60-year term may actually trade in the market place at £66,000 because a lessee may persuade a purchaser of this interest that a statutory right to lease extension will enable him to acquire one at a premium of around £6,700. The difference between what the interest would be worth (£75,000) after extension and what the purchaser is paying for the flat (£66,000) allows more than enough room for payment of the £6,700 premium including an element of profit for time and trouble. The consequent effects of this are that the marriage value to the landlord is reduced and, if £66,000 instead of £62,000 were put into the calculations shown above, the premium payable for a new lease would actually reduce to £4,300.

The state of affairs highlighted above should theoretically be disregarded when valuing the diminution in value of the landlord's interest. Schedule 6, para 3(2)(b) directs that the statutory right to a lease extension be disregarded in practice. However, valuers may find it difficult to find evidence to support valuations ignoring the statutory right, because the available evidence will inevitably reflect the existence of the Act.[31]

The market for short leases existing with the knowledge of the Act is still young, but as it matures it can be expected that the comparative value of short and shortening leases will rise because of the expectation of a problem-free route to an extended new lease.

31 Particularly once the market has had two to three years' experience of the Act, and pre-Act transactions are consigned to the archives.

20.7 Valuation of intermediate leases

20.7.1 The price payable

Where there is an intermediate leasehold interest which is a concurrent tenancy intermediate between the interest of the competent landlord and the tenant's lease,[32] the price payable to the owner of that interest is the aggregate of the diminution in value of the interest and any amount of compensation which is payable.[33] The diminution in value is the difference between the value of the intermediate lease prior to the grant of the new lease and the value of that interest once the new lease is granted, in each case valued at the valuation date.[34]

20.7.2 Valuation of a minor intermediate lease

Many of these intermediate leases will be of inconsequential capital value because they will be virtually co-terminus with the tenant's lease.[35] In such a case, the 1993 Act provides for a formula based on the gilts market[36] and this will need to be followed in any case where the expectation of possession is less than one month and the profit rent in respect of the intermediate lease is no more than £5 per annum.[37] If the minor intermediate lease comprises property other than the tenant's flat, the rent payable must be apportioned to the flat to determine if there is a profit rent.[38]

20.7.3 Valuation of any other intermediate lease

A more valuable intermediate lease is less likely than in the case of collective enfranchisement. If one exists, the price must be calculated along similar lines to the valuation of the landlord's interest, subject to such modifications as are appropriate for the sale of the interest in question subject to the tenant's lease.[39]

---

32 See Sch 13(1) and s 40(4)(c).

33 Schedule 13(6); the diminution in value is determined in accordance with Sch 6, para 7 and any compensation by virtue of para 9. Any compensation is calculated in the same way as compensation for loss for the landlord (see 20.4).

34 Schedule 6, para 7. The intermediate interest is subject to a deemed surrender and re-grant (see 16.2.2). The valuation date is when all the terms of acquisition are agreed or determined by the leasehold valuation tribunal (Sch 6, para 1). It will be valued as if it was a concurrent lease (see s 101(8)).

35 There will often be a nominal reversion of, say, 10 days.

36 This is the same as that used for a collective enfranchisement (Sch 6, para 8(2),(6) and (7)). It is based on the yield from two-and-a-half per cent consolidated stock.

37 Such an interest is defined as a minor intermediate lease (Sch 6, para 8(3)). Profit rent, as might be expected, is the amount received by the intermediate lessee less the amount paid under that lease (Sch 6, para 8(4)). Expectation of possession is defined in Sch 6, para 8(8) and (9).

38 Schedule 6, para 8(4).

39 Schedule 6, para 8(1).

20.7.4 Apportioning marriage value

In calculating the value of an intermediate lease, any marriage value which is payable to the landlord will be apportioned. Where the premium payable for the grant of the new lease includes an amount for marriage value and there is an intermediate lease, the landlord's share of marriage value must be divided between the landlord and the owners of the intermediate leasehold interests in proportion to the amounts by which the value of their respective interests will be diminished in consequence of the grant of the new lease.[40] It is up to the landlord to pay to any intermediate lessee the share of the marriage value as so determined.[41]

40 Schedule 6, para 10(1)–(2).

41 Schedule 6, para 10(4).

CHAPTER TWENTY-ONE

ENFRANCHISEMENT OF LEASEHOLD HOUSES

21.1 The valuation amendments

As we have seen in chapter seventeen, the 1993 Act extends the right of enfranchisement given in the Leasehold Reform Act 1967 to all houses provided that qualifying criteria are met. Valuers experienced in the sector will already be familiar with the 1967 Act valuation guide-lines and examples of the 'old' and 'new' methods have been set out in chapter eighteen.[1]

Subject to several exceptions,[2] any house held on a qualifying lease by a qualifying tenant, notwithstanding its rateable value, may now be subject to enfranchisement by virtue of Chapter III of the 1993 Act. The principles of valuation are an extension of the existing 1967 Act rules and Sch 15 to the 1993 Act sets out the full amendment to s 9 of the 1967 Act for the avoidance of doubt. Of most interest to valuers is the new amendment at s 9(1)(c):

> 'If in determining the price so payable there falls to be taken into account any marriage value arising by virtue of the coalescence of the freehold and leasehold interests, the share of the marriage value to which the tenant is to be regarded as being entitled shall not exceed one half of it.'[3]

The effect of this amendment is to give the landlord a minimum of 50 per cent share of any marriage value for all houses which were, and are to be, valued in accordance with the 'new' method (ie s 9(1A) but does not alter the basis of valuation for houses valued under the 'old' method under s 9(1).

Another factor to be taken into account is the additional head of claim by way of compensation.[4] In the same way that the collective enfranchisement and individual lease extension provide for the landlord to receive compensation for loss of development rights, detrimental effect upon his retained land, etc, so the amendments to the 1967 Act now bring in this similar compensation if required.

---

1 See 18.3.2 and 18.3.3.

2 See 17.2.5.

3 See 17.4.2.

4 See 17.4.3.

The 1993 Act does not give houses, previously excluded by virtue of an excessive rateable value, the alternative of a right to an extended 50-lease. For this reason and the fact that they would be excluded from statutory protection at the end of the term, the valuation for houses with a rateable value in excess of £1,500 in London (£750 elsewhere) will have a slightly different valuation than those which we have been familiar with previously. The difference comes in the 10 per cent deduction normally made in s 9(1A) valuations for the risk that the tenant will claim rights under Part I of the 1954 Act to remain in property at the end of the current lease.

21.2 An example

The application of the 1993 Act amendments can be best demonstrated with a worked example.

WORKED EXAMPLE EIGHT

Indicative valuation under 1993 Act amendment to Leasehold Reform Act 1967
A large detached house in Kensington, London W8. The house is held on a lease having 35 years unexpired at a ground rent of £1,000 per annum and with a rateable value of £2,750. The freehold vacant possession value of the house would be £1,250,000, and its value on a 35-year lease, presently £650,000. Both of these sums to be obtained through comparable evidence.

(a) Freeholder's interest				
Ground rent		£1,000 pa		
Years purchase for 35 years @ 7%[5]	×	12.974		
			£ 12,974	
Capital value of reversion to freehold vacant possession value		£1,250,000		
Deferred for 35 years @ 7%	×	.0936		
			£117,000	
				£129,974
(b) Marriage value				
Freehold vacant possession value		£1,250,000		
Less freeholder's interest		£ 129,974		
Less lessees's interest		£ 650,000		
Gain on marriage		£ 470,026		
Share at 50%				£235,013

5 It is unclear at this stage whether tribunals will continue their disposition towards investment yields between six and eight per cent.

(c) Compensation		£Nil
		£364,987
Enfranchisement price	say	**£365,000**

21.3 The potential profit

An enfranchisement price of £365,000 would give an enfranchising lessee a 'profit' of £235,000. It follows that the higher the value of the property, the greater the profit element to the lessee. These large amounts of profit on high value houses can be expected to lead to an increase in the comparative value of short leases. The £650,000 valuation which was obtained from comparable evidence for **Worked Example Eight** above may rise, thus closing the marriage value gap as vendors become less reluctant to allow their purchasers an instant 'profit' once they have satisfied the residency requirement.

One can understand how this amendment to the 1967 Act has been greeted by lessees and strongly objected to by the small number of landlords in the market who have an interest in leasehold houses at the higher end of the value spectrum.

PART SIX

PROCEDURAL, CONSEQUENTIAL AND MISCELLANEOUS PROVISIONS

CHAPTER TWENTY-TWO

PROCEDURAL MATTERS

22.1 Notices

22.1.1 Form of the notice

The procedures for collective enfranchisement and for obtaining a lease extension depend on commencement by notice with a counter-notice in response.[1] Apart from the obvious need for any such notice to be in writing,[2] there are currently no requirements as to the form of such notices. They may be sent by post[3] but this is permissive and not mandatory. Personal delivery of the notice will suffice. It may be advisable to post notices given under the 1993 Act using the recorded delivery service which will provide evidence of delivery where necessary. No doubt it will also be common practice to ask the recipient to acknowledge receipt and provide a copy of the notice to be signed and returned as evidence that the intended recipient has the notice.

Although there is a statutory power for the Secretary of State to prescribe the form of any notice required or authorised to be given including the particulars which the notice must contain,[4] no regulations have been made[5] nor are there apparently any plans to do so at present.

22.1.2 Signing the notice

As has been noted, an initial notice under s 13 must be signed by every qualifying tenant who gives the notice and a tenant's notice under s 42 seeking a lease extension must be signed by the tenant by whom it is given.[6] Personal signature is more likely to bring to the attention of the tenant the commitment involved in proceeding and prevents, in a collective enfranchisement, any

---

1 For the statutory requirements as to content of such notices see 6.1.10 and 13.1.2 respectively.

2 Section 99(1)(a).

3 Section 99(1)(b).

4 Section 99(6).

5 Neither at the date the 1993 Act came into force (1 November 1993) nor at the date when this text states the law. Prescribed forms are said to be inconsistent with current policy to deregulate as far as possible.

6 Section 99(5)(a) (and see 6.1.8 and 13.1.1).

attempt to use the name of qualifying tenants without their knowledge and agreement. The potential liability for costs will no doubt be drawn to the attention of clients at this time. The only substitute for personal signature of these notices would be under a power of attorney.

Any other notice by any tenant or tenants must be signed by or on behalf of the tenant by whom it is given.[7] There are no specific provisions relating to the signing of counter-notices or other notices by a landlord or the reversioner.

22.1.3 *Address for service*

Notices by a tenant to an immediate landlord in respect of premises which are subject to the Landlord and Tenant Act 1987[8] may be validly given to the address furnished by the landlord[9] unless a different address in England and Wales has been subsequently notified.[10] An initial notice, tenant's notice and all counter-notices must contain an address at which notices may be given. Thereafter, notices can be validly given to that address unless and until a new address is notified by written notice.[11] These provisions also apply to any notices in proceedings before the court or the leasehold valuation tribunal.[12]

22.2 County court jurisdiction

22.2.1 *The extent of the jurisdiction*

All jurisdiction which the 1993 Act confers on a court is exercised by a county court, which will be the county court in whose area the premises concerned are situate. This jurisdiction extends not only to any jurisdiction expressly conferred on a court but also to any question arising under or by virtue of the Act which is not one expressed to fall within the jurisdiction of a leasehold valuation tribunal.[13]

22.2.2 *Power to join proceedings*

Where county court proceedings are brought under the Act, other proceedings may be joined even if those other proceedings would otherwise be outside the

---

7 Section 99(5)(b). Solicitors or agents should expressly state that the notice is given on behalf of the tenant or tenants by whom it is given.

8 This will be most premises since the 1987 Act applies to premises which consist of or include a dwelling held under a tenancy outside the Landlord and Tenant Act 1954 (1987 Act, s 46).

9 By due notification under s 48; or, if this has not been done, to the address given in the latest rent demand by virtue of s 47.

10 Section 99(3).

11 Section 99(2).

12 Section 99(4).

13 Section 90(1) and (2).

county court's jurisdiction. There is a similar power in respect of the High Court; the High Court has no original jurisdiction under the Act but does have jurisdiction to hear and determine any proceedings which are joined to others where the High Court does enjoy jurisdiction.[14]

22.2.3 *New county court rules*

With regard to most applications to be made, existing county court rules cover the procedure to be adopted. Thus, an application to court will be covered by CCR Ord 3, r 4 which sets out the procedure to be followed, including the documents which must be filed. Service of any court application will normally be posted by court staff under CCR Ord 7.

It is understood that new rules will be made to cover applications where the landlord cannot be found.[15] These will be contained in amendments to CCR Ord 43, r 14 which already cover similar applications under the Landlord and Tenant Acts. A new sub-paragraph will be inserted.[16]

Payments into court may be required under the Act.[17] The procedure will be governed by amendments to CCR Ord 49 which already deal with payments into court under the Leasehold Reform Act 1967; the amendments will extend the procedure to the 1993 Act. In outline, the procedure is as follows.

1 The tenant files an affidavit with the court which made the vesting order or the court for the district where the premises are situate stating the reasons for the payment, with supporting details of the property and the name of the landlord.
2 The court gives notice to the landlord and any other relevant person of the proposed payment in.

Finally, CCR Ord 49, r 8(3) will be amended to prescribe the procedure when proceedings are transferred by the county court to the leasehold valuation tribunal[18] and will be based on the analogous procedure under the Leasehold Reform Act 1967. Notice of the transfer is given by the court to all parties and copies of all relevant documents are sent to the tribunal.

22.2.4 *Power to approve new leases*

There may be cases where a tenant, with the right to a new lease, is willing to accept a new lease on terms which restrict his statutory rights. The court is given power to approve a new lease where the terms exclude or modify the

---

14 Section 90(4) and (3).

15 Under s 26(3) (see 7.8.1 and 14.7.1).

16 It is understood that the necessary amendments will be made to the CCR in early 1994. The court has no discretion to refuse the landlord's application to be joined as a party.

17 By virtue of ss 27(3), 51(3) and Sch 8, para 4.

18 Under s 91(4) (see 22.3.3).

entitlement to participate in a later collective enfranchisement or the right to acquire a further lease under the Act.[19]

22.3 Jurisdiction of leasehold valuation tribunals

22.3.1 Constitution

The jurisdiction conferred on a leasehold valuation tribunal is to be exercised by a rent assessment committee constituted under the 1993 Act.[20] This follows the pattern set under the 1967 Act.[21] At least one member of the tribunal will be a chartered surveyor, valuer or other person with experience in the valuation of land.[22] When determining matters under the 1993 Act, there are no statutory restrictions which limit the determination to within the figures and submissions of the parties. Thus, as under the 1967 Act[23] a leasehold valuation tribunal does not have to rely upon the evidence presented; it may use its own knowledge and experience, giving the parties the opportunity to comment on additional evidence or other valuation approaches which the tribunal intends to adopt.[24]

22.3.2 Extent of the jurisdiction

A leasehold valuation tribunal's work under the 1993 Act extends beyond valuation matters, although all valuation issues are included. The most important task of the tribunal will be to determine the terms of acquisition, where they cannot be agreed, of any new lease or freehold acquired by collective enfranchisement.[25] This will not just be the amount of any purchase price or premium but also, in a collective enfranchisement, the nature and extent of the freehold to be acquired, the rights to be granted over any property, the apportionment of conditions where a reversionary interest is severed and the provisions to be contained in any conveyance. In the case of lease renewal, all the terms to be contained in the lease are subject to the tribunal's jurisdiction. It is specifically provided that the tribunal may determine that the extent of the property to be acquired by enfranchisement or lease renewal is to be less extensive than that specified in an initial notice or tenant's notice.[26]

---

19 Section 93(4)–(6). See also 16.3.2. Such a lease must comply with most of the provisions governing the grant of any new lease unless express provision to the contrary is made (s 93(8)).

20 Sections 91(1) and 101(1). It is to be known as a leasehold valuation tribunal (s 91(3)).

21 Housing Act 1980, s 142(1). See also the Landlord and Tenant Act 1987, ss 13 and 31.

22 Housing Act 1980, Sch 22, para 1, applied by s 91(10). In practice, another member is usually a lawyer and the third a lay person.

23 See Hague, *Leasehold Enfranchisement*, 2nd edn, 1987, Sweet & Maxwell, 16–08.

24 *British Petroleum Pension Trust v Blake* (1982) 264 EG 721, LT.

25 Section 91(2) (a). For the definition of terms of acquisition in a collective enfranchisement or lease renewal respectively, see ss 24(8) and 48(7).

26 Section 91(9).

The tribunal will also determine[27] the terms of any leaseback[28] and any extra sum payable after a breach of the duty of disclosure.[29] The amount of the relevant costs payable is also a matter for the tribunal and not the court, including the extent of liability on a withdrawal or deemed withdrawal; and the apportionment of costs or any other amount is within the remit of the tribunal. The actual costs incurred in relation to the leasehold valuation proceedings are not recoverable by any court order.[30]

22.3.3 *Transfer of proceedings*

Whenever in any proceedings before the court there is a question or issue within the jurisdiction of a leasehold valuation tribunal, the determination of that question is to be transferred to the tribunal by the court. The remaining proceedings can be adjourned or disposed of and the decision of the tribunal may be given effect to by court order if it relates to any matter to be determined by the court.[31]

22.3.4 *Procedure*

The procedure before a leasehold valuation tribunal is governed largely by the Rent Assessment Committee (England and Wales) (Leasehold Valuation Tribunal) Regulations 1993[32] and applications must comply with these regulations.[33] These regulations replace the 1981 Regulations[34] and apply to proceedings before a tribunal under the 1967, 1987 and 1993 Acts.[35] Reference should be made to those regulations for the details of the procedure to be followed. Practitioners familiar with the superseded regulations will find that the provisions are substantially repeated in the 1993 Regulations. The main difference is in Sch 1 relating to the particulars to be included in any application. Instead of a series of statutory forms being prescribed, Sch 1 only lists the particulars which must be included in an application. In other aspects, the procedure will be the same. The provisions as to the hearing, non-appearance, inspection of the property, adjournments and recording the decision are, in substance, the same except that 21 days' notice of the hearing

27 Section 91(2)(b)–(e).
28 Under s 36 and Sch 9 (see 9.5).
29 Under s 18(2) (see 6.5.3).
30 Section 91(8) and see 9.2.4 and 16.7.1.
31 Section 91(4). See 22.2.3 for the amendment to the CCR, under the power in s 91(5), prescribing the procedure for such transfers.
32 SI 1993/2408, set out in Appendix 3 below and in force on 1 November 1993.
33 Section 91(6).
34 SI 1981/271, revoked as from 1 November 1993.
35 Applications covered are those under the Leasehold Reform Act 1967, s 21, the Landlord and Tenant Act 1987, ss 13 and 31, as well as collective enfranchisement and the grant of a new lease under the 1993 Act.

must now be given.[36] Hearings will normally be in public[37] and parties can appear by counsel, a solicitor or by any other person authorised to appear.[38] Before the hearing, the tribunal must take all reasonable steps to ensure that copies of all documents received from one party are supplied to the others and that any document the tribunal has as a result of its own enquiries are supplied to all parties.[39] The rule that the decision must contain no reference to the decision being by a majority or the opinion of a minority has been dropped from the new regulations.[40]

In a collective enfranchisement the nominee purchaser is the party to the proceedings and the parties cannot include the participating tenants.[41]

Where a matter is referred to the tribunal, the tribunal may, by notice in writing served on the tenant or landlord, nominee purchaser or superior landlord,[42] require the recipient to give to the tribunal within a specified period of not less than 14 days such information as the tribunal may reasonably require.[43]

22.3.5 Costs and appeals

There is no power for the tribunal to make an order for costs, nor does the liability for paying the landlord's costs extend to costs before a tribunal, nor are they recoverable by order of any court.[44] Each party must bear its own costs. An appeal lies from a decision of the leasehold valuation tribunal to the lands tribunal only.[45]

22.3.6 Jurisdiction in respect of Crown leases

Although leases with a Crown interest are exempt from the Act[46] it has been indicated that in many cases a collective enfranchisement or new lease will be offered where, but for the Crown interest, the tenant or tenants would be

---

36 SI 1993/2408, reg 5(2); previously it was 14 days.
37 Ibid, reg 5(5).
38 Ibid, reg 6.
39 Ibid, reg 9.
40 See ibid, reg 11; it would seem that the decision, which must contain the reasons, may now refer to these matters but need not do so.
41 Section 91(7); the reversioner will be a party and other relevant landlords can choose to be separately represented (see 5.9.2 and Sch 1, para 7(1)(b)). A relevant landlord can require by notice that the reversioner applies to the tribunal to determine the terms of acquisition of any interest of that landlord (Sch 1, para 7(3)).
42 Which will include the reversioner.
43 Housing Act 1980, Sch 22, para 7 applied and extended by s 91(10) and (11)(a). Such notice must contain a statutory statement of the fine payable in the event of non-compliance (SI 1993/2408, reg 13).
44 Sections 33(5), 60(5) and 91(8).
45 Housing Act 1980, Sch 22, para 2 applied by s 91(10), which prohibits an appeal or case stated to the High Court.
46 See 3.4.7 and 11.3.3.

entitled under the Act. In such cases, where a leasehold valuation tribunal would have had jurisdiction, all parties can agree that the issue be determined by the tribunal. The Act accords jurisdiction in such cases.[47]

22.4 Orders becoming final

It will frequently be necessary to calculate when an order or decision of the court or leasehold valuation tribunal 'becomes final' since the next stage of the procedure may be calculated from that date. The Act provides[48] that if an order is not appealed against, the order is treated as becoming final on the expiry of the time for bringing an appeal. If an appeal is made and is not successful, the decision becomes final when the appeal is determined – unless there is a right of further appeal, in which case the decision becomes final when the time-limit for any further appeal expires. If an appeal is abandoned or otherwise ceases to have effect, the order or decision appealed against becomes final at that time.

22.5 Enforcement of obligations

The court has a residual power where any person has defaulted on their obligations under the Act. First, a notice must be served on the person in question requiring the default to be made good. If there is no compliance within a period of 14 days, application to the court can be made. The court then has power to order that the default be made good within such time-limit as the court specifies.[49]

---

47 Section 88.
48 Section 101(9).
49 Section 92.

CHAPTER TWENTY-THREE

ESTATE MANAGEMENT SCHEMES

23.1 Context

23.1.1 Background

In a considerable number of cases, a large number of separate premises containing flats will be held from a common landlord as part of an estate. This is particularly true in London but such estates are found elsewhere in England and Wales. In the case of leasehold houses, a large majority were probably held as part of an estate at the time of the enactment of the Leasehold Reform Act 1967 ('the 1967 Act') which introduced the concept of the retention of management powers by the common landlord of an estate area. This was done for the general benefit of the residents of the area to enable a continuing unified system of management after enfranchisement of houses. This is achieved at a cost to any individual who secured the freehold of a house, where a management scheme is in place, of control on the use or redevelopment of the property and the imposition of obligations for maintenance, repair and appearance.

The precedent of the 1967 Act is not the only reason for the provision for the establishment of estate management schemes under the 1993 Act. Considerable concern was expressed in Parliament on the impact of collective enfranchisement and the right to a new lease on the appearance and future of the estates. It was thought that there was a real risk not only that exercise of these rights would be detrimental to the appearance of an area but that a scheme which merely permitted the former common landlord to set up a management scheme might be inadequate. The new rights given by the 1993 Act could eventually and rapidly result in a landlord losing all or most of the investment interest[1] in the estate and there would therefore be little incentive for an estate management scheme to be set up or, if set up, to be continued by the landlord. The concept of an estate management scheme in the 1993 Act therefore builds on the principles applied under the 1967 Act but the procedure is different and there are greater powers for persons and bodies other than the

1 See 2.3.1.

former common landlord.[2] Although, perhaps, a majority of flats will not be in an area where a scheme would be appropriate, there will be considerable scope for the establishment of schemes in areas covered by the historic estates.

23.1.2 Main features of estate management schemes

The procedure for establishing an estate management scheme differs substantially from the approach of the 1967 Act. However, since both the 1967 and 1993 Acts have time-limits dating from the enactment of the legislation for an application to establish a scheme, the 1967 Act procedure is now obsolete.[3] The basis on which a scheme may be approved and the contents and obligations of a scheme once established are much more similar to the 1967 Act.

The main features of an estate management scheme under the 1993 Act are as follows.

1 Application for the approval of a scheme is submitted to a leasehold valuation tribunal.[4]
2 Application can be made in the first instance by the common landlord or by two landlords of neighbouring areas. If, however, no application is made or scheme established within the time limit, there is a further short period when a local planning authority or the Historic Buildings and Monuments Commission can separately or jointly apply to establish a scheme.
3 A scheme can only be approved if the leasehold valuation tribunal is satisfied that it is in the general interest for the landlord to retain powers of management in order to maintain adequate standards of appearance and amenity and regulate redevelopment.
4 A proposed scheme must be extensively advertised and interested persons served with notice of the application. There is a right for interested persons to appear before and make representations to the tribunal.
5 Existing estate management schemes under the 1967 Act can be amended by the tribunal to extend it to property enfranchised under the 1993 Act.

---

2 The intention on estate management schemes was to reintroduce the provisions of s 19 of the 1967 Act, but with improvement, particularly a more simplified procedure. The aim was to ensure that schemes were no more onerous than under the 1967 Act, while allowing positive covenants to be enforced without frustrating enfranchisement (HL Deb, Vol 545, cols 1713–1714). See also HC Deb, Standing Committee B, cols 271–286, 26 November 1992, especially col 273.

3 Under the 1967 Act, establishment of a scheme originally had to be by application to the Minister for a certificate before 1 January 1970; in relation to an area comprising property in the increased rateable value limits, the time-limit was extended to 31 July 1976.

4 This is a more straightforward procedure than the two-stage process under the 1967 Act of applying first to the Minister for a certificate and then to the High Court for approval.

23.2 The scope of estate management schemes

23.2.1 *Definition*

The term 'estate management scheme' is the title given to a scheme approved by a leasehold valuation tribunal for a defined area which is occupied directly or indirectly under leases held from one landlord.[5] It is designed to secure that the landlord retains powers of management in respect of enfranchised property[6] and have rights against the house or premises arising from the exercise of the powers of management.[7] A scheme can be made to extend to property where the landlord's interest is disposed of without formal enfranchisement procedures under the 1993 or 1967 Act (as extended) and so facilitate disposals of the freehold to tenants which are negotiated without statutory formality.[8]

23.2.2 *Contents*

Although the content of any particular scheme will depend on the circumstances, any scheme may provide for all or any of the following matters.[9]

1 Regulating the redevelopment, use or appearance of property in which tenants have acquired the landlord's interest.[10] If the approach under the 1967 Act is followed, requirements to submit plans and pay landlord's surveyor's costs will be permitted but any consents required from a landlord for redevelopment will be subject to the proviso that consent must not be unreasonably withheld. Use restrictions, particularly to residential use only, can be included in a scheme even if the conveyance of the freehold contained restrictive covenants in similar form. In appropriate cases, schemes are likely to include detailed restrictions regulating appearance and alterations.
2 Imposing on owners or occupiers obligations to carry out works of maintenance, repair, renewal or replacement in relation to the property[11]

5 The only other property which can be included is property occupied by the landlord or by his licencees or presently unoccupied.
6 This will either be a 'house' where the freehold is acquired by the extended rights given by the 1993 Act (see 17.2) or 'premises' which have been collectively enfranchised (s 69(a) and (b)).
7 Section 69(1)(i) and (ii).
8 Section 69(6).
9 Section 69(2) and (3). The wording of s 69(3) is very similar to that in the Leasehold Reform Act 1967, s 19(8) and the decisions reported on schemes established under the 1967 Act will undoubtedly be used as guidance by a tribunal under the 1993 Act. See Hague, *Leasehold Enfranchisement*, 2nd edn, 1987, Sweet & Maxwell, 10–15 to 10–24 for a very full and helpful discussion of both reported and unreported cases.
10 A proposed right of repurchase for development purposes was not within the identical wording of s 19(8)(a) of the 1967 Act (*Re Calthorpe Estate, Birmingham* (1973) 26 P & CR 120).
11 Under the 1967 Act, it was held that such obligations must be limited to the external or internal structural parts of the property (*Re Sherwood Close (Barnes) Management Co's Application* [1972] Ch 208).

they use or enjoy or an obligation to pay a charge for costs incurred by the landlord.[12]

3 Empowering the landlord to do works of maintenance, repair, renewal or replacement if the scheme is not complied with.[13]

4 Providing for inspection by the landlord and for recovery of any sums due by means of a charge on the property; in the enforcement of any charge, the landlord has mortgagee powers.[14]

5 Making different provision for different parts of the area of the scheme.

An estate management scheme must make provision for variation or termination and for excluding part of the area in the event of a change of circumstances. Such changes may be possible by or with the approval of the leasehold valuation tribunal.[15]

23.2.3 Transfer of management powers

A scheme, once established, does not terminate if a landlord disposes of the remaining interest in the property within the area. Consequently, it must always be possible to identify from the scheme who is to be treated as the landlord. To cover the real possibility that a landlord may wish to relinquish the management powers, a scheme must make provision for transfer. This may be to a local authority, or any other body, including one established for that very purpose.[16] The process of transfer can be regulated by the scheme and a leasehold valuation tribunal can be required to either effect or approve a transfer.[17]

23.3 Establishment of a scheme

23.3.1 Application for approval – procedure

A scheme is established by application to a leasehold valuation tribunal for

12 This does not empower the creation of accumulation or sinking funds to cover anticipated expenditure. An attempt to permit such funds was defeated (See HC Deb, Vol 545, cols 1716–1722, the Government Minister, Lord Strathclyde, arguing that it would perpetuate the landlord and tenant relationship in respect of service charges).

13 This may be a straightforward default power or the operation of any provisions of the scheme can be made conditional on the landlord doing these works or providing services or amenities of any description.

14 This will mean powers to take possession, of sale and leasing and of appointing a receiver under the Law of Property Act 1925, ss 99–101. Hague (above) points out (at 10–21, p 214) that where the scheme includes such a charge and provision there may be difficulties in obtaining advances from a building society on properties subject to such a potential charge. He suggests a proviso which postpones any charge under the scheme to any other mortgage or charge created before the charge under the scheme has arisen. See *Re Abbots Park Estate (No 2)* [1972] 1 WLR 1597.

15 Section 69(2).

16 References to a landlord, therefore, include a local authority or body who has taken a transfer of rights and powers under a scheme (s 69(7)).

17 Section 69(4) and (5).

approval made either by the landlord or by two or more persons as landlords of neighbouring areas or a representative body. Application must be made within a period of two years of the 1993 Act coming into force, namely by 31 October 1995; in practice, application needs to be made before the completion of the first enfranchisement and may be 'triggered' by the first application by a tenant.[18]

An application will not be considered unless there has been adequate notice to interested persons.[19] Although the section permits such notice by advertisement or otherwise, on similar wording under the 1967 Act the Minister usually required notice to each of the tenants by post. It is thought that the tribunals are likely to adopt a similar attitude. It is provided that each local planning authority within whose area any part of the scheme falls and, for schemes in England, the Historic Buildings and Monuments Commission, are persons interested.[20] Notices should be given to them as well as to the tenants, together with such other advertisements which are appropriate in a particular case. The notices must set out the provision intended to be made by the scheme and invite representations to the tribunal.[21] A tribunal must afford to persons who have made representations an opportunity to appear and address the tribunal when the application is being considered.[22]

23.3.2 Basis of approval

A leasehold valuation tribunal will not approve a scheme unless it is satisfied that, to maintain adequate standards of amenity and appearance and to regulate future development, it is in the general interest that the landlord should retain powers of management and have the rights as proposed. In making its decision, a tribunal is to pay regard primarily to the likely benefits resulting from the scheme to the area as a whole and the extent that it is reasonable to impose, to achieve those benefits, obligations on the tenants acquiring the freehold. In balancing these two primary considerations a tribunal is also to have regard to past development and present character of the area, to architectural or historic considerations, to neighbouring areas and to any other general circumstances.[23]

A tribunal can approve a scheme as originally submitted or with modifications to the extent of the area or to the provisions contained in it. Such modifications must be proposed or agreed to by the applicant. Approval will be given if the scheme appears to be fair and practical and not to give the landlord

---

18 Sections 70(1), 71(1) and (3).

19 Section 70(4).

20 Section 70(5). See s 70(14) for the definition of local planning authority.

21 This is within a time-limit which appears to the tribunal to be reasonable.

22 Section 70(6).

23 Section 70(2) and (3). In requiring that the tribunal 'shall' have regard to these matters, it was hoped that heritage matters would be given proper consideration (HL Deb, Vol 545, col 1714 and Vol 544, col 136).

a degree of control out of proportion to that previously exercised or required for the purposes of the scheme.[24] From similar wording under the 1967 Act, it is clear that although a scheme must broadly reflect the existing lease provisions, suitable new powers of management can be included provided they are not out of proportion to those previously exercised and a scheme does not need to be perfect to be considered fair and practical.[25] Once approved, a scheme can and should be registered as a local land charge; once registered a scheme becomes enforceable against the owners and occupiers of the property to which it relates.[26]

23.3.3 Refusal of approval

A tribunal can declare that no scheme can be approved for the area after due consideration of the matters to which it is to have regard and the provision which it is practical to make. The only other basis for dismissing the application apart from making such a declaration is if the applicant is unwilling to agree a suitable scheme or is not proceeding with the matter with due dispatch.[27]

23.3.4 Application by two or more landlords

An application by two or more landlords of neighbouring areas can be approved where the tribunal decides that the joint area could have been treated as a single unit if there had been a common landlord and if it is satisfied that the joint applicants are willing to co-operate in management and administration. On approval of such a joint scheme, conditions for securing co-operation can be inserted into the scheme.[28]

23.3.5 Application by a representative body

Application can also be made for approval of a scheme by a representative body, either alone or, more likely, jointly with the landlord or two or more landlords of adjoining areas.[29] A representative body is one which represents the interest of owners and occupiers within the area and tenants who are entitled to acquire the interest of their landlords or any body which appears suitable to the tribunal. A scheme can confer on a representative body the rights

24 Section 70(7) and (8).

25 *Re Dulwich College Estate's Application* (1973) 231 EG 845.

26 Section 70(11) and (12)(a). The provisions for compensation for non-registration in s 10 of the Local Land Charges Act 1975 do not apply (s 70(13)).

27 Section 70(9) and (10). There is similar provision in s 19(4) of the 1967 Act; Hague (above) comments (at 10–13, p 208) that a declaration leading to dismissal did not occur in practice in applications to the High Court under that Act.

28 Section 71(1) and (2).

29 Section 71(3). With leave of the tribunal, an existing application can be proceeded with by a representative body or landlord(s) alone or jointly without regard to who made the application in the first place. There may be practical difficulties in a representative body proceeding alone; for comment on the analogous provisions in the 1967 Act, see Hague (above) at 10–24, p 216.

and powers which a landlord would otherwise have or rights to participate in management and administration of a scheme.[30]

23.3.6 *Crown estates*

The appropriate authority in relation to Crown estates may make an application for the approval of an estate management scheme. This may be done where, but for the existence of the Crown interest, the right to a collective enfranchisement or the enfranchisement of a house would be given by the 1993 Act.[31] This will enable estate management schemes to be established and management powers retained where the Crown voluntarily allows an enfranchisement.[32]

23.3.7 *Applications out of time*

Under the 1967 Act, the time-limits for application for a scheme were absolute but under the 1993 Act a late application can be made in very exceptional circumstances. Such applications, after 31 October 1995, require the consent of the Secretary of State given in the six-month period prior to the application being made. Consent will only be given if the Secretary of State is satisfied that:[33]

1 the proposed late application could not have been made before the expiry of the two-year period; and/or
2 any earlier, in-time application would probably have been dismissed but a change of circumstances now means an application would probably be granted; and
3 adequate notice of the application for consent has been given to all interested persons.

It is thought that few applications are likely to meet these conditions. Any application for consent must be in writing and comply with any procedural requirements then made by statutory instrument.

23.4 Applications by public bodies

23.4.1 *Arises only in default in respect of conservation areas*

The 1993 Act permits a local planning authority or the Historic Buildings and Monuments Commission, separately or jointly, to make application for the

30 Section 71(4)–(5).
31 Sections 94(6)–(8) and (11).
32 See, further, 3.4.7.
33 Section 72. In moving the amendment to permit late applications, reference was particularly made to new developments or the refurbishing of an estate which is incomplete when the Act came into force (HL Deb, Vol 545, col 1728 (Lord Strathclyde)).

approval of a scheme within a conservation area.[34] This is a default power; such application can only be made after 31 October 1995 when the time-limit for a landlord's application expires and will only be approved where the tribunal considers that an in-time application by a landlord would have been successful.[35] Consequently, an application can only be made where no scheme has been approved for the area or an earlier application has been withdrawn or dismissed and if there is no subsisting request by the landlord for consent for a late application.[36]

23.4.2 Time-limit

An application by a public body is also subject to a time-limit; there is only a six-month window of opportunity, the period normally commencing once the time-limit for the landlord has expired.[37] Exceptionally, the six-month period will be dated from the time any outstanding application by a landlord is withdrawn or dismissed and the six-month period can be extended in the event of an application by a landlord for consent to a late application.

23.4.3 Powers conferred

A scheme approved on application by a public body may confer on the applicants the rights and powers which might have been conferred on the landlord. The effect is otherwise similar to a scheme approved on application by a landlord with the important exception that neither an approved scheme nor the possibility of an application being made can result in the adjustment of the price on enfranchisement.[38]

23.5 Effect on enfranchisement claims

23.5.1 Suspension of pending claims

When an application for approval of a scheme[39] is made, any current enfranchisement claims are effectively suspended. In the case of a notice under

34 The Commission can only apply after consultation with the local planning authority; there are also provisions to cover proposed schemes which cross planning authority boundaries (s 73(5)–(6)). 'Conservation area' has the meaning given to it by the Planning (Listed Buildings and Conservation Areas) Act 1990, s 70(14).

35 Section 73(1)–(2).

36 Under s 72 (see 23.3.6).

37 Section 73(3); this will mean that the period will normally be 1 November 1995 to 30 April 1996.

38 See s 73(7)–(11) and especially s 73(10); see also 23.5.3.

39 Or a request for consent to a late application is made under s 72.

the 1967 Act where the entitlement arises by virtue of the amendments in the 1993 Act, no further steps need be taken towards the execution of a conveyance except those which appear to the landlord to be reasonable in the circumstances.[40] Where an initial notice is given either before or after the application, no proceedings are to be brought[41] or further steps taken to determine the terms of the acquisition by the nominee purchaser beyond those which appear to the landlord to be reasonable in the circumstances. A counter-notice must be given if this has not yet been done but the landlord need not, if the claim is admitted, give the details of his counter-proposals.[42]

Once an application for a scheme is withdrawn or dismissed, or a scheme is approved, the section ceases to apply[43] and the enfranchisement claim, if not withdrawn, will resume.[44] If a complete counter-notice has not been given in response to the initial notice the reversioner must give a further counter-notice within a period of two months.[45]

23.5.2 Power to withdraw

The making of the application also triggers a right of withdrawal where a tenant of a house or a nominee purchaser gave notice before the application was made. This can be done by a further notice by the tenant to the landlord or by the nominee purchaser to the reversioner.[46] In either case, the withdrawal does not give rise to the requirement to pay any costs.[47]

23.5.3 Effect on price

Once a scheme is approved and registered as a local land charge, any subsequent acquisition of a freehold becomes subject to the scheme. The price payable, either under s 9 of the 1967 Act or Sch 6 to the 1993 Act in the case of a collective enfranchisement shall be adjusted so far as appropriate, if at all; but not in relation to a scheme approved on application by a public body.[48]

---

40 Section 74(1)(b)(i) and (2)(a).

41 Except under ss 22 and 23 (court proceedings to determine validity of a claim or to deal with a claim by the landlord to resist on the basis of an intention to redevelop (see 7.2 and 7.3).

42 Section 74(3)(b)–(c); the counter-notice must comply with s 21(2) but not 21(3); it is not required if the initial notice is withdrawn. The provisions were explained as a suspension of the process of determination of the terms of the proposed acquisition (HC Deb, Standing Committee B, cols 284–285, 26 November 1992).

43 Section 74(5). This also applies where a request for consent for a late application is withdrawn or refused (s 74(6)).

44 Without prejudice to anything done in the meantime (s 74(7)).

45 Section 74(8). The standard provisions apply to the giving of such a further counter-notice (s 74(9)).

46 Section 74(2)(b) and 3(a) respectively.

47 Either under s 9(4) of the 1967 Act or s 33 (see 9.2.1).

48 Section 70(12)(b)–(c) (s 73(10)). The idea is to prevent a landlord who failed to promote his own scheme from benefiting from one promoted by a public body (HL Deb, Vol 544, col 137 and Vol 545, col 1715).

23.6 Variation of existing schemes

23.6.1 Jurisdiction

Management schemes established under the 1967 Act will contain provisions for termination or variation or exclusion of part of the area of a scheme.[49] Applications for any such changes are now to be made to the leasehold valuation tribunal and not the High Court.[50]

23.6.2 Power to extend existing schemes

Existing schemes can be extended with approval of the tribunal to cover houses which receive the right to enfranchise under the 1993 Act amendments.[51] They cannot be extended to cover flats but can be further amended in the future.[52] Applications must comply with the regulations made.[53]

---

49 1967 Act, s 19(6).

50 Section 75(1). For this purpose, a leasehold valuation tribunal means a rent assessment committee within s 142(2) of the Housing Act 1980 and not one constituted under the Rent Act 1977, Sch 10 (s 75(5)).

51 Under s 69(1)(a) and the new 1967 Act, ss 1A and 1B, introduced by ss 63 and 64 (see 17.2.1 and 17.2.4).

52 Section 75(2)–(3).

53 Sections 75(4) and (5). The Rent Assessment Committee (England and Wales) (Leasehold Valuation Tribunal) Regulations 1993, SI 1993/2408, are set out in Appendix 2.

CHAPTER TWENTY-FOUR

THE RIGHT OF MANAGEMENT AUDIT

24.1 Outline of the provisions

24.1.1 The concept

The 1993 Act confers a right of management audit upon tenants of dwellings under long leases who pay a service charge.[1] The tenants who are given this right are termed 'qualifying tenants' but the definition is not the same as that for the rights of collective enfranchisement or lease renewal. On the whole, the definition is wider. The idea is to enable such tenants to have the right to, and to pay for, an audit of the management accounts to ascertain whether the service charges levied upon them are being used to discharge the management functions in an efficient and effective manner. The exercise is largely information gathering at the expense of the tenants, who will pay both for the audit and for any actual costs incurred by the landlord who may properly charge these to management expenses. However, the intention is to measure management standards by approved codes of management practice. Regard can be had to any such approved codes when the auditor determines whether the management is efficient and effective. An audit which reveals shortcomings, inefficiencies or unjustified payments will then provide the tenants with evidence to enforce covenants in their leases, challenge the validity of service charges levied and (it is hoped) ensure that the codes of practice are observed in the future. The 1993 Act does not give any new remedies for problems which the audit may reveal.

24.1.2 The legislative framework

The right of audit is contained in Chapter V of the 1993 Act.[2] It is exercisable normally by two-thirds of tenants subject to a common service charge but may

1 Service charge for audit purposes has the meaning under the Landlord and Tenant Act 1985, s 18(1), namely an amount payable by a tenant of a dwelling as part of or in addition to the rent which is payable, directly or indirectly, for services, repairs, maintenance or insurance or the landlord's costs of management where the whole or part of the payment varies or may vary according to the costs incurred.

2 Sections 76–84. There was very little debate on these provisions; none at all in the Standing Committee (see HC Deb, Standing Committee B, col 286) and very little of substance in the House of Lords (see HC Deb, Vol 544, cols 143–146 and Vol 545, cols 215–216).

be exercised by one of two such tenants[3] or even a single tenant. The audit is undertaken by a qualified and independent professional appointed by the tenants. The audit is commenced by notice and the auditor is given the necessary rights of access and inspection.

The right of audit must be seen in the context of the existing provisions in the Landlord and Tenant Act 1985 ('the 1985 Act') relating to service charges. By that Act, service charge costs are only recoverable to the extent that they are reasonably incurred and only then if they have been provided to a reasonable standard;[4] by an amendment there is power to apply to court for an order that some costs are not recoverable if they do not meet these standards.[5] The right of audit gives additional powers to ascertain the true state of affairs and test the accuracy of any summary of relevant costs provided under the 1985 Act.[6]

24.2 The right

24.2.1 Nature of the right

The right is given to qualifying tenants, normally two or more, who occupy dwellings held on long leases from the same landlord.[7] The right is to an audit to be carried out on their behalf of the management of the premises and any appurtenant property.

24.2.2 Right exercised by qualifying tenants

For the purposes of management audit, a qualifying tenant is a tenant of a dwelling under a long lease[8] where a service charge is payable under the lease. It need not be at a low rent and may be a house or a flat; in practice, most will be flats. Occupation of a dwelling under a business lease does not qualify.[9] Although a dwelling can only have one qualifying tenant at any time, a person

---

3 But not both at the same time; once one notice is given, no subsequent notice can be given for a period of 12 months (see 24.5).

4 1985 Act, ss 18 and 19.

5 Ibid, s 20C, inserted by the Landlord and Tenant Act 1987, s 41.

6 1985 Act, s 22.

7 Section 76(1).

8 Long lease is defined as one within s 7(a)–(c) and a shared ownership lease, whatever the share of the tenant under it (s 77(2)). The clarification as to the meaning of a long lease by way of exception or extension contained in s 7(2)–(5) would not appear to have been incorporated into the definition for the purposes of management audit.

9 Section 77(1)(a). A business lease is one within the Landlord and Tenant Act 1985, Part II (s 101(1)).

may be a qualifying tenant of two or more dwellings at the same time. Joint tenants will together constitute the qualifying tenant and any one or more can sign the notice requiring an audit.[10]

Where the premises consist of three or more dwellings let to qualifying tenants of the same landlord, the right is exercisable by not less than two-thirds of those tenants. If the premises consist of or include only two dwellings let to qualifying tenants, either or both together can exercise the right.[11] A single qualifying tenant has the right to an audit if there is no other dwelling in the premises let to a qualifying tenant apart from that let to him.[12]

24.2.3 The premises

The audit is of the relevant premises and appurtenant property as defined.[13] The premises are the buildings in relation to which the management functions[14] are discharged where the costs are covered by common service charge contributions,[15] payable under the leases of the qualifying tenants.[16] Appurtenant property is any property not part of the premises but covered by the discharge of management functions.

24.3 The nature of the audit

24.3.1 Purposes

The audit is carried out for the twin, linked purposes of ascertaining the extent to which the landlord is discharging the management functions owed to the qualifying tenants in an efficient and effective manner and the extent to which the sums payable by those tenants are being applied in an efficient and effective manner.[17] To achieve such an audit, there is need for a standard by which the landlord's procedures and performance can be measured. Rather than providing a regulation there is power for the Secretary of State to approve one

10 Section 77(3)–(6). If two or more leases of the same dwelling have qualifying tenants, then it is the tenant under the superior lease which does not qualify.

11 Section 76(2). The right is linked to the number of dwellings let to qualifying tenants not to the number of flats, units or dwellings. Thus, if there are premises with 10 flats or units and only two are dwellings let on long leases to qualifying tenants, either can exercise the right of audit. The cost should encourage co-operation.

12 Section 76(4)–(5) and (7). The provisions apply to audit on behalf of a single tenant with any necessary modifications.

13 Section 76(3) and (6).

14 Defined in s 84 to include functions in respect to provision of services or the repair, maintenance or insurance of the property.

15 Defined in s 76(8).

16 Or under the lease of the single qualifying tenant where appropriate.

17 Section 78(1).

or more codes of practice;[18] it is specifically provided that regard should be had to any applicable provisions of an approved code when determining whether the obligations of any landlord are being discharged in an efficient and effective manner.[19]

24.3.2 The auditor

The auditor is appointed by the qualifying tenants seeking the audit.[20] The auditor must be a qualified accountant[21] or a qualified surveyor[22] and cannot be a tenant of any property within the relevant premises, nor, although it would be unlikely for the tenants to wish to appoint such a person, an officer, partner agent or employee of the landlord.[23] The auditor has the freedom to appoint persons to assist in the audit as he thinks fit.[24]

23.3.3. The rights which are exercisable

The rights conferred on an auditor are as follows.

1 A right to a written summary of costs incurred or to be incurred in connection with the service charge. This is the summary which a tenant is entitled to by virtue of the 1985 Act[25] with the right to inspecting and taking copies or extracts from the accounts or other documents supporting such summary.[26]

2 A right to inspect any other document the sight of which is reasonably required for the carrying out of the audit with a right to take copies or extracts.[27]

3 A right to inspect any common parts in the relevant premises or appurtenant property.[28]

---

18 Under s 87 (see 25.3). It is understood that the Royal Institution of Chartered Surveyors is preparing two codes of management practice to be submitted to the Secretary of State for approval.

19 Section 78(2).

20 Either by not less than two-thirds of the qualifying tenants or, where there are just two dwellings, by either or both such tenants.

21 This means a person eligible for appointment as a company auditor within the Companies Act 1989; this definition is achieved by reference in s 78(4)(a) to the Landlord and Tenant Act 1987, s 28, which, by amendment by Regulations (SI 1991/1997, reg 2, Sch, para 60) further refers to s 25 of the 1989 Companies Act.

22 A fellow or professional associate of either the Royal Institution of Chartered Surveyors or the Incorporated Society of Valuers and Auctioneers; or a person who satisfies requirements made by regulation (s 78(5)).

23 Section 78(3) and (4); the Landlord and Tenant Act 1987, s 28(4)–(6).

24 Section 78(6). Such assistants have the right to carry out the same inspections, and have the same rights to copies and extracts as are given to the auditor (s 79(8)).

25 See 1985 Act, ss 21(1) and 18(2).

26 Section 79(2)(a).

27 Section 79(2)(b)–(c).

28 Section 79(4).

24.4 Exercise of the right of audit

24.4.1 Exercisable by notice

The right of management audit is exercised by the giving of a notice to the landlord by the auditor which must be signed by each of the tenants on whose behalf it is given.[29] The notice must state the full name of each tenant and the address of the dwelling, the name and address of the auditor, specify any documents or description of documents which the auditor is entitled to have or wishes to inspect[30] and the date[31] on which the auditor proposes any inspection.[32] Inevitably, the documents may need to be described in general terms in the notice. The notice may be given direct to the landlord or to any person receiving rent on behalf of the landlord who must forward it to the landlord as soon as may be.[33]

24.4.2 Exercisable against agents

If a person other than the landlord has the responsibility for either the discharge of management functions or the application of the service charges levied or the right to enforce payment of any service charge, then an audit can be applied to such a person.[34] A management agent will be covered by this provision. Notice should be given to such 'relevant person' at, so far as is reasonably practical, the same time as the notice to the landlord, giving a copy of that additional notice to the landlord.[35]

24.4.3 Audit procedure – landlord's response

A landlord has one month to respond to the audit notice. Within this period the written summary of costs incurred or to be incurred in connection with the service charge[36] must be supplied to the auditor and facilities afforded to permit inspection of the supporting documents which are the basis of the summary.[37] Similar inspection facilities must be made available in respect of any other documents requested, unless an objection is made and reasons given for the

---

29 Sections 79(3)(a) and 80(1) and (2).

30 Within s 79(2) (see 23.3.3).

31 This must be a date not less than one month nor more than two months from the giving of the notice (s 80(4)).

32 Section 80(3).

33 Section 80(5).

34 Section 79(7); defining 'relevant person'.

35 Section 79(3)(b). It is not possible to have an audit of an agent or other relevant person without serving the landlord.

36 See 23.3.3.

37 Section 81(1)(a).

refusal.[38] An agent or other relevant person has the same duty and a similar right to object.[39] In the face of any such objection, or in any case where the landlord has failed to comply, the auditor may apply to the court within the period of not less than two nor more than four months from the audit notice. If the court is satisfied that the documents are covered by the right of audit it can make an order requiring compliance by either the landlord or the relevant person.[40]

The landlord's response should also approve the date proposed in the audit notice for inspection of the common parts. If this is not acceptable or convenient for the landlord, an alternative date can be proposed within the two-month period from the audit notice.[41] Once again, a court order can be sought within the same time-limits to secure compliance with the inspection request.[42]

24.4.4 Assistance of a superior landlord

There may be cases where some of the information required for a landlord to comply with a request for the written summary of costs incurred or to be incurred in connection with the service charge are in the possession of a superior landlord. In such a case, the landlord is to make a written request for that information and the superior landlord has a duty to comply within one month. In respect of any documents in possession of a superior landlord, the landlord is to inform the auditor of the fact and the name and address of that landlord. The auditor may then give notice and the superior landlord is to allow inspection.[43] The court's power to order compliance apply to a superior landlord in such a case.[44]

24.4.5 Termination of responsibility

A landlord may dispose of his interest during an audit; an agent or other relevant person may cease to be responsible for discharging management functions. In either case, if some responsibility for discharge of the obligations arising out of the audit notice remains[45] then the requirements of complying with the audit remains to that extent.[46] After a disposal the new landlord who takes over management is responsible for the obligations arising out of the audit notice as if notice had been given and to the extent as is appropriate to reflect

38 Section 81(1)(b).
39 Section 81(3).
40 Section 81(4), (5) and (7). The use of the word 'may' in 'may make an order' probably gives a court discretion whether or not to order.
41 Section 81(1)(c) and (2).
42 Section 81(6) and (7).
43 Section 82(1) and (2).
44 Section 82(3) (see 24.4.3).
45 This could be for the period up to the date of disposal or the date of ceasing to act as an agent.
46 Section 83(2) and (4).

the degree of responsibility.[47] Enquiries about any management audit notices received becomes yet another concern of a proposed transferee when a disposal of a landlord's interest is being negotiated.

24.4.6 Costs of the audit

The costs of the audit are a matter for negotiation between the auditor and the appointing tenants. Costs cannot be recovered as such from the landlord. The landlord cannot charge for making available any facilities for inspection; but any costs actually incurred in making the facilities available may be treated as part of the management costs and added to the service charge.[48]

24.5 Further audit restricted

Once an audit notice has been given, either to a landlord or a relevant person, then no further audit notice can be given during the 12-month period from the date of the earlier audit notice by or on behalf of any persons who, in relation to the earlier notice, were qualifying tenants of the constituent dwellings.[49]

47 Section 83(1) and (3). The date of disposal becomes the date from which time for compliance is calculated. There is no obligation in the statute for the assigning landlord to inform the would-be assignee of the audit. The burden is, therefore, on any assignee to deal with the matters by pre-contract enquiry.

48 Section 79(6).

49 Section 83(5).

CHAPTER TWENTY-FIVE

MISCELLANEOUS STATUTORY CHANGES

25.1 Amendments to the Landlord and Tenant Act 1987

25.1.1 Compulsory acquisition of landlord's interest

Three amendments are made to Part III of the Landlord and Tenant Act 1987 which is concerned with the compulsory acquisition by tenants of their landlord's interest.[1] The first is to bring the number of tenants who are needed for the right to exist or to be exercised in line with the 1993 Act. Thus, for compulsory acquisition to be available, two-thirds of the total number of flats must be held by qualifying tenants.[2] Secondly, the requisite majority of tenants proceeding is increased from 'more than 50%' to 'not less than two-thirds'.[3] Finally, the conditions for the making of acquisition orders are eased with the removal of the requirement that the appointment of a manager under Part II of the 1987 Act would not be an adequate remedy.[4]

25.1.2 Variation of leases

There is also a short but significant amendment to Part IV of the 1987 Act.[5] By that Act, any party to a long lease may apply to the court for a variation of the lease on the ground that it fails to make satisfactory provision in respect of certain specified matters.[6] One of these is the computation of any service charge; but in this regard a lease only failed to make satisfactory provision if (inter alia) the aggregate amounts would *exceed* the whole of the expenditure.[7] The amendment now made substitutes 'either exceed or be less than' for the

---

1 Section 85.

2 Section 85(2), substituting a new s 25(2)(c) into the 1987 Act; s 25(3) is deleted. This constitutes a general easing and simplification of the previous position where over 90 per cent of the flats had to be let on long leases if there were 10 flats or more, 100 per cent in the case of three or fewer flats and all but one flat in premises with four to nine flats.

3 Section 85(3), amending s 27(4) of the 1987 Act.

4 Section 85(4), deleting s 29(2)(c) of the 1987 Act.

5 Section 86, introduced at Report Stage in the House of Lords by the Earl of Lytton with Government acquiescence (HL Deb, Vol 545, cols 1882–1884).

6 1987 Act, s 35(1) and (2).

7 1987 Act, s 35(2)(f) and (4), emphasis supplied.

word 'exceed'.[8] This will, seemingly, permit a court to vary payments in cases where current service charge recovery is less than actual expenditure and now gives landlords with inadequate service charge recovery the possibility of varying leases in their favour. The provision was described by the Government Minister accepting the amendment as removing ambiguity relating to the consequential effects of enfranchisement on part of a development.[9] However, the amendment produced would appear to have a more wide ranging effect than the statements made in Parliament would suggest and the issue of compensation payable to tenants in respect of loss sustained by any variation may be a difficult one for a court to assess.[10]

25.2 Accommodation for persons with mental disorders

During the passage of the legislation, concern was expressed about the ability of developers and landlords effectively to exclude, by restrictive covenant, occupation of dwellings by persons with mental disorders. The House of Lords inserted into the Bill a clause which became s 89.[11] Any agreement which relates to a lease[12] of any property which is or includes a dwelling shall be void if it has the effect of prohibiting or imposing restrictions on the occupation of it by persons with mental disorders or the provision of accommodation within the dwelling for them.[13] Only agreements on or after 1 November 1993 are caught by the section; but after that date the provision operates against agreements relating to both flats and houses, both in and outside of leases and to agreements made before a lease is created.

25.3 Codes of practice

25.3.1 Power to approve codes of practice

The Secretary of State is given power to approve any code of practice submitted to him for approval which appears to him to be designed to promote

8 Section 86, amending s 35(4)(c) of the 1987 Act.

9 HL, Vol 545, cols 1882–1884. The Minister gave the assurance, in response to questions about the effect of the change, that 'nobody will end up paying more'. However, if the effect is to permit a court to increase service charge recovery to 100 per cent from a figure less than that, it would seem that tenants may end up paying more.

10 Compensation for loss is payable if the court so orders under s 38(10) of the 1987 Act; see also the comments of Lord Coleraine at HL Deb, Vol 545, col 1883. For a recent article on the point, see (1993) 137 Sol Jo 960–961 (G Sherriff).

11 The clause was proposed by Lords Rix and Renton and received so much support (HL Deb, Vol 545, cols 1892–1896) that the Government brought forward its own clause at Third Reading (HL Deb, Vol 546, cols 216–217).

12 Licences to occupy are not included.

13 Within the meaning of the Mental Health Act 1983.

desirable practices in the management of residential property.[14] Part of the code or more than one can be approved providing that satisfactory arrangements are made to publicise the terms of an approved code.[15] The 1993 Act specifically envisages that an approved code might make provision for resolution of disputes, competitive tendering for repair and other works and the administration of trusts in respect of sums paid by way of service charges.[16]

25.3.2 Consequence of failure to comply with approved practice

As with most codes, a failure to observe the provisions of an approved code does not incur liability to proceedings. However, an approved code is admissible as evidence and any provision which the court considers relevant to any question arising in proceedings can be taken into account by a court or tribunal.[17]

14 Section 87(1). An approved code will extend to dwellings let on licences as well as leases (s 87(9)).
15 Section 87(2)–(4).
16 Section 87(6)(b).
17 Section 87(7) (see also s 78(2) and 24.3.1).

APPENDICES

Appendix 1 – Statute

Leasehold Reform, Housing and Urban Development Act 1993

(1993 c 28)

ARRANGEMENT OF SECTIONS

PART I

LANDLORD AND TENANT

CHAPTER I

COLLECTIVE ENFRANCHISEMENT IN CASE OF TENANTS OF FLATS

Preliminary

Procedure following giving of initial notice

Applications to court or leasehold valuation tribunal

Termination of acquisition procedures

Determination of price and costs of enfranchisement

Completion of acquisition

Supplemental

CHAPTER II

INDIVIDUAL RIGHT OF TENANT OF FLAT TO ACQUIRE NEW LEASE

Preliminary

Preliminary inquiries by qualifying tenant

The tenant's notice

Procedure following giving of tenant's notice

Applications to court of leasehold valuation tribunal

Termination or suspension of acquisition procedures

Grant of new lease

Costs incurred in connection with new lease

Landlord's right to terminate new lease

Supplemental

CHAPTER III

ENFRANCHISEMENT UNDER LEASEHOLD REFORM ACT 1967

Extension of right to enfranchise

Provision of accommodation for persons with mental disorders

CHAPTER VII

GENERAL

SCHEDULES

PART I

LANDLORD AND TENANT

CHAPTER I

COLLECTIVE ENFRANCHISEMENT IN CASE OF TENANTS OF FLATS

Preliminary

1. The right to collective enfranchisement

(1) This Chapter has effect for the purpose of conferring on qualifying tenants of flats contained in premises to which this Chapter applies on the relevant date the right, exercisable subject to and in accordance with this Chapter, to have the freehold of those premises acquired on their behalf –

(a) by a person or persons appointed by them for the purpose, and
(b) at a price determined in accordance with this Chapter;

and that right is referred to in this Chapter as 'the right to collective enfranchisement'.

(2) Where the right to collective enfranchisement is exercised in relation to any such premises ('the relevant premises') –

(a) the qualifying tenants by whom the right is exercised shall be entitled, subject to and in accordance with this Chapter, to have acquired, in like manner, the freehold of any property which is not comprised in the relevant premises but to which this paragraph applies by virtue of subsection (3); and
(b) section 2 has effect with respect to the acquisition of leasehold interests to which paragraph (a) or (b) or subsection (1) of that section applies.

(3) Subsection (2)(a) applies to any property if the freehold of it is owned by the person who owns the freehold of the relevant premises and at the relevant date either –

(a) it is appurtenant property which is demised by the lease held by a qualifying tenant of a flat contained in the relevant premises; or
(b) it is property which any such tenant is entitled under the terms of the lease of his flat to use in common with the occupiers of other premises (whether those premises are contained in the relevant premises or not).

(4) The right of acquisition in respect of the freehold of any such property as is mentioned in subsection (3)(b) shall, however, be taken to be satisfied with respect to that property if, on the acquisition of the relevant premises in pursuance of this Chapter, either –

(a) there are granted by the freeholder –
   (i) over that property, or
   (ii) over any other property,
   such permanent rights as will ensure that thereafter the occupier of the flat referred to in that provision has as nearly as may be the same rights as those enjoyed in relation to that property on the relevant date by the qualifying tenant under the terms of his lease; or
(b) there is acquired from the freeholder the freehold of any other property over which any such permanent rights may be granted.

(5) A claim by qualifying tenants to exercise the right to collective enfranchisement may be made in relation to any premises to which this Chapter applies despite the fact that

those premises are less extensive than the entirety of the premises in relation to which those tenants are entitled to exercise that right.

(6) Any right or obligation under this Chapter to acquire any interest in property shall not extend to underlying minerals in which that interest subsists if –
 (a) the owner of the interest requires the minerals to be excepted, and
 (b) proper provision is made for the support of the property as it is enjoyed on the relevant date.

(7) In this section –
 'appurtenant property', in relation to a flat, means any garage, outhouse, garden, yard or appurtenances belonging to, or usually enjoyed with, the flat;
 'the freeholder' means the person who owns the freehold of the relevant premises;
 'the relevant premises' means any such premises as are referred to in subsection (2).

(8) In this Chapter 'the relevant date', in relation to any claim to exercise the right to collective enfranchisement, means the date on which notice of the claim is given under section 13.

2. Acquisition of leasehold interests

(1) Where the right to collective enfranchisement is exercised in relation to any premises to which this Chapter applies ('the relevant premises'), then, subject to and in accordance with this Chapter –
 (a) there shall be acquired on behalf of the qualifying tenants by whom the right is exercised every interest to which this paragraph applies by virtue of subsection (2); and
 (b) those tenants shall be entitled to have acquired on their behalf any interest to which this paragraph applies by virtue of subsection (3);
and any interest so acquired on behalf of those tenants shall be acquired in the manner mentioned in paragraphs (a) and (b) of section 1(1).

(2) Paragraph (a) of subsection (1) above applies to the interest of the tenant under any lease which is superior to the lease held by a qualifying tenant of a flat contained in the relevant premises.

(3) Paragraph (b) of subsection (1) above applies to the interest of the tenant under any lease (not falling within subsection (2) above) under which the demised premises consist of or include –
 (a) any common parts of the relevant premises, or
 (b) any property falling within section 1(2)(a) which is to be acquired by virtue of that provision,
where the acquisition of that interest is reasonably necessary for the proper management or maintenance of those common parts, or (as the case may be) that property, on behalf of the tenants by whom the right to collective enfranchisement is exercised.

(4) Where the demised premises under any lease falling within subsection (2) or (3) include any premises other than –
 (a) a flat contained in the relevant premises which is held by a qualifying tenant,
 (b) any common parts of those premises, or
 (c) any such property as is mentioned in subsection (3)(b),
the obligation or (as the case may be) right under subsection (1) above to acquire the interest of the tenant under the lease shall not extend to his interest under the lease in any such other premises.

(5) Where the qualifying tenant of a flat is a public sector landlord and the flat is let under a secure tenancy, then if –

(a) the condition specified in subsection (6) is satisfied, and

(b) the lease of the qualifying tenant is directly derived out of a lease under which the tenant is a public sector landlord,

the interest of that public sector landlord as tenant under that lease shall not be liable to be acquired by virtue of subsection (1) to the extent that it is an interest in the flat or in any appurtenant property; and the interest of a public sector landlord as tenant under any lease out of which the qualifying tenant's lease is indirectly derived shall, to the like extent, not be liable to be so acquired (so long as the tenant under every lease intermediate between that lease and the qualifying tenant's lease is a public sector landlord).

(6) The condition referred to in subsection (5)(a) is that either –

(a) the qualifying tenant is the immediate landlord under the secure tenancy, or

(b) he is the landlord under a lease which is superior to the secure tenancy and the tenant under that lease, and the tenant under every lease (if any) intermediate between it and the secure tenancy, is also a public sector landlord;

and in subsection (5) 'appurtenant property' has the same meaning as in section 1.

(7) In this section 'the relevant premises' means any such premises as are referred to in subsection (1).

3. Premises to which this Chapter applies

(1) Subject to section 4, this Chapter applies to any premises if –

(a) they consist of a self-contained building or part of a building and the freehold of the whole of the building or of that part of the building is owned by the same person;

(b) they contain two or more flats held by qualifying tenants; and

(c) the total number of flats held by such tenants is not less than two-thirds of the total number of flats contained in the premises.

(2) For the purposes of this section a building is a self-contained building if it is structurally detached, and a part of a building is a self-contained part of a building if –

(a) it constitutes a vertical division of the building and the structure of the building is such that that part could be redeveloped independently of the remainder of the building; and

(b) the relevant services provided for occupiers of that part either –

(i) are provided independently of the relevant services provided for occupiers of the remainder of the building, or

(ii) could be so provided without involving the carrying out of any works likely to result in a significant interruption in the provision of any such services for occupiers of the remainder of the building;

and for this purpose 'relevant services' means services provided by means of pipes, cables or other fixed installations.

4. Premises excluded from right

(1) This Chapter does not apply to premises falling within section 3(1) if –

(a) any part or parts of the premises is or are neither –

(i) occupied, or intended to be occupied, for residential purposes, nor

(ii) comprised in any common parts of the premises; and

(b) the internal floor area of that part or of those parts (taken together) exceeds 10 per cent of the internal floor area of the premises (taken as a whole).

(2) Where in the case of any such premises any part of the premises (such as, for example, a garage, parking space or storage area) is used, or intended for use, in conjunction with a particular dwelling contained in the premises (and accordingly is not comprised in any common parts of the premises), it shall be taken to be occupied, or intended to be occupied, for residential purposes.

(3) For the purpose of determining the internal floor area of a building or of any part of a building, the floor or floors of the building or part shall be taken to extend (without interruption) throughout the whole of the interior of the building or part, except that the area of any common parts of the building or part shall be disregarded.

(4) This Chapter does not apply to premises falling within section 3(1) if the premises are premises with a resident landlord and do not contain more than four units.

5. Qualifying tenants

(1) Subject to the following provisions of this section, a person is a qualifying tenant of a flat for the purposes of this Chapter if he is tenant of the flat under a long lease at a low rent.

(2) Subsection (1) does not apply where –
- (a) the lease is a business lease; or
- (b) the immediate landlord under the lease is a charitable housing trust and the flat forms part of the housing accommodation provided by it in the pursuit of its charitable purposes; or
- (c) the lease was granted by sub-demise out of a superior lease other than a long lease at a low rent, the grant was made in breach of the terms of the superior lease, and there has been no waiver of the breach by the superior landlord;

and in paragraph (b) 'charitable housing trust' means a housing trust within the meaning of the Housing Act 1985 which is a charity within the meaning of the Charities Act 1993.

(3) No flat shall have more than one qualifying tenant at any one time.

(4) Accordingly –
- (a) where a flat is for the time being let under two or more leases to which subsection (1) applies, any tenant under any of those leases which is superior to that held by any other such tenant shall not be a qualifying tenant of the flat for the purposes of this Chapter; and
- (b) where a flat is for the time being let to joint tenants under a lease to which subsection (1) applies, the joint tenants shall (subject to paragraph (a) and subsection (5)) be regarded for the purposes of this Chapter as jointly constituting the qualifying tenant of the flat.

(5) Where apart from this subsection –
- (a) a person would be regarded for the purposes of this Chapter as being (or as being among those constituting) the qualifying tenant of a flat contained in any particular premises consisting of the whole or part of a building, but
- (b) that person would also be regarded for those purposes as being (or as being among those constituting) the qualifying tenant of each of two or more other flats contained in those premises,

then, whether that person is tenant of the flats referred to in paragraphs (a) and (b) under a single lease or otherwise, there shall be taken for those purposes to be no qualifying tenant of any of those flats.

(6) For the purposes of subsection (5) in its application to a body corporate any flat let to an associated company (whether alone or jointly with any other person or persons) shall be treated as if it were so let to that body; and for this purpose 'associated company' means another body corporate which is (within the meaning of section 736 of the Companies Act 1985) that body's holding company, a subsidiary of that body or another subsidiary of that body's holding company.

6. Qualifying tenants satisfying residence condition

(1) For the purposes of this Chapter a qualifying tenant of a flat satisfies the residence condition at any time when the condition specified in subsection (2) is satisfied with respect to him.

(2) That condition is that the tenant has occupied the flat as his only or principal home –
(a) for the last twelve months, or
(b) for periods amounting to three years in the last ten years,
whether or not he has used it also for other purposes.

(3) For the purposes of subsection (2) –
(a) any reference to the tenant's flat includes a reference to part of it; and
(b) it is immaterial whether at any particular time the tenant's occupation was in right of the lease by virtue of which he is a qualifying tenant or in right of some other lease or otherwise;
but any occupation by a company or other artificial person, or (where the tenant is a corporation sole) by the corporator, shall not be regarded as occupation for the purposes of that subsection.

(4) In the case of a lease held by joint tenants –
(a) the condition specified in subsection (2) need only be satisfied with respect to one of the joint tenants; and
(b) subsection (3) shall apply accordingly (the reference to the lease by virtue of which the tenant is a qualifying tenant being read for this purpose as a reference to the lease by virtue of which the joint tenants are a qualifying tenant).

7. Meaning of 'long lease'

(1) In this Chapter 'long lease' means (subject to the following provisions of this section) –
(a) a lease granted for a term of years certain exceeding 21 years, whether or not it is (or may become) terminable before the end of that term by notice given by or to the tenant or by re-entry, forfeiture or otherwise;
(b) a lease for a term fixed by law under a grant with a covenant or obligation for perpetual renewal (other than a lease by sub-demise from one which is not a long lease) or a lease taking effect under section 149(6) of the Law of Property Act 1925 (leases terminable after a death or marriage);
(c) a lease granted in pursuance of the right to buy conferred by Part V of the Housing Act 1985 or in pursuance of the right to acquire on rent to mortgage terms conferred by that Part of that Act; or
(d) a shared ownership lease, whether granted in pursuance of that Part of that Act or otherwise, where the tenant's total share is 100 per cent.

(2) A lease terminable by notice after a death or marriage is not to be treated as a long lease for the purposes of this Chapter if –

(a) the notice is capable of being given at any time after the death or marriage of the tenant;

(b) the length of the notice is not more than three months; and

(c) the terms of the lease preclude both –

(i) its assignment otherwise than by virtue of section 92 of the Housing Act 1985 (assignments by way of exchange), and

(ii) the sub-letting of the whole of the premises comprised in it.

(3) Where the tenant of any property under a long lease at a low rent, on the coming to an end of that lease, becomes or has become tenant of the property or part of it under any subsequent tenancy (whether by express grant or by implication of law), then that tenancy shall be deemed for the purposes of this Chapter (including any further application of this subsection) to be a long lease irrespective of its terms.

(4) Where –

(a) a lease is or has been granted for a term of years certain not exceeding 21 years, but with a covenant or obligation for renewal without payment of a premium (but not for perpetual renewal), and

(b) the lease is or has been renewed on one or more occasions so as to bring to more than 21 years the total of the terms granted (including any interval between the end of a lease and the grant of a renewal),

this Chapter shall apply as if the term originally granted had been one exceeding 21 years.

(5) References in this Chapter to a long lease include –

(a) any period during which the lease is or was continued under Part I of the Landlord and Tenant Act 1954 or under Schedule 10 to the Local Government and Housing Act 1989;

(b) any period during which the lease was continued under the Leasehold Property (Temporary Provisions) Act 1951.

(6) Where in the case of a flat there are at any time two or more separate leases, with the same landlord and the same tenant, and –

(a) the property comprised in one of those leases consists of either the flat or a part of it (in either case with or without any appurtenant property), and

(b) the property comprised in every other lease consists of either a part of the flat (with or without any appurtenant property) or appurtenant property only,

then in relation to the property comprised in such of those leases as are long leases, this Chapter shall apply as it would if at that time –

(i) there were a single lease of that property, and

(ii) that lease were a long lease;

but this subsection has effect subject to the operation of subsections (3) to (5) in relation to any of the separate leases.

(7) In this section –

'appurtenant property' has the same meaning as in section 1;

'shared ownership lease' means a lease –

(a) granted on payment of a premium calculated by reference to a percentage of the value of the demised premises or the cost of providing them, or

(b) under which the tenant (or his personal representatives) will or may be entitled to a sum calculated by reference, directly or indirectly, to the value of those premises; and 'total share', in relation to the interest of a tenant under a shared ownership lease, means his initial share plus any additional share or shares in the demised premises which he has acquired.

8. Leases at a low rent

(1) For the purposes of this Chapter a lease of a flat is a lease at a low rent if either no rent was payable under it in respect of the flat during the initial year or the aggregate amount of rent so payable during that year did not exceed the following amount, namely –

(a) where the lease was entered into before 1st April 1963, two-thirds of the letting value of the flat (on the same terms) on the date of the commencement of the lease;

(b) where –

(i) the lease was entered into either on or after 1st April 1963 but before 1st April 1990, or on or after 1st April 1990 in pursuance of a contract made before that date, and

(ii) the flat has a rateable value at the date of the commencement of the lease or else at any time before 1st April 1990,

two-thirds of the rateable value of the flat on the appropriate date; or

(c) in any other case, £1,000 if the flat is in Greater London or £250 if elsewhere.

(2) For the purposes of subsection (1) –

(a) 'the initial year', in relation to any lease, means the period of one year beginning with the date of the commencement of the lease;

(b) 'the appropriate date' means the date of the commencement of the lease or, if the flat in question did not have a rateable value on that date, the date on which the flat first had a rateable value;

(c) section 25(1), (2) and (4) of the Rent Act 1977 (rateable value etc) shall apply, with any necessary modifications, for the purpose of determining the amount of the rateable value of a flat on a particular date;

(d) 'rent' means rent reserved as such, and there shall be disregarded any part of the rent expressed to be payable in consideration of services to be provided, or of repairs, maintenance or insurance to be effected by the landlord, or to be payable in respect of the cost thereof to the landlord under the lease or a superior landlord; and

(e) there shall be disregarded any term of the lease providing for suspension or reduction of rent in the event of damage to property demised, or for any penal addition to the rent in the event of a contravention of or non-compliance with the terms of the lease or an agreement collateral thereto.

(3) In subsection (1)(a) above the reference to letting value shall be construed in like manner as, under the law of England and Wales, the reference to letting value is to be construed where it appears in the proviso to section 4(1) of the Leasehold Reform Act 1967 (meaning of 'low rent').

(4) Accordingly, in determining the letting value of a flat at any time for the purposes of subsection (1)(a) above, regard shall be had to whether, and (if so) in what amount, a premium might then have been lawfully demanded as the whole or part of the consideration for the letting.

(5) Where, by virtue of section 7(4), a lease which has been renewed on one or more occasions is to be treated as a long lease for the purposes of this Chapter, then for the

purpose of determining under this section whether it is for those purposes a long lease at a low rent –

(a) the lease shall be deemed to have been entered into on the date of the last renewal of the lease; and

(b) that date shall be deemed to be the date of the commencement of the lease.

(6) Subsection (2)(a) above shall have effect in relation to any shared ownership lease falling within section 7(1)(d) as if the reference to the date of commencement of the lease were a reference to the date on which the tenant's total share became 100 per cent; and section 7(7) shall apply for the interpretation of this subsection.

(7) In this section any reference to a flat let under a lease includes a reference to any appurtenant property (within the meaning of section 1) which on the relevant date is let with the flat to the tenant under the lease.

9. The reversioner and other relevant landlords for the purposes of this Chapter

(1) Where, in connection with any claim to exercise the right to collective enfranchisement in relation to any premises, it is not proposed to acquire any interests other than –

(a) the freehold of the premises, or

(b) any other interests of the person who owns the freehold of the premises,

that person shall be the reversioner in respect of the premises for the purposes of this Chapter.

(2) Where, in connection with any such claim, it is proposed to acquire interests of persons other than the person who owns the freehold of the premises to which the claim relates, then –

(a) the reversioner in respect of the premises shall for the purposes of this Chapter be the person identified as such by Part I of Schedule 1 to this Act; and

(b) the person who owns the freehold of the premises, and every person who owns any leasehold interest which it is proposed to acquire under or by virtue of section 2(1)(a) or (b), shall be a relevant landlord for those purposes.

(3) Subject to the provisions of Part II of Schedule 1, the reversioner in respect of any premises shall, in a case to which subsection (2) applies, conduct on behalf of all the relevant landlords all proceedings arising out of any notice given with respect to the premises under section 13 (whether the proceedings are for resisting or giving effect to the claim in question).

(4) Schedule 2 (which makes provision with respect to certain special categories of landlords) has effect for the purposes of this Chapter.

10. Premises with a resident landlord

(1) For the purposes of this Chapter any premises falling within section 3(1) are at any time premises with a resident landlord if –

(a) the premises are not, and do not form part of, a purpose-built block of flats; and

(b) the freeholder, or an adult member of the freeholder's family –

  (i) at that time occupies a flat contained in the premises as his only or principal home, and

  (ii) has so occupied such a flat throughout a period of not less than twelve months ending with that time.

(2) Where any premises falling within section 3(1) would at any time ('the relevant time') be premises with a resident landlord but for the fact that subsection (1)(b)(ii)

above does not apply, the premises shall nevertheless be treated for the purposes of this Chapter as being at that time premises with a resident landlord if –

(a) immediately before the date when the freeholder acquired his interest in the premises the premises were (or, had this Chapter then been in force, would have been) such premises for the purposes of this Chapter; and

(b) the freeholder, or an adult member of the freeholder's family –

(i) entered into occupation of a flat contained in the premises within the period of 28 days beginning with that date, and

(ii) has occupied such a flat as his only or principal home throughout the period beginning with the time when he so entered into occupation and ending with the relevant time.

(3) In paragraph (b) of each of subsections (1) and (2) any reference to a flat includes a reference to a unit (other than a flat) which is used as a dwelling.

(4) Where the freehold interest in any premises is held on trust, subsections (1) and (2) shall apply as if, in paragraph (b) of each of those subsections, any reference to the freeholder were instead a reference to a person having an interest under the trust (whether or not also a trustee).

(5) For the purposes of this section a person is an adult member of another's family if that person is –

(a) the other's wife or husband; or

(b) a son or daughter or a son-in-law or daughter-in-law of the other, or of the other's wife or husband, who has attained the age of 18; or

(c) the father or mother of the other, or of the other's wife or husband;

and in paragraph (b) any reference to a person's son or daughter includes a reference to any stepson or stepdaughter of that person, and 'son-in-law' and 'daughter-in-law' shall be construed accordingly.

(6) In this section –

'the freeholder', in relation to any premises, means the person who owns the freehold of the premises;

'purpose-built block of flats' means a building which as constructed contained two or more flats.

Preliminary inquiries by tenants

11. Right of qualifying tenant to obtain information about superior interests etc

(1) A qualifying tenant of a flat may give –

(a) to his immediate landlord, or

(b) to any person receiving rent on behalf of his immediate landlord,

a notice requiring the recipient to give the tenant (so far as known to the recipient) the name and address of the person who owns the freehold of the relevant premises and the name and address of every other person who has an interest to which subsection (2) applies.

(2) In relation to a qualifying tenant of a flat, this subsection applies to the following interests, namely –

(a) the freehold of any property not contained in the relevant premises –

(i) which is demised by the lease held by the tenant, or

(ii) which the tenant is entitled under the terms of his lease to use in common with other persons; and

(b) any leasehold interest in the relevant premises or in any such property which is superior to that of the tenant's immediate landlord.

(3) Any qualifying tenant of a flat may give to the person who owns the freehold of the relevant premises a notice requiring him to give the tenant (so far as known to him) the name and address of every person, apart from the tenant, who is –

(a) a tenant of the whole of the relevant premises, or
(b) a tenant or licensee of any separate set or sets of premises contained in the relevant premises, or
(c) a tenant or licensee of the whole or any part of any common parts so contained or of any property not so contained –
  (i) which is demised by the lease held by a qualifying tenant of a flat contained in the relevant premises, or
  (ii) which any such qualifying tenant is entitled under the terms of his lease to use in common with other persons.

(4) Any such qualifying tenant may also give –

(a) to the person who owns the freehold of the relevant premises, or
(b) to any person falling within subsection (3)(a), (b) or (c),

a notice requiring him to give the tenant –

(i) such information relating to his interest in the relevant premises or (as the case may be) in any such property as is mentioned in subsection (3)(c), or
(ii) (so far as known to him) such information relating to any interest derived (wither directly or indirectly) out of that interest,

as is specified in the notice, where the information is reasonably required by the tenant in connection with the making of a claim to exercise the right to collective enfranchisement in relation to the whole or part of the relevant premises.

(5) Where a notice is given by a qualifying tenant under subsection (4), the following rights shall be exercisable by him in relation to the recipient of the notice, namely –

(a) a right, on giving reasonable notice, to be provided with a list of documents to which subsection (6) applies;
(b) a right to inspect, at any reasonable time and on giving reasonable notice, any documents to which that subsection applies; and
(c) a right, on payment of a reasonable fee, to be provided with a copy of any documents which are contained in any list provided under paragraph (a) or have been inspected under paragraph (b).

(6) This subsection applies to any document in the custody or under the control of the recipient of the notice under subsection (4) –

(a) sight of which is reasonably required by the qualifying tenant in connection with the making of such a claim as is mentioned in that subsection; and
(b) which, on a proposed sale by a willing seller to a willing buyer of the recipient's interest in the relevant premises or (as the case may be) in any such property as is mentioned in subsection (3)(c), the seller would be expected to make available to the buyer (whether at or before contract or completion).

(7) Any person who –

(a) is required by a notice under any of subsections (1) to (4) to give any information to a qualifying tenant, or
(b) is required by a qualifying tenant under subsection (5) to supply any list of documents, to permit the inspection of any documents or to supply a copy of any documents,

shall comply with that requirement within the period of 28 days beginning with the date of the giving of the notice referred to in paragraph (a) or (as the case may be) with the date of the making of the requirement referred to in paragraph (b).

(8) Where –
- (a) a person has received a notice under subsection (4), and
- (b) within the period of six months beginning with the date of receipt of the notice, he –
  - (i) disposes of any interest (whether legal or equitable) in the relevant premises otherwise than by the creation of an interest by way of security for a loan, or
  - (ii) acquires any such interest (otherwise than by way of security for a loan),

then (unless that disposal or acquisition has already been notified to the qualifying tenant in accordance with subsection (7)) he shall notify the qualifying tenant of that disposal or acquisition within the period of 28 days beginning with the date when it occurred.

(9) In this section –

'document' has the same meaning as in Part I of the Civil Evidence Act 1968;

'the relevant premises', in relation to any qualifying tenant of a flat, means –
- (a) if the person who owns the freehold interest in the flat owns the freehold of the whole of the building in which the flat is contained, that building, or
- (b) if that person owns the freehold of part only of that building, that part of the building;

and any reference to an interest in the relevant premises includes an interest in part of those premises.

12. Right of qualifying tenant to obtain information about other matters

(1) Any notice given by a qualifying tenant under section 11(4) shall, in addition to any other requirement imposed in accordance with that provision, require the recipient to give the tenant –
- (a) the information specified in subsection (2) below; and
- (b) (so far as known to the recipient) the information specified in subsection (3) below.

(2) The information referred to in subsection (1)(a) is –
- (a) whether the recipient has received in respect of any premises containing the tenant's flat –
  - (i) a notice under section 13 in the case of which the relevant claim is still current, or
  - (ii) a copy of such a notice; and
- (b) if so, the date on which the notice under section 13 was given and the name and address of the nominee purchaser for the time being appointed for the purposes of section 15 in relation to that claim.

(3) The information referred to in subsection (1)(b) is –
- (a) whether the tenant's flat is comprised in any property in the case of which any of paragraphs (a) to (d) of section 31(2) is applicable; and
- (b) if paragraph (b) or (d) of that provision is applicable, the date of the application in question.

(4) Where –
- (a) within the period of six months beginning with the date of receipt of a notice given by a tenant under section 11(4), the recipient of the notice receives in respect of any premises containing the tenant's flat –

(i) a notice under section 13, or
(ii) a copy of such a notice, and

(b) the tenant is not one of the qualifying tenants by whom the notice under section 13 is given,

the recipient shall, within the period of 28 days beginning with the date of receipt of the notice under section 13 or (as the case may be) the copy, notify the tenant of the date on which the notice was given and of the name and address of the nominee purchaser for the time being appointed for the purposes of section 15 in relation to the relevant claim.

(5) Where –
(a) the recipient of a notice given by a tenant under section 11(4) has, in accordance with subsection (1) above, informed the tenant of any such application as is referred to in subsection (3)(b) above; and
(b) within the period of six months beginning with the date of receipt of the notice, the application is either granted or refused by the Commissioners of Inland Revenue or is withdrawn by the applicant,

the recipient shall, within the period of 28 days beginning with the date of the granting, refusal or withdrawal of the application, notify the tenant that it has been granted, refused or withdrawn.

(6) In this section 'the relevant claim', in relation to a notice under section 13, means the claim in respect of which that notice is given; and for the purposes of subsection (2) above any such claim is current if –
(a) that notice continues in force in accordance with section 13(11), or
(b) a binding contract entered into in pursuance of that notice remains in force, or
(c) where an order has been made under section 24(4)(a) or (b) or 25(6)(a) or (b) with respect to any such premises as are referred to in subsection (2)(a) above, any interests which by virtue of the order fall to be vested in the nominee purchaser have yet to be so vested.

The initial notice

13. Notice by qualifying tenants of claim to exercise right

(1) A claim to exercise the right to collective enfranchisement with respect to any premises is made by the giving of notice of the claim under this section.

(2) A notice given under this section ('the initial notice') –
(a) must be given to the reversioner in respect of those premises; and
(b) must be given by a number of qualifying tenants of flats contained in the premises as at the relevant date which –
(i) is not less than two-thirds of the total number of such tenants, and
(ii) is not less than one-half of the total number of flats so contained;

and not less than one-half of the qualifying tenants by whom the notice is given must satisfy the residence condition.

(3) The initial notice must –
(a) specify and be accompanied by a plan showing –
(i) the premises of which the freehold is proposed to be acquired by virtue of section 1(1),
(ii) any property of which the freehold is proposed to be acquired by virtue of section 1(2)(a), and
(iii) any property of the person who owns the freehold of the specified premises over which it is proposed that rights (specified in the notice) should be granted by him in connection with the acquisition of the freehold of the

specified premises or of any such property so far as falling within section 1(3)(a);

(b) contain a statement of the grounds on which it is claimed that the specified premises are, on the relevant date, premises to which this Chapter applies;

(c) specify –
  (i) any leasehold interest proposed to be acquired under or by virtue of section 2(1)(a) or (b), and
  (ii) any flats or other units contained in the specified premises in relation to which it is considered that any of the requirements in Part II of Schedule 9 to this Act are applicable;

(d) specify the proposed purchase price for each of the following, namely –
  (i) the freehold interest in the specified premises,
  (ii) the freehold interest in any property specified under paragraph (a)(ii), and
  (iii) any leasehold interest specified under paragraph (c)(i);

(e) state the full names of all the qualifying tenants of flats contained in the specified premises and the addresses of their flats, and contain the following particulars in relation to each of those tenants, namely –
  (i) such particulars of his lease as are sufficient to identify it, including the date on which the lease was entered into, the term for which it was granted and the date of the commencement of the term,
  (ii) such further particulars as are necessary to show that the lease is a lease at a low rent, and
  (iii) if it is claimed that he satisfies the residence condition, particulars of the period or periods falling within the preceding ten years for which he has occupied the whole or part of his flat as his only or principal home;

(f) state the full name or names of the person or persons appointed as the nominee purchaser for the purposes of section 15, and an address in England and Wales at which notices may be given to that person or those persons under this Chapter; and

(g) specify the date by which the reversioner must respond to the notice by giving a counter-notice under section 21.

(4) In a case where the tenant's lease is held by joint tenants, subsection (3)(e)(iii) shall have effect as if any reference to the tenant were a reference to any joint tenant by virtue of whose occupation of the flat in question it is claimed that the residence condition is satisfied.

(5) The date specified in the initial notice in pursuance of subsection (3)(g) must be a date falling not less than two months after the relevant date.

(6) A notice shall not be given under this section with respect to any premises unless the qualifying tenants by whom it is given have obtained a valuation prepared by a qualified surveyor in respect of –
  (a) the freehold interest in the specified premises,
  (b) the freehold interest in any property specified under subsection (3)(a)(ii), and
  (c) any leasehold interest specified under subsection (3)(c)(i),

and any such notice must contain a statement confirming that they have done so and state the name of the surveyor in question.

(7) For the purposes of subsection (6) a person is a qualified surveyor if –
  (a) he is a fellow or professional associate of the Royal Institution of Chartered Surveyors or of the Incorporated Society of Valuers and Auctioneers or satisfies such other requirement or requirements as may be prescribed by regulations made by the Secretary of State; and

(b) he is reasonably believed by the qualifying tenants to have ability in, and experience of, the valuation of premises of the particular kind, and in the particular area, in question;

and any valuation prepared for the purposes of that subsection must be prepared in conformity with the provisions of Schedule 6 so far as relating to the determination of the price payable under this Chapter for the interest in question.

(8) Where any premises have been specified in a notice under this section, no subsequent notice which specifies the whole or part of those premises may be given under this section so long as the earlier notice continues in force.

(9) Where any premises have been specified in a notice under this section and –

(a) that notice has been withdrawn, or is deemed to have been withdrawn, under or by virtue of any provision of this Chapter or under section 74(3), or

(b) in response to that notice, an order has been applied for and obtained under section 23(1),

no subsequent notice which specifies the whole or part of those premises may be given under this section within the period of twelve months beginning with the date of the withdrawal or deemed withdrawal of the earlier notice or with the time when the order under section 23(1) becomes final (as the case may be).

(10) In subsections (8) and (9) any reference to a notice which specifies the whole or part of any premises includes a reference to a notice which specifies any premises which contain the whole or part of those premises; and in those subsections and this 'specifies' means specifies under subsection (3)(a)(i).

(11) Where a notice is given in accordance with this section, then for the purposes of this Chapter the notice continues in force as from the relevant date –

(a) until a binding contract is entered into in pursuance of the notice, or an order is made under section 24(4)(a) or (b) or 25(6)(a) or (b) providing for the vesting of interests in the nominee purchaser;

(b) if the notice is withdrawn or deemed to have been withdrawn under or by virtue of any provision of this Chapter or under section 74(3), until the date of the withdrawal or deemed withdrawal, or

(c) until such other time as the notice ceases to have effect by virtue of any provision of this Chapter.

(12) In this Chapter 'the specified premises', in relation to a claim made under this Chapter, means –

(a) the premises specified in the initial notice under subsection (3)(a)(i), or

(b) if it is subsequently agreed or determined under this Chapter that any less extensive premises should be acquired in pursuance of the notice in satisfaction of the claim, those premises;

and similarly references to any property or interest specified in the initial notice under subsection (3)(a)(ii) or (c)(i) shall, if it is subsequently agreed or determined under this Chapter that any less extensive property or interest should be acquired in pursuance of the notice, be read as references to that property or interest.

(13) Schedule 3 to this Act (which contains restrictions on participating in the exercise of the right to collective enfranchisement, and makes further provision in connection with the giving of notices under this section) shall have effect.

Participating tenants and nominee purchaser

14. The participating tenants

(1) In relation to any claim to exercise the right to collective enfranchisement, the participating tenants are (subject to the provisions of this section and Part I of Schedule 3) the following persons, namely –

(a) in relation to the relevant date, the qualifying tenants by whom the initial notice is given; and

(b) in relation to any time falling after that date, such of those qualifying tenants as for the time being remain qualifying tenants of flats contained in the specified premises.

(2) Where the lease by virtue of which a participating tenant is a qualifying tenant of his flat is assigned to another person the assignee of the lease shall, within the period of 14 days beginning with the date of the assignment, notify the nominee purchaser –

(a) of the assignment, and

(b) as to whether or not the assignee is electing to participate in the proposed acquisition.

(3) Where a qualifying tenant of a flat contained in the specified premises –

(a) is not one of the persons by whom the initial notice was given, and

(b) is not such an assignee of the lease of a participating tenant as is mentioned in subsection (2),

then (subject to paragraph 8 of Schedule 3) he may elect to participate in the proposed acquisition, but only with the agreement of all the persons who are for the time being participating tenants; and, if he does so elect, he shall notify the nominee purchaser forthwith of this election.

(4) Where a person notifies the nominee purchaser under subsection (2) or (3) of his election to participate in the proposed acquisition, he shall be regarded as a participating tenant for the purposes of this Chapter –

(a) as from the date of the assignment or agreement referred to in that subsection; and

(b) so long as he remains a qualifying tenant of a flat contained in the specified premises.

(5) Where a participating tenant dies, his personal representatives shall, within the period of 56 days beginning with the date of death, notify the nominee purchaser –

(a) of the death of the tenant, and

(b) as to whether or not the personal representatives are electing to withdraw from participation in the proposed acquisition;

and, unless the personal representatives of a participating tenant so notify the nominee purchaser that they are electing to withdraw from participation in that acquisition, they shall be regarded as a participating tenant for the purposes of this Chapter –

(i) as from the date of the death of the tenant, and

(ii) so long as his lease remains vested in them.

(6) Where in accordance with subsection (4) or (5) any assignee or personal representatives of a participating tenant ('the tenant') is or are to be regarded as a participating tenant for the purposes of this Chapter, any arrangements made between the nominee purchaser and the participating tenants and having effect immediately before the date of the assignment or (as the case may be) the date of death shall have effect as from that date –

(a) with such modifications as are necessary for substituting the assignee or (as the case may be) the personal representatives as a party to the arrangements in the place of the tenant; or

(b) in the case of an assignment by a person who remains a qualifying tenant of a flat contained in the specified premises, with such modifications as are necessary for adding the assignee as a party to the arrangements.

(7) Where the nominee purchaser receives a notification under subsection (2), (3) or (5), he shall, within the period of 28 days beginning with the date of receipt of the notification –

(a) give a notice under subsection (8) to the reversioner in respect of the specified premises, and

(b) give a copy of that notice to every other relevant landlord.

(8) A notice under this subsection is a notice stating –

(a) in the case of a notification under subsection (2) –

(i) the date of the assignment and the name and address of the assignee,

(ii) that the assignee has or (as the case may be) has not become a participating tenant in accordance with subsection (4), and

(iii) if he has become a participating tenant (otherwise than in a case to which subsection (6)(b) applies), that he has become such a tenant in place of his assignor;

(b) in the case of a notification under subsection (3), the name and address of the person who has become a participating tenant in accordance with subsection (4); and

(c) in the case of a notification under subsection (5) –

(i) the date of death of the deceased tenant,

(ii) the names and addresses of the personal representatives of the tenant, and

(iii) that in accordance with that subsection those persons are or (as the case may be) are not to be regarded as a participating tenant.

(9) Every notice under subsection (8) –

(a) shall identify the flat with respect to which it is given; and

(b) if it states that any person or persons is or are to be regarded as a participating tenant, shall be signed by the person or persons in question.

(10) In this section references to assignment include an assent by personal representatives and assignment by operation of law, where the assignment is –

(a) to a trustee in bankruptcy, or

(b) to a mortgagee under section 89(2) of the Law of Property Act 1925 (foreclosure of leasehold mortgage),

and references to an assignee shall be construed accordingly.

(11) Nothing in this section has effect for requiring or authorising anything to be done at any time after a binding contract is entered into in pursuance of the initial notice.

15. The nominee purchaser: appointment and replacement

(1) The nominee purchaser shall conduct on behalf of the participating tenants all proceedings arising out of the initial notice, with a view to the eventual acquisition by him, on their behalf, of such freehold and other interests as fall to be so acquired under a contract entered into in pursuance of that notice.

(2) In relation to any claim to exercise the right to collective enfranchisement with respect to any premises, the nominee purchaser shall be such person or persons as may

for the time being be appointed for the purposes of this section by the participating tenants; and in the first instance the nominee purchaser shall be the person or persons specified in the initial notice in pursuance of section 13(3)(f).

(3) The appointment of any person as the nominee purchaser, or as one of the persons constituting the nominee purchaser, may be terminated by the participating tenants by the giving of a notice stating that the person's appointment is to terminate on the date on which the notice is given.

(4) Any such notice must be given –
- (a) to the person whose appointment is being terminated, and
- (b) to the reversioner in respect of the specified premises.

(5) Any such notice must in addition either –
- (a) specify the name or names of the person or persons constituting the nominee purchaser as from the date of the giving of the notice, and an address in England and Wales at which notices may be given to that person or those persons under this Chapter; or
- (b) state that the following particulars will be contained in a further notice given to the reversioner within the period of 28 days beginning with that date, namely –
  - (i) the name of the person or persons for the time being constituting the nominee purchaser,
  - (ii) if falling after that date, the date of appointment of that person or of each of those persons, and
  - (iii) an address in England and Wales at which notices may be given to that person or those persons under this Chapter;

and the appointment of any person by way of replacement for the person whose appointment is being terminated shall not be valid unless his name is specified, or is one of those specified, under paragraph (a) or (b).

(6) Where the appointment of any person is terminated in accordance with this section, anything done by or in relation to the nominee purchaser before the date of termination of that person's appointment shall be treated, so far as necessary for the purpose of continuing its effect, as having been done by or in relation to the nominee purchaser as constituted on or after that date.

(7) Where the appointment of any person is so terminated, he shall not be liable under section 33 for any costs incurred in connection with the proposed acquisition under this Chapter at any time after the date of termination of his appointment; but if –
- (a) at any such time he is requested by the nominee purchaser for the time being to supply to the nominee purchaser, at an address in England and Wales specified in the request, all or any documents in his custody or under his control that relate to that acquisition, and
- (b) he fails without reasonable cause to comply with any such request or is guilty of any unreasonable delay in complying with it,

he shall be liable for any costs which are incurred by the nominee purchaser, or for which the nominee purchaser is liable under section 33, in consequence of the failure.

(8) Where –
- (a) two or more persons together constitute the nominee purchaser, and
- (b) the appointment of any (but not both or all) of them is terminated in accordance with this section without any person being appointed by way of immediate replacement,

the person or persons remaining shall for the time being constitute the nominee purchaser.

(9) Where –
  (a) a notice given under subsection (3) contains such a statement as is mentioned in subsection (5)(b), and
  (b) as a result of the termination of the appointment in question there is no nominee purchaser for the time being,

the running of any period which –
  (i) is prescribed by or under this Part for the giving of any other notice or the making of any application, and
  (ii) would otherwise expire during the period beginning with the date of the giving of the notice under subsection (3) and ending with the date when the particulars specified in subsection (5)(b) are notified to the reversioner,

shall (subject to subsection (10)) be suspended throughout the period mentioned in paragraph (ii).

(10) If –
  (a) the circumstances are as mentioned in subsection (9)(a) and (b), but
  (b) the particulars specified in subsection (5)(b) are not notified to the reversioner within the period of 28 days specified in that provision,

the initial notice shall be deemed to have been withdrawn at the end of that period.

(11) A copy of any notice given under subsection (3) or (5)(b) shall be given by the participating tenants to every relevant landlord (other than the reversioner) to whom the initial notice or a copy of it was given in accordance with section 13 and Part II of Schedule 3; and, where a notice under subsection (3) terminates the appointment of a person who is one of two or more persons together constituting the nominee purchaser, a copy of the notice shall also be so given to every other person included among those persons.

(12) Nothing in this section applies in relation to the termination of the appointment of the nominee purchaser (or of any of the persons constituting the nominee purchaser) at any time after a binding contract is entered into in pursuance for the initial notice; and in this Chapter references to the nominee purchaser, so far as referring to anything done by or in relation to the nominee purchaser at any time falling after such a contract is so entered into, are references to the person or persons constituting the nominee purchaser at the time when the contract is entered into or such other person as is for the time being the purchaser under the contract.

16. The nominee purchaser: retirement or death

(1) The appointment of any person as the nominee purchaser, or as one of the persons constituting the nominee purchaser, may be terminated by that person by the giving of a notice stating that he is resigning his appointment with effect from 21 days after the date of the notice.

(2) Any such notice must be given –
  (a) to each of the participating tenants; and
  (b) to the reversioner in respect of the specified premises.

(3) Where the participating tenants have received any such notice, they shall, within the period of 56 days beginning with the date of the notice, give to the reversioner a notice informing him of the resignation and containing the following particulars, namely –
  (a) the name or names of the person or persons for the time being constituting the nominee purchaser,

(b) if falling after that date, the date of appointment of that person or of each of those persons, and
(c) an address in England and Wales at which notices may be given to that person or those persons under this Chapter;

and the appointment of any person by way of replacement for the person resigning his appointment shall not be valid unless his name is specified, or is one of those specified, under paragraph (a).

(4) Subsections (6) to (8) of section 15 shall have effect in connection with a person's resignation of his appointment in accordance with this section as they have effect in connection with the termination of a person's appointment in accordance with that section.

(5) Where the person, or one of the persons, constituting the nominee purchaser dies, the participating tenants shall, within the period of 56 days beginning with the date of death, give to the reversioner a notice informing him of the death and containing the following particulars, namely –

(a) the name or names of the person or persons for the time being constituting the nominee purchaser,
(b) if falling after that date, the date of appointment of that person or of each of those persons, and
(c) an address in England and Wales at which notices may be given to that person or those persons under this Chapter;

and the appointment of any person by way of replacement for the person who has died shall not be valid unless his name is specified, or is one of those specified, under paragraph (a).

(6) Subsections (6) and (8) of section 15 shall have effect in connection with the death of any such person as they have effect in connection with the termination of a person's appointment in accordance with that section.

(7) If –

(a) the participating tenants are required to give a notice under subsection (3) or (5), and
(b) as a result of the resignation or death referred to in that subsection there is no nominee purchaser for the time being,

the running of any period which –

(i) is prescribed by or under this Part for the giving of any other notice or the making of any application, and
(ii) would otherwise expire during the period beginning with the relevant date and ending with the date when the particulars specified in that subsection are notified to the reversioner,

shall (subject to subsection (8)) be suspended throughout the period mentioned in paragraph (ii); and for this purpose 'the relevant date' means the date of the notice of resignation under subsection (1) or the date of death (as the case may be).

(8) If –

(a) the circumstances are as mentioned in subsection (7)(a) and (b), but
(b) the participating tenants fail to give a notice under subsection (3) or (as the case may be) subsection (5) within the period of 56 days specified in that subsection,

the initial notice shall be deemed to have been withdrawn at the end of that period.

(9) Where a notice under subsection (1) is given by a person who is one of two or more persons together constituting the nominee purchaser, and copy of the notice shall be

given by him to every other person included among those persons; and a copy of any notice given under subsection (3) or (5) shall be given by the participating tenants to every relevant landlord (other than the reversioner) to whom the initial notice or a copy of it was given in accordance with section 13 and Part II of Schedule 3.
(10) Nothing in this section applies in relation to the resignation or death of the nominee purchaser (or any of the persons together constituting the nominee purchaser) at any time after a binding contract is entered into in pursuance of the initial notice.

Procedure following giving of initial notice

17. Access by relevant landlords for valuation purposes

(1) Once the initial notice or a copy of it has been given in accordance with section 13 or Part II of Schedule 3 to the reversioner or to any other relevant landlord, that person and any person authorised to act on his behalf shall, in the case of –
(a) any part of the specified premises, or
(b) any part of any property specified in the notice under section 13(3)(a)(ii),
in which he has a freehold or leasehold interest which is included in the proposed acquisition by the nominee purchaser, have a right of access thereto for the purpose of enabling him to obtain a valuation of that interest in connection with the notice.

(2) Once the initial notice has been given in accordance with section 13, the nominee purchaser and any person authorised to act on his behalf shall have a right of access to –
(a) any part of the specified premises, or
(b) any part of any property specified in the notice under section 13(3)(a)(ii),
where such access is reasonably required by the nominee purchaser in connection with any matter arising out of the notice.

(3) A right of access conferred by this section shall be exercisable at any reasonable time and on giving not less than 10 days' notice to the occupier of any premises to which access is sought (or, if those premises are unoccupied, to the person entitled to occupy them).

18. Duty of nominee purchaser to disclose existence of agreements affecting specified premises etc

(1) If at any time during the period beginning with the relevant date and ending with the valuation date for the purposes of Schedule 6 –
(a) there subsists between the nominee purchaser and a person other than a participating tenant any agreement (of whatever nature) providing for the disposal of a relevant interest, or
(b) if the nominee purchaser is a company, any person other than a participating tenant holds any share in that company by virtue of which a relevant interest may be acquired,
the existence of that agreement or shareholding shall be notified to the reversioner by the nominee purchaser as soon as possible after the agreement or shareholding is made or established or, if in existence on the relevant date, as soon as possible after that date.

(2) If –
(a) the nominee purchaser is required to give any notification under subsection (1) but fails to do so before the price payable to the reversioner or any other relevant landlord in respect of the acquisition of any interest of his by the nominee purchaser is determined for the purposes of Schedule 6, and
(b) it may reasonably be assumed that, had the nominee purchaser given the notification, it would have resulted in the price so determined being increased by

an amount referable to the existence of any agreement or shareholding falling within subsection (1)(a) or (b),

the nominee purchaser and the participating tenants shall be jointly and severally liable to pay the amount to the reversioner or (as the case may be) the other relevant landlord.

(3) In subsection (1) 'relevant interest' means any interest in, or in any part of, the specified premises or any property specified in the initial notice under section 13(3)(a)(ii).

(4) Paragraph (a) of subsection (1) does not, however, apply to an agreement if the only disposal of such an interest for which it provides is one consisting in the creation of an interest by way of security for a loan.

19. Effect of initial notice as respects subsequent transactions by freeholder etc

(1) Where the initial notice has been registered in accordance with section 97(1), then so long as it continues in force –

(a) the person who owns the freehold of the specified premises shall not –

(i) make any disposal severing his interest in those premises or in any property specified in the notice under section 13(3)(a)(ii), or

(ii) grant out of that interest any lease under which, if it had been granted before the relevant date, the interest of the tenant would to any extent have been liable on that date to acquisition by virtue of section 2(1)(a) or (b); and

(b) other relevant landlord shall grant out of his interest in the specified premises or in any property so specified any such lease as is mentioned in paragraph (a)(ii);

and any transaction shall be void to the extent that it purports to effect any such disposal or any such grant of a lease as is mentioned in paragraph (a) or (b).

(2) Where the initial notice has been so registered and at any time when it continues in force –

(a) the person who owns the freehold of the specified premises disposes of his interest in those premises or in any property specified in the notice under section 13(3)(a)(ii), or

(b) any other relevant landlord disposes of any interest of his specified in the notice under section 13(3)(c)(i),

subsection (3) below shall apply in relation to that disposal.

(3) Where this subsection applies in relation to any such disposal as is mentioned in subsection (2)(a) or (b), all parties shall for the purposes of this Chapter be in the same position as if the person acquiring the interest under the disposal –

(a) had become its owner before the initial notice was given (and was accordingly a relevant landlord in place of the person making the disposal), and

(b) had been given any notice or copy of a notice given under this Chapter to that person, and

(c) had taken all steps which that person had taken;

and, if any subsequent disposal of that interest takes place at any time when the initial notice continues in force, this subsection shall apply in relation to that disposal as if any reference to the person making the disposal included any predecessor in title of his.

(4) Where immediately before the relevant date there is in force a binding contract relating to the disposal to any extent –

(a) by the person who owns the freehold of the specified premises, or

(b) by any other relevant landlord,

of any interest of his falling within subsection (2)(a) or (b), then, so long as the initial notice continues in force, the operation of the contract shall be suspended so far as it relates to any such disposal.

(5) Where –

(a) the operation of a contract has been suspended under subsection (4) ('the suspended contract'), and

(b) a binding contract is entered into in pursuance of the initial notice,

then (without prejudice to the general law as to the frustration of contracts) the person referred to in paragraph (a) or (b) of that subsection shall, together with all other persons, be discharged from the further performance of the suspended contract so far as it relates to any such disposal as is mentioned in subsection (4).

(6) In subsections (4) and (5) any reference to a contract (except in the context of such a contract as is mentioned in subsection (5)(b)) includes a contract made in pursuance of an order of any court; but those subsections do not apply to any contract providing for the eventuality of a notice being given under section 13 in relation to the whole or part of the property in which any such interest as is referred to in subsection (4) subsists.

20. Right of reversioner to require evidence of tenant's right to participate

(1) The reversioner in respect of the specified premises may, within the period of 21 days beginning with the relevant date, give the nominee purchaser a notice requiring him, in the case of any person by whom the initial notice was given, to deduce the title of that person to the lease by virtue of which it is claimed that he is a qualifying tenant of a flat contained in the specified premises.

(2) The nominee purchaser shall comply with any such requirement within the period of 21 days beginning with the date of the giving of the notice.

(3) Where –

(a) the nominee purchaser fails to comply with a requirement under subsection (1) in the case of any person within the period mentioned in subsection (2), and

(b) the initial notice would not have been given in accordance with section 13(2)(b) if –

(i) that person, and

(ii) any other person in the case of whom a like failure by the nominee purchaser has occurred,

had been neither included among the persons who gave the notice nor included among the qualifying tenants of the flats referred to in that provision,

the initial notice shall be deemed to have been withdrawn at the end of that period.

21. Reversioner's counter-notice

(1) The reversioner in respect of the specified premises shall give a counter-notice under this section to the nominee purchaser by the date specified in the initial notice in pursuance of section 13(3)(g).

(2) The counter-notice must comply with one of the following requirements, namely –

(a) state that the reversioner admits that the participating tenants were on the relevant date entitled to exercise the right to collective enfranchisement in relation to the specified premises;

(b) state that, for such reasons as are specified in the counter-notice, the reversioner does not admit that the participating tenants were so entitled;

(c) contain such a statement as is mentioned in paragraph (a) or (b) above but state that an application for an order under subsection (1) of section 23 is to be made by such appropriate landlord (within the meaning of that section) as is specified in the counter-notice, on the grounds that he intends to redevelop the whole or a substantial part of the specified premises.

(3) If the counter-notice complies with the requirement set out in subsection (2)(a), it must in addition –

(a) state which (if any) of the proposals contained in the initial notice are accepted by the reversioner and which (if any) of those proposals are not so accepted, and specify –

(i) in relation to any proposal which is not so accepted, the reversioner's counter-proposal, and

(ii) any additional leaseback proposals by the reversioner;

(b) if (in a case where any property specified in the initial notice under section 13(3)(a)(ii) is property falling within section 1(3)(b)) any such counter-proposal relates to the grant of rights or the disposal of any freehold interest in pursuance of section 1(4), specify –

(i) the nature of those rights and the property over which it is proposed to grant them, or

(ii) the property in respect of which it is proposed to dispose of any such interest,

as the case may be;

(c) state which interests (if any) the nominee purchaser is to be required to acquire in accordance with subsection(4) below;

(d) state which rights (if any) the person who owns the freehold of the specified premises, or any other relevant landlord, desires to retain –

(i) over any property in which he has any interest which is included in the proposed acquisition by the nominee purchaser, or

(ii) over any property in which he has any interest which the nominee purchaser is to be required to acquire in accordance with subsection (4) below,

on the grounds that the rights are necessary for the proper management or maintenance of property in which he is to retain a freehold or leasehold interest; and

(e) include a description of any provisions which the reversioner or any other relevant landlord considers should be included in any conveyance to the nominee purchaser in accordance with section 34 and Schedule 7.

(4) The nominee purchaser may be required to acquire on behalf of the participating tenants the interest in any property of the person who owns the freehold of the specified premises or of any other relevant landlord, if the property –

(a) would for all practical purposes cease to be of use and benefit to him, or

(b) would cease to be capable of being reasonably managed or maintained by him,

in the event of his interest in the specified premises or (as the case may be) in any other property being acquired by the nominee purchaser under this Chapter.

(5) Where a counter-notice specified any interest in pursuance of subsection (3)(c), the nominee purchaser or any person authorised to act on his behalf shall, in the case of any part of the property in which that interest subsists, have a right of access thereto for the purpose of enabling the nominee purchaser to obtain, in connection with the proposed acquisition by him, a valuation of that interest; and subsection (3) of section 17 shall apply in relation to the exercise of that right as it applies in relation to the exercise of a right of access conferred by that section.

(6) Every counter-notice must specify an address in England and Wales at which notices may be given to the reversioner under this Chapter.

(7) The reference in subsection (3)(a)(ii) to additional leaseback proposals is a reference to proposals which relate to the leasing back, in accordance with section 36 and Schedule 9, of flats or other units contained in the specified premises and which are made either –
- (a) in respect of flats or other units in relation to which Part II of that Schedule is applicable but which were not specified in the initial notice under section 13(3)(c)(ii), or
- (b) in respect of flats or other units in relation to which Part III of that Schedule is applicable.

(8) Schedule 4 (which imposes requirements as to the furnishing of information by the reversioner about the exercise of rights under Chapter II with respect to flats contained in the specified premises) shall have effect.

Applications to court or leasehold valuation tribunal

22. Proceedings relating to validity of initial notice

(1) Where –
- (a) the reversioner in respect of the specified premises has given the nominee purchaser a counter-notice under section 21 which (whether it complies with the requirement set out in subsection (2)(b) or (c) of that section) contains such a statement as is mentioned in subsection (2)(b) of that section, but
- (b) the court is satisfied, on an application made by the nominee purchaser, that the participating tenants were on the relevant date entitled to exercise the right to collective enfranchisement in relation to the specified premises,

the court shall by order make a declaration to that effect.

(2) Any application for an order under subsection (1) must be made not later than the end of the period of two months beginning with the date of the giving of the counter-notice to the nominee purchaser.

(3) If on any such application the court makes an order under subsection (1), then (subject to subsection (4)) the court shall make an order –
- (a) declaring that the reversioner's counter-notice shall be of no effect, and
- (b) requiring the reversioner to give a further counter-notice to the nominee purchaser by such date as is specified in the order.

(4) Subsection (3) shall not apply if –
- (a) the counter-notice complies with the requirement set out in section 21(2)(c), and
- (b) either –
  - (i) an application for an order under section 23(1) is pending, or
  - (ii) the period specified in section 23(3) as the period for the making of such an application has not expired.

(5) Subsections (3) to (5) of section 21 shall apply to any further counter-notice required to be given by the reversioner under subsection (3) above as if it were a counter-notice under that section complying with the requirement set out in subsection (2)(a) of that section.

(6) If an application by the nominee purchaser for an order under subsection (1) is dismissed by the court, the initial notice shall cease to have effect at the time when the order dismissing the application becomes final.

23. Tenants' claim liable to be defeated where landlord intends to redevelop

(1) Where the reversioner in respect of the specified premises has given a counter-notice under section 21 which complies with the requirement set out in subsection (2)(c) of that section, the court may, on the application of any appropriate landlord, by order declare that the right to collective enfranchisement shall not be exercisable in relation to those premises by reason of that landlord's intention to redevelop the whole or a substantial part of the premises.

(2) The court shall not make an order under subsection (1) unless it is satisfied –
- (a) that not less than two-thirds of all the long leases on which flats contained in the specified premises are held are due to terminate within the period of five years beginning with the relevant date; and
- (b) that for the purposes of redevelopment the applicant intends, once the leases in question have so terminated –
  - (i) to demolish or reconstruct, or
  - (ii) to carry out substantial works of construction on,

  the whole or a substantial part of the specified premises; and
- (c) that he could not reasonably do so without obtaining possession of the flats demised by those leases.

(3) Any application for an order under subsection (1) must be made within the period of two months beginning with the date of the giving of the counter-notice to the nominee purchaser; but, where the counter-notice is one falling within section 22(1)(a), such an application shall not be proceeded with until such time (if any) as an order under section 22(1) becomes final.

(4) Where an order under subsection (1) is made by the court, the initial notice shall cease to have effect on the order becoming final.

(5) Where an application for an order under subsection (1) is dismissed by the court, the court shall make an order –
- (a) declaring that the reversioner's counter-notice shall be of no effect, and
- (b) requiring the reversioner to give a further counter-notice to the nominee purchaser by such date as is specified in the order.

(6) Where –
- (a) the reversioner has given such a counter-notice as is mentioned in subsection (1), but
- (b) either –
  - (i) no application for an order under that subsection is made within the period referred to in subsection (3), or
  - (ii) such an application is so made but is subsequently withdrawn,

then (subject to subsection (8)), the reversioner shall give a further counter-notice to the nominee purchaser within the period of two months beginning with the appropriate date.

(7) In subsection (6) 'the appropriate date' means –
- (a) if subsection (6)(b)(i) applies, the date immediately following the end of the period referred to in subsection (3); and
- (b) if subsection (6)(b)(ii) applies, the date of withdrawal of the application.

(8) Subsection (6) shall not apply if any application has been made by the nominee purchaser under section 22(1).

(9) Subsections (3) to (5) of section 21 shall apply to any further counter-notice required to be given by the reversioner under subsection (5) or (6) above as if it were a counter-notice under that section complying with the requirement set out in subsection (2)(a) of that section.

(10) In this section 'appropriate landlord', in relation to the specified premises, means –
(a) the reversioner or any other relevant landlord; or
(b) any two or more persons falling within paragraph (a) who are acting together.

24. Applications where terms in dispute or failure to enter contract

(1) Where the reversioner in respect of the specified premises has given the nominee purchaser –
(a) a counter-notice under section 21 complying with the requirement set out in subsection (2)(a) of that section, or
(b) a further counter-notice required by or by virtue of section 22(3) or section 23(5) or (6),
but any of the terms of acquisition remain in dispute at the end of the period of two months beginning with the date on which the counter-notice or further counter-notice was so given, a leasehold valuation tribunal may, on the application of either the nominee purchaser or the reversioner, determine the matters in dispute.

(2) Any application under subsection (1) must be made not later than the end of the period of six months beginning with the date on which the counter-notice or further counter-notice was given to the nominee purchaser.

(3) Where –
(a) the reversioner has given the nominee purchaser such a counter-notice or further counter-notice as is mentioned in subsection (1)(a) or (b), and
(b) all of the terms of acquisition have been either agreed between the parties or determined by a leasehold valuation tribunal under subsection (1),
but a binding contract incorporating those terms has not been entered into by the end of the appropriate period specified in subsection (6), the court may, on the application of either the nominee purchaser or the reversioner, make such order under subsection (4) as it thinks fit.

(4) The court may under this subsection make an order –
(a) providing for the interests to be acquired by the nominee purchaser to be vested in him on the terms referred to in subsection (3);
(b) providing for those interests to be vested in him on those terms, but subject to such modifications as –
(i) may have been determined by a leasehold valuation tribunal, on the application of either the nominee purchaser or the reversioner, to be required by reason of any change in circumstances since the time when the terms were agreed or determined as mentioned in that subsection, and
(ii) are specified in the order; or
(c) providing for the initial notice to be deemed to have been withdrawn at the end of the appropriate period specified in subsection (6);
and Schedule 5 shall have effect in relation to any such order as is mentioned in paragraph (a) or (b) above.

(5) Any application for an order under subsection (4) must be made not later than the end of the period of two months beginning immediately after the end of the appropriate period specified in subsection (6).

(6) For the purposes of this section the appropriate period is –

(a) where all of the terms of acquisition have been agreed between the parties, the period of two months beginning with the date when those terms were finally so agreed;

(b) where all or any of those terms have been determined by a leasehold valuation tribunal under subsection (1) –

(i) the period of two months beginning with the date when the decision of the tribunal under that subsection becomes final, or

(ii) such other period as may have been fixed by the tribunal when making its determination.

(7) In this section 'the parties' means the nominee purchaser and the reversioner and any relevant landlord who has given to those persons a notice for the purposes of paragraph 7(1)(a) of Schedule 1.

(8) In this Chapter 'the terms of acquisition', in relation to a claim made under this Chapter, means the terms of the proposed acquisition by the nominee purchaser, whether relating to –

(a) the interests to be acquired,

(b) the extent of the property to which those interests relate or the rights to be granted over any property,

(c) the amounts payable as the purchase price for such interests,

(d) the apportionment of conditions or other matters in connection with the severance of any reversionary interest, or

(e) the provisions to be contained in any conveyance,

or otherwise, and includes any such terms in respect of any interest to be acquired in pursuance of section 1(4) or 21(4).

25. Applications where reversioner fails to give counter-notice or further counter-notice

(1) Where the initial notice has been given in accordance with section 13 but –

(a) the reversioner has failed to give the nominee purchaser a counter-notice in accordance with section 21(1), or

(b) if required to give the nominee purchaser a further counter-notice by or by virtue of section 22(3) or section 23(5) or (6), the reversioner has failed to comply with that requirement,

the court may, on the application of the nominee purchaser, make an order determining the terms on which he is to acquire, in accordance with the proposals contained in the initial notice, such interests and rights as are specified in it under section 13(3).

(2) The terms determined by the court under subsection (1) shall, if Part II of Schedule 9 is applicable, include terms which provide for the leasing back, in accordance with section 36 and that Part of that Schedule, of flats or other units contained in the specified premises.

(3) The court shall not make any order on an application made by virtue of paragraph (a) of subsection (1) unless it is satisfied –

(a) that the participating tenants were on the relevant date entitled to exercise the right to collective enfranchisement in relation to the specified premises; and

(b) if applicable, that the requirements of Part II of Schedule 3 were complied with as respects the giving of copies of the initial notice.

(4) Any application for an order under subsection (1) must be made not later than the end of the period of six months beginning with the date by which the counter-notice or

further counter-notice referred to in that subsection was to be given to the nominee purchaser.

(5) Where –
(a) the terms of acquisition have been determined by an order of the court under subsection (1), but
(b) a binding contract incorporating those terms has not been entered into by the end of the appropriate period specified in subsection (8),
the court may, on the application of either the nominee purchaser or the reversioner, make such order under subsection (6) as it thinks fit.

(6) The court may under this subsection make an order –
(a) providing for the interests to be acquired by the nominee purchaser to be vested in him on the terms referred to in subsection (5);
(b) providing for those interests to be vested in him on those terms, but subject to such modifications as –
(i) may have been determined by a leasehold valuation tribunal, on the application of either the nominee purchaser or the reversioner, to be required by reason of any change in circumstances since the time when the terms were determined as mentioned in that subsection, and
(ii) are specified in the order; or
(c) providing for the initial notice to be deemed to have been withdrawn at the end of the appropriate period specified in subsection (8);
and Schedule 5 shall have effect in relation to any such order as is mentioned in paragraph (a) or (b) above.

(7) Any application for an order under subsection (6) must be made not later than the end of the period of two months beginning immediately after the end of the appropriate period specified in subsection (8).

(8) For the purposes of this section the appropriate period is –
(a) the period of two months beginning with the date when the order of the court under subsection (1) becomes final, or
(b) such other period as may have been fixed by the court when making that order.

26. Applications where relevant landlord cannot be found

(1) Where not less than two-thirds of the qualifying tenants of flats contained in any premises to which this Chapter applies desire to make a claim to exercise the right to collective enfranchisement in relation to those premises but –
(a) (in a case to which section 9(1) applies) the person who owns the freehold of the premises cannot be found or his identity cannot be ascertained, or
(b) (in a case to which section 9(2) applies) each of the relevant landlords is someone who cannot be found or whose identity cannot be ascertained,
the court may, on the application of the qualifying tenants in question, make a vesting order under this subsection –
(i) with respect to any interests of that person (whether in those premises or in any other property) which are liable to acquisition on behalf of those tenants by virtue of section 1(1) or (2)(a) or section 2(1), or
(ii) with respect to any interests of those landlords which are so liable to acquisition by virtue of any of those provisions,
as the case may be.

(2) Where in a case to which section 9(2) applies –

(a) not less than two-thirds of the qualifying tenants of flats contained in any premises to which this Chapter applies desire to make a claim to exercise the right to collective enfranchisement in relation to those premises, and
(b) paragraph (b) of subsection (1) does not apply, but
(c) a notice of that claim or (as the case may be) a copy of such a notice cannot be given in accordance with section 13 or Part II of Schedule 3 to any person to whom it would otherwise be required to be so given because he cannot be found or his identity cannot be ascertained,

the court may, on the application of the qualifying tenants in question, make an order dispensing with the need to give such a notice or (as the case may be) a copy of such a notice to that person.

(3) If that person is the person who owns the freehold of the premises, then on the application of those tenants, the court may, in connection with an order under subsection (2), make an order appointing any other relevant landlord to be the reversioner in respect of the premises in place of that person; and if it does so references in this Chapter to the reversioner shall apply accordingly.

(4) The court shall not make an order on any application under subsection (1) or (2) unless it is satisfied –
(a) that on the date of the making of the application the premises to which the application relates were premises to which this Chapter applies; and
(b) that on that date the applicants would not have been precluded by any provision of this Chapter from giving a valid notice under section 13 with respect to those premises.

(5) Before making any such order the court may require the applicants to take such further steps by way of advertisement or otherwise as the court thinks proper for the purpose of tracing the person or persons in question; and if, after an application is made for a vesting order under subsection (1) and before any interest is vested in pursuance of the application, the person or (as the case may be) any of the persons referred to in paragraph (a) or (b) of that subsection is traced, then no further proceedings shall be taken with a view to any interest being so vested, but (subject to subsection (6)) –
(a) the rights and obligations of all parties shall be determined as if the applicants had, at the date of the application, duly given notice under section 13 of their claim to exercise the right to collective enfranchisement in relation to the premises to which the application relates; and
(b) the court may give such directions as the court thinks fit as to the steps to be taken for giving effect to those rights and obligations, including directions modifying or dispensing with any of the requirements of this Chapter or of regulations made under this Part.

(6) An application for a vesting order under subsection (1) may be withdrawn at any time before execution of a conveyenace under section 27(3) and, after it is withdrawn, subsection (5)(a) above shall not apply; but where any step is taken (whether by the applicants or otherwise) for the purpose of giving effect to subsection (5)(a) in the case of any application, the application shall not afterwards be withdrawn except –
(a) with the consent of every person who is the owner of any interest the vesting of which is sought by the applicants, or
(b) by leave of the court,

and the court shall not give leave unless it appears to the court just to do so by reason of matters coming to the knowledge of the applicants in consequence of the tracing of any such person.

(7) Where an order has been made under subsection (2) dispensing with the need to give a notice under section 13, or a copy of such a notice, to a particular person with respect to any particular premises, then if –

(a) a notice is subsequently given under that section with respect to those premises, and
(b) in reliance on the order, the notice or a copy of the notice is not to be given to that person,

the notice must contain a statement of the effect of the order.

(8) Where a notice under section 13 contains such a statement in accordance with subsection (7) above, then in determining for the purposes of any provision of this Chapter whether the requirements of section 13 or Part II of Schedule 3 have been complied with in relation to the notice, those requirements shall be deemed to have been complied with so far as relating to the giving of the notice or a copy of it to the person referred to in subsection (7) above.

(9) Rules of court shall make provision –

(a) for requiring notice of any application under subsection (3) to be served by the persons making the application on any person who the applicants know or have reason to believe is a relevant landlord; and
(b) for enabling persons served with any such notice to be joined as parties to the proceedings.

27. Supplementary provisions relating to vesting orders under section 26(1)

(1) A vesting order under section 26(1) is an order providing for the vesting of any such interests as are referred to in paragraph (i) or (ii) of that provision –

(a) in such person or persons as may be appointed for the purpose by the applicants for the order, and
(b) on such terms as may be determined by a leasehold valuation tribunal to be appropriate with a view to the interests being vested in that person or those persons in like manner (so far as the circumstances permit) as if the applicants had, at the date of their application, given notice under section 13 of their claim to exercise the right to collective enfranchisement in relation to the premises with respect to which the order is made.

(2) If a leasehold valuation tribunal so determines in the case of a vesting order under section 26(1), the order shall have effect in relation to interests which are less extensive than those specified in the application on which the order was made.

(3) Where any interests are to be vested in any person or persons by virtue of a vesting order under section 26(1), then on his or their paying into court the appropriate sum in respect of each of those interests there shall be executed by such person as the court may designate a conveyance which –

(a) is in a form approved by a leasehold valuation tribunal, and
(b) contains such provisions as may be so approved for the purpose of giving effect so far as possible to the requirements of section 34 and Schedule 7;

and that conveyance shall be effective to vest in the person or persons to whom the conveyance is made the interests expressed to be conveyed, subject to and in accordance with the terms of the conveyance.

(4) In connection with the determination by a leasehold valuation tribunal of any question as to the interests to be conveyed by any such conveyance, or as to the rights with or subject to which they are to be conveyed, it shall be assumed (unless the contrary

is shown) that any person whose interests are to be conveyed ('the transferor') has no interest in property other than those interests and, for the purpose of excepting them from the conveyance, any minerals underlying the property in question.

(5) The appropriate sum which in accordance with subsection (3) is to be paid into court in respect of any interest is the aggregate of –

(a) such amount as may be determined by a leasehold valuation tribunal to be the price which would be payable in respect of that interest in accordance with Schedule 6 if the interest were being acquired in pursuance of such a notice as is mentioned in subsection (1)(b); and

(b) any amounts or estimated amounts determined by such a tribunal as being, at the time of execution of the conveyance, due to the transferor from any tenants of his of premises comprised in the premises in which that interest subsists (whether due under or in respect of their leases or under or in respect of agreements collateral thereto).

(6) Where any interest is vested in any person or persons in accordance with this section, the payment into court of the appropriate sum in respect of that interest shall be taken to have satisfied any claims against the applicants for the vesting order under section 26(1), their personal representatives or assigns in respect of the price payable under this Chapter for the acquisition of that interest.

(7) Where any interest is so vested in any person or persons, section 32(5) shall apply in relation to his or their acquisition of that interest as it applies in relation to the acquisition of any interest by a nominee purchaser.

Termination of acquisition procedures

28. Withdrawal from acquisition by participating tenants

(1) At any time before a binding contract is entered into in pursuance of the initial notice, the participating tenants may withdraw that notice by the giving of a notice to that effect under this section ('a notice of withdrawal').

(2) A notice of withdrawal must be given –

(a) to the nominee purchaser;

(b) to the reversioner in respect of the specified premises; and

(c) to every other relevant landlord who is known or believed by the participating tenants to have given to the nominee purchaser a notice under paragraph 7(1) or (4) of Schedule 1;

and, if by virtue of paragraph (c) a notice of withdrawal falls to be given to any person falling within that paragraph, it shall state that he is a recipient of the notice.

(3) The nominee purchaser shall, on receiving a notice of withdrawal, give a copy of it to every relevant landlord who –

(a) has given to the nominee purchaser such a notice as is mentioned in subsection (2)(c); and

(b) is not stated in the notice of withdrawal to be a recipient of it.

(4) Where a notice of withdrawal is given by the participating tenatns under subsection (1) –

(a) those persons, and

(b) (subject to subsection (5)) every other person who is not a participating tenant for the time being but has at any time been such a tenant,

shall be liable –

(i) to the reversioner, and

(ii) to every other relevant landlord,

for all relevant costs incurred by him in pursuance of the initial notice down to the time when the notice of withdrawal or a copy of it is given to him in accordance with subsection (2) or (3).

(5) A person falling within paragraph (b) of subsection (4) shall not be liable for any costs by virtue of that subsection if –

(a) the lease in respect of which he was a participating tenant has been assigned to another person; and

(b) that other person has become a participating tenant in accordance with section 14(4);

and in paragraph (a) above the reference to an assignment shall be construed in accordance with section 14(10).

(6) Where any liability for costs arises under subsection (4) –

(a) it shall be a joint and several liability of the persons concerned; and

(b) the nominee purchaser shall not be liable for any costs under section 33.

(7) In subsection (4) 'relevant costs', in relation to the reversioner or any other relevant landlord, means costs for which the nominee purchaser would (apart from subsection (6)) be liable to that person under section 33.

29. Deemed withdrawal of initial notice

(1) Where, in a case falling within paragraph (a) of subsection (1) of section 22 –

(a) no application for an order under that subsection is made within the period specified in subsection (2) of that section, or

(b) such an application is so made but is subsequently withdrawn,

the initial notice shall be deemed to have been withdrawn –

(i) (if paragraph (a) above applies) at the end of that period, or

(ii) (if paragraph (b) above applies) on the date of the withdrawal of the application.

(2) Where –

(a) in a case to which subsection (1) of section 24 applies, no application under that subsection is made within the period specified in subsection (2) of that section, or

(b) in a case to which subsection (3) of that section applies, no application for an order under subsection (4) of that section is made within the period specified in subsection (5) of that section,

the initial notice shall be deemed to have been withdrawn at the end of the period referred to in paragraph (a) or (b) above (as the case may be).

(3) Where, in a case falling within paragraph (a) or (b) of subsection (1) of section 25, no application for an order under that subsection is made within the period specified in subsection (4) of that section, the initial notice shall be deemed to have been withdrawn at the end of that period.

(4) Where, in a case to which subsection (5) of section 25 applies, no application for an order under subsection (6) of that section is made within the period specified in subsection (7) of that section, the initial notice shall be deemed to have been withdrawn at the end of that period.

(5) The following provisions, namely –

(a) section 15(10),

(b) section 16(8),

(c) section 20(3),

(d) section 24(4)(c), and
(e) section 25(6)(c),
also make provision for a notice under section 13 to be deemed to have been withdrawn at a particular time.

(6) Where the initial notice is deemed to have been withdrawn at any time by virtue of any provision of this Chapter, subsections (4) and (5) of section 28 shall apply for the purposes of this section in like manner as they apply where a notice of withdrawal is given under that section, but as if the reference in subsection (4) of that section to the time when a notice or copy is given as there mentioned were a reference to the time when the initial notice is so deemed to have been withdrawn.

(7) Where the initial notice is deemed to have been withdrawn by virtue of section 15(10) or 16(8) –
(a) the liability for costs arising by virtue of subsection (6) above shall be a joint and several liability of the persons concerned; and
(b) the nominee purchaser shall not be liable for any costs under section 33.

(8) In the provisions applied by subsection (6), 'relevant costs', in relation to the reversioner or any other relevant landlord, means costs for which the nominee purchaser is, or would (apart from subsection (7)) be, liable to that person under section 33.

30. Effect on initial notice or subsequent contract of institution of compulsory acquisition procedures

(1) A notice given under section 13 shall be of no effect if on the relevant date –
(a) any acquiring authority has, with a view to the acquisition of the whole or part of the specified premises for any authorised purpose –
(i) served notice to treat on any relevant person, or
(ii) entered into a contract for the purchase of the interest of any such person in the premises or part of them, and
(b) the notice to treat or contract remains in force.

(2) In subsection (1) 'relevant person', in relation to the specified premises, means –
(a) the person who owns the freehold of the premises; or
(b) any other person who owns any leasehold interest in the premises which is specified in the initial notice under section 13(3)(c)(i).

(3) A notice given under section 13 shall not specify under subsection (3)(a)(ii) or (c)(i) of that section any property or leasehold interest in property if on the relevant date –
(a) any acquiring authority has, with a view to the acquisition of the whole or part of the property for any authorised purpose –
(i) served notice to treat on the person who owns the freehold of, or any such leasehold interest in, the property, or
(ii) entered into a contract for the purchase of the interest of any such person in the property or part of it, and
(b) the notice to treat or contract remains in force.

(4) A notice given under section 13 shall cease to have effect if, before a binding contract is entered into in pursuance of the notice, any acquiring authority serves, with a view to the acquisition of the whole or part of the specified premises for any authorised purpose, notice to treat as mentioned in subsection (1)(a).

(5) Where any such authority so serves notice to treat at any time after a binding contract is entered into in pursuance of the notice given under section 13 but before

completion of the acquisition by the nominee purchaser under this Chapter, then (without prejudice to the general law as to the frustration of contracts) the parties to the contract shall be discharged from the further performance of the contract.

(6) Where subsection (4) or (5) applies in relation to the initial notice or any contract entered into in pursuance of it, then on the occasion of the compulsory acquisition in question the compensation payable in respect of any interest in the specified premises (whether or not the one to which the relevant notice to treat relates) shall be determined on the basis of the value of the interest –

(a) (if subsection (4) applies) subject to and with the benefit of the rights and obligations arising from the initial notice and affecting that interest; or
(b) (if subsection (5) applies) subject to and with the benefit of the rights and obligations arising from the contract and affecting that interest.

(7) In this section –

(a) 'acquiring authority', in relation to the specified premises or any other property, means any person or body of persons who has or have been, or could be, authorised to acquire the whole or part of those premises or that property compulsorily for any purpose; and
(b) 'authorised purpose', in relation to any acquiring authority, means any such purpose.

31. Effect on initial notice of designation for inheritance tax purposes and applications for designation

(1) A notice given under section 13 shall be of no effect if on the relevant date the whole or any part of –

(a) the specified premises, or
(b) any property specified in the notice under section 13(3)(a)(ii), is qualifying property.

(2) For the purposes of this section the whole or any part of the specified premises, or of any property specified as mentioned in subsection (1), is qualifying property if –

(a) it has been designated under section 31(1)(b), (c) or (d) of the Inheritance Tax Act 1984 (designation and undertakings relating to conditionally exempt transfers), whether with or without any other property, and no chargeable event has subsequently occurred with respect to it; or
(b) an application to the Board for it to be so designated is pending; or
(c) it is the property of a body not established or conducted for profit and a direction has been given in relation to it under section 26 of that Act (gifts for public benefit), whether with or without any other property; or
(d) an application to the Board for a direction to be so given in relation to it is pending.

(3) For the purposes of subsection (2) an application is pending as from the time when it is made to the Board until such time as it is either granted or refused by the Board or withdrawn by the applicant; and for this purpose an application shall not be regarded as made unless and until the applicant has submitted to the Board all such information in support of the application as is required by the Board.

(4) A notice given under section 13 shall cease to have effect if, before a binding contract is entered into in pursuance of the notice, the whole or any part of –

(a) the specified premises, or

(b) any property specified in the notice under section 13(3)(a)(ii), becomes qualifying property.

(5) Where a notice under section 13 ceases to have effect by virtue of subsection (4) above –

(a) the nominee purchaser shall not be liable for any costs under section 33; and

(b) the person who applied or is applying for designation or a direction shall be liable –

(i) to the qualifying tenants by whom the notice was given for all reasonable costs incurred by them in the preparation and giving of the notice; and

(ii) to the nominee purchaser for all reasonable costs incurred in pursuance of the notice by him or by any other person who has acted as the nominee purchaser.

(6) Where it is claimed that subsection (1) or (4) applies in relation to a notice under section 13, the person making the claim shall, at the time of making it, furnish the nominee purchaser with evidence in support of it; and if he fails to do so he shall be liable for any costs which are reasonably incurred by the nominee purchaser in consequence of the failure.

(7) In subsection (2) –

(a) paragraphs (a) and (b) apply to designation under section 34(1)(a), (b) or (c) of the Finance Act 1975 or section 77(1)(b), (c) or (d) of the Finance Act 1976 as they apply to designation under section 31(1)(b), (c) or (d) of the Inheritance Tax Act 1984; and

(b) paragraphs (c) and (d) apply to a direction under paragraph 13 of Schedule 6 to the Finance Act 1975 as they apply to a direction under section 26 of that Act of 1984.

(8) In this section –

'the Board' means the Commissioners of Inland Revenue;

'chargeable event' means –

(a) any event which in accordance with any provision of Chapter II of Part II of the Inheritance Tax Act 1984 (exempt transfers) is a chargeable event, including any such provision as applied by section 78(3) of that Act (conditionally exempt occasions); or

(b) any event which would have been a chargeable event in the circumstances mentioned in section 79(3) of that Act (exemption from ten-yearly charge).

Determination of price and costs of enfranchisement

32. Determination of price

(1) Schedule 6 to this Act (which relates to the determination of the price payable by the nominee purchaser in respect of each of the freehold and other interests to be acquired by him in pursuance of this Chapter) shall have effect.

(2) The lien of the owner of any such interest (as vendor) on the specified premises, or (as the case may be) on any other property, for the price payable shall extend –

(a) to any amount which, at the time of the conveyance of that interest, are due to him from any tenants of his of premises comprised in the premises in which that interest subsists (whether due under or in respect of their leases or under or in respect of agreements collateral thereto); and

(b) to any amount payable to him by virtue of section 18(2); and

(c) to any costs payable to him by virtue of section 33.

(3) Subsection (2)(a) does not apply in relation to amounts due to the owner of any such interest from tenants of any premises which are to be comprised in the premises demised by a lease granted in accordance with section 36 and Schedule 9.

(4) In subsection (2) the reference to the specified premises or any other property includes a reference to a part of those premises or that property.

(5) Despite the fact that in accordance with Schedule 6 no payment or only a nominal payment is payable by the nominee purchaser in respect of the acquisition by him of any interest he shall nevertheless be deemed for all purposes to be a purchaser of that interest for a valuable consideration in money or money's worth.

33. Costs of enfranchisement

(1) Where a notice is given under section 13, then (subject to the provisions of this section and sections 28(6), 29(7) and 31(5)) the nominee purchaser shall be liable, to the extent that they have been incurred in pursuance of the notice by the reversioner or by any other relevant landlord, for the reasonable costs of and incidental to any of the following matters, namely –

(a) any investigation reasonably undertaken –

(i) of the question whether any interest in the specified premises or other property is liable to acquisition in pursuance of the initial notice, or

(ii) of any other question arising out of that notice;

(b) deducing, evidencing and verifying the title to any such interest;

(c) making out and furnishing such abstracts and copies as the nominee purchaser may require;

(d) any valuation of any interest in the specified premises or other property;

(e) any conveyance of any such interest;

but this subsection shall not apply to any costs if on a sale made voluntarily a stipulation that they were to be borne by the purchaser would be void.

(2) For the purposes of subsection (1) any costs incurred by the reversioner or any other relevant landlord in respect of professional services rendered by any person shall only be regarded as reasonable if and to the extent that costs in respect of such services might reasonably be expected to have been incurred by him if the circumstances had been such that he was personally liable for all such costs.

(3) Where by virtue of any provision of this Chapter the initial notice ceases to have effect at any time, then (subject to subsection (4)) the nominee purchaser's liability under this section for costs incurred by any person shall be a liability for costs incurred by him down to that time.

(4) The nominee purchaser shall not be liable for any costs under this section if the initial notice ceases to have effect by virtue of section 23(4) or 30(4).

(5) The nominee purchaser shall not be liable under this section for any costs which a party to any proceedings under this Chapter before a leasehold valuation tribunal incurs in connection with the proceedings.

(6) In this section references to the nominee purchaser include references to any person whose appointment has terminated in accordance with section 15(3) or 16(1); but this section shall have effect in relation to such a person subject to section 15(7).

(7) Where by virtue of this section or of this section and section 29(6) taken together, two or more persons are liable for any costs, they shall be jointly and severally liable for them.

Completion of acquisition

34. Conveyance to nominee purchaser

(1) Any conveyance executed for the purposes of this Chapter, being a conveyance to the nominee purchaser of the freehold of the specified premises or of any other property, shall grant to the nominee purchaser an estate in fee simple absolute in those premises or that property, subject only to such incumbrances as may have been agreed or determined under this Chapter to be incumbrances subject to which that estate should be granted, having regard to the following provisions of this Chapter.

(2) Any such conveyance shall, where the nominee purchaser is to acquire any leasehold interest in the specified premises or (as the case may be) in the other property to which the conveyance relates, provide for the disposal to the nominee purchaser of any such interest.

(3) Any conveyance executed for the purposes of this Chapter shall have effect under section 2(1) of the Law of Property Act 1925 (conveyances overreaching certain equitable interests etc) to overreach any incumbrance capable of being overreached under section 2(1) –

(a) as if, where the interest conveyed is settled land for the purposes of the Settled Land Act 1925, the conveyance were made under the powers of that Act, and
(b) as if the requirements of section 2(1) as to payment of the capital money allowed any part of the purchase price paid or applied in accordance with section 35 below or Schedule 8 to this Act to be so paid or applied.

(4) For the purposes of this section 'incumbrances' includes –

(a) rentcharges, and
(b) (subject to subsection (5)) personal liabilities attaching in respect of the ownership of land or an interest in land though not charged on that land or interest.

(5) Burdens originating in tenure, and burdens in respect of the upkeep or regulation for the benefit of any locality of any land, building, structure, works, ways or watercourse shall not be treated as incumbrances for the purposes of this section; but any conveyance executed for the purposes of this Chapter shall be made subject to any such burdens.

(6) A conveyance executed for the purposes of this Chapter shall not be made subject to any incumbrance capable of being overrreached by the conveyance, but shall be made subject (where they are not capable of being overreached) to –

(a) rentcharges redeemable under sections 8 to 10 of the Rentcharges Act 1977, and
(b) those falling within paragraphs (c) and (d) of section 2(3) of that Act (estate rentcharges and rentcharges imposed under certain enactments),

except as otherwise provided by subsections (7) and (8) below.

(7) Where any land is to be conveyed to the nominee purchaser by a conveyance executed for the purposes of this Chapter, subsection (6) shall not preclude the person who owns the freehold interest in the land from releasing, or procuring the release of, the land from any rentcharge.

(8) The conveyance of any such land ('the relevant land') may, with the agreement of the nominee purchaser (which shall not be unreasonably withheld), provide in accordance with section 190(1) of the Law of Property Act 1925 (charging of rentcharges on land without rent owner's consent) that a rentcharge –

(a) shall be charged exclusively on other land affected by it in exoneration of the relevant land, or

(b) shall be apportioned between other land affected by it and the relevant land.

(9) Except to the extent that any departure is agreed to by the nominee purchaser and the person whose interest is to be conveyed, any conveyance executed for the purposes of this Chapter shall –

(a) as respects the conveyance of any freehold interest, conform with the provisions of Schedule 7, and

(b) as respects the conveyance of any leasehold interest, conform with the provisions of paragraph 2 of that Schedule (any reference in that paragraph to the freeholder being read as a reference to the person whose leasehold interest is to be conveyed).

(10) Any such conveyance shall in addition contain a statement that it is a conveyance executed for the purposes of this Chapter; and any such statement shall comply with such requirements as may be prescribed by rules made in pursuance of section 144 of the Land Registration Act 1925 (power to make general rules).

35. Discharge of existing mortgages on transfer to nominee purchaser

(1) Subject to the provisions of Schedule 8, where any interest is acquired by the nominee purchaser in pursuance of this Chapter, the conveyance by virtue of which it is so acquired shall, as regards any mortgage to which this section applies, be effective by virtue of this section –

(a) to discharge the interest from the mortgage, and from the operation of any order made by a court for the enforcement of the mortgage, and

(b) to extinguish any term of years created for the purposes of the mortgage,

and shall do so without the persons entitled to or interested in the mortgage or in any such order or term of years becoming parties to or executing the conveyance.

(2) Subject to subsections (3) and (4), this section applies to any mortgage of the interest so acquired (however created or arising) which –

(a) is a mortgage to secure the payment of money or the performance of any other obligation by the person from whom the interest is so acquired or any other person; and

(b) is not a mortgage which would be overreached apart from this section.

(3) This section shall not apply to any such mortgage if it has been agreed between the nominee purchaser and the reversioner or (as the case may be) any other relevant landlord that the interest in question should be acquired subject to the mortgage.

(4) In this section and Schedule 8 'mortgage' includes a charge or lien; but neither this section nor that Schedule applies to a rentcharge.

36. Nominee purchaser required to grant leases back to former freeholder in certain circumstances

(1) In connection with the acquisition by him of the freehold of the specified premises, the nominee purchaser shall grant to the person from whom the freehold is acquired

such leases of flats or other units contained in those premises as are required to be so granted by virtue of Part II or III of Schedule 9.

(2) Any such lease shall be granted so as to take effect immediately after the acquisition by the nominee purchaser of the freehold of the specified premises.

(3) Where any flat or other unit demised under any such lease ('the relevant lease') is at the time of that acquisition subject to any existing lease, the relevant lease shall take effect as a lease of the freehold reversion in respect of the flat or other unit.

(4) Part IV of Schedule 9 has effect with respect to the terms of a lease granted in pursuance of Part II or III of that Schedule.

37. Acquisition of interests from local authorities etc

Schedule 10 to this Act (which makes provision with respect to the acquisition of interests from local authorities etc in pursuance of this Chapter) shall have effect.

Supplemental

38. Interpretation of Chapter I

(1) In this Chapter (unless the context otherwise requires) –
'conveyance' includes assignment, transfer and surrender, and related expressions shall be construed accordingly;
'the initial notice' means the notice given under section 13;
'the nominee purchaser' shall be construed in accordance with section 15;
'the participating tenants' shall be construed in accordance with section 14;
'premises with a resident landlord' shall be construed in accordance with section 10;
'public sector landlord' means any of the persons listed in section 171(2) of the Housing Act 1985;
'qualifying tenant' shall be construed in accordance with section 5;
'the relevant date' has the meaning given by section 1(8);
'relevant landlord' and 'the reversioner' shall be construed in accordance with section 9;
'the right to collective enfranchisement' means the right specified in section 1(1);
'secure tenancy' has the meaning given by section 79 of the Housing Act 1985;
'the specified premises' shall be construed in accordance with section 13(12);
'the terms of acquisition' has the meaning given by section 24(8);
'unit' means –
- (a) a flat;
- (b) any other separate set of premises which is constructed or adapted for use for the purposes of a dwelling; or
- (c) a separate set of premises let, or intended for letting, on a business lease.

(2) Any reference in this Chapter (however expressed) to the acquisition or proposed acquisition by the nominee purchaser is a reference to the acquisition or proposed acquisition by the nominee purchaser, on behalf of the participating tenants, of such freehold and other interests as fall to be so acquired under a contract entered into in pursuance of the initial notice.

(3) Any reference in this Chapter to the interest of a relevant landlord in the specified premises is a reference to the interest in those premises by virtue of which he is, in accordance with section 9(2)(b), a relevant landlord.

(4) Any reference in this Chapter to agreement in relation to all or any of the terms of acquisition is a reference to agreement subject to contract.

CHAPTER II

INDIVIDUAL RIGHT OF TENANT OF FLAT TO ACQUIRE NEW LEASE

Preliminary

39. Right of qualifying tenant of flat to acquire new lease

(1) This Chapter has effect for the purpose of conferring on a tenant of a flat, in the circumstances mentioned in subsection (2), the right, exercisable subject to and in accordance with this Chapter, to acquire a new lease of the flat on payment of a premium determined in accordance with this Chapter.

(2) Those circumstances are that on the relevant date for the purposes of this Chapter –
- (a) the tenant is a qualifying tenant of the flat; and
- (b) the tenant has occupied the flat as his only or principal home –
  - (i) for the last three years, or
  - (ii) for periods amounting to three years in the last ten years,

  whether or not he has used it also for other purposes.

(3) The following provisions, namely –
- (a) section 5 (with the omission of subsections (5) and (6)),
- (b) section 7, and
- (c) section 8,

shall apply for the purposes of this Chapter as they apply for the purposes of Chapter I; and references in this Chapter to a qualifying tenant of a flat shall accordingly be construed by reference to those provisions.

(4) For the purposes of this Chapter a person can be (or be among those constituting) the qualifying tenant of each of two or more flats at the same time, whether he is tenant of those flats under one lease or under two or more separate leases.

(5) For the purposes of subsection (2)(b) above –
- (a) any reference to the tenant's flat includes a reference to part of it; and
- (b) it is immaterial whether at any particular time the tenant's occupation was in right of the lease by virtue of which he is a qualifying tenant or in right of some other lease or otherwise;

but any occupation by a company or other artificial person, or (where the tenant is a corporation sole) by the corporator, shall not be regarded as occupation for the purposes of that provision.

(6) In the case of a lease held by joint tenants –
- (a) the condition in subsection (2)(b) need only be satisfied with respect to one of the joint tenants; and
- (b) subsection (5) shall apply accordingly (the reference to the lease by virtue of which the tenant is a qualifying tenant being read for this purpose as a reference to the lease by virtue of which the joint tenants are a qualifying tenant).

(7) The right conferred by this Chapter on a tenant to acquire a new lease shall not extend to underlying minerals comprised in his existing lease if –
- (a) the landlord requires the minerals to be excepted, and
- (b) proper provision is made for the support of the premises demised by that existing lease as they are enjoyed on the relevant date.

(8) In this Chapter 'the relevant date', in relation to a claim by a tenant under this Chapter, means the date on which notice of the claim is given to the landlord under section 42.

40. The landlord for the purposes of this Chapter

(1) In this Chapter 'the landlord', in relation to the lease held by a qualifying tenant of a flat, means the person who is the owner of that interest in the flat which for the time being fulfils the following conditions, namely –

(a) it is an interest in reversion expectant (whether immediately or not) on the termination of the tenant's lease, and

(b) it is either a freehold interest or a leasehold interest whose duration is such as to enable that person to grant a new lease of that flat in accordance with this Chapter,

and is not itself expectant (whether immediately or not) on an interest which fulfils those conditions.

(2) Where in accordance with subsection (1) the immediate landlord under the lease of a qualifying tenant of a flat is not the landlord in relation to that lease for the purposes of this Chapter, the person who for those purposes is the landlord in relation to it shall conduct on behalf of all the other landlords all proceedings arising out of any notice given by the tenant with respect to the flat under section 42 (whether the proceedings are for resisting or giving effect to the claim in question).

(3) Subsection (2) has effect subject to the provisions of Schedule 11 to this Act (which makes provision in relation to the operation of this chapter in cases to which that subsection applies).

(4) In this section and that Schedule –

(a) 'the tenant' means any such qualifying tenant as is referred to in subsection (2) and 'the tenant's lease' means the lease by virtue of which he is a qualifying tenant;

(b) 'the competent landlord' means the person who, in relation to the tenant's lease, is the landlord (as defined by subsection (1)) for the purposes of this Chapter;

(c) 'other landlord' means any person (other than the tenant or a trustee for him) in whom there is vested a concurrent tenancy intermediate between the interest of the competent landlord and the tenant's lease.

(5) Schedule 2 (which makes provision with respect to certain special categories of landlords) has effect for the purposes of this Chapter.

Preliminary inquiries by qualifying tenant

41. Right of qualifying tenant to obtain information about superior interests etc

(1) A qualifying tenant of a flat may give –

(a) to his immediate landlord, or

(b) to any person receiving rent on behalf of his immediate landlord,

a notice requiring the recipient to state whether the immediate landlord is the owner of the freehold interest in the flat and, if not, to give the tenant such information as is mentioned in subsection (2) (so far as known to the recipient).

(2) That information is –

(a) the name and address of the person who owns the freehold interest in the flat;

(b) the duration of the leasehold interest in the flat of the tenant's immediate landlord and the extent of the premises in which it subsists; and

(c) the name and address of every person who has a leasehold interest in the flat which is superior to that of the tenant's immediate landlord, the duration of any such interest and the extent of the premises in which it subsists.

(3) If the immediate landlord of any such qualifying tenant is not the owner of the freehold interest in the flat, the tenant may also –

(a) give to the person who is the owner of that interest a notice requiring him to give the tenant such information as is mentioned in paragraph (c) of subsection (2) (so far as known to that person);

(b) give to any person falling within that paragraph a notice requiring him to give the tenant –

(i) particulars of the duration of his leasehold interest in the flat and the extent of the premises in which it subsists, and

(ii) (so far as known to him) such information as is mentioned in paragraph (a) of that subsection and, as regards any other person falling within paragraph (c) of that subsection, such information as is mentioned in that paragraph.

(4) Any notice given by a qualifying tenant under this section shall, in addition to any other requirement imposed in accordance with subsections (1) to (3), require the recipient to state –

(a) whether he has received in respect of any premises containing the tenant's flat –

(i) a notice under section 13 in the case of which the relevant claim under Chapter I is still current, or

(ii) a copy of such a notice; and

(b) if so, the date on which the notice under section 13 was given and the name and address of the nominee purchaser for the time being appointed for the purposes of section 15 in relation to that claim.

(5) For the purposes of subsection (4) –

(a) 'the relevant claim under Chapter I', in relation to a notice under section 13, means the claim in respect of which that notice is given; and

(b) any such claim is current if –

(i) that notice continues in force in accordance with section 13(11), or

(ii) a binding contract entered into in pursuance of that notice remains in force, or

(iii) where an order has been made under section 24(4)(a) or (b) or 25(6)(a) or (b) with respect to any such premises as are referred to in subsection (4)(a) above, any interests which by virtue of the order fall to be vested in the nominee purchaser for the purposes of Chapter I have yet to be so vested.

(6) Any person who is required to give any information by virtue of a notice under this section shall give that information to the qualifying tenant within the period of 28 days beginning with the date of the giving of the notice.

The tenant's notice

42. Notice by qualifying tenant of claim to exercise right

(1) A claim by a qualifying tenant of a flat to exercise the right to acquire a new lease of the flat is made by the giving of notice of the claim under this section.

(2) A notice given by a tenant under this section ('the tenant's notice') must be given –

(a) to the landlord, and

(b) to any third party to the tenant's lease.

(3) The tenant's notice must –

(a) state the full name of the tenant and the address of the flat in respect of which he claims a new lease under this Chapter;
(b) contain the following particulars, namely –
  (i) sufficient particulars of that flat to identify the property to which the claim extends,
  (ii) such particulars of the tenant's lease as are sufficient to identify it, including the date on which the lease was entered into, the term for which it was granted and the date of the commencement of the term,
  (iii) such further particulars as are necessary to show that the tenant's lease is, in accordance with section 8 (as that section applies in accordance with section 39(3)), a lease at a low rent, and
  (iv) particulars of the period or periods falling within the preceding ten years for which the tenant has occupied the whole or part of the flat as his only or principal home;
(c) specify the premium which the tenant proposes to pay in respect of the grant of a new lease under this Chapter and, where any other amount will be payable by him in accordance with any provision of Schedule 13, the amount which he proposes to pay in accordance with that provision;
(d) specify the terms which the tenant proposes should be contained in any such lease;
(e) state the name of the person (if any) appointed by the tenant to act for him in connection with this claim, and an address in England and Wales at which notices may be given to any such person under this Chapter; and
(f) specify the date by which the landlord must respond to the notice by giving a counter-notice under section 45.

(4) If the tenant's lease is held by joint tenants, the reference to the tenant in subsection (3)(b)(iv) shall be read as a reference to any joint tenant with respect to whom it is claimed that the condition in section 39(2)(b) is satisfied.

(5) The date specified in the tenant's notice in pursuance of subsection (3)(f) must be a date falling not less than two months after the date of the giving of the notice.

(6) Where a notice under this section has been given with respect to any flat, no subsequent notice may be given under this section with respect to the flat so long as the earlier notice continues in force.

(7) Where a notice under this section has been given with respect to a flat and –
(a) that notice has been withdrawn, or is deemed to have been withdrawn, under or by virtue of any provision of this Chapter, or
(b) in response to that notice, an order has been applied for and obtained under section 47(1),

no subsequent notice may be given under this section with respect to the flat within the period of twelve months beginning with the date of the withdrawal or deemed withdrawal of the earlier notice or with the time when the order under section 47(1) becomes final (as the case may be).

(8) Where a notice is given in accordance with this section, then for the purposes of this Chapter the notice continues in force as from the relevant date –
(a) until a new lease is granted in pursuance of the notice;
(b) if the notice is withdrawn, or is deemed to have been withdrawn, under or by virtue of any provision of this Chapter, until the date of the withdrawal or deemed withdrawal; or
(c) until such other time as the notice ceases to have effect by virtue of any provision of this Chapter;

but this subsection has effect subject to section 54.

(9) Schedule 12 (which contains restrictions on terminating a tenant's lease where he has given a notice under this section amd makes other provision in connection with the giving of notices under this section) shall have effect.

43. General provisions as respects effect of tenant's notice

(1) Where a notice has been given under section 42 with respect to any flat, the rights and obligations of the landlord and the tenant arising from the notice shall enure for the benefit of and be enforceable against them, their personal representatives and assigns to the like extent (but no further) as rights and obligations arising under a contract for leasing freely entered into between the landlord and the tenant.

(2) Accordingly, in relation to matters arising out of any such notice, references in this Chapter to the landlord and the tenant shall, in so far as the context permits, include their respective personal representatives and assigns.

(3) Notwithstanding anything in subsection (1), the righs and obligations of the tenant shall be assignable with, but shall not be capable of subsisting apart from, the lease of the entire flat; and, if the tenant's lease is assigned without the benefit of the notice, the notice shall accordingly be deemed to have been withdrawn by the tenant as at the date of the assignment.

(4) In the event of any default by the landlord or the tenant in carrying out the obligations arising from the tenant's notice, the other of them shall have the like rights and remedies as in the case of a contract freely entered into.

(5) In a case to which section 40(2) applies, the rights and obligations of the landlord arising out of the tenant's notice shall, so far as their interests are affected, be rights and obligations respectively of the competent landlord and of each of the other landlords, and references to the landlord in subsections (1) and (2) above shall apply accordingly.

(6) In subsection (5) 'competent landlord' and 'other landlord' have the meaning given by section 40(4); and subsection (5) has effect without prejudice to the operation of section 40(2) or Schedule 11.

Procedure following giving of tenant's notice

44. Access by landlords for valuation purposes

(1) Once the tenant's notice or a copy of it has been given in accordance with section 42 or Part I of Schedule 11 –

(a) to the landlord for the purposes of this Chapter, or

(b) to any other landlord (as defined by section 40(4)),

that landlord and any person authorised to act on his behalf shall have a right of access to the flat to which the notice relates for the purpose of enabling that landlord to obtain, in connection with the notice, a valuation of his interest in the flat.

(2) That right shall be exercisable at any reasonable time and on giving not less than 3 days' notice to the tenant.

45. Landlord's counter-notice

(1) The landlord shall give a counter-notice under this section to the tenant by the date specified in the tenant's notice in pursuance of section 42(3)(f).

(2) The counter-notice must comply with one of the following requirements –
- (a) state that the landlord admits that the tenant had on the relevant date the right to acquire a new lease of his flat;
- (b) state that, for such reasons as are specified in the counter-notice, the landlord does not admit that the tenant had such a right on that date;
- (c) contain such a statement as is mentioned in paragraph (a) or (b) above but state that the landlord intends to make an application for an order under section 47(1) on the grounds that he intends to redevelop any premises in which the flat is contained.

(3) If the counter-notice complies with the requirement set out in subsection (2)(a), it must in addition –
- (a) state which (if any) of the proposals contained in the tenant's notice are accepted by the landlord and which (if any) of those proposals are not so accepted; and
- (b) specify, in relation to each proposal which is not accepted, the landlord's counter-proposal.

(4) The counter-notice must specify an address in England and Wales at which notices may be given to the landlord under this Chapter.

(5) Where the counter-notice admits the tenant's right to acquire a new lease of his flat, the admission shall be binding on the landlord as to the matters mentioned in section 39(2)(a) and (b), unless the landlord shows that he was induced to make the admission by misrepresentation or the concealment of material facts; but the admission shall not conclude any question whether the particulars of the flat stated in the tenant's notice in pursuance of section 42(3)(b)(i) are correct.

Applications to court or leasehold valuation tribunal

46. Proceedings relating to validity of tenant's notice

(1) Where –
- (a) the landlord has given the tenant a counter-notice under section 45 which (whether it complies with the requirement set out in subsection (2)(b) or (c) of that section) contains such a statement as is mentioned in subsection (2)(b) of that section, and
- (b) the court is satisfied, on an application made by the landlord, that on the relevant date the tenant had no right under this Chapter to acquire a new lease of his flat,

the court shall by order make a declaration to that effect.

(2) Any application for an order under subsection (1) must be made not later than the end of the period of two months beginning with the date of the giving of the counter-notice to the tenant; and if, in a case falling within paragraph (a) of that subsection, either –
- (a) no application for such an order is made by the landlord within that period, or
- (b) such an application is so made but is subsequently withdrawn,

section 49 shall apply as if the landlord had not given the counter-notice.

(3) If on any such application the court makes such a declaration as is mentioned and in subsection (1), the tenant's notice shall cease to have effect on the order becoming final.

(4) If, however, any such application is dismissed by the court, then (subject to subsection (5)) the court shall make an order –
- (a) declaring that the landlord's counter-notice shall be of no effect, and
- (b) requiring the landlord to give a further counter-notice to the tenant by such date as is specified in the order.

(5) Subsection (4) shall not apply if –
(a) the counter-notice complies with the requirement set out in section 45(2)(c), and
(b) either –
(i) an application for an order under section 47(1) is pending, or
(ii) the period specified in section 47(3) as the period for the making of such an application has not expired.

(6) Subsection (3) of section 45 shall apply to any further counter-notice required to be given by the landlord under subsection (4) above as if it were a counter-notice under that section complying with the requirement set out in subsection (2)(a) of that section.

47. Application to defeat tenant's claim where landlord intends to redevelop

(1) Where the landlord has given the tenant a counter-notice under section 45 which complies with the requirement set out in subsection (2)(c) of that section, the court may, on the application of the landlord, by order declare that the right to acquire a new lease shall not be exercisable by the tenant by reason of the landlord's intention to redevelop any premises in which the tenant's flat is contained; and on such an order becoming final the tenant's notice shall cease to have effect.

(2) The court shall not make an order under subsection (1) unless it is satisfied –
(a) that the tenant's lease of his flat is due to terminate within the period of five years beginning with the relevant date; and
(b) that for the purposes of redevelopment the landlord intends, once the lease has so terminated –
(i) to demolish or reconstruct, or
(ii) to carry out substantial works of construction on,
the whole or a substantial part of any premises in which the flat is contained; and
(c) that he could not reasonably do so without obtaining possession of the flat.

(3) Any application for an order under subsection (1) must be made within the period of two months beginning with the date of the giving of the counter-notice to the tenant; but, where the counter-notice is one falling within section 46(1)(a), such an application shall not be proceeded with until such time (if any) as any order dismissing an application under section 46(1) becomes final.

(4) Where an application for an order under subsection (1) is dismissed by the court, the court shall make an order –
(a) declaring that the landlord's counter-notice shall be of no effect, and
(b) requiring the landlord to give a further counter-notice to the tenant by such date as is specified in the order.

(5) Where –
(a) the landlord has given such a counter-notice as is mentioned in subsection (1), but
(b) either –
(i) no application for an order under that subsection is made within the period referred to in subsection (3), or
(ii) such an application is so made but is subsequently withdrawn,
then (subject to subsection (7)), the landlord shall give a further counter-notice to the tenant within the period of two months beginning with the appropriate date.

(6) In subsection (5) 'the appropriate date' means –
(a) if subsection (5)(b)(i) applies, the date immediately following the end of the period referred to in subsection (3); and

(b) if subsection (5)(b)(ii) applies, the date of withdrawal of the application.

(7) Subsection (5) shall not apply if any application has been made by the landlord for an order under section 46(1).

(8) Subsection (3) of section 45 shall apply to any further counter-notice required to be given by the landlord under subsection (4) or (5) above as if it were a counter-notice under that section complying with the requirement set out in subsection (2)(a) of that section.

48. Applications where terms in dispute or failure to enter into new lease

(1) Where the landlord his given the tenant –
- (a) a counter-notice under section 45 which complies with the requirement set out in subsection (2)(a) of that section, or
- (b) a further counter-notice required by or by virtue of section 46(4) or section 47(4) or (5),

but any of the terms of acquisition remain in dispute at the end of the period of two months beginning with the date when the counter-notice or further counter-notice was so given, a leasehold valuation tribunal may, on the application of either the tenant or the landlord, determine the matters in dispute.

(2) Any application under subsection (1) must be made not later than the end of the period of six months beginning with the date on which the counter-notice or further counter-notice was given to the tenant.

(3) Where –
- (a) the landlord has given the tenant such a counter-notice or further counter-notice as is mentioned in subsection (1)(a) or (b), and
- (b) all the terms of acquisition have been either agreed between those persons or determined by a leasehold valuation tribunal under subsection (1),

but a new lease has not been entered into in pursuance of the tenant's notice by the end of the appropriate period specified in subsection (6), the court may, on the application of either the tenant or the landlord, make such order as it thinks fit with respect to the performance or discharge of any obligations arising out of that notice.

(4) Any such order may provide for the tenant's notice to be deemed to have been withdrawn at the end of the appropriate period specified in subsection (6).

(5) Any application for an order under subsection (3) must be made not later than the end of the period of two months beginning immediately after the end of the appropriate period specified in subsection (6).

(6) For the purposes of this section the appropriate period is –
- (a) where all of the terms of acquisition have been agreed between the tenant and the landlord, the period of two months beginning with the date when those terms were finally so agreed; or
- (b) where all or any of those terms have been determined by a leasehold valuation tribunal under subsection (1) –
  - (i) the period of two months beginning with the date when the decision of the tribunal under subsection (1) becomes final, or
  - (ii) such other period as may have been fixed by the tribunal when making its determination.

(7) In this Chapter 'the terms of acquisition', in relation to a claim by a tenant under this Chapter, means the terms on which the tenant is to acquire a new lease of his flat, whether they relate to the terms to be contained in the lease or to the premium or any other amount payable by virtue of Schedule 13 in connection with the grant of the lease, or otherwise.

49. Applications where landlord fails to give counter-notice or further counter-notice

(1) Where the tenant's notice has been given in accordance with section 42 but –
- (a) the landlord has failed to give the tenant a counter-notice in accordance with section 45(1), or
- (b) if required to give a further counter-notice to the tenant by or by virtue of section 46(4) or section 47(4) or (5), the landlord has failed to comply with that requirement,

the court may, on the application of the tenant, make an order determining, in accordance with the proposals contained in the tenant's notice, the terms of acquisition.

(2) The court shall not make such an order on an application made by virtue of paragraph (a) of subsection (1) unless it is satisfied –
- (a) that on the relevant date the tenant had the right to acquire a new lease of his flat; and
- (b) if applicable, that the requirements of Part I of Schedule 11 were complied with as respects the giving of copies of the tenant's notice.

(3) Any application for an order under subsection (1) must be made not later than the end of the period of six months beginning with the date by which the counter-notice or further counter-notice referred to in that subsection was required to be given.

(4) Where –
- (a) the terms of acquisition have been determined by an order of the court under this section, but
- (b) a new lease has not been entered into in pursuance of the tenant's notice by the end of the appropriate period specified in subsection (7),

the court may, on the application of either the tenant or the landlord, make such order as it thinks fit with respect to the performance or discharge of any obligations arising out of that notice.

(5) Any such order may provide for the tenant's notice to be deemed to have been withdrawn at the end of the appropriate period specified in subsection (7).

(6) Any application for an order under subsection (4) must be made not later than the end of the period of two months beginning immediately after the end of the appropriate period specified in subsection (7).

(7) For the purposes of this section the appropriate period is –
- (a) the period of two months beginning with the date when the order of the court under subsection (1) becomes final, or
- (b) such other period as may have been fixed by the court when making that order.

50. Applications where landlord cannot be found

(1) Where –
- (a) a qualifying tenant of a flat desires to make a claim to exercise the right to acquire a new lease of his flat, but
- (b) the landlord cannot be found or his identity cannot be ascertained,

the court may, on the application of the tenant, make a vesting order under this subsection.

(2) Where –

(a) a qualifying tenant of a flat desires to make such a claim as is mentioned in subsection (1), and

(b) paragraph (b) of that subsection does not apply, but

(c) a copy of a notice of that claim cannot be given in accordance with Part I of Schedule 11 to any person to whom it would otherwise be required to be so given because that person cannot be found or his identity cannot be ascertained,

the court may, on the application of the tenant, make an order dispensing with the need to give a copy of such a notice to that person.

(3) The court shall not make an order on any application under subsection (1) or (2) unless it is satisfied –

(a) that on the date of the making of the application the tenant had the right to acquire a new lease of his flat; and

(b) that on that date he would not have been precluded by any provision of this Chapter from giving a valid notice under section 42 with respect to his flat.

(4) Before making any such order the court may require the tenant to take such further steps by way of advertisement or otherwise as the court thinks proper for the purpose of tracing the person in question; and if, after an application is made for a vesting order under subsection (1) and before any lease is executed in pursuance of the application the landlord is traced, then no further proceedings shall be taken with a view to a lease being so executed, but (subject to subsection (5)) –

(a) the rights and obligations of all parties shall be determined as if the tenant had, at the date of the application, duly given notice under section 42 of his claim to exercise the right to acquire a new lease of his flat; and

(b) the court may give such directions as the court thinks fit as to the steps to be taken for giving effect to those rights and obligations, including directions modifying or dispensing with any of the requirements of thie Chapter or of regulations made under this Part.

(5) An application for a vesting order under subsection (1) may be withdrawn at any time before execution of a lease under section 51(3) and, after it is withdrawn, subsection (4)(a) above shall not apply; but where any step is taken (whether by the landlord or the tenant) for the purpose of giving effect so subsection (4)(a) in the case of any application, the application shall not afterwards be withdrawn except –

(a) with the consent of the landlord, or

(b) by leave of the court,

and the court shall not give leave unless it appears to the court just to do so by reason of matters coming to the knowledge of the tenant in consequence of the tracing of the landlord.

(6) Where an order has been made under subsection (2) dispensing with the need to give a copy of a notice under section 42 to a particular person with respect to any flat, then if –

(a) a notice is subsequently given under that section with respect to that flat, and

(b) in reliance on the order, a copy of the notice is not to be given to that person,

the notice must contain a statement of the effect of the order.

(7) Where a notice under section 42 contains such a statement in accordance with subsection (6) above, then in determining for the purposes of any provision of this

Chapter whether the requirements of Part I of Schedule 11 have been complied with in relation to the notice, those requirements shall be deemed to have been complied with so far as relating to the giving of a copy of the notice to the person referred to in subsection (6) above.

51. Supplementary provisions relating to vesting orders under section 50(1)

(1) A vesting order under section 50(1) is an order providing for the surrender of the tenant's lease of his flat and for the granting to him of a new lease of it on such terms as may be determined by a leasehold valuation tribunal to be appropriate with a view to the lease being granted to him in like manner (so far as the circumstances permit) as if he had, at the date of his application, given notice under section 42 of his claim to exercise the right to acquire a new lease of his flat.

(2) If a leasehold valuation tribunal so determines in the case of a vesting order under section 50(1), the order shall have effect in relation to property which is less extensive than that specified in the application on which the order was made.

(3) Where any lease is to be granted to a tenant by virtue of a vesting order under section 50(1), then on his paying into court the appropriate sum there shall be executed by such person as the court may designate a lease which –

(a) is in a form approved by a leasehold valuation tribunal, and

(b) contains such provisions as may be so approved for the purpose of giving effect so far as possible to section 56(1) and section 57 (as that section applies in accordance with subsections (7) and (8) below);

and that lease shall be effective to vest in the person to whom it is granted the property expressed to be demised by it, subject to and in accordance with the terms of the lease.

(4) In connection with the determination by a leasehold valuation tribunal of any question as to the property to be demised by any such lease, or as to the rights with or subject to which it is to be demised, it shall be assumed (unless the contrary is shown) that the landlord has no interest in property other than the property to be demised and, for the purpose of excepting them from the lease, any minerals underlying that property.

(5) The appropriate sum to be paid into court in accordance with subsection (3) is the aggregate of –

(a) such amount as may be determined by a leasehold valuation tribunal to be the premium which is payable under Schedule 13 in respect of the grant of the new lease;

(b) such other amount or amounts (if any) as may be determined by such a tribunal to be payable by virtue of that Schedule in connection with the grant of that lease; and

(c) any amounts or estimated amounts determined by such a tribunal as being, at the time of execution of that lease, due to the landlord from the tenant (whether due under or in respect of the tenant's lease of his flat or under or in respect of any agreement collateral thereto).

(6) Where any lease is granted to a person in accordance with this section, the payment into court of the appropriate sum shall be taken to have satisfied any claims against the tenant, his personal representatives or assigns in respect of the premium and any other amounts payable as mentioned in subsection (5)(a) and (b).

(7) Subject to subsection (8), the following provisions, namely –

(a) sections 57 to 59, and

(b) section 61 and Schedule 14,

shall, so far as capable of applying to a lease granted in accordance with this section, apply to such a lease as they apply to a lease granted under section 56; and subsections (6) and (7) of that section shall apply in relation to a lease granted in accordance with this section as they apply in relation to a lease granted under that section.

(8) In its application to a lease granted in accordance with this section –
- (a) section 57 shall have effect as if –
  - (i) any reference to the relevant date were a reference to the date of the application under section 50(1) in pursuance of which the vesting order under that provision was made, and
  - (ii) in subsection (5) the reference to section 56(3)(a) were a reference to subsection (5)(c) above; and
- (b) section 58 shall have effect as if –
  - (i) in subsection (3) the second reference to the landlord were a reference to the person designated under subsection (3) above, and
  - (ii) subsections (6)(a) and (7) were omitted.

Termination or suspension of acquisition procedures

52. Withdrawal by tenant from acquisition of new lease

(1) At any time before a new lease is entered into in pursuance of the tenant's notice, the tenant may withdraw that notice by the giving of a notice to that effect under this section ('a notice of withdrawal').

(2) A notice of withdrawal must be given –
- (a) to the landlord for the purposes of this Chapter;
- (b) to every other landlord (as defined by section 40(4)); and
- (c) to any third party to the tenant's lease.

(3) Where a notice of withdrawal is given by the tenant to any person in accordance with subsection (2), the tenant's liability under section 60 for costs incurred by that person shall be a liability for costs incurred by him down to the time when the notice is given to him.

53. Deemed withdrawal of tenant's notice

(1) Where –
- (a) in a case to which subsection (1) of section 48 applies, not application under that subsection is made within the period specified in subsection (2) of that section, or
- (b) in a case to which subsection (3) of that section applies, no application for an order under that subsection is made within the period specified in subsection (5) of that section,

the tenant's notice shall be deemed to have been withdrawn at the end of the period referred to in paragraph (a) or (b) above (as the case may be).

(2) Where, in a case falling within paragraph (a) or (b) of subsection (1) of section 49, no application for an order under that subsection is made within the period specified in subsection (3) of that section, the tenant's notice shall be deemed to have been withdrawn at the end of that period.

(3) Where, in a case to which subsection (4) of section 49 applies, no application for an order under that subsection is made within the period specified in subsection (6) of that section, the tenant's notice shall be deemed to have been withdrawn at the end of that period.

(4) The following provisions, namely –
(a) section 43(3),
(b) section 48(4), and
(c) section 49(5),
also make provision for a notice under section 42 to be deemed to have been withdrawn at a particular time.

54. Suspension of tenant's notice during currency of claim under Chapter I

(1) If, at the time when the tenant's notice is given –
(a) a notice has been given under section 13 with respect to any premises containing the tenant's flat, and
(b) the relevant claim under Chapter I is still current,
the operation of the tenant's notice shall be suspended during the currency of that claim; and so long as it is so suspended no further notice shall be given, and no application shall be made, under this Chapter with a view to resisting or giving effect to the tenant's claim.

(2) If, at any time when the tenant's notice continues in force, a notice is given under section 13 with respect to any premises containing the tenant's flat, then, as from the date which is the relevant date for the purposes of Chapter I in relation to that notice under section 13, the operation of the tenant's notice shall be suspended during the currency of the relevant claim under Chapter I; and so long as it is so suspended no further notice shall be given, and no application shall be made or proceeded with, under this Chapter with a view to resisting or giving effect to the tenant's claim.

(3) Where the operation of the tenant's notice is suspended by virtue of subsection (1) or (2), the landlord shall give the tenant a notice informing him of its suspension –
(a) (if it is suspended by virtue of subsection (1)) not later than the date specified in the tenant's notice in pursuance of section 4293)(f); or
(b) (if it is suspended by virtue of subsection (2)) as soon as possible after the date referred to in that subsection;
and any such notice shall in addition inform the tenant of the date on which the notice under section 13 was given and of the name and address of the nominee purchaser for the time being appointed for the purposes of section 15 in relation to the relevant claim under Chapter I.

(4) Where –
(a) the operation of the tenant's notice is suspended by virtue of subsection (1), and
(b) as a result of the relevant claim under Chapter I ceasing to be current, the operation of the tenant's notice subsequently ceases to be so suspended and the tenant's notice thereupon continues in force in accordance with section 42(8),
then, as from the date when that claim ceases to be current ('the termination date'), this Chapter shall apply as if there were substituted for the date specified in the tenant's notice in pursuance of section 42(3)(f) such date as results in the period of time intervening between the termination date and that date being equal to the period of time intervening between the relevant date and the date originally so specified.

(5) Where –
(a) the operation of the tenant's notice is suspended by virtue of subsection (2), and
(b) its suspension began in circumstances falling within subsection (6), and
(c) as a result of the relevant claim under Chapter I ceasing to be current, the operation of the tenant's notice subsequently ceases to be so suspended and the tenant's notice thereupon continues in force in accordance with section 42(8),

any relevant period shall be deemed to have begun on the date when that claim ceases to be current.

(6) The circumstances referred to in subsection (5)(b) are that the suspension of the operation of the tenant's notice began –

- (a) before the date specified in the tenant's notice in pursuance of section 42(3)(f) and before the landlord had given the tenant a counter-notice under section 45; or
- (b) after the landlord had given the tenant a counter-notice under section 45 complying with the requirement set out in subsection (2)(b) or (c) of that section but –
  - (i) before any application had been made for an order under section 46(1) or 47(1), and
  - (ii) before the period for making any such application had expired; or
- (c) after an order had been made under section 46(4) or 47(4) but –
  - (i) before the landlord had given the tenant a further counter-notice in accordance with the order, and
  - (ii) before the period for giving any such counter-notice had expired.

(7) Where –

- (a) the operation of the tenant's notice is suspended by virtue of subsection (2), and
- (b) its suspension began otherwise than in circumstances falling within subsection (6), and
- (c) as a result of the relevant claim under Chapter I ceasing to be current, the operation of the tenant's notice subsequently ceases to be so suspended and the tenant's notice thereupon continues in force in accordance with section 42(8),

any relevant period shall be deemed to have begun on the date on which the tenant is given a notice under subsection (8) below or, if earlier, the date on which the tenant gives the landlord a notice informing him of the circumstances by virtue of which the operation of the tenant's notice has ceased to be suspended.

(8) Where subsection (4), (5) or (7) applies, the landlord shall, as soon as possible after becoming aware of the circumstances by virtue of which the operation of the tenant's notice has ceased to be suspended as mentioned in that subsection, give the tenant a notice informing him that, as from the date when the relevant claim under Chapter I ceased to be current, the operation of his notice is no longer suspended.

(9) Subsection (8) shall not, however, require the landlord to give any such notice if he has received a notice from the tenant under subsection (7).

(10) In subsections (5) and (7) 'relevant period' means any period which –

- (a) is prescribed by or under this Part for the giving of any notice, or the making of any application, in connection with the tenant's notice; and
- (b) was current at the time when the suspension of the operation of the tenant's notice began.

(11) For the purposes of this section –

- (a) 'the relevant claim under Chapter I', in relation to a notice under section 13, means the claim in respect of which that notice is given; and
- (b) any such claim is current if –
  - (i) that notice continues in force in accordance with section 13(11), or
  - (ii) a binding contract entered into in pursuance of that notice remains in force, or
  - (iii) where an order has been made under section 24(4)(a) or (b) or 25(6)(a) or (b) with respect to any such premises as are referred to in subsection (1) or

(2) above (as the case may be), any interests which by virtue of the order fall to be vested in the nominee purchaser for the purposes of Chapter I have yet to be so vested.

55. Effect on tenant's notice of institution of compulsory acquisition procedures

(1) A notice given by a tenant under section 42 shall be of no effect if on the relevant date –

(a) any person or body of persons who has or have been, or could be, authorised to acquire the whole or part of the tenant's flat compulsorily for any purpose has or have, with a view to its acquisition for that purpose –

(i) served notice to treat on the landlord or the tenant, or

(ii) entered into a contract for the purchase of the interest or either of them in the flat or part of it, and

(b) the notice to treat or contract remains in force.

(2) A notice given by a tenant under section 42 shall cease to have effect if, before a new lease is entered into in pursuance of it, any such person or body of persons as is mentioned in subsection (1) serves or serve notice to treat as mentioned in that subsection.

(3) Where subsection (2) applies in relation to a notice given by a tenant under section 42, then on the occasion of the compulsory acquisition in question the compensation payable in respect of any interest in the tenant's flat (whether or not the one to which the relevant notice to treat relates) shall be determined on the basis of the value of the interest subject to and with the benefit of the rights and obligations arising from the tenant's notice and affecting that interest.

Grant of new lease

56. Obligation to grant new lease

(1) Where a qualifying tenant of a flat has under this Chapter a right to acquire a new lease of the flat and gives notice of his claim in accordance with section 42, then except as provided by this Chapter the landlord shall be bound to grant to the tenant, and the tenant shall be bound to accept –

(a) in substitution for the existing lease, and

(b) on payment of the premium payable under Schedule 13 in respect of the grant,

a new lease of the flat at a peppercorn rent for a term expiring 90 years after the term date of the existing lease.

(2) In addition to any such premium there shall be payable by the tenant in connection with the grant of any such new lease such amounts to the owners of any intermediate leasehold interests (within the meaning of Schedule 13) as are so payable by virtue of that Schedule.

(3) A tenant shall not be entitled to require the execution of any such new lease otherwise than on tendering to the landlord, in addition to the amount of any such premium and any other amounts payable by virtue of Schedule 13, the amount so far as ascertained –

(a) of any sums payable by him by way of rent or recoverable from him as rent in respect of the flat up to the date of tender;

(b) of any sums for which at that date the tenant is liable under section 60 in respect of costs incurred by any relevant person (within the meaning of that section); and

(c) of any other sums due and payable by him to any such person under or in respect of the existing lease;

and, if the amount of any such sums is not or may not be fully ascertained, on offering reasonable security for the payment of such amount as may afterwards be found to be payable in respect of them.

(4) To the extent that any amount tendered to the landlord in accordance with subsection (3) is an amount due to a person other than the landlord, that amount shall be payable to that person by the landlord; and that subsection has effect subject to paragraph 7(2) of Schedule 11.

(5) No provision of any lease prohibiting, restricting or otherwise relating to a sub-demise by the tenant under the lease shall have effect with reference to the granting of any lease under this section.

(6) It is hereby declared that nothing in any of the provisions specified in paragraph 1(2) of Schedule 10 (which impose requirements as to consent or consultation or other restrictions in relation to disposals falling within those provisions) applies to the granting of any lease under this section.

(7) For the purposes of subsection (6), paragraph 1(2) of Schedule 10 has effect as if the reference to section 79(2) of the Housing Act 1988 (which is not relevant in the context of subsection (6)) were omitted.

57. Terms on which new lease is to be granted

(1) Subject to the provisions of this Chapter (and in particular to the provisions as to rent and duration contained in section 56(1)), the new lease to be granted to a tenant under section 56 shall be a lease on the same terms as those of the existing lease, as they apply on the relevant date, but with such modifications as may be required or appropriate to take account –

(a) of the omission from the new lease of property included in the existing lease but not comprised in the flat;

(b) of alterations made to the property demised since the grant of the existing lease; or

(c) in a case where the existing lease derives (in accordance with section 7(6) as it applies in accordance with section 39(3)) from more than one separate leases, of their combined effect and of the differences (if any) in their terms.

(2) Where during the continuance of the new lease the landlord will be under any obligation for the provision of services, or for repairs, maintenance or insurance –

(a) the new lease may require payments to be made by the tenant (whether as rent or otherwise) in consideration of those matters or in respect of the cost thereof to the landlord; and

(b) (if the terms of the existing lease do not include any provision for the making of any such payments by the tenant or include provision only for the payment of a fixed amount) the terms of the new lease shall make, as from the term date of the existing lease, such provision as may be just –

(i) for the making by the tenant of payments related to the cost from time to time to the landlord, and

(ii) for the tenant's liability to make those payments to be enforceable by distress, re-entry or otherwise in like manner as if it were a liability for payment of rent.

(3) Subject to subsection (4), provision shall be made by the terms of the new lease or by an agreement collateral thereto for the continuance, with any suitable adaptations, of any agreement collateral to the existing lease.

(4) For the purposes of subsections (1) and (3) there shall be excluded from the new lease any term of the existing lease or of any agreement collateral thereto in so far as that term –
(a) provides for or relates to the renewal of the lease,
(b) confers any option to purchase or right of pre-emption in relation to the flat demised by the existing lease, or
(c) provides for the termination of the existing lease before its term date otherwise than in the event of a breach of its terms;
and there shall be made in the terms of the new lease or any agreement collateral thereto such modifications as may be required or appropriate to take account of the exclusion of any such term.

(5) Where the new lease is granted after the term date of the existing lease, then on the grant of the new lease there shall be payable by the tenant to the landlord, as an addition to the rent payable under the existing lease, any amount by which, for the period since the term date or the relevant date (whichever is the later), the sums payable to the landlord in respect of the flat (after making any necessary apportionment) for the matters referred to in subsection (2) fall short in total of the sums that would have been payable for such matters under the new lease if it had been granted on that date; and section 56(3)(a) shall apply accordingly.

(6) Subsections (1) to (5) shall have effect subject to any agreement between the landlord and tenant as to the terms of the new lease or any agreement collateral thereto; and either of them may require that for the purposes of the new lease any term of the existing lease shall be excluded or modified in so far as –
(a) it is necessary to do so in order to remedy a defect in the existing lease; or
(b) it would be unreasonable in the circumstances to include, or include without modification, the term in question in view of changes occurring since the date of commencement of the existing lease which affect the suitability on the relevant date of the provisions of that lease.

(7) The terms of the new lease shall –
(a) make provision in accordance with section 59(3); and
(b) reserve to the person who is for the time being the tenant's immediate landlord the right to obtain possession of the flat in question in accordance with section 61.

(8) In granting the new lease the landlord shall not be bound to enter into any covenant for title beyond that implied from the grant, and a person entering into any covenant required of him as landlord shall be entitled to limit his personal liability to breaches of that covenant for which he is responsible.

(9) Where any person –
(a) is a third party to the existing lease, or
(b) (not being the landlord or tenant) is a party to any agreement collateral thereto,
then (subject to any agreement between him and the landlord and the tenant) he shall be made a party to the new lease or (as the case may be) to an agreement collateral thereto, and shall accordingly join in its execution; but nothing in this section has effect so as to require the new lease or (as the case may be) any such collateral agreement to provide for him to discharge any function at any time after the term date of the existing lease.

(10) Where –

(a) any such person ('the third party') is in accordance with subsection (9) to discharge any function down to the term date of the existing lease, but
(b) it is necessary or expedient in connection with the proper enjoyment by the tenant of the property demised by the new lease for provision to be made for the continued discharge of that function after that date,

the new lease or an agreement collateral thereto shall make provision for that function to be discharged after that date (whether by the third party or by some other person).

(11) The new lease shall contain a statement that it is a lease granted under section 56; and any such statement shall comply with such requirements as may be prescribed by rules made in pursuance of section 144 of the Land Registration Act 1925 (power to make general rules).

58. Grant of new lease where interest of landlord or tenant is subject to a mortgage

(1) Subject to subsection (2), a qualifying tenant shall be entitled to be granted a new lease under section 56 despite the fact that the grant of the existing lease was subsequent to the creation of a mortgage on the landlord's interest and not authorised as against the persons interested in the mortgage; and a lease granted under that section –
(a) shall be deemed to be authorised as against the persons interested in any mortgage on the landlord's interest (however created or arising), and
(b) shall be binding on those persons.

(2) A lease granted under section 56 shall not, by virtue of subsection (1) above, be binding on the persons interested in any such mortgage if the existing lease –
(a) is granted after the commencement of this Chapter, and
(b) being granted subsequent to the creation of the mortgage, would not, apart from that subsection, be binding on the persons interested in the mortgage.

(3) Where –
(a) a lease is granted under section 56, and
(b) any person having a mortgage on the landlord's interest is thereby entitled to possession of the documents of title relating to that interest,

the landlord shall, within one month of the execution of the lease, deliver to that person a counterpart of it duly executed by the tenant.

(4) Where the existing lease is, immediately before its surrender on the grant of a lease under section 56, subject to any mortgage, the new lease shall take effect subject to the mortgage in substitution for the existing lease; and the terms of the mortgage, as set out in the instrument creating or evidencing it, shall accordingly apply in relation to the new lease in like manner as they applied in relation to the existing lease.

(5) Where –
(a) a lease granted under section 56 takes effect subject to any such subsisting mortgage on the existing lease, and
(b) at the time of execution of the new lease the person having the mortgage is thereby entitled to possession of the documents of title relating to the existing lease,

he shall be similarly entitled to possession of the documents of title relating to the new lease; and the tenant shall deliver the new lease to him within one month of the date on which the lease is received from Her Majesty's Land Registry following its registration.

(6) Where –

(a) the landlord fails to deliver a counterpart of the new lease in accordance with subsection (3), or

(b) the tenant fails to deliver the new lease in accordance with subsection (5),

the instrument creating or evidencing the mortgage in question shall apply as if the obligation to deliver a counterpart or (as the case may be) deliver the lease were included in the terms of the mortgage as set out in that instrument.

(7) A landlord granting a lease under section 56 shall be bound to take such steps as may be necessary to secure that the lease is not liable in accordance with subsection (2) to be defeated by persons interested in a mortgage on his interest; but a landlord is not obliged, in order to grant a lease for the purposes of that section, to acquire a better title than he has or could require to be vested in him.

59. Further renewal, but no security of tenure, after grant of new lease

(1) The right to acquire a new lease under this Chapter may be exercised in relation to a lease of a flat despite the fact that the lease is itself a lease granted under section 56; and the provisions of this Chapter shall, with any necessary modifications, apply for the purposes of or in connection with any claim to exercise that right in relation to a lease so granted as they apply for the purposes of or in connection with any claim to exercise that right in relation to a lease which has not been so granted.

(2) Where a lease has been granted under section 56 –

(a) none of the statutory provisions relating to security of tenure for tenants shall apply to the lease;

(b) after the term date of the lease none of the following provisions, namely –

(i) section 1 of the Landlord and Tenant Act 1954 or Schedule 10 to the Local Government and Housing Act 1989 (which make provision for security of tenure on the ending of long residential tenancies), or

(ii) Part II of that Act of 1954 (business tenancies),

shall apply to any sub-lease directly or indirectly derived out of the lease; and

(c) after that date no person shall be entitled by virtue of any such sub-lease to retain possession under –

(i) Part VII of the Rent Act 1977 (security of tenure for protected tenancies etc) or any enactment applying or extending that Part of that Act,

(ii) the Rent (Agriculture) Act 1976, or

(iii) Part I of the Housing Act 1988 (assured tenancies etc).

(3) Where a lease has been granted under section 56, no long lease created immediately or derivatively by way of sub-demise under the lease shall confer on the sub-tenant, as against the tenant's landlord, any right under this Chapter to acquire a new lease (and for this purpose 'long lease' shall be construed in accordance with section 7).

(4) Any person who –

(a) grants a sub-lease to which subsection (2)(b) and (c) will apply, or

(b) negotiates with a view to the grant of such a sub-lease by him or by a person for whom he is acting as agent,

shall inform the other party that the sub-lease is to be derived out of a lease granted under section 56, unless either he knows that the other party is aware of it or he himself is unaware of it.

(5) Where any lease contains a statement to the effect that it is a lease granted under section 56, the statement shall be conclusive for the purposes of subsections (2) to (4) in favour of any person who is not a party to the lease, unless the statement appears from the lease to be untrue.

Costs incurred in connection with new lease

60. Costs incurred in connection with new lease to be paid by tenant

(1) Where a notice is given under section 42, then (subject to the provisions of this section) the tenant by whom it is given shall be liable, to the extent that they have been incurred by any relevant person in pursuance of the notice, for the reasonable costs of and incidental to any of the following matters, namely –

(a) any investigation reasonably undertaken of the tenant's right to a new lease;
(b) any valuation of the tenant's flat obtained for the purpose of fixing the premium or any other amount payable by virtue of Schedule 13 in connection with the grant of a new lease under section 56;
(c) the grant of a new lease under that section;

but this subsection shall not apply to any costs if on a sale made voluntarily a stipulation that they were to be borne by the purchaser would be void.

(2) For the purposes of subsection (1) any costs incurred by a relevant person in respect of professional services rendered by any person shall only be regarded as reasonable if and to the extent that costs in respect of such services might reasonably be expected to have been incurred by him if the circumstances had been such that he was personally liable for all such costs.

(3) Where by virtue of any provision of this Chapter the tenant's notice ceases to have effect, or is deemed to have been withdrawn, at any time, then (subject to subsection (4)) the tenant's liability under this section for costs incurred by any person shall be a liability for costs incurred by him down to that time.

(4) A tenant shall not be liable for any costs under this section if the tenant's notice ceases to have effect by virtue of section 47(1) or 55(2).

(5) A tenant shall not be liable under this section for any costs which a party to any proceedings under this Chapter before a leasehold valuation tribunal incurs in connection with the proceedings.

(6) In this section 'relevant person', in relation to a claim by a tenant under this Chapter, means the landlord for the purposes of this Chapter, any other landlord (as defined by section 40(4)) or any third party to the tenant's lease.

Landlord's right to terminate new lease

61. Landlord's right to terminate new lease on grounds of redevelopment

(1) Where a lease of a flat ('the new lease') has been granted under section 56 but the court is satisfied, on an application made by the landlord –

(a) that for the purposes of redevelopment the landlord intends –
  (i) to demolish or reconstruct, or
  (ii) to carry out substantial works of construction on,

  the whole or a substantial part of any premises in which the flat is contained, and
(b) that he could not reasonably do so without obtaining possession of the flat,

the court shall by order declare that the landlord is entitled as against the tenant to obtain possession of the flat and the tenant is entitled to be paid compensation by the landlord for the loss of the flat.

(2) An application for an order under this section may be made –

(a) at any time during the period of 12 months ending with the term date of the lease in relation to which the right to acquire a new lease was exercised; and

(b) at any time during the period of five years ending with the term date of the new lease.

(3) Where the new lease is not the first lease to be granted under section 56 in respect of a flat, subsection (2) shall apply as if paragraph (b) included a reference to the term date of any previous lease granted under that section in respect of the flat, but paragraph (a) shall be taken to be referring to the term date of the lease in relation to which the right to acquire a new lease was first exercised.

(4) Where an order is made under this section, the new lease shall determine, and compensation shall become payable, in accordance with Schedule 14 to this Act; and the provisions of that Schedule shall have effect as regards the measure of compensation payable by virtue of any such order and the effects of any such order where there are sub-leases, and as regards other matters relating to orders and applications under this section.

(5) Except in subsection (1)(a) or (b), any reference in this section to the flat held by the tenant under the new lease includes any premises let with the flat under that lease.

Supplemental

62. Interpretation of Chapter II

(1) In this Chapter –

'the existing lease', in relation to a claim by a tenant under this Chapter, means the lease in relation to which the claim is made;

'the landlord', in relation to such a claim, has the meaning given by section 40(1);

'mortgage' includes a charge or lien;

'qualifying tenant' shall be construed in accordance with section 39(3);

'the relevant date' (unless the context otherwise requires) has the meaning given by section 39(8);

'the tenant's notice' means the notice given under section 42;

'the terms of acquisition' shall be construed in accordance with section 48(7);

'third party', in relation to a lease, means any person who is a party to the lease apart from the tenant under the lease and his immediate landlord.

(2) Subject to subsection (3), references in this Chapter to a flat, in relation to a claim by a tenant under this Chapter, include any garage, outhouse, garden, yard and appurtenances belonging to, or usually enjoyed with, the flat and let to the tenant with the flat on the relevant date (or, in a case where an application is made under section 50(1), on the date of the making of the application).

(3) Subsection (2) does not apply –

(a) to any reference to a flat in section 47 or 55(1); or

(b) to any reference to a flat (not falling within paragraph (a) above) which occurs in the context of a reference to any premises containing the flat.

(4) In the application of section 8 for the purposes of this Chapter (in accordance with section 39(3)) references to a flat shall be construed in accordance with subsection (2) above, instead of in accordance with subsection (7) of section 8.

CHAPTER III

ENFRANCHISEMENT UNDER LEASEHOLD REFORM ACT 1967

Extension of right to enfranchise

63. Extension of right to enfranchise to houses whose value or rent exceeds applicable limit

After section 1 of the Leasehold Reform Act 1967 there shall be inserted –

> **'1A. Right to enfranchisement only in case of houses whose value or rent exceeds limit under s 1 or 4**
>
> (1) Where subsection (1) of section 1 above would apply in the case of the tenant of a house but for the fact that the applicable financial limit specified in subsection (1)(a)(i) or (ii) or (as the case may be) subsection (5) or (6) of that section is exceeded, this Part of this Act shall have effect to confer on the tenant the same right to acquire the freehold of the house and premises as would be conferred by subsection (1) of that section if that limit were not exceeded.
>
> (2) Where a tenancy of any property is not a tenancy at a low rent in accordance with section 4(1) below but is a tenancy falling within section 4A(1) below, the tenancy shall nevertheless be treated as a tenancy at a low rent for the purposes of this Part of this Act so far as it has effect for conferring on any person a right to acquire the freehold of a house and premises.'

64. Tenancies terminable after death or marriage

(1) The following section shall be inserted in the Leasehold Reform Act 1967 after the section 1A inserted by section 63 above –

> **'1B. Right to enfranchisement only in case of certain tenancies terminable after death or marriage**
>
> Where a tenancy granted so as to become terminable by notice after a death or marriage –
>
> (a) is (apart from this section) a long tenancy in accordance with section 3(1) below, but
>
> (b) was granted before 18th April 1980 or in pursuance of a contract entered into before that date,
>
> then (notwithstanding section 3(1)) the tenancy shall be a long tenancy for the purposes of this Part of this Act only so far as this Part has effect for conferring on any person a right to acquire the freehold of a house and premises.'

(2) In section 3(1) of that Act (meaning of 'long tenancy') –

(a) after 'and includes' there shall be inserted 'both a tenancy taking effect under section 149(6) of the Law of Property Act 1925 (leases terminable after a death or marriage) and'; and

(b) in the proviso (which prevents certain categories of tenancies terminable after death or marriage being long tenancies), for the words from 'if either' onwards there shall be substituted 'if –

(a) the notice is capable of being given at any time after the death or marriage of the tenant;

(b) the length of the notice is not more than three months; and

(c) the terms of the tenancy preclude both –

(i) its assignment otherwise than by virtue of section 92 of the Housing Act 1985 (assignments by way of exchange), and

(ii) the sub-letting of the whole of the premises comprised in it.'

65. Additional 'low rent' test

After section 4 of the Leasehold Reform Act 1967 there shall be inserted –

> **'4A. Alternative rent limits for purposes of section 1A(2)**
>
> (1) For the purposes of section 1A(2) above a tenancy of any property falls within this subsection if either no rent was payable under it in respect of the property during the initial year or the aggregate amount of rent so payable during that year did not exceed the following amount, namely –
>
> (a) where the tenancy was entered into before 1st April 1963, two-thirds of the letting value of the property (on the same terms) on the date of the commencement of the tenancy;
>
> (b) where –
>
> (i) the tenancy was entered into either on or after 1st April 1963 but before 1st April 1990, or on or after 1st April 1990 in pursuance of a contract made before that date, and
>
> (ii) the property had a rateable value at the date of the commencement of the tenancy or else at any time before 1st April 1990,
>
> two-thirds of the rateable value of the property on the relevant date; or
>
> (c) in any other case, £1,000 if the property is in Greater London or £250 if elsewhere.
>
> (2) For the purposes of subsection (1) above –
>
> (a) 'the initial year', in relation to any tenancy, means the period of one year beginning with the date of the commencement of the tenancy;
>
> (b) 'the relevant date' means the date of the commencement of the tenancy or, if the property did not have a rateable value on that date, the date on which it first had a rateable value; and
>
> (c) paragraphs (b) and (c) of section 4(1) above shall apply as they apply for the purposes of section 4(1);
>
> and it is hereby declared that in subsection (1) above the reference to the letting value of any property is to be construed in like manner as the reference in similar terms which appears in the proviso to section 4(1) above.
>
> (3) Section 1(7) above applies to any amount referred to in subsection (1)(c) above as it applies to the amount referred to in subsection (1)(a)(ii) of that section.'

66. Price payable by tenant on enfranchisement by virtue of section 63 or 64

(1) In section 9 of the Leasehold Reform Act 1967 (purchase price and costs of enfranchisement etc), after subsection (1B) there shall be inserted –

> '(1C) Notwithstanding subsection (1) above, the price payable for a house and premises where the right to acquire the freehold arises by virtue of any one or more of the provisions of sections 1A and 1B above shall be determined in accordance with subsection (1A) above; but in any such case –
>
> (a) if in determining the price so payable there falls to be taken into account any marriage value arising by virtue of the coalescence of the freehold and leasehold interests, the share of the marriage value to which the tenant is to be regarded as being entitled shall not exceed one-half of it; and
>
> (b) section 9A below has effect for determining whether any additional amount is payable by way of compensation under that section;
>
> and in a case where the provision (or one of the provisions) by virtue of which the right to acquire the freehold arises in section 1A(1) above, subsection (1A) above

shall apply with the omission of the assumption set out in paragraph (b) of that subsection.'

(2) Section 9 of that Act, as amended by this section and with the omission of repealed provisons, is set out in Schedule 15 to this Act.

(3) After section 9 of that Act there shall be inserted –

'9A. Compensation payable in cases where right to enfranchisement arises by virtue of section 1A or 1B

(1) If, in a case where the right to acquire the freehold of a house and premises arises by virtue of any one or more of the provisions of sections 1A and 1B above, the landlord will suffer any loss or damage to which this section applies, there shall be payable to him such amount as is reasonable to compensate him for that loss or damage.

(2) This section applies to –

(a) any diminution in value of any interest of the landlord in other property resulting from the acquisition of his interest in the house and premises; and

(b) any other loss or damage which results therefrom to the extent that it is referable to his ownership of any interest in other property.

(3) Without prejudice to the generality of paragraph (b) of subsection (2) above, the kinds of loss falling within that paragraph include loss of development value in relation to the house and premises to the extent that it is referable as mentioned in that paragraph.

(4) In subsection (3) above 'development value', in relation to the house and premises, means any increase in the value of the landlord's interest in the house and premises which is attributable to the possibility of demolishing, reconstructing, or carrying out substantial works of construction on, the whole or a substantial part of the house and premises.

(5) In relation to any case falling within subsection (1) above –

(a) any reference (however expressed) –

(i) in section 8 or 9(3) or (5) above, or

(ii) in any of the following provisions of this Act,

to the price payable under section 9 above shall be construed as including a reference to any amount payable to the landlord under this section; and

(b) for the purpose of determining any such separate price as is mentioned in paragraph 7(1)(b) of Schedule 1 to this Act, this section shall accordingly apply (with any necessary modifications) to each of the superior interests in question.'

Exceptions to right to enfranchise

67. Exclusion of right to enfranchise in case of houses let by charitable housing trusts

(1) Section 1 of the Leasehold Reform Act 1967 (tenants entitled to enfranchisement or extension) shall be amended as follows.

(2) In subsection (3) (excepted cases) there shall be added at the end –

'or, in the case of any right to which subsection (3A) below applies, at any time when the tenant's immediate landlord is a charitable housing trust and the house forms part of the housing accommodation provided by the trust in the pursuit of its charitable purposes.'

(3) After subsection (3) there shall be inserted –

'(3A) For the purposes of subsection (3) above this subsection applies as follows –

(a) where the tenancy was created after the commencement of Chapter III of Part I of the Leasehold Reform, Housing and Urban Development Act 1993, this subsection applies to any right to acquire the freehold of the house and premises; but

(b) where the tenancy was created before that commencement, this subsection applies only to any such right exercisable by virtue of any one or more of the provisions of sections 1A and 1B below;

and in that subsection 'charitable housing trust' means a housing trust within the meaning of the Housing Act 1985 which is a charity within the meaning of the Charities Act 1993.'

68. Exclusion of right in case of property transferred for public benefit etc

After section 32 of the Leasehold Reform Act 1967 there shall be inserted –

'32A. Property transferred for public benefit etc

(1) A notice of a person's desire to have the freehold of a house and premises under this Part shall be of no effect if at the relevant time the whole or any part of the house and premises is qualifying property and either –

(a) the tenancy was created after the commencement of Chapter III of Part I of the Leasehold Reform, Housing and Urban Development Act 1993; or

(b) (where the tenancy was created before that commencement) the tenant would not be entitled to have the freehold if either or both of sections 1A and 1B above were not in force.

(2) For the purposes of this section the whole or any part of the house and premises is qualifying property if –

(a) it has been designated under section 31(1)(b), (c) or (d) of the Inheritance Tax Act 1984 (designation and undertakings relating to conditionally exempt transfers), whether with or without any other property, and no chargeable event has subsequently occurred with respect to it; or

(b) an application to the Board for it to be so designated is pending; or

(c) it is the property of a body not established or conducted for profit and a direction has been given in relation to it under section 26 of that Act (gifts for public benefit), whether with or without any other property; or

(d) an application to the Board for a direction to be so given in relation to it is pending.

(3) For the purposes of subsection (2) above an application is pending as from the time when it is made to the Board until such time as it is either granted or refused by the Board or withdrawn by the applicant; and for this purpose an application shall not be regarded as made unless and until the applicant has submitted to the Board all such information in support of the application as is required by the Board.

(4) A notice of a person's desire to have the freehold of a house and premises under this Part shall cease to have effect if –

(a) before completion of the conveyance in pursuance of the tenant's notice, the whole or any part of the house and premises becomes qualifying property; and

(b) the condition set out in subsection (1)(a) or (as the case may be) subsection (1)(b) above is satisfied.

(5) Where a tenant's notice ceases to have effect by virtue of subsection (4) above –

(a) section 9(4) above shall not apply to require the tenant to make any payment to the landlord in respect of costs incurred by reason of the notice; and

(b) the person who applied or is applying for designation or a direction shall be liable to the tenant for all reasonable costs incurred by the tenant in connection with his claim to acquire the freehold of the house and premises.

(6) Where it is claimed that subsection (1) or (4) above applies in relation to a tenant's notice, the person making the claim shall, at the time of making it, furnish the tenant with evidence in support of it; and if he fails to do so he shall be liable for any costs which are reasonably incurred by the tenant in consequence of the failure.

(7) In subsection (2) above –

(a) paragraphs (a) and (b) apply to designation under section 34(1)(a), (b) or (c) of the Finance Act 1975 or section 77(1)(b), (c) or (d) of the Finance Act 1976 as they apply to designation under section 31(1)(b), (c) or (d) of the Inheritance Tax Act 1984; and

(b) paragraphs (c) and (d) apply to a direction under paragraph 13 of Schedule 6 to the Finance Act 1975 as they apply to a direction under section 26 of that Act of 1984.

(8) In this section –

'the Board' means the Commissioners of Inland Revenue;

'chargeable event' means –

(a) any event which in accordance with any provision of Chapter II of Part II of the Inheritance Tax Act 1984 (exempt transfers) is a chargeable event, including any such provision as applied by section 78(3) of that Act (conditionally exempt occasions); or

(b) any event which would have been a chargeable event in the circumstances mentioned in section 79(3) of that Act (exemption from ten-yearly charge).'

CHAPTER IV

ESTATE MANAGEMENT SCHEMES IN CONNECTION WITH ENFRANCHISEMENT

69. Estate management schemes

(1) For the purposes of this Chapter an estate management scheme is a scheme which (subject to sections 71 and 73) is approved by a leasehold valuation tribunal under section 70 for an area occupied directly or indirectly under leases held from one landlord (apart from property occupied by him or his licensees or for the time being unoccupied) and which is designed to secure that in the event of tenants –

(a) acquiring the landlord's interest in their house and premises ('the house') under Part I of the Leasehold Reform Act 1967 by virtue of any one or more of the provisions of sections 1A and 1B of that Act (as inserted by sections 63 and 64 above), or

(b) acquiring the landlord's interest in any premises ('the premises') in accordance with Chapter I of this Part of this Act, the landlord will –
  (i) retain powers of management in respect of the house or premises, and
  (ii) have rights against the house or premises in respect of the benefits arising from the exercise elsewhere of his powers of management.

(2) An estate management scheme may make different provision for different parts of the area of the scheme, and shall include provision for terminating or varying all or any of the provisions of the scheme, or excluding part of the area, if a change of circumstances makes it appropriate, or for enabling it to be done by or with the approval of a leasehold valuation tribunal.

(3) Without prejudice to any other provision of this section, an estate management scheme may provide for all or any of the following matters –
(a) for regulating the redevelopment, use or appearance of property in which tenants have acquired the landlord's interest as mentioned in subsection (1)(a) or (b);
(b) for empowering the landlord for the time being to carry out works of maintenance, repair, renewal or replacement in relation to any such property or carry out work to remedy a failure in respect of any such property to comply with the scheme, or for making the operation of any provisions of the scheme conditional on his doing so or on the provision or maintenance by him of services, facilities or amenities of any description;
(c) for imposing on persons from time to time occupying or interested in any such property obligations in respect of the carrying out of works of maintenance, repair, renewal or replacement in relation to the property or property used or enjoyed by them in common with others, or in respect of costs incurred by the landlord for the time being on any matter referred to in this paragraph or in paragraph (b) above;
(d) for the inspection from time to time of any such property on behalf of the landlord for the time being, and for the recovery by him of sums due to him under the scheme in respect of any such property by means of a charge on the property;

and the landlord for the time being shall have, for the enforcement of any charge imposed under the scheme, the same powers and remedies under the Law of Property Act 1925 and otherwise as if he were a mortgagee by deed having powers of sale and leasing and of appointing a receiver.

(4) Except as provided by the scheme, the operation of an estate management scheme shall not be affected by any disposition or devolution of the landlord's interest in the property within the area of the scheme or in parts of that property; but the scheme –
(a) shall include provision for identifying the person who is for the purposes of the scheme to be treated as the landlord for the time being; and
(b) shall also include provision for transferring, or allowing the landlord for the time being to transfer, all or any of the powers and rights conferred by the scheme on the landlord for the time being to a local authority or other body, including a body constituted for the purpose.

(5) Without prejudice to the generality of paragraph (b) of subsection (4), an estate management scheme may provide for the operation of any provision for transfer included in the scheme in accordance with that paragraph to be dependent –
(a) on a determination of a leasehold valuation tribunal effecting or approving the transfer;
(b) on such other circumstances as the scheme may provide.

(6) An estate management scheme may extend to property in which the landlord's interest is disposed of otherwise than as mentioned in subsection (1)(a) or (b) (whether

residential property or not), so as to make that property, or allow it to be made, subject to any such provision as is or might be made by the scheme for property in which tenants acquire the landlord's interest as mentioned in either of those provisions.

(7) In this Chapter references to the landlord for the time being shall have effect, in relation to powers and rights transferred to a local authority or other body as contemplated by subsection (4)(b) above, as references to that authority or body.

70. Approval by leasehold valuation tribunal of estate management scheme

(1) A leasehold valuation tribunal may, on an application made by a landlord for the approval of a scheme submitted by him to the tribunal, approve the scheme as an estate management scheme for such area falling within section 69(1) as is specified in the scheme; but any such application must (subject to section 72) be made within the period of two years beginning with the date of the coming into force of this section.

(2) A leasehold valuation tribunal shall not approve a scheme as an estate management scheme for any area unless it is satisfied that, in order to maintain adequate standards of appearance and amenity and regulate redevelopment within the area in the event of tenants acquiring the interest of the landlord in any property as mentioned in section 69(1)(a) or (b), it is in the general interest that the landlord should retain such powers of management and have such rights falling within section 69(1)(i) and (ii) as are conferred by the scheme.

(3) In considering whether to approve a scheme as an estate management scheme for any area, a leasehold valuation tribunal shall have regard primarily to –
- (a) the benefit likely to result from the scheme to the area as a whole (including houses or premises likely to be acquired from the landlord as mentioned in section 69(1)(a) or (b)); and
- (b) the extent to which it is reasonable to impose, for the benefit of the area, obligations on tenants so acquiring the interest of their landlord;

but the tribunal shall also have regard to the past development and present character of the area and to architectural or historical considerations, to neighbouring areas and to the circumstances generally.

(4) A leasehold valuation tribunal shall not consider any application for it to approve a scheme unless it is satisfied that the applicant has, by advertisement or otherwise, given adequate notice to persons interested –
- (a) informing them of the application for approval of the scheme and the provision intended to be made by the scheme, and
- (b) inviting them to make representations to the tribunal about the application within a time which appears to the tribunal to be reasonable.

(5) In subsection (4) 'persons interested' includes, in particular, in relation to any application for the approval of a scheme for any area ('the scheme area') within a conservation area –
- (a) each local planning authority within whose area any part of the scheme area falls, and
- (b) if the whole of the scheme area is in England, the Historic Buildings and Monuments Commission for England.

(6) Where representations about an application are made under subsection (4)(b), the tribunal shall afford to the persons making those representations an opportunity to appear and be heard by the tribunal at the time when the application is considered by it.

(7) Subject to the preceding provisions of this section, a leasehold valuation tribunal shall, after considering the application, approve the scheme in question either –

(a) as originally submitted, or

(b) with any relevant modifications proposed or agreed to by the applicant,

if the scheme (with those modifications, if any) appears to the tribunal –

(i) to be fair and practicable, and

(ii) not to give the landlord a degree of control out of proportion to that previously exercised by him or to that required for the purposes of the scheme.

(8) In subsection (7) 'relevant modifications' means modifications relating to the extent of the area to which the scheme is to apply or to the provisions contained in it.

(9) If, having regard to –

(a) the matters mentioned in subsection (3), and

(b) the provision which it is practicable to make by a scheme,

the tribunal thinks it proper to do so, the tribunal may declare that no scheme can be approved for the area in question in pursuance of the application.

(10) A leasehold valuation tribunal shall not dismiss an application for the approval of a scheme unless –

(a) it makes such a declaration as is mentioned in subsection (9); or

(b) in the opinion of the tribunal the applicant is unwilling to agree to a suitable scheme or is not proceeding in the matter with due despatch.

(11) A scheme approved under this section as an estate management scheme for an area shall be a local land charge, notwithstanding section 2(a) or (b) of the Local Land Charges Act 1975 (matters which are not local land charges), and for the purposes of that Act the landlord for that area shall be treated as the originating authority as respects any such charge.

(12) Where such a scheme is registered in the appropriate local land charges register –

(a) the provisions of the scheme relating to property of any description shall so far as they respectively affect the persons from time to time occupying or interested in that property be enforceable by the landlord for the time being against them, as if each of them had covenanted with the landlord for the time being to be bound by the scheme; and

(b) in relation to any acquisition such as is mentioned in section 69(1)(a) above, section 10 of the Leasehold Reform Act 1967 (rights to be conveyed on enfranchisement) shall have effect subject to the provisions of the scheme, and the price payable under section 9 of that Act shall be adjusted so far as is appropriate (if at all); and

(c) in relation to any acquisition such as is mentioned in section 69(1)(b) above, section 34 of, and Schedule 7 to, this Act shall have effect subject to the provisions of the scheme, and any price payable under Schedule 6 to this Act shall be adjusted so far as is appropriate (if at all).

(13) Section 10 of the Local Land Charges Act 1975 (compensation for non-registration etc) shall not apply to schemes which, by virtue of subsection (11) above, are local land charges.

(14) In this section and in section 73 'conservation area' and 'local planning authority' have the same meaning as in the Planning (Listed Buildings and Conservation Areas) Act 1990; and in connection with the latter expression –

(a) the expression 'the planning Acts' in the Town and Country Planning Act 1990 shall be treated as including this Act; and
(b) paragraphs 4 and 5 of Schedule 4 to the Planning (Listed Buildings and Conservation Areas) Act 1990 (further provisions as to exercise of functions by different authorities) shall apply in relation to functions under or by virtue of this section or section 73 of this Act as they apply in relation to functions under section 69 of that Act.

71. Applications by two or more landlords or by representative bodies

(1) Where, on a joint application made by two or more persons as landlords of neighbouring areas, it appears to a leasehold valuation tribunal –
(a) that a scheme could in accordance with subsections (1) and (2) of section 70 be approved as an estate management scheme for those areas, treated as a unit, if the interests of those persons were held by a single person, and
(b) that the applicants are willing to be bound by the scheme to co-operate in the management of their property in those areas and in the administration of the scheme,

the tribunal may (subject to the provisions of section 70 and subsection (2) below) approve the scheme under that section as an estate management scheme for those areas as a whole.

(2) Any such scheme shall be made subject to conditions (enforceable in such manner as may be provided by the scheme) for securing that the landlords and their successors co-operate as mentioned in subsection (1)(b) above.

(3) Where it appears to a leasehold valuation tribunal –
(a) that a scheme could, on the application of any landlord or landlords, be approved under section 70 as an estate management scheme for any area or areas, and
(b) that any body of persons –
(i) is so constituted as to be capable of representing for the purposes of the scheme the persons occupying or interested in property in the area or areas (other than the landlord or landlords or his or their licensees), or such of them as are or may become entitled to acquire their landlord's interest as mentioned in section 69(1)(a) or (b), and
(ii) is otherwise suitable,

an application for the approval of the scheme under section 70 may be made to the tribunal by the representative body alone or by the landlord or landlords alone or by both jointly and, by leave of the tribunal, may be proceeded with by the representative body or by the landlord or landlords despite the fact that the body or landlord or landlords in question did not make the application.

(4) Without prejudice to section 69(4)(b), any such scheme may with the consent of the landlord or landlords, or on such terms as to compensation or otherwise as appear to the tribunal to be just –
(a) confer on the representative body any such rights or powers under the scheme as might be conferred on the landlord or landlords for the time being, or
(b) enable the representative body to participate in the administration of the scheme or in the management by the landlord or landlords of his or their property in the area or areas.

(5) Where any such scheme confers any rights or powers on the representative body in accordance with subsection (4) above, section 70(11) and (12)(a) shall have effect with such modifications (if any) as are provided for in the scheme.

72. Applications after expiry of two-year period

(1) An application for the approval of a scheme for an area under section 70 (including an application in accordance with section 71(1) or (3)) may be made after the expiry of the period mentioned in subsection (1) of that section if the Secretary of State has, not more than six months previously, consented to the making of such an application for that area or for an area within which that area falls.

(2) The Secretary of State may give consent under subsection (1) to the making of an application ('the proposed application') only where he is satisfied –
- (a) that either or both of the conditions mentioned in subsection (3) apply; and
- (b) that adequate notice has been given to persons interested informing them of the request for consent and the purpose of the request.

(3) The conditions referred to in subsection (2)(a) are –
- (a) that the proposed application could not have been made before the expiry of the period mentioned in section 70(1); and
- (b) that –
  - (i) any application for the approval under section 70 of a scheme for the area, or part of the area, to which the proposed application relates would probably have been dismissed under section 70(10(a) had it been made before the expiry of that period; but
  - (ii) because of a change in any of the circumstances required to be considered under section 70(3) the proposed application would, if made following the giving of consent by the Secretary of State, probably be granted.

(4) A request for consent under subsection (1) must be in writing and must comply with such requirements (if any) as to the form of, or the particulars to be contained in, any such request as the Secretary of State may by regulations prescribe.

(5) The procedure for considering a request for consent under subsection (1) shall be such as may be prescribed by regulations made by the Secretary of State.

73. Applications by certain public bodies

(1) Where it appears to a leasehold valuation tribunal after the expiry of the period mentioned in section 70(1) that a scheme could, on the application of any landlord or landlords within that period, have been approved under section 70 as an estate management scheme for any area or areas within a conservation area, an application for the approval of the scheme under that section may, subject to subsections (2) and (3) below, be made to the tribunal by one or more bodies constituting the relevant authority for the purposes of this section.

(2) An application under subsection (1) may only be made if –
- (a) no scheme has been approved under section 70 for the whole or any part of the area or areas to which the application relates ('the scheme area'); and
- (b) any application which has been made in accordance with section 70(1), 71(1) or 71(3) for the approval of a scheme for the whole or any part of the scheme area has been withdrawn or dismissed; and
- (c) no request for consent under section 72(1) which relates to the whole or any part of the scheme area is pending or has been granted within the last six months.

(3) An application under subsection (1) above must be made within the period of six months beginning –
- (a) with the date on which the period mentioned in section 70(1) expires, or

(b) if any application has been made as mentioned in subsection (2)(b) above, with the date (or, as the case may be, the latest date) on which any such application is withdrawn or dismissed,

whichever is the later; but if at any time during that period of six months a request of a kind mentioned in subsection (2)(c) above is pending or granted, an application under subsection (1) above may, subject to subsection (2) above, be made within the period of –

(i) six months beginning with the date on which the request is withdrawn or refused, or

(ii) twelve months beginning with the date on which the request is granted,

as the case may be.

(4) A scheme approved on an application under subsection (1) may confer on the applicant or applicants any such rights or powers under the scheme as might have been conferred on the landlord or landlords for the time being.

(5) For the purposes of this section the relevant authority for the scheme area is –

(a) where that area falls wholly within the area of a local planning authority –

(i) that authority; or

(ii) subject to subsection (6), that authority acting jointly with the Historic Buildings and Monuments Commission for England ('the Commission'); or

(iii) subject to subsection (6), the Commission; or

(b) in any other case –

(i) all of the local planning authorities within each of whose areas any part of the scheme area falls, acting jointly; or

(ii) subject to subsection (6), one or more of those authorities acting jointly with the Commission; or

(iii) subject to subsection (6), the Commission.

(6) The Commission may make, or join in the making of, an application under subsection (1) only if –

(a) the whole of the scheme area is in England; and

(b) they have consulted any local planning authority within whose area the whole or any part of the scheme area falls.

(7) Where a scheme is approved on an application under subsection (1) by two or more bodies acting jointly, the scheme shall, if the tribunal considers it appropriate, be made subject to conditions (enforceable in such manner as may be provided by the scheme) for securing that those bodies co-operate in the administration of the scheme.

(8) Where a scheme is approved on an application under subsection (1) –

(a) section 70(11) and (12)(a) shall (subject to subsection (9) below) have effect as if any reference to the landlord, or the landlord for the time being, for the area for which an estate management scheme has been approved were a reference to the applicant or applicants; and

(b) section 70(12)(b) and (c) shall each have effect with the omission of so much of that provision as relates to the adjustment of any such price as is there mentioned.

(9) A scheme so approved shall not be enforceable by a local planning authority in relation to any property falling outside the authority's area; and in the case of a scheme approved on a joint application made by one or more local planning authorities and the Commission, the scheme may provide for any of its provisions to be enforceable in relation to property falling within the area of a local planning authority either by the authority alone, or by the Commission alone, or by the authority and the Commission acting jointly, as the scheme may provide.

(10) For the purposes of –
(a) section 9(1A) of the Leasehold Reform Act 1967 (purchase price on enfranchisement) as it applies in relation to any acquisition such as is mentioned in section 69(1)(a) above, and
(b) paragraph 3 of Schedule 6 to this Act as it applies in relation to any acquisition such as is mentioned in section 69(1)(b) above (including that paragraph as it applies by virtue of paragraph 7 or 11 of that Schedule),

it shall be assumed that any scheme approved under subsection (1) and relating to the property in question had not been so approved, and accordingly any application for such a scheme to be approved, and the possibility of such an application being made, shall be disregarded.

(11) Section 70(14) applies for the purposes of this section.

74. Effect of application for approval on claim to acquire freehold

(1) Subject to subsections (5) and (6), this subsection applies where –
(a) an application ('the scheme application') is made for the approval of a scheme as an estate management scheme for any area or a request ('the request for consent') is made for consent under section 72(1) in relation to any area, and
(b) whether before or after the making of the application or request –
(i) the tenant of a house in that area gives notice of his desire to have the freehold under Part I of the Leasehold Reform Act 1967, being entitled to do so by virtue only of either or both of the sections of that Act referred to in section 69(1)(a) above, or
(ii) a notice is given under section 13 above in respect of any premises in the area.

(2) Where subsection (1) applies by virtue of paragraph (b)(i) of that subsection, then –
(a) no further steps need be taken towards the execution of a conveyance to give effect to section 10 of the 1967 Act beyond those which appear to the landlord to be reasonable in the circumstances; and
(b) if the notice referred to in subsection (1)(b)(i) ('the tenant's notice') was given before the making of the scheme application or the request for consent, that notice may be withdrawn by a further notice given by the tenant to the landlord.

(3) Where subsection (1) applies by virtue of paragraph (b)(ii) of that subsection, then –
(a) if the notice referred to in that provision ('the initial notice') was given before the making of the scheme application or the request for consent, the notice may be withdrawn by a further notice given by the nominee purchaser to the reversioner;
(b) unless the initial notice is so withdrawn, the reversioner shall, if he has not already given the nominee purchaser a counter-notice under section 21, give him by the date referred to in subsection (1) of that section a counter-notice which complies with one of the requirements set out in subsection (2) of that section (but in relation to which subsection (3) of that section need not be complied with); and
(c) no proceedings shall be brought under Chapter I in pursuance of the initial notice otherwise than under section 22 or 23, and, if the court under either of those sections makes an order requiring the reversioner to give a further counter-notice to the nominee purchaser, the date by which it is to be given shall be such date as falls two months after subsection (1) above ceases to apply;

but no other counter-notice need be given under Chapter I, and (subject to the preceding provisions of this subsection) no further steps need be taken towards the final determination (whether by agreement or otherwise) of the terms of the proposed acquisition by the nominee purchaser beyond those which appear to the reversioner to be reasonable in the circumstances.

(4) If the tenant's notice or the initial notice is withdrawn in accordance with subsection (2) or (3) above, section 9(4) of the 1967 Act or (as the case may be) section 33 above shall not have effect to require the payment of any costs incurred in pursuance of that notice.

(5) Where the scheme application is withdrawn or dismissed, subsection (1) does not apply at any time falling after –

(a) the date of the withdrawal of the application, or

(b) the date when the decision of the tribunal dismissing the application becomes final,

as the case may be; and subsection (1) does not apply at any time falling after the date on which a scheme is approved for the area referred to in that subsection, or for any part of it, in pursuance of the scheme application.

(6) Where the request for consent is withdrawn or refused, subsection (1) does not apply at any time falling after the date on which the request is withdrawn or refused, as the case may be; and where the request is granted, subsection (1) does not apply at any time falling more than six months after the date on which it is granted (unless that subsection applies by virtue of an application made in reliance on the consent).

(7) Where, in accordance with subsection (5) or (6), subsection (1) ceases to apply as from a particular date, it shall do so without prejudice to –

(a) the effect of anything done before that date in pursuance of subsection (2) or (3); or

(b) the operation of any provision of this Part, or of regulations made under it, in relation to anything so done.

(8) If, however, no notice of withdrawal has been given in accordance with subsection (3) before the date when subsection (1) so ceases to apply and before that date either –

(a) the reversioner has given the nominee purchaser a counter-notice under section 21 complying with the requirement set out in subsection (2)(a) of that section, or

(b) section 23(6) would (but for subsection (3) above) have applied to require the reversioner to give a further counter-notice to the nominee purchaser,

the reversioner shall give a further counter-notice to the nominee purchaser within the period of two months beginning with the date when subsection (1) ceases to apply.

(9) Subsections (3) to (5) of section 21 shall apply to any further counter-notice required to be given by the reversioner under subsection (8) above as if it were a counter-notice under that section complying with the requirement set out in subsection (2)(a) of that section; and sections 24 and 25 shall apply in relation to any such counter-notice as they apply in relation to one required by section 22(3).

(10) In this section –

'the 1967 Act' means the Leasehold Reform Act 1967; and

'the nominee purchaser' and 'the reversioner' have the same meaning as in Chapter I of this Part of this Act;

and references to the approval of a scheme for any area include references to the approval of a scheme for two or more areas in accordance with section 71 or 73 above.

75. Variation of existing schemes

(1) Where a scheme under section 19 of the Leasehold Reform Act 1967 (estate management schemes in connection with enfranchisement under that Act) includes, in

pursuance of subsection (6) of that section, provision for enabling the termination or variation of the scheme, or the exclusion of part of the area of the scheme, by or with the approval of the High Court, that provision shall have effect –

(a) as if any reference to the High Court were a reference to a leasehold valuation tribunal, and
(b) with such modifications (if any) as are necessary in consequence of paragraph (a).

(2) A scheme under that section may be varied by or with the approval of a leasehold valuation tribunal for the purpose of, or in connection with, extending the scheme to property within the area of the scheme in which the landlord's interest may be acquired as mentioned in section 69(1)(a) above.

(3) Where any such scheme has been varied in accordance with subsection (2) above, section 19 of that Act shall apply as if the variation had been effected under provisions included in the scheme in pursuance of subsection (6) of that section (and accordingly the scheme may be further varied under provisions so included).

(4) Any application made under or by virtue of this section to a leasehold valuation tribunal shall comply with such requirements (if any) as to the form of, or the particulars to be contained in, any such application as the Secretary of State may by regulations prescribe.

(5) In this section any reference to a leasehold valuation tribunal is a reference to such a rent assessment committee as is mentioned in section 142(2) of the Housing Act 1980 (leasehold valuation tribunals).

CHAPTER V

TENANTS' RIGHT TO MANAGEMENT AUDIT

76. Right to audit management by landlord

(1) This Chapter has effect to confer on two or more qualifying tenants of dwellings held on leases from the same landlord the right, exercisable subject to and in accordance with this Chapter, to have an audit carried out on their behalf which relates to the management of the relevant premises and any appurtenant property by or on behalf of the landlord.

(2) That right shall be exercisable –

(a) where the relevant premises consist of or include two dwellings let to qualifying tenants of the same landlord, by either or both of those tenants; and
(b) where the relevant premises consist of or include three or more dwellings let to qualifying tenants of the same landlord, by not less than two-thirds of those tenants;

and in this Chapter the dwellings let to those qualifying tenants are referred to as 'the constituent dwellings'.

(3) In relation to an audit on behalf of two or more qualifying tenants –

(a) 'the relevant premises' means so much of –
    (i) the building or buildings containing the dwellings let to those tenants, and
    (ii) any other building or buildings,

as constitutes premises in relation to which management functions are discharged in respect of the costs of which common service charge contributions are payable under the leases of those qualifying tenants; and

(b) 'appurtenant property' means so much of any property not contained in the relevant premises as constitutes property in relation to which any such management functions are discharged.

(4) This Chapter also has effect to confer on a single qualifying tenant of a dwelling the right, exercisable subject to and in accordance with this Chapter, to have an audit carried out on his behalf which relates to the management of the relevant premises and any appurtenant property by or on behalf of the landlord.

(5) That right shall be exercisable by a single qualifying tenant of a dwelling where the relevant premises contain no other dwelling let to a qualifying tenant apart from that let to him.

(6) In relation to an audit on behalf of a single qualifying tenant –

(a) 'the relevant premises' means so much of –

(i) the building containing the dwelling let to him, and

(ii) any other building or buildings,

as constitutes premises in relation to which management functions are discharged in respect of the costs of which a service charge is payable under his lease (whether as a common service charge contribution or otherwise); and

(b) 'appurtenant property' means so much of any property not contained in the relevant premises as constitutes property in relation to which any such management functions are discharged.

(7) The provisions of sections 78 to 83 shall, with any necessary modifications, have effect in relation to an audit on behalf of a single qualifying tenant as they have effect in relation to an audit on behalf of two or more qualifying tenants.

(8) For the purposes of this section common service charge contributions are payable by two or more persons under their leases if they may be required under the terms of those leases to contribute to the same costs by the payment of service charges.

77. Qualifying tenants

(1) Subject to the following provisions of this section, a tenant is a qualifying tenant of a dwelling for the purposes of this Chapter if –

(a) he is a tenant of the dwelling under a long lease other than a business lease; and

(b) any service charge is payable under the lease.

(2) For the purposes of subsection (1) a lease is a long lease if –

(a) it is a lease falling within any of paragraphs (a) to (c) of subsection (1) of section 7; or

(b) it is a shared ownership lease (within the meaning of that section), whether granted in pursuance of Part V of the Housing Act 1985 or otherwise and whatever the share of the tenant under it.

(3) No dwelling shall have more than one qualifying tenant at any one time.

(4) Accordingly –

(a) where a dwelling is for the time being let under two or more leases falling within subsection (1), any tenant under any of those leases which is superior to that held by any other such tenant shall not be a qualifying tenant of the dwelling for the purposes of this Chapter; and

(b) where a dwelling is for the time being let to joint tenants under a lease falling within subsection (1), the joint tenants shall (subject to paragraph (a)) be regarded for the purposes of this Chapter as jointly constituting the qualifying tenant of the dwelling.

(5) A person can, however, be (or be among those constituting) the qualifying tenant of each of two or more dwellings at the same time, whether he is tenant of those dwellings under one lease or under two or more separate leases.

(6) Where two or more persons constitute the qualifying tenant of a dwelling in accordance with subsection (4)(b), any one or more of those persons may sign a notice under section 80 on behalf of both or all of them.

78. Management audits

(1) The audit referred to in section 76(1) is an audit carried out for the purposes of ascertaining –
- (a) the extent to which the obligations of the landlord which –
  - (i) are owed to the qualifying tenants of the constituent dwellings, and
  - (ii) involve the discharge of management functions in relation to the relevant premises or any appurtenant property,

  are being discharged in an efficient and effective manner; and
- (b) the extent to which sums payable by those tenants by way of service charges are being applied in an efficient and effective manner;

and in this Chapter any such audit is referred to as a 'management audit'.

(2) In determining whether any such obligations as are mentioned in subsection (1)(a) are being discharged in an efficient and effective manner, regard shall be had to any applicable provisions of any code of practice for the time being approved by the Secretary of State under section 87.

(3) A management audit shall be carried out by a person who –
- (a) is qualified for appointment by virtue of subsection (4); and
- (b) is appointed –
  - (i) in the circumstances mentioned in section 76(2)(a), by either or both of the qualifying tenants of the constituent dwellings, or
  - (ii) in the circumstances mentioned in section 76(2)(b), by not less than two-thirds of the qualifying tenants of the constituent dwellings;

and in this Chapter any such person is referred to as 'the auditor'.

(4) A person is qualified for appointment for the purposes of subsection (3) above if –
- (a) he has the necessary qualification (within the meaning of subsection (1) of section 28 of the 1985 Act (meaning of 'qualified accountant')) or is a qualified surveyor;
- (b) he is not disqualified from acting (within the meaning of that subsection); and
- (c) he is not a tenant of any premises contained in the relevant premises.

(5) For the purposes of subsection (4)(a) above a person is a qualified surveyor if he is a fellow or professional associate of the Royal Institution of Chartered Surveyors or of the Incorporated Society of Valuers and Auctioneers or satisfies such other requirement or requirements as may be prescribed by regulations made by the Secretary of State.

(6) The auditor may appoint such persons to assist him in carrying out the audit as he thinks fit.

79. Rights exercisable in connection with management audits

(1) Where the qualifying tenants of any dwellings exercise under section 80 their right to have a management audit carried out on their behalf, the rights conferred on the auditor by subsection (2) below shall be exercisable by him in connection with the audit.

(2) The rights conferred on the auditor by this subsection are –
(a) a right to require the landlord –
(i) to supply him with such a summary as is referred to in section 21(1) of the 1985 Act (request for summary of relevant costs) in connection with any service charges payable by the qualifying tenants of the constituent dwellings, and
(ii) to afford him reasonable facilities for inspecting, or taking copies of or extracts from, the accounts, receipts and other documents supporting any such summary;
(b) a right to require the landlord or any relevant person to afford him reasonable facilities for inspecting any other documents sight of which is reasonably required by him for the purpose of carrying out the audit; and
(c) a right to require the landlord or any relevant person to afford him reasonable facilities for taking copies of or extracts from any documents falling within paragraph (b).

(3) The rights conferred on the auditor by subsection (2) shall be exercisable by him –
(a) in relation to the landlord, by means of a notice under section 80; and
(b) in relation to any relevant person, by means of a notice given to that person at (so far as is reasonably practicable) the same time as a notice under section 80 is given to the landlord;
and, where a notice is given to any relevant person in accordance with paragraph (b) above, a copy of that notice shall be given to the landlord by the auditor.

(4) The auditor shall also be entitled, on giving notice in accordance with section 80, to carry out an inspection of any common parts comprised in the relevant premises or any appurtenant property.

(5) The landlord or (as the case may be) any relevant person shall –
(a) where facilities for the inspection of any documents are required under subsection (2)(a)(ii) or (b), make those facilities available free of charge;
(b) where any documents are required to be supplied under subsection (2)(a)(i) or facilities for the taking of copies or extracts are required under subsection (2)(a)(ii) or (c), be entitled to supply those documents or (as the case may be) make those facilities available on payment of such reasonable charge as he may determine.

(6) The requirement imposed on the landlord by subsection (5)(a) to make any facilities available free of charge shall not be construed as precluding the landlord from treating as part of his costs of management any costs incurred by him in connection with making those facilities so available.

(7) In this Chapter 'relevant person' means a person (other than the landlord) who –
(a) is charged with responsibility –
(i) for the discharge of any such obligations as are mentioned in section 78(1)(a), or
(ii) for the application of any such service charges as are mentioned in section 78(1)(b); or

(b) has a right to enforce payment of any such service charges.

(8) In this Chapter references to the auditor in the context of –
(a) being afforded any such facilities as are mentioned in subsection (2), or
(b) the carrying out of any inspection under subsection (4),
shall be read as including a person appointed by the auditor under section 78(6).

80. Exercise of right to have a management audit

(1) The right of any qualifying tenants to have a management audit carried out on their behalf shall be exercisable by the giving of a notice under this section.

(2) A notice given under this section –
(a) must be given to the landlord by the auditor, and
(b) must be signed by each of the tenants on whose behalf it is given.

(3) Any such notice must –
(a) state the full name of each of those tenants and the address of the dwelling of which he is a qualifying tenant;
(b) state the name and address of the auditor;
(c) specify any documents or description of documents –
  (i) which the landlord is required to supply to the auditor under section 79(2)(a)(i), or
  (ii) in respect of which he is required to afford the auditor facilities for inspection or for taking copies or extracts under any other provision of section 79(2); and
(d) if the auditor proposes to carry out an inspection under section 79(4), state the date on which he proposes to carry out the inspection.

(4) The date specified under subsection (3)(d) must be a date falling not less than one month nor more than two months after the date of the giving of the notice.

(5) A notice is duly given under this section to the landlord of any qualifying tenants if it is given to a person who receives on behalf of the landlord the rent payable by any such tenants; and a person to whom such a notice is so given shall forward it as soon as may be to the landlord.

81. Procedure following giving of notice under section 80

(1) Where the landlord is given a notice under section 80, then within the period of one month beginning with the date of the giving of the notice, he shall –
(a) supply the auditor with any document specified under subsection (3)(c)(i) of that section, and afford him, in respect of any document falling within section 79(2)(a)(ii), any facilities specified in relation to it under subsection (3)(c)(ii) of section 80;
(b) in the case of every other document or description of documents specified in the notice under subsection (3)(c)(ii) of that section, either –
  (i) afford the auditor facilities for inspection or (as the case may be) taking copies or extracts in respect of that document or those documents, or
  (ii) give the auditor a notice stating that he objects to doing so for such reasons as are specified in the notice; and
(c) if a date is specified in the notice under subsection (3)(d) of that section, either approve the date or propose another date for the carrying out of an inspection under section 79(4).

(2) Any date proposed by the landlord under subsection (1)(c) must be a date falling not later than the end of the period of two months beginning with the date of the giving of the notice under section 80.

(3) Where a relevant person is given a notice under section 79 requiring him to afford the auditor facilities for inspection or taking copies or extracts in respect of any documents or description of documents specified in the notice, then within the period of one month beginning with the date of the giving of the notice, he shall, in the case of every such document or description of documents, either –

(a) afford the auditor the facilities required by him; or

(b) give the auditor a notice stating that he objects to doing so for such reasons as are specified in the notice.

(4) If by the end of the period of two months beginning with –

(a) the date of the giving of the notice under section 80, or

(b) the date of the giving of such a notice under section 79 as is mentioned in subsection (3) above,

the landlord or (as the case may be) a relevant person has failed to comply with any requirement of the notice, the court may, on the application of the auditor, make an order requiring the landlord or (as the case may be) the relevant person to comply with that requirement within such period as is specified in the order.

(5) The court shall not make an order under subsection (4) in respect of any document or documents unless it is satisfied that the document or documents falls or fall within paragraph (a) or (b) of section 79(2).

(6) If by the end of the period of two months specified in subsection (2) no inspection under section 79(4) has been carried out by the auditor, the court may, on the application of the auditor, make an order providing for such an inspection to be carried out on such date as is specified in the order.

(7) Any application for an order under subsection (4) or (6) must be made before the end of the period of four months beginning with –

(a) in the case of an application made in connection with a notice given under section 80, the date of the giving of that notice; or

(b) in the case of an application made in connection with such a notice under section 79 as is mentioned in subsection (3) above, the date of the giving of that notice.

82. Requirement relating to information etc held by superior landlord

(1) Where the landlord is required by a notice under section 80 to supply any summary falling within section 79(2)(a), and any information necessary for complying with the notice so far as relating to any such summary is in the possession of a superior landlord –

(a) the landlord shall make a written request for the relevant information to the person who is his landlord (and so on, if that person is himself not the superior landlord);

(b) the superior landlord shall comply with that request within the period of one month beginning with the date of the making of the request; and

(c) the landlord who received the notice shall then comply with it so far as relating to any such summary within the time allowed by section 81(1) or such further time, if any, as is reasonable.

(2) Where –

(a) the landlord is required by a notice under section 80 to afford the auditor facilities for inspection or taking copies or extracts in respect of any documents or description of documents specified in the notice, and
(b) any of the documents in question is in the custody or unde the control of a superior landlord,

the landlord shall on receiving the notice inform the auditor as soon as may be of that fact and of the name and address of the superior landlord, and the auditor may then give the superior landlord a notice requiring him to afford the facilities in question in respect of the document.

(3) Subsections (3) to (5) and (7) of section 81 shall, with any necessary modifications, have effect in relation to a notice given to a superior landlord under subsection (2) above as they have effect in relation to any such notice given to a relevant person as is mentioned in subsection (3) of that section.

83. Supplementary provisions

(1) Where –
(a) a notice has been given to a landlord under section 80, and
(b) at a time when any obligations arising out of the notice remain to be discharged by him –
(i) he disposes of the whole or part of his interest as landlord of the qualifying tenants of the constituent dwellings, and
(ii) the person acquiring any such interest of the landlord is in a position to discharge any of those obligations to any extent,

that person shall be responsible for discharging those obligations to that extent, as if he had been given the notice under that section.

(2) If the landlord is, despite any such disposal, still in a position to discharge those obligations to the extent referred to in subsection (1), he shall remain responsible for so discharging them; but otherwise the person referred to in that subsection shall be responsible for so discharging them to the exclusion of the landlord.

(3) Where a person is so responsible for discharging any such obligations (whether with the landlord or otherwise) –
(a) references to the landlord in section 81 shall be read as including, or as, references to that person to such extent as is appropriate to reflect his responsibility for discharging those obligations; but
(b) in connection with the discharge of any such obligations by that person, that section shall apply as if any reference to the date of the giving of the notice under section 80 were a reference to the date of the disposal referred to in subsection (1).

(4) Where –
(a) a notice has been given to a relevant person under section 79, and
(b) at a time when any obligations arising out of the notice remain to be discharged by him, he ceases to be a relevant person, but
(c) he is, despite ceasing to be a relevant person, still in a position to discharge those obligations to any extent,

he shall nevertheless remain responsible for discharging those obligations to that extent; and section 81 shall accordingly continue to apply to him as if he were still a relevant person.

(5) Where –
(a) a notice has been given to a landlord under section 80, or

(b) a notice has been given to a relevant person under section 79,

then during the period of twelve months beginning with the date of that notice, no subsequent such notice may be given to the landlord or (as the case may be) that person on behalf of any persons who, in relation to the earlier notice, were qualifying tenants of the constituent dwellings.

84. Interpretation of Chapter V

In this Chapter –

'the 1985 Act' means the Landlord and Tenant Act 1985;

'appurtenant property' shall be construed in accordance with section 76(3) or (6);

'the auditor', in relation to a management audit, means such a person as is mentioned in section 78(3);

'the constituent dwellings' means the dwellings referred to in section 76(2)(a) or (b) (as the case may be);

'landlord' means immediate landlord;

'management audit' means such audit as is mentioned in section 78(1);

'management functions' includes functions with respect to the provision of services or the repair, maintenance or insurance of property;

'relevant person' has the meaning given by section 79(7);

'the relevant premises' shall be construed in accordance with section 76(3) or (6);

'service charge' has the meaning given by section 18(1) of the 1985 Act.

CHAPTER VI

MISCELLANEOUS

Compulsory acquisition of landlord's interest

85. Amendment of Part III of Landlord and Tenant Act 1987

(1) Part III of the Landlord and Tenant Act 1987 (compulsory acquisition by tenants of their landlord's interest) shall be amended as follows.

(2) In section 25 (compulsory acquisition of landlord's interest by qualifying tenants) –

(a) for subsection (2)(c) there shall be substituted –

'(c) the total number of flats held by such tenants is not less than two-thirds of the total number of flats contained in the premises.'; and

(b) subsection (3) shall be omitted.

(3) In section 27(4) (meaning of requisite majority in relation to qualifying tenants), for 'more than 50 per cent' there shall be substituted 'not less than two-thirds'.

(4) In section 29(2) (conditions for making acquisition orders), the words from 'and (c)' onwards shall be omitted.

Variation of leases

86. Variation of leases under Part IV of Landlord and Tenant Act 1987

In section 35(4) of the Landlord and Tenant Act 1987 (variation of lease on grounds that it fails to make satisfactory provision with respect to the computation of a service charge), in paragraph (c), for 'exceed' there shall be substituted 'either exceed or be less than'.

Codes of practice

87. Approval by Secretary of State of codes of management practice

(1) The Secretary of State may, if he considers it appropriate to do so, by order—
  (a) approve any code of practice—
    (i) which appears to him to be designed to promote desirable practices in relation to any matter or matters directly or indirectly concerned with the management of residential property by relevant persons; and
    (ii) which has been submitted to him for his approval;
  (b) approve any modifications of any such code which have been so submitted; or
  (c) withdraw his approval for any such code or modifications.

(2) The Secretary of State shall not approve any such code or any modifications of any such code unless he is satisfied that arrangements have been made for the text of the code or the modifications to be published in such manner as he considers appropriate for bringing the provisions of the code or the modifications to the notice of those likely to be affected by them (which, in the case of modifications of a code, may include publication of a text of the code incorporating the modifications).

(3) The power of the Secretary of State under this section to approve a code of practice which has been submitted to him for his approval includes power to approve a part of any such code; and references in this section to a code of practice may accordingly be read as including a reference to a part of a code of practice.

(4) At any one time there may be two or more codes of practice for the time being approved under this section.

(5) A code of practice approved under this section may make different provision with respect to different cases or descriptions of cases, including different provision for different areas.

(6) Without prejudice to the generality of subsections (1) and (5) –
  (a) a code of practice approved under this section may, in relation to any such matter as is referred to in subsection (1), make provision in respect of relevant persons who are under an obligation to discharge any function in connection with that matter as well as in respect of relevant persons who are not under such an obligation; and
  (b) any such code may make provision with respect to –
    (i) the resolution of disputes with respect to residential property between relevant persons and the tenants of such property;
    (ii) competitive tendering for works in connection with such property; and
    (iii) the administration of trusts in respect of amounts paid by tenants by way of service charges.

(7) A failure on the part of any person to comply with any provision of a code of practice for the time being approved under this section shall not of itself render him liable to any proceedings; but in any proceedings before a court or tribunal –
  (a) any code of practice approved under this section shall be admissible in evidence; and
  (b) any provision of any such code which appears to the court or tribunal to be relevant to any question arising in the proceedings shall be taken into account in determining that question.

(8) For the purposes of this section –

(a) 'relevant person' means any landlord of residential property or any person who discharges management functions in respect of such property, and for this purpose 'management functions' includes functions with respect to the provision of services or the repair, maintenance or insurance of such property;

(b) 'residential property' means any building or part of a building which consists of one or more dwellings let on leases, but references to residential property include –

(i) any garage, outhouse, garden, yard and appurtenances belonging to or usually enjoyed with such dwellings,

(ii) any common parts of any such building or part, and

(iii) any common facilities which are not within any such building or part; and

(c) 'service charge' means an amount payable by a tenant of a dwelling as part of or in addition to the rent –

(i) which is payable, directly or indirectly, for services, repairs, maintenance or insurance or any relevant person's costs of management, and

(ii) the whole or part of which varies or may vary according to the costs or estimated costs incurred or to be incurred by any relevant person in connection with the matters mentioned in sub-paragraph (i).

(9) This section applies in relation to dwellings let on licences to occupy as it applies in relation to dwellings let on leases, and references in this section to landlords and tenants of residential property accordingly include references to licensors and licensees of such property.

Jurisdiction of leasehold valuation tribunals in relation to enfranchisement etc of Crown land

88. Jurisdiction of leasehold valuation tribunals in relation to enfranchisement etc of Crown land

(1) This section applies where any tenant under a lease from the Crown is proceeding with a view to acquiring the freehold or an extended lease of a house and premises in circumstances in which, but for the existence of any Crown interest in the land subject to the lease, he would be entitled to acquire the freehold or such an extended lease under Part I of the Leasehold Reform Act 1967.

(2) Where –

(a) this section applies in accordance with subsection (1), and

(b) any question arises in connection with the acquisition of the freehold or an extended lease of the house and premises which is such that, if the tenant were proceeding as mentioned in that subsection in pursuance of a claim made under Part I of that Act, a leasehold valuation tribunal constituted for the purposes of that Part of that Act would have jurisdiction to determine it in proceedings under that Part, and

(c) it is agreed between –

(i) the appropriate authority and the tenant, and

(ii) all other persons (if any) whose interests would fall to be represented in proceedings brought under that Part for the determination of that question by such a tribunal,

that that question should be determined by such a tribunal,

a rent assessment committee constituted for the purposes of this section shall have jurisdiction to determine that question.

(3) A rent assessment committee shall, when constituted for the purposes of this section, be known as a leasehold valuation tribunal.

(4) Paragraphs 1 to 3 of Schedule 22 to the Housing Act 1980 (provisions relating to leasehold valuation tribunals constituted for the purposes of Part I of the Leasehold Reform Act 1967) shall apply to a leasehold valuation tribunal constituted for the purposes of this section.

(5) Any application made to such a leasehold valuation tribunal must comply with such requirements (if any) as to the form of, or the particulars to be contained in, any such application as the Secretary of State may by regulations prescribe.

(6) For the purposes of this section 'lease from the Crown' means a lease of land in which there is, or has during the subsistence of the lease been, a Crown interest superior to the lease; and 'Crown interest' and 'the appropriate authority' in relation to a Crown interest mean respectively –

- (a) an interest comprised in the Crown Estate, and the Crown Estate Commissioners;
- (b) an interest belonging to Her Majesty in right of the Duchy of Lancaster, and the Chancellor of the Duchy;
- (c) an interest belonging to the Duchy of Cornwall, and such person as the Duke of Cornwall or the possessor for the time being of the Duchy appoints;
- (d) any other interest belonging to a government department or held on behalf of Her Majesty for the purposes of a government department, and the Minister in charge of that department.

(7) In this section any reference to a leasehold valuation tribunal constituted for the purposes of Part I of the Leasehold Reform Act 1967 is a reference to such a rent assessment committee as is mentioned in section 142(2) of the Housing Act 1980 (leasehold valuation tribunals).

Provision of accommodation for persons with mental disorders

89. Avoidance of provisions preventing occupation of leasehold property by persons with mental disorders

(1) Any agreement relating to a lease of any property which comprises or includes a dwelling (whether contained in the instrument creating the lease or not and whether made before the creation of the lease or not) shall be void in so far as it would otherwise have the effect of prohibiting or imposing any restriction on –

- (a) the occupation of the dwelling, or of any part of the dwelling, by persons with mental disorders (within the meaning of the Mental Health Act 1983), or
- (b) the provision of accommodation within the dwelling for such persons.

(2) Subsection (1) applies to any agreement made after the coming into force of this section.

CHAPTER VII

GENERAL

90. Jurisdiction of county courts

(1) Any jurisdiction expressed to be conferred on the court by this Part shall be exercised by a county court.

(2) There shall also be brought in a county court any proceedings for determining any question arising under or by virtue of any provision of Chapter I or II or this Chapter which is not a question falling within its jurisdiction by virtue of subsection (1) or one falling within the jurisdiction of a leasehold valuation tribunal by virtue of section 91.

(3) Where, however, there are brought in the High Court any proceedings which, apart from this subsection, are proceedings within the jurisdiction of the High Court, the High Court shall have jurisdiction to hear and determine any proceedings joined with those proceedings which are proceedings within the jurisdiction of a county court by virtue of subsection (1) or (2).

(4) Where any proceedings are brought in a county court by virtue of subsection (1) or (2), the court shall have jurisdiction to hear and determine any other proceedings joined with those proceedings, despite the fact that, apart from this subsection, those other proceedings would be outside the court's jurisdiction.

91. Jurisdiction of leasehold valuation tribunals

(1) any jurisdiction expressed to be conferred on a leasehold valuation tribunal by the provisions of this Part (except section 75 or 88) shall be exercised by a rent assessment committee constituted for the purposes of this section; and any question arising in relation to any of the matters specified in subsection (2) shall, in default of agreement, be determined by such a rent assessment committee.

(2) Those matters are –
- (a) the terms of acquisition relating to –
  - (i) any interest which is to be acquired by a nominee purchaser in pursuance of Chapter I, or
  - (ii) any new lease which is to be granted to a tenant in pursuance of Chapter II,

  including in particular any matter which needs to be determined for the purposes of any provision of Schedule 6 or 13;
- (b) the terms of any lease which is to be granted in accordance with section 36 and Schedule 9;
- (c) the amount of any payment falling to be made by virtue of section 18(2);
- (d) the amount of any costs payable by any person or persons by virtue of any provision of Chapter I or II and, in the case of costs to which section 33(1) or 60(1) applies, the liability of any person or persons by virtue of any such provision to pay any such costs; and
- (e) the apportionment between two or more persons of any amount (whether of costs or otherwise) payable by virtue of any such provision.

(3) A rent assessment committee shall, when constituted for the purposes of this section, be known as a leasehold valuation tribunal; and in the following provisions of this section references to a leasehold valuation tribunal are (unless the context otherwise requires) references to such a committee.

(4) Where in any proceedings before a court there falls for determination any question falling within the jurisdiction of a leasehold valuation tribunal by virtue of Chapter I or II or this section, the court –
- (a) shall by order transfer to such a tribunal so much of the proceedings as relate to the determination of that question; and
- (b) may then dispose of all or any remaining proceedings, or adjourn the disposal of all or any such proceedings pending the determination of that question by the tribunal, as it thinks fit;

and accordingly once that question has been so determined the court shall, if it is a question relating to any matter falling to be determined by the court, give effect to the determination in an order of the court.

(5) Without prejudice to the generality of any other statutory provision –

(a) the power to make regulations under section 74(1)(b) of the Rent Act 1977 (procedure of rent assessment committees) shall extend to prescribing the procedure to be followed consequent on a transfer under subsection (4) above; and

(b) rules of court may prescribe the procedure to be followed in connection with such a transfer.

(6) Any application made to a leasehold valuation tribunal under or by virtue of this Part must comply with such requirements (if any) as to the form of, or the particulars to be contained in, any such application as the Secretary of State may by regulations prescribe.

(7) In any proceedings before a leasehold valuation tribunal which relate to any claim made under Chapter I, the interests of the participating tenants shall be represented by the nominee purchaser, and accordingly the parties to any such proceedings shall not include those tenants.

(8) No costs which a party to any proceedings under or by virtue of this Part before a leasehold valuation tribunal incurs in connection with the proceedings shall be recoverable by order of any court (whether in consequence of a transfer under subsection (4) or otherwise).

(9) A leasehold valuation tribunal may, when determining the property in which any interest is to be acquired in pursuance of a notice under section 13 or 42, specify in its determination property which is less extensive than that specified in that notice.

(10) Paragraphs 1 to 3 and 7 of Schedule 22 to the Housing Act 1980 (provisions relating to leasehold valuation tribunals constituted for the purposes of Part I of the Leasehold Reform Act 1967) shall apply to a leasehold valuation tribunal constituted for the purposes of this section; but –

(a) in relation to any proceedings which relate to a claim made under Chapter I of this Part of this Act, paragraph 7 of that Schedule shall apply as if the nominee purchaser were included among the persons on whom a notice is authorised to be served under that paragraph; and

(b) in relation to any proceedings on an application for a scheme to be approved by a tribunal under section 70, paragraph 2(a) of that Schedule shall apply as if any person appearing before the tribunal in accordance with subsection (6) of that section were a party to the proceedings.

(11) In this section –

'the nominee purchaser' and 'the participating tenants' have the same meaning as in Chapter I;

'the terms of acquisition' shall be construed in accordance with section 24(8) or section 48(7), as appropriate;

and the reference in subsection (10) to a leasehold valuation tribunal constituted for the purposes of Part I of the Leasehold Reform Act 1967 shall be construed in accordance with section 88(7) above.

92. Enforcement of obligations under Chapters I and II

(1) The court may, on the application of any person interested, make an order requiring any person who has failed to comply with any requirement imposed on him under or by virtue of any provision of Chapter I or II to make good the default within such time as is specified in the order.

(2) An application shall not be made under subsection (1) unless –

(a) a notice has been previously given to the person in question requiring him to make good the default, and
(b) more than 14 days have elapsed since the date of the giving of that notice without his having done so.

93. Agreements excluding or modifying rights of tenant under Chapter I or II

(1) Except as provided by this section, any agreement relating to a lease (whether contained in the instrument creating the lease or not and whether made before the creation of the lease or not) shall be void in so far as it –
(a) purports to exclude or modify –
(i) any entitlement to participate in the making or a claim to exercise the right to collective enfranchisement under Chapter I,
(ii) any right to acquire a new lease under Chapter II, or
(iii) any right to compensation under section 61; or
(b) provides for the termination or surrender of the lease in the event of the tenant becoming a participating tenant for the purposes of Chapter I or giving a notice under section 42; or
(c) provides for the imposition of any penalty or disability on the tenant in that event.

(2) Subsection (1) shall not be taken to preclude a tenant from surrendering his lease, and shall not –
(a) invalidate any agreement for the acquisition on behalf of a tenant of an interest superior to his lease, or for the acquisition by a tenant of a new lease, on terms different from those provided by Chapters I and II; or
(b) where a tenant has become a participating tenant for the purposes of Chapter I or has given a notice under section 42, invalidate –
(i) any agreement that the notice given under section 13 or (as the case may be) section 42 shall cease to have effect, or
(ii) any provision of such an agreement excluding or restricting for a period not exceeding three years any such entitlement or right as is mentioned in subsection (1)(a)(i) or (ii); or
(c) where a tenant's right to compensation under section 61 has accrued, invalidate any agreement as to the amount of the compensation.

(3) Where –
(a) a tenant having the right to acquire a new lease under Chapter II –
(i) has entered into an agreement for the surrender of his lease without the prior approval of the court, or
(ii) has entered into an agreement for the grant of a new lease without any of the terms of acquisition (within the meaning of that Chapter) having been determined by a leasehold valuation tribunal under that Chapter, or
(b) a tenant has been granted a new lease under Chapter II or by virtue of subsection (4) below and, on his landlord claiming possession for the purposes of redevelopment, enters into an agreement without the prior approval of the court for the surrender of the lease,

then on the application of the tenant a county court, or any court in which proceedings are brought on the agreement, may, if in its opinion the tenant is not adequately recompensed under the agreement for his rights under Chapter II, set aside or vary the agreement and give such other relief as appears to it to be just having regard to the situation and conduct of the parties.

(4) Where a tenant has the right to acquire a new lease under Chapter II, there may with the approval of the court be granted to him in satisfaction of that right a new lease on

such terms as may be approved by the court, which may include terms excluding or modifying –

(a) any entitlement to participate in the making of a claim to exercise the right to collective enfranchisement under Chapter I, or

(b) any right to acquire a further lease under Chapter II.

(5) Subject to the provisions specified in subsection (6) and to subsection (7), a lease may be granted by virtue of subsection (4), and shall if so granted be binding on persons entitled to any interest in or charge on the landlord's estate –

(a) despite the fact that, apart from this subsection, it would not be authorised against any such persons, and

(b) despite any statutory or other restrictions on the landlord's power of leasing.

(6) The provisions referred to in subsection (5) are –

(a) section 36 of the Charities Act 1993 (restrictions on disposition of charity land); and

(b) paragraph 8(2)(c) of Schedule 2 to this Act.

(7) Where the existing lease of the tenant is granted after the commencement of Chapter II and, the grant being subsequent to the creation of a charge on the landlord's estate, the existing lease is not binding on the persons interested in the charge, a lease granted by virtue of subsection (4) shall not be binding on those persons.

(8) Where a lease is granted by virtue of subsection (4), then except in so far as provision is made to the contrary by the terms of the lease, the following provisions shall apply in relation to the lease as they apply in relation to a lease granted under section 56, namely –

(a) section 58(3), (5) and (6);

(b) section 59(2) to (5); and

(c) section 61 and Schedule 14;

and subsections (5) to (7) of section 56 shall apply in relation to the lease as they apply in relation to a lease granted under that section.

94. Crown land

(1) Subject to subsection (2), Chapters I and II shall apply to a lease from the Crown if (and only if) there has ceased to be a Crown interest in the land subject to it.

(2) Where a tenant under a lease from the Crown would, but for the existence of any Crown interest, be entitled to acquire a new lease under Chapter II, then if –

(a) that Crown interest is superior to the interest of the person who for the purposes of Chapter II is the landlord in relation to the lease, and

(b) either –

(i) that landlord is entitled to grant such a new lease without the concurrence of the appropriate authority, or

(ii) the appropriate authority notifies that landlord that, as regards any Crown interest affected, the authority will concur in granting such a new lease,

subsection (1) shall apply as if there had ceased to be any Crown interest in the land subject to the lease, and Chapter II shall apply accordingly.

(3) The restriction imposed by section 3(2) of the Crown Estate Act 1961 (general provisions as to management) on the term for which a lease may be granted by the Crown Estate Commissioners shall not apply where –

(a) the lease is granted by way of renewal of a long lease at a low rent, and
(b) it appears to the Crown Estate Commissioners that, but for the existence of any Crown interest, there would be a right to acquire a new lease under Chapter II of this Part of this Act.

(4) Where, in the case of land belonging –
(a) to Her Majesty in right of the Duchy of Lancaster, or
(b) to the Duchy of Cornwall,
it appears to the appropriate authority that a tenant under a long lease at a low rent would, but for the existence of any Crown interest, be entitled to acquire a new lease under Chapter II, then a lease corresponding to that to which the tenant would be so entitled may be granted to take effect wholly or partly out of the Crown interest by the same person and with the same formalities as in the case of any other lease of such land.

(5) In the case of land belonging to the Duchy of Cornwall, the purposes authorised by section 8 of the Duchy of Cornwall Management Act 1863 for the advancement of parts of such gross sums as are there mentioned shall include the payment to tenants under leases from the Crown of sums corresponding to those which, but for the existence of any Crown interest, would be payable by way of compensation under section 61 above.

(6) The appropriate authority in relation to any area occupied under leases from the Crown may make an application for the approval under section 70 of a scheme for that area which is designed to secure that, in the event of tenants udner those leases acquiring freehold interests in such circumstances as are mentioned in subsection (7) below, the authority will –
(a) retain powers of management in respect of the premises in which any such freehold interests are acquired, and
(b) have rights against any such premises in respect of the benefits arising from the exercise elsewhere of the authority's powers of management.

(7) The circumstances mentioned in subsection (6) are cicrumstances in which, but for the existence of any Crown interest, the tenants acquiring any such freehold interests would be entitled to acquire them as mentioned in section 69(1)(a) or (b).

(8) Subject to any necessary modifications –
(a) subsections (2) to (7) of section 69 shall apply in relation to any such scheme as is mentioned in subsection (6) above as they apply in relation to an estate management scheme; and
(b) section 70 shall apply in relation to the approval of such a scheme as it applies in relation to the approval of a scheme as an estate management scheme.

(9) Subsection (10) applies where –
(a) any tenants under leases from the Crown are proceeding with a view to acquiring the freehold of any premises in circumstances in which, but for the existence of any Crown interest, they would be entitled to acquire the freehold under Chapter I, or
(b) any tenant under a lease from the Crown is proceeding with a view to acquiring a new lease of his flat in circumstances in which, but for the existence of any Crown interest, he would be entitled to acquire such a lease under Chapter II.

(10) Where –
(a) this subsection applies in accordance with subsection (9), and
(b) any question arises in connection with the acquisition of the freehold of those premises or any such new lease which is such that, if the tenants or tenant were proceeding as mentioned in that subsection in pursuance of a claim made under

Chapter I or (as the case may be) Chapter II, a leasehold valuation tribunal would have jurisdiction to determine it in proceedings under that Chapter, and

(c) it is agreed between –
  (i) the appropriate authority and the tenants or tenant, and
  (ii) all other persons (if any) whose interests would fall to be represented in proceedings brought under that Chapter for the determination of that question by a leasehold valuation tribunal,

that that question should be determined by such a tribunal,

a leasehold valuation tribunal shall have jurisdiction to determine that question; and references in this subsection to a leasehold valuation tribunal are to such a tribunal constituted for the purposes of section 91.

(11) For the purposes of this section 'lease from the Crown' means a lease of land in which there is, or has during the subsistence of the lease been, a Crown interest superior to the lease; and 'Crown interest' and 'the appropriate authority' in relation to a Crown interest mean respectively –

(a) an interest comprised in the Crown Estate, and the Crown Estate Commissioners;
(b) an interest belonging to Her Majesty in right of the Duchy of Lancaster, and the Chancellor of the Duchy;
(c) an interest belonging to the Duchy of Cornwall, and such person as the Duke of Cornwall or the possessor for the time being of the Duchy appoints;
(d) any other interest belonging to a government department or held on behalf of Her Majesty for the purposes of a government department, and the Minister in charge of that department.

(12) For the purposes of this section 'long lease at a low rent' shall be construed in accordance with sections 7 and 8.

95. Saving for National Trust

Chapters I and II shall not prejudice the operation of section 21 of the National Trust Act 1907, and accordingly there shall be no right under Chapter I or II to acquire any interest in or new lease of any property if an interest in the property is under that section vested inalienably in the National Trust for Places of Historic Interest or Natural Beauty.

96. Property within cathedral precinct

There shall be no right under Chapter I or II to acquire any interest in or lease of any property which for the purposes of the Care of Cathedrals Measure 1990 is within the precinct of a cathedral church.

97. Registration of notices, applications and orders under Chapters I and II

(1) No lease shall be registrable under the Land Charges Act 1972 or be taken to be an estate contract within the meaning of that Act by reason of any rights or obligations of the tenant or landlord which may arise under Chapter I or II, and any right of a tenant arising from a notice given under section 13 or 42 shall not be an overriding interest within the meaning of the Land Registration Act 1925; but a notice given under section 13 or 42 shall be registrable under the Land Charges Act 1972, or may be the subject of a notice or caution under the Land Registration Act 1925, as if it were an estate contract.

(2) The Land Charges Act 1972 and the Land Registration Act 1925 –

(a) shall apply in relation to an order made under section 26(1) or 50(1) as they apply in relation to an order affecting land which is made by the court for the purpose of enforcing a judgment or recognisance; and

(b) shall apply in relation to an application for such an order as they apply in relation to other pending land actions.

(3) The persons applying for such an order in respect of any premises shall be treated for the purposes of section 57 of the Land Registration Act 1925 (inhibitions) as persons interested in relation to any registered land containing the whole or part of those premises.

98. Power to prescribe procedure under Chapters I and II

(1) Where a claim to exercise the right to collective enfranchisement under Chapter I is made by the giving of a notice under section 13, or a claim to exercise the right to acquire a new lease under Chapter II is made by the giving of a notice under section 42, then except as otherwise provided by Chapter I or (as the case may be) Chapter II –

(a) the procedure for giving effect to the notice, and

(b) the rights and obligations of all parties in relation to the investigation of title and other matters arising in giving effect to the notice,

shall be such as may be prescribed by regulations made by the Secretary of State and, subject to or in the absence of provision made by any such regulations, shall be as nearly as may be the same as in the case of a contract of sale or leasing freely negotiated between the parties.

(2) Regulations under this section may, in particular, make provision –

(a) for a person to be discharged from performing any obligations arising out of a notice under section 13 or 42 by reason of the default or delay of some other person;

(b) for the payment of a deposit –

(i) by a nominee purchaser (within the meaning of Chapter I) on exchange of contracts, or

(ii) by a tenant who has given a notice under section 42; and

(c) with respect to the following matters, namely –

(i) the person with whom any such deposit is to be lodged and the capacity in which any such person is to hold it, and

(ii) the circumstances in which the whole or part of any such deposit is to be returned or forfeited.

99. Notices

(1) Any notice required or authorised to be given under this Part –

(a) shall be in writing; and

(b) may be sent by post.

(2) Where in accordance with Chapter I or II an address in England and Wales is specified as an address at which notices may be given to any person or persons under that Chapter –

(a) any notice required or authorised to be given to that person or those persons under that Chapter may (without prejudice to the operation of subsection (3)) be given to him or them at the address so specified; but

(b) if a new address in England and Wales is so specified in substitution for that address by the giving of a notice to that effect, any notice so required or authorised to be given may be given to him or them at that new address instead.

(3) Where a tenant is required or authorised to give any notice under Chapter I or II to a person who –

(a) is the tenant's immediate landlord, and
(b) is such a landlord in respect of premises to which Part VI of the Landlord and Tenant Act 1987 (information to be furnished to tenants) applies,

the tenant may, unless he has been subsequently notified by the landlord of a different address in England and Wales for the purposes of this section, give the notice to the landlord –

(i) at the address last furnished to the tenant as the landlord's address for service in accordance with section 48 of that Act (notification of address for service of notices on landlord); or
(ii) if no such address has been furnished, at the address last furnished to the tenant as the landlord's address in accordance with section 47 of that Act (landlord's name and address to be contained in demands for rent).

(4) Subsections (2) and (3) apply to notices in proceedings under Chapter I or II as they apply to notices required or authorised to be given under that Chapter.

(5) Any notice which is given under Chapter I or II by any tenants or tenant must –
(a) if it is a notice given under section 13 or 42, be signed by each of the tenants, or (as the case may be) by the tenant, by whom it is given; and
(b) in any other case, be signed by or on behalf of each of the tenants, or (as the case may be) by or on behalf of the tenant, by whom it is given.

(6) The Secretary of State may by regulations prescribe –
(a) the form of any notice required or authorised to be given under this Part; and
(b) the particulars which any such notice must contain (whether in addition to, or in substitution for, any particulars required by virtue of any provision of this Part).

100. Orders and regulations

(1) Any power of the Secretary of State to make orders or regulations under this Part –
(a) may be so exercised as to make different provision for different cases or descriptions of cases, including different provision for different areas; and
(b) includes power to make such procedural, incidental, supplementary and transitional provision as may appear to the Secretary of State necessary or expedient.

(2) Any power of the Secretary of State to make orders or regulations under this Part shall be exercisable by statutory instrument which (except in the case of regulations making only such provision as is mentioned in section 99(6)) shall be subject to annulment in pursuance of a resolution of either House of Parliament.

101. General interpretation of Part I

(1) In this Part –

'business lease' means a tenancy to which Part II of the Landlord and Tenant Act 1954 applies;

'common parts', in relation to any building or part of a building, includes the structure and exterior of that building or part and any common facilities within it;

'the court' (unless the context otherwise requires) means, by virtue of section 90(1), a county court;

'disposal' means a disposal whether by the creation or the transfer of an interest, and includes the surrender of a lease and the grant of an option or right of pre-emption, and 'acquisition' shall be construed accordingly (as shall expressions related to either of these expressions);

'dwelling' means any building or part of a building occupied or intended to be occupied as a separate dwelling;

'flat' means a separate set of premises (whether or not on the same floor) –

(a) which forms part of a building, and

(b) which is constructed or adapted for use for the purposes of a dwelling, and

(c) either the whole or a material part of which lies above or below some other part of the building;

'interest' includes estate;

'lease' and 'tenancy', and related expressions, shall be construed in accordance with subsection (2);

'rent assessment committee' means a rent assessment committee constituted under Schedule 10 to the Rent Act 1977;

'the term date', in relation to a lease granted for a term of years certain, means (subject to subsection (6)) the date of expiry of that term, and, in relation to a tenancy to which any of the provisions of section 102 applies, shall be construed in accordance with those provisions.

(2) In this Part 'lease' and 'tenancy' have the same meaning, and both expressions include (where the context so permits) –

(a) a sub-lease or sub-tenancy, and

(b) an agreement for a lease or tenancy (or for a sub-lease or sub-tenancy),

but do not include a tenancy at will or at sufferance; and the expressions 'landlord' and 'tenant', and references to letting, to the grant of a lease or to covenants or the terms of a lease, shall be construed accordingly.

(3) In this Part any reference (however expressed) to the lease held by a qualifying tenant of a flat is a reference to a lease held by him under which the demised premises consist of or include the flat (whether with or without one or more other flats).

(4) Where two or more persons jointly constitute either the landlord or the tenant or qualifying tenant in relation to a lease of a flat, any reference in this Part to the landlord or to the tenant or qualifying tenant is (unless the context otherwise requires) a reference to both or all of the persons who jointly constitute the landlord or the tenant or qualifying tenant, as the case may require.

(5) Any reference in this Part to the date of the commencement of a lease is a reference to the date of commencement of the term of the lease.

(6) In the case of a lease which derives (in accordance with section 7(6)) from more than one separate leases, references in this Part to the date of the commencement of the lease or to the term date shall, if the terms of the separate leases commenced at different dates or those leases have different term dates, have effect as references to the date of the commencement, or (as the case may be) to the term date, of the lease comprising the flat in question (or the earliest date of commencement or earliest term date of the leases comprising it).

(7) For the purposes of this Part property is let with other property if the properties are let either under the same lease or under leases which, in accordance with section 7(6), are treated as a single lease.

(8) For the purposes of this Part any lease which is reversionary on another lease shall be treated as if it were a concurrent lease intermediate between that other lease and any interest superior to that other lease.

(9) For the purposes of this Part an order of a court or a decision of a leasehold valuation tribunal is to be treated as becoming final –

(a) if not appealed against, on the expiry of the time for bringing an appeal; or
(b) if appealed against and not set aside in consequence of the appeal, at the time when the appeal and any further appeal is disposed of –
  (i) by the determination of it and the expiry of the time for bringing a further appeal (if any), or
  (ii) by its being abandoned or otherwise ceasing to have effect.

102. Term date and other matters relating to periodical tenancies

(1) Where either of the following provisions (which relate to continuation tenancies) applies to a tenancy, namely –
(a) section 19(2) of the Landlord and Tenant Act 1954 ('the 1954 Act'), or
(b) paragraph 16(2) of Schedule 10 to the Local Government and Housing Act 1989 ('the 1989 Act'),
the tenancy shall be treated for the relevant purposes of this Part as granted to expire –
(i) on the date which is the term date for the purposes of the 1954 Act (namely, the first date after the commencement of the 1954 Act on which, apart from the 1954 Act, the tenancy could have been brought to an end by a notice to quit given by the landlord under the tenancy), or
(ii) on the date which is the term date for the purposes of Schedule 10 to the 1989 Act (namely, the first date after the commencement of Schedule 10 to the 1989 Act on which, apart from that Schedule, the tenancy could have been brought to an end by such a notice to quit),
as the case may be.

(2) Subject to subsection (1), where under section 7(3) a tenancy created or arising as a tenancy from year to year or other periodical tenancy is to be treated as a long lease, then for the relevant purposes of this Part, the term date of that tenancy shall be taken to be the date (if any) on which the tenancy is to terminate by virtue of a notice to quit given by the landlord under the tenancy before the relevant date for those purposes, or else the earliest date on which it could as at that date (in accordance with its terms and apart from any enactment) be brought to an end by such a notice to quit.

(3) Subject to subsection (1), in the case of a tenancy granted to continue as a periodical tenancy after the expiry of a term of years certain, or to continue as a periodical tenancy if not terminated at the expiry of such a term, any question whether the tenancy is at any time to be treated for the relevant purposes of this Part as a long lease, and (if so) with what term date, shall be determined as it would be if there had been two tenancies, as follows –
(a) one granted to expire at the earliest time (at or after the expiry of that term of years certain) at which the tenancy could (in accordance with its terms and apart from any enactment) be brought to an end by a notice to quit given by the landlord under the tenancy; and
(b) the other granted to commence at the expiry of the first (and not being one to which subsection (1) applies).

(4) In this section 'the relevant purposes of this Part' means the purposes of Chapter I or, to the extent that section 7 has effect for the purposes of Chapter II in accordance with section 39(3), the purposes of that Chapter.

103. Application of Part I to Isles of Scilly

This Part applies to the Isles of Scilly subject to such exceptions, adaptations and modifications as the Secretary of State may by order direct.

PART IV

SUPPLEMENTAL

186. Financial provisions
(1) There shall be paid out of money provided by Parliament –
(a) any expenses of the Secretary of Sate incurred in consequence of this Act; and
(b) any increase attributable to this Act in the sums payable out of money so provided under any other enactment.

(2) There shall be paid into the Consolidated Fund any increase attributable to this Act in the sums payable into that Fund under any other enactment.

187. Amendments and repeals
(1) The enactments mentioned in Schedule 21 to this Act shall have effect subject to the amendments there specified (being minor amendments and amendments consequential on the provisions of this Act).

(2) The enactments mentioned in Schedule 22 to this Act (which include some that are spent or no longer of practical utility) are hereby repealed to the extent specified in the third column of that Schedule.

188. Short title, commencement and extent
(1) This Act may be cited as the Leasehold Reform, Housing and Urban Development Act 1993.

(2) This Act, except –
(a) this section;
(b) sections 126 and 127, 135 to 140, 149 to 151, 181(1), (2) and (4) and 186; and
(c) the repeal in section 80(1) of the Local Government and Housing Act 1989,
shall come into force on such day as the Secretary of State may by order made by statutory instrument appoint; and different days may be so appointed for different provisions or for different purposes.

(3) An order under subsection (2) may contain such transitional provisions and savings (whether or not involving the modification of any statutory provision) as appear to the Secretary of Sate necessary or expedient in connection with the provisions thereby brought into force by the order.

(4) The following, namely –
(a) Part I of the Act;

. . .

extend to England and Wales only.

. . .

(7) This Part, except this section, paragraph 3 of Schedule 21 and the repeals in the House of Commons Disqualification Act 1975 and the Northern Ireland Assembly Disqualification Act 1975, does not extend to Northern Ireland.

SCHEDULES

Section 9

SCHEDULE 1

CONDUCT OF PROCEEDINGS BY REVERSIONER ON BEHALF OF OTHER LANDLORDS

PART I

THE REVERSIONER

Freeholder to be reversioner

1. Subject to paragraphs 2 to 4, the reversioner in respect of any premises is the person who owns the freehold of those premises.

Replacement of freeholder by other relevant landlord

2. The court may, on the application of all the relevant landlords of any premises, appoint to be the reversioner in respect of those premises (in place of the person designated by paragraph 1) such person as may have been determined by agreement between them.

3. If it appears to the court, on the application of a relevant landlord of any premises –
   (a) that the respective interests of the relevant landlords of those premises, the absence or incapacity of the person referred to in paragraph 1 or other special circumstances require that some person other than the person there referred to should act as the reversioner in respect of the premises, or
   (b) that the person referred to in that paragraph is unwilling to act as the reversioner,

the court may appoint to be the reversioner in respect of those premises (in place of the person designated by paragraph 1) such person as it thinks fit.

4. The court may also, on the application of any of the relevant landlords or of the nominee purchaser, remove the reversioner in respect of any premises and appoint another person in his place, if it appears to the court proper to do so by reason of any delay or default, actual or apprehended, on the part of the reversioner.

5. A person appointed by the court under any of paragraphs 2 to 4 –
   (a) must be a relevant landlord; but
   (b) may be so appointed on such terms and conditions as the court thinks fit.

PART II

CONDUCT OF PROCEEDINGS ON BEHALF OF OTHER LANDLORDS

Acts of reversioner binding on other landlords

6.—(1) Without prejudice to the generality of section 9(3) –

   (a) any notice given by or to the reversioner under this Chapter or section 74(3) following the giving of the initial notice shall be given or received by him on behalf of all the relevant landlords; and
   (b) the reversioner may on behalf and in the name of all or (as the case may be) any of those landlords –

(i) deduce, evidence or verify the title to any property;
(ii) negotiate and agree with the nominee purchaser the terms of acquisition;
(iii) execute any conveyance for the purpose of transferring any interest to the nominee purchaser;
(iv) receive the price payable for the acquisition of any interest;
(v) take or defend any legal proceedings under this Chapter in respect of matters arising out of the initial notice.

(2) Subject to paragraph 7 –
(a) the reversioner's acts in relation to matters within the authority conferred on him by section 9(3), and
(b) any determination of the court or a leasehold valuation tribunal under this Chapter in proceedings between the reversioner and the nominee purchaser,
shall be binding on the other relevant landlords and on their interests in the specified premises or any other property; but in the event of dispute the reversioner or any of the other relevant landlords may apply to the court for directions as to the manner in which the reversioner should act in the dispute.

(3) If any of the other relevant landlords cannot be found, or his identity cannot be ascertained, the reversioner shall apply to the court for directions and the court may make such order as it thinks proper with a view to giving effect to the rights of the participating tenants and protecting the interests of other persons, but subject to any such directions –
(a) the reversioner shall proceed as in other cases;
(b) any conveyance executed by the reversioner on behalf of that relevant landlord which identifies the interest to be conveyed shall have the same effect as if executed in his name; and
(c) any sum paid as the price for the acquisition of that relevant landlord's interest, and any other sum payable to him by virtue of Schedule 6, shall be paid into court.

(4) The reversioner, if he acts in good faith and with reasonable care and diligence, shall not be liable to any of the other relevant landlords for any loss or damage caused by any act or omission in the exercise or intended exercise of the authority conferred on him by section 9(3).

Other landlords acting independently

7.—(1) Notwithstanding anything in section 9(3) or paragraph 6, any of the other relevant landlords shall, at any time after the giving by the reversioner of a counter-notice under section 21 and on giving notice of his intention to do so to both the reversioner and the nominee purchaser, be entitled –
(a) to deal directly with the nominee purchaser in connection with any of the matters mentioned in sub-paragraphs (i) to (iii) of paragraph 6(1)(b) so far as relating to the acquisition of any interest of his;
(b) to be separately represented in any legal proceedings in which his title to any property comes in question, or in any legal proceedings relating to the terms of acquisition so far as relating to the acquisition of any interest of his.

(2) If the nominee purchaser so requires by notice given to the reversioner and any of the other relevant landlords, that landlord shall deal directly with the nominee purchaser for the purpose of deducing, evidencing or verifying the landlord's title to any property.

(3) Any of the other relevant landlords may by notice given to the reversioner require him to apply to a leasehold valuation tribunal for the determination by the tribunal of

any of the terms of acquisition so far as relating to the acquisition of any interest of the landlord.

(4) Any of the other relevant landlords may also, on giving notice to the reversioner and the nominee purchaser, require that the price payable for the acquisition of his interest shall be paid by the nominee purchaser to him, or to a person authorised by him to receive it, instead of to the reversioner; but if, after being given proper notice of the time and method of completion with the nominee purchaser, either –

(a) he fails to notify the reversioner of the arrangements made with the nominee purchaser to receive payment, or
(b) having notified the reversioner of those arrangements, the arrangements are not duly implemented,

the reversioner shall be authorised to receive the payment for him, and the reversioner's written receipt for the amount payable shall be a complete discharge to the nominee purchaser.

Obligations of other landlords to reversioner

8.—(1) It shall be the duty of each of the other relevant landlords –

(a) (subject to paragraph 7) to give the reversioner all such information and assistance as he may reasonably require; and
(b) after being given proper notice of the time and method of completion with the nominee purchaser, to ensure that all deeds and other documents that ought on his part to be delivered to the nominee purchaser on completion are available for the purpose, including in the case of registered land the land certificate and any other documents necessary to perfect the nominee purchaser's title;

and, if any of the other relevant landlords fails to comply with this sub-paragraph, that relevant landlord shall indemnify the reversioner against any liability incurred by the reversioner in consequence of the failure.

(2) Each of the other relevant landlords shall make such contribution as shall be just to the costs and expenses properly incurred by the reversioner in pursuance of section 9(3) which are not recoverable or not recovered form the nominee purchaser or any other person.

Applications made by other landlords under section 23(1)

9. The authority given to the reversioner by section 9(3) shall not extend to the bringing of proceedings under section 23(1) on behalf of any of the other relevant landlords, or preclude any of those landlords from bringing proceedings under that provision on his own behalf.

Sections 9 and 40

SCHEDULE 2

SPECIAL CATEGORIES OF LANDLORDS

Interpretation

1.—(1) In this Schedule –

'Chapter I landlord' means a person who is, in relation to a claim made under Chapter I, the reversioner or any other relevant landlord within the meaning of that Chapter;

'Chapter II landlord' means a person who is, in relation to a claim made under Chapter II, the landlord within the meaning of that Chapter or any of the other landlords (as defined by section 40(4));

'debenture holders' charge' means a charge (whether a floating charge or not) in favour of the holders of a series of debentures issued by a company or other body of persons, or in favour of trustees for such debenture holders;

'mortgage' includes a charge or lien, and related expressions shall be construed accordingly;

'the relevant notice' means –

(a) in relation to a Chapter I landlord, the notice given under section 13, and

(b) in relation to a Chapter II landlord, the notice given under section 42.

(2) In paragraphs 5 to 8 any reference to a premium payable on the grant of a lease includes a reference to any other amount payable by virtue of Schedule 13 in connection with its grant.

Mortgagee in possession of landlord's interest

2.—(1) Where –

(a) the interest of a Chapter I or Chapter II landlord is subject to a mortgage, and

(b) the mortgagee is in possession,

all such proceedings arising out of the relevant notice as would apart from this sub-paragraph be taken by or in relation to that landlord ('the mortgagor') shall, as regards his interest, be conducted by and through the mortgagee as if he were that landlord; but this sub-paragraph shall not, in its application to a Chapter I landlord, affect the operation in relation to the mortgagee of section 35 or Schedule 8.

(2) Where sub-paragraph (1) above applies to a Chapter I landlord, then (without prejudice to the generality of that sub-paragraph) any application under section 23(1) that would otherwise be made by the mortgagor (whether alone or together with any other person or persons) shall be made by the mortgagee as if he were the mortgagor.

(3) Where –

(a) the interest of a Chapter I landlord is subject to a mortgage, and

(b) a receiver appointed by the mortgagee or by order of any court is in receipt of the rents and profits,

the person referred to in paragraph (a) shall not make any application under section 23(1) without the consent of the mortgagee, and the mortgagee may by notice given to that person require that, as regards his interest, this paragraph shall apply, either generally or so far as it relates to section 23, as if the mortgagee were a mortgagee in possession.

(4) Where –

(a) the interest of a Chapter I or Chapter II landlord is subject to a mortgage, and

(b) the mortgagee is in possession or a receiver appointed by the mortgagee or by order of any court is in receipt of the rents and profits,

the relevant notice or a copy of it shall be regarded as duly given to that landlord if it is given to the mortgagee or to any such receiver; but whichever of the landlord, the mortgagee and any such receiver are not the recipient of the notice shall be given a copy of it by the recipient.

(5) Sub-paragraph (4) has effect in relation to a debenture holders' charge as if any reference to the mortgagee were a reference to the trustees for the debenture holders; but, where the relevant notice is given to a Chapter I or Chapter II landlord whose interest is subject to any such charge and there is no trustee for the debenture holders, the landlord shall forthwith send it or a copy of it to any receiver appointed by virtue of the charge.

(6) Where –

(a) a Chapter I or Chapter II landlord is given the relevant notice or a copy of it, and
(b) his interest is subject to a mortgage to secure the payment of money,

then (subject to sub-paragraph (7)), the landlord shall forthwith inform the mortgagee (unless the notice was given to him or a receiver appointed by virtue of the mortgage) that the notice has been given, and shall give him such further information as may from time to time be reasonably required from the landlord by the mortgagee.

(7) Sub-paragraph (6) does not apply to a debenture holders' charge.

Landlord's interest vested in custodian trustee

3. Where the interest of a Chapter I or Chapter II landlord is vested in a person as custodian trustee, then for the purposes of Chapter I or (as the case may be) Chapter II the interest shall be deemed to be vested in the managing trustees or committee of management as owners of that interest, except as regards the execution of any instrument disposing of or otherwise affecting that interest.

Landlord under a disability

4. Where a Chapter I or Chapter II landlord is incapable by reason of mental disorder (within the meaning of the Mental Health Act 1983) of managing and administering his property and affairs, then for the purposes of Chapter I or (as the case may be) Chapter II –

(a) the landlord's receiver appointed under Part VII of that Act or Part VIII of the Mental Health Act 1959, or
(b) (if no such receiver is acting for him) any person authorised in that behalf,

shall, under an order of the authority having jurisdiction under Part VII of the Mental Health Act 1983, take the place of the landlord.

Landlord's interest held on trust for sale

5.—(1) Where the interest of a Chapter I landlord is held on trust for sale, any sum payable to the landlord by way of the price payable for the interest on its acquisition in pursuance of Chapter I shall be dealt with as if it were proceeds of sale arising under the trust.

(2) Where the interest of a Chapter II landlord is held on trust for sale –

(a) any sum payable to the landlord by way of a premium on the grant of a new lease under Chapter II or section 933(4) shall be dealt with as if it were proceeds of sale arising under the trust; and
(b) the purposes authorised –
    (i) by section 73 of the Settled Land Act 1925, as applied by section 28 of the Law of Property Act 1925, for the application of capital money, and
    (ii) by section 71 of the Settled Land Act 1925, as applied as aforesaid, as purposes for which money may be raised by mortgage,

shall include the payment of compensation by the landlord on the termination of a new lease granted under Chapter II or section 93(4) (whether the payment is made in pursuance of an order under section 61 or in pursuance of an agreement made in conformity with paragraph 5 of Schedule 14 without an application having been made under that section).

Landlord's interest subject to a settlement

6. Where the interest of a Chapter II landlord is subject to a settlement (within the meaning of the Settled Land Act 1925), the purposes authorised –

(a) by section 73 of that Act for the application of capital money, and
(b) by section 71 of that Act as purposes for which money may be raised by mortgage,

shall include the payment of compensation as mentioned in paragraph 5(2)(b) above.

University or college landlords

7.—(1) Where a Chapter I landlord is a university or college to which the Universities and College Estates Act 1925 applies, any sum payable to the landlord by way of the price payable for any interest on its acquisition in pursuance of Chapter I shall be dealt with as if it were an amount payable by way of consideration on a sale effected under that Act.

(2) Where a Chapter II landlord is a university or college to which that Act applies –
(a) any sum payable to the landlord by way of a premium on the grant of a new lease under Chapter II or section 93(4) shall be dealt with as if it were an amount payable by way of consideration on a sale effected under that Act; and
(b) the purposes authorised –
(i) by section 26 of that Act for the application of capital money, and
(ii) by section 31 of that Act as purposes for which money may be raised by mortgage,

shall include the payment of compensation as mentioned in paragraph 5(2)(b) above.

Ecclesiastical landlords

8.—(1) The provisions of this paragraph shall have effect as regards Chapter I or Chapter II landlords who are ecclesiastical landlords; and in this paragraph 'ecclesiastical landlord' means –
(a) a capitular body within the meaning of the Cathedrals Measure 1963 having an interest as landlord in property, or
(b) a diocesan board of finance having an interest as landlord in property belonging to the board as diocesan glebe land.

(2) In relation to an interest of an ecclesiastical landlord, the consent of the Church Commissioners shall be required to sanction –
(a) the provisions to be contained in a conveyance in accordance with section 34 and Schedule 7, or in any lease granted under section 56, and the price or premium payable, except as regards matters determined by the court or a leasehold valuation tribunal;
(b) any exercise of the ecclesiastical landlord's rights under section 61, except as aforesaid, and any agreement for the payment of compensation to a tenant in conformity with paragraph 5 of Schedule 14 without an application having been made under that section; and
(c) any grant of a lease in pursuance of section 93(4);

and the Church Commissioners shall be entitled to appear and be heard in any proceedings under this Part to which an ecclesiastical landlord is a party or in which he is entitled to appear and be heard.

(3) Where a capitular body has an interest in property which forms part of the endowment of a cathedral church –
(a) any sum payable to that body by way of –
(i) the price payable for any interest in the property on its acquisition in pursuance of Chapter I, or

(ii) A premium on the grant of a new lease under Chapter II or section 93(4), shall be treated as part of that endowment; and

(b) the powers conferred by sections 21 and 23 of the Cathedrals Measure 1963 in relation to the investment in the acquisition of land of money forming part of the endowment of a cathedral church shall extend to the application of any such money in the payment of compensation as mentioned in paragraph 5(2)(b) above.

(4) In the case of a diocesan board of finance –

(a) no consent or concurrence other than that of the Church Commissioners under sub-paragraph (2) above shall be required to a disposition under this Part of the interest of the diocesan board of finance in property (including a grant of a new lease in pursuance of section 93(4));

(b) any sum payable to the diocesan board of finance by way of –

(i) the price payable for any interest in property on its acquisition in pursuance of Chapter I, or

(ii) a premium on the grant of a new lease of property under Chapter II or section 93(4),

shall be paid to the Church Commissioners to be applied for purposes for which the proceeds of any such disposition of property by agreement would be applicable under any enactment or Measure authorising such a disposition or disposing of the proceeds of such a disposition; and

(c) any sum required for the payment of compensation as mentioned in paragraph 5(2)(b) above may be paid by the Church Commissioners on behalf of the diocesan board of finance out of any money held by them.

(5) In this paragraph 'diocesan board of finance' and 'diocesan glebe land' have the same meaning as in the Endowments and Glebe Measure 1976.

Section 13

SCHEDULE 3

THE INITIAL NOTICE: SUPPLEMENTARY PROVISIONS

PART I

RESTRICTIONS ON PARTICIPATION BY INDIVIDUAL TENANTS, EFFECT OF CLAIMS ON OTHER NOTICES, FORFEITURES ETC

Prior notice by tenant terminating lease

1. A qualifying tenant of a flat shall not participate in the giving of a relevant notice of claim if the notice is given –

(a) after the tenant has given notice terminating the lease of the flat (other than a notice that has been superseded by the grant, express or implied, of a new tenancy); or

(b) during the subsistence of an agreement for the grant to the tenant of a future tenancy of the flat, where the agreement is one to which paragraph 17 of Schedule 10 to the Local Government and Housing Act 1989 applies.

Prior notice by landlord terminating lease

2.—(1) A qualifying tenant of a flat shall not participate in the giving of a relevant notice of claim if the notice is given more than four months after a landlord's notice terminating the tenant's lease of the flat has been given under section 4 of the Landlord and Tenant Act 1954 or served under paragraph 4(1) of Schedule 10 to the Local Government and Housing Act 1989 (whether or not the notice has effect to terminate the lease).

(2) Where in the case of any qualifying tenant of a flat –
(a) any such landlord's notice is given or served as mentioned in sub-paragraph (1), but
(b) that notice was not given or served more than four months before the date when a relevant notice of claim is given,
the landlord's notice shall cease to have effect on that date.

(3) If –
(a) any such landlord's notice ceases to have effect by virtue of sub-paragraph (2), but
(b) the claim made in pursuance of the relevant notice of claim is not effective,
then sub-paragraph (4) shall apply to any landlord's notice terminating the tenant's lease of the flat which –
(i) is given under section 4 of the Landlord and Tenant Act 1954 or served under paragraph 4(1) of Schedule 10 of the Local Government and Housing Act 1989, and
(ii) is so given or served within one month after the expiry of the period of currency of that claim.

(4) Where this sub-paragraph applies to a landlord's notice, the earliest date which may be specified in the notice as the date of termination shall be –
(a) in the case of a notice given under section 4 of that Act of 1954 –
(i) the date of termination specified in the previous notice, or
(ii) the date of expiry of the period of three months beginning with the date of the giving of the new notice,
whichever is the later; or
(b) in the case of a notice served under paragraph 4(1) of Schedule 10 to that Act of 1989 –
(i) the date of termination specified in the previous notice, or
(ii) the date of expiry of the period of four months beginning with the date of service of the new notice,
whichever is the later.

(5) Where –
(a) by virtue of sub-paragraph (4) a landlord's notice specifies as the date of termination of a lease a date earlier than six months after the date of the giving of the notice, and
(b) the notice proposes a statutory tenancy,
section 7(2) of the Landlord and Tenant Act 1954 shall apply in relation to the notice with the substitution, for references to the period of two months ending with the date of termination specified in the notice and the beginning of that period, of references to the period of three months beginning with the date of the giving of the notice and the end of that period.

Orders for possession and pending proceedings for forfeiture etc

3.—(1) A qualifying tenant of a flat shall not participate in the giving of a relevant notice of claim if at the time when it is given he is obliged to give up possession of his flat in pursuance of an order of a court or will be so obliged at a date specified in such an order.

(2) Except with the leave of the court, a qualifying tenant of a flat shall not participate in the giving of a relevant notice of claim at a time when any proceedings are pending to enforce a right of re-entry or forfeiture terminating his lease of the flat.

(3) Leave shall only be granted under sub-paragraph (2) if the court is satisfied that the tenant does not wish to participate in the giving of such a notice of claim solely or mainly for the purpose of avoiding the consequences of the breach of the terms of his lease in respect of which proceedings are pending.

(4) If –
- (a) leave is so granted, and
- (b) a relevant notice of claim is given,

the tenant's lease shall be deemed for the purposes of the claim to be a subsisting lease despite the existence of those proceedings and any order made afterwards in those proceedings; and, if the claim is effective, the court in which those proceedings were brought may set aside or vary any such order to such extent and on such terms as appear to that court to be appropriate.

Institution of compulsory purchase procedures

4.—(1) A qualifying tenant of a flat shall not participate in the giving of a relevant notice of claim if on the date when the notice is given –
- (a) any person or body of persons who has or have been, or could be, authorised to acquire the whole or part of the flat compulsorily for any purpose has or have, with a view to its acquisition for that purpose –
  - (i) served a notice to treat on that tenant, or
  - (ii) entered into a contract for the purchase of his interest in the whole or part of the flat; and
- (b) the notice to treat or contract remains in force.

(2) Where –
- (a) a relevant notice of claim is given, and
- (b) during the currency of the claim any such person or body of persons as is mentioned in sub-paragraph (1)(a) serves or serve, in relation to the flat held by a participating tenant, notice to treat as mentioned in that provision,

the tenant shall cease to be entitled to participate in the making of the claim by virtue of being a qualifying tenant of the flat, and shall accordingly cease to be a participating tenant in respect of the flat.

Notice terminating lease given by tenant or landlord during currency of claim

5. Where a relevant notice of claim is given, any notice terminating the lease of any flat held by a participating tenant, whether it is –
- (a) a notice given by the tenant, or
- (b) a landlord's notice given under section 4 of the Landlord and Tenant Act 1954 or served under paragraph 4(1) of Schedule 10 to the Local Government and Housing Act 1989,

shall be of no effect if it is given or served during the currency of the claim.

Initial notice operates to prevent termination of tenant's lease by other means

6.—(1) Where a relevant notice of claim is given, then during the currency of the claim and for three months thereafter the lease of any flat held by a participating tenant shall not terminate –
- (a) by effluxion of time, or

(b) in pursuance of a notice to quit given by the landlord, or
(c) by the termination of a superior lease;
but if the claim is not effective, and but for this sub-paragraph the lease would have so terminated before the end of those three months, the lease shall so terminate at the end of those three months.

(2) Sub-paragraph (1) shall not be taken to prevent an earlier termination of the lease in any manner not mentioned in that sub-paragraph, and shall not affect –
(a) the power under section 146(4) of the Law of Property Act 1925 (relief against forfeiture of leases) to grant a tenant relief against the termination of a superior lease, or
(b) any right of the tenant to relief under section 16(2) of the Landlord and Tenant Act 1954 (relief where landlord proceeding to enforce covenants) or under paragraph 9 of Schedule 5 to that Act (relief in proceedings brought by superior landlord).

(3) The reference in sub-paragraph (2) to section 16(2) of, and paragraph 9 of Schedule 5 to, the Landlord and Tenant Act 1954 includes a reference to those provisions as they apply in relation to Schedule 10 to the Local Government and Housing Act 1989.

Restriction on proceedings against participating tenant to enforce right of re-entry or forfeiture

7.—(1) Where a relevant notice of claim is given, then during the currency of the claim –
(a) no proceedings to enforce any right of re-entry or forfeiture terminating the lease of any flat held by a participating tenant shall be brought in any court without the leave of that court; and
(b) leave shall only be granted if the court is satisfied that the tenant is participating in the making of the claim solely or mainly for the purpose of avoiding the consequences of the breach of the terms of his lease in respect of which proceedings are proposed to be brought.

(2) If leave is granted under sub-paragraph (1), the tenant shall cease to be entitled to participate in the making of the claim by virtue of being a qualifying tenant of the flat referred to in that sub-paragraph, and shall accordingly cease to be a participating tenant in respect of the flat.

Restrictions for purposes of s 14(3) on tenant electing to become participating tenant during currency of claim

8.—(1) Where a relevant notice of claim is given, a qualifying tenant of a flat may not subsequently make an election under section 14(3)
(a) if he was prohibited from participating in the giving of the notice by virtue of paragraph 1, 2(1), 3(1) or 4(1) above; or
(b) at a time when he would be so prohibited from participating in the giving of a relevant notice of claim, if such a notice were to be given then.

(2) Where a relevant notice of claim is given, then except with the leave of the court, a qualifying tenant of a flat may not subsequently make an election under section 14(3) at a time when any proceedings are pending to enforce a right of re-entry or forfeiture terminating his lease of the flat.

(3) Leave shall only be granted under sub-paragraph (2) if the court is satisfied that the tenant does not wish to make such an election solely or mainly for the purpose of

avoiding the consequences of the breach of the terms of his lease in respect of which proceedings are pending.

(4) If –
(a) leave is so granted, and
(b) the tenant makes such an election,
the tenant's lease shall be deemed for the purposes of the claim to be a subsisting lease despite the existence of those proceedings and any order made afterwards in those proceedings; and, if the claim is effective, the court in which those proceedings were brought may set aside or vary any such order to such extent and on such terms as appear to that court to be appropriate.

(5) References in this paragraph and paragraph 9 below to making an election under section 14(3) are references to making such an election to participate in the making of the claim in respect of which the relevant notice of claim is given.

Effect of tenant's election on certain notices given by landlord

9.—(1) This paragraph applies to a qualifying tenant of a flat who, following the giving of a relevant notice of claim, makes an election under section 14(3).

(2) Where in the case of any such tenant –
(a) a landlord's notice terminating the tenant's lease of the flat has been given or served as mentioned in paragraph 2(1) above (whether or not the notice has effect to terminate the lease), but
(b) that notice was not given or served more than four months before the date when the tenant makes his election under section 14(3),
the landlord's notice shall cease to have effect on that date.

(3) If –
(a) any such landlord's notice ceases to have effect by virtue of sub-paragraph (2) above, but
(b) the claim made in pursuance of the relevant notice of claim is not effective,
then paragraph 2(4) above shall apply to any landlord's notice terminating the tenant's lease of the flat which –
(i) is given under section 4 of the Landlord and Tenant Act 1954 or served under paragraph 4(1) of Schedule 10 to the Local Government and Housing Act 1989, and
(ii) is so given or served within one month after the expiry of the period of currency of that claim;
and paragraph 2(5) above shall apply accordingly.

(4) Paragraph 8(5) above applies for the purposes of this paragraph.

Interpretation

10.—(1) For the purposes of this Part of this Schedule –
(a) 'relevant notice of claim', in relation to any flat, means a notice under section 13 in the case of which the specified premises contain that flat, and references to participating in the giving of such a notice are references to being one of the persons by whom the notice is given;
(b) references to a notice under section 13 include, in so far as the context permits, references to a notice purporting to be given under that section (whether by persons who are qualifying tenants or not);

(c) references to a claim being effective are references to a binding contract being entered into for the acquisition of the freehold and other interests falling to be acquired in pursuance of the claim or to the making of an order under section 24(4)(a) or (b) or 25(6)(a) or (b) which provides for the vesting of those interests; and

(d) references to the currency of a claim are –

(i) where the claim is made by a valid notice under section 13, references to the period during which the notice continues in force in accordance with subsection (11) of that section, or

(ii) where the claim is made by a notice which is not a valid notice under section 13, references to the period beginning with the giving of the notice and ending with the time when the notice is set aside by the court or is withdrawn or when it would (if valid) cease to have effect or be deemed to have been withdrawn.

(2) For the purposes of sub-paragraph (1)(d) the date when a notice is set aside, or would (if valid) cease to have effect, in consequence of an order of a court shall be taken to be the date when the order becomes final.

PART II

PROCEDURE FOR GIVING COPIES TO RELEVANT LANDLORDS

Application of Part II

11. This Part of this Schedule has effect where a notice under section 13 is given in a case to which section 9(2) applies.

Qualifying tenants to give copies of initial notice

12.—(1) The qualifying tenants by whom the initial notice is given shall, in addition to giving the initial notice to the reversioner in respect of the specified premises, give a copy of the notice to every other person known or believed by them to be a relevant landlord of those premises.

(2) The initial notice shall state whether copies are being given in accordance with sub-paragraph (1) to anyone other than the recipient and, if so, to whom.

Recipient of notice or copy to give further copies

13.—(1) Subject to sub-paragraph (2), a recipient of the initial notice or of a copy of it (including a person receiving a copy under this sub-paragraph) shall forthwith give a copy to any person who –

(a) is known or believed by him to be a relevant landlord, and

(b) is not stated in the recipient's copy of the notice, or known by him, to have received a copy.

(2) Sub-paragraph (1) does not apply where the recipient is neither the reversioner nor another relevant landlord.

(3) Where a person gives any copies of the initial notice in accordance with sub-paragraph (1), he shall –

(a) supplement the statement under paragraph 12(2) by adding any further persons to whom he is giving copies or who are known to him to have received one; and

(b) notify the qualifying tenants by whom the initial notice is given of the persons added by him to that statement.

Consequences of failure to comply with paragraph 12 or 13

14.—(1) Where –

(a) a relevant landlord of the specified premises does not receive a copy of the initial notice before the end of the period specified in it in pursuance of section 13(3)(g), but

(b) he was given a notice under section 11 by any of the qualifying tenants by whom the initial notice was given and, in response to the notice under that section, notified the tenant in question of his interest in the specified premises,

the initial notice shall cease to have effect at the end of that period.

(2) Where –

(a) sub-paragraph (1) does not apply, but

(b) any person fails without reasonable cause to comply with paragraph 12 or 13 above, or is guilty of any unreasonable delay in complying with either of those paragraphs,

he shall be liable for any loss thereby occasioned to the qualifying tenants by whom the initial notice was given or to the reversioner or any other relevant landlord.

PART III

OTHER PROVISIONS

Inaccuracies or misdescription in initial notice

15.—(1) The initial notice shall not invalidated by any inaccuracy in any of the particulars required by section 13(3) or by any misdescription of any of the property to which the claim extends.

(2) Where the initial notice –

(a) specifies any property or interest which was not liable to acquisition under or by virtue of section 1 or 2, or

(b) fails to specify any property or interest which is so liable to acquisition,

the notice may, with the leave of the court and on such terms as the court may think fit, be amended so as to exclude or include the property or interest in question.

(3) Where the initial notice is so amended as to exclude any property or interest, references to the property or interests specified in the notice under any provision of section 13(3) shall be construed accordingly; and, where it is so amended as to include any property or interest, the property or interest shall be treated as if it had been specified under the provision of that section under which it would have fallen to be specified if its acquisition had been proposed at the relevant date.

Effect on initial notice of tenant's lack of qualification to participate

16.—(1) It is hereby declared that, where at the relevant date any of the persons by whom the initial notice is given –

(a) is not a qualifying tenant of a flat contained in the specified premises, or

(b) is such a qualifying tenant but is prohibited from participating in the giving of the notice by virtue of Part I of this Schedule, or

(c) (if it is claimed in the notice that he satisfies the residence condition) does not satisfy that condition, the notice shall not be invalidated on that account, so long as the notice was in fact properly given by a sufficient number of qualifying tenants of flats contained in the premises as at the relevant date, and not less than one-half of the qualifying tenants by whom it was so given then satisfied the residence condition.

(2) For the purposes of sub-paragraph (1) a sufficient number is a number which –
- (a) is not less than two-thirds of the total number of qualifying tenants of flats contained in the specified premises as at the relevant date, and
- (b) is not less than one-half of the total number of flats so contained.

Section 21

SCHEDULE 4

INFORMATION TO BE FURNISHED BY REVERSIONER ABOUT EXERCISE OF RIGHTS UNDER CHAPTER II

Information to accompany counter-notice

1.—(1) This paragraph applies where before the date of the giving of a counter-notice under section 21 the reversioner or any other relevant landlord –
- (a) has received –
  - (i) a notice given under section 42 with respect to any flat contained in the specified premises (being a notice to which section 54(1) or (2) applies on that date), or
  - (ii) a copy of such a notice, or
- (b) has given any counter-notice under section 45 in response to any such notice.

(2) A copy of every notice which, or a copy of which, has been received as mentioned in sub-paragraph (1)(a), and a copy of every counter-notice which has been given as mentioned in sub-paragraph (1)(b), shall either –
- (a) accompany any counter-notice given under section 21, or
- (b) be given to the nominee purchaser by the reversioner as soon as possible after the date of the giving of any such counter-notice.

Continuing duty to furnish information

2.—(1) Subject to sub-paragraph (3), this paragraph applies where on or after the date of the giving of a counter-notice under section 21 the reversioner or any other relevant landlord receives –
- (a) a notice given under section 42 with respect to any flat continued in the specified premises or a copy of such a notice, or
- (b) any notice of withdrawal given under section 52 and relating to any notice under section 42 of which a copy has already been furnished to the nominee purchaser under this Schedule.

(2) A copy of every notice which, or a copy of which, is received as mentioned in sub-paragraph (1)(a) or (b) shall be given to the nominee purchaser by the reversioner as soon as possible after the time when the notice or copy is received by the reversioner of (as the case may be) the other relevant landlord.

(3) This paragraph does not apply if the notice or copy is received by the reversioner or (as the case may be) the other relevant landlord otherwise than at a time when –
- (a) the initial notice continues in force, or
- (b) a binding contract entered into in pursuance of that notice remains in force, or

(c) where an order has been made under section 24(4)(a) or (b) or 25(6)(a) or (b) with respect to the specified premises, any interests which by virtue of the order fall to be vested in the nominee purchaser have yet to be so vested.

Duty of other landlords to furnish copies to reversioner

3.—(1) Without prejudice to the generality of paragraph 8(1)(a) of Schedule 1, the duty imposed by that provision shall extend to requiring any relevant landlord (other than the reversioner) who –

(a) receives a relevant notice or a copy of such a notice, or
(b) gives a relevant counter-notice,

to furnish a copy of the notice or counter-notice to the reversioner as soon as possible after the time when the notice or copy is received or (as the case may be) the counter-notice is given by the relevant landlord.

(2) In this paragraph 'relevant notice' and 'relevant counter-notice' mean respectively any notice of which a copy is required to be given to the nominee purchaser by the reversioner in accordance with this Schedule and any counter-notice of which a copy is required to be so given.

Sections 24 and 25

SCHEDULE 5

VESTING ORDERS UNDER SECTIONS 24 AND 25

Interpretation

1.—(1) In this Schedule 'as vesting order' means an order made by the court under section 24(4)(a) or (b) or section 25(6)(a) or (b).

(2) In this Schedule 'the relevant terms of acquisition', in relation to any such order, means the terms of acquisition referred to in section 24(4)(a) or (b) or section 25(6)(a) or (b), as the case may be.

Execution of conveyance

2.—(1) Where any interests are to be vested in the nominee purchaser by virtue of a vesting order, then on his paying into court the appropriate sum in respect of each of those interests there shall be executed by such person as the court may designate a conveyance which –

(a) is in a form approved by a leasehold valuation tribunal, and
(b) contains such provisions as may be so approved for the purpose of giving effect to the relevant terms of acquisition.

(2) The conveyance shall be effective to vest in the nominee purchaser the interests expressed to be conveyed, subject to and in accordance with the terms of the conveyance.

The appropriate sum

3.—(1) In the case of any vesting order, the appropriate sum which in accordance with paragraph 2(1) is to be paid into court in respect of any interest is the aggregate of –

(a) such amount as is fixed by the relevant terms of acquisition as the price which is payable in accordance with Schedule 6 in respect of that interest; and
(b) any amounts or estimated amounts determined by a leasehold valuation tribunal as being, at the time of execution of the conveyance, due to the transferor from any tenants of his of premises comprised in the premises in which that interest

subsists (whether due under or in respect of their leases or under or in respect of agreements collateral thereto).

(2) In this paragraph 'the transferor', in relation to any interest, means the person from whom the interest is to be acquired by the nominee purchaser.

Effect of payment of appropriate sum into court

4. Where any interest is vested in the nominee purchaser in accordance with this Schedule, the payment into court of the appropriate sum in respect of that interest shall be taken to have satisfied any claims against the nominee purchaser or the participating tenants, or the personal representatives or assigns of any of them, in respect of the price payable under this Chapter for the acquisition of that interest.

Supplemental

5.—(1) In the provisions specified in sub-paragraph (2) references to a binding contract being entered into in pursuance of the initial notice shall be read as including references to the making of a vesting order.

(2) Those provisions are
(a) section 14(11);
(b) section 15(12) (except so far as it provides for the interpretation of references to the nominee purchaser);
(c) section 16(10);
(d) section 19(5)(b);
(e) section 28(1);
(f) section 30(4); and
(g) section 31(4).

(3) Where, at any time after a vesting order is made but before the interests falling to be vested in the nominee purchaser by virtue of the order have been so vested, any acquiring authority (within the meaning of section 30) serves notice to treat as mentioned in subsection (1)(a) of that section, the vesting order shall cease to have effect.

(4) Where sub-paragraph (3) applies to any vesting order, then on the occasion of the compulsory acquisition in question the compensation payable in respect of any interest in the specified premises (whether or not the one to which the notice to treat relates) shall be determined on the basis of the value of the interest subject to and with the benefit of the rights and obligations arising from the initial notice and affecting the interest.

(5) In section 38(2) (except so far as it provides for the interpretation of references to the proposed acquisition by the nominee purchaser) the reference to a contract entered into in pursuance of the initial notice shall be read as including a reference to a vesting order.

Section 32

SCHEDULE 6

PURCHASE PRICE PAYABLE BY NOMINEE PURCHASER

PART I

GENERAL

Interpretation and operation of Schedule

1.—(1) In this Schedule –
'the freeholder' means the person who owns the freehold of the specified premises;

'intermediate leasehold interest' means the interest of the tenant under a lease which is superior to the lease held by a qualifying tenant of a flat contained in the specified premises, to the extent that –
(a) any such interest is to be acquired by the nominee purchaser by virtue of section 2(1)(a), and
(b) it is an interest in the specified premises;

'the valuation date' means the date when the interest in the specified premises which is to be acquired by the nominee purchaser from the freeholder is determined either by agreement or by a leasehold valuation tribunal under this Chapter.

(2) Parts II to IV of this Schedule have effect subject to the provisions of Parts V and VI (which relate to interests with negative values).

PART II

FREEHOLD OF SPECIFIED PREMISES

Price payable for freehold of specified premises

2.—(1) Subject to the provisions of this paragraph, the price payable by the nominee purchaser for the freehold of the specified premises shall be the aggregate of –
(a) the value of the freeholder's interest in the premises as determined in accordance with paragraph 3,
(b) the freeholder's share of the marriage value as determined in accordance with paragraph 4, and
(c) any amount of compensation payable to the freeholder under paragraph 5.

(2) Where the amount arrived at in accordance with sub-paragraph (1) is a negative amount, the price payable by the nominee purchaser for the freehold shall be nil.

Value of freeholder's interest

3.—(1) Subject to the provisions of this paragraph, the value of the freeholder's interest in the specified premises is the amount which at the valuation date that interest might be expected to realise if sold on the open market by a willing seller (with neither the nominee purchaser nor any participating tenant buying or seeking to buy) on the following assumptions –
(a) on the assumption that the vendor is selling for an estate in fee simple –
  (i) subject to any leases subject to which the freeholder's interest in the premises is to be acquired by the nominee purchaser, but
  (ii) subject also to any intermediate or other leasehold interests in the premises which are to be acquired by the nominee purchaser;
(b) on the assumption that this Chapter and Chapter II confer no right to acquire any interest in the specified premises or to acquire any new lease (except that this shall not preclude the taking into account of a notice given under section 42 with respect to a flat contained in the specified premises where it is given by a person other than a participating tenant);
(c) on the assumption that any increase in the value of any flat held by a participating tenant which is attributable to an improvement carried out at his own expense by the tenant or by any predecessor in title is to be disregarded; and
(d) on the assumption that (subject to paragraphs (a) and (b)) the vendor is selling

with and subject to the rights and burdens with and subject to which the conveyance to the nominee purchaser of the freeholder's interest is to be made, and in particular with and subject to such permanent or extended rights and burdens as are to be created in order to give effect to Schedule 7.

(2) It is hereby declared that the fact that sub-paragraph (1) requires assumptions to be made as to the matters specified in paragraphs (a) to (d) of that sub-paragraph does not preclude the making of assumptions as to other matters where those assumptions are appropriate for determining the amount which at the valuation date the freeholder's interest in the specified premises might be expected to realise if sold as mentioned in that sub-paragraph.

(3) In determining that amount there shall be made such deduction (if any) in respect of any defect in title as on a sale of the interest on the open market might be expected to be allowed between a willing seller and a willing buyer.

(4) Where a lease of any flat or other unit contained in the specified premises is to be granted to the freeholder in accordance with section 36 and Schedule 9, the value of his interest in those premises at the valuation date so far as relating to the flat or other unit shall be taken to be the difference as at the date between –

(a) the value of his freehold interest in it, and
(b) the value of his interest in it under that lease, assuming it to have been granted to him at that date;

and each of those values shall, so far as is appropriate, be determined in like manner as the value of the freeholder's interest in the whole of the specified premises is determined for the purposes of paragraph 2(1)(a).

(5) The value of the freeholder's interest in the specified premises shall not be increased by reason of –

(a) any transaction which –
    (i) is entered into on or after the date of the passing of this Act (otherwise than in pursuance of a contract entered into before that date), and
    (ii) involves the creation or transfer of an interest superior to (whether or not preceding) any interest held by a qualifying tenant of a flat contained in the specified premises; or
(b) any alteration on or after that date of the terms on which any such superior interest is held.

(6) Sub-paragraph (5) shall not have the effect of preventing an increase in value of the freeholder's interest in the specified premises in a case where the increase is attributable to any such leasehold interest with a negative value as is mentioned in paragraph 14(2).

Freeholder's share of marriage value

4.—(1) The marriage value is the amount referred to in sub-paragraph (2), and the freeholder's share of the marriage value is –

(a) such proportion of that amount as is determined by agreement between the reversioner and the nominee purchaser or, in default of agreement, as is determined by a leasehold valuation tribunal to be the proportion which in its opinion would have been determined by an agreement made at the valuation date between the parties on a sale on the open market by a willing seller, or

(b) 50 per cent of that amount,
whichever is the greater.

(2) The marriage value is any increase in the aggregate value of the freehold and every intermediate leasehold interest in the specified premises, when regarded as being (in consequence of their being acquired by the nominee purchaser) interests under the control of the participating tenants, as compared with the aggregate value of those interests when held by the persons from whom they are to be so acquired, being an increase in value –

(a) which is attributable to the potential ability of the participating tenants, once those interests have been so acquired, to have new leases granted to them without payment of any premium and without restriction as to length of term, and
(b) which, if those interests were being sold to the nominee purchaser on the open market by willing sellers, the nominee purchaser would have to agree to share with the sellers in order to reach agreement as to price.

(3) For the purposes of sub-paragraph (2) the value of the freehold or any intermediate leasehold interest in the specified premises when held by the person from whom it is to be acquired by the nominee purchaser and its value when acquired by the nominee purchaser –

(a) shall be determined on the same basis as the value of the interest is determined for the purposes of paragraph 2(1)(a) or (as the case may be) paragraph 6(1)(b)(i); and
(b) shall be so determined as at the valuation date.

(4) Accordingly, in so determining the value of an interest when acquired by the nominee purchaser –

(a) the same assumptions shall be made under paragraph 3(1) (or, as the case may be, under paragraph 3(1) as applied by paragraph 7(1)) as are to be made under that provision in determining the value of the interest when held by the person from whom it is to be acquired by the nominee purchaser; and
(b) any merger or other circumstances affecting the interest on its acquisition by the nominee purchaser shall be disregarded.

Compensation for loss resulting from enfranchisement

5.—(1) Where the freeholder will suffer any loss or damage to which this paragraph applies, there shall be payable to him such amount as is reasonable to compensate him for that loss or damage.

(2) This paragraph applies to –

(a) any diminution in value of any interest of the freeholder in other property resulting from the acquisition of his interest in the specified premises; and
(b) any other loss of damage which results therefrom to the extent that it is referable to his ownership of any interest in other property.

(3) Without prejudice to the generality of paragraph (b) of sub-paragraph (2), the kinds of loss falling within that paragraph include loss of development value in relation to the specified premises to the extent that it is referable as mentioned in that paragraph.

(4) In sub-paragraph (3) 'development value', in relation to the specified premises, means any increase in the value of the freeholder's interest in the premises which is attributable to the possibility of demolishing, reconstructing, or carrying out substantial works of construction on, the whole or a substantial part of the premises.

(5) Where the freeholder will suffer loss or damage to which this paragraph applies, then in determining the amount of compensation payable to him under this paragraph, it shall not be material that –

(a) the loss or damage could to any extent be avoided or reduced by the grant to him, in accordance with section 36 and Schedule 9, of a lease granted in pursuance of Part III of that Schedule, and

(b) he is not requiring the nominee purchaser to grant any such lease.

PART III

INTERMEDIATE LEASEHOLD INTERESTS

Price payable for intermediate leasehold interests

6.—(1) Where the nominee purchaser is to acquire one or more intermediate leasehold interests –

(a) a separate price shall be payable for each of those interests, and

(b) (subject to the provisions of this paragraph) that price shall be the aggregate of –

(i) the value of the interest as determined in accordance with paragraph 7, and

(ii) any amount of compensation payable to the owner of that interest in accordance with paragraph 8.

(2) Where in the case of any intermediate leasehold interest the amount arrived at in accordance with sub-paragraph (1)(b) is a negative amount, the price payable by the nominee purchaser for the interest shall be nil.

Value of intermediate leasehold interests

7.—(1) Subject to sub-paragraph (2), paragraph 3 shall apply for determining the value of any intermediate leasehold interest for the purposes of paragraph 6(1)(b)(i) with such modifications as are appropriate to relate that paragraph to a sale of the interest in question subject (where applicable) to any leases intermediate between that interest and any lease held by a qualifying tenant of a flat contained in the specified premises.

(2) The value of an intermediate leasehold interest which is the interest of the tenant under a minor intermediate lease shall be calculated by applying the formula set out in sub-paragraph (7) instead of in accordance with sub-paragraph (1).

(3) 'A minor intermediate lease' means a lease complying with the following requirements, namely –

(a) it must have an expectation of possession of not more than one month, and

(b) the profit rent in respect of the lease must be not more than £5 per year;

and, in the case of a lease which is in immediate reversion on two or more leases, those requirements must be complied with in connection with each of the sub-leases.

(4) Where a minor intermediate lease is in immediate reversion on two or more leases –

(a) the formula set out in sub-paragraph (7) shall be applied in relation to each of those sub-leases (and sub-paragraphs (5) and (6) shall also so apply); and

(b) the value of the interest of the tenant under the minor intermediate lease shall accordingly be the aggregate of the amounts calculated by so applying the formula.

(5) 'Profit rent' means an amount equal to that of the rent payable under the lease on which the minor intermediate lease is in immediate reversion, less that of the rent payable under the minor intermediate lease.

(6) Where the minor intermediate lease or that on which it is in immediate reversion comprises property other than a flat held by a qualifying tenant, then in sub-paragraph (5) the reference to the rent payable under it means so much of that rent as is apportioned to any such flat.

(7) The formula is –

$$P = £\frac{R}{Y} - \frac{R}{Y(1 + Y)^n}$$

where –

P = the price payable;

R = the profit rent;

Y = the yield (expressed as a decimal fraction) from 2½ per cent Consolidated Stock;

n = the period, expressed in years (taking any part of a year as a whole year), of the remainder of the term of the minor intermediate lease as at the valuation date.

(8) In calculating the yield from 2½ per cent Consolidated Stock, the price of that stock shall be taken to be the middle market price at the close of business on the last trading day in the week before the valuation date.

(9) For the purposes of this paragraph the expectation of possession carried by a lease in relation to a lease ('the sub-lease') on which it is in immediate reversion is the expectation of possession which it carries at the valuation date after the sub-lease, on the basis that –

(a) (subject to sub-paragraph (10)) where the sub-lease is a lease held by a qualifying tenant of a flat contained in the specified premises, it terminates at the valuation date if its term date fell before then, or else it terminates on its term date; and

(b) in any other case, the sub-lease terminates on its term date.

(10) In a case where before the relevant date for the purposes of this Chapter the landlord of any such qualifying tenant as is mentioned in sub-paragraph (9)(a) had given notice to quit terminating the tenant's sub-lease on a date earlier than that date, the date specified in the notice to quit shall be substituted for the date specified in that provision.

Compensation for loss on acquisition of interest

8. Sub-paragraphs (1) to (4) of paragraph 5 shall apply in relation to the owner of any intermediate leasehold interest as they apply in relation to the freeholder.

Owners of intermediate interests entitled to part of marriage value

9.—(1) This paragraph applies where –

(a) the price payable for the freehold of the specified premises includes an amount in respect of the freeholder's share of the marriage value, and

(b) the nominee purchaser is to acquire any intermediate leasehold interests.

(2) The amount payable to the freeholder in respect of his share of the marriage value shall be divided between the freeholder and the owners of the intermediate leasehold

interests in proportion to the value of their respective interests in the specified premises (as determined for the purposes of paragraph 2(1)(a) or paragraph 6(1)(b)(i), as the case may be).

(3) Where the owner of an intermediate leasehold interest is entitled in accordance with sub-paragraph (2) to any part of the amount payable to the freeholder in respect of the freeholder's share of the marriage value, the amount to which he is so entitled shall be payable to him by the freeholder.

PART IV

OTHER INTERESTS TO BE ACQUIRED

Price payable for other interests

10.—(1) Where the nominee purchaser is to acquire any freehold interest in pursuance of section 1(2)(a) or (4) or section 21(4), then (subject to sub-paragraph (3) below) the price payable for that interest shall be the aggregate of –

(a) the value of the interest as determined in accordance with paragraph 11,
(b) any share of the marriage value to which the owner of the interest is entitled under paragraph 12, and
(c) any amount of compensation payable to the owner of the interest in accordance with paragraph 13.

(2) Where the nominee purchaser is to acquire any leasehold interest by virtue of section 2(1) other than an intermediate leasehold interest, or he is to acquire any leasehold interest in pursuance of section 21(4), then (subject to sub-paragraph (3) below) the price payable for that interest shall be the aggregate of –

(a) the value of the interest as determined in accordance with paragraph 11, and
(b) any amount of compensation payable to the owner of the interest in accordance with paragraph 13.

(3) Where in the case of any interest the amount arrived at in accordance with sub-paragraph (1) or (2) is a negative amount, the price payable by the nominee purchaser for the interest shall be nil.

Value of other interests

11.—(1) In the case of any such freehold interest as is mentioned in paragraph 10(1), paragraph 3 shall apply for determining the value of the interest with such modifications as are appropriate to relate it to a sale of the interest subject (where applicable) to any leases intermediate between that interest and any lease held by a qualifying tenant of a flat contained in the specified premises.

(2) In the case of any such leasehold interest as is mentioned in paragraph 10(2), then –

(a) (unless paragraph (b) below applies) paragraph 3 shall apply as mentioned in sub-paragraph (1) above;
(b) if it is the interest of the tenant under a minor intermediate lease within the meaning of paragraph 7, sub-paragraphs (2) to (10) of that paragraph shall apply with such modifications as are appropriate for determining the value of the interest.

(3) In its application in accordance with sub-paragraph (1) or (2) above, paragraph 3(6) shall have effect as if the reference to paragraph 14(2) were a reference to paragraph 18(2).

Marriage value

12.—(1) Where any such freehold interest as is mentioned in paragraph 10(1) is an interest in any such property as is mentioned in section 1(3)(a) –

(a) sub-paragraphs (2) to (4) of paragraph 4 shall apply with such modifications as are appropriate for determining the marriage value in connection with the acquisition by the nominee purchaser of that interest; and

(b) sub-paragraph (1) of that paragraph shall apply with such modifications as are appropriate for determining the share of the marriage value to which the owner of that interest is entitled.

(2) Where –

(a) the owner of any such freehold interest is entitled to any share of the marriage value in respect of any such property, and

(b) the nominee purchaser is to acquire any leasehold interests in that property superior to any lease held by a participating tenant,

the amount payable to the owner of the freehold interest in respect of his share of the marriage value in respect of that property shall be divided between the owner of that interest and the owners of the leasehold interests in proportion to the value of their respective interests in that property (as determined for the purposes of paragraph 10(1) or (2), as the case may be).

(3) Where the owner of any such leasehold interest ('the intermediate landlord') is entitled in accordance with sub-paragraph (2) to any part of the amount payable to the owner of any freehold interest in respect of his share of the marriage value in respect of any property, the amount to which the intermediate landlord is so entitled shall be payable to him by the owner of that freehold interest.

Compensation for loss on acquisition of interest

13. Sub-paragraphs (1) to (4) of paragraph 5 shall apply in relation to the owner of any such freehold or leasehold interest as is mentioned in paragraph 10(1) or (2) and to the acquisition of that interest as they apply in relation to the freeholder and to the acquisition of his interest in the specified premises (and accordingly any reference in those provisions of paragraph 5 to the specified premises shall be read for this purpose as a reference to the property in which any such freehold or leasehold interest subsists).

PART V

VALUATION ETC OF INTERESTS IN SPECIFIED PREMISES WITH NEGATIVE VALUES

Valuation of freehold and intermediate leasehold interests

14.—(1) Where –

(a) the value of the freeholder's interest in the specified premises (as determined in accordance with paragraph 3), or

(b) the value of any intermediate leasehold interest (as determined in accordance with paragraph 7),

is a negative amount, the value of the interest for the relevant purposes shall be nil.

(2) Where sub-paragraph (1) applies to any intermediate leasehold interest whose value is a negative amount ('the negative interest'), then for the relevant purposes any interests in the specified premises superior to the negative interest and having a positive value shall be reduced in value –

(a) beginning with the interest which is immediately superior to the negative interest and continuing (if necessary) with any such other superior interests in order of proximity to the negative interest;
(b) until the aggregate amount of the reduction is equal to the negative amount in question; and
(c) without reducing the value of any interest to less than nil.

(3) In a case where sub-paragraph (1) applies to two or more intermediate leasehold interests whose values are negative amounts, sub-paragraph (2) shall apply separately in relation to each of those interests –
(a) beginning with the interest which is inferior to every other of those interests and then in order of proximity to that interest; and
(b) with any reduction in the value of any interest for the relevant purposes by virtue of any prior application of sub-paragraph (2) being taken into account.

(4) For the purposes of sub-paragraph (2) an interest has a positive value if (apart from that sub-paragraph) its value for the relevant purposes is a positive amount.

(5) In this part of this Schedule 'the relevant purposes' –
(a) as respects the freeholder's interest in the specified premises, means the purposes of paragraph 2(1)(a); and
(b) as respects any intermediate leasehold interest, means the purposes of paragraph 6(1)(b)(i).

Calculation of marriage value

15.—(1) Where (as determined in accordance with paragraph 4(3) and (4)) the value of any interest –
(a) when held by the person from whom it is to be acquired by the nominee purchaser, or
(b) when acquired by the nominee purchaser,
is a negative amount, then for the purposes of paragraph 4(2) the value of the interest when so held or acquired shall be nil.

(2) Where sub-paragraph (1) above applies to any intermediate leasehold interest whose value when held or acquired as mentioned in paragraph (a) or (b) of that sub-paragraph is a negative amount, paragraph 14(2) to (4) shall apply for determining for the purposes of paragraph 4(2) the value when so held or acquired or other interests in the specified premises, as if –
(a) any reference to paragraph 14(1) were a reference to sub-paragraph (1) above; and
(b) any reference to the relevant purposes were, as respects any interest, a reference to the purposes of paragraph 4(2) as it applies to the interest when so held or acquired.

(3) References in paragraph 16 or 17 to paragraph 14(2) or (3) do not extend to that provision as it applies in accordance with sub-paragraph (2) above.

Apportionment of marriage value

16.—(1) Where paragraph 14(1) applies to an interest, the value of the interest for the purposes of paragraph 9(2) shall be nil, unless sub-paragraph (2) below applies.

(2) In a case where paragraph 14(1) applies to the freeholder's interest in the specified premises and to every intermediate leasehold interest –
(a) sub-paragraph (1) above shall not apply for the purposes of paragraph 9(2); and

(b) any division falling to be made on the proportional basis referred to in paragraph 9(2) shall be so made in such a way as to secure that the greater the negativity of an interest's value the smaller the share in respect of the interest.

(3) In a case where –

(a) paragraph 14(2) operates to reduce the value of any such superior interest as is there mentioned ('the superior interest'), and

(b) after the operation of that provision there remains any interest whose value for the relevant purposes is a positive amount,

the value of the superior interest for the purposes of paragraph 9(2) shall be the value which (in accordance with paragraph 14(2)) it has for the relevant purposes.

(4) In a case where –

(a) paragraph 14(2) operates to reduce the value of any such superior interest as is there mentioned ('the superior interest'), but

(b) after the operation of that provision there remains no such interest as is mentioned in sub-paragraph (3)(b) above,

the value of the superior interest for the purposes of paragraph 9(2) shall be the value which it has for the relevant purposes apart from paragraph 14(2).

Adjustment of compensation

17.—(1) Where –

(a) paragraph 14(2) operates to reduce the value of any such superior interest as is there mentioned ('the superior interest'), and

(b) apart from this paragraph any amount of compensation is payable under paragraph 8 to the owner of any relevant inferior interest in respect of that interest,

there shall be payable to the owner of the superior interest so much of the amount of compensation as is equal to the amount of the reduction or, if less than that amount, the whole of the amount of compensation.

(2) Where –

(a) paragraph 14(2) operates to reduce the value of two or more such superior interests as are there mentioned ('the superior interests'), and

(b) apart from this paragraph any amount of compensation is payable under paragraph 8 to the owner of any relevant inferior interest in respect of that interest,

sub-paragraph (1) shall apply in the first instance as if the reference to the owner of the superior interest were to the owner of such of the superior interests as is furthest from the negative interest, and then, as respects any remaining amount of compensation, as if that reference were to the owner of such of the superior interests as is next furthest from the negative interest, and so on.

(3) In sub-paragraph (1) or (2) 'relevant inferior interest', in relation to any interest whose value is reduced as mentioned in that sub-paragraph ('the superior interest'), means –

(a) the negative interest on account of which any such reduction is made, or

(b) any other interest intermediate between that negative interest and the superior interest;

but sub-paragraph (1) shall apply in the first instance in relation to any amount of compensation payable to the owner of that negative interest, and then, for the purpose of offsetting (so far as possible) any reduction remaining to be offset in accordance with sub-paragraph (1) or (2), in relation to any amount of compensation payable to the owner of the interest immediately superior to that negative interest, and so on in order of proximity to it.

(4) To the extent that an amount of compensation is payable to the owner of any interest by virtue of this paragraph –

(a) paragraph 2(1)(c) or 6(1)(b)(ii) shall have effect as if it were an amount of compensation payable to him, as owner of that interest, in accordance with paragraph 5 or 8, as the case may be; and

(b) the person who would otherwise have been entitled to it in accordance with paragraph 8 shall accordingly not be so entitled.

(5) In a case where paragraph 14(2) applies separately in relation to two or more negative interests in accordance with paragraph 14(3), the preceding provisions of this paragraph shall similarly apply separately in relation to the reductions made on account of each of those interests, and shall so apply –

(a) according to the order determined by paragraph 14(3)(a); and

(b) with there being taken into account any reduction in the amount of compensation payable to any person under paragraph 8 which results from the prior application of the preceding provisions of this paragraph.

PART VI

VALUATION ETC OF OTHER INTERESTS WITH NEGATIVE VALUES

Valuation of freehold and leasehold interests

18.—(1) Where –

(a) the value of any freehold interest (as determined in accordance with paragraph 11(1)), or

(b) the value of any leasehold interest (as determined in accordance with paragraph 11(2)),

is a negative amount, the value of the interest for the relevant purposes shall be nil.

(2) Where, in the case of any property, sub-paragraph (1) applies to any leasehold interest in the property whose value is a negative amount ('the negative interest'), then for the relevant purposes any interests in the property superior to the negative interest and having a positive value shall, if they are interests which are to be acquired by the nominee purchaser, be reduced in value –

(a) beginning with the interest which is nearest to the negative interest and continuing (if necessary) with any such other superior interests in order of proximity to the negative interest;

(b) until the aggregate amount of the reduction is equal to the negative amount in question; and

(c) without reducing the value of any interest to less than nil.

(3) In a case where sub-paragraph (1) applies to two or more leasehold interests in any property whose values are negative amounts, sub-paragraph (2) shall apply separately in relation to each of those interests –

(a) beginning with the interest which is inferior to every other of those interests and then in order of proximity to that interest; and

(b) with any reduction in the value of any interest for the relevant purposes by virtue of any prior application of sub-paragraph (2) being taken into account.

(4) For the purposes of sub-paragraph (2) an interest has a positive value if (apart from that sub-paragraph) its value for the relevant purposes is a positive amount.

(5) In this Part of this Schedule 'the relevant purposes' –
(a) as respects any freehold interest, means the purposes of paragraph 10(1)(a); and
(b) as respects any leasehold interest, means the purposes of paragraph 10(2)(a).

Calculation of marriage value

19.—(1) Where (as determined in accordance with paragraph 4(3) and (4)) the value of any interest –
(a) when held by the person from whom it is to be acquired by the nominee purchaser, or
(b) when acquired by the nominee purchaser,
is a negative amount, then for the purposes of paragraph 4(2) the value of the interest when so held or acquired shall be nil.

(2) Where, in the case of any property, sub-paragraph (1) above applies to any leasehold interest in the property whose value when held or acquired as mentioned in paragraph (a) or (b) of that sub-paragraph is a negative amount, paragraph 18(2) to (4) shall apply for determining for the purposes of paragraph 4(2) the value when so held or acquired of other interests in the property, as if –
(a) any reference to paragraph 18(1) were a reference to sub-paragraph (1) above; and
(b) any reference to the relevant purposes were, as respects any interest, a reference to the purposes of paragraph 4(2) as it applies to the interest when so held or acquired.

(3) In this paragraph any reference to any provision of paragraph 4 is a reference to that provision as it applies in accordance with paragraph 12(1).

(4) References in paragraph 20 or 21 to paragraph 18(2) or (3) do not extend to that provision as it applies in accordance with sub-paragraph (2) above.

Apportionment of marriage value

20.—(1) Where paragraph 18(1) applies to any interest in any property to which paragraph 12(1) applies, the value of the interest for the purposes of paragraph 12(2) shall be nil, unless sub-paragraph (2) below applies.

(2) Where, in the case of any property, paragraph 18(1) applies to every interest which is to be acquired by the nominee purchaser –
(a) sub-paragraph (1) above shall not apply for the purposes of paragraph 12(2); and
(b) any division falling to be made on the proportional basis referred to in paragraph 12(2) shall be so made in such a way as to secure that the greater the negativity of an interest's value the smaller the share in respect of the interest.

(3) Where in the case of any property –
(a) paragraph 18(2) operates to reduce the value of any such superior interest as is there mentioned ('the superior interest'), and
(b) after the operation of that provision there remains any interest which is to be acquired by the nominee purchaser and whose value for the relevant purposes is a positive amount,
the value of the superior interest for the purposes of paragraph 12(2) shall be the value which (in accordance with paragraph 18(2) it has for the relevant purposes.

(4) Where in the case of any property –
(a) paragraph 18(2) operates to reduce the value of any such superior interest as is there mentioned ('the superior interest'), but

(b) after the operation of that provision there remains no such interest as is mentioned in sub-paragraph (3)(b) above,

the value of the superior interest for the purposes of paragraph 12(2) shall be the value which it has for the relevant purposes apart from paragraph 18(2).

Adjustment of compensation

21.—(1) Where in the case of any property –

(a) paragraph 18(2) operates to reduce the value of any such superior interest as is there mentioned ('the superior interest'), and

(b) apart from this paragraph any amount of compensation is payable by virtue of paragraph 13 to the owner of any relevant inferior interest in respect of that interest,

there shall be payable to the owner of the superior interest so much of the amount of compensation as is equal to the amount of the reduction or, if less than that amount, the whole of the amount of compensation.

(2) Where in the case of any property –

(a) paragraph 18(2) operates to reduce the value of two or more such superior interests as are there mentioned ('the superior interests'), and

(b) apart from this paragraph any amount of compensation is payable by virtue of paragraph 13 to the owner of any relevant inferior interest in respect of that interest,

sub-paragraph (1) shall apply in the first instance as if the reference to the owner of the superior interest were to the owner of such of the superior interests as is furthest from the negative interest, and then, as respects any remaining amount of compensation, as if that reference were to the owner of such of the superior interests as is next furthest from the negative interest, and so on.

(3) In sub-paragraph (1) or (2) 'relevant inferior interest', in relation to any interest whose value is reduced as mentioned in that sub-paragraph ('the superior interest'), means –

(a) the negative interest on account of which any such reduction is made, or

(b) any other interest in the property in question which is to be acquired by the nominee purchaser and is intermediate between that negative interest and the superior interest;

but sub-paragraph (1) shall apply in the first instance in relation to any amount of compensation payable to the owner of that negative interest, and then, for the purpose of offsetting (so far as possible) any reduction remaining to be offset in accordance with sub-paragraph (1) or (2), in relation to any amount of compensation payable to the owner of such interest falling within paragraph (b) above as is nearest to that negative interest, and so on in order of proximity to it.

(4) To the extent that an amount of compensation is payable to the owner of any interest by virtue of this paragraph –

(a) paragraph 10(1)(c) or (as the case may be) paragraph 10(2)(b) shall have effect as if it were an amount of compensation payable to him, as owner of that interest, in accordance with paragraph 13; and

(b) the person who would otherwise have been entitled to it in accordance with paragraph 13 shall accordingly not be so entitled.

(5) In a case where paragraph 18(2) applies separately in relation to two or more negative interests in accordance with paragraph 18(3), the preceding provisions of this

paragraph shall similarly apply separately in relation to the reductions made on account of each of those interests, and shall so apply –

(a) according to the order determined by paragraph 18(3)(a); and

(b) with there being taken into account any reduction in the amount of compensation payable to any person by virtue of paragraph 13 which results from the prior application of the preceding provisions of this paragraph.

Section 34

SCHEDULE 7

CONVEYANCE TO NOMINEE PURCHASER ON ENFRANCHISEMENT

Interpretation

1. In this Schedule –

(a) 'the relevant premises' means, in relation to such a conveyance as is mentioned in section 34(1), the premises of which the freehold is to be conveyed by means of the conveyance;

(b) 'the freeholder', in relation to any such conveyance, means the person whose freehold interest in the relevant premises is to be conveyed by means of the conveyance;

(c) 'other property' means property of which the freehold is not to be acquired by the nominee purchaser under this Chapter; and

(d) 'the appropriate time' means the time when the freehold of the relevant premises is to be conveyed to the nominee purchaser.

General

2.—(1) The conveyance shall not exclude or restrict the general words implied in conveyances under section 62 of the Law of Property Act 1925, or the all-estate clause implied under section 63 of the Act, unless –

(a) the exclusion or restriction is made for the purpose of preserving or recognising any existing interest of the freeholder in tenant's incumbrances or any existing right or interest of any other person, or

(b) the nominee purchaser consents to the exclusion or restriction.

(2) The freeholder shall not be bound –

(a) to convey to the nominee purchaser any better title than that which he has or could require to be vested in him, or

(b) to enter into any covenant for title other than such covenant as under section 76(1)(F) of the Law of Property Act 1925 is implied in the case of a person conveying, and expressed to convey, as trustee or mortgagee.

(3) In this paragraph 'tenant's incumbrances' includes any interest directly or indirectly derived out of a lease, and any incumbrance on a lease or any such interest (whether or not the same matter is an incumbrance also on any interest reversionary on the lease); and 'incumbrances' has the same meaning as it has for the purposes of section 34 of this Act.

Rights of support, passage of water etc

3.—(1) This paragraph applies to rights of any of the following descriptions, namely –

(a) rights of support for a building or part of a building;

(b) rights to the access of light and air to a building or part of a building;
(c) rights to the passage of water or of gas or other piped fuel, or to the drainage or disposal of water, sewage, smoke or fumes, or to the use or maintenance of pipes or other installations for such passage, drainage or disposal;
(d) rights to the use or maintenance of cables or other installations for the supply of electricity, for the telephone or for the receipt directly or by landline of visual or other wireless transmissions;

and the provisions required to be included in the conveyance by virtue of sub-paragraph (2) are accordingly provisions relating to any such rights.

(2) The conveyance shall include provisions having the effect of –
(a) granting with the relevant premises (so far as the freeholder is capable of granting them) –
(i) all such easements and rights over other property as are necessary to secure as nearly as may be for the benefit of the relevant premises the same rights as exist for the benefit of those premises immediately before the appropriate time, and
(ii) such further easements and rights (if any) as are necessary for the reasonable enjoyment of the relevant premises; and
(b) making the relevant premises subject to the following easements and rights (so far as they are capable of existing in law), namely –
(i) all easements and rights for the benefit of other property to which the relevant premises are subject immediately before the appropriate time, and
(ii) such further easements and rights (if any) as are necessary for the reasonable enjoyment of other property, being property in which the freeholder has an interest at the relevant date.

Rights of way

4. Any such conveyance shall include –
(a) such provisions (if any) as the nominee purchaser may require for the purpose of securing to him and the persons deriving title under him rights of way over other property, so far as the freeholder is capable of granting them, being rights of way that are necessary for the reasonable enjoyment of the relevant premises; and
(b) such provisions (if any) as the freeholder may require for the purpose of making the relevant premises subject to rights of way necessary for the reasonable enjoyment of other property, being property in which he is to retain an interest after the acquisition of the relevant premises.

Restrictive covenants

5.—(1) As regards restrictive covenants, the conveyance shall include –
(a) such provisions (if any) as the freeholder may require to secure that the nominee purchaser is bound by, or to indemnify the freeholder against breaches of, restrictive covenants which –
(i) affect the relevant premises otherwise than by virtue of any lease subject to which the relevant premises are to be acquired or any agreement collateral to any such lease, and
(ii) are immediately before the appropriate time enforceable for the benefit of other property; and
(b) such provisions (if any) as the freeholder or the nominee purchaser may require to secure the continuance (with suitable adaptations) of restrictions arising by virtue of any such lease or collateral agreement as is mentioned in paragraph (a)(i), being either –

(i) restrictions affecting the relevant premises which are capable of benefiting other property and (if enforceable only by the freeholder) are such as materially to enhance the value of the other property, or
(ii) restrictions affecting other property which are such as materially to enhance the value of the relevant premises; and
(c) such further restrictions as the freeholder may require to restrict the use of the relevant premises in a way which –
(i) will not interfere with the reasonable enjoyment of those premises as they have been enjoyed during the currency of the leases subject to which they are to be acquired, but
(ii) will materially enhance the value of other property in which the freeholder has an interest at the relevant date.

(2) In this paragraph 'restrictive covenant' means a covenant or agreement restrictive of the user of any land or building.

Section 35

SCHEDULE 8

DISCHARGE OF MORTGAGES ETC: SUPPLEMENTARY PROVISIONS

Construction

1. In this Schedule –
'the consideration payable' means the consideration payable for the acquisition of the relevant interest;
'the landlord' means the person from whom the relevant interest is being acquired;
'the relevant interest' means any such interest as is mentioned in paragraph 2(1).

Duty of nominee purchaser to redeem mortgages

2.—(1) Where in accordance with section 35(1) a conveyance will operate to discharge any interest from a mortgage to secure the payment of money, it shall be the duty of the nominee purchaser to apply the consideration payable, in the first instance, in or towards the redemption of any such mortgage (and, if there are more than one, then according to their priorities).

(2) If any amount payable in accordance with sub-paragraph (1) to the person entitled to the benefit of a mortgage is not so paid, nor paid into court in accordance with paragraph 4, the relevant interest shall remain subject to the mortgage as regards the amount in question, and to the extent section 35(1) shall not apply.

(3) subject to sub-paragraph (4), sub-paragraph (1) shall not apply to a debenture holders' charge, that is to say, a charge (whether a floating charge or not) in favour of the holders of a series of debentures issued by a company or other body of persons, or in favour of trustees for such debenture holders; and any such charge shall be disregarded in determining priorities for the purposes of sub-paragraph (1).

(4) Sub-paragraph (3) shall not have effect in relation to a charge in favour of trustees for debenture holders which, at the date of the conveyance by virtue of which the relevant interest is acquired by the nominee purchaser, is (as regards that interest) a specific and not a floating charge.

Determination of amounts due in respect of mortgages

3.—(1) For the purpose of determining the amount payable in respect of any mortgage under paragraph 2(1) –

(a) a person entitled to the benefit of a mortgage to which that provision applies shall not be permitted to exercise any right to consolidate that mortgage with a separate mortgage on other property; and

(b) if the landlord or any participating tenant is himself entitled to the benefit of a mortgage to which that provision applies, it shall rank for payment as it would if another person were entitled to it, and the nominee purchaser shall be entitled to retain the appropriate amount in respect of any such mortgage of a participating tenant.

(2) For the purpose of discharging any interest from a mortgage to which paragraph 2(1) applies, a person may be required to accept three months or any longer notice of the intention to pay the whole or part of the principal secured by the mortgage, together with interest to the date of payment, notwithstanding that the terms of the security make other provision or no provision as to the time and manner of payment; but he shall be entitled, if he so requires, to receive such additional payment as is reasonable in the circumstances –

(a) in respect of the costs of re-investment or other incidental costs and expenses; and

(b) in respect of any reduction in the rate of interest obtainable on re-investment.

Payments into court

4.—(1) Where under section 35(1) any interest is to be discharged from a mortgage and, in accordance with paragraph 2(1), a person is or may be entitled in respect of the mortgage to receive the whole or part of the consideration payable, then if –

(a) for any reason difficulty arises in ascertaining how much is payable in respect of the mortgage, or

(b) for any reason mentioned in sub-paragraph (2) below difficulty arises in making a payment in respect of the mortgage,

the nominee purchaser may pay into court on account of the consideration payable the amount, if known, of the payment to be made in respect of the mortgage or, if that amount is not known, the whole of that consideration or such lesser amount as the nominee purchaser thinks right in order to provide for that payment.

(2) Payment may be made into court in accordance with sub-paragraph (1)(b) where the difficulty arises for any of the following reasons, namely –

(a) because a person who is or may be entitled to receive payment cannot be found or his identity cannot be ascertained;

(b) because any such person refuses or fails to make out a title, or to accept payment and give a proper discharge, or to take any steps reasonably required of him to enable the sum payable to be ascertained and paid; or

(c) because a tender of the sum payable cannot, by reason of complications in the title to it or the want of two or more trustees or for other reasons, be effected, or not without incurring or involving unreasonable cost or delay.

(3) Without prejudice to sub-paragraph (1)(a), the whole or part of the consideration payable shall be paid into court by the nominee purchaser if, before execution of the conveyance referred to in paragraph 2(1), notice is given to him –

(a) that the landlord, or a person entitled to the benefit of a mortgage on the relevant interest, requires him to do so for the purpose of protecting the rights of persons so entitled, or for reasons related to the bankruptcy or winding up of the landlord, or

(b) that steps have been taken to enforce any mortgage on the relevant interest by the bringing of proceedings in any court, or by the appointment of a receiver, or otherwise;

and where payment into court is to be made by reason only of a notice under this sub-paragraph, and the notice is given with reference to proceedings in a court specified in the notice other than a county court, payment shall be made into the court so specified.

Savings

5.—(1) Where any interest is discharged by section 35(1) from a mortgage (without the obligations secured by the mortgage being satisfied by the receipt of the whole or part of the consideration payable), the discharge of that interest from the mortgage shall not prejudice any right or remedy for the enforcement of those obligations against other property comprised in the same or any other security, nor prejudice any personal liability as principal or otherwise of the landlord or any other person.

(2) Nothing in this Schedule or section 35 shall be construed as preventing a person from joining in the conveyance referred to in paragraph 2(1) for the purpose of discharging the relevant interest from any mortgage without payment or for a lesser payment than that to which he would otherwise be entitled; and, if he does so, the persons to whom the consideration payable ought to be paid shall be determined accordingly.

Section 36

SCHEDULE 9

GRANT OF LEASES BACK TO FORMER FREEHOLDER

PART I

GENERAL

1.—(1) In this Schedule –

'the appropriate time' means the time when the freehold of the specified premises is acquired by the nominee purchaser;

'the demised premises', in relation to a lease granted or to be granted in pursuance of Part II or III of this Schedule, means –

(a) the flat or other unit demised or to be demised under the lease, or

(b) in the case of such a lease under which two or more units are demised, both or all of those units or (if the context so permits) any of them;

'the freeholder' means the person who owns the freehold of the specified premises immediately before the appropriate time;

'housing association' has the meaning given by section 1(1) of the Housing Associations Act 1985;

'intermediate landlord', in relation to a flat or other unit let to a tenant, means a person who holds a leasehold interest in the flat or other unit which is superior to that held by the tenant's immediate landlord;

'other property' means property other than the demised premises.

(2) In this Schedule any reference to a flat or other unit, in the context of the grant of a lease of it, includes any yard, garden, garage, outhouses and appurtenances belonging to or usually enjoyed with it and let with it immediately before the appropriate time.

PART II

MANDATORY LEASEBACK

Flats etc let under secure tenancies

2.—(1) This paragraph applies where immediately before the appropriate time any flat contained in the specified premises is let under a secure tenancy and either –

(a) the freeholder is the tenant's immediate landlord, or
(b) the freeholder is a public sector landlord and every intermediate landlord of the flat (as well as the immediate landlord under the secure tenancy) is also a public sector landlord.

(2) Sub-paragraph (1)(b) has effect whether any such intermediate landlord, or the immediate landlord under the secure tenancy, is or is not a qualifying tenant of the flat.

(3) Where this paragraph applies, the nominee purchaser shall grant to the freeholder a lease of the flat in accordance with section 36 and paragraph 4 below.

(4) In this paragraph any reference to a flat includes a reference to a unit (other than a flat) which is used as a dwelling.

Flats etc let by housing associations under tenancies other than secure tenancies

3.—(1) This paragraph applies where immediately before the appropriate time any flat contained in the specified premises is let by a housing association under a tenancy other than a secure tenancy and –
(a) the housing association is the freeholder, and
(b) the tenant is not a qualifying tenant of the flat.

(2) Where this paragraph applies, the nominee purchaser shall grant to the freeholder (that is to say, the housing association) a lease of the flat in accordance with section 36 and paragraph 4 below.

(3) In this paragraph any reference to a flat includes a reference to a unit (other than a flat) which is used as a dwelling.

Provisions as to terms of lease

4.—(1) Any lease granted to the freeholder in pursuance of paragraph 2 or 3, and any agreement collateral to it, shall conform with the provisions of part IV of this Schedule except to the extent that any departure from those provisions is agreed to by the nominee purchaser and the freeholder with the approval of a leasehold valuation tribunal.

(2) A leasehold valuation tribunal shall not approve any such departure from those provisions unless it appears to the tribunal that it is reasonable in the circumstances.

(3) In determining whether any such departure is reasonable in the circumstances, the tribunal shall have particular regard to the interests of the tenant under the secure tenancy referred to in paragraph 2(1) or (as the case may be) under the housing association tenancy referred to in paragraph 3(1).

(4) Subject to the preceding provisions of this paragraph, any such lease or agreement as is mentioned in sub-paragraph (1) may include such terms as are reasonable in the circumstances.

PART III

RIGHT OF FREEHOLDER TO REQUIRE LEASEBACK OF CERTAIN UNITS

Flats without qualifying tenants and other units

5.—(1) Subject to sub-paragraph (3), this paragraph applies to any unit contained in the specified premises which is not immediately before the appropriate time a flat let to a person who is a qualifying tenant of it.

(2) Where this paragraph applies, the nominee purchaser shall, if the freeholder by notice requires him to do so, grant to the freeholder a lease of the unit in accordance with section 36 and paragraph 7 below.

(3) This paragraph does not apply to a flat or other unit to which paragraph 2 or 3 applies.

Flat etc occupied by resident landlord

6.—(1) This paragraph applies where immediately before the appropriate time –
(a) the specified premises are premises with a resident landlord; and
(b) the freeholder is the person by virtue of whose occupation of a flat or other unit contained in those premises they are premises with a resident landlord; and
(c) the freeholder is a qualifying tenant of that flat or other unit ('the relevant unit').

(2) Where this paragraph applies –
(a) the nominee purchaser shall, if the freeholder by notice requires him to do so, grant to him a lease of the relevant unit in accordance with section 36 and paragraph 7 below; and
(b) any lease of that unit held by the freeholder immediately before the appropriate time shall be deemed to have been surrendered by him on the grant of the lease referred to in paragraph (a).

(3) Sections 5, 7 and 8 shall apply for the purpose of determining whether, for the purposes of sub-paragraph (1)(c) above, the freeholder is a qualifying tenant of a unit other than a flat as they apply for the purpose of determining whether a person is a qualifying tenant of a flat.

Provisions as to terms of lease

7.—(1) Any lease granted to the freeholder in pursuance of paragraph 5 or 6, and any agreement collateral to it, shall conform with the provisions of Part IV of this Schedule except to the extent that any departure from those provisions –
(a) is agreed to by the nominee purchaser and the freeholder; or
(b) is directed by a leasehold valuation tribunal on an application made by either of those persons.

(2) A leasehold valuation tribunal shall not direct any such departure from those provisions unless it appears to the tribunal that it is reasonable in the circumstances.

(3) In determining whether any such departure is reasonable in the circumstances, the tribunal shall have particular regard to the interests of any person who will be the tenant of the flat or other unit in question under a lease inferior to the lease to be granted to the freeholder.

(4) Subject to the preceding provisions of this paragraph, any such lease or agreement as is mentioned in sub-paragraph (1) may include such terms as are reasonable in the circumstances.

PART IV

TERMS OF LEASE GRANTED TO FREEHOLDER

Duration of lease and rent

8. The lease shall be a lease granted for a term of 999 years at a peppercorn rent.

General rights to be granted

9. The lease shall not exclude or restrict the general words implied under section 62 of the Law of Property Act 1925, unless the exclusion or restriction is made for the purpose of preserving or recognising an existing right or interest of any person.

Rights of support, passage of water etc

10.—(1) This paragraph applies to rights of any of the following descriptions, namely –
- (a) rights of support for a building or part of a building;
- (b) rights to the access of light and air to a building or part of a building;
- (c) rights to the passage of water or of gas or other piped fuel, or to the drainage or disposal of water, sewage, smoke or fumes, or to the use or maintenance of pipes or other installations for such passage, drainage or disposal; and
- (d) rights to the use or maintenance of cables or other installations for the supply of electricity, for the telephone or for the receipt directly or by landline of visual or other wireless transmissions;

and the provisions required to be included in the lease by virtue of sub-paragraph (2) are accordingly provisions relating to any such rights.

(2) The lease shall include provisions having the effect of –
- (a) granting with the demised premises (so far as the lessor is capable of granting them) –
  - (i) all such easements and rights over other property as are necessary to secure as nearly as may be for the benefit of the demised premises the same rights as exist for the benefit of those premises immediately before the appropriate time, and
  - (ii) such further easements and rights (if any) as are necessary for the reasonable enjoyment of the demised premises; and
- (b) making the demised premises subject to the following easements and rights (so far as they are capable of existing in law), namely –
  - (i) all easements and rights for the benefit of other property to which the demised premises are subject immediately before the appropriate time, and
  - (ii) such further easements and rights (if any) as are necessary for the reasonable enjoyment of other property, being property in which the lessor acquires an interest at the appropriate time.

Rights of way

11. The lease shall include –
- (a) such provisions (if any) as the lessee may require for the purpose of securing to him, and persons deriving title under him, rights of way over other property (so far as the lessor is capable of granting them), being rights of way that are necessary for the reasonable enjoyment of the demised premises; and
- (b) such provisions (if any) as the lessor may require for the purpose of making the demised premises subject to rights of way necessary for the reasonable enjoyment

of other property, being property in which the lessor acquires an interest at the appropriate time.

Common use of premises and facilities

12. The lease shall include, so far as the lessor is capable of granting them, the like rights to use in common with others any premises, facilities or services as are enjoyed immediately before the appropriate time by any tenant of the demised premises.

Covenants affecting demised premises

13. The lease shall include such provisions (if any) as the lessor may require to secure that the lessee is bound by, or to indemnify the lessor against breaches of, restrictive covenants (that is to say, covenants or agreements restrictive of the use of any land or premises) affecting the demised premises immediately before the appropriate time and enforceable for the benefit of other property.

Covenants by lessor

14.—(1) The lease shall include covenants by the lessor –
- (a) to keep in repair the structure and exterior of the demised premises and of the specified premises (including drains, gutters and external pipes) and to make good any defect affecting that structure;
- (b) to keep in repair any other property over or in respect of which the lessee has rights by virtue of this Schedule;
- (c) to ensure, so far as practicable, that the services which are to be provided by the lessor and to which the lessee is entitled (whether alone or in common with others) are maintained at a reasonable level, and to keep in repair any installation connected with the provision of any of those services.

(2) The lease shall include a covenant requiring the lessor –
- (a) to insure the specified premises for their full reinstatement value against destruction or damage by fire, tempest, flood or any other cause against the risk of which it is the normal practice to insure;
- (b) to rebuild or reinstate the demised premises or the specified premises in the case of any such destruction or damage.

Covenants by lessee

15. The lease shall include a covenant by the lessee to ensure that the interior of the demised premises is kept in good repair (including decorative repair).

Contributions by lessee

16.—(1) The lease may require the lessee to bear a reasonable part of the costs incurred by the lessor in discharging or insuring against the obligations imposed by the covenants required by paragraph 14(1) or in discharging the obligation imposed by the covenant required by paragraph 14(2)(a).

(2) Where a covenant required by paragraph 14(1) or (2)(a) has been modified to any extent in accordance with paragraph 4 or 7, the reference in sub-paragraph (1) above to the obligations or (as the case may be) the obligation imposed by that covenant shall be read as a reference to the obligations or obligation imposed by that covenant as so modified.

Assignment and sub-letting of premises

17.—(1) Except where the demised premises consist of or include any unit let or intended for letting on a business lease, the lease shall not include any provision prohibiting or restricting the assignment of the lease or the sub-letting of the whole or part of the demised premises.

(2) Where the demised premises consist of or include any such unit as is mentioned in sub-paragraph (1), the lease shall contain a prohibition against –
- (a) assigning or sub-letting the whole or part of any such unit, or
- (b) altering the user of any such unit,

without the prior written consent of the lessor (such consent not to be unreasonably withheld).

Restriction on terminating lease

18. The lease shall not include any provision for the lease to be terminated otherwise than by forfeiture on breach of any term of the lease by the lessee.

Section 37

SCHEDULE 10

ACQUISITION OF INTERESTS FROM LOCAL AUTHORITIES ETC

Disapplication of provisions relating to disposals by local authorities etc

1.—(1) It is hereby declared that nothing in any of the provisions specified in sub-paragraph (2) (which impose requirements as to consent or consultation or other restrictions in relation to disposals falling within those provisions) applies to any disposal of a freehold or leasehold interest in any premises which is made in pursuance of this Chapter.

(2) The provisions referred to in sub-paragraph (1) are –
- (a) sections 32 and 43 of the Housing Act 1985 (disposals of land by local authorities) and section 133 of the Housing Act 1988 (certain subsequent disposals);
- (b) section 9(1) and (1A) of the Housing Associations Act 1985 (disposals by registered and unregistered housing associations);
- (c) section 79(1) and (2) of the Housing Act 1988 (disposals by housing action trusts) and section 81 of that Act (certain subsequent disposals); and
- (d) section 105(1) of that Act (disposals subsequent to change of landlord of secure tenants).

Provisions relating to secure tenants following leaseback

2.—(1) This paragraph applies where a lease is granted to a public sector landlord in pursuance of paragraph 2 of Schedule 9.

(2) Where –
- (a) immediately before the appropriate time the public sector landlord was the immediate landlord under a secure tenancy of a flat contained in the demised premises, and
- (b) that tenancy continues in force after the grant of the lease referred to in sub-paragraph (1),

the tenant shall be deemed to have continued without interruption as tenant of the landlord under the secure tenancy, despite the disposal of the landlord's interest which immediately preceded the grant of the lease referred to in that sub-paragraph.

(3) Where –
(a) immediately before the appropriate time a person was a successor in relation to a secure tenancy of a flat contained in the demised premises, and
(b) that person is, in connection with the grant of the lease referred to in sub-paragraph (1) granted a new secure tenancy of that flat which is a tenancy for a term certain,

then for the purposes of sections 87 to 90 of the Housing Act 1985 (succession on death of tenant) that person shall also be a successor in relation to the new tenancy.

(4) Where –
(a) immediately before the appropriate time a person was the tenant under a secure tenancy of a flat contained in the demised premises, and
(b) that person is, in connection with the grant of the lease referred to in sub-paragraph (1), granted a new secure tenancy of that flat,

then, for the purpose of determining whether either of the conditions referred to in sub-paragraph (5) is satisfied, the new tenancy shall not be regarded as a new letting of the flat but shall instead be regarded as a continuation of the secure tenancy referred to in paragraph (a) above.

(5) Those conditions are –
(a) the condition specified in sub-paragraph (1)(b) of paragraph 5 of Schedule 5 to the Housing Act 1985 (exception to the right to buy in case of letting in connection with employment); and
(b) the condition specified in sub-paragraph (1)(b) of paragraph 11 of that Schedule (exception to the right to buy in case of letting for occupation by person of pensionable age etc).

(6) In this paragraph –
(a) any reference to a secure tenancy of a flat is a reference to a secure tenancy of a flat whether with or without any yard, garden, garage, outhouses or appurtenances belonging to or usually enjoyed with it; and
(b) any reference to a flat includes a reference to a unit (other than a flat) which is used as a dwelling.

(7) In this paragraph –
(a) 'the appropriate time' and 'the demised premises' have the same meaning as in Schedule 9; and
(b) 'successor' has the same meaning as in section 88 of the Housing Act 1985.

Section 40

SCHEDULE 11

PROCEDURE WHERE COMPETENT LANDLORD IS NOT TENANT'S IMMEDIATE LANDLORD

PART I

PROCEDURE IN RELATION TO TENANT'S NOTICE

Tenant's notice may be given to any of the other landlords

1. The tenant's notice under section 42 shall be regarded as given to the competent landlord for the purposes of subsection (2)(a) of that section if it is given to any of the

other landlords instead; and references in this Chapter to the relevant date shall be construed accordingly.

Tenant to give copies of notice

2.—(1) Where the tenant's notice is given to the competent landlord, the tenant shall give a copy of the notice to every person known or believed by him to be one of the other landlords.

(2) Where the tenant's notice is, in accordance with paragraph 1, given to one of the other landlords, the tenant shall give a copy of the notice to every person (apart from the recipient of the notice) known or believed by the tenant to be either the competent landlord or one of the other landlords.

(3) The tenant's notice shall state whether copies are being given in accordance with this paragraph to anyone other than the recipient and, if so, to whom.

Recipient of notice or copy to give further copies

3.—(1) Subject to sub-paragraph (2), a recipient of the tenant's notice or of a copy of it (including a person receiving a copy under this sub-paragraph) –
- (a) shall forthwith give a copy to any person who –
  - (i) is known or believed by him to be the competent landlord or one of the other landlords, and
  - (ii) is not stated in the recipient's copy of the notice, or known by him, to have received a copy; and
- (b) if he knows who is, or he believes himself to be, the competent landlord, shall –
  - (i) give a notice to the tenant stating who is the person thought by him to be the competent landlord, and
  - (ii) give a copy of it to that person (if not himself) and to every person known or believed by him to be one of the other landlords.

(2) Sub-paragraph (1) does not apply where the recipient is neither the competent landlord nor one of the other landlords.

(3) Where a person gives any copies of the tenant's notice in accordance with sub-paragraph (1)(a), he shall –
- (a) supplement the statement under paragraph 2(3) by adding any further persons to whom he is giving copies or who are known by him to have received one; and
- (b) notify the tenant of the persons added by him to that statement.

Consequences of failure to comply with paragraph 2 or 3

4.—(1) Where –
- (a) the competent landlord or any of the other landlords does not receive a copy of the tenant's notice before the end of the period specified in it in pursuance of section 42(3)(i), but
- (b) he was given a notice under section 41 by the tenant and, in response to the notice under that section, notified the tenant of his interest in the tenant's flat,

the tenant's notice shall cease to have effect at the end of that period.

(2) Where –
- (a) sub-paragraph (1) does not apply, but

(b) any person fails without reasonable cause to comply with paragraph 2 or 3 above, or is guilty of any unreasonable delay in complying with either of those paragraphs,

he shall be liable for any loss thereby occasioned to the tenant or to the competent landlord or any of the other landlords.

PART II

CONDUCT OF PROCEEDINGS BY COMPETENT LANDLORD ON BEHALF OF OTHER LANDLORDS

Counter-notice to specify other landlords

5. Any counter-notice given to the tenant by the competent landlord must specify the other landlords on whose behalf he is acting.

Acts of competent landlord binding on other landlords

6.—(1) Without prejudice to the generality of section 40(2) –

(a) any notice given under this Chapter by the competent landlord to the tenant,

(b) any agreement for the purposes of this Chapter between that landlord and the tenant, and

(c) any determination of the court or a leasehold valuation tribunal under this Chapter in proceedings between that landlord and the tenant,

shall be binding on the other landlords and on their interests in the property demised by the tenant's lease or any other property; but in the event of dispute the competent landlord or any of the other landlords may apply to the court for directions as to the manner in which the competent landlord should act in the dispute.

(2) Subject to paragraph 7(2), the authority given to the competent landlord by section 40(2) shall extend to receiving on behalf of any other landlord any amount payable to that person by virtue of Schedule 13.

(3) If any of the other landlords cannot be found, or his identity cannot be ascertained, the competent landlord shall apply to the court for directions and the court may make such order as it thinks proper with a view to giving effect to the rights of the tenant and protecting the interests of other persons; but, subject to any such directions, the competent landlord shall proceed as in other cases.

(4) The competent landlord, if he acts in good faith and with reasonable care and diligence, shall not be liable to any of the other landlords for any loss or damage caused by any act or omission in the exercise or intended exercise of the authority given to him by section 40(2).

Other landlords acting independently

7.—(1) Notwithstanding anything in section 40(2), any of the other landlords shall, at any time after the giving by the competent landlord of a counter-notice under section 45 and on giving notice to both the competent landlord and the tenant of his intention to be so represented, be entitled to be separately represented –

(a) in any legal proceedings in which his title to any property comes in question, or

(b) in any legal proceedings relating to the determination of any amount payable to him by virtue of Schedule 13.

(2) Any of the other landlords may also, on giving notice to the competent landlord and

the tenant, require that any amount payable to him by virtue of Schedule 13 shall be paid by the tenant to him, or to a person authorised by him to receive it, instead of to the competent landlord; but if, after being given proper notice of the time and method of completion with the tenant, either –

(a) he fails to notify the competent landlord of the arrangements made with the tenant to receive payment, or

(b) having notified the competent landlord of those arrangements, the arrangements are not duly implemented,

the competent landlord shall be authorised to receive the payment for him, and the competent landlord's written receipt for the amount payable shall be a complete discharge to the tenant.

Obligations of other landlords to competent landlord

8.—(1) It shall be the duty of each of the other landlords (subject to paragraph 7) to give the competent landlord all such information and assistance as he may reasonably require; and, if any of the other landlords fails to comply with this sub-paragraph, that landlord shall indemnify the competent landlord against any liability incurred by him in consequence of the failure.

(2) Each of the other landlords shall make such contribution as shall be just to costs and expenses which are properly incurred by the competent landlord in pursuance of section 40(2) but are not recoverable or not recovered from the tenant.

Applications made by other landlords under section 47(1)

9.—(1) The authority given to the competent landlord by section 40(2) shall not extend to the bringing of proceedings under section 47(1) on behalf of any of the other landlords, or preclude any of those landlords from bringing proceedings under that provision on his own behalf as if he were the competent landlord.

(2) In section 45(2)(c) any reference to the competent landlord shall include a reference –

(a) to any of the other landlords, or

(b) to any two or more of the following, namely the competent landlord and the other landlords, acting together;

and in section 47(1) and (2) references to the landlord shall be construed accordingly; but if any of the other landlords intend to make such an application as is mentioned in section 45(2)(c), whether alone or together with any other person or persons, his name shall be stated in the counter-notice.

Deemed surrender and re-grant of leases of other landlords

10.—(1) Where a lease is executed under section 56 or 93(4) or in pursuance of any order made under this Chapter, then (subject to sub-paragraph (3)) that instrument shall have effect for the creation of the tenant's new lease of his flat, and for the operation of the rights and obligations conferred and imposed by it, as if there had been a surrender and re-grant of any subsisting lease intermediate between the interest of the competent landlord and the existing lease; and the covenants and other provisions of that instrument shall be framed and take effect accordingly.

(2) Section 57(2) shall apply to the new lease on the basis that account is to be taken of obligations imposed on any of the other landlords by virtue of that or any superior lease; and section 59(3) shall apply on the basis that the reference there to the tenant's landlord

includes the immediate landlord from whom the new lease will be held and all superior landlords, including any superior to the competent landlord.

(3) Where a lease of the tenant's flat superior to the existing lease is vested in the tenant or a trustee from him, the new lease shall include an actual surrender of that superior lease without a re-grant, and it shall accordingly be disregarded for the purposes of the preceding provisions of this paragraph.

Discharge of existing mortgages

11. Where by reason of section 58(2) it is necessary to make any payment to discharge the tenant's flat from a mortgage affecting the interest of any landlord, then if the competent landlord is not the landlord liable or primarily liable in respect of the mortgage, he shall not be required to make that payment otherwise than out of money made available for the purpose by the landlord so liable, and it shall be the duty of that landlord to provide for the mortgage being discharged.

Section 42

SCHEDULE 12

THE TENANT'S NOTICE: SUPPLEMENTARY PROVISIONS

PART I

EFFECT OF TENANT'S NOTICE ON OTHER NOTICES, FORFEITURES ETC

Prior notice by tenant terminating lease

1. A notice given by a qualifying tenant of a flat under section 42 shall be of no effect if it is given –
   (a) after the tenant has given notice terminating the lease of the flat (other than a notice that has been superseded by the grant, express or implied, of a new tenancy); or
   (b) during the subsistence of an agreement for the grant to the tenant of a future tenancy of the flat, where the agreement is one to which paragraph 17 of Schedule 10 to the Local Government and Housing Act 1989 applies.

Prior notice by landlord terminating lease

2.—(1) Subject to sub-paragraph (2), a notice given by a qualifying tenant of a flat under section 42 shall be of no effect if it is given more than two months after a landlord's notice terminating the tenant's lease of the flat has been given under section 4 of the Landlord and Tenant Act 1954 or served under paragraph 4(1) of Schedule 10 to the Local Government and Housing Act 1989 (whether or not the notice has effect to terminate the lease).

(2) Sub-paragraph (1) does not apply where the landlord gives his written consent to a notice being given under section 42 after the end of those two months.

(3) Where in the case of a qualifying tenant of a flat who gives notice under section 42 –
   (a) any such landlord's notice is given or served as mentioned in sub-paragraph (1), but
   (b) that notice was not given or served more than two months before the date on which the notice under section 42 is given to the landlord,

the landlord's notice shall cease to have effect on that date.

(4) If –

(a) any such landlord's notice ceases to have effect by virtue of sub-paragraph (3), but

(b) the claim made by the tenant by the giving of his notice under section 42 is not effective,

then sub-paragraph (5) shall apply to any landlord's notice terminating the tenant's lease of the flat which –

(i) is given under section 4 of the Landlord and Tenant Act 1954 or served under paragraph 4(1) of Schedule 10 to the Local Government and Housing Act 1989, and

(ii) is so given or served within one month after the expiry of the period of currency of that claim.

(5) Where this sub-paragraph applies to a landlord's notice, the earliest date which may be specified in the notice as the date of termination shall be –

(a) in the case of a notice given under section 4 of that Act of 1954 –

(i) the date of termination specified in the previous notice, or

(ii) the date of expiry of the period of three months beginning with the date of the giving of the new notice,

whichever is the later; or

(b) in the case of a notice served under paragraph 4(1) of Schedule 10 to that Act of 1989 –

(i) the date of termination specified in the previous notice, or

(ii) the date of expiry of the period of four months beginning with the date of service of the new notice,

whichever is the later.

(6) Where –

(a) by virtue of sub-paragraph (5) a landlord's notice specifies as the date of termination of a lease a date earlier than six months after the date of the giving of the notice, and

(b) the notice proposes a statutory tenancy,

section 7(2) of the Landlord and Tenant Act 1954 shall apply in relation to the notice with the substitution, for references to the period of two months ending with the date of termination specified in the notice and the beginning of that period, of references to the period of three months beginning with the date of the giving of the notice and the end of that period.

Orders for possession and pending proceedings for forfeiture etc

3.—(1) A notice given by a qualifying tenant of a flat under section 42 shall be of no effect if at the time when it is given he is obliged to give up possession of his flat in pursuance of an order of a court or will be so obliged at a date specified in such an order.

(2) Except with the leave of the court, a qualifying tenant of a flat shall not give a notice under section 42 at a time when any proceedings are pending to enforce a right of re-entry or forfeiture terminating his lease of the flat.

(3) Leave shall only be granted under sub-paragraph (2) if the court is satisfied that the tenant does not wish to give such a notice solely or mainly for the purpose of avoiding the consequences of the breach of the terms of his lease in respect of which proceedings are pending.

(4) If –

(a) leave is so granted, and

(b) the tenant by such a notice makes a claim to acquire a new lease of his flat,

the tenant's lease shall be deemed for the purposes of the claim to be a subsisting lease despite the existence of those proceedings and any order made afterwards in those proceedings; and, if the claim is effective, the court in which those proceedings were brought may set aside or vary any such order to such extent and on such terms as appear to that court to be appropriate.

Notice terminating lease given by tenant or landlord during currency of claim

4. Where by a notice given under section 42 a tenant makes a claim to acquire a new lease of a flat, any notice terminating the tenant's lease of the flat, whether it is –

(a) a notice given by the tenant, or

(b) a landlord's notice given under section 4 of the Landlord and Tenant Act 1954 or served under paragraph 4(1) of Schedule 10 to the Local Government and Housing Act 1989,

shall be of no effect if it is given or served during the currency of the claim.

Tenant's notice operates to prevent termination of lease

5.—(1) Where by a notice under section 42 a tenant makes a claim to acquire a new lease of a flat, then during the currency of the claim and for three months thereafter the lease of the flat shall not terminate –

(a) by effluxion of time, or

(b) in pursuance of a notice to quit given by the immediate landlord of the tenant, or

(c) by the termination of a superior lease;

but if the claim is not effective, and but for this sub-paragraph the lease would have so terminated before the end of those three months, the lease shall so terminate at the end of those three months.

(2) Sub-paragraph (1) shall not be taken to prevent an earlier termination of the lease in any manner not mentioned in that sub-paragraph, and shall not affect –

(a) the power under section 146(4) of the Law of Property Act 1925 (relief against forfeiture of leases) to grant a tenant relief against the termination of a superior lease, or

(b) any right of the tenant to relief under section 16(2) of the Landlord and Tenant Act 1954 (relief where landlord proceeding to enforce covenants) or under paragraph 9 of Schedule 5 to that Act (relief in proceedings brought by superior landlord).

Restriction on proceedings to enforce right of re-entry or forfeiture

6. Where by a notice under section 42 a tenant makes a claim to acquire a new lease of a flat, then during the currency of the claim –

(a) no proceedings to enforce any right of re-entry or forfeiture terminating the lease of the flat shall be brought in any court without the leave of that court, and

(b) leave shall only be granted if the court is satisfied that the notice was given solely or mainly for the purpose of avoiding the consequences of the breach of the terms of the tenant's lease in respect of which proceedings are proposed to be brought;

but where leave is granted, the notice shall cease to have effect.

Effect of notice under section 16(2) of Landlord and Tenant Act 1954 on tenant's notice

7.—(1) A tenant who, in proceedings to enforce a right of re-entry or forfeiture or a right to damages in respect of a failure to comply with any terms of his lease, applies for relief under section 16 of the Landlord and Tenant Act 1954 is not thereby precluded from making a claim to acquire a new lease under this Chapter; but if he gives notice under section 16(2) of that Act (under which the tenant is relieved from any order for recovery of possession or for payment of damages, but the tenancy is cut short), any notice given by him under section 42 with respect to property comprised in his lease shall be of no effect or, if already given, shall cease to have effect.

(2) Sub-paragraph (1) shall apply in relation to proceedings relating to a superior tenancy with the substitution for the references to section 16 and to section 16(2) of the Landlord and Tenant Act 1954 of references to paragraph 9 and to paragraph 9(2) of Schedule 5 to that Act.

Interpretation

8.—(1) For the purposes of this Part of this Schedule –
- (a) references to a notice under section 42 include, in so far as the context permits, references to a notice purporting to be given under that section (whether by a qualifying tenant or not), and references to the tenant by whom a notice is given shall be construed accordingly;
- (b) references to a claim being effective are references to a new lease being acquired in pursuance of the claim; and
- (c) references to the currency of a claim are –
  - (i) where the claim is made by a valid notice under section 42, references to the period during which the notice continues in force in accordance with subsection (8) of that section, or
  - (ii) where the claim is made by a notice which is not a valid notice under section 42, references to the period beginning with the giving of the notice and ending with the time when the notice is set aside by the court or is withdrawn or when it would (if valid) cease to have effect or be deemed to have been withdrawn.

(2) For the purposes of sub-paragraph (1)(c) the date when a notice is set aside, or would (if valid) cease to have effect, in consequence of an order of a court shall be taken to be the date when the order becomes final.

(3) The references in this Schedule –
- (a) to section 16 of the Landlord and Tenant Act 1954 and subsection (2) of that section, and
- (b) to paragraph 9 of Schedule 5 to that Act and sub-paragraph (2) of that paragraph,

include references to those provisions as they apply in relation to Schedule 10 to the Local Government and Housing Act 1989 (security of tenure on ending of long residential tenancies).

PART II

OTHER PROVISIONS

9.—(1) The tenant's notice shall not be invalidated by any inaccuracy in any of the particulars required by section 42(3) or by any misdescription of any of the property to which the claim extends.

(2) Where the tenant's notice –

(a) specifies any property which he is not entitled to have demised to him under a new lease granted in pursuance of this Chapter, or

(b) fails to specify any property which he is entitled to have so demised to him,

the notice may, with the leave of the court and on such terms as the court may think fit, be amended so as to exclude or include the property in question.

Section 56

SCHEDULE 13

PREMIUM AND OTHER AMOUNTS PAYABLE BY TENANT ON GRANT OF NEW LEASE

PART I

GENERAL

1. In this Schedule –

'intermediate at leasehold interest' means the interest of any person falling within section 40(4)(c), to the extent that it is an interest in the tenant's flat subsisting immediately before the grant of the new lease;

'the valuation date' means the date when all of the terms of acquisition (apart from those relating to the premium and any other amounts payable by virtue of this Schedule in connection with the grant of the new lease) have been determined either by agreement or by a leasehold valuation tribunal under this Chapter.

PART II

PREMIUM PAYABLE IN RESPECT OF GRANT OF NEW LEASE

Premium payable by tenant

2. The premium payable by the tenant in respect of the grant of the new lease shall be the aggregate of –

(a) the diminution in value of the landlord's interest in the tenant's flat as determined in accordance with paragraph 3,

(b) the landlord's share of the marriage value as determined in accordance with paragraph 4, and

(c) any amount of compensation payable to the landlord under paragraph 5.

Diminution in value of landlord's interest

3.—(1) The diminution in value of the landlord's interest is the difference between –

(a) the value of the landlord's interest in the tenant's flat prior to the grant of the new lease; and

(b) the value of his interest in the flat once the new lease is granted.

(2) Subject to the provisions of this paragraph, the value of any such interest of the landlord as is mentioned in sub-paragraph (1)(a) or (b) is the amount which at the valuation date that interest might be expected to realise if sold on the open market by a willing seller (with the tenant not buying or seeking to buy) on the following assumptions –

(a) on the assumption that the vendor is selling for an estate in fee simple or (as the case may be) such other interest as is held by the landlord, subject to the relevant lease and any intermediate leasehold interests;

(b) on the assumption that Chapter I and this Chapter confer no right to acquire any interest in any premises containing the tenant's flat or to acquire any new lease;
(c) on the assumption that any increase in the value of the flat which is attributable to an improvement carried out at his own expense by the tenant or by any predecessor in title is to be disregarded; and
(d) on the assumption that (subject to paragraph (b)) the vendor is selling with and subject to the rights and burdens with and subject to which the relevant lease has effect or (as the case may be) is to be granted.

(3) In sub-paragraph (2) 'the relevant lease' means either the tenant's existing lease or the new lease, depending on whether the valuation is for the purposes of paragraph (a) or paragraph (b) of sub-paragraph (1).

(4) It is hereby declared that the fact that sub-paragraph (2) requires assumptions to be made as to the matters specified in paragraphs (a) to (d) of that sub-paragraph does not preclude the making of assumptions as to other matters where those assumptions are appropriate for determining the amount which at the valuation date any such interest of the landlord as is mentioned in sub-paragraph (1)(a) or (b) might be expected to realise if sold as mentioned in sub-paragraph (2).

(5) In determining any such amount there shall be made such deduction (if any) in respect of any effect in title as on a sale of that interest on the open market might be expected to be allowed between a willing seller and a willing buyer.

(6) The value of any such interest of the landlord as is mentioned in sub-paragraph (1)(a) or (b) shall not be increased by reason of –
(a) any transaction which –
(i) is entered into on or after the date of the passing of this Act (otherwise than in pursuance of a contract entered into before that date), and
(ii) involves the creation or transfer of an interest superior to (whether or not preceding) any interest held by the tenant; or
(b) any alteration on or after that date of the terms on which any such superior interest is held.

Landlord's share of marriage value

4.—(1) The marriage value is the amount referred to in sub-paragraph (2), and the landlord's share of the marriage value is –
(a) such proportion of that amount as is determined by agreement between the landlord and the tenant or, in default of agreement, as is determined by a leasehold valuation tribunal to be the proportion which in its opinion would have been determined by an agreement made at the valuation date between the parties on a sale on the open market by a willing seller, or
(b) 50 per cent of that amount,

whichever is the greater.

(2) The marriage value is the difference between the following amounts, namely –
(a) the aggregate of –
(i) the value of the interest of the tenant under his existing lease,
(ii) the value of the landlord's interest in the tenant's flat prior to the grant of the new lease, and
(iii) the values prior to the grant of that lease of all intermediate leasehold interests (if any); and
(b) the aggregate of –
(i) the value of the interest to be held by the tenant under the new lease,

(ii) the value of the landlord's interest in the tenant's flat once the new lease is granted, and
(iii) the values of all intermediate leasehold interests (if any) once that lease is granted.

(3) For the purposes of sub-paragraph (2) –
(a) the value of any interest of the tenant shall be determined as at the valuation date;
(b) the value of any such interest of the landlord as is mentioned in paragraph (a) or paragraph (b) of that sub-paragraph is the amount determined for the purposes of paragraph 3(1)(a) or paragraph 3(1)(b) (as the case may be); and
(c) the value of any intermediate leasehold interest shall be determined in accordance with paragraph 8, and shall be so determined as at the valuation date.

Compensation for loss arising out of grant of new lease

5.—(1) Where the landlord will suffer any loss or damage to which this paragraph applies, there shall be payable to him such amount as is reasonable to compensate him for that loss or damage.

(2) This paragraph applies to –
(a) any diminution in value of any interest of the landlord in any property other than the tenant's flat which results from the grant to the tenant of the new lease; and
(b) any other loss or damage which results therefrom to the extent that it is referable to the landlord's ownership of any such interest.

(3) Without prejudice to the generality of paragraph (b) of sub-paragraph (2), the kinds of loss falling within that paragraph include loss of development value in relation to the tenant's flat to the extent that it is referable as mentioned in that paragraph.

(4) In sub-paragraph (3) 'development value', in relation to the tenant's flat, means any increase in the value of the landlord's interest in the flat which is attributable to the possibility of demolishing, reconstructing, or carrying out substantial works of construction affecting, the flat (whether together with any other premises or otherwise).

PART III

AMOUNTS PAYABLE TO OWNERS OF INTERMEDIATE LEASEHOLD INTERESTS

Amount payable to owner of intermediate interest

6. In connection with the grant of the new lease to the tenant there shall be payable by the tenant to the owner of any intermediate leasehold interest an amount which is the aggregate of –
(a) the diminution in value of that interest as determined in accordance with paragraph 7; and
(b) any amount of compensation payable to him under paragraph 9.

Diminution in value of intermediate interest

7.—(1) The diminution in value of any intermediate leasehold interest is the difference between –
(a) the value of that interest prior to the grant of the new lease; and
(b) the value of that interest once the new lease is granted.

(2) Each of those values shall be determined, as at the valuation date, in accordance with paragraph 8.

Value of intermediate interests

8.—(1) Subject to sub-paragraph (2), paragraph 3(2) to (6) shall apply for determining the value of any intermediate leasehold interest for the purposes of any provision of this Schedule with such modifications as are appropriate to relate those provisions of paragraph 3 to a sale of the interest in question subject to the tenant's lease for the time being and to any leases intermediate between the interest in question and that lease.

(2) The value of an intermediate leasehold interest which is the interest of the tenant under a minor intermediate lease shall be calculated by applying the formula set out in sub-paragraph (6) instead of in accordance with sub-paragraph (1).

(3) 'A minor intermediate lease' means a lease complying with the following requirements, namely –

(a) it must have an expectation of possession of not more than one month, and
(b) the profit rent in respect of the lease must be not more than £5 per year.

(4) 'Profit rent' means an amount equal to that of the rent payable under the lease on which the minor intermediate lease is in immediate reversion, less that of the rent payable under the minor intermediate lease.

(5) Where the minor intermediate lease or that on which it is in immediate reversion comprises property other than the tenant's flat, then in sub-paragraph (4) the reference to the rent payable under it means so much of that rent as is apportioned to that flat.

(6) The formula is –

$$P = £\frac{R}{Y} - \frac{R}{Y(1 + Y)^n}$$

where –

P = the price payable;
R = the profit rent;
Y = the yield (expressed as a decimal fraction) from 2½ per cent Consolidated Stock;
n = the period, expressed in years (taking any part of a year as a whole year), of the remainder of the term of the minor intermediate lease as at the valuation date.

(7) In calculating the yield from 2½ per cent Consolidated Stock, the price of that stock shall be taken to be the middle market price at the close of business on the last trading day in the week before the valuation date.

(8) For the purposes of this paragraph the expectation of possession carried by a lease is the expectation which it carries at the valuation date of possession after the tenant's lease, on the basis that –

(a) (subject to sub-paragraph (9)) the tenant's lease terminates at the valuation date if its term date fell before then, or else it terminates on its term date; and
(b) any other lease terminates on its term date.

(9) In a case where before the relevant date for the purposes of this Chapter the immediate landlord of the tenant had given notice to quit terminating the tenant's lease on a date earlier than that date, the date specified in the notice to quit shall be substituted for the date specified in sub-paragraph (8)(a) above.

Compensation for loss arising out of grant of new lease

9. Paragraph 5 shall apply in relation to the owner of any intermediate leasehold interest as it applies in relation to the landlord.

Owners of intermediate interests entitled to part of marriage value

10.—(1) This paragraph applies in a case where –
(a) the premium payable by the tenant in respect of the grant of the new lease includes an amount in respect of the landlord's share of the marriage value, and
(b) there are any intermediate leasehold interests.

(2) The amount payable to the landlord in respect of his share of the marriage value shall be divided between the landlord and the owners of any such intermediate interests in proportion to the amounts by which the values of their respective interests in the flat will be diminished in consequence of the grant of the new lease.

(3) For the purposes of sub-paragraph (2) –
(a) the amount by which the value of the landlord's interest in the flat will be so diminished is the diminution in value of that interest as determined for the purposes of paragraph 2(a); and
(b) the amount by which the value of any intermediate leasehold interest will be so diminished is the diminution in value of that interest as determined for the purposes of paragraph 6(a).

(4) Where the owner of any intermediate leasehold interest is entitled in accordance with sub-paragraph (2) to any part of the amount payable to the landlord in respect of the landlord's share of the marriage value, the amount to which he is so entitled shall be payable to him by the landlord.

Section 61

SCHEDULE 14

PROVISIONS SUPPLEMENTARY TO SECTION 61

1.—(1) This Schedule has effect where a tenant of a flat is entitled to be paid compensation under section 61, or would be so entitled on the landlord obtaining an order for possession, or where an application for such an order is dismissed or withdrawn.

(2) In this Schedule –
'application for possession' means a landlord's application under section 61;
'the new lease' has the same meaning as in that section; and
'order for possession' means an order made under that section;
and (except in the case of the reference in paragraph 5(1)(b) to the flat as a dwelling) references to the flat held by the tenant under the new lease shall be construed in accordance with subsection (5) of that section.

2.—(1) Where an order for possession is made –
(a) the new lease shall determine, and
(b) the compensation payable to the tenant by virtue of the order shall become payable,

on such date as may, when the amount of compensation has been determined either by agreement between the landlord and the tenant or by a leasehold valuation tribunal, be fixed by order of the court made on the application of either the landlord or the tenant.

(2) Where the application for possession was made by virtue of section 61(2)(a), then –

(a) (unless paragraph (b) below applies) an order of the court under this paragraph shall not fix a date earlier than the term date of the lease in relation to which the right to acquire a new lease was exercised;

(b) in a case where section 61(2)(a) applies in accordance with section 61(3), an order of the court under this paragraph shall not fix a date earlier than the term date of the lease in relation to which that right was first exercised.

(3) In fixing the date referred to in sub-paragraph (1) the court shall have regard to the conduct of the parties and to the extent to which the landlord has made reasonable preparations for proceeding with the redevelopment (including the obtaining of, or preparations relating to the obtaining of, any requisite permission or consent, whether from any authority whose permission or consent is required under any enactment or from the owner of an interest in any property).

(4) The court may by order direct that the whole or part of the compensation payable to the tenant shall be paid into court, if the court thinks it expedient to do so for the purpose of ensuring that the sum paid is available for meeting any mortgage on the tenant's interest in the flat in question, or for the purpose of division, or for any other purpose.

3.—(1) On the termination of a lease under an order for possession there shall terminate also any immediate or derivative sub-lease, and the tenant shall be bound to give up possession of the flat in question to the landlord except in so far as he is precluded from doing so by the rights of other persons to retain possession under or by virtue of any enactment.

(2) Where a sub-lease of property comprised in the lease has been created after the date of the application for possession, no person shall in respect of that sub-lease be entitled under any of the following provisions (which relate to retaining possession on the termination of a superior tenancy), namely –

(a) subsection (2) of section 137 of the Rent Act 1977, or any enactment (including subsection (5) of that section) applying or extending it,

(b) subsection (2) of section 9 of the Rent (Agriculture) Act 1976 as extended by subsection (5) of that section, or

(c) section 18(1) of the Housing Act 1988,

to retain possession of that property after the termination of the lease under the order for possession.

(3) In exercising its jurisdiction under section 61 or this Schedule the court shall assume that the landlord, having obtained an order for possession, will not be precluded from obtaining possession by the right of any person to retain possession by virtue of –

(a) Part VII of the Rent Act 1977 or any enactment applying or extending that Part of that Act,

(b) the Rent (Agriculture) Act 1976, or

(c) Part I of the Housing Act 1988,

or otherwise.

(4) A person in occupation of any property under a sub-lease liable to terminate under sub-paragraph (1) may, with the leave of the court, appear and be heard on any application for possession or any application under paragraph 2.

4. Where an order has been made by a county court under paragraph 2, that court or another county court shall have jurisdiction to hear and determine any proceedings brought by virtue of the order to recover possession of the property or to recover the compensation.

5.—(1) The amount payable to a tenant, by virtue of an order for possession, by way of compensation for loss of his flat shall be the amount which at the valuation date the new lease, if sold on the open market by a willing seller, might be expected to realise on the following assumptions –

(a) on the assumption that Chapter I and this Chapter confer no right to acquire any interest in any premises containing the tenant's flat or to acquire any new lease;

(b) on the assumption that the vendor is selling –

(i) subject to the rights of any person who will on the termination of the lease be entitled to retain possession as against the landlord, but otherwise with vacant possession, and

(ii) subject to any restriction that would be required (in addition to any imposed by the terms of the lease) to limit the uses of the flat to those to which it has been put since the commencement of the lease and to preclude the erection of any new dwelling or any other building not ancillary to the flat as a dwelling; and

(c) on the assumption that (subject to paragraphs (a) and (b)) the vendor is selling with and subject to the rights and burdens with and subject to which the flat will be held by the landlord on the termination of the lease.

(2) It is hereby declared that the fact that sub-paragraph (1) requires assumptions to be made as to the matters specified in paragraphs (a) to (c) of that sub-paragraph does not preclude the making of assumptions as to other matters where those assumptions are appropriate for determining the amount which at the valuation date the new lease might be expected to realise if sold as mentioned in that sub-paragraph.

(3) In determining any such amount there shall be made such deduction (if any) in respect of any defect in title as on a sale of that interest on the open market might be expected to be allowed between a willing seller and a willing buyer.

(4) In this paragraph 'the valuation date' means the date when the amount of the compensation payable to the tenant is determined as mentioned in paragraph 2(1).

6.—(1) Part I of the Landlord and Tenant Act 1927 (compensation for improvements on termination of business tenancies) shall not apply on the termination of the new lease or any sub-lease in accordance with this Schedule; and a request for a new tenancy under section 26 of the Landlord and Tenant Act 1954 in respect of the new lease or any sub-lease shall be of no effect if made after the application for possession, or, if already made, shall cease to have effect on the making of that application.

(2) Where a sub-lease terminating with the new lease in accordance with paragraph 3 is one to which Part II of the Landlord and Tenant Act 1954 applies, the compensation payable to the tenant shall be divided between him and the sub-tenant in such proportions as may be just, regard being had to their respective interests in the flat in question and to any loss arising from the termination of those interests and not incurred by imprudence.

(3) Where the amount of the compensation payable to the tenant is agreed between him and the landlord without the consent of a sub-tenant entitled under sub-paragraph (2) to a share in the compensation, and is shown by the sub-tenant to be less than might reasonably have been obtained by the tenant, the sub-tenant shall be entitled under sub-paragraph (2) to recover from the tenant such increased share as may be just.

7.—(1) The landlord shall not be concerned with the application of the amount payable to the tenant by way of compensation under an order for possession, but (subject to any statutory requirements as to payment of capital money arising under a settlement or a disposition on trust for sale and to any order under paragraph 2(4) for payment into court) the written receipt of the tenant shall be a complete discharge for the amount payable.

(2) The landlord shall be entitled to deduct from the amount so payable to the tenant –
(a) the amount of any sum recoverable as rent in respect of the flat up to the termination of the new lease; and
(b) the amount of any other sums due and payable by the tenant to the landlord under or in respect of the lease or any agreement collateral thereto.

8.—(1) Where a landlord makes an application for possession, and it is made to appear to the court that in relation to matters arising out of that application (including the giving up of possession of the flat or the payment of compensation) the landlord or the tenant has been guilty of any unreasonable delay or default, the court may –
(a) by order revoke or vary, and direct repayment of sums paid under, any provision made by a previous order as to payment of the costs of proceedings taken in the court on or with reference to the application; or
(b) where costs have not been awarded, award costs.

(2) Where an application for possession is dismissed or withdrawn, and it is made to appear to the court –
(a) that the application was not made in good faith, or
(b) that the landlord had attempted in any material respect to support by misrepresentation or the concealment of material facts a request to the tenant to deliver up possession without an application for possession,

the court may order that no further application for possession of the flat made by the landlord shall be entertained if it is made within the period of five years beginning with the date of the order.

9. Where –
(a) the new lease is held on trust for sale, and
(b) compensation is paid by the landlord on the termination of the new lease (whether the payment is made in pursuance of an order for possession or in pursuance of an agreement made in conformity with paragraph 5 above without an application having been made under section 61),

the sum received shall be dealt with as if it were proceeds of sale arising under the trust.

10. Where –
(a) the tenant under the new lease is a university or college to which the Universities and College Estates Act 1925 applies, and
(b) compensation is paid as mentioned in paragraph 9(b) above,

the sum received shall be dealt with as if it were an amount payable by way of consideration on a sale effected under that Act.

11. Where –
(a) the tenant under the new lease is a capitular body within the meaning of the Cathedrals Measure 1963 and the lease comprises property which forms part of the endowment of a cathedral church, and
(b) compensation is paid as mentioned in paragraph 9(b) above,

the sum received shall be treated as part of that endowment.

12.—(1) Where –
(a) the tenant under the new lease is a diocesan board of finance and the lease comprises diocesan glebe land, and
(b) compensation is paid as mentioned in paragraph 9(b) above,

the sum received shall be paid to the church commissioners to be applied for purposes for which the proceeds of any disposition of property by agreement would be applicable under any enactment or Measure authorising such a disposition or disposing of the proceeds of such a disposition.

(2) In this paragraph 'diocesan board of finance' and 'diocesan glebe land' have the same meaning as in the Endowments and Glebe Measure 1976.

Section 66

SCHEDULE 15

SECTION 9 OF THE LEASEHOLD REFORM ACT 1967, AS AMENDED

9. Purchase price and costs of enfranchisement, and tenant's right to withdraw

(1) Subject to subsection (2) below, the price payable for a house and premises on a conveyance under section 8 above shall be the amount which at the relevant time the house and premises, if sold in the open market by a willing seller (with the tenant and members of his family who reside in the house not buying or seeking to buy), might be expected to realise on the following assumptions:–

(a) on the assumption that the vendor was selling for an estate in fee simple, subject to the tenancy but on the assumption that this Part of this Act conferred no right to acquire the freehold, and if the tenancy has not been extended under this Part of this Act, on the assumption that (subject to the landlord's rights under section 17 below) it was to be so extended;

(b) on the assumption that (subject to paragraph (a) above) the vendor was selling subject, in respect of rent charges to which section 11(2) below applies, to the same annual charge as the conveyance to the tenant is to be subject to, but the purchaser would otherwise be effectively exonerated until the termination of the tenancy from any liability or charge in respect of tenant's incumbrances; and

(c) on the assumption that (subject to paragraphs (a) and (b) above) the vendor was selling with and subject to the rights and burdens with and subject to which the conveyance to the tenant is to be made, and in particular with and subject to such permanent or extended rights and burdens as are to be created in order to give effect to section 10 below.

The reference in this subsection to members of the tenant's family shall be construed in accordance with section 7(7) of this Act.

(1A) Notwithstanding the foregoing subsection, the price payable for a house and premises, –

(i) the rateable value of which was above £1,000 in Greater London and £500 elsewhere on 31st March 1990, or,

(ii) which had no rateable value on that date and R exceeded £16,333 under the formula in section 1(1)(a) above (and section 1(7) above shall apply to that amount as it applies to the amount referred to in subsection (1)(a)(ii) of that section)

shall be the amount which at the relevant time the house and premises, if sold in the open market by a willing seller, might be expected to realise on the following assumptions: –

(a) on the assumption that the vendor was selling for an estate in fee simple, subject to the tenancy, but on the assumption that this Part of this Act conferred no right to acquire the freehold or an extended lease and, where the tenancy has been extended under this Part of this Act, that the tenancy will terminate on the original term date;

(b) on the assumption that at the end of the tenancy the tenant has the right to remain in possession of the house and premises

(i) if the tenancy is such a tenancy as is mentioned in subsection (2) or subsection (3) of section 186 of the Local Government and Housing Act 1989, or is a tenancy which is a long tenancy at a low rent for the purposes of Part I of the Landlord and Tenant Act 1954 in respect of which the landlord is not able to serve a notice under section 4 of that Act specifying a date of termination earlier than 15th January 1999, under the provisions of Schedule 10 to the Local Government and Housing Act 1989; and

(ii) in any other case under the provisions of Part I of the Landlord and Tenant Act 1954;

(c) on the assumption that the tenant has no liability to carry out any repairs, maintenance or redecorations under the terms of the tenancy of Part I of the Landlord and Tenant Act 1954;

(d) on the assumption that the price be diminished by the extent to which the value of the house and premises has been increased by any improvement carried out by the tenant or his predecessors in title at their own expense;

(e) on the assumption that (subject to paragraph (a) above) the vendor was selling subject, in respect of rentcharges to which section 11(2) below applies, to the same annual charge as the conveyance to the tenant is to be subject to, but the purchaser would otherwise be effectively exonerated until the termination of the tenancy from any liability or charge in respect of tenant's incumbrances; and

(f) on the assumption that (subject to paragraphs (a) and (b) above) the vendor was selling with and subject to the rights and burdens with and subject to which the conveyance to the tenant is to be made, and in particular with and subject to such permanent or extended rights and burdens as are to be created in order to give effect to section 10 below.

(1B) For the purpose of determining whether the rateable value of the house and premises is above £1,000 in Greater London, or £500 elsewhere, the rateable value shall be adjusted to take into account any tenant's improvements in accordance with Schedule 8 to the Housing Act 1974.

(1C) Notwithstanding subsection (1) above, the price payable for a house and premises where the right to acquire the freehold arises by virtue of any one or more of the provisions of sections 1A and 1B above shall be determined in accordance with subsection (1A) above; but in any such case –

(a) if in determining the price so payable there falls to be taken into account any marriage value arising by virtue of the coalescence of the freehold and leasehold interests, the share of the marriage value to which the tenant is to be regarded as being entitled shall not exceed one-half of it; and

(b) section 9A below has effect for determining whether any additional amount is payable by way of compensation under that section;

and in a case where the provision (or one of the provisions) by virtue of which the right to acquire the freehold arises is section 1A(1) above, subsection (1A) above shall apply with the omission of the assumption set out in paragraph (b) of that subsection.

(2) The price payable for the house and premises shall be subject to such deduction (if any) in respect of any defect in the title to be conveyed to the tenant as on a sale in

the open market might be expected to be allowed between a willing seller and a willing buyer.

(3) On ascertaining the amount payable, or likely to be payable, as the price for a house and premises in accordance with this section (but not more than one month after the amount payable has been determined by agreement or otherwise), the tenant may give written notice to the landlord that he is unable or unwilling to acquire the house and premises at the price he must pay; and thereupon –

(a) the notice under section 8 above of his desire to have the freehold shall cease to have effect, and he shall be liable to make such compensation as may be just to the landlord in respect of the interference (if any) by the notice with the exercise by the landlord of his power to dispose of or deal with the house and premises or any neighbouring property; and

(b) any further notice given under that section with respect to the house or any part of it (with or without other property) shall be void if given within the following three years.

(4) Where a person gives notice of his desire to have the freehold of a house and premises under this Part of this Act, then unless the notice lapses under any provision of this Act excluding his liability, there shall be borne by him (so far as they are incurred in pursuance of the notice) the reasonable costs of or incidental to any of the following matters:–

(a) any investigation by the landlord of that person's right to acquire the freehold;

(b) any conveyance or assurance of the house and premises or any part thereof or of any outstanding estate or interest therein;

(c) deducing, evidencing and verifying the title to the house and premises or any estate or interest therein;

(d) making out and furnishing such abstracts and copies as the person giving the notice may require;

(e) any valuation of the house and premises;

but so that this subsection shall not apply to any costs if on a sale made voluntarily a stipulation that they were to be borne by the purchaser would be void.

(5) The landlord's lien (as vendor) on the house and premises for the price payable shall extend –

(a) to any sums payable by way of rent or recoverable as rent in respect of the house and premises up to the date of the conveyance; and

(b) to any sums for which the tenant is liable under subsection (4) above; and

(c) to any other sums due and payable by him to the landlord under or in respect of the tenancy or any agreement collateral thereto.

. . .

Section 187(1)

SCHEDULE 21

MINOR AND CONSEQUENTIAL AMENDMENTS

Land Registration Act 1925 (c 21)

1. In section 49(1) of the Land Registration Act 1925 (rules to provide for notices of other rights, interests and claims), there shall be added at the end –

'(k) orders made under section 26(1) or 50(1) of the Leasehold Reform, Housing and Urban Development Act 1993 which in the case of unregistered land may be protected by registration under the Land Charges Act 1972 and which, notwithstanding section 59 of this Act, it may be deemed expedient to protect by notice instead of by caution.'

. . .

Leasehold Reform Act 1967 (c 88)

4. In subsection (1A) of section 21 of the Leasehold Reform Act 1967 (jurisdiction of leasehold valuation tribunals), for the words from 'be' onwards there shall be substituted the words 'comply with any requirements imposed by regulations under subsection (4A)(a) or (b) below'.

Land Compensation Act 1973 (c 26)

5. After section 12 of the Land Compensation Act 1973 (tenants entitled to enfranchisement or extension under Leasehold Reform Act 1967) there shall be inserted the following section –

'12A Tenants participating in collective enfranchisement, or entitled to individual lease extension, under Part I of Leasehold Reform, Housing and Urban Development Act 1993

(1) A tenancy to which subsection (2) or (3) below applies ('a qualifying tenancy') shall be treated as an owner's interest as defined in section 2(4) above whether or not the unexpired term on the date of service of the notice of claim is of the length there specified.

(2) This subsection applies to a tenancy if the tenant, on the relevant date –
- (a) is in respect of the tenancy a qualifying tenant for the purposes of Chapter I of Part I of the 1993 Act (collective enfranchisement); and
- (b) by virtue of the tenancy, either –
  - (i) is a participating tenant in relation to a claim to exercise the right to collective enfranchisement under that Chapter; or
  - (ii) is one of the participating tenants on whose behalf the acquisition by the nominee purchaser has been made in pursuance of such a claim.

(3) This subsection applies to a tenancy if the tenant, on the relevant date and in respect of the tenancy, is a qualifying tenant for the purposes of Chapter II of Part I of the 1993 Act (individual right to acquire new lease) who –
- (a) has on or before that date given notice under section 42 of the Act (notice by qualifying tenant of claim to exercise right); and
- (b) has not acquired a new lease before that date.

(4) If no claim is made in respect of a qualifying tenancy before the claimant has ceased to be entitled to it in consequence of a lease being granted to him by the nominee purchaser or, as the case may be, under Chapter II of Part I of the 1993 Act, the claimant may make a claim in respect of the qualifying tenancy as if he were still entitled to it.

(5) No claim shall be made by virtue of subsection (4) above after the claimant has ceased to be entitled to the lease referred to in that subsection, but such a claim may be made before the first claim day if it is made before the claimant had disposed of that lease and after he has made a contract for disposing of it.

(6) Compensation shall not be payable before the first claim day on any claim made by virtue of subsection (5) above.

(7) Any notice of a claim made by virtue of this section shall contain, in addition to the matters mentioned in section 3 above, a statement that is is made in respect of a qualifying tenancy as defined in this section and, if made by virtue of subsection (4) or (5) above, sufficient particulars to show that it falls within that subsection.

(8) In relation to a claim made by virtue of subsection (4) above, section 4(4)(a) above shall have effect as if the reference to the date of service of notice of the claim were a reference to the relevant date.

(9) In this section –
- (a) 'the 1993 Act' means the Leasehold Reform, Housing and Urban Development Act 1993; and
- (b) 'participating tenant', 'nominee purchaser' and 'the acquisition by the nominee purchaser' shall be construed in accordance with sections 14, 15 and 38(2) of that Act respectively.'

. . .

Rent Act 1977 (c 42)

7. In subsection (1)(b) of section 74 of the Rent Act 1977 (regulations), for the words from 'by rent officers' onwards there shall be substituted the words –
'(i) by rent officers under this Act; and
(ii) by rent assessment committees whether under this Act or otherwise; and'.

. . .

National Heritage Act 1983 (c 47)

9. After subsection (2A) of section 33 of the National Heritage Act 1983 (general functions of the Historic Buildings and Monuments Commission for England) there shall be inserted the following subsection –

'(2B) In relation to England, the Commission may make, or join in the making of, applications under section 73(1) of the Leasehold Reform, Housing and Urban Development Act 1993, and may exercise, or participate in the exercise of, any rights or powers conferred by a scheme approved under section 70 of that Act.'

. . .

Landlord and Tenant Act 1987 (c 31)

26. In subsection (2) of section 4 of the Landlord and Tenant Act 1987 (relevant disposals), after paragraph (d) there shall be inserted the following paragraph –

'(da) a disposal of any freehold or leasehold interest in pursuance of Chapter I of Part I of the Leasehold Reform, Housing and Urban Development Act 1993;'

27. In subsection (2) of section 13 of that Act (determination by rent assessment committees of questions relating to purchase notices), for the words from 'be' to 'particulars,' there shall be substituted the words 'comply with such requirements (if any) as to the form of, or the particulars to be contained in, any such application'.

. . .

Planning (Listed Buildings and Conservation Areas) Act 1990 (c 9)

30.—(1) In subsection (1) of section 72 of the Planning (Listed Buildings and Conservation Areas) Act 1990 (general duty as respects conservation areas in exercise of planning functions), for the words 'powers under' there shall be substituted the words 'functions under or by virtue of'.

(2) In subsection (2) of that section there shall be added at the end 'and sections 70 and 73 of the Leasehold Reform, Housing and Urban Development Act 1993'.

31. In paragraphs 2 and 4 of Schedule 4 to that Act (further provisions as to exercise of functions by different authorities), for the words 'and 8' there shall be substituted the words '8 and 8A'.

Section 187(2)

SCHEDULE 22

REPEALS

Chapter	Short title	Extent of repeal
	. . .	
1980 c 51	The Housing Act 1980	In section 141, '3', In Schedule 21, paragraph 3
	. . .	
1987 c 31	The Landlord and Tenant Act 1987	Section 25(3) In section 29(2), the words from 'and (c)' onwards

Appendix 2 – Statutory Instruments

The Leasehold Reform (Collective Enfranchisement and Lease Renewal) Regulations 1993

(SI 1993/2407)

The Secretary of State, as respects England, and the Secretary of State for Wales, as respects Wales, in exercise of the powers conferred on them by sections 98 and 100(1) of the Leasehold Reform, Housing and Urban Development Act 1993 and all other powers enabling them in that behalf, hereby make the following Regulations –

Citation, commencement and interpretation

1.—(1) These Regulations may be cited as the Leasehold Reform (Collective Enfranchisement and Lease Renewal) Regulations 1993 and shall come into force on 1st November 1993.

(2) In these Regulations references to sections and Schedules without more are references to sections of and Schedules to the Leasehold Reform, Housing and Urban Development Act 1993.

Procedure for collective enfranchisement

2. In a transaction undertaken to give effect to an initial notice the nominee purchaser, the reversioner and any relevant landlord shall, unless they otherwise agree, be bound by Schedule 1 to these Regulations.

Procedure for lease renewal

3. In a transaction undertaken to give effect to a tenant's notice, the landlord and the tenant shall, unless they otherwise agree, be bound by Schedule 2 to these Regulations.

Notices

4. Any notice, statement, answer or document required or authorised to be given under these Regulations –

(a) shall be in writing, and
(b) may be sent by post.

Regulation 2

SCHEDULE 1

COLLECTIVE ENFRANCHISEMENT

Interpretation

1. In this Schedule –

'counter-notice' means a notice given under section 21, and 'further counter-notice' means a notice required by or by virtue of section 22(3) or section 23(5) or (6);
'qualifying tenant' shall be construed in accordance with section 5;
'the relevant date' has the meaning given by section 1(8);
'terms of acquisition' has the meaning given by section 24(8).

Evidence that residence condition satisfied

2.—(1) The reversioner may require the nominee purchaser to give him evidence of the occupation on which a qualifying tenant who is claimed in the initial notice to satisfy the residence condition relies, by giving him notice within the period of twenty-one days beginning with the relevant date.

(2) The nominee purchaser shall comply with any such requirement by giving a statutory declaration made by that qualifying tenant to the reversioner within the period of twenty-one days beginning with the date the notice is given.

Delivery of proof of title

3.—(1) Sub-paragraph (2) applies where the reversioner has given a counter-notice complying with section 21(2)(a) (admitting the right to collective enfranchisement) or a further counter-notice, or, if no such counter-notice or further counter-notice is given, the nominee purchaser has applied to the court for an order under section 25(1) (applications where reversioner fails to give counter-notice or further counter-notice).

(2) Subject to paragraph 5, the nominee purchaser may require the reversioner to deduce title to the interests proposed to be acquired in accordance with section 13(3)(a) and (c)(i) (matters specified in the initial notice) and to any interest in relation to which the reversioner has made proposals in accordance with section 21(3)(b) and (c) (matters specified in counter-notice), or to any less extensive interest which it has been agreed or determined by a leasehold valuation tribunal will be acquired, by giving him notice.

(3) The reversioner shall comply with any such requirement by giving the nominee purchaser –

(a) in the case of an interest registered in the register of title kept at her Majesty's Land Registry, all particulars and information which have to be given or may be required to be given on a sale of registered land pursuant to section 110 of the Land Registration Act 1925 (provisions as between vendor and purchaser), and
(b) in the case of any other interest, an epitome of title,

within the period of twenty-eight days beginning with the date the notice is given.

Requisitions

4.—(1) Subject to paragraph 5, the nominee purchaser shall give to the reversioner a statement of any objections to or requisitions on the proof of title within the period of fourteen days beginning with the date the proof is given (whether or not within the time required).

(2) The reversioner shall give to the nominee purchaser an answer to any statement of objections or requisitions within the period of fourteen days beginning with the date the statement is given.

(3) The nominee purchaser shall give to the reversioner a further statement of any objections to or comments on the answer within the period of seven days beginning with the date the answer is given.

(4) Any objection or requisition not included in any statement given within the period referred to in sub-paragraph (1) shall be deemed waived, and any matter which could have been raised in a statement so given shall be deemed not to be a defect in title for the purposes of paragraph 3(3) of Schedule 6 and as it is applied by paragraph 7(1) and by paragraph 11(1) of that Schedule (effect of defect in title on valuation of interest to be acquired).

(5) Any objection not included in any further statement given within the period specified in sub-paragraph (3) shall be deemed waived and any matter which could have been raised in a further statement so given shall be deemed not to be a defect in title for the purposes of paragraph 3(3) of Schedule 6 and as it is applied as described in sub-paragraph (4).

(6) If no further statement is given within the time specified in sub-paragraph (3), the reversioner's answer shall be considered satisfactory.

Relevant landlords acting independently

5.—(1) Sub-paragraph (2) applies where –
- (a) a relevant landlord has given notice in accordance with paragraph 7(1)(a) of Schedule 1 (relevant landlord's entitlement to act independently of the reversioner) of his intention to deal directly with the nominee purchaser in connection with deducing, evidencing or verifying his title, or
- (b) the nominee purchaser has given notice in accordance with paragraph 7(2) of Schedule 1 (nominee purchaser's entitlement to require a relevant landlord to deal directly with him) to a relevant landlord.

(2) Any notice, statement or further statement given –
- (a) under paragraph 3 requiring proof of that relevant landlord's title, or
- (b) under paragraph 4 raising requisitions, or making objections to or comments on that relevant landlord's title,

shall be given to him and not to the reversioner, and he will be under a duty to comply with any such notice or respond to any such statement instead of the reversioner.

Preparation of contract

6.—(1) The reversioner shall prepare the draft contract and give it to the nominee purchaser within the period of twenty-one days beginning with the date the terms of acquisition are agreed or determined by a leasehold valuation tribunal.

(2) The nominee purchaser shall give to the reversioner a statement of any proposals for amending the draft contract within the period of fourteen days beginning with the date the draft contract is given.

(3) If no statement is given by the nominee purchaser within the time specified in sub-paragraph (2) he shall be deemed to have approved the draft.

(4) The reversioner shall give to the nominee purchaser an answer, giving any

objections to or comments on the proposals in the statement, within the period of fourteen days beginning with the date the statement is given.

(5) If no answer is given by the reversioner within the time specified in sub-paragraph (4), he shall be deemed to have agreed to the nominee purchaser's proposals for amendments to the draft contract.

Payment of deposit

7.—(1) The reversioner may require the nominee purchaser to pay a deposit on exchange of contracts in pursuance of the initial notice.

(2) The amount of the deposit required shall be £500, or 10 per cent of the purchase price agreed or determined by a leasehold valuation tribunal to be payable for the interests to be acquired, whichever is the greater.

(3) The nominee purchaser shall pay the deposit so required to the reversioner's solicitor or licensed conveyancer as stakeholder.

Cancellation of land charges etc

8. Where the initial notice has been registered as a land charge or a notice or caution has been registered in respect of it under section 97(1), and either it is withdrawn, deemed to have been withdrawn or otherwise ceases to have effect, the nominee purchaser shall at the request of the reversioner without delay take all steps necessary to procure cancellation of the registration.

Regulation 3

SCHEDULE 2

LEASE RENEWAL

Interpretation

1. In this Schedule –

'counter-notice' means a notice given under section 45, and 'further counter-notice' means a notice required by or by virtue of section 46(4) or section 47(4) or (5);
'flat' shall be construed in accordance with section 62(2);
'the landlord' has the meaning given by section 40(1);
'lease' means a lease granted to give effect to a tenant's notice;
'the relevant date' has the meaning given by section 39(8);
'tenant' means a tenant who has given a tenant's notice;
'terms of acquisition' has the meaning given by section 48(7).

Payment of deposit

2.—(1) The landlord may give to the tenant a notice requiring him to pay a deposit on account of the premium payable for the lease at any time when the tenant's notice continues in force under section 42(8).

(2) The amount of the deposit shall be £250, or 10 per cent of the amount proposed in the tenant's notice as payable on the grant of the lease in accordance with Schedule 13 (premium and other amounts payable by tenant on grant of new lease), whichever is the greater.

(3) The tenant shall pay the deposit so required to the landlord's solicitor or licensed conveyancer as stakeholder within the period of fourteen days beginning with the date the notice is given.

Return of deposit

3.—(1) Subject to sub-paragraph (3), the tenant may give to the landlord a notice requiring him to procure the return of the deposit to the tenant at any time after the tenant's notice is withdrawn, deemed to have been withdrawn or otherwise ceases to have effect.

(2) The landlord shall comply with any such requirement within the period of fourteen days beginning with the date the notice is given.

(3) The landlord shall be entitled to have deducted from the deposit any amount due to him from the tenant in accordance with section 60 (tenant's liability for landlord's costs).

Evidence of tenant's right to a lease

4.—(1) The landlord may require the tenant to –
(a) deduce title to his tenancy, and
(b) give evidence by statutory declaration of the occupation on which he relies in the tenant's notice by giving him notice with the period of twenty-one days beginning with the relevant date.

(2) The tenant shall comply with any such requirement within the period of twenty-one days beginning with the date the notice is given.

Delivery of proof of title

5.—(1) Sub-paragraph (2) applies where the landlord has given a counter-notice complying with section 45(2)(a) (admitting the right to a new lease) or a further counter-notice, or, if no such counter-notice or further counter-notice is given, the tenant has applied to the court for an order under section 49(1) (applications where landlord fails to give counter-notice or further counter-notice).

(2) The tenant may require the landlord to deduce title to his interest in the flat to which the tenant's notice relates by giving him notice.

(3) The landlord shall comply with any such requirement by giving the tenant –
(a) in the case of an interest registered in the register of title kept at Her Majesty's Land Registry, all particulars and information which have to be given or may be required to be given on a sale of registered land pursuant to section 110 of the Land Registration Act 1925 (provisions as between vendor and purchaser), and
(b) subject to sub-paragraph (4), in the case of any other, an epitome of title,
within the period of twenty-eight days beginning with the date the notice is given.

(4) In a case where the landlord is not the freeholder, and the title to the freehold or any leasehold reversion to the landlord's title (if any) is not registered at Her Majesty's Land Registry, the landlord shall use his best endeavours to obtain an epitome of that title and shall also give it to the tenant.

Requisitions

6.—(1) The tenant shall give to the landlord a statement of any objections to or requisitions on the proof of title within the period of fourteen days beginning with the date the proof is given (whether or not within the time required).

(2) The landlord shall give to the tenant an answer to any statement of objections or requisitions within the period of fourteen days beginning with the date the statement is given.

(3) The tenant shall give to the landlord a further statement of any objections to or comments on the answer within the period of seven days beginning with the date the answer is given.

(4) Any objection or requisition not included in any statement given within the period referred to in sub-paragraph (1) shall be deemed waived, and any matter which could have been raised in a statement so given shall be deemed not to be a defect in title for the purposes of paragraph 3(5) of Schedule 13 and as it is applied by paragraph 8(1) of that Schedule (effect of defect in title on calculation of diminution in value of landlord's interest or any intermediate leasehold interest).

(5) Any objection not included in any further statement given within the period specified in sub-paragraph (3) shall be deemed waived and any matter which could have been raised in a further statement so given shall be deemed not to form a defect in the title for the purposes of paragraph 3(5) of Schedule 13 and as it is applied as described in sub-paragraph (4).

(6) If no further statement is given within the time specified in sub-paragraph (3), the landlord's answer shall be considered satisfactory.

Preparation of lease

7.—(1) The landlord shall prepare a draft lease and give it to the tenant within the period of fourteen days beginning with the date the terms of acquisition are agreed or determined by a leasehold evaluation tribunal.

(2) The tenant shall give to the landlord a statement of any proposals for amending the draft lease within the period of fourteen days beginning with the date the draft lease is given.

(3) If no statement is given by the tenant within the time specified in sub-paragraph (2), he shall be deemed to have approved the draft lease.

(4) The landlord shall give to the tenant an answer giving any objections to or comments on the proposals in the statement within the period of fourteen days beginning with the date the statement is given.

(5) If no answer is given by the landlord within the time specified in sub-paragraph (4), he shall be deemed to have approved the amendments to the draft lease proposed by the tenant.

(6) The landlord shall prepare the lease and as many counterparts as he may reasonably require and shall give the counterpart or counterparts to the tenant for execution a reasonable time before the completion date.

(7) The tenant shall give the counterpart or counterparts of the lease, duly executed, to the landlord and the landlord shall give the lease, duly executed, to the tenant, on the completion date or as soon as possible afterwards.

Completion

8.—(1) Subject to sub-paragraph (2), after the draft lease is approved or deemed to have been approved, either the landlord or the tenant may give the other notice requiring him to complete the grant of the lease on the first working day after the expiration of twenty-one days beginning with the date the notice is given.

(2) Sub-paragraph (1) shall not apply if the date for completion would fall after the expiry of the appropriate period specified for the purposes of section 48 or 49 (applications where terms in dispute or failure to enter into new lease, and applications where landlord fails to give counter-notice or further counter-notice), and in that event the date for completion shall be such day as the landlord and tenant agree in writing or the court orders under section 48(3) or 49(4) (order of the court on failure to enter into new lease).

(3) The landlord shall by notice inform any other landlord who has given notice in accordance with paragraph 7(2) of Schedule 11 (other landlords acting independently) of the date for completion as soon as possible after notice has been given in accordance with sub-paragraph (1) or the date for completion agreed or ordered by the court in accordance with sub-paragraph (2).

(4) Completion shall take place at the office of the landlord's solicitor or licensed conveyancer.

Cancellation of land charges etc

9. Where a tenant's notice has been registered under section 97(1) as a land charge or a notice or caution has been registered in respect of it, and it is withdrawn, deemed to have been withdrawn or otherwise ceases to have effect, the tenant shall at the request of the landlord without delay take all steps necessary to procure cancellation of the registration.

The Rent Assessment Committee (England and Wales) (Leasehold Valuation Tribunal) Regulations 1993

(SI 1993/2408)

The Secretary of State for the Environment, as respects England, and the Secretary of State for Wales, as respects Wales, in exercise of the powers conferred upon them by section 21(4A) of the Leasehold Reform Act 1967, section 74(1) of the Rent Act 1977, sections 13(2) and 31(5) of the Landlord and Tenant Act 1987, and sections 75(4), 88(5) and 91(6) of the Leasehold Reform, Housing and Urban Development Act 1993 and of all other powers enabling them in that behalf, and after consultation with the Council on Tribunals, hereby make the following Regulations:

1. Citation and commencement

These Regulations may be cited as the Rent Assessment Committee (England and Wales) (Leasehold Valuation Tribunal) Regulations 1993 and shall come into force on 1st November 1993.

2. Interpretation

In these Regulations –

'application' means an application to a tribunal under section 21(1) (jurisdiction of leasehold valuation tribunals) of the Leasehold Reform Act 1967, or under section 13 (determination by leasehold valuation tribunals of questions relating to purchase notices) or section 31 (determination by leasehold valuation tribunals of terms where acquisition order) of the Landlord and Tenant Act 1987, or under or by virtue of Part I of the 1993 Act (collective enfranchisement and grant of new lease) and includes, except where the contrary is indicated, a scheme application;

'party' includes (as regards a scheme application) two or more landlords or a representative body under section 71 (applications by two or more landlords or by a representative body) of the 1993 Act, and the relevant authority for the purposes of section 73 (applications by certain public bodies) of that Act;

'person making representations' means such a person as is mentioned in section 70(6) of the 1993 Act;

'scheme application' means an application under Chapter IV of Part I of the 1993 Act, or under section 19 of the Leasehold Reform Act 1967 (retention of management powers for general benefit of neighbourhood) as it has effect by virtue of section 75 (variation of existing schemes) of the 1993 Act;

'the 1993 Act' means the Leasehold Reform, Housing and Urban Development Act 1993; and

'tribunal' means a leasehold valuation tribunal.

3. Applications

(1) The particulars to be included in an application, except a scheme application, are those specified in Schedule 1 to these Regulations.

(2) The particulars to be included in a scheme application are those specified in Schedule 2 to these Regulations.

4. On receipt of an application the tribunal shall send a copy of it and of each of the documents which accompanied it to each person named in it as a respondent.

5. Hearings
(1) A hearing shall be on the date and at the time and place appointed by the tribunal.

(2) The tribunal shall give notice of the appointed date, time and place to the parties not less that 21 days (or such shorter period as the parties may agree) before the appointed date, and the tribunal shall send a copy of the notice –

(a) to any other person who has indicated to the tribunal an intention to appear at the hearing; and

(b) in the case of a scheme application, to any person making representations.

(3) The notice shall contain a statement that an appeal to the Lands Tribunal may only be made by a person who appeared before the tribunal in proceedings to which he was a party.

(4) The tribunal may, where they consider it appropriate, arrange that an application shall be heard together with any one or more other applications.

(5) A hearing shall be in public unless, for special reasons, the tribunal decide that a hearing or part of a hearing shall be held in private.

6. At a hearing –

(a) the tribunal shall determine the procedure (subject to these Regulations), and the order in which the persons appearing before them are to be heard;

(b) a person appearing before the tribunal may do so either in person or by a representative authorised by him, whether or not that representative is of counsel or a solicitor; and

(c) a person appearing before the tribunal may give evidence on his own behalf, call witnesses, and cross-examine any witnesses called by any other person appearing.

7. Non-appearance

If a party or person mentioned in regulation 5(2) does not appear at a hearing, the tribunal may proceed with the hearing if they are satisfied that notice has been given to that party or person in accordance with these Regulations.

8. Adjournment

(1) The tribunal may postpone or adjourn a hearing at their discretion either of their own motion, or at the request of the parties or of one or more of the persons appearing before them, but they shall not do so at the request of one party or person except where they consider it reasonable to do so having regard to the grounds for the request, the time at which the request is made and the convenience of the other persons appearing before them.

(2) The tribunal shall give reasonable notice of any postponed or adjourned hearing to the persons appearing before them.

9. Documents

(1) Before the date of a hearing, the tribunal shall take all reasonable steps to ensure that each of the parties and persons making representations is given –

(a) a copy of, or sufficient extracts from or particulars of, any document relevant to the proceedings which has been received from a party or person making

representations (other than a document already in the possession of that party or one of which he has previously been supplied with a copy); and
(b) a copy of any document which embodies the results of any enquiries made by or for the tribunal for the purposes of the proceedings.

(2) At the hearing, if a person appearing before the tribunal does not have in his possession a relevant document or a copy of, or sufficient extracts from or particulars of, a relevant document, then unless –
(a) that person consents to the continuation of the hearing; or
(b) the tribunal consider that that person has a sufficient opportunity to deal with the document without an adjournment of the hearing,
the tribunal shall adjourn the hearing for a period which they consider will give that person a sufficient opportunity to deal with the document.

10. Inspections

(1) The tribunal may (subject to the necessary consent being obtained) inspect the house, premises or area which are the subject of the proceedings.

(2) An inspection may be made before, during or after the close of a hearing, as the tribunal may decide, and the tribunal shall give the persons appearing before them an opportunity to attend.

(3) Notice of an inspection shall be given as if it were notice of a hearing, but the requirements for notice may be dispensed with or relaxed with the consent of the persons appearing before the tribunal or if the tribunal are satisfied that such persons have received sufficient notice.

(4) Where an inspection is made after the close of a hearing, the tribunal shall, if they consider it expedient to do so on account of any matter arising from the inspection, reopen the hearing; and if the hearing is to be reopened regulation 5(2) shall apply as it applied to the original hearing, except that its requirements may be dispensed with or relaxed with the consent of the parties and persons mentioned in regulations 5(2) or if the tribunal are satisfied that such parties and persons have received sufficient notice.

(5) This regulation shall apply, so far as is reasonable and practicable, to any comparable house, premises or area to which the attention of the tribunal is directed.

11. Decisions

(1) The decision of the tribunal shall be recorded in a document signed by the chairman of the tribunal (or, in the event of his absence or incapacity, by another member of the tribunal) which shall contain the reasons for the decision.

(2) The chairman (or in the event of his absence or incapacity, another member of the tribunal) shall have power, by certificate under his hand, to correct any clerical mistakes in the document or any errors arising in it from an accidental slip or omission.

(3) A copy of the document and of any such correction shall be sent by the tribunal to each party and person making representations.

12. Attendance by member of Council on Tribunals

Nothing in these Regulations shall prevent a member of the Council on Tribunals in that capacity from attending any hearing or inspection or from being present during the tribunal's deliberations as to their decision; but a member of the Council on Tribunals may not take part in such deliberations.

13. Information required by tribunal

(1) Where a tribunal require information to be given under paragraph 7 of Schedule 22 to the Housing Act 1980, the notice shall contain a statement to the effect that any person who fails without reasonable cause to comply with the notice is liable on summary conviction to a fine not exceeding level 3 on the standard scale.

(2) Paragraph (1) above shall not apply in the case of a notice addressed to an appropriate authority in relation to a Crown interest.

14. Notices

Where any notice or other document is required under these Regulations to be given or sent by the tribunal, it shall be sufficient compliance with these Regulations if the notice or other document is sent by pre-paid post or by facsimile transmission addressed to the person for whom it is intended at his usual or last known address or (if a person has appointed an agent to act on his behalf) to his agent at the address of the agent supplied to the tribunal.

15. Amendments

(1) Regulation 2(2) of the Rent Assessment Committees (England and Wales) Regulations 1971 is amended by the addition, at the end of the definition of 'committee' of the words –

'or by section 75, 88 or 91 (jurisdiction of leasehold valuation tribunals) of the Leasehold Reform, Housing and Urban Development Act 1993'.

(2) The Rent Assessment Committee (England and Wales) (Leasehold Valuation Tribunal) (Amendment) Regulations 1987, and the Rent Assessment Committee (England and Wales) (Leasehold Valuation Tribunal) (Amendment) Regulations 1988, are each amended by the omission of the following –

(a) in article 2, the definition of 'the 1981 Regulations';
(b) article 4; and
(c) the Schedule.

16. Revocation

The Rent Assessment Committee (England and Wales) (Leasehold Valuation Tribunal) Regulations 1981 are hereby revoked.

Regulation 3(1)

SCHEDULE 1

PARTICULARS TO BE INCLUDED IN APPLICATIONS

1. The Address of the property which is the subject of the application.

2. A statement of the purpose of the application, identifying the relevant statutory provision.

3. The name and address of the applicant.

4. The name, address and profession of the applicant's representative, if any.

5. Whether the applicant is the reversioner or other freeholder or landlord, nominated person, nominee purchaser, or tenant; or, if none of the former, the capacity in which the applicant makes the application.

6. The name and address of the respondent and whether the respondent is the reversioner or other freeholder or landlord, nominated person, nominee purchaser or tenant; or, if none of the former, the capacity of the respondent.

7. If the respondent is not the freeholder, the name and address of the freeholder.

8. The name and address of any intermediate landlord, which the applicant knows or could reasonably obtain.

9. The name and address of any person having a mortgage or other charge over an interest in the property held by the freeholder or other landlord, which the applicant knows or could reasonably obtain.

10. Copies of –
  (a) any lease;
  (b) any notice served by any party;
  (c) any application to court or court order; and
  (d) any other document
which are relevant to the application and which the applicant has or could reasonably obtain.

11. Any terms which have already been determined or agreed between the parties, including a copy of any draft conveyance or lease.

12. Any terms which are in dispute.

13. If an amount or price is in dispute, the amount or price which the applicant considers to be appropriate.

14. If the application is for determination of the amount of compensation payable under section 17 or 18 of the Leasehold Reform Act 1967, details of the circumstances under which the claim for compensation arises.

15. If the application includes an application for determination of the amount of a sub-tenant's share of compensation under section 21(2) of the Leasehold Reform Act 1967, the name and address of the sub-tenant, and a copy of any agreement for a sub-tenancy.

16. If the application is made under section 13 of the Landlord and Tenant Act 1987, the date on which the landlord acquired the property, and the terms of acquisition, including the sums paid.

17. If the application is made under the Landlord and Tenant Act 1987 or under the 1993 Act, a map or plan showing the property and any appurtenant property which is relevant to the application.

18. If the application is for apportionment of an amount under section 91(2) (e) of the 1993 Act, the circumstances by which the need for apportionment arises, and the apportionment which the applicant considers to be appropriate.

19. If the application relates to the grant of leases back to a former freeholder under Schedule 9 to the 1993 Act, the name and address of any secure tenant, tenant under housing association tenancy, or sub-tenant to whose interests the tribunal is required to have particular regard.

20. The date of the application.

Regulation 3(2)

SCHEDULE 2

PARTICULARS TO BE INCLUDED IN SCHEME APPLICATIONS

1. A statement of the purpose of the scheme application, identifying the relevant statutory provision.

2. The name and address of the applicant.

3. The name, address and profession of the applicant's representative, if any.

4. Where the applicant is not a natural person, whether the applicant is a representative body within the meaning of that expression in section 71(3) of the 1993 Act, or a relevant authority within the meaning of that expression in section 73(5) of that Act.

5. In the case of an application under section 70 of the 1993 Act, a copy of any advertisement or other document showing compliance with the requirements of subsection (4) of that section.

6. A description of the area for which the scheme is proposed, including identification of the area by a map or plan.

7. The proposed provisions of the scheme.

8. Where any modification is proposed relating to the extent of the area of an existing scheme, or approval is sought for variation of an existing scheme, a description of the proposed modification, including identification by a map or plan of the area to which the modification or variation relates, and of any part of an area proposed to be excluded or (as the case may be) included.

9. Where any modification to the provisions of the scheme is proposed by the applicant (as to which see section 70(7) of the 1993 Act), a description of the proposed modification, including where relevant identification by a map or plan of the area to which the modification relates.

10. In the case of an application under section 70 of the 1993 Act, a copy of any consent given by the Secretary of State under section 72(1) of that Act.

11. The date of the application.

The Leasehold Reform (Notices) (Amendment) Regulations 1993

(SI 1993/2409)

The Secretary of State for the Environment, as respects England, and the Secretary of State for Wales, as respects Wales, in exercise of the powers conferred by section 66 of the Landlord and Tenant Act 1954 as applied by section 22(5) of the Leasehold Reform Act 1967 and now vested in them and of all other powers enabling them in that behalf, hereby make the following Regulations: –

1. Citation and commencement

These Regulations may be cited as the Leasehold Reform (Notices) (Amendment) Regulations 1993 and shall come into force on 1st November 1993.

2. Amendments

(1) The Appendix to the Leasehold Reform (Notices) Regulations 1967 is amended in accordance with the following provisions of this regulation.

(2) In Form 1 (notice of leaseholder's claim) –

(a) for paragraphs 3 and 4 of the Schedule substitute –

'Note 7. 3. *Particulars of the tenancy of the house and premises sufficient to identify the instrument creating the tenancy and to show that the tenancy is and has at the material times been a long tenancy or treated as a long tenancy.*

Note 7A. 4. *Particulars of the tenancy of the house and premises sufficient to show that the tenancy is and has at the material times been a tenancy at a low rent or treated at a low rent.*';

(b) after paragraph 6 insert –

'Note 7B. 6A. *Additional particulars sufficient to show that the value of the house and premises does not exceed the applicable financial limit specified in section 1(1) (a) (i) or (ii), (5) or (6) of the Act. (These are not required where the right to have the freehold is claimed in reliance on any one or more of the provisions in section 1A or 1B of the Act.)*

Note 7C. 6B. *Additional particulars sufficient to show whether the house and premises are to be valued in accordance with section 9(1) or section 9(1A) of the Act. (These are not required where the right to have the freehold is claimed in reliance on any one or more of the provisions in section 1A or 1B of the Act.)*'; and

(c) at the end of Note 7 insert –

'In addition to the provisions of section 3 of the Act, section 174(a) of the Housing Act 1985 provides for certain tenancies granted pursuant to the right to buy to be treated as long tenancies. Section 1B of the Act also provides for certain tenancies terminable on death or marriage to be long tenancies for the limited right described in Note 7B.

7A. In addition to the provisions of section 4 of the Act, section 174(b) of the Housing Act 1985 provides for certain shared ownership leases granted pursuant to the right to buy to be treated as tenancies at a low rent. Section 1A(2) of the Act also provides for certain tenancies at a low rent for the limited right described in Note 7B.

7B. A claimant who relies on any one or more of the provisions in section 1A or 1B of the Act has the right to have the freehold at a price determined in accordance with section 9(1C) of the Act, but not the right to have an extended lease. Section 1A(1) applies to a tenancy of a house and premises the value of which exceeds the applicable financial limit. (Sections 1A(2) and 1B are described in Notes 7A and 7 respectively.)

7C. If section 175 of the Housing Act 1985 (leases granted pursuant to the right to buy etc) applies to a tenancy, the price payable for the house and premises is not determined in accordance with section 9(1).'.

(3) In Form 3 (notice of leaseholder's claim under section 28(1)(b)(ii)) –

(a) for paragraphs 3 and 4 of the Schedule substitute –

'Note 5. 3. *Particulars of the tenancy of the house and premises sufficient to identify the instrument creating the tenancy and to show that the tenancy is and has at the material times been a long tenancy, or treated as a long tenancy.*

Note 5A. 4. *Particulars of the tenancy of the house and premises sufficient to show that the tenancy is and has at the material times been a tenancy at a low rent, or treated as a tenancy at a low rent.*';

(b) after paragraph 6 of the Schedule insert –

'Note 5B. 6A. *Additional particulars sufficient to show that the value of the house and premises does not exceed the applicable financial limit specified in section 1(1)(a)(i) or (ii), (5) or (6) of the Act. (These are not required where the right to acquire the freehold is claimed in reliance on any one or more of the provisions in section 1A or 1B of the Act.)*

Note 5C. 6B. *Additional particulars sufficient to show whether the house and premises are to be valued in accordance with section 9(1) or section 9(1A) of the Act. (These are not required where the right to acquire the freehold is claimed in reliance on any one or more of the provisions in section 1A or 1B of the Act.)*'; and

(c) at the end of Note 5 insert—

'In addition to the provisions of section 3 of the Act, section 174(a) of the Housing Act 1985 provides for certain tenancies granted pursuant to the right to buy to be treated as long tenancies. Section 1B of the Act also provides for certain tenancies terminable on death or marriage to be long tenancies for the limited right described in Note 5B.

5A. In addition to the provisions of section 4 of the Act, section 174(b) of the Housing Act 1985 provides for certain shared ownership leases granted pursuant to the right to buy to be treated as tenancies at a low rent. Section 1A(2) of the Act also provides for certain tenancies to be treated as tenancies at a low rent for the limited right described in Note 5B.

5B. A claimant who relies on any one or more of the provisions in section 1A or 1B of the Act has the right to have the freehold at a price determined in accordance with section 9(1C) of the Act, but not the right to have an extended lease. Section 1A(1) applies to a tenancy of a house and premises the value of which exceeds the applicable financial limit. (Sections 1A(2) and 1B are described in Notes 5A and 5 respectively.)

5C. If section 175 of the Housing Act 1985 (leases granted pursuant to the right to buy etc) applies to a tenancy, the price payable for the house and premises is not determined in accordance with section 9(1).'.

4. Transitional

These Regulations shall not apply in a case where a notice under section 8 or 14 of the Leasehold Reform Act 1967 (tenant's notice of desire to have the freehold or an extended lease) was given before these Regulations came into force.

Appendix 3

TABLE OF PARLIAMENTARY DEBATES

Note: The First Reading of Bills in both Houses are formal. Since the Second Reading debates are concerned with the principle of the proposed legislation, ministerial statements tend to be concerned with the general policy and purpose. Clauses receive detailed consideration in the Committee and Report stages.

With the exception of Standing Committee B, references are to the volumes of the House of Commons Official Report, Parliamentary Debates (Hansard) and to the parallel House of Lords, Official Report, Parliamentary Debates (Hansard), London, HMSO.

	DATE	REFERENCE
HOUSE OF COMMONS		
Second Reading	3 November 1992	Vol 213, Cols 152–254.
Committee Stage	Considered in Standing Committee B in 25 sittings. The provisions of Part I were debated in the first 10 sittings between 10 November and 1 December 1992 Cols 3–371.	
Report	9 February 1993	Vol 218, Cols 832–952, 988–1026
Third Reading	10 February 1993	Vol 218, Cols 1026–1038.
HOUSE OF LORDS		
Second Reading	23 February 1993	Vol 543, Cols 85–176.
Committee Stage	9 March 1993	Vol 543, Cols 930–959; 1016–1058;
	15 March 1993	Vol 543, Cols 1228–1246; 1255–1286; 1300–1332.
	22 March 1993	Vol 544, Cols 9–28; 40–77; 79–154.
	29 March 1993	Vol 544, Cols 598–661; 674–712.
Report	11 May 1993	Vol 545, Cols 1184–1205; 1216–1251; 1252–1272.
	18 May 1993	Vol 545, Cols 1651–1732.
	20 May 1993	Vol 545, Cols 1860–1915; 1926–1964.

	DATE	REFERENCE
Third Reading	25 May 1993	Vol 546, Cols 176–252.

HOUSE OF COMMONS

Consideration of Lords Amendments	14 June 1993	Vol 226, Cols 645–701.

HOUSE OF LORDS

Consideration of Commons Reason and Amendments	8 July 1993	Vol 547, Cols 1522–1533.

INDEX

References are to paragraph numbers.